Photography
A Cultural History

SECOND EDITION

Mary Warner Marien

Laurence King Publishing

First published in Great Britain 2002

Second edition published 2006 by
Laurence King Publishing Ltd
71 Great Russell Street
London WC1B 3BP
Tel: + 44 20 7430 8850
Fax: + 44 20 7430 8880
email: enquiries@laurenceking.co.uk
www.laurenceking.co.uk

A catalogue record for this book is available from
the British Library.

ISBN-13: 978–1–85669–493–3
ISBN-10: 1–85669–493–3

Printed in China

Every effort has been made to contact the copyright
holders, but should there be any errors or omissions,
Laurence King Publishing Ltd would be pleased to
insert the appropriate acknowledgement in any
subsequent printing of this publication.

Commissioning Editor: Kara Hattersley-Smith
Senior Editor: Jessica Spencer
Picture Researcher: Emma Brown
Interior Designer: Ian Hunt Design
Cover Designer: Pentagram

Front cover: Eva Besnyo, *John Fernhout and his
Rolleiflex by the Baltic Sea*, 1932. Collection Hague
Municipal Museum.

Back cover: Boris Mikhailov, *Untitled* from the *Case
History* series, 1997–98. Courtesy the artist.

Frontispiece: Lewis Carroll, *Alice Liddell as
"The Beggar Maid,"* c. 1859. Hand-colored albumen
print. Sotheby's Picture Library, London.

CONTENTS

CHAPTER EIGHT
Into the New Millennium

Preface

Despite the impressive increase in college photography courses during the last decades of the twentieth century, autodidacts such as myself make up the bulk of photohistorians. Like many others, I became a photographic historian in my parents' living room, while looking at copies of *Life* magazine. We photohistorians revel in our passionate preferences. If I thought I could get away with it, I would have filled this book with my favorite pictures, such as those that French photographer Robert Doisneau made of Paris in the 1950s and 1960s. I have not yet found a tactic to show Doisneau's work in my survey, nor have I included him here in the second edition, even though, in a portrait pinned above my desk, a broadly grinning Doisneau points directly at me, prompting me to keep on trying (Fig. 1).

In writing this book, I have tried to survey photography's history in such a way that readers can gauge the medium's manifold developments, and appreciate the historical and cultural contexts in which photographers lived and worked. Some readers may long for a comprehensive taxonomy of photography, a unified field with movements and ideas carefully delineated like kingdoms, phyla, orders, and species. Indeed, this sort of categorization is a practical, if sometimes blunt, instrument with which to create order and highlight dominant ideas and visual approaches. Yet it is crucial to remember that people living in a particular era do not synchronize their thoughts. They interpret, refine, resist, oppose, or ignore the prevalent attitudes of their time. Years of teaching have brought home to me the dangers of homogenizing subtly distinctive viewpoints or creating periods so watertight that they leave no residue in the next chapter.

My students have taught me that, contrary to conventional wisdom, they do not dislike history, but are instead hungry for it. Consequently, I have tried to sketch the political and economic events that shaped the circumstances in which photography was practiced, while paying special attention to the particular ideas generated by and about photography in each period. Each chapter concludes with a "Philosophy and Practice" section, centered on how beliefs shaped photographic practice. In addition, the Focus boxes in this book discuss particular ideas and historical moments.

Photography generates its own special excitement, in part because it quickly reacts to encompass fresh material and new analytic tools, underscoring its vital, interdisciplinary character. Although photography was a Western discovery, students are rightly curious about its many manifestations in the wider world. To serve that interest, I have both incorporated recent research into non-Western photographers and Western visions of the non-Western world as they were directed towards science, anthropology, journalism, and art.

I am mindful that, despite the existence of several lengthy published histories, comprehensive surveys of photography in India and China (countries that make up more than one-third of the world's population) have yet to be written. As the numbers of photographers and historians from these countries increase, so too does the opportunity for comprehensive historical recall. Although photography became a business in its first decade, the photographic archives of business and industry have scarcely been mined, and the history of advertising photography, which has shaped the modern experience internationally, remains mostly unwritten.

Influential photographers have often led long lives traversing eras during which many changes took place. For example, Alfred Stieglitz (1864–1946) was born one year before the American Civil War ended, and he died one year after World War II. Having taught an introductory course, I realized that newcomers to the field appreciate an overview of individual careers such as that of Stieglitz, even if this requires occasionally disrupting the chronological order of the presentation. Hence I have included a number of Portrait boxes that concentrate the mind on certain influential photographers.

I have discovered in the classroom that today's students are puzzled by the lengthy struggle waged through the nineteenth and twentieth centuries to have photography accepted as an art form. I have narrated that contest, not simply as a large-scale attempt to achieve parity with painting, but as it relates to wider social issues, such as the ascent of a professional, moneyed

middle class and the rise of consumer culture.

At present, globalization encourages a convergence and blurring of photographic genres: photojournalists show their work in art galleries; artists create new magazines to foster social change; practitioners from developing countries depict indigenous motifs using digital tools. The computer, invented, as its name suggests, to facilitate computations, has instead spun a technology and a communications web that are actively investigated and refined by photographers from many fields. Along with my student-colleagues, I am intrigued by emerging technologies, and I have concluded this survey with a review of the digital tools as well as the emerging trends that are shaping the new millennium.

NEW TO THIS EDITION

The second edition incorporates more new and exciting research, such as the conclusions we can draw from the fact that Victorian photographer

1
GERARD MONICO,
Robert Doisneau, 1986.

Roger Fenton took not one but two photographs in the so-called "Valley of Death." It has also benefited from the continuing post-1989 opening up of Soviet archives. It offers new sections on the rise of constructed narratives and the impact of fashion photography during the late twentieth century.

The last chapter has been completely revised to account for developments during the early years of the third millennium, such as the escalation of vernacular photography through the agency of camera phones and photo-blogs. It discusses recent changes in feminist photography, current photography in the Arab world and in China, and considers the ways in which contemporary society envisions itself in relation to war and war imagery.

This edition also benefits from a completely revised timeline and expanded glossary and bibliography.

ACKNOWLEDGMENTS

For the second edition of this book, many people generously contributed their time and advice, including Geoff Batchen, Bissy Genova, Roy Flukinger, Frank Macomber, and Larry Schaaf. In addition, I owe a special debt to A. P. Balachandran for his continuing help in finding Indian photographers and locating information on the history of photography in India. Millagros Trelles, a Peruvian graduate student of my friend Dale Tussing, readily took on the task of updating my information on the Peruvian Truth Commission's photographic exhibitions. Like all of us interested in photographic history, I constantly relied on the George Eastman House Database, maintained by Andrew Eskind. As always, my spouse and live-in editor Michael Marien, provided good counsel and information faster than Google.

I also wish to thank the following reviewers who made useful comments for the development of the second edition: Peter B. Hales, University of Illinois at Chicago; James Housefield, Texas State University; Ellen Land-Weber, Humboldt State University; Greta Jennings Murphy, Northern Arizona University; Virginia Vanneman, Pensacola Junior College. Thanks also to Elizabeth Ferrer and Lia Strasser.

For the second edition, as for the first, the staff at Laurence King Publishing Ltd., made the task lighter. Lee Ripley Greenfield's enthusiasm for the project energized me; Kara Hattersley-Smith ably and patiently guided the planning phase; and Jessica Spencer's formidable tactical and scheduling skills steered the project home. I am in awe of Matthew Taylor's copy-editing, Emma's Brown's fortitude in finding images, and Ian Hunt's savvy design work. Thanks are also due to Jamie Ambrose for her work on the timeline and to Victoria Robinson for the index.

My greatest debt is to a legion of people whom I have never met, whose on-going research and writing on photography's history shaped the first edition, and refreshed the second. Without their research and insights, I could not have conceived the first edition, nor revised this one. I humbly dedicate this book to the international community of photographers, scholars, and critics whose efforts expand and perfect our field.

MARY WARNER MARIEN
Syracuse University
Syracuse, New York
February 2006

Introduction

One of photography's oldest dreams lay stranded on the floor (Fig. 2), snubbed by the museum crowd who refused to be taken in by it, and skirted by schoolchildren who guessed that it was a trick to lure them into trouble. The neatly stacked pile of images that sophisticates and students shunned was made up of identical photographs picturing rain-fattened clouds taken by Felix Gonzalez-Torres (1957–1996). The Cuban-born artist was indifferent to the orthodox purity of art media and eager to explore the poetics of the mundane. In the past, he had put photographs of an elegantly rumpled bed on public billboards, or

2
FELIX GONZALEZ-TORRES, *Untitled (Aparición)*, 1991. Offset print on paper.

invited gallery visitors to open and consume shinily wrapped candies that he had spilled onto thick carpets.

Had some of his cloud pictures found their way onto the waiting school bus, the watchful security staff were instructed to summon the curator, who would then replenish the stack. By giving away his work, Gonzalez-Torres mocked the belief that art should be precious or rare.

About a decade after photography was disclosed to the world in 1839, commentators began to ponder how to gather and distribute information cheaply or freely through camerawork. Ever since, the potential for the wide dissemination of photographs through photographic reproductions has thrilled and perplexed social pundits. Inexhaustibly free, a work of art and of science, ephemeral and permanent, neglected but controlled, Gonzalez-Torres's stacked images condensed an enduring wish for open access to the world of visual experience. The work also summarized what the photographer and critic Allan Sekula called the "goofy inconsistency" of assertions made about the medium.[1]

By 1850, photography was deeply at odds with itself. It was conjectured to be variously an art, a danger to art, a science, a revolutionary means of education, a mindless machine, and a threat to social order. For some, photography augured a modern, bloodless class revolution achievable through the democratic dissemination of knowledge hitherto available only to the well-to-do. Others envisioned a monstrous social degeneration in which the middle class, sated with visual fantasies of reality, would repudiate accepted values and become a breed of narcissistic, self-justifying voyeurs.

Advocates of photography's potential tended to ignore the ways in which the photograph was not an objective view but a series of choices. Yet then and now, a photographer makes many decisions in the process of creating an image, including deciding the distance from the subject, height of the camera, angle of vision, and presence or absence of background information. Will the photograph ultimately stand on its own, or will it find its place in a series of pictures? Should the image contain sharply delineated detail, or be blurred by the lens or by atmospheric conditions? How will tones of black and white, or hues of color, figure in the composition? Will artificial lighting be used instead of natural light, or along with natural light, to emphasize elements in the picture? Will the photograph be printed or will it exist as digital information, or both? Will the photograph be enhanced or altered by digital means or presented just as it appeared when looked at through the lens or on the viewing screen? These components are part of the visual considerations that the photographer bears in mind, and which viewers use to interpret a photographic image.

I believe we have to approach photography as both a visual language and a cluster of expectations and ideas. The far-reaching social dialogue about photography did not fluctuate at the same speed as technological invention. From the first, people responded to the *idea* of photography. For Lady Elizabeth Eastlake, writing in 1857, photography portended a proliferation of images that fed what she called the "craving or rather necessity for cheap, prompt, and correct facts," but which was antithetical to progress in the finer things, such as art.[2] Henry James's famous 1890 short story "The Real Thing" pointed out that mass media encouraged the general public's "perversity—an innate preference for the represented subject over the real one."[3] Writing on photography in 1927, the otherwise perceptive German critic Siegfried Kracauer lambasted "the blizzard of photographs," especially in the illustrated magazines and newspapers, calling it a "secretion of the capitalist mode of production" that swept away the dams of memory and annihilated meaning.[4]

Historian Daniel Boorstin warned in 1961 that we are threatened by a "new peculiarly American menace. It is not the menace of class war, of ideology, of poverty, of disease, of illiteracy, of demagoguery, or of tyranny, though these now plague most of the world. It is the menace of unreality."[5] The state of photography emerged as a central intellectual concern in the late 1970s and the 1980s, when the medium came to symbolize both the mass media and the experience of mediated reality.

Sounding the alarm, art critic Thomas Lawson ominously declared that "the camera, in all its manifestations, is our god, dispensing what we mistakenly take to be truth."[6]

In the early twentieth century, the piquant blend of psychology and desire that erupted in Surrealist art unexpectedly vaulted from the gallery to the illustrated newspaper, where momentary collisions of fact and symbol, subsequently called "grab shots," have dominated the place "above the fold" ever since. From the events of September 11, 2001 to the 2004 South Asia tsunami (Fig. 3), and 2005's hurricanes in the American South and earthquake in Pakistan and adjacent areas, we have come to recognize how an affecting symbolism can be wrung from family photographs arrayed as impromptu posters of the missing, memorials to those who were lost, and as declarations of patriotism. Straightaway, vernacular images were transformed into public media, and private symbols crystallized into social symbols of anxiety and hopefulness.

Our time is characterized by such mergers. Art, photojournalism, social documentary, and scientific imaging are converging, blurring traditional boundaries and energizing photographic practice. Photojournalists routinely show their work in art galleries, and artists launch magazines to circulate photographs that depict the modern world and encourage social change. Writing a round-up piece for *The New York Times* at the end of 2003, critic Roberta Smith exclaimed that "ours feels like the most promising moment since the 1980s, thanks to scores of young artists who are reducing to dust and reimagining the deeply entrenched polarities that dominated so much of 20th century art. Fluent in many mediums, they are erasing the distinctions between digital and hand-crafted, political and personal, theory and practice, spirit and flesh, sight and sound, subject and form."[7] When the critic John Berger wrote that "the relation between what we see and what we know is never settled,"[8] he pinpointed the underlying, unresolved energy that animates photography and keeps it engaging new audiences. Always fascinating, photography continues both to reflect and to shape our world.

3
BAZUKI MUHAMMAD,
Tsunami Survivor from Sweden Volunteers at the Hospital in Phuket, Thailand, January 4, 2005.

R. Schellenberg del. sc.

CHAPTER ONE

The Origins of Photography (to 1839)

**1.0
JOHANN KASPAR
LAVATER,** *Silhouette
Machine,* **c. 1780.
Engraving from
Lavater's** *Essays on
Physiognomy.*
**Gernsheim Collection.
Harry Ransom
Humanities Research
Center, University of
Texas at Austin.**

The Swiss scientist
J. K. Lavater was a major
proponent of the silhou-
ette form. The shadow
cast by sunlight or a
candle was traced on to
paper. The image was
filled in by hand, or used
by the artist as a tem-
plate to cut a silhouette
from black paper. The
silhouette's popularity
drew on the increasingly
widespread conception
that human character
could be read through
the study of facial
features.

Photography was presented to the world
on August 19, 1839, at a joint meeting of
the Academy of Science and the Academy
of Fine Arts in Paris. Claiming a sore
throat, Louis-Jacques-Mandé Daguerre
(1787–1851), the specified inventor, did
not make the initial presentation. He
left the demonstration and technical discussion to François Arago (1786–1853),
a scientist and member of the Chamber
of Deputies, the lower house of the
French government. For his accomplishment, Daguerre was awarded a lifelong
pension from the French government.
The only requirement placed upon him
was that he fully reveal his method,
which he did in his booklet *Historique et
description du procédé du Daguerréotype
et du Diorama* (*History and Description
of the Process of the Daguerreotype and the
Diorama*) (1839). The text was quickly
translated into many languages and
published around the world.

Tradition still casts Daguerre as the
originator of photography, a consensus
initiated by François Arago almost two
centuries ago. Yet the history of the
development of photography is a more
complicated tale, involving partial successes, missed opportunities, good fortune, and false starts. It centers on basic

questions about how the elements of
history, especially the history of technology, are reckoned and ordered. The
oft-repeated story of the presentation of
photography in 1839 says little about the
precursors of the medium, the specific
course of invention, the social environment in which the medium was conceived, or about others who contributed
to Daguerre's work or who formulated
different photographic processes.

The basic ingredients of photography—a light-tight box, lenses, and
light-sensitive substances—had been
known for hundreds of years before they
were combined. If the invention of
photography had depended solely on
the availability of materials, it could have
taken place during the late Renaissance.
Indeed, all but the light-sensitive material
was present in a technique for astronomical observation that used some European
cathedrals like cameras. Beginning in
the sixteenth century, the dark interiors of
churches such as Santa Maria del Fiore in
Florence, Italy, and Saint-Sulpice in Paris,
France, were punctuated with a small
hole in the roof, which worked like a lens
to focus an image of the sun on the floor
below, where its movements were measured and used to establish the modern

calendar. Ironically, these gauges verified Galileo's theory that the sun, not the earth, was the center of our universe, an idea repudiated by the Catholic Church.[1] With the cathedral serving as a camera, a light-sensitive material might have been found in silver. Silversmithing was an advanced art in the Renaissance, and the perception that silver darkens when exposed to light was an ancient commonplace. If someone ever tried placing a polished silver plate on the floor of the cathedral, however, to see whether it would register the sun's image, no record of that experiment has survived.

Before the end of the eighteenth century, imagining the photographic process seems to have been difficult. Unlike other transformational technologies, such as air travel and automobiles, photography was not foreseen in the centuries before it was invented. Looking back on what was widely perceived as the medium's abrupt appearance, American essayist and medical doctor Oliver Wendell Holmes (1809–1894) remarked that "in all the prophecies of dreaming enthusiasts, in all the random guesses of the future conquests over matter, we do not remember any prediction of such an inconceivable wonder. … No Century of Inventions includes this among its possibilities."[2] In utopian and speculative fiction written prior to 1800, only the 1760 novel *Giphantie*, by French writer Charles François Tiphaigne de la Roche (1723–1774), anticipated something like the detailed transcription of the observable world that would occur with photography. In *Giphantie*, a narrator visits the hollow of the earth's center, where a group of spirits creates highly illusionistic paintings. A canvas is smeared with a mysterious viscous material and placed before a desired scene. Like a mirror, it records every color and detail. After an hour's drying time in a dark place, the picture becomes permanent. Arguably, *Giphantie* anticipated the use of light-sensitive chemicals, but the story did not involve a light-tight box, lenses — or a human operator.

Although it seems that the invention of photography should be related to the start of the Industrial Revolution, its connection to the technical, social, and political changes that accompanied the initial mechanization of production during the late eighteenth and early nineteenth century in Europe is not easy to establish.

The desire for reliable visual reproductions has been linked to the needs of expanding commerce and industry, and the wish of the emerging middle class for realistic portraits. But around 1800, when the first documentable experiments attempted to record the visible world by means of light-sensitive materials, these trends were not clearly discernible to contemporaries. It is as if photography was invented twice: once during a period of largely concealed and scattered technological development, from the turn of the eighteenth century to 1839, and then again in the decades after disclosure, when it would be ceaselessly reinvented by the social uses to which it was put and the cultural dialogue surrounding it. A similar lag between invention and social use occurred with the fax machine, which had working prototypes in the 1920s, but which did not come into widespread use until the late twentieth century, when business and science demands for quick, global transmissions increased.

BEFORE PHOTOGRAPHY

Describing the late eighteenth century, historian Eric Hobsbawm persuasively depicted a world that was largely rural, in which there was no urban, mass culture pressing for realistic, multiple images.[3] Even in Britain, where industrialism was most advanced, the stream of reports, novels, and documents describing the Industrial Revolution did not appear until the 1830s and 1840s. In the early nineteenth century, the visual arts were dominated by Neoclassical idealism and Romantic expression. Naturalistic depiction of reality was occasionally pursued, for example, in the style of German landscape painting known as Biedermeier, or British watercolors such as those of John Sell Cotman (1782–1842), although this trend did not yet seem influential. While the British artist John Constable (1776–1837) struggled to render his observations of the changing light effects of sun and clouds in the rural landscape, his successful contemporary Joseph Mallord William Turner (1775–1851) produced fantastical medleys of color unfettered by mere depiction. Similarly, during the 1820s, French artist Eugène Delacroix (1798–1863) was fascinated with expressionistic color and theatrical lighting effects, and was less interested in realism. By the mid-1830s, when many painters became more concerned with the appearance of mundane reality, as in the work of the Barbizon School of artists such as Théodore Rousseau (1812–1867), photography had been invented by several people.

The invention of photography—or photographies, since several different image-making methods were created— did not depend directly on the impetus of a particular visual tradition, or even a demonstrable social need. Instead, the climate of congenial attitudes toward material progress, research, and innovation encouraged its conception. Around 1800, western European countries began to define government's role as fostering economic development through the expansion of industry and commerce. Social progress was understood to flow from the intellectual freedom of individuals seeking to solve scientific problems that would lead to practical applications. Those with the most to gain from this attitude toward change were the educated classes, as well as entrepreneurs, manufacturers, and enlightened landlords— people making up a growing middle class whose status was based on their achievements and earnings.[4]

The primary elements of the photographic process began to be linked and experimented with in an era when practical, commercially feasible applications of scientific experiments were encouraged by national policy and cultural values. Independent entrepreneurs and business people started to believe that

their investments in research might be rewarded. Much of the history of early experiments in photography shows cultural attitudes prompting resourceful individuals to resolve technical puzzles. Not every inventor sought financial gain and acclaim, but each of the originators whose stories we know believed in tinkering with devices and testing formulas. In 1839, when the medium was disclosed, the industrializing world was anxious to see how it might be applied to portraiture, record-keeping, political persuasion, academic investigation, and travel accounts. But around 1800, when scattered inventors began attempting to record optical reality by chemical and optical means, that cultural readiness for photography's later uses is not apparent.

TECHNOLOGICAL AND ARTISTIC FOREBEARS

Because our culture places great value on the imaginative art of the past, it is sometimes forgotten that one of the most common uses for visual depictions in the centuries before photography was to copy the observable world and to communicate visual information in an uninflected manner. Routine commissions for landscapes and portraits did not generally call for the artist's personal interpretation or stylistic flair. Similarly, engravers and etchers, who produced multiple images from drawings cut into a wooden or metal plate, were expected faithfully to copy historic monuments, machines and devices, animals and botanical specimens, and even works of art.

Contraptions to help artists produce images had existed for centuries. French

1.1
ABRAHAM BOSSE,
Engraving Depicting Artist at Work.

The subject of the portrait sits behind a screen composed of vertical and horizontal strings that form equal-sized squares. To assure that the likeness has the correct proportions for the sitter's face, the artist, who also has a similar screen on his drawing table, copies details into each square.

printmaker Abraham Bosse (1602–1676), who wrote and lectured on perspective, showed how artists could achieve greater fidelity by employing a screen with equally spaced squares (Fig. 1.1)[5]. This simple device was particularly useful in foreshortening—that is, contracting the image of an object or human figure so as to create the appearance of perspective. A variant of the technique, employing graph paper, is used today.

The PANTOGRAPH, familiar since the seventeenth century, and still available as a drafting tool and as a child's toy, helped artists copy, enlarge, or reduce drawings. French engraver Gilles-Louis Chrétien (1754–1811) adapted the pantograph to engraving in 1786, calling his invention the PHYSIONOTRACE (Fig. 1.2). The physionotrace mechanized a technique for making profiles (Fig. 1.3) that can be traced back to the time of Louis XIV (1638–1715; r. 1643–1715). Not only did the physionotrace permit users to make multiple copies, but it also allowed color to be applied.[6] SILHOUETTES, or shadow

1.2 (above)
ARTIST UNKNOWN, *Gilles-Louis Chrétien's Physionotrace.* **Drawing, c. 1786. Bibliothèque Nationale de France, Paris.**

Chrétien adapted the pantograph's tracing procedures to portraiture. In the upper section of the device, the artist viewed the sitter through an eyepiece, moving it to trace the profile. A stylus in the lower frame tracked the eyepiece movements exactly, registering them in ink on paper. The portrait was transferred to a copper plate, etched, and used to make multiple images.

1.3
ARTIST UNKNOWN, *Gilbert Motier, Marquis de La Fayette,* *1895;* (below image) *D'après le physionotrace de Quenedey.* **Aquatint, colored, after physionotrace drawing. Marquis de Lafayette Print Collection. David Bishop Skillman Library. Lafayette College Library, Easton, Pennsylvania.**

Gilbert Motier Marquis de
LA FAYETTE.

1.4
ARTIST UNKNOWN,
Bernie (Silhouette portrait), 1790s. Ink on paper mounted on 5 1/3 x 4 1/8 in. (13.5 x 10.6 cm) paper. Hans P. Kraus, Jr. Collection, New York.

portraits, were part entertainment and part artistic venture. Silhouette makers primarily served the bourgeoisie, but they also sold profile portraits on the streets and at parties. Some dextrously cut dark paper while observing a subject standing in profile; others used a candle to project the outline of a subject's head on to a sheet of paper (Figs. 1.0, 1.4).

The public acceptance of the silhouette, usually a single image, and the physionotrace, which produced multiple, engraved images, accompanied the growth of the middle classes in eighteenth-century Europe, and their taste for likenesses rendered without the idealization and ornament flaunted in aristocratic portraits. A seemingly neutral descriptive approach to portraits in all media began to distinguish middle-class likenesses from those created for the upper classes. In addition to being quicker to produce than a painting, and certainly less expensive, the silhouette and the physionotrace responded to the middle-class view of itself as a distinct social group. Such portraits exemplified a sense of individualism and accomplishment among professionals and business people, expressed not simply through the ownership of portraits but also through a preference for likenesses that accentuated such personal features as the shape of the nose and the slant of the forehead. Treatises on physiognomy, the study of physical features as a means

to deduce human character, appealed to a middle class seeking new ways, beyond pedigree, to understand temperament and personal achievement. As they evolved, mechanical aids to drawing became more exact, emphasizing outlines and contours rather than shading, or atmospheric effects, or personal interpretation. A similar idea of a neutral representation found favor in the sciences, especially biology, botany, and geology, which sought methods to convey visual data objectively.

The drawing aid with the most direct effect on photography was the CAMERA OBSCURA, literally, a "dark room." Actually, the camera obscura was originally a darkened, room-size chamber, in which a tiny opening in one wall acted like a lens, focusing an upside-down image of the scene outside on to the opposite wall. Over time, the room-sized chamber was made smaller and portable (Fig. 1.5). It was equipped with lenses, and constructed with an internal mirror so that the upside-down image was righted and could be traced on a piece of paper placed on a translucent glass plate installed in the top of the device. Like other machines to aid drawing, the camera obscura did not encourage imagination or personal style, and usually produced stiff, formal images (Fig. 1.6). It could help artists to trace the outlines of shapes, but it obviously could not copy the religious, historical, or mythological

1.5
GEORG BRANDER,
Table Camera Obscura, 1769. Engraving. Gernsheim Collection. Harry Ransom Humanities Research Center, University of Texas at Austin.

Light rays bearing a likeness of the Greek figure holding a harp enter the camera obscura (shown in the lower half of this engraving) through the lens, bounce off a mirror (rendered in fig. 2 as a slanted line), and are reflected onto a piece of translucent glass onto which a man has placed a thin paper sheet. He can see the reflection well enough to trace it. (At the top of this engraving is shown a fold-out camera.)

1.6 (above)
THOMAS SANDBY,
Windsor from the
Goswells, 1770. Camera
obscura drawing.
The Royal Collection.
© 2002 Her Majesty
Queen Elizabeth II.

English artist Thomas
Sandby (1721–1798)
used a camera obscura
to create this view on
four pieces of paper
overlapped to present a
wide panorama. In
his expert hands, the
strength of the device is
apparent, especially in
the proper perspective
accorded the concen-
trated buildings in
the distance. Since the
camera obscura involves
tracing an image, it is
inadequate in rendering
atmospheric effects
such as cloudiness.

1.7 (right)
CORNELIUS VARLEY,
Artist Sketching with a
Wollaston Camera
Lucida, 1830. Engraving.
Gernsheim Collection.
Harry Ransom Humani-
ties Research Center,
University of Texas
at Austin.

The British watercolor
artist Cornelius Varley
(1781–1873) not only
used the camera lucida,
but also came up with
his own improvement
in 1811, called Varley's
Graphic Telescope. This
employed a cylindrical
telescope to create the
illusion that the image
of a scene existed on a
sheet of drawing paper.

scenes that were central to art production
until the nineteenth century.

An even more transportable and
lightweight aid to drawing was patented
in 1806 by British scientist William
Hyde Wollaston (1766–1828). Simple, if
somewhat awkward to use, the CAMERA
LUCIDA, or light room, consisted of a
rod to which was affixed a glass prism
having two silvered sides that reflected
the scene at which it was aimed. A
person wishing to draw a scene would
attach the camera lucida to a drawing
table and adjust the prism so as to
reflect an image directly into the eye.
Looking down, the user then moved the
prism slightly to create the illusion of
the scene existing on the drawing paper.
The would-be artist could then trace
the outlines of the scene directly on to
the drawing paper, while looking up
occasionally to check the actual scene.
The camera lucida was useful to travelers who wanted to record topographic
or architectural views (Figs. 1.7, 1.8).

There were, in sum, two general
categories of drawing aids. The first,
such as the camera lucida, helped artists
produce a single image. The second,
such as the physionotrace, yielded multiple copies. The development of these
devices in the years prior to photography
indicates different needs, not a concerted social demand. For example,
landscape artists used drawing devices
to make a visual record as part of the
preparation for a painting. Travelers
employed these tools to render mementos of a scene. In either case, the user
did not ordinarily intend to make multiple copies of the image, like copy-artists,
engravers, and printers. Similarly, when
photography was invented by a number
of individuals, some created systems
that produced unique single images,
and others fashioned techniques that
could make multiple copies.

Drawn by C. Varley for G. Dolland, with the Camera Lucida.

THE INVENTION OF
"PHOTOGRAPHIES"

The history of the first photographs
has been made to fit into the widely
accepted notion that invention is regular
and progressive, with each experiment
building in an orderly, successful
way on the achievements of the past.
However, none of photography's pioneers reported making headway in that
fashion. Even limiting the standard history of the medium's inception to a few
celebrated European efforts in the late
eighteenth and early nineteenth centuries, so as then to imply a link to the
Industrial Revolution, has not produced

Villa Melzi

5th Oct.r 1833

a neat chronology of inventions. The camera has been seen as an image-making machine, swiftly spewing out pictures just as mechanized looms produced cloth for a new market. But the swift camera started to take shape only after 1855, through the combined effect of technological changes, the development of networks for the production and consumption of images, and the emergence of a mass market public. The first photographs were much closer to pre-industrial craft production, in which single, unique objects were made by hand.

ANTOINE FLORENCE AND THE QUESTION OF SIMULTANEOUS INVENTION

French artist and cartographer Antoine Hércules Romuald Florence (1804–1879) traveled through the interior of Brazil with German naturalist Baron Georg von Lansdorff (1774–1852) to record the area's peoples and natural settings. After the 1824–29 expedition he settled in a remote part of the province of São Paulo, where he painted views and portraits. In 1830, while

trying to publish a book on animal sounds, he became frustrated by the lack of nearby printing shops, and invented his own printing technique, which he called *poligraphie*, meaning "multiple writing." Soon after, Florence conceived photography after noticing that certain fabrics faded when exposed to light. According to Boris Kossoy, Florence was successful because he was removed from centers of scientific learning, and had to think unconventionally.[7] With the aid of the local druggist, Florence experimented with the camera obscura to see if he could make its images permanent. Unsuccessful, he investigated the print-making potential of glass plates that were covered with a dark mixture of gum arabic and soot. Like an engraver, he scratched designs into the plates, and then placed them on paper that had been made light-sensitive through a treatment with silver chloride, which darkens in the presence of light. The paper's light-sensitivity could be halted by the application of an ammonia solution, which stopped the darkening action.

Florence's diaries show precise drawings of small cameras and of printing frames that used sunlight to print an image. In 1832, he began using the term *photographie* for his process, deriving it from the Greek words for light and writing.[8] He used his photographic technique to produce diplomas, tags, and labels, but appears not to have fared well in reproducing camera images. When Daguerre's photography was announced in 1839, Florence realized that his humble efforts could not compete, and he directed his energies toward other aspects of the printing business.[9] Writing to newspapers in São Paulo and Rio de Janeiro, he modestly declared that he would not "dispute anyone's discovery … because two people can have the same idea."[10]

The notion of simultaneous invention—that two or more people can develop the same concept at about the same time—was mentioned by Florence and by another of photography's pioneers, William Henry Fox Talbot (1800–1877), whose experiments are discussed later in the chapter.[11] Simultaneous invention makes it difficult to construct a linear chronology of photography and suggests, moreover, that there may have been other successful yet unknown attempts to invent photography. If Florence, living in a remote area, could originate a way to reproduce labels using a light-sensitive silver compound, others elsewhere in the world may have had similar partial success. It is probable that, while the work of individuals such as Florence will become better known, the precise history of photography's invention will never be fully ascertained.

THE PROBLEM OF PERMANENCE: WEDGWOOD AND DAVY

Many histories of photography trace the development of European photography through the research of Thomas Wedgwood (1771–1805) and Humphry Davy (1778–1829), both of whom—unlike Florence—were in touch with up-to-date scientific inquiry. Wedgwood, son of Josiah Wedgwood (1730–1795), the British amateur scientist and pottery manufacturer who helped popularize Neoclassicism with his designs, attended meetings of the Lunar Society, a distinguished group that included physician–scientist Erasmus Darwin (1731–1802), inventor James Watt

(1736–1819), and the political theorist and scientist Joseph Priestley (1733–1804). The group kept abreast of scientific discoveries in Europe and America, and deliberately sought practical applications for new findings. Thomas Wedgwood's special interest was the new, or French, chemistry developed by Antoine-Laurent Lavoisier (1743–1794), who mandated repeated testing of hypotheses in the laboratory, a practice he helped to establish as the standard for the field. The new chemists were animated by the sense that they were discovering the world afresh.

An enthusiasm for science, especially the new chemistry, prompted Wedgwood and his friend Davy, then a humble apothecary's apprentice, to experiment with light-sensitive materials. They sought to fix the image of an object's shadow cast on paper or leather that had been made light-sensitive by immersion in a silver nitrate solution, and they also attempted to capture images formed in a camera obscura. In addition, they tried to copy paintings on glass, by letting light pass through the glass on to light-sensitive paper. Unknown to them, silver nitrate was not sufficiently light-sensitive to hold the image projected inside the camera obscura. The more direct approach, shadow images of objects and paintings on glass, did leave a photographic imprint, although it was not permanent, since the silver nitrate continued to react to light until the surface darkened. In his 1802 report on their work, Davy announced that "nothing but a method of preventing the unshaded part of the delineation from being coloured by exposure to the day is wanting, to render the process as useful as it is elegant."[12] Wedgwood was prevented by illness from taking part in further joint experiments, and Davy moved on in other scientific directions, eventually becoming the president of the Royal Society.

Although Wedgwood and Davy's experiments in fixing a light-induced image were less successful than the later efforts of Florence, their publication in the influential *Journals of the Royal Institution of Great Britain* (1802) meant that they could be consulted by scientists and later historians of photography (Florence's contribution was not recognized until 1970). Even so, their work did not become a stepping stone for subsequent successful attempts to stabilize an image through photochemical reactions. In that sense, it was as isolated as that of Florence in Brazil.

THE "SUN WRITING" OF NIÉPCE

Another precursor of photography was the "sun writing" developed in France by Joseph Nicéphore Niépce (1765–1833). Born to a family of people who had worked for French royalty, Niépce received a fine education, and he came of age with high expectations. The French Revolution, which began in 1789, altered his prospects, and, from the seclusion of a country estate, he sought ways of making a living. With his brother Claude, he spent years perfecting an internal combustion engine intended to power riverboats. Dubbed the *pyréolophore*, this engine was intended to rival the new onboard steam engine, by burning vegetable oil or other similar substances; it received a French patent in 1807. Like many would-be entrepreneurs who saw the development of new machines and processes as the source of prosperity, Niépce turned his attention to the potential of the lithographic process.

LITHOGRAPHY, a technique for reproducing images, uses drawings on a flat surface, usually a smooth stone (ancient Greek: *lithos*), rather than a metal or wood recessed surface, as in engraving and etching. It was perfected in 1798 by the German actor and writer Alois Senefelder (1771–1834). For communicating information, the lithograph had several advantages. It could yield quite a large number of prints, and it could render tones and shadows more subtly than etching and engraving, which got their effects of light and dark from the closeness of individual lines scratched into the surface of the plate. Lithography appealed to painters, who could work directly on the lithographic stone without having laboriously to cut lines into the surface. But it also intrigued early nineteenth-century entrepreneurs, who saw in lithography a process that could surpass existing methods for illustration. In the early 1800s, lithography aroused the kind of get-rich-quick excitement generated in small computer and software companies in the late twentieth century.

Lacking the ability to draw on the lithographic stone, Niépce began to experiment with ways to produce an image through the action of light upon photosensitive materials. His early efforts, begun in 1816, involved the use of paper made light-sensitive by the application of a silver chloride solution. After exposing the photosensitive paper in a camera obscura, he experienced some of the very same problems as Wedgwood and Davy. The image was too indistinct, and the action of the light could not be thoroughly stopped. Moreover, the tones of the image were reversed: dark became light, and light became dark, to create what was later known as a NEGATIVE. Niépce tried, without success, to use the negative as it is used today, that is, printing it to create a POSITIVE image, in which the tones are re-reversed and thereby corrected. He also failed to alter the reversed dark and light areas through chemical means.

Undaunted, Niépce continued to try out various light-sensitive materials. He does not seem to have known about the experiments of Wedgwood and Davy; nor, like them, did he encounter many past investigations of such materials. An obscure 1727 paper on the effects of light on silver nitrate by German scientist Johann Heinrich Schulze (1687–1744) might have been difficult to locate, but experiments with light-sensitive materials conducted by Swedish chemist Carl Wilhelm Scheele (1742–1786), published in 1777, and the work of Swiss librarian and botanist Jean Senebier (1742–1809), published in 1782, would have been available to a researcher living in an academic and intellectual capital such as early nineteenth-century Paris. The discovery by British scientist John Herschel (1792–1871), published in 1819, that hyposulphite of soda dissolved silver chloride, thereby stopping its reaction to light, also seems to have been unknown to Niépce, although he did receive advice about photosensitive materials from French chemist Louis-Nicolas Vauquelin (1763–1829). Niépce's approach to photography was thus largely independent of the research of others.[13]

Beginning in 1822, Niépce shifted his interests to copying engravings by means of the action of light. To do so, he saturated an engraving with oil to make it more transparent. He then placed it on a pewter plate that had been coated with bitumen of Judea, a substance known to harden when exposed to light. After light exposure, the areas beneath dark parts of the engraving, the lines, remained soft, while those beneath the light parts of the engraving, the spaces between the lines, hardened. The plate was rinsed with lavender oil, washing away the soft areas. What remained was an engraving plate, whose grooved areas Niépce had further etched with acid, and then printed (Fig. 1.9).

Finding this procedure more encouraging than his experiment with silver chloride, Niépce put a similarly prepared plate in a camera obscura and exposed it in a window at his estate, Le Gras, near Chalon-sur-Saône. After about eight hours, he removed the plate and washed it with a mixture of oil of lavender and petroleum oil, and rinsed away those soluble areas of the plate

1.9
JOSEPH NICÉPHORE NIÉPCE, *Cardinal d'Amboise***, 1826. Heliograph on pewter plate (reproduction of an engraving). Musée Nicéphore Niépce, Chalon-sur-Saône, France.**

A seventeenth-century image of Cardinal d'Amboise was one of the most popular and commercially successful engravings in France. Niépce copied the image onto a pewter plate by photographic means as an experiment to show that the process would make it possible to print multiple copies, although he never seems to have done so.

1.10
JOSEPH NICÉPHORE NIÉPCE, *View from the Window at Gras*, c. 1826. Heliograph. Gernsheim Collection. Harry Ransom Humanities Research Center, University of Texas at Austin.

Rediscovered in 1952 by photographic historians Alison Gernsheim and Helmut Gernsheim, the image still obscurely shows—on the left—an upper story of the Niépce residence that served as a pigeon house and, in the center, a slanted roof of a barn. Because the picture was exposed for about eight hours while the sun changed position, sunlight appears to be shining on the roof and on both ends of the buildings. Experiments conducted in 2002 confirmed Niépce's technique.

where the bitumen of Judea had received less light. The resulting plate contained a poor but visible negative of the scene outside the window where the camera obscura had been placed. The image itself was reversed laterally—that is, left to right. Niépce then took the plate and exposed it to iodine fumes. The iodine did not fully reverse the tones, but it created greater contrasts.[14] In effect, Niépce made what is now called a DIRECT POSITIVE image, one that, as the name implies, produces a photograph without a separate negative. Because there was no negative from which to print copies, the image could not be reproduced. Though not completely stable, Niépce's *View from the Window at Gras* (c. 1826) is considered to be the world's first permanent photograph (Fig. 1.10).

In 1827, Niépce brought examples of his process, called heliography, from the Greek words for sun and writing, to London, where he was visiting his brother Claude, who still hoped to get financial backing for the combustion engine to power riverboats. Claude's ill-health and the increasing financial strains on the family prompted Niépce to seek funding for his photographic process. He managed to get the attention and support of Francis Bauer (1758–1840), a Fellow of the Royal Society, for whom he prepared a short "Notice sur l'héliographie" ("Notice on Heliography") (December 8, 1827), describing the process in general terms. His failure to generate interest in the process may have been due to Niépce's cautious concealment of his exact technique. Before returning to France in February 1828, Niépce left many heliographs of engravings and the *View from the Window at Gras* with Francis Bauer.

THE COLLABORATION OF NIÉPCE AND DAGUERRE

While traveling through Paris on his journey to Britain, Niépce met with Daguerre, at that time known as a painter, designer of stage sets, and co-proprietor of the Diorama, a distinctive kind of theater that presented realistic special effects to thrill audiences (Fig. 1.11). To plan his stage illusions, especially the impression of deeply recessed theatrical space, Daguerre employed the camera obscura. He also made some ineffectual attempts to capture photochemically the images produced by the camera obscura.

Daguerre and Niépce were introduced by Charles Chevalier (1804–1859), a Parisian maker of optical instruments and devices such as the camera obscura, with whom both men did business. After his disappointing trip to England, coupled with the death of his brother Claude in February 1828, Niépce redoubled his efforts to find a photochemical method to obtain permanent camera obscura images. He moved from using pewter plates to highly polished silver plates, and to copper plates covered with silver. He continued to use bitumen of Judea, which yielded better picture quality when employed on a silver backing.

Niépce had decided to work with Daguerre to improve the photographic process, even though, as the photographic historians Alison and Helmut Gernsheim concluded, Daguerre could not produce a successful photograph to show Niépce. In a contract signed by

both on December 14, 1829, Daguerre promised to give Niépce an improved camera obscura, and Niépce agreed to show Daguerre the means by which he was able to capture camera obscura images, which he did at his estate. Daguerre later admitted that the camera obscura he gave to Niépce was ineffective in producing clearer images. When Niépce died suddenly in 1833, Daguerre took up his research.

DAGUERRE AND THE LATENT IMAGE

Daguerre's personal circumstances were very different from Niépce's. Born into a petit-bourgeois family, he lacked much formal education. Nevertheless, his outgoing personality and drive to succeed contrasted with Niépce's docile yet mistrustful attitude toward others. Daguerre was poised to take advantage of social forces in the 1830s. In France, the hold of upper-class landowning interests remained strong, but was challenged by the growing power of middle-class commercial and industrial development. Business people, bureaucrats, and managers were part of an emerging elite based not on birth but on intelligence and hard work. Daguerre's humble beginnings and rise to prominence as

1.11
LOUIS-JACQUES-MANDÉ DAGUERRE, *Landscape with Gothic Ruins and Figures,* **1821. Brown ink and wash drawing. George Eastman House, Rochester, New York.**

Daguerre's watercolor of the mists and shadows in a ruined Gothic church gives a sense of the dramatic style of the Diorama's entertainment. Through carefully planned shifting lighting, transparent paintings on thin fabric, and sound effects, audiences were given the impression of being in a ruin, on an alpine hill, or near a waterfall.

In what may be the oldest surviving daguerreotype, Daguerre carefully arranged plaster casts, a wicker-wrapped bottle, and a framed print to show the remarkable ability of the new medium. Ranging from black to white, with many tones in between, the daguerreotype also demonstrated the ability to render different surface textures clearly.

a co-owner of the Diorama in Paris and, subsequently, in London made him something of a class hero.

By 1835, Daguerre's experiments with Niépce's materials—silver plates, silver-plated copper plates, and iodine—led to his concentrating on the creation of a LATENT IMAGE, that is, an image that had been registered on the silver surface of a plate, but which was not yet visible. Like Niépce, who treated *View from the Window* with iodine fumes, Daguerre realized that treatments after exposure could bring out the image more effectively. Where Niépce started with a visible image, and intensified the tones using iodine fumes to give the picture greater contrast, Daguerre found that there was a latent image on the exposed silver plate, which could be treated with mercury fumes, further developing the picture, and making it visible. Soon after, in 1837, he discovered that a solution of common table salt dissolved in hot water would stop the light-sensitive material from continuing to react (Fig. 1.12).

In the end, Daguerre's photographic process was so simple that he, like Niépce before him, began to worry about someone stealing it, and robbing

him of both his place in history and his long-sought financial reward. To make a DAGUERREOTYPE, a copper sheet plated with silver was given a high polish. The plate, as it was called, was placed with the silver side down over a closed box containing iodine. The iodine fumes fused with the silver to create silver iodide, which is light-sensitive. The plate was then fitted into a camera obscura adapted for it and exposed to light. Exposure times varied, but the earliest daguerreotypes took about four to five minutes (Fig. 1.13), according to one of the reports sent to the French Chamber of Deputies. The plate, with its latent image, was then put in a special box and exposed to mercury fumes, which blended with the silver to produce a visible image. The still light-reactive image was thoroughly washed with a sodium chloride (table salt) solution, which stopped the response to light, and then carefully rinsed with plain water.

With his success, Daguerre renegotiated the contract he had made with Niépce, which was held by Niépce's son Isidore (1805–1868). In 1837, Daguerre demanded and received the right to call himself the inventor of the process, and to have the process bear his name.

1.13
LOUIS-JACQUES-MANDÉ DAGUERRE,
View of the Boulevard du Temple, c. 1839.
Daguerreotype.
Bayerisches Nationalmuseum, Munich, Germany.

Early daguerreotypes made city streets seem deserted, because carriages and pedestrians moved too quickly to be registered on the daguerreotype plate. The man on the corner with his foot raised has probably stopped to spend some time having his shoes polished; hence his image and that of the bootblack were recorded.

Isidore Niépce secured his father's legacy by getting Daguerre to agree that accounts of both photographic processes would be published together. Additionally, Daguerre and Isidore Niépce arranged to market the processes by subscription—that is, by selling shares to the public. However, an initial attempt in 1838 to convince the public to buy shares in the new business failed. Paradoxically, Daguerre's reputation for creating optical illusions at the Diorama seems to have made the public suspicious of his methods. For a second attempt in late 1838, Daguerre prepared a broadsheet describing his research and that of Niépce. He subtly promoted his own process, while paying sentimental, faintly belittling attention to Niépce's early efforts. The broadsheet boasted that the daguerreotype required only three to thirty minutes' outdoor exposure to light, and speculated on future uses. Daguerre considered that the daguerreotype would be used by the "leisured class," making renderings of country houses, and providing the means to "form collections of all kinds."

"The little work it entails," he concluded, "will greatly please ladies."[15]

At about the same time, Daguerre attempted to persuade prominent scientists and artists to endorse his photographic process. When the astronomer and politician François Arago saw the daguerreotype, he soon set about securing French government assistance for the process. Government support for science and invention was an important feature of French intellectual life.[16] With the sponsorship of a member of the French Academy of Science, and the approval of the Academy, a French citizen could approach the relevant government department for funds. Arago, a liberal and progressive member of the Chamber of Deputies, had already sponsored bills for the development of the railroad and the telegraph. While he may have seen in Daguerre's process a counterpart of his own attempts to measure the intensity of light, he also recognized that the ingredients of the daguerreotype process were sufficiently simple and easily available that the procedure could be quickly copied.

Since copyright would not readily secure rights to the process, Arago cleverly suggested that the government provide Daguerre and Isidore Niépce with pensions, and that the new process be magnanimously given to the world by France.

On January 7, 1839, Arago made a statement to the French Academy of Science describing the process in the most general terms, and emphasizing the originality of Daguerre's invention. The day before, H. Gaucheraud, a journalist writing for the *Gazette de France*, previewed the new process, suggesting that the fine detail of the daguerreotype would not substantially challenge drawing and painting, because the appearance of the daguerreotype was much closer to the look of engravings and of mezzotints, a printing process able to produce a greater range of tones than etchings and engravings.[17]

RESPONSES TO THE ANNOUNCEMENT OF THE DAGUERREOTYPE

News of Daguerre's invention was quickly broadcast, and caught the attention of those who recalled related experiments and those who were working on similar photographic processes. Francis Bauer, to whom Niépce had given some heliographs, quickly organized a British exhibit of these works, in an effort to publicize his acquaintance's earlier accomplishments. In a March 1839 paper on photography, John Herschel recalled that a book by Elizabeth Fulhame, *View to a New Art of Dying* [sic] *and Painting* (1794), proposed capturing and retaining images on cloth through the interaction of light and certain metals.[18] The historian of photography Pierre G. Harmant has revealed that, from 1839 on, twenty-four persons claimed to have invented photography.[19] Among them was Hippolyte Bayard (1801–1887), who attempted to deduce Daguerre's process before the specific information was released to the public.

BAYARD'S DIRECT POSITIVE PROCESS

Bayard, a minor official in the French Ministry of Finance with no scientific training, responded to the 1839 announcement of Daguerre's method by making photographic experiments. He aimed at making a direct positive print, such as that produced by Niépce and Daguerre, but one that he and others considered to be a simpler and more elegant process than theirs. Bayard completely darkened light-sensitive paper that had been soaked in sodium chloride by exposing it to light. He then took the blackened paper and soaked it again, this time in a solution of potassium iodide. When this paper was placed in a camera obscura and exposed, the light bleached the paper according to its intensity. Like the daguerreotype, Bayard's unnamed process produced a single, unique print that could not be used as a negative to make multiple copies.

Hoping to share Daguerre's success, Bayard showed his images to Arago, who was disconcerted by the prospect of another inventor. Doubtless aware of such famous challenges to discovery as the struggle between British scientist Joseph Priestley and French scientist A.-L. Lavoisier for the discovery of oxygen, Arago secured some small funds to enable Bayard to continue his experiments, but asked him not to announce his findings. Although Bayard exhibited about thirty of his direct positive prints on July 14, 1839, lack of official recognition prevented him from achieving Daguerre's celebrity. Using his direct positive process, Bayard created a comic yet critical response to his nation's neglect of his work. In an image he titled *Self-Portrait as a Drowned Man*, Bayard photographed himself feigning death by suicide (Fig. 1.14). Although Bayard's melodramatic pretense did not earn him the honor he desired, he did not drown himself, but went on to make further photographs, some of which, like his *Self-Portrait*, teased the viewer into thinking about what could be represented in photography, and what could not (see p. 33; Fig. 2.10).

HERSCHEL'S "PHOTOGRAPHIC SPECIMENS"

In Britain, meanwhile, John Herschel, like many scientists, became intrigued with the recent announcement of the daguerreotype, even though the precise formula and materials had not been divulged. Two decades before, in 1819,

1.14
HIPPOLYTE BAYARD,
Self-Portrait as a Drowned Man, 1840.
Direct paper positive.
Société Française de Photographie, Paris.

Playing on the Romantic notion of the misunderstood artist who commits suicide, Bayard penned a note on the back of this photograph, suggesting that he ended his life in penniless despair. Noting the darkness of his hands and face, Bayard added that these indicated decomposition, since no one even came to the morgue to claim his body![20]

Herschel had explored the properties of a chemical called hyposulphite of soda, discovering that it would dissolve silver salts. "HYPO" (now the term for sodium thiosulfate), used today in the development process of black-and-white photography, got its nickname from Herschel's nineteenth-century work. Another of Herschel's early photographic experiments was his 1831 exploration of the light reactions of platinum salts.

A few weeks after Daguerre's announcement, Herschel began to try his luck with photography. In his notebook for January 29, 1839, he wrote: "Expts [experiments] tried within the last few days since hearing of Daguerre's *secret* & that Fox Talbot has also got something of same kind."[21] On the very next day, with no understanding of Daguerre's process, but a wealth of knowledge about light-sensitive chemicals and lenses, Herschel succeeded in fixing a camera image and conceived of making prints from a negative image. On February 7, 1839, he showed some of his images at the Royal Society. Writing to his friend and colleague Talbot a few days later, he referred to his "photographic specimens" (Fig. 1.15), thus coining the word "photographic", which quickly evolved into "photography," the general term for the medium. (The term *photographie* employed by Florence may have been used earlier, but his work was unknown in Europe.)

Herschel's photographic investigations continued into the 1840s. He experimented with the possibilities of color photography, using vegetable dyes; he also used iron salts to create a process he dubbed CYANOTYPE, which produced an image in which the dominant tones were deep Prussian blue and white (Fig. 1.16). Herschel was one of the first to voice the democratic potential

The results of early photographic experiments were often faint. Few of these indistinct images have survived. One of Herschel's earliest images, this silver-based photograph depicts through a window the telescope used by his famous father, the astronomer William Herschel.

of photography: of the cyanotype he wrote that every person might be a printer and a publisher.[22] While it never became a major form of photography, the simplicity and low cost of the cyanotype made it a commercial success in the 1840s, and a favorite at the end of the nineteenth century for amateurs and scientists working in the field. Until the advent of digital image processing, it was widely used to produce blueprints for architects and builders.

TALBOT'S PHOTOGENIC DRAWING

"Change rules supreme in the affairs of men," reflected Herschel's friend and scientific colleague Talbot, upon hearing about the daguerreotype. Talbot had conceived fixing light-induced images as early as 1833, and had also had some modest success the following year, well before Daguerre achieved provable results. Musing intently, Talbot reflected on the quirk of fate by which, "after having devoted much labour and attention to the perfecting of this invention, and having now brought it, as I think, to a

point in which it deserved the notice of the scientific world, — that exactly at the moment that I was then engaged in drawing up an account of it, to be presented to the Royal Society, the same invention should be announced in France."[23] As historian Gail Buckland observed, "Talbot was staggered."[24] He had no way of knowing whether his method was the same as that developed by Daguerre, but he sensed the prospect of losing his claim to be the first to capture a camera image.

Talbot, a multi-talented British scientist, classical scholar, and linguist, was educated at Cambridge University and lived at the family estate of Lacock Abbey. He dated his photographic efforts to 1833, when he got disappointing results using a camera lucida as an aid to drawing scenes near Lake Como in Italy. "After various fruitless attempts I laid aside the instrument and came to the conclusion that its use required a previous knowledge of drawing which unfortunately I did not possess," he recalled. "I then thought of trying again

1.16 (above)
JOHN HERSCHEL. *Untitled,* 1842. Cyanotype. Harry Ransom Humanities Research Center.

Herschel copied an engraving of a fashionable nineteenth-scene, in which a figure, often a woman, clasps a book whose contents seem to have prompted languid daydreaming.

a method which I had tried many years before," he continued: "This method was, to take a *camera obscura* and to throw the image of the objects on a piece of paper in its focus—fairy pictures, creations of a movement, and destined as rapidly to fade away. It was during these thoughts that the idea occurred to me—how charming it would be if it were possible to cause these natural images to imprint themselves durably, and remain fixed upon the paper."[25]

By 1834, Talbot had experimented with two methods of fixing a photochemically induced image. The least-known was similar to that concocted by Florence. While staying in Geneva, Switzerland, Talbot prepared glass plates by darkening them with candle smoke, and varnishing the surface so that the soot would stay in place. He then drew or wrote on the plates with a tool that cut through the black coating, and placed them over paper that had been made light-sensitive. When exposed to light, the lines of drawing or writing were transferred to the paper. He suggested that the technique could be used by friends to share letters and images.[26]

In addition, Talbot formulated a method of sensitizing paper similar to the procedure of Wedgwood and Davy, although he later claimed not to have read their published results from 1802. Aware of the light-sensitivity of silver compounds, Talbot discovered that the strength of a solution of ordinary table salt (sodium chloride) in water was key to making images and then stopping the action of light. He first soaked paper in a weak solution, and allowed it to dry. He then applied a solution of silver nitrate, which reacted with the sodium chloride to form light-sensitive silver chloride. He did not put the sensitized paper in a camera obscura, but placed an object to be copied, such as a leaf, lace, or fern frond directly on the paper, sometimes flattened it down with a piece of glass to make greater contact with the paper, and then exposed the sandwiched object to light. When the object was removed, a pale rendering of its shape remained on the paper. Depending on the strength of the sunlight to which it was exposed, from ten minutes to thirty minutes were necessary to make a print. The area surrounding the image darkened due to exposure to light.

After the object was removed from the paper, Talbot had to prevent the light area from darkening in response to further exposure. He tried various chemicals to inhibit the continuing action of light upon the paper, among them potassium iodide, and a strong solution of table salt. Because of the use of table salt, both in sensitizing the paper and in fixing its image, the process would eventually be called a SALT PRINT. Talbot referred to his work as "PHOTOGENIC DRAWING"—that is, light-caused drawing—or "sciagraphy"—that is, shadow writing (Fig. 1.17). Prints such as these are still made today, and they are often called shadowgraphs or photograms.

Although he jotted a reminder message in his notebook for May 1834, telling himself to "Patent Photogenic Drawing," Talbot did not do so.[27] Since each sheet of paper used in his technique had to be processed separately, the results were uneven and labor-intensive. Perhaps Talbot was waiting until he could perfect the reliability and consistency of photogenic drawing. He continued to experiment, and in 1835, he managed to make a picture after exposing sensitized paper in a small camera (Fig. 1.18). In February of that year, Talbot noted that his photogenic drawings might be used to yield what he called a second drawing. In other words, he conceived of the photogenic drawing not simply as an end in itself, but also as a negative from which positive prints might be made, although he did not actually use the term or print from one of his early photogenic drawings.

1.17
WILLIAM HENRY FOX TALBOT, *Leaf with Serrated Edge,* **c. 1839. Photogenic drawing negative. National Museum of Photography, Film and Television, Bradford, England.**

In Talbot's photogenic drawing process, a negative image was produced. The leaf was placed on light-sensitized paper and exposed to the sun. Where the light could reach it directly, the paper turned dark. Where the leaf hindered light from exposing the paper, a pale silhouette, complete with well-rendered veins, was left on the paper. The technique became the basis for multiple photographic prints.

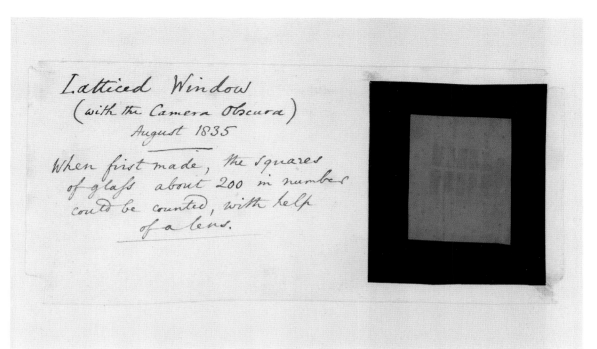

1.18
WILLIAM HENRY
FOX TALBOT, *Latticed
Window Taken with
the Camera Obscura*,
August 1835. Photogenic
drawing negative,
mounted on blackened
paper. National Museum
of Photography, Film
and Television, Bradford,
England.

Of this photograph of
a Gothic window at his
estate, Talbot wrote that
"When first made, the
squares of glass about
200 in number could
be counted, with help
of a lens."

In 1841, after improving the capability of photogenic drawings to make multiple copies, Talbot would patent a photographic process he called the CALOTYPE. The name derived from *kalos*, the Greek word for "beauty." Like the daguerreotype, it made use of the latent image, the invisible picture on the negative that had to be further developed after exposure in the camera. Unlike the daguerreotype, with its single, unique picture, the calotype produced a negative, from which many prints could be made. Thus the calotype would become the basis for modern photographic reproduction. But in the mid-1830s, before the announcement of the daguerreotype, Talbot was losing interest in his photographic experiments. He returned to his classical studies for more than three years, until Daguerre's announcement spurred him to demonstrate not only that his method was original, but also that it had generated photographs before 1839.

THE POLITICS OF INVENTION

Talbot read about Daguerre's image-making process within days of the January 7, 1839, announcement, and quickly moved to make his own work known. He wrote to Arago, claiming prior invention, and prepared a paper giving "Some Account of the Art of Photogenic Drawing, or, the Process by which Natural Objects May be Made to Delineate Themselves without the Aid of the Artist's Pencil," which he read at the Royal Society on January 31, 1839. The first exhibit of his photogenic drawings took place as part of the regular Friday evening lecture of the Royal Institution on January 25, 1839. Scientist Michael Faraday (1791–1867) spoke about Daguerre's invention, and then urged the audience to examine a display of Talbot's work. *The Literary Gazette* (Saturday, February 2, 1839) recorded that the purpose of the exhibition was to establish Talbot's claim to original invention, should he be challenged by Daguerre. The journal went on to exclaim that "No human hand has hitherto traced such lines as these drawings displayed; and what man may hereafter do, now that Dame Nature has become his drawing mistress, it is impossible to predict."[28] *The Magazine of Science, and School of Arts* copied Talbot's photogenic drawings in ink for the cover of its April 27, 1839, edition (Fig. 1.19).

While photography itself had not been predicted, many of the nineteenth-century uses of photography were soon foreseen after its disclosure in 1839. Arago, for instance, thought that it could aid archeological research and restoration, and also be employed as a kind of objective retina (*rétine physique*) that would assist scientists in studying the properties of light.[29] He thought it might

1.19
ARTIST UNKNOWN,
The Magazine of Science, and School of Arts, 1839. Photogenic drawings on magazine cover, new series, vol. 1, no. 4, April 27, 1839.

Samples of Talbot's photogenic drawings could not be printed in magazines or newspapers, but had to be copied by hand in ink and engraved.

THE

MAGAZINE OF SCIENCE,

And School of Arts.

4.]   NEW EDITION.   1½*d.*

FAC-SIMILES OF PHOTOGENIC DRAWINGS.

be used to record the art painted and incised on the walls of ancient Egyptian buildings—a task begun in the nineteenth century, yet still far from complete at the beginning of the twenty-first century.

In his arguments for making the daguerreotype a French gift to the world, Arago also anticipated the mistrust and wrangling that would follow the near-simultaneous announcements of two competing photographic processes.

Talbot, for example, was very wary of showing the French his process. Writing to Herschel in February 1839, he suggested "that it might be best not to disclose at present the washing out process, the retransfer, & c. until brought to a state more worthy of publication, inasmuch as the Parisians would hardly be able to discover it immediately if it is not part of Daguerre's process, & I wish to show them that we could do something here which they could not imitate as yet."[30]

In France, Arago hastened to establish Daguerre as the exclusive inventor of photography. He saw to it that Talbot and Herschel, along with other well-known scientists, were boldly invited to Paris to see the daguerreotype and, presumably, to witness its exceptional rendering ability. Talbot refused, but asked Herschel, who was already planning a visit there, to view Daguerre's work. "I shall be glad to hear from you, what you think of them," he wrote: "Whatever their merit, which no doubt is very great, I think that in one respect our English method must have the advantage." "To obtain a second copy of the same view," Talbot continued, "Daguerre must return to the same locality & set up his instrument a second time; for he cannot copy from his metallic plate, being opaque."[31]

When Herschel saw Daguerre's pictures, he reported back to Talbot that "it is hardly saying too much to call them miraculous." The daguerreotypes, he wrote, "surpass anything I could have conceived as within the bounds of reasonable expectation ... Every gradation of light & shade is given with a softness & fidelity which sets all painting at an immeasurable distance." Herschel also added that the exposure time needed for Daguerre's process was very short.[32] In effect, Talbot's respected colleague and friend was compelled to acknowledge the visual superiority of the daguerreotype, a difference in quality so great that it seemed to trivialize Talbot's objection that the daguerreotype could not make multiple copies.

When Daguerre's Diorama burned to the ground in March 1839, Arago strengthened his efforts to award him a pension and to claim the invention of photography for France. He wrote to the minister of the interior hinting that various nations had made Daguerre tempting offers, which the inventor refused. Arago also arranged a display of daguerreotypes for the Chamber of Deputies, and showed the process to the Chamber of Peers. In addition, he orchestrated the major themes of various formal reports presented to these two chambers. In the Chamber of Deputies, Arago stressed the potential scientific importance of Daguerre's invention to the science of photometry (measuring the properties of light) and astronomy. His friend and scientific colleague

Joseph Louis Gay-Lussac (1778–1850) reiterated the notion in the Chamber of Peers. Both attempted to raise national pride and rouse a rivalry with Britain by pressing the need to make photography a French cultural achievement. Arago and Gay-Lussac stirred memories of the contest between British and French linguists to translate the Rosetta Stone, which led to the modern understanding of Egyptian hieroglyphics, and they alluded to the dispute between France and England as to the origin of the Gothic style in architecture. At a time when memories of the Napoleonic Wars between the two countries were still fresh, clear claim to the invention of photography would be read as evidence of national superiority.

In this effort to make Daguerre the sole inventor, reports on his process made to the Chamber of Deputies, Chamber of Peers, and the French Academy of Science distanced his achievement from that of Niépce. Arago insisted that the daguerreotype was "entièrement neuf" (entirely new), and that Daguerre's work of genius was threatened by the efforts of would-be geniuses.[33] From January to August 1839, when the process had its first public demonstration, Daguerre's reputation as an original intellect steadily grew. During that period, no details of his process were revealed, enveloping the daguerreotype and its inventor in irresistible mystery. Indeed, although he was required to produce a booklet describing the daguerreotype process in detail, Daguerre never revealed exactly how he developed it, but allowed tales of fortuitous accidents and miraculous visual events to fill in the blanks. In the end, he and Isidore Niépce secured government pensions, with Daguerre receiving the larger share.

The excitement following the first public demonstration of Daguerre's process, at the joint meeting of the Academy of Science and the Academy of Fine Arts in Paris on August 19, 1839, was captured by Marc-Antoine Gaudin (1804–1880), a maker of optical instruments:

We all felt an extraordinary emotion and unknown sensations which made us madly gay ... Everyone wanted to copy the view offered by his window, and very happy was he who at first attempt obtained a silhouette of roofs against the sky: he was in ecstasies over the stove-pipes; he did not cease to count

FOCUS
The Stranger

A mythical inventor of photography arrived late on the scene during the 1850s. Accounts of photography's history, published in journals aimed at a general audience, recounted the appearance of "the Stranger," a bedraggled man who enters the Paris shop of optical instrument-maker Charles Chevalier in January 1826. The Stranger wants to purchase a camera obscura, but his poverty prevents him from buying the best instrument. The Stranger recounts his attempts to fix the images in a camera obscura, and shows Chevalier some photographs. As he is about to depart the shop, the Stranger leaves a vial of a secret brown liquid with Chevalier, telling him that it is the substance that produces photographs. The Stranger does not leave instructions for its use, and when he does not return to the shop, Chevalier asks Daguerre to try the brown liquid. Daguerre has no success, but his attempts use up the mysterious substance.

As the story of the Stranger moved from source to source, it grew in complexity. The Stranger became poorer, and his physical needs became more urgent. Conjectures were added. Why did the Stranger not return to Chevalier's shop? Did he end his days in a charity hospital, shivering with cold and hunger? Did he plunge himself into the Seine, discouraged that Daguerre, not he, had got credit for photography? For a person of genius, the later stories concluded, life's disappointments are sharper than for the rest of us.

Like Hippolyte Bayard's self-portrait of himself as a drowned man (see Fig. 1.14), the story of the Stranger was infused with notions of doomed Romantic genius. Indeed, it has been speculated that Bayard's disheartening experience in gaining acceptance for his photographic process may be the origin of the story (Fig. 1.20).

L'inconnu montrant une épreuve photographique à M. Charles Chevalier. Dessin de M. Gustave Janet.

1.20
ARTIST UNKNOWN,
"The Stranger," from Francis Wey, *Comment le soleil est devenu peintre: histoire du daguerréotype et de la photographie*. Musée des Familles, June 1853. Wood engraving. Widener Library, Harvard University, Cambridge, Massachusetts.

the tiles on the roofs and the bricks of the chimneys; he was astonished to see the cement between each brick; in a word, the poorest picture caused him unutterable joy, inasmuch as the process was then new and appeared deservedly marvellous.[34]

In January 1839, there was not one, but several photographies. Some had failed or were destined to be forgotten. Some, like Daguerre's process, produced single images; others, like Talbot's, were potentially capable of making multiple prints. The quality of those images produced on metal and paper differed as well. The daguerreotype rendered a startlingly detailed picture on a mirror-like silver surface. The paper processes produced images that were less distinct, with large contrasting areas of dark and light. Because the paper absorbed the light-sensitive chemicals, the result often looked like a monochrome watercolor, sunk into the paper's fabric. The daguerreotype, by comparison, seemed to have lifelike, three-dimensional qualities. It yielded a wide range of gray tones, where the paper processes, depending on the type and purity of chemical used, included tawny orange, gray-violet, and sepia-brown.

PHILOSOPHY AND PRACTICE: NATURE'S AUTOMATIC WRITING

The pioneers of photography portrayed it as a way to generate pictures independent of the physical talent and mental effort of the camera operator. Talbot, Daguerre, and Niépce all shied away from explaining photography as an invention that makes images through human agency. Each insisted that photography originated in nature and was disclosed by nature. Talbot wrote that photography depicts its images "by optical and chemical means *alone*"; the image is "impressed by Nature's hand." Daguerre put it this way: "the daguerreotype is not an instrument which serves to draw nature; but a chemical and physical process which gives her the power to reproduce herself." Niépce defined his accomplishment as "spontaneous reproduction, by the action of light." The initial legal agreement, drawn up by Niépce and Daguerre, spoke of Niépce's attempts

"to fix the images which nature offers, without the assistance of a draughtsman."[35] Of course, photography's inventors observed the medium's verisimilitude and its reliable visual reproduction, but they stressed its apparent spontaneity: "auto-graphy," nature's automatic writing. These modest, even self-effacing descriptions would trouble photography for generations in its attempts to legitimize itself as a fine art medium.

Beginning with the earliest written accounts, photography was described in different terms than the machines, instruments, and processes of the Industrial Revolution. By situating photography in nature and in natural history, rather than in human history, its pioneers distanced the medium from the history of other innovations. For example, the words "invention" and "discovery" were (and still are) used interchangeably in reference to photography, while other technological achievements are usually unequivocally called inventions. It would be bizarre to think of the railroad or the telegraph, for example, as having been discovered; but photography, considered as a natural phenomenon, much like magnetism, has been understood to be discovered, then applied to human use.

In this way the medium was integrated with Western notions of empiricism, especially its core belief that knowledge should be based on disinterested observation, not personal opinion. The shared cultural imagining of photography—that is, the idea of photography, rather than its practical applications—emphasized photography as a natural *and* neutral vision. The camera image was thought to be like the picture on the retina of the human eye, confirming an eighteenth-century proposition that the retinal image is completely independent of the subject's thoughts and feelings. Photography's neutral vision was conceived not only as a boon to science, but also as a socially symbolic anticipation of a future in which the world could be better known by more people—a means to democratize knowledge. But that very concept of democratic neutrality or objectivity would also soon create a backlash that denigrated the individual photographer's ability to be a discerning interpreter of ideas.

CHAPTER TWO

The Second Invention of Photography (1839–1854)

During the months following Daguerre and Arago's first presentation in 1839, photography and its potential were energetically discussed in Britain, Europe, Russia, and the United States, as well as some parts of Asia and Latin America (Fig. 2.1). But the basic outlines of photography's practical uses and social meanings—its second invention—took more than a decade to emerge.

THE SECOND INVENTION

One of the earliest indications of photography's transition from an invention to an active agent in the social world was the patenting of both the calotype and the daguerreotype processes. In the summer of 1839, Daguerre was quietly working with an agent in Britain to patent his process there, and to assign the manufacture of his camera and supplies to a French firm run by Alphonse Giroux (active 1840s). Daguerre received the patent, restricting the making of daguerreotypes in Britain to those who paid to do so. Similarly, Talbot patented the calotype process in 1841, although he charged only commercial photographers to use it. In part, the patenting

of the daguerreotype and the calotype was motivated by nationalistic competition, but it also indicated the transformation of photography from an invention into a property with commercial promise.

Daguerre's instruction manual arrived in the United States in September 1839, but news of the invention had come months earlier. In April 1839, when few people had seen a photograph, *The New Yorker* was sufficiently confident in the medium's future to extol both Daguerre's contrivance and Talbot's photogenic drawing. The article humorously proposed that photography would conquer the other arts: "The Dagueroscope [sic] and the Photogenic revolution are to keep you all down, ye painters, engravers, and, alas!, the harmless race, the sketchers."[1] On a more serious note, the article discussed photography as a modern innovation, situating it among the "phastasmagoria of inventions [that] passes rapidly before us."[2] Another commentator, who had never seen a daguerreotype, nonetheless praised it as "more like some marvel of a fairy tale or delusion of necromancy than a practical reality."[3]

In the 1840s, as photography began to proliferate as a craft, a fledgling

2.0
GEORGE PHILLIPS BOND & JOHN ADAMS WHIPPLE, *Moon,* **c. 1851. Daguerreotype. Harvard College Observatory, Cambridge, Massachusetts.**

The Great Refractor telescope was thought to be the largest in the world at the time that astronomer Bond and daguerreotype portraitist Whipple amazed their colleagues with views that clearly captured the lined and cratered surface of the moon. The technical achievement of their moon photographs was recognized at the Crystal Palace Exhibition in London in 1851 (see p. 29).

2.1
THÉODORE MAURISSET, *La Daguerréotypomanie*, 1840. Lithograph on card. National Gallery of Canada/Musée des Beaux-Arts du Canada, Ottawa.

Théodore Maurisset's (1803–1868) lithograph *La Daguerréotypomanie* ("Daguerreotypomania") is a fantasy on the future of the daguerreotype. It foretells the effects of mass-produced photographs, the appearance of aerial photography, and the demise of engravers, who are invited to rent gallows near the center of the picture, on which to end their useless lives.

LA DAGUERREOTYPOMANIE.

industry, a means of record-keeping, and an aspiring art form, it also became a topic in newspapers, magazines, and other areas of public debate, where it was regularly called an "art-science." The term recognized that photographic images were not only generated by a mix of science and art, but also applied in both activities. The ambiguous character of photography in its early years was fostered by the equally uncertain definitions of art and science. Art could mean a skill or a craft, as well as specific media such as painting, sculpture, and engraving. Science referred to areas of knowledge such as biology and geology, and also to techniques for making experiments and observations, such as objective scrutiny and recording.[4] To many observers, photography seemed a science wedded to a craft, fundamentally dependent on the photographer's knowledge of chemistry and willingness to experiment. Images that appear primarily aesthetic might result from scientific inquiry.

For example, the Austrian scientist Anton Georg Martin (1812–1882) studied photography soon after it was announced, and used it to picture an ordinary farmyard in winter (Fig. 2.2). Martin's aim, indicated by a note on the back of the image, was to experiment with exposure time, light, and equipment.[5] Those who took up the new medium found themselves refitting traditional visual arts subjects, such as landscape, to photography's capabilities. The blending of custom and camera-work is evident in French photographer Alexandre Clausel's (1802–1884) *Landscape near Troyes*, in which a transitory moment is anchored within a carefully chosen point of view whose symmetry and balance derive from the rules of artistic composition (Fig. 2.3).

Writing in *The Athenaeum*, an anonymous author expressed the absence of a distinct category for photography. Describing a meeting of the Calotype Club in London, which was founded in 1847, the writer noted that the members had "associated together for the purpose of pursuing their experiments in this art-science (we scarcely know the word fittest completely to designate it)."[6] The "art-science" label survived into the 1850s. In an early issue of *La Lumière*, France's first photographic magazine, Francis Wey (1812–1882) announced that the journal would be "neutral ground" for photography, which inherently embraced both science and art.[7] There is little evidence that this

2.2
ANTON GEORG
MARTIN, *Vienna:
Winter Landscape*, 1841.
Daguerreotype.
Museum für Kunst und
Gewerbe, Hamburg,
Germany.

categorization was unsettling; instead, the term "art-science" seemed productively vague, expressing an interplay between the humanities and the sciences, and the broad interests of people who took up the new medium. Images such as those produced by William

Henry Fox Talbot's friend the botanist and scientific illustrator Anna Atkins could be simultaneously aesthetically pleasing and scientific, without any perceived contradiction (see Fig. 2.14).

Although the daguerreotype was primarily adopted when exact renderings

2.3
ALEXANDRE
CLAUSEL, *Landscape
near Troyes, France*,
c. 1855. Daguerreotype.
George Eastman House,
Rochester, New York.

Although the daguerreo-
type was widely under-
stood to be useful
primarily in recording
facts, Clausel produced
a poetic rendering of
light and water, taking
advantage of the
daguerreotype's range
of gray tones.

in portraiture and in science were desired, and the calotype used when softer effects and multiple copies were wanted, no rigid conventions governed their use. Thus, despite the daguerreotype's superior detail and sharp focus, the calotype's ability to make multiple copies, and to be retouched on the negative, made it valuable to scientists as well. Similarly, the daguerreotype could occasionally be made to approximate landscape painting, as Alexandre Clausel convincingly did through his well-balanced composition and attentive use of many middle-gray tones that evoke the look of multiple thin layers of paint. Especially in the early years of its second invention, photography was flexible and experimental, neither a sharply delimited art form nor quite the product of science.

Reactions to early photography ranged from the exuberant to the cautious. American poet and short-story writer Edgar Allan Poe (1809–1849), the subject of a haunting 1849 portrait (Fig. 2.4), wrote three articles on photography for popular magazines in 1840. Describing the daguerreotype's "most

American poet and fiction writer Edgar Allan Poe is shown in a daguerreotype portrait made just days after a suicide attempt.

miraculous beauty," Poe opined that "all language must fall short of conveying any just idea of the truth ... but the closest scrutiny of the photogenic drawing discloses only a more absolute truth, a more perfect identity of aspect with the thing represented." He urged readers to imagine a "positively perfect mirror" that "is *infinitely* more accurate in its representation than any painting by human hands."[8]

Despite *The New Yorker* magazine's playful 1839 foreboding that photography would stifle art, few painters saw early photography as a threat. Still, when John Jabez Edwin Mayall (1810–1901), an American photographer working in London, proposed that the daguerreotype was capable of illustrating history, an editorial response in an 1847 issue of *The Athenaeum* corrected him: "At best, he [Mayall] can only hope to get a mere naturalist's rendering. Ideality is unattainable,—and imagination supplanted by the presence of fact."[9] Nevertheless, Mayall went on to document history—or at least a photographic version of it. His mammoth plate daguerreotype, one of fourteen made of *The Crystal Palace at Hyde Park, London*, depicted the interior of Joseph Paxton's (1801–1865) remarkable large metal and glass structure which housed the Great Exhibition of the Works of Industry of All Nations in 1851 (Fig. 2.5).

Because the photograph was commonly conceived as nature delineating nature, some found it lacking in imagination. *The New Yorker*'s anonymous commentator was convinced that "Nature is only become handmaid to Art, not her mistress ... Painters need not despair; their labours will be as much in request as ever, but in a higher field: the finer qualities of taste and invention will be called into action more powerfully: and the mechanical process will be only abridged and rendered more perfect."[10]

Many of photography's modern applications emerged in the 1840s and early 1850s, together with an equally enduring dialogue about visual representation and multiple imaging. The medium's expansion was inextricably associated with world-shaping forces. Industrial capitalism created a middle class of professionals, such as scientists, who began to use photography in their

FOCUS
Iron, Glass, and Photography

The Great Exhibition, dubbed the "Crystal Palace Exhibition" by the press, opened in London in May 1851. This early world's fair brimmed with excitement for technological progress and material prosperity. Nearly 800 examples from six countries were exhibited. The Crystal Palace, visted by about 6 million people, boasted Britain's lead in industrial production and promoted the idea that modern mass manufacturing and engineering could be applied in the cause of economic and social betterment. For example, a model, modular house for the working class was on display.[11] Observers noted the resemblance of Joseph Paxton's building to a glass house, the space used by photographers, and associated both structures with social advancement (Fig. 2.5).

Included in the Crystal Palace displays were cameras, other photographic equipment, and photographs. Commercial portraits and landscape photographs were shown with photographic equipment, while art photography was displayed in the Fine Arts Court. Roughly the same number of daguerreotypes and calotypes were shown.[12]

The connections between technological progress, social advancement, modern architecture, and the new medium of photography also occurred in France, where Hector Horeau (1801–1872), an architect, egyptologist, and publisher of prints based on early photographs, was an avid proponent of glass and iron building construction. His philosophy for public works emphasized education and communication for the working class, an idea also expressed by proponents of photography. Ironically, Horeau had successfully competed in the contest to design the Crystal Palace, only to be replaced a month later by Paxton.

2.5
J. J. MAYALL, *The Crystal Palace at Hyde Park, London*, 1851. Daguerreotype. The J. Paul Getty Museum, Los Angeles, California.

work. The rapid growth of cities facilitated the exchange of ideas among people interested in the medium of photography, and the shift of populations from the countryside to the cities accentuated the desire for observable personal identity, fueling the market for photographic portraits. Whereas in small towns and villages people were usually known to their neighbors, in the burgeoning cities strangers gawked at strangers, sizing them up in an instant. In this milieu of unstable social identity, photography offered sitters a chance to fix an outward appearance for all time.

As the medium's capacities grew during its first dozen years, photography also provided a way to enact a public personality through which sitters might be known and remembered. While urban populations increased, rural peoples, traditional occupations, and unpolluted landscapes emerged as sentimental and nostalgic subjects in the visual arts, and, ultimately, in photography. Meanwhile, the expansion of Western powers into Asia, Africa, and Latin America provided fresh vistas to be photographed, and a persuasive visual means to rationalize foreign adventurism. The new image-making method altered the way in which people related to visual media. By the mid-1850s, photography, which had initially seemed a wondrous phenomenon, had become a routine part of Western life.

TALBOT AND *THE PENCIL OF NATURE*

While Daguerre took little part in the development of photography after 1839, Talbot continued his efforts. His 1839 account of photogenic drawing conceived the photographic image as a kind of *"natural magic"*[13] with potential for both science and art. He went on to explore both these aspects.

In 1835 Talbot had produced what may be the world's first photomicrograph—that is, a photograph of a magnified small object. Talbot believed that photography would "be especially useful for naturalists since one can copy the most difficult things, for instance

2.6
WILLIAM HENRY FOX TALBOT, *The Open Door,* **1844, plate 5 from** *The Pencil of Nature,* **1844–46. Salt print from a calotype negative.**

Describing this image, Talbot wrote that the seventeenth-century Dutch school of painting had already commended scenes from everyday life, and he suggested that photographers could use the camera to create similarly evocative views.

2.7
WILLIAM HENRY FOX TALBOT, *Articles of China,* **plate 3 from** *The Pencil of Nature,* **1844–46. Calotype. Fox Talbot Collection. National Museum of Photography, Film and Television, Bradford, England.**

Images in *The Pencil of Nature* inventoried books, glassware, and china, demonstrating photography's ability to present neutral information in pictorial form, and its potential as evidence.

crystallizations and minute parts of plants, with a great deal of ease,"[14] but he was also interested in its art applications. He considered *The Open Door* (Fig. 2.6), in which he emulated seventeenth-century Dutch painting of scenes from everyday life, an example "of the early beginnings of a new art."[15] Larry Schaaf has observed that the photograph draws on the doorway as a traditional symbol of the passage between life and light, and death and darkness.[16]

The Open Door was included as Plate 5 in Talbot's book *The Pencil of Nature,* which he published in six sections, between 1844 and 1846. One of the first books illustrated with actual photographs rather than engraved versions, *The Pencil of Nature* contained twenty-four calotype images. Since the calotype process created a negative, from which positive prints could be made, actual calotypes were tipped in (pasted at the corners to the page). Each image was accompanied by an explanatory text. *The Pencil of Nature* demonstrated the breadth of Talbot's investigation into the applications of photography. Some

images, such as *Articles of China,* showed photography's record-keeping ability (Fig. 2.7), while others demonstrated how photography could variously depict biological specimens, architecture, and sculpture, and reproduce sketches and engravings. Talbot even suggested that in the future photographs might be taken in the dark, making possible secret surveillance.

Throughout the 1840s, Talbot mingled art, science, and what would eventually be called documentary photography, in such works as the series of haystack studies produced on his property. Early on, he understood photography's ability to present a sequence of images, the meaning of which proceeded not just from one example, but from all of them and from their arrangement. As the French Impressionist painter Claude Monet (1840–1926) would do later in the nineteenth century, Talbot studied the effects of light, and he also delighted in the configuration of geometric shapes found in the natural and built environments. *The Haystack* is a virtuoso piece, taken when the light best revealed the prickly surface of the stack and as shadows define its sturdy geometry (Fig. 2.8). Talbot also thought to include a visually teasing conflict between the leaning ladder and its upright shadow.

Talbot also pursued commercial experiments with photography. Exploiting the calotype's ability to furnish multiple prints, he founded a photographic studio and printing establishment in Reading, a town about 40 miles west of London (Fig. 2.9). The business was part of the mid-century industrialization of photography; here Talbot produced *The Pencil of Nature* as well as other views for sale.

BAYARD: THE DOUBTING CAMERA

After Hippolyte Bayard produced his *Self-Portrait as a Drowned Man* (see Fig. 1.14), he continued to test the limits of photographic representation, exploring ways in which it could be misleading or unsettling (Fig. 2.10). Some contemporary viewers recognized Bayard's unusual approach; Francis Wey wrote that Bayard's images united "the impression of reality with the fantasy of dreams."[17] Ultimately, Bayard took up both daguerreotype and calotype photography, in which he enjoyed professional success. In some photographs,

he lingered on the textural richness and attractive shapes of such ordinary objects as leaves, tools, stone, and straw. But a teasing sense continued to inform his work: what the eye sees, and what the photograph records, may not be trustworthy.

PHOTOGRAPHY AND THE SCIENCES

Though few early photographers were as multi-faceted in their interests as Talbot, as early as May of 1839 scientists had attempted to employ Talbot's photogenic drawings in their work.

THE MICROSCOPE AND THE TELESCOPE

After witnessing Daguerre's Paris presentation of his invention and studying directly with Daguerre, the Viennese physicist and mathematician Andreas Ritter von Ettingshausen (1796–1878) created startlingly detailed microscopic images (Fig. 2.11). Ettingshausen was a member of an informal circle of artists, mathematicians, and scientists who explored photography, but, like many of its early users and advocates, he did not pursue the new invention throughout his scientific career. The scientist Léon

**2.8
WILLIAM HENRY FOX TALBOT, *The Haystack* from *The Pencil of Nature*. Glasgow University Library, Department of Special Collections.**

Published in Talbot's *Pencil of Nature*, the plate *The Haystack* became especially popular with the public, perhaps because the new medium of photography was used to pay homage to an agricultural practice that endured into the modern era.

2.9
PHOTOGRAPHER UNKNOWN, *Untitled* (Panorama showing Talbot's Reading establishment), c. 1845. Calotype. National Museum of Photography, Film and Television, Bradford, England.

Talbot's establishment in Reading produced multiple copies of photographs in the glasshouse seen in the rear, as well as outside in the sunlight, as here. Talbot can be seen on the far right, removing a lens cap from a camera.

2.10
HIPPOLYTE BAYARD, *Self-Portrait with Plaster Casts*, 1850. Gelatin silver print. National Gallery of Canada/Musée des Beaux-Arts du Canada, Ottawa.

Unlike other early photographers, Bayard sometimes jested with the idea that the photograph was a mirror of reality, as in this image of apparently weightless, gravity-defying plaster casts of statues.

2.11 (above)
ANDREAS RITTER VON ETTINGSHAUSEN, *Section of Climatis,* **March 4, 1840. Daguerreotype. Ezra Mack, New York.**

This cross-section seemed to record the plant's cell structure. However, the lens magnifying the specimen in this early experiment distorted the cells' shape and size.

2.12 (right)
LÉON FOUCAULT, Microscopic studies, plates 21, 22, 23, 24, from Alfred Donné's *Cours de Microscopie,* **1845. Engravings from daguerreotypes. The J. Paul Getty Museum, Los Angeles, California.**

Foucault (1819–1868), who would later do distinguished research into the speed of light, became involved with photography while still a medical student. He helped to produce eighty-six microscopic daguerreotypes, which were then engraved for the textbook *Cours de Microscopie* (*Course in Microscopy*) (1845), written by his mentor, the physicist Alfred Donné (1801–1878) (Fig. 2.12). Because the daguerrean process was a tricky, time-consuming way to make duplicates, during its early years the usual course for reproducing daguerreotypes in both scientific and artistic illustrations was to hand-copy the image on to an engraving plate.

Beginning in the early 1840s, several daguerreotype experiments reduced printed matter to a size so small that it had to be read with a microscope. This microform technique promised to condense rare books and manuscripts to an easily transportable and storable size. Celestial photographs were also tried, although the dim light of distant stars,

2.14
ANNA ATKINS, *Poppy,* c. 1852. Cyanotype.
Victoria & Albert Museum, London.

In the nineteenth century, several amateur women scientists prepared botanical specimens for scientific study. Beginning in 1843, Anna Atkins published about a dozen copies of *British Algae: Cyanotype Impressions*, which contained nearly 400 cyanotype pictures. She sent the book to friends and researchers, such as William Henry Fox Talbot.

2.13
WILHELM & FRIEDRICH LANGENHEIM,
Seven Daguerreotypes Showing Eclipse of the Sun, May 26, 1854.
Daguerreotypes.
Gilman Paper Company Collection, New York.

with the obvious exception of the sun, made clear and detailed photographs difficult. Daguerre himself made a faint image of the moon to prove the potential benefits of the medium to his sponsor, the astronomer and politician François Arago. In 1845, with Arago's encouragement, Foucault and another French scientist, Hippolyte Fizeau, had some success in photographing the sun with sunspots. The result was published as a lithograph in Arago's *Astronomie populaire* (1858). In America, George Phillips Bond (1825–1865) and John Adams Whipple (1822–1891) made daguerreotype views of the moon (Fig. 2.0). Philadelphia photographers and dealers in photographic equipment Wilhelm Langenheim (1807–1874) and his brother Friedrich (1809–1879) recorded eight phases of the solar eclipse of 1854 (Fig. 2.13).

BIOLOGY

In the nineteenth century, many men and women of the upper classes were active amateur scientists. They collected and classified biological specimens and attempted to preserve them for further study. Those who could draw or work in

watercolor also rendered copies of their finds. For more than a decade, scientific illustrator Anna Atkins (1799–1871) created impeccable cyanotype impressions of algae species and other specimens. A member of the Botanical Society of London and an accomplished book illustrator, Atkins used the technique developed by John Herschel to combine scientific exactitude with aesthetic sensitivity to form and presentation (Fig. 2.14). Because her prints were originals and bore a one-to-one relationship to their subjects, they were thought to constitute persuasive documentation. Similar work was done by Thereza Llewelyn (1834–1926), whose photogenic rendering of a maidenhair fern surrounds her portrait by her father, John Dillwyn Llewelyn (Fig. 2.15). He had been introduced to photography by his wife, Emma Thomasina Talbot (William Henry Fox Talbot's first cousin), and was typical of the amateur photographers who experimented with the technical and chemical aspects of photography, while making a variety of landscape images and family pictures. Like many amateurs, he benefited from meetings with others, and exchanges, often by mail, of information

2.15
JOHN DILLWYN
LLEWELYN, *Thereza,*
c. 1853. Salted paper
print. Gilman Paper
Company Collection,
New York.

An amateur scientist,
Thereza Llewelyn was
interested in botany and
astronomy. This portrait
was intended to show
her at work and to
indicate symbolically
her accomplishments,
through the presence
of books, biological
samples, and scientific
instruments.

2.16
GEORGE SHADBOLT,
Watching the Newts,
c. mid-1850s. Salted
paper print. George
Eastman House,
Rochester, New York.

Observing newts, small
aquatic salamanders
that cannot be seen in
the photograph, seems
like an odd subject for
an image. But in the
context of the amateur
photography practiced
by the middle and upper
classes, it conveys not
only the scientific interests of educated people
but also their available
leisure time to pursue
hobbies such as biology
and photography.

and photographs from men and women with similar interests. Another British amateur, active in both scientific and artistic photography, was George Shadbolt (1819–1901). The country paths and venerable trees in his *Watching the Newts* (Fig. 2.16) are characteristic of British amateur subject matter, which generally ignored industrial and urban views in favor of ancient buildings and traditional agricultural pursuits.

ANTHROPOLOGY AND MEDICINE

From the first, practitioners of anthropology and medicine saw in photography a good opportunity to generate historical and research archives. The notion was still in force at the end of the century when Robert Sommer, a German professor of psychiatry, proclaimed that photography should "replace the written record (or at least supplement it)," because the medium "is uncontaminated by the interpretive problems inherent in language."[18]

Hugh Welch Diamond (1806–1886), a British medical doctor and active amateur, photographed still lifes and took pictures of antiquarian interest. He also made photographs of mental patients (Fig. 2.17). He professed that mentally ill patients could look at photographs of themselves and better understand their afflictions. For Diamond, the photograph was a transparent medium that allowed the therapist and the patient accurately to interpret the language of nature. "The picture speaks for itself," he asserted.[19] Diamond maintained that "the Photographer secures with unerring accuracy the external phenomena of each passion, as the really certain indication of internal derangement, and exhibits to the eye the well known sympathy which exists between the diseased brain and the organs and features of the body."[20] Addressing the Royal Society in 1856, he stressed that photography's scientific objectivity would give it historical importance. "Photography," he concluded, "gives permanence to these remarkable cases ... and makes them observable not only now but for ever."[21] Because these photographs were understood to be both effective therapeutic and educational instruments, patients were obliged to pose for them.

Dr. Diamond was one of the first photographers to experiment with the

COLLODION PROCESS, or wet-plate process, a new negative–positive process published by Frederick Scott Archer (1813–1857) in 1851. Although still time-consuming, the wet-plate process used glass, rather than paper, to support the light-sensitive material. It boasted a greater sensitivity and shorter exposure time than previous processes, including the albumen glass-plate negatives, devised in the late 1840s by Claude Félix Abel de St. Victor Niépce (1805–1870), a relative of Joseph Nicéphore Niépce. The wet-plate process furnished multiple images that were free from the imprint of texture rendered by the paper negatives.

Most photographs of mental patients were intended for scientific study, but in rare instances some were used to raise money for the asylum. A French example, mounted individual daguerreotypes in a poster-like format, publicized a lottery to benefit patients (Fig. 2.18). Photography was also used during its first decade to describe, compare, and rank "racial" types. The notion of race was renewed in the late eighteenth and early nineteenth centuries, when it was

2.17
HUGH WELCH DIAMOND, *Seated Woman with Bird*, c. 1855. Albumen print. The J. Paul Getty Museum, Los Angeles, California.

Most of Diamond's photographs were of women patients. He adapted the new medium to continue a series of engraved patient portraits, started by his predecessor, as superintendent of the Surrey County Lunatic Asylum.

37

PHOTOGRAPHY AND THE SCIENCES

2.18
PHOTOGRAPHER UNKNOWN, *Untitled* (Lottery announcement), 1852. The J. Paul Getty Museum,
Los Angeles, California.

The heading, "Galerie Historique," and the phrase, "au bénéfice des originaux," have ironic meanings.
A regular gallery presented portraits of famous individuals, not asylum inmates. The phrase "au bénéfice des
originaux" means both for the benefit of those pictured and for the benefit of eccentric or unusual people.[22]

used to describe innate qualities of nations and ethnicities, sometimes with the aim of arousing nationalistic feeling. With the rapid colonization of the non-Western world, human diversity was increasingly discussed and classified.

The French photographer E. Thiésson (active 1840s) produced annotated images of the residents of Sofala, a town in Mozambique (Fig. 2.19), and of the Botocudo people in Brazil. Thiésson omitted names and personal details in an attempt to accentuate the scientific objectivity of his photographs. He developed a specific visual vocabulary, posing his subjects from the side and from the front, and using a plain background. The appearance of neutrality and the distance of subjects from the camera were conventions that developed slowly and unevenly during photography's first decades, as ethnographers concocted a standard, "styleless" style to connote truth. In fact, many early images of non-Westerners employed the customs of middle-class portraiture, as in a subtle daguerreotype by the Philadelphia photographers Wilhelm and Friedrich Langenheim (Fig. 2.20). With its simple background, three-quarter profile, and the sitter's contemplative pose, the

2.19 (above)
E. THIÉSSON, *Native Woman of Sofala*, 1845. Daguerreotype. Gift of Eastman Kodak Co. George Eastman House, Rochester, New York.

The side or profile view of non-Western subjects appeared first in early daguerreotypes. It became the standard visual technique for photographing non-Western peoples, and anticipated the so-called "mug shot" in police photography.

2.20 (below)
WILHELM & FRIEDRICH LANGENHEIM, *African Youth*, 1848. Daguerreotype. Peabody Museum, Harvard University, Cambridge, Massachusetts.

FOCUS
Photography, Race, and Slavery

The Langenheim daguerreotype (see Fig. 2.20) was probably in the collection of the Swiss-born naturalist Louis Agassiz (1807–1873), who came to the United States in 1846. The founder of Harvard University's museum of comparative zoology, Agassiz was an avid proponent of photographic data and perhaps the best-known scientist in mid-nineteenth-century America.[23] His ethnological interests led him to authorize a Southern colleague to commission front, back, and side views of slaves from a North Carolina plantation in 1850. Agassiz hoped to provide visual evidence for his theory that the races were created separately at different times and in different parts of the world, an idea that slavery's proponents felt would

scientifically justify racial inequality. Agassiz's colleague hired J. T. Zealy (active 1850s), who ran photographic studios in Columbia, South Carolina, and Petersburg, Virginia, to make a series of fifteen daguerreotypes.

In two images of a slave named Jack, the key assumption of middle-class portraiture—that personal character was expressed through physical appearance—vies with the desire to record objectively a generic physical type (Figs. 2.21 and 2.22). Zealy's subjects were identified not by their African names, but by their slave names and the names of the plantations on which they served. In the first picture, Jack is romantically lit, emphasizing facial features that make him appear noble, pensive, and

2.21
J. T. ZEALY, *Jack*, 1850s. Daguerreotype. Peabody Museum of Art, Archaeology & Ethnology, Harvard University, Cambridge, Massachusetts.

...ting. His eyes are fixed beyond the camera. But
...cond, side view, his personality traits are dimin-
...d the romantic side light of the first image is
...ntensify anatomical features that would substan-
...ssiz's thesis. Although the photographs were
...compare and contrast physical types, no images
...arably posed white men and women accompanied
...guerreotypes.
...nain purpose of Zealy's slave photographs was
...ice viewers of the truth of a racial theory. But
...raise questions about the authorship of images.
...n Agassiz commissioned them as part of his field-
...was not there when the images were made.

A colleague communicated to the photographer what
the aim of the photographs was to be and labeled the final
prints, yet Zealy actually made the exposures. Obviously,
the subjects of these photographs had no say in their
representation.

Today, Zealy's name is appended to the images,
because in contemporary law and ethics photographers
are understood to be the originators of their work. But
in nineteenth-century terms, Zealy was, in this instance,
an operator—that is, a person who exposed and/or developed photographs for those who conceived the pictures.
The images were sent to Agassiz; they were not Zealy's
property to keep, copy, or distribute.

2.22
J. T. ZEALY, *Jack*
(from the side),
1850s. Daguerreotype.
Peabody Museum of
Art, Archaeology &
Ethnology, Harvard
University, Cambridge,
Massachusetts.

image wavers between anthropological record and formal portraiture.

Some medical evidence was collected in early photographs, yet highly detailed, sometimes hand-colored engravings continued to be used because they revealed fine points of anatomical structures more clearly than photographs.[24] Patients were photographed according to the conventions of portraiture, rather than to show only wounds and diseases. They seldom posed in clinical settings, but were pictured in surroundings such as those used for middle-class portraits, and their faces were usually identifiable (Fig. 2.23). Modern protocols for photographing illness — concealing personal identity and emphasizing symptoms — did not become prevalent until the later nineteenth century. In many respects, the patients in early medical photographs resembled the portraits that doctors took of themselves.[25] As the medical profession grew in numbers and prestige throughout the second half of the nineteenth century, however, largely owing to the increasing use of antiseptics and anesthesia, so too did the rhetoric of therapy and medical education. This in turn fostered more revealing medical imaging that focused on wounds, marks, or dysfunctions. The explicitness of photographs picturing American Civil War casualties (see Fig. 3.35) far exceeded the decorum afforded patients a decade earlier.

Performing History? The Dr. Morton Controversy

Where art conventions influenced early photographic practice, a contradictory blend of old ideas and new expectations was created. A series of daguerreotypes taken in Boston, Massachusetts, by the firm of Southworth and Hawes combined notions associated with older media, such as printmaking and painting, with emergent ideas about the purpose of photography. As a result, it was not immediately clear whether these photographs showed the actual surgery in which ether was first used to relieve pain during an operation, or whether the event was reenacted for the camera (Fig. 2.24).

Dr. William T. G. Morton, the discoverer of ether and the man who first used it in surgery, could not be identified in the pictures, nor could the original patient. The suggestion that these images were reenactments did not invalidate them, however. The *tableau vivant*, or living picture, was a popular entertainment in which people donned costumes to recreate historic scenes or famous works of art. Moreover, the visual arts traditionally sanctioned artists who were not present at historical events to depict those events, even to embellish such scenes. If the surgery scene employed artistic license, this would not make it a falsification calculated to deceive viewers. The views may simply have been made to commemorate the historical event, or as devices with which to petition Congress for an award to Dr. Morton.

Certain viewers interpreted the presence of medical instruments in cases as evidence of an authentic operating room. Others also argued that, if the daguerreotypes were reenactments, they would have emulated the original surgery more closely, in which the patient probably sat in an operating chair. Skeptics also observed that participants appeared to be posing for the camera in a manner not possible during actual surgery. Some scholars observed that Dr. John Collins Warren, shown

2.24
ALBERT SANDS SOUTHWORTH & JOSIAH JOHNSON HAWES, *Early Operation Using Ether for Anesthesia*,
1847. Daguerreotype. The J. Paul Getty Museum, Los Angeles, California.

Although photography was quickly associated with truthful experience, photographers also borrowed from the
art tradition of commemorating historical events. Here an early, but not the first, use of anesthesia is registered
both as a document of an actual operation and as a symbolic acclamation of a milestone in medicine. To modern
eyes, however, the surgeons in street clothes and the general indifference to hygiene evident in the room do not
indicate progress.

with his hands on the patient's draped
leg, may have asked Southworth and
Hawes to pose the scene so as to emulate Rembrandt's famous painting *The
Anatomy Lesson of Dr. Tulp.*[26]

By modern hygiene standards, the
surgeon and his colleagues, mostly in
street clothes, and the patient, still in
his stockings, seem prepared not for
surgery but for photography. Moreover,
the statue visible in the upper right-
hand corner appears outlandish in an
operating room. But medical historians
pointed out that, if the image recorded
the pre-operation application of anesthesia in an anteroom, then the poses, garb,
setting, and even that statue, would
be plausible.

Eventually, another photograph
was found that convincingly showed
the subsequent post-operative scene,
thus clearing up the mystery. A real
surgery, though not the first use of
anesthesia, had taken place before the
camera of Southworth and Hawes.
While the first surgery under ether was
not photographed, in the public memory these later images came to stand
for that momentous event. In effect,
these daguerreotypes were at once commemorative, documentary, scientific,
symbolic, and aesthetic. This rich multi-
plicity, a result of the mixing of science
and art in early photography, did not
persist long. The tensions between
realism and symbolism were taken up

again in the twentieth century in such art movements as Surrealism and Conceptual Art, as well as in advertising (see Chapter Five).

RECORDING EVENTS WITH THE CAMERA

Although both the calotype and the daguerreotype processes were too slow to record rapid action, early attempts were made to photograph public events on the spot. For example, Hermann Biow (1804–1850), a portrait photographer living in the German city of Hamburg, is credited with photographing the ruins of the great fire that devastated the city between May 5 and May 8, 1842 (Fig. 2.25). George N. Barnard, an American who would become famous for his American Civil War photographs (see Fig. 3.17), used the daguerrean process to record a lakeside granary fire in Oswego, New York (Fig. 2.26).

In Hamburg and Oswego, the photographers happened to be nearby when these dramatic scenes occurred, but had no preconceived plan to make, sell, or publish their daguerreotypes. By contrast, when historic happenings were anticipated, photographers could arrange to be present. In France, a remarkable pair of "before and after" daguerreotypes were made with the explicit intention of rushing them to publication as wood engravings. During the revolution of 1848, middle-class demands for greater political influence and the right to vote flared up into street conflicts that led to the abdication of King Louis-Philippe and the establishment of a provisional government, which declared a republic. A daguerreotypist named Eugène Thibault (active 1840–1870) was commissioned by the weekly Paris journal *L'Illustration* to photograph the barricades prior to and after a skirmish between the revolutionaries and French troops. The resulting images were published on July 1, 1848 (Figs. 2.27, 2.28).

While painters and printmakers could enhance their images with sharply rendered scenes of gallantry and heroism, photographers were hard-pressed to express the full historical significance or emotional impact of events. The London photographer W. E. Kilburn (active 1846–1862) took daguerreotypes of a meeting of the Chartists, a loose coalition of working-

2.25
HERMANN BIOW,
Ruins of Hamburg Fire,
1842. Daguerreotype.
Museum für
Hamburgische
Geschichte, Hamburg,
Germany.

Biow was able to make forty-six daguerreotypes of the destruction. Often cited as the first efforts of photojournalism, the photographs were not originally intended for publication in a newspaper.

GEORGE N.
BARNARD, *Burning of Oswego Mills*, July 5, 1853. Daguerreotype. George Eastman House, Rochester, New York.

The inadequacy of the daguerreotype to render action is apparent. The fast-moving flames are indistinct, and the bodies of workers on the barge in the foreground are transparent like ghosts. Barnard later sold copies of this photograph to the public.

2.27
EUGÈNE THIBAULT, *The Revolution of 1848: Before the Attack*, 1848. Daguerreotype. Count Geofroy de Beaufort Collection.

2.28
EUGÈNE THIBAULT, *The Revolution of 1848: After the Attack*, 1848. Daguerreotype. Count Geoffroy de Beauffort Collection.

In the foreground of figure 2.27, many cobblestones appear to be missing. They were often removed and stacked near the barricades to be thrown at the advancing troops.

2.29
W. E. KILBURN,
*The Great Chartist
Meeting on Kennington
Common*, April 10, 1848.
Daguerreotype. Royal
Archives © 2002 Her
Majesty Queen
Elizabeth II.

Photographs of histori-
cal events sometimes
failed to find a visually
striking event or symbol
with which to represent
the occasion. Kilburn's
image does not show
the importance of the
scene to viewers.

class people seeking political and
economic reforms, on April 10, 1848.
But his static views fail to convey the
exhilaration of the assembly and the
speeches in defiance of the government
(Fig. 2.29).

WAR AND PHOTOGRAPHY

IMAGING WAR

Early photographers faced both philosophical and technical difficulties when
they attempted to document the facts,
causes, and the experience of conflict.
Both the daguerreotype and the calotype
required lengthy preparation of materials prior to exposure in the camera and
a cumbersome development process;
neither was able to register the rapid
action of battle. In having to conceive
the war photograph without scenes of
active conflict, photographers fell back
on visual conventions established in
other media, and on the public's expectations of what war pictures should look
like. War photographers had to cope

with the lack of an established market
or viewing space for their work, and the
fact that, unlike painters and engravers,
they were restricted to what happened in
front of the lens. Artists in other media
could devise patriotic symbols and emotionally affecting scenes, but the war
photographer was faced with transforming the real into the symbolic, and with
finding or staging heart-rending incidents. These and other perplexities sur-
faced in the first photographed wars.

The Mexican–American War coincided with the rise of American newspapers. Daily papers in cities benefited
not only from new high-speed presses
but also from news carried across the
nation by couriers and sometimes by
telegraph. Public interest in the war
accelerated the appearance of wood-
engraving illustrations in newspapers,
and increased the popularity of lithographs. But these images were not based
on photographs, nor was there a call to
make them more authentic by copying
camerawork. In the long term, however,
the war brought about a change in

FOCUS
The Mexican–American War

In 1836, led by American residents, the Mexican province of Texas declared itself an independent republic. The separation was the final result of long-running quarrels between the two nations about land rights and financial reparations due to Americans for property lost during civil unrest in Mexico in the 1830s. Peace negotiations were hampered by the American residents' campaign to have Texas annexed by the USA (Texas eventually achieved statehood on December 29, 1845). Relations between Mexico and the United States were further troubled by the escalating American desire to "manifest destiny" by acquiring more North American soil, including the Mexican territories of California and New Mexico. Further, the prospect of Texas's entry into the Union as a state in which slavery was legal intensified the national debate about the future of slavery. After skirmishes with Mexican troops early in 1846, the United States declared war. The war ended in 1848 with the treaty of Guadalupe Hildalgo, in which Mexico ceded extensive territories including most of what became Arizona, California, Colorado, Nevada, and New Mexico.

The fifty or so anonymous photographs remaining from the conflict—often called the first photographed war—show the faltering beginnings of a war photography largely cut off from battle scenes and troop movements. Some general tendencies are apparent: as happened in many subsequent conflicts, for example, photographs of soldiers were made either before they left for the war or in military encampments. Disruptions in trade and transportation caused shortages of photographic materials near the front, yet scarce supplies did not keep photographers from boasting their ability to make images. Photographers also made images of war heroes, along with a few landscapes and town views. One of the best-preserved examples is the daguerreotype of Brigadier General John Ellis Wool, accompanied by his staff, on a street in the Mexican town of Saltillo (Fig. 2.30). Because of the daguerreotype's long exposure time, the group had to pause to have a photograph taken. Still, some blurring occurred on the left side of the image.

2.30
PHOTOGRAPHER
UNKNOWN, *General Wool and Staff, Calle Real, Saltillo, Mexico*, c. 1847. Daguerreotype. Amon Carter Museum, Fort Worth, Texas.

DEATH OF MAJOR RINGGOLD.
OF THE FLYING ARTILLERY.
AT THE BATTLE OF PALO-ALTO, (TEXAS) MAY 8TH 1846.

2.31
ARTIST UNKNOWN,
Death of Major Ringgold of the Flying Artillery, at the Battle of Palo-Alto (Texas), May 8, 1846, 1846. Lithograph. Amon Carter Museum, Fort Worth, Texas.

Painters and printmakers frequently embellished death scenes of major figures. Ringgold's white horse bows low so that a well-dressed, unruffled aide can catch the falling body of his mortally wounded master. Mindful of his wounds, Ringgold points toward heaven, as his wide-eyed mount, now burdened with an empty saddle (the traditional military symbol of death), seems about to weep.

journalism that affected photography. For the first time, war correspondents dispatched from major American papers could send back reports that were rushed into print. Speedier reporting by war correspondents eroded the domination of the Washington, D.C., newspapers and the military as major sources of war information. The Mexican–American War also fostered an appetite for up-to-date news. Within a decade, communications systems were specifically developed to transport both images and text describing distant hostilities. In Britain, for example, topical images of the Crimean War (1853–56) would be displayed for viewing and sale (see pp. 99–104).

During and after the Mexican–American War, patriotic themes dominated the images produced for the press and the market. A popular hand-colored lithograph portraying the melodramatic death of Major Samuel Ringgold could not have been matched by the camera without overt staging (Fig. 2.31). Early war photographs, however, were not always innocent of manipulation. The amputation scene in an intriguing Mexican daguerreotype was probably restaged for the camera. It shows a

sergeant who has just been operated on, presumably by Dr. Pedro Van der Linden, Inspector General of Mexico's Military Medical Corps[27] (Fig. 2.32). Van der Linden, on the far right, is holding an amputated lower leg. Other participants point to the patient's stump, and someone has added a sign noting the place and date. It seems unlikely that this image was made immediately after the operation; more probably it was reenacted later. Historian Gina Rodriguez Hernández believes that the group was arranged for the camera, because the participants appear too clean for battlefront surgery.[28] Van der Linden recounted being interrupted by North American soldiers while performing an amputation. Thrusting out his bloody hands, he pleaded for humanitarian respect, and, as his story goes, the Americans not only retreated, but became his protectors and received his medical services.

A daguerreotypist accompanying the United States troops may have made the picture to commemorate the brief eruption of peace during combat.[29] Posed like a history painting, the image evokes the same sort of contradictions

2.32
PHOTOGRAPHER UNKNOWN,
Amputation,
Mexican–American War, Cerro Gordo, 1847. Daguerreotype. National Institute of Anthropology and History, Mexico City, Mexico.

A damaged daguerreotype made in Mexico pays homage to a brief pause in the conflict to allow a doctor to perform a grisly amputation. Proof of the battlefield surgery is evidenced by the patient raising his bloody stump, and by the surgeon's presentation to the camera of the severed limb.

surrounding the Southworth and Hawes daguerreotypes of the first uses of surgical anesthesia.

BRITISH CONFLICTS IN ASIA

John McCosh (1805–1885; occasionally spelt MacCosh) is the earliest war photographer whose name is known. He took photographs not of troops but of fellow officers in India, where he served as a surgeon with the East India Company during the Second Sikh War (1848–49),

a conflict between the Sikh minority and the British. McCosh made calotype photographs as a hobby in the mid-1840s. In addition to portraits of military colleagues, he also photographed local people, emphasizing "racial" physical characteristics. During the Second Burma War (1852–53), between the Burmese and the British, McCosh produced large photographs, such as his view within the city of Prome (Fig. 2.33).

2.33
JOHN McCOSH,
Artillery in front of Stone Dragons, Prome, Burma, 1852. Calotype. National Army Museum, Chelsea, London.

Images such as John McCosh's 1852 photograph of British artillery in front of the Stone Dragons in the Burmese city of Prome confidently juxtapose non-Western culture with symbols of imperialist might.

EXPEDITIONARY AND TRAVEL PHOTOGRAPHY

The global expansion of European and American power spurred the growth of photographic practice. Despite its unwieldy equipment and technical limitations, photography was seen as an important tool for information gathering. John Herschel had unsuccessfully suggested that photographic equipment be included in an 1839 British expedition to the Antarctic; then in 1842, American photographer Edward Anthony (1811–1888) accompanied a government survey of the northeast boundary of the United States and Canada.[30] None of Anthony's daguerreotypes survives, however. Despite modest success, the era's enthusiasm for exploration found a strong symbol in the camera. In 1846 the journal *Art Union* called it "an indispensable accompaniment to all exploring expeditions," which would "greatly ... abbreviate the toils and diminish the dangers of those who may follow" in the tracks of the explorer.[31]

EGYPT AND THE HOLY LAND

As early as 1839, François Arago had urged the use of the new medium of photography in copying the hieroglyphic inscriptions on ancient Egyptian buildings. He was envisioning a continuation of the extensive French documentation of ancient Egypt begun under Napoleon, but, although Egypt was one of the first sites to attract daguerrean photographers, they did not fulfill Arago's hope for a systematic visual survey of Egyptian antiquities. Instead, they composed views that responded to the European taste for picturesque ruins. The picturesque, meaning literally like a picture, was a broad aesthetic category in nineteenth-century thought. In general, it meant that a natural scene was composed in such a way that it stirred fine feelings or thoughts in the viewer, just as a painting or a sketch might do. By selecting such topics and designing scenes reminiscent of prints and paintings, photographers validated their efforts and won public acceptance.

2.34
HECTOR HOREAU,
Medinet Habu, plate 18 from *Panorama d'Égypte et de Nubie*, 1841. Aquatint from daguerreotype by Joly de Lotbinière. Resource Collections of the Getty Center for the History of Art and the Humanities, Los Angeles, California.

Because the daguerreotype was a unique image that did not produce a negative, it could only be copied by the daguerrean process. To produce copies, engraving and lithography were used. Views derived from daguerreotypes were sometimes printed (as here) using aquatint, an engraving process able to mimic the tonal range of daguerreotypes.

2.35
N. M. P. LEREBOURS,
Portail de Notre Dame de Paris (detail),
plate 43 from *Excursions Daguerriennes*,
1840–44. Engraving after a daguerreotype.
George Eastman House, Rochester, New York.

The photographic camera and operator, and a human subject leaning on the left side of the portal on the right, were probably added to this view of Notre-Dame, Paris, to provide both human interest and a sense of scale. This print is one of the earliest pictures to show a photographer at work.

Early photographers took advantage of the fact that several regions of the Middle East contained both ancient monuments and biblical sites. While on a Grand Tour of Greece, Egypt, and the Holy Land, the Swiss-born Canadian Pierre-Gustave Joly de Lotbinière (1798–1865) made daguerreotypes of Egyptian architecture. His work became the basis for the AQUATINTS issued by the architect and egyptologist Hector Horeau in *Panorama d'Égypte et de Nubie* (*Panorama of Egypt and Nubia*) (1841) (Fig. 2.34). Similarly, French publisher Noël Marie Paymal Lerebours (1807–1873) relied on daguerreotypes when he assembled a multi-volume work titled *Excursions Daguerriennes, representant les vues et les monuments les plus remarquables du globe* (*Daguerrian Excursions, Showing the World's Most Remarkable Views and Monuments*) (1840–44). Lerebours, who bought daguerreotypes and commissioned others for his publications, calculated that prospective buyers would not appreciate a straightforward transcription of daguerreotype views, so he adjusted harsh shadows and other elements to make his scenes more appealing to contemporary taste (Fig. 2.35).

Lerebours's *Excursions Daguerriennes* discounted the efforts of the many anonymous photographers who contributed daguerreotypes, and credited the publisher for conceptualizing, organizing, and printing the work. In the era of early photography, conceptualization was routinely prized over the actual taking and making of a photograph. In the portrait studio, for instance, the photographer might pose a client and arrange the lighting, while an assistant actually exposed and developed the image. For a long time, Scottish photographer David Octavius Hill was bestowed more distinction for the art direction of his pictures than his partner,

Robert Adamson, was given for the execution of them (see p. 72).

Among more than a hundred travel subjects included in *Excursions Daguerriennes* is a view of the Propylaea, or gateway to the Athenian Acropolis, taken by Lotbinière (Fig. 2.36). Greek photographers, too, photographed ancient remains, but daguerreotypes taken by Greeks of their homeland in the early 1840s do not survive.[32] A remarkable daguerreotype of a general view of the Acropolis from the hill of Philopappus was taken later by Greek painter Philippos Margaritis (1810–1892)[33] (Fig. 2.37).

The Holy Land was another destination for many early photographers, and the site for one of the first planned attempts to use photography as a form of persuasion. When working on a new edition of *Evidence of the Truth of the Christian Religion*, Alexander Keith (1791–1880) asked his son the medical doctor George Skene Keith (1819–1910), of Edinburgh, to make daguerreotypes that would show the veracity of the Bible. An earlier edition contained drawings probably not done on the site,[34] but for the new edition, published in 1844, George Keith took about thirty daguerreotypes, eighteen of which were made into engravings for the book, in order to "convince the unprejudiced inquirer or the rational and sincere believer, that it is impossible that his

2.36
JOLY DE LOTBINIÈRE, *View of the Propylaea of the Acropolis, Athens,* 1839, *from Excursions Daguerriennes,* 1840–44. Engraving after a daguerreotype. George Eastman House, Rochester, New York.

The gateway, or Propylaea, of the Athenian Acropolis was a portal through which well-to-do Europeans longed to pass as part of their Classical education. In this engraved version, the shadows on the columns have been noticeable softened in comparison with the original image, in which the deep shadows seem almost to cut the columns into pieces.

2.37
PHILIPPOS MARGARITIS, *Untitled* (Acropolis: general view from the Hill of Philopappus, southwest), 1865.
Daguerreotype. The J. Paul Getty Museum, Los Angeles, California.

This daguerreotype reveals more pronounced contrasts and greater detail than would an engraving after a daguerreotype (see Fig. 2.36). Margaritis learned the daguerreotype process from the traveling French photographer Philippe Perraud (born 1815).

faith be false."[35] Keith's images were accompanied by biblical quotations (Fig. 2.38). Not all Western photographers focused exclusively on places and buildings important to Christian belief. Among nearly a hundred daguerreotypes made by the French nobleman Joseph-Philibert Girault de Prangey (1804–1892), an admirer and student of Islamic architecture, are images of such famous buildings as the Dome of the Rock (Fig. 2.39).

Different methods of producing light-sensitive paper for photographs were also employed by travelers. French writer, amateur egyptologist, and student of Arabic literature Maxime Du Camp (1822–1894) adapted the process for an extended trip with writer Gustave Flaubert (1821–1880) to Egypt, Nubia,

and the Holy Land. Du Camp was commissioned by the French Ministry of Public Education to photograph Egypt's monuments. Flaubert, then largely unknown, held a commission from the Department of Agriculture to study crop production and trade. These commissions functioned like passports, allowing travelers to circumvent questions and delays.

After many struggles with the medium, Du Camp managed to make more than 200 paper negatives, 125 of which were printed, mounted on paper, and bound with an introduction. The photographs were printed by Louis Désiré Blanquart-Evrard (1802–1872), who perfected the calotype and also increased its yield. Blanquart-Evrard coated the light-sensitive paper with whey and albumen, derived from milk and eggs respectively. The coating allowed the so-called ALBUMEN PAPER to be prepared ahead of time, which quickly led to the commercialization of its production. With another entrepreneur, Blanquart-Evrard also operated a photographic printing factory, a further sign of photography's impending transition from a handicraft to an industrial process.

Unlike volumes that depended on engravings or aquatints based on daguerreotypes, Du Camp's *Égypte, Nubie, Palestine et Syrie* (*Egypt, Nubia, Palestine, and Syria*) (1852) contained reproductions of actual photographs, one of the first travel books to do so. Breaking with the newly established style of adjusting shadows and adding human figures to daguerreotype-based travel pictures, Du Camp chose more neutral views of ancient Egyptian art and architecture (Fig. 2.40). Having defined his goal as an accurate account of ancient Egyptian monuments, he

2.39
J. P. GIRAULT DE PRANGEY, *The Dome of the Rock and the Wailing Wall* (laterally reversed view), c. 1850.
Daguerreotype. Bibliothèque Nationale de France, Paris.

Since Girault de Prangey was excluded from Islamic sacred buildings, many of his views are taken at a distance.
His photograph of the Dome of the Rock, Jerusalem, shows the mosque and, in front of it, the Wailing Wall,
sacred to Jews.

made precise measurements of buildings as well as photographing them. He also recorded contemporary Arab culture, only to have most of these pictures rejected by his publisher, who thought they had no commercial value. Toward the end of his journey, Du Camp traded his photographic equipment for yards of embroidered fabric and never resumed his photographic work.

Not every photographer in Egypt was as committed to scientific detachment and neutral description as Du Camp. John B. Greene (1832–1856), born in France of an American family, actively pursued the study of both photography and ancient cultures, becoming one of the earliest archeologists to use the new medium in his work. Some of his images parallel those of Du Camp in depicting ancient Egyptian architecture, sculpture, and inscriptions with legibility and precision; other works seem more like evocative watercolors than

2.40
MAXIME DU CAMP, *Colossus of Memnon*, 1850. Salt print from paper negative. Gernsheim Collection. Harry Ransom Humanities Research Center, University of Texas at Austin.

In his Egyptian views, Du Camp chose points of view that created a sense of order, and conveyed a clear idea of the monument. The human figure standing in the lap of the colossus may seem comical, but was probably asked to stand there to give the viewer a sense of scale.

systematic records (Fig. 2.41). More than ninety of Greene's Egyptian images were published by Blanquart-Evrard in *Le Nil: Paysage, explorations photographiques* (*The Nile: Landscape and Photographic Explorations*) (1854).

The idea of the photographic series—that is, of creating and arranging images in meaningful sequences—was increasingly adopted in historical, archeological, travel, scientific, medical, and even art photography. During the medium's earliest years, compilations of dissimilar and unrelated images, such as those found in Lerebours's *Excursions Daguerriennes* and Talbot's *The Pencil of Nature*, were prevalent. But as photography proliferated, the arrangements of related images were published more frequently. Photographic series expanded the notion of photography from that of an image-making process to something akin to writing. Nineteenth-century albums and books containing interrelated pictures underscored the photographer's skill in building up what the twentieth century would know as the photographic essay. Slowly, commentators began to concede that some photography—series, aesthetic endeavors, and scientific improvements—involved intellectual exertion, a claim that would serve to distance professional and serious amateur photographers from itinerant and part-time practitioners.

THE HISTORIC MONUMENTS COMMISSION

In its historical and civic interest, as well as its convenient stillness and large masses, architecture was suited to photography. Moreover, as historian Janet Buerger observed, in the medium's early period, cityscapes were more popular in photography than in any previous art medium. The growth of urban areas during the mid-nineteenth century doubtless helped make the city an object

2.41
JOHN B. GREENE, *The Banks of the Nile at Thebes,* **1854. Salted paper print from a waxed paper negative. George Eastman House, Rochester, New York.**

Early photographic materials were so sensitive to the light of the sky that the upper regions of photographs tended to be overexposed. Consequently, some photographers selected angles that diminished the prominence of the sky. Others, such as Greene in this Egyptian scene, deliberately used the blankness to create a sense of emptiness.

of increased interest. Photographers often chose to picture the enduring monuments from the past with which the public customarily identified cities. For example, Frederick von Martens (1809–1875), a French photographer of German descent who made photographs for Lerebours, invented a rotating camera. His panoramic view of Paris sweeps down the Seine River to the Cathedral of Notre-Dame, which was enclosed in scaffolding for repairs (Fig. 2.42).

A grand series of architectural photographs was undertaken by the Historic Monuments Commission of the French Ministry of the Interior. Formed prior to the disclosure of photography to the world, the commission was charged with listing, surveying, and making recommendations for the historically correct restoration of French medieval and Gothic architecture. This task seemed urgent for several reasons. The aftermath of the French Revolution, the expansion of urban populations, and the industrial disruption of the country-side all nurtured a sense that the future would be markedly different from the past. In turn, this recognition of rapidly passing time heightened public apprecia-tion of history and historical landmarks, many of which had been very seriously neglected or damaged. Moreover, French medieval and Gothic buildings were cherished symbols of cultural achieve-ment, intensified by France's political and economic rivalry with Britain.

This politically charged atmosphere helped to revitalize the Historic Monuments Commission, which, by 1850, was considering whether to use photography in its architectural inven-tory. It might have been expected that the commission would choose the

daguerreotype, a French invention that rendered a more detailed image than did the British calotype. Yet the commis-sion rejected the daguerreotype's cold metallic tinge in favor of the softer forms produced by the calotype. Further, a leading member of the commission complained that people of taste had not fully accepted the daguerreotype, because its mass of details was more distracting than artful. By contrast, the calotype's less sharply defined shapes and details and its evocative shadows more eloquently expressed nostalgia for the medieval past. The large size of the calotype was also an attractive feature, as was its ability to produce negatives from which multiple copies could be made.[36]

The photographic enterprise, which came to be known collectively as the Missions Héliographiques, employed several French photographers, the first of whom was Hippolyte Bayard, then vice-president of the recently founded professional association the Société Héliographique. Like many early photo-graphic organizations, it did not special-ize in any one kind of photographic practice. It encouraged artistic, scien-tific, and technical discussions, and published a journal. Within this group, and others similar to it in Europe and America, scientists created what would be called artistic photographs, and artists freely experimented with the chemistry of photography.

Five members of the Société Héliographique (Edouard Baldus, Hippolyte Bayard, Gustave Le Gray, Henri Le Secq, O. Mestral), were chosen by the Historic Monuments Commission, among them Edouard Baldus (1813–1889), who brought a remarkable inventiveness to the task.

Typically, Missions Héliographiques photographers were assigned areas of France and particular monuments. Among Baldus's destinations was the church of Saint-Trophîme in Arles, a city in the south of France. In the adjacent medieval cloister, the self-styled "painter-photographer" Baldus cleverly devised an image-making process that went beyond the scope of his camera's vision. He created a large print of the *Cloister of Saint-Trophîme, Arles* (1851) by joining many negatives, and by retouching them where necessary (Fig. 2.43). In this effort, Baldus defined the photograph not as the pure product of a single camera exposure, but as a flexible basis for picture-making. Throughout its subsequent history, photographers would juggle two notions, either aligning themselves with the idea of the inherently unique value of the unretouched negative and print, or maintaining that camerawork is, and should be, multifold, embracing not only the pure print but also all manipulations of the images.

Henri Le Secq (1818–1882), another of the Missions Héliographiques

photographers, was also a painter and antiquarian. His undertakings for the Historic Monuments Commission often produced finely detailed registers of architecture and sculpture, as in the *Tour des Rois* (*Tower of Kings*) from the south tower of Reims Cathedral (1851) (Fig. 2.44). In his other work, Le Secq orchestrated images in which deep shadows mute detail and create such

**2.43 (below and right)
EDOUARD BALDUS,**
Cloister of Saint-Trophîme, Arles, 1851.
Partly hand-painted paper print. Musée National des Monuments Français, Paris.

Rather than accept the modest range of his lens, which could not encompass the full scope of the cloister, Baldus made ten sharply focused negatives and subtly connected them (see the white lines in the thumbnail, right). He retouched the joins, and accentuated tones across the negative's surface. The image of the vault directly above where Baldus would have stood is not a camera image at all, but a hand-painted negative, carefully affixed to the rest.[37]

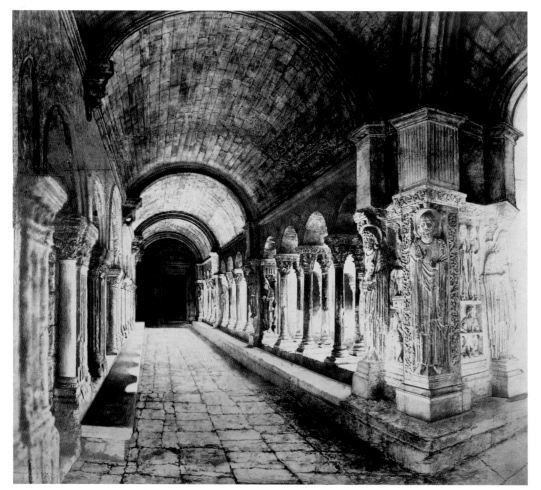

**2.44 (opposite)
HENRI LE SECQ,**
Tower of Kings, Reims Cathedral, 1851. Salted paper print. The J. Paul Getty Museum, Los Angeles, California.

The photographic journal *La Lumière* praised this image by Le Secq as having been reported stone by stone.[38] Le Secq recorded the tower from an angle few visitors would have seen, and thereby showed details that could not be viewed from the ground. The scaffolding on the left side of the picture indicates that restoration has already begun; it was carried out between 1845 and 1864.

2.45
HENRI LE SECQ,
Farmyard Scene, near St. Leu-d'Esserent,
c. 1852. Cyanotype print from paper negative.
Museum Purchase.
George Eastman House,
Rochester, New York.

sharp contrasts that the photograph even approaches abstraction (Fig. 2.45); he also made ingenious still-life photographs.

The subject matter of the Historic Monuments Commission was taken up by other photographers without official appointments to the commission,

notably Charles Nègre (1820–1880). Nègre, a painter, progressed from daguerreotype to paper photography in the late 1840s. He made architectural photographs and a unique series of street photographs, including images of organ grinders, rag pickers, and chimney sweeps (Fig. 2.46).

2.46
CHARLES NÈGRE,
Chimney Sweeps Walking. Salted paper print. National Gallery of Canada.

Photographs of workers going about their chores are rare in early photography, and Nègre's are among the first. From the look of the chimney sweeps' feet, it appears that Nègre asked his subjects to stop momentarily in order to record their appearance. The background areas of the photograph have been retouched, to diminish the details of the buildings so as to emphasize the sweeps.

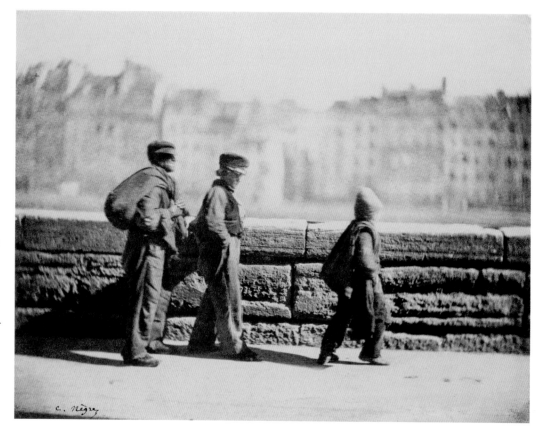

PORTRAITURE AND THE CAMERA

A wide range of photographic practice developed rapidly in the medium's early years. Yet neither landscape, nor still life, nor the variety of scientific practice acquired quite the aura of magic that the portrait photograph did. At first, Daguerre thought that portraits were impracticable, and the otherwise imaginative François Arago likewise declared that there was little hope that the technique could be used for portraiture. In the earliest daguerreotypes (Fig. 2.47), sitters tended to move or blink during the long exposure time required, blurring the images. It was some time, too, before the modern smile became an omnipresent convention. The chemistry making possible shorter exposure times improved swiftly, and devices to hold heads still were soon invented, bringing on a rush of daguerrean portraits (Fig. 2.48). The detailed, silver-surfaced daguerreotype was resolutely preferred to the more atmospheric calotype prints. American scientist, inventor, and artist Samuel F. B. Morse

(1791–1872) was in Paris when Daguerre's invention was first announced. In March 1839, in exchange for an invitation to see how the telegraph worked, Daguerre showed Morse his photographic process. Morse's interest in camera images, however, had predated that of Daguerre. About thirty years earlier, he had unsuccessfully attempted to fix images obtained in a camera obscura.

Once instructions for making the daguerreotype became available, Morse was among the first to make images. Although occasionally frustrated by the unpredictable medium, he is reputed to have produced an extraordinary image of members of the Yale University class of 1810, as they gathered in August 1840 for their thirtieth reunion (Fig. 2.49). The frame surrounding the collection of portraits measures only 3¼ by 4¼ inches, and each image is only ½-inch square. It is not known if the images were somehow reduced in size from larger portraits, or whether the ingenious maker used a special camera to make diminutive originals, which were then rephotographed.[39]

2.47
ROBERT CORNELIUS (attrib.), *Seated Couple*, c. 1840. Daguerreotype. Floyd & Marion Rinhart Collection, Ohio State University Libraries, Columbus, Ohio.

Early photographs required an exposure time of two minutes or more. The stern expressions and wide-open eyes of sitters sometimes resulted from their attempts to keep still and not blink.

2.48
HONORÉ DAUMIER,
Nouveau procédé employé pour obtenir des poses gracieuses, c. 1856. Lithograph on paper. National Gallery of Canada/Musée des Beaux-Arts du Canada, Ottawa.

Cartoons spoofing the inconveniences of early portrait photography soon appeared. Many studios employed vise-like equipment, hidden by the sitter's hair and body in the final picture, to steady the head.

2.49 (below)
S. F. B. MORSE (?),
Graduates of Yale, Class of 1810, 1840. Daguerreotype.

The earliest daguerreotype portraits are often rigidly frontal. The sitter sat beneath a skylight, while reflectors directed more light on selected features (Fig. 2.50). Given the discomfort involved, the *Daguerrean Journal* suggested that resolute indifference was "the best expression for a Daguerreotype."[40]

Subsequently, viewers could pore over daguerreotypes with magnifying lenses, marveling at the details of representation, especially the outlines of family resemblance and the contrast between youth and age.

In London, in March 1841, Richard Beard (1802–1885) opened a daguerreotype studio, the first licensed public source for daguerreotypes in Britain. It was quickly followed by the studio of another licensee, the London firm of French entrepreneur Jean-François-Antoine Claudet (1797–1867). In 1851, Claudet enlarged his London offices, establishing what he called the "Temple to Photography," a studio decorated with painted portrait medallions of artists, scientists, and photographic pioneers. Claudet's attempt to claim for photography the status of both a science and an art would be variously repeated throughout the nineteenth century.

Claudet's portrait work quickly diversified: he added backdrops and studio props, and he grouped his sitters in aesthetically pleasing arrangements. His 1851 daguerreotype *The Geography Lesson* shows a man standing before a globe, and children with books, the central one of which shows a print of a classical building (Fig. 2.51). The image is a daguerreotype using the STEREOGRAPHY technique—that is, produced by two

2.50
GEORGE
CRUIKSHANK,
*Photographic
Phenomena*, 1842.
Paper print. Gernsheim
Collection. Humanities
Research Center,
University of Texas
at Austin.

PHOTOGRAPHIC PHENOMENA, OR THE NEW SCHOOL
OF PORTRAIT-PAINTING.

" Sit, cousin Percy ; sit, good cousin Hotspur !"—HENRY IV.
" My lords, be seated."—*Speech from the Throne.*

2.51
J. F. A. CLAUDET,
The Geography Lesson,
1851. Stereoscopic
daguerreotype.
Gernsheim Collection.
Harry Ransom
Humanities Research
Center, University of
Texas at Austin.

Claudet specialized in
intricate arrangements
of his sitters. The image
being viewed by this
group might well be a
photograph produced
in engraved form by
a publisher such as
Lerebours.[41]

cameras spaced to imitate human binocular vision. In a special viewer, the two stereographic images appeared to be a single three-dimensional scene. Though obviously posed, Claudet's picture is not far-fetched. Books such as Lerebours's *Daguerrian Excursions* were used to teach geography to a generation of children.

In Berlin, Gustav Oehme (1817–1881), an optician who studied with Daguerre, set up a photography studio. He seems to have arranged the family in his 1847 group portrait to maximize the appearance of casual good-naturedness (Fig. 2.52). The necessity for clients to hold a pose is nevertheless evident on the right, where the girl is steadied by the woman next to her. Photographers and sitters abandoned rigid appearances as soon as technical improvements permitted: clients learned to appear joyful, studious, or reflective, and smiles and signs of congeniality

swept through photographic practice. In the literature of the time, the idea of enacting an emotion for the camera was not felt to conflict with the notion that photographs rendered truth to experience. The photographic studio emerged as a new social space in which sitters could compose and record an image of how they desired to appear for acquaintances, strangers, and posterity.

COLORING THE IMAGE

When the Russian daguerreotypist Aleksei Grekov (1779/80–1850s) titled his 1840 booklet *A Painter without a Brush and Paint, Photographing Any Images, Portraits, Landscapes, etc., in Their True and Faithful Colour in a Few Minutes,* he was referring to the gray scale of the daguerreotype, not to hues on the color spectrum.[42] However, daguerreotypes were sometimes hand-tinted, to avoid the gray tones that

2.52
GUSTAV OEHME,
Group Portrait in Oehme's Studio, Berlin, April 11, 1847. Daguerreotype. Robert Lebeck Collection. Rheinisches Bildarchiv, Cologne, Germany.

By the late 1840s, sitters preferred to appear casual and affectionate. Smiles began to replace the stern faces of the early 1840s.

**2.53
PHOTOGRAPHER
UNKNOWN,** *James
Warner Woolsey, Nevada
City, Miner, with Nugget
Weighing over Eight
Pounds,* 1849–50.
Daguerreotype. Mrs.
Philip Kendall Bekeart
Collection.

The hand-painted gold
nugget conveys the
sitter's good fortune
during the California
gold rush. His carefully
curled locks and trim
moustache seem to
suggest that his luck has
allowed him to afford a
fine barber. When men
set out for the gold rush,
they were frequently
photographed wearing
rough cloths and hold-
ing a pick and shovel.

**2.54 (below)
J. A. MOULIN,** *Étude:
Séduction,* c. 1852.
Paper print. Bibliothèque
Nationale de France,
Paris.

Paris photographer
Jacques-Antoine Moulin
(c. 1800–c. 1869),
who specialized in
académies, was adept at
contriving poses that
used suggestive drapery
and exotic settings.

customers identified with illness and
death.[43] French critic Francis Wey
denounced the unrelenting gray of the
daguerreotype portrait as "fried fish
pasted on to metal plaques."[44] Some
photographers attempted to create
daguerreotypes that would be automatically colored by chemical reactions to
light rays.

Color was not always a simple, realistic addition to a photograph. In a portrait of James Warner Woolsey, the gold
nugget was subsequently wash-painted
to achieve a symbolic quality (Fig. 2.53).
The color was applied by an artist painting directly on to the daguerreotype,
probably with a thin camel-hair brush.
Soft pastel colors were often added to
warm the skin tones in erotic daguerreotypes, the market for which expanded
when stereographic daguerreotypes
began to be produced. The creation of
so-called *académies*, photographs of
nudes and semi-nude women, profess-
edly made for the use of artists, provided
some daguerreotypists and calotypists
with additional income, as did frankly
erotic photographs (Fig. 2.54). Pictured

singly or in groups, the nude female figure substantially outnumbered male nudes (Fig. 2.55). The capability of the paper photograph to make multiple prints allowed the output of nude photographs to increase rapidly: as historian Elizabeth Anne McCauley has shown, despite some attempts at censorship, soft-core pornographic photographs were one of the first mass-market products.[45]

As materials became more widely available and reliable, photographic practice grew. An 1848 American article declared that "in our great cities, a daguerreotypist is to be found in almost every square; and there is scarcely a county in any state that has not one or more of these industrious individuals busy at work catching 'the shadow' ere the 'substance fade.'"[46] The idea of securing the shadow, or image, before the sitter deceased was not always possible; it sometimes meant commissioning images of dead people. The custom of

making a deathbed image, through making a death mask or painting, was democratized through photography and became a routine practice among the mid-nineteenth-century middle classes. Because of the high mortality rate, infants and children were the frequent subjects of such photographs, which were not, as today, considered ghoulish (Fig. 2.56). The post-mortem photograph became widespread in America and throughout Europe. Later, when most people had photographs of their family and friends, the practice declined.

THE PHOTOGRAPHY STUDIO

A European observer remarked that "American daguerreotypists go to enormous expense for their rooms, which are most elegantly furnished ... Everything is ... united to distract the mind of the visitor from his cares and give to his countenance an expression of calm contentment."[47] In the biggest

2.55
EUGÈNE DURIEU,
Académie de l'Album Delacroix réunissant,
1853–54. Paper print.
Bibliothèque Nationale de France, Paris.

The painter Eugène Delacroix commissioned several photographic studies for his work, such as this male nude. Delacroix maintained that photography was too unimaginative to be a genuine art.

2.56
PHOTOGRAPHER
UNKNOWN, *Father
and Mother Holding
a Dead Child*,
c. 1850–1860s.
Daguerreotype. Strong
Museum, Rochester,
New York.

Post-mortem photo-
graphy flourished in
photography's early
decades, among clients
who preferred to capture
an image of a deceased
loved one rather than
have no photograph
at all.

2.57
AUGUSTUS WASHINGTON, *John Brown*, c. 1846–47. Quarter-plate daguerreotype. National Portrait Gallery, Smithsonian Institution, Washington, D.C.

Washington may have met Brown through their mutual anti-slavery activities
in New England. One of the earliest American photographers of African and
Asian descent, Washington worked in Hartford, Connecticut, a stronghold of the
abolitionist movement.

2.58
ALEXANDER S. THOMAS, *James Presley Ball*, late 1850s–early 1860s. Daguerreotype.
Cincinnati Art Museum. Gift of James M. Marrs, M.D. Photo: Walsh 11/1999.

Ball created a six-hundred-yard painted panorama based on his 1855 anti-slavery
pamphlet, *Ball's Splendid Mammoth Pictorial Tour of the United States Comprising
Views of the African Slave Trade; of Northern and Southern Cities, of Cotton and Sugar
Plantations; of the Mississippi, Ohio and Susquehanna Rivers, Niagara Falls, etc.*

American cities, daguerrean studios began to rival part-time and itinerant photographers. The historian Alan Trachtenberg observed that "sitters were encouraged to will themselves into the desired self-expression," thereby creating "a role and a mask."[48] Salon owners might employ fashion and hair stylists, while less expensive venues too began to provide visual symbols of personal achievement and economic success for their portraits. Plain backgrounds were replaced by painted backdrops, such as garden scenes, and studio props such as columns, chairs, tables, rugs, books, sculptures, and flowers were added to reflect the sitter's interests, attitudes, or aspirations.

The shift from relatively unaffected pictures to images in which sitters used the new medium to enact an appearance gave photographers more leeway in which to design photographic representations. As one example, Augustus Washington's (1820/1821–1875) powerful portrait of American abolitionist John Brown depends on the orchestration of Brown's hands (Fig. 2.57). One is raised in the position of vow-making or challenge, while the other grasps a flag thought to be that of the Subterranean Pass Way, Brown's unrealized scheme for an organization such as the Underground Railroad, which assisted runaway slaves. Washington, the son of a former slave and an Asian woman, was an active abolitionist. He eventually emigrated to Liberia, the African country acquired by the American Colonization Society, which promoted the repatriation of freed slaves. Washington prospered in Africa, running several photographic studios, farming sugarcane, and serving in the Liberian Congress.

Like Washington, other African-American photographers catered to both white and black customers. At least fifty black daguerreotypists are known to have practiced in the United States during photography's first decade.[49] J. P. (James Presley) Ball (1825–1904), also an active abolitionist, began his career in Cincinnati, Ohio, and soon built the city's largest and most successful photographic practice in a studio he called the "Great Daguerrian Gallery of the West" (Fig. 2.58). During his long life, he attracted a wide clientele, including celebrities such as Frederick Douglass and Charles Dickens. He worked in a variety of photographic processes and established studios in Montana, Washington, and perhaps also in Hawaii, where he died.

CELEBRITY PHOTOGRAPHY

Numerous photographic studios attracted customers by exhibiting images of celebrities. Studios offered free daguerreotypes to celebrities from all walks of life in exchange for the right to exhibit their likenesses, and to reproduce them, mostly as engravings or lithographs. In the mid-1840s, John Plumbe (1809–1857), an American photographer who was born in Wales, devised a plan to mass-produce celebrity photographs by offering subscribers a daily portrait of the rich and famous.[50] Though this scheme failed, early photographers encouraged the public taste for celebrity likenesses. Realistic images of political figures helped to shift the public's perception of politics away from events and toward personalities. Lithographs based on photographs also featured well-known public people, as in a print showing Daniel Webster's 1850 address to the United States Senate. This was part of the fiery debate that led to the Compromise of 1850, which allowed slavery to continue in the states where it existed, but not in the newly acquired state of California. To create the lithograph, engraved versions of daguerreotype portraits were affixed to hand-drawn bodies, with the disturbing result that the senators' out-of-scale heads look like an arrangement of fruit (Fig. 2.59).

THE FIRM OF SOUTHWORTH AND HAWES

The Boston photographic establishment run by Albert Sands Southworth (1811–1894) and Josiah Johnson Hawes (1808–1901) exhibited large daguerreotypes of political and cultural celebrities, along with scenes of Boston's economic prosperity and historical heritage (Figs. 2.60 and 2.61). Southworth and Hawes specialized in large—that is, whole-plate—daguerreotypes (usually $6\frac{1}{2}$ inches wide by $8\frac{1}{2}$ inches high) that cost about $15. At a time when commonplace daguerreotypes sold for about $2, and some were even advertised for as low

2.59 (above)
PHOTOGRAPHER
UNKNOWN, *Daniel Webster Addressing the U.S. Senate in the Great Debate on the Compromise Measures of 1850*, 1850. Lithograph made from daguerreotypes by Eliphalet M. Brown. Library of Congress, Washington, D.C.

The heads of the senators listening to Daniel Webster were copied from daguerreotypes made by Eliphalet Brown, who later accompanied Commodore Matthew C. Perry to Japan (see p. 124).

2.60
ALBERT SANDS
SOUTHWORTH & JOSIAH
JOHNSON HAWES,
McKay's Shipyard, East Boston, c. 1855. Daguerreotype. Museum of Fine Arts, Boston, Massachusetts.

**2.61
ALBERT SANDS
SOUTHWORTH &
JOSIAH JOHNSON
HAWES,** *Harriet
Beecher Stowe,*
c. 1850. Quarter-plate
daguerreotype.
Metropolitan Museum,
New York.

Stowe's *Uncle Tom's
Cabin* was published in
installments in 1850, the
same year as this photo-
graph. Photographs
of well-known persons
were displayed in
photographic studios
to encourage business.
Celebrities often were
offered free photo-
graphs in exchange for
permission to exhibit
their image.

as 25 cents,[51] Southworth and Hawes
boasted that they did no cheap work.

The notion of the daguerreotypist
as an artist was forcefully advanced by
Albert Sands Southworth, in his self-
portrait and in his writing (Fig. 2.62).
He maintained that "the artist, even in
photography, must go beyond discovery
and the knowledge of facts. He must
create and invent truths, and produce
new developments of facts." Playing on
the mid-nineteenth-century interest in
character study, Southworth described

the role of the photographer as catching
"the whole character of the sitter ... at
first sight." Southworth affirmed that
"Nature is not all to be represented as it is,
but as it ought to be, and might possibly
have been."[52]

THE CALOTYPE PORTRAIT:
HILL AND ADAMSON

The absence of specialization in early
photography produced remarkable
hybrids. The work of David Octavius
Hill (1802–1870) and Robert Adamson

2.62
**ALBERT SANDS
SOUTHWORTH,**
Self-Portrait, c. 1848.
Daguerreotype. Gilman
Paper Company
Collection, New York.

Southworth contrived
a dramatically lit picture,
with a delicate, rich
progression of gray
tones. Back-lighted, as
were many of his clients,
Southworth showed
himself in the guise
of a thoughtful, long-
suffering, Romantic
painter.

(1821–1848) in Scotland encompassed landscape, portraiture, and ethnographic recording. Hill was originally a landscape painter and lithographer, who was asked to create a commemorative painting showing the clergymen who participated in the 1843 independence movement that freed the Scottish Church from the Church of England. Daunted by the thought of sketching the 400 people present, he asked Edinburgh engineer turned photographer Robert Adamson to photograph the participants. Trading on

the traditional understanding of the commemorative painting, Hill included portraits of persons who were not present at the original event in the work, finished twenty years later, titled *The Signing of the Deed of Demission*.[53] Like the print of Daniel Webster speaking to the Senate (see Fig. 2.59), the painting relinquished perspective and enlarged the proportions of the heads so that the faces would show clearly. But with the calotypes generated during their brief collaboration, Hill and Adamson were more visually inventive.

2.63
DAVID OCTAVIUS HILL & ROBERT ADAMSON, *Dr. Alexander Keith*, c. 1843. Paper print. Scottish National Portrait Gallery, Edinburgh.

Hill and Adamson developed a style of male portraiture that emphasized Reverend Keith's head and hands, parts of the body thought to express inner character (see also p. 52). Perhaps because their images incorporated aesthetic values also found in paintings, there were few objections to their non-naturalistic use of photography.

They turned the calotype's formal qualities to their advantage. Rather than imitating the itemizing detail of the daguerreotype, Hill and Adamson composed within the softer forms resulting from the calotype's paper negative. Adapting artistic principles of light and shade (CHIAROSCURO), they orchestrated the surface with large areas of shadow, which suppressed fine detail. They posed sitters artfully, and used intense, unnaturalistic lighting to create theatrical effects (Fig. 2.63). Viewers compared Hill and Adamson's style to the light and shadow effects in Rembrandt's works, a resemblance that Talbot had also remarked in relation to his early work.[54] Hill was especially pleased with what others, particularly proponents of the daguerreotype, found inferior in the calotype process. He admitted that "The rough surface, and unequal texture throughout of the paper is the main cause of the Calotype failing in details, before the process of Daguerreotypy [sic]." Of calotypes, he wrote that "they look like the imperfect work of a man—and not the much diminished perfect work of God."[55]

The exposure time for Hill and Adamson's calotypes could be as long as two minutes. They photographed outdoors, usually in direct sunlight, often using monuments in Edinburgh's Greyfriars' churchyard as a backdrop. They encouraged sitters to enrich their portraits with expressive props, such as books or drawing implements. In addition to their portrait work, Hill and Adamson made some of the earliest anthropological photographs in the nearby fishing village of Newhaven (Fig. 2.64), whose waning traditional way of life contrasted with that of industrializing Edinburgh. These and other prints by Hill and Adamson appealed to the yearning for simpler, pre-industrial times. They were sold singly or in albums, through booksellers and galleries, thus extending the market for photographs.

When the images were shown at the Royal Scottish Academy, Adamson was listed as executing the photographs, while Hill gave artistic direction. This information was perhaps intended to convince painters that photographs might be shown in their gallery. But it also indicates the split between

2.64
DAVID OCTAVIUS HILL & ROBERT ADAMSON, *Mrs. Elizabeth Hall and Unknown Woman (Newhaven Fishwives)*, c. 1845. Salted paper print. Scottish National Portrait Gallery, Edinburgh.

FOCUS
The First Police Pictures?

An exceptional early series of 220 photographic portraits of itinerant people was made by Swiss photographer and lithographer Carl Durheim (1810–1890) from 1852 to 1853. During a large-scale Swiss government operation, stateless, itinerant people were held in open confinement in the city of Bern, and forced to adopt a more settled life. They had been poor tradespeople who moved from town to town, subsisting as tinkers and grinders, or by making baskets (Fig. 2.65).

The images were intended to be transformed from paper photographs into lithographs and distributed to the police so they could identify any of the itinerants who strayed from Bern. Thinking that it would make identification easier, the photographer tried to show as much of the person's body as possible. Although police pictures did not become routine until the 1880s, occasional portraits of criminals were made in the late 1850s and 1860s. The slow development was caused by the absence of an accepted format with which to standardize them and of a network through which to circulate them.

2.65
CARL DURHEIM, *Katharina Josephine Wächter*, 1852–53. Salted paper print. Swiss Federal Archive, Bern.

conceptualization and implementation in early photography. For about a century after Hill's death in 1870, their collaborative work was largely credited to Hill's imagination as a painter, rather than to Adamson's technical virtuosity.[56]

THE REALITY EFFECT

Unlike painting and engraving, photography left relatively few visible traces of its manufacture. Compared with brushstrokes and a network of lines, the daguerreotype seemed like a smooth mirror that did not betray how it was made. As a result, the photograph was seen as an automatic recording device that required no interpretation. Increasingly the photograph was believed to be what the average person would have seen standing in the same spot at the same time as the photographer. Stereoscopic daguerreotypes, such as *The Geography Lesson* (see Fig. 2.51), added the illusion of three-dimensionality. The fact that photographers such as Baldus (see p. 58) manipulated and retouched negatives did not significantly affect the public's belief in photographic truth. Neither did the increasing use of calculated poses and studio props in portrait photography.

Belief in the medium's objective reflection of reality was reinforced by photographers' efforts to intensify the appearance of truth. For example, while ornate backgrounds and symbolic objects continued to be used, some photographers returned to the plain backgrounds of the earliest daguerreotypes, and had the sitter look directly into the camera. This technique made the photograph seem unaffected. By using bust shots, facial features were enlarged, sometimes to life size, giving the impression of a personal encounter, as if the viewer personally knew the sitter well enough to enter his or her private space.

With the increased "reality effect" came a lasting dilemma, detectable in many early photographs: the tension between visual intensity taken as truth and the larger, societal significance of a subject. This problem is evident in what may be the first daguerreotypes of Native Americans. During the 1840s, St. Louis photographer Thomas M. Easterly photographed the Sauk and

the Fox, who were resettled by the U.S. government to the Nemaha Reservation in what is now the state of Kansas. His image of the chief Keokuk (Fig. 2.66) uses impressive detail, a simple backdrop, and restrained hand-coloring to connote immediacy and truthfulness. Yet this image was far from historically comprehensive. At the time it was made, Keokuk had been appointed by United States Indian Affairs officials to replace a more rebellious leader. He and other Sauk and Fox companions were in St. Louis to give an entertainment performance of so-called war dances at a circus. Like the photograph of the 1848 Chartist meeting (see Fig. 2.29), Keokuk's portrait does not lie, but nor does it tell the full story. In public discussions and literature, the capacity of the photograph to seem whole and complete, while omitting relevant truths, was rarely addressed directly. Nevertheless, the conflicts in society's understanding of photography and the problems of truth-telling found some expression in mid-nineteenth-century literature.

2.66
THOMAS EASTERLY, *Keokuk, or the Watchful Fox,* **1847. Hand-colored quarter-plate daguerreotype. Missouri Historical Society, St. Louis, Missouri.**

Easterly's portrait of *Keokuk, or the Watchful Fox,* a chief of the Sauk and Fox, concentrated on the sitter's worn face and distinctive clothing. He relied on a plain, neutral background to accentuate the sitter's pensive look, while he highlighted the exotic elements of Native American apparel.

PHOTOGRAPHY AND FICTION

In overwrought language and outlandish plots, popular fiction played on the visual veracity of photography, suggesting that the medium could reach beneath the surface to penetrate the minds of sitters. It could thwart villains and make straight the path of true love. This good magic was complemented by stories of bad photographic magic, in which Svengali-like daguerreotypists spied on newlyweds and lured innocents from their families. In such stories, the mysterious and compelling powers of hypnotism and mesmerism (a variety of hypnotism thought to be induced by magnetic fields, in vogue during photography's early years) were merged with photography. Some sitters reported that they felt drawn to the camera's eye, or unnerved by the experience of being photographed, as if they were being scrutinized, or compelled to act like a marionette. In a daguerreotype of a hypnotism session, most of the participants appear unaware of the camera's presence, as though they are in what was termed a "magnetic sleep" (Fig. 2.67).

The best-known story about photography's double-life as a recorder of reality and a mysterious generator of insights into character is Nathaniel Hawthorne's *The House of the Seven Gables*. By 1851, when Hawthorne published the novel, public perception of photography's relationship to truth had emerged as a pivotal metaphor for knowledge and ignorance. The story's central character, Mr. Holgrave, is a daguerreotypist. His portraits have special powers, extending human sight into insight, and revealing what ordinary vision cannot bring into focus: the moral character of individuals.

The nineteenth-century trust in character reading of facial features and human gestures, which predated the invention of photography, soon transferred to photography. In *The House of the Seven Gables*, that faith was enhanced by the association of magic with daguerrean realism. Belief in the extraordinary powers of photography was manifest in sitters' requests to photographers, such

2.67
JOHN ADAMS
WHIPPLE, *Hypnotism*,
c. 1845. Daguerreotype,
no. 113. Gilman Paper
Company Collection,
New York.

Hypnotism and photography were both associated with magic and mystery in the public mind. John Adams Whipple was the Boston scientist who, with George Phillips Bond, successfully made daguerreotype views of the moon in about 1851 (see Fig. 2.0).

as the one that photographers use tokens of the dead, for example a scarf or hat, to summon forth the image of the departed one for a photograph.[57] Fiction gave voice to the way in which growing public confidence in photographic representation was mixed with wariness about its power.

PHILOSOPHY AND PRACTICE: A THREAT TO ART?

Photography is arguably the most historically aware visual medium. The writing of its history began with the disclosure of the medium to the world in 1839, and persisted as a preoccupation throughout nineteenth-century photographic literature. Isidore Niépce, son of Joseph Nicéphore Niépce, attempted to assert his father's place in history with a slim 1841 volume called *Historique de la découverte improprement nommé daguerréotype* (*History of the Discovery Improperly Called Daguerreotype*). In the same year, Robert Hunt (1807–1887), a geologist and staunch advocate of photography from the first, published *A Popular Treatise on the Art of Photography*, which served to introduce the public to both photographic history and techniques.

Despite the historical interests of photography's proponents, subjects with no evident scientific, archival, artistic, or commercial value were neglected. Child laborers, for instance, are largely absent from early photography. Images of working men and women, except when stiffly posed with tools or clothed in quaint ethnic and regional costume, are also uncommon. Scenes of ordinary activities such as preparing food are exceedingly rare, unless these activities are performed in an exotic culture.

Photography's association with the broad technological changes taking place in the industrializing world was firmly fixed within the medium's first decade. Both its proponents and its critics likened photography to such major modern inventions as the steam engine and the telegraph. Writing in 1840 about Italian Renaissance art, British critic Francis Palgrave (1788–1861) produced a vituperative aside on modern inventions, including photography:

"Steam-engine and furnace, the steel plate, the roller, the press, the Daguerreotype, the Voltaic battery, and the lens, are the antagonist principles of art."[58] By contrast, an unnamed commentator for an 1843 issue of the *Edinburgh Review* effused that photography "is indeed as great a step in the fine arts, as the steam-engine was in the mechanical arts ... and ... it will take the highest rank among the inventions of the present age." Yet this writer urged his readers to make a clear distinction between the linear, cumulative development of science and technology, and what constitutes genuine advancement in art. Progress in art, the reviewer declared, was not endlessly incremental: "It would be hazardous to assert that Apelles and Zeuxis were surpassed by Reynolds and Lawrence, and still more so that Praxiteles and Phidias must have yielded the palm to Canova and Chantrey."[59]

As belief in the objectivity of photography took hold, the medium was belittled as a potential art form. Influential British critic John Ruskin (1819–1900) contradicted himself on the matter of the daguerreotype. After calling it a blessing in 1845, less than a year later he found it a matter of serious concern. Acknowledging the daguerreotype as "the most marvellous invention of the century," Ruskin worried about its effects on viewers' perceptions of art: "As regards art, I wish it had never been discovered, it will make the eye too fastidious to accept mere handling."[60]

Photography, for Ruskin, was so wedded to minute appearances that it could not express the personality and soul of the artist. His was a new twist on an old theme: after an October 1839 exhibition of daguerreotypes at the Academy of Arts in St. Petersburg, Russia, one reviewer reported that "the daguerreotype is a useless means of making portraits," because "mathematical verisimilitude and lifeless precision do not do justice to a portrait, for which one needs expression and life; these can only be conveyed by the animating strength of talent and thought of an individual — no machine can do this."[61] Similarly, Eugène Delacroix, who sometimes used photographs as aids for his work, called the camera a machine that makes pictures untrue to human perception.

Where the mind filters and emphasizes, the machine does not. It cannot engage the world as the mind can, and its intractable verisimilitude prevented the dialogue of soul to soul that Delacroix deemed the central activity of art.[62]

Criticism of photography's mechanical simplicity merged easily with passionate contemporary reproach of the damaging social effects inherent in mass culture. In France, Flaubert recoiled from what he called "a whorish century," filled with "fake materials, fake luxury, fake pride." Literary critic C.-A. Sainte-Beuve (1804–1869) decried the advent of industrial literature, which he thought was served up to satisfy base emotions, rather than edify.[63] In this intellectual atmosphere, photographic verisimilitude became a bludgeon in the hands of photography's critics. French critic Etienne-Jean Delécluze (1781–1863) saw photography as a science imposing its mode of dogged imitation on art.[64] Advocates of photography responded by suggesting that photography could improve public taste, particularly through art reproduction, which was attempted early in the 1840s[65] (Fig. 2.68).

The friction between photography's advocates and detractors may have spurred French photographer Gustave Le Gray (1820–1882) to outline a special aesthetic appreciation for photography, drawing on the principles of painting. A skilled photographic technician and chemist who worked for the Historic Monuments Commission, Le Gray advanced the idea that profuse photographic detail did not have artistic merit. With critics such as Francis Wey and photographers such as Hill and Adamson, Le Gray advocated a theory of sacrifices, that is, of giving up particulars, and composing the picture surface either with sharply defined tonal areas, or through softness.[66] As early as 1853, the English painter and photographer William Newton (1785–1869) similarly advocated the development of an art photography that consciously worked against the glut of details produced by "chemical Photography." He proposed rendering a subject a little out of focus.[67] Le Gray's support of the new medium and his excitement about its possibilities are expressed in his treatises; where some critics considered that photography would lower public appreciation

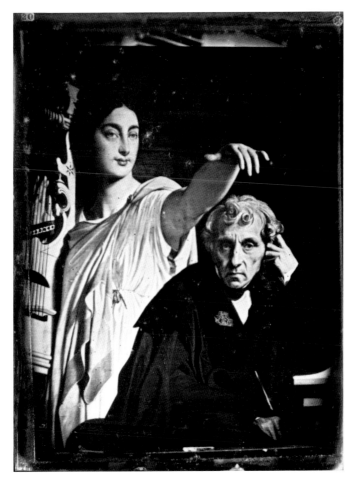

2.68
PHOTOGRAPHER UNKNOWN, *Ingres' Painting of Cherubini and his Muse*, 1841–42. Daguerreotype. The J. Paul Getty Museum, Los Angeles, California.

The use of photography for art reproduction was advocated from the first. Photographs of statues and buildings were generally more satisfactory than photographs of paintings, because early photographic chemicals were not sensitive to a full range of colors.

2.69
GUSTAVE LE GRAY,
Forest of Fontainebleau,
c. 1851. Daguerreotype.
The J. Paul Getty
Museum, Los Angeles,
California.

Le Gray was not inter-
ested in imitating paint-
ing, but became aware
of photography's poten-
tial as light work, that
is, as the major medium
for understanding
the effects of light on
form. The appearance
of bright patches of
form-dissolving light
is similar to what the
French Impressionist
painters would achieve
a decade later.

for art, he argued that it would advance
taste by allowing the public to study the
fullness of nature.[68]

In the *Forest of Fontainebleau* (c. 1851)
(Fig. 2.69), Le Gray pictured a spot that
was a favorite of the Barbizon School
painters, such as Jean-Baptiste-Camille
Corot (1796–1875) and Jean-François
Millet (1814–1875), who sought new
artistic subjects in the commonplace
landscape of the village of Barbizon,
near Paris. The Barbizon group was not
only an art faction; it was also associated
with democratic freedom, because its
subject, nature, was free to all and could
be understood without having had a
classical education.

Le Gray filled the frame of his
Barbizon view with impressions of fil-
tered woodland light and, in the monochromatic palette available to him,
rendered the rich varieties of green,
from verdant lichen patches to silvery
leaves. His approach to photography
combined science and art. He experimented with techniques to render delicate gradations of tone, and he invented

his own dry WAXED PAPER PROCESS,
which kept the paper sensitive for two
weeks, and allowed the photographer
to develop it up to a week after exposure.
Le Gray's famous seascapes reveal the
extent of his resistance to the idea that
photography was merely an automatic
recording of scenes before the lens.
He manipulated the photograph in a
number of ways. He sometimes photographed dramatic cloud formations
separately from sea views, merging the
resulting two negatives, and printing
the sky and the sea separately. To complete the picture, he carefully retouched
the horizon line where the two negatives
met. *Mediterranean Sea at Sète* merged
one negative of the sea and one of the
sky, creating a dramatic image with
blazing light in the center of the picture
(Fig. 2.70). Le Gray's concern with the
overall aesthetic harmony of the print
also led him to retouch clouds, subtract
figures, accentuate horizontal or vertical
elements, and vignette scenes—that
is, to darken the edges of the print to
emphasize the center. The technique

of printing more than one negative to create a single picture, as Baldus had done in the cloister of Saint-Trophîme in Arles (see Fig. 2.43), became known as COMBINATION PRINTING. Like the out-of-focus photograph and the photograph to which paint has been added, combination printing challenged the notion of photography as an unadulterated transcription of optical reality.

The most profound changes arising in the first fifteen years of photography were less visible than the profusion of images generated by the new medium and the debate about its worth as art. Faith in photography as an impartial image-maker began to alter the human relationship to memory. No prior medium fully presaged the common photograph's ability to externalize remembrance, or to produce images conceived of as genuinely akin to actual experience. The sense of a personal encounter, of being there, connected individual experience with national and scientific events. At the same time, what twentieth-century French philosopher Michel Foucault (1926–1984) called "compulsive visibility" began to play a much larger part in human affairs.[69] Societal, scientific, and even personal progress started to be understood as dependent on increased visibility of data in all fields of government and in intellectual inquiry.

As the notion that something might be photographed hardened into the expectation that it ought to be photographed, the public began to perceive a natural claim to see images of all sorts. By the mid-1850s, this perception gave impetus to the making and marketing of a great array of pictures, from individual portraits to scientific images and the first efforts of photojournalism. The assumption that one would own a single photograph of oneself eventually yielded to the notion that one desired to own, or at least to see, many photographic images, including those of strangers and far-off events. During photography's first fifteen years, the stage was set for the intense commercialization and dissemination of photography, which in turn sharpened the question of photography as a fine art, while deepening its acceptance as a chronicler.

2.70
GUSTAVE LE GRAY, *Mediterranean Sea at Sète*, 1856–59. Albumen silver print from two glass negatives. Gilman Paper Company, New York.

Printed from two separate glass negatives, Le Gray's seascape emphasizes the brilliant sheen of sun on water. The place where the two negatives were joined is barely perceptible along the horizon line.

CHAPTER THREE

The Expanding Domain (1854–1880)

**3.0
WILLIAM PRYOR
FLOYD, *Photographers'
Studios* (Floyd's studio
among other studios,
Queen's Road, Hong
Kong), late 1860s–early
1870s. Albumen print.
Gift of Mrs. W. F.
Spinney, 1923. Peabody
Essex Museum, Salem,
Massachusetts.**

Photography studios
flourished in areas
where colonial forces
traded. Western photog-
raphers frequently hired
Asian assistants, who
soon set up their own
rival businesses.

"It is now more than fifteen years ago that specimens of our new and mysterious art were first exhibited to our wondering gaze," recalled Lady Elizabeth Eastlake (1809–1893) in a review of photography written in 1857. "Since then," she continued, "photography has become a household word and a household want; it is used alike by art and science, by love, business, and justice; it is found in the most sumptuous salon, and in the dingiest attic."[1] Photographic images were displayed in shop windows, and newspapers used photographic sources for their illustrations. At the same time, with the continued spread of photography, the development of new applications, and the intense commercialization of the medium in the late 1850s, amazement at its ability to capture appearances declined. As photography became more commonplace, the medium's societal and artistic impact was more frequently debated.

The rapid commercialization of photography sprang from the interaction of social needs and technical inventions. The convenience of the collodion, or wet plate, process, and the resulting availability of low-priced prints stimulated the market for portraits of family, friends, and public figures. As the telegraph, railroad, steamship, and the clipper speeded up communications, commerce, and travel, the desire for portraits and views kept pace. For instance, in the months leading up to the outbreak of the American Civil War in 1861, the market for inexpensive portraits of people in the news grew at an unparalleled rate.[2] In Britain, the views of Egypt by British photographer Francis Frith (1822–1898) were anticipated keenly. At the same time, the growing market for low-priced photographs intensified the contrast between the so-called "cheap johns" who churned these out and those who hoped to elevate photography to the status of a fine art.

THE STEREOGRAPH

Chief among the low-priced photographs that burgeoned in the later nineteenth century was the stereograph. Stereographic photographs helped turn photography into an industry, by stoking the viewer's desire to see more of the world. The principle of the stereograph was known before the invention of photography, and applied to daguerreotypes (see Fig. 2.51). Stereographs became immensely popular from the mid-1850s to the early twentieth century, with improvements in the technology of paper photography, and with the development of special cameras that used two lenses. During the 1840s, stereographic daguerreotypes had been made by joining images produced by two separate cameras, but the new stereographic camera produced two simultaneous images, photographed as if one were seen with the left eye and the other with the right (Fig. 3.1). Placed in a special viewer, the images recombined to give the illusion of receding space. Given their ease of production, photographers and publishers quickly sought ways of mass-producing and distributing stereographs. One of the largest nineteenth-century photographic supply houses and publishers of photographs, E. and H. T. Anthony & Co. in New York, was said to have stereographs of 50,000 different subjects, including views of Broadway traffic.[3] Producers of stereographs manufactured millions of images, and set up the distribution networks with which to market them (Fig. 3.2).

To twenty-first-century viewers, stereographs may seem airless, static, and artificial. But to nineteenth-century viewers, the stereograph was a quite unprecedented leap forward in realistic representation, which opened up great expectations. In a swooning 1859 essay on "The Stereoscope and the Stereograph," Oliver Wendell Holmes (see p. 2), the well-known Boston area physician, photographer, and writer on photography, noted that when looking at the image, "the mind feels its way into the very depths of the picture," awestruck at its inexhaustible detail.[4] Holmes had a knack for describing the physical feelings experienced when using the viewing instrument: "The shutting out of surrounding objects, and the concentration of the whole attention … produce a dreamlike exaltation of the faculties, a kind of clairvoyance, in which we seem to leave the body behind us and sail away into one strange scene after another, like disembodied spirits."[5] Holmes thought the stereograph surpassed painting in its intense illusionism and in its potential to broadcast knowledge to a wide audience. It would become "the card of introduction to make all mankind acquaintances," and it would simulate the feeling of being present at natural wonders such as the Alps, and human marvels such as the pyramids. For Holmes, the stereograph was a watershed moment in the progress of human history:

Form is henceforth divorced from matter. … Give us a few negatives of things worth seeing. … There is only one Coliseum or Pantheon; but how many millions of potential negatives have they shed — representatives of billions of pictures. … Every

3.1
PHOTOGRAPHER UNKNOWN, *Untitled* (Stereoscopes in use), c. 1860s. Stereograph. George Eastman House, Rochester, New York.

Stereographs were viewed in stereoscopes. Although viewers could exchange pictures, they could not simultaneously look through the device and see the three-dimensional effect.

3258 The Fresh View Agent soliciting.

1440. BROADWAY, N. Y., FROM 18th ST.

3.2
PHOTOGRAPHER UNKNOWN, *Looking up Broadway from the Corner of Broome Street,* 1868. Stereograph. Albumen silver print, 1868–71. Library of Congress, Washington, D.C.

So-called instantaneous views depicted bustling city life, a favorite subject for the stereograph. The technical characteristics of stereographic cameras allowed them to fix activity without blurring the action.

conceivable object of Nature and Art will soon scale off its surface for us. ... The time will come when a man who wishes to see any object, natural or artificial will go to the Imperial, National, or City Stereographic Library and call for its skin or form. ... We do now distinctly propose the creation of a comprehensive and systematic stereographic library, where all men can find the special forms they particularly desire to see as artists, or as scholars, or as mechanics, or in any other capacity.[6]

The growth of science and its organizing systems, particularly in such areas of public interest as geology, geography, biology, and ethnography, helped to stimulate the stereograph market, as did colonial expansion and global commerce. Behind the eagerness for stereographs was the ideal of democratic access to information. "What an educational revolution is here, my countrymen," wrote a critic in an 1858 issue of the British journal *The Athenaeum.* "Why our Tommys and Harrys will know the world's surface as well as a circumnavigator. ... What a stock of knowledge our Tommys and Harrys will begin life with! Perhaps in ten years or so the question will be seriously discussed ... whether it will be any use to travel now that you can send out your artist to bring home Egypt in his carpetbag to amuse the drawing room with."[7] Stereography

thus concocted a pleasing combination of education and entertainment that presaged what the late twentieth century would call infotainment. In the words of a French commentator, photography increasingly seemed capable of "enlightening the masses so as to elevate and amend them."[8]

Stereographs were produced and marketed through a global network of publishers and dealers. The public's desire to collect "stereos," as they were called, created a boom and bust economy in the images as photographers and publishers attempted to entice the public with new subjects to view. Sometimes a photographer or publisher created a best-selling stereo or set of stereo cards, at other times the images moldered in warehouses while the company that issued them went bankrupt. The vogue highlighted the issue of images as property. When stereographs were pirated from one publishing house and published by another, civil penalties were seldom applied and copyright laws proved inadequate.

Demand led more photographers to carry stereo cameras along with their regular equipment. Moreover, ambitious photographers started to conceive the image with reference to the stereograph's ability to render depth. In landscape photography, for example, the

3.3
ANDRÉ ADOLPHE
EUGÈNE DISDÉRI,
Princess Buonaparte
Gabrielli, c. 1862. Uncut
carte-de-visite cards.
Gernsheim Collection.
Harry Ransom
Humanities Research
Center, University of
Texas at Austin.

Cartes-de-visite were
inexpensively produced
by the thousands.
Ordinary people traded
and collected images
of family and friends,
as well as pictures of
people they did not
know. The *carte* or card
photograph was used as
promotional material by
politicians and celebri-
ties. Inadvertently, the
cartes also promoted the
notion that the public
has the right to look at
the rich and famous.

photographers picked or even composed
scenes in which an object such as a
fallen tree or wedge patterns of dark and
light would lead the eye from the foreground to the middle ground, and then
on to distant hills (see Fig. 3.75).

Portraits were seldom done in the
stereo format, because the illusion of
deep pictorial space would have been
distracting. But almost every other subject was conceivable as a stereograph.
The market swelled with sets of stereographs devoted to such themes as travel,
religion, urban vistas, and architecture.
Romance and courtship were depicted
by photographers who contrived stories
and used actors to perform scenes.
Pornographic stereos were available for
beholding in small, discreet viewing
devices. When photographers from
the North and the South went forth to
photograph the American Civil War
(1861–1865), they often brought along
a stereographic camera. Because these

cameras were lighter and more portable
than the standard view camera, photographers sometimes used them to make
images that they did not intend to issue
as stereographs.

THE *CARTE-DE-VISITE*

Whereas the appeal of the stereograph
is easy to understand, the success of the
CARTE-DE-VISITE, or "card photograph"
as it was called in the United States,
is less obviously apparent. Perfected
and patented in 1854 by French photographer André Adolphe Eugène Disdéri
(1819–1889), the *carte-de-visite* was a
small portrait photograph originally
intended to be pasted to the back of a
regular visiting card (4 by 2½ inches)
(Fig. 3.3). Like the stereographic camera,
the standard *carte-de-visite* camera had
more than one lens. But whereas the
stereo camera took two pictures at the
same time, the *carte-de-visite* camera was
constructed so that up to eight different

images of the sitter could be exposed on one photographic plate.

The cheapness of the *carte-de-visite* portrait, resulting from its efficient means of production, partly explains its rapid acceptance. Many *cartes-de-visite* were full-length portraits, or bust-length shots, rather than close-up studies of the face. The distance from the camera, especially in the full-length portraits, eliminated the need and expense of careful lighting and time-consuming retouching. The success of the *carte-de-visite* also derived from the liberal use of fancy furniture and painted backdrops calculated to make the sitter appear rich. Like the later daguerreotypes, *cartes-de-visite* encouraged sitters to construct an image of self-satisfaction and financial prosperity. Some photographers even stocked lavish clothing, which they rented to sitters for the photographic moment.

The vogue for *carte-de-visite* photographs was, like that for stereographs, propelled by a collecting urge. People amassed *cartes* of famous people much as they accumulated stereos of notable natural wonders, placing them in plush albums. Such renowned figures as France's Emperor Napoleon III, President Abraham Lincoln in the United States, and members of Britain's royal family recognized the public's craving to possess their likenesses, and willingly posed for photographers. Speculation in *carte* subjects ran high, and overproduction was common, resulting in an even more precarious market than that for the stereograph. The vogue lasted about ten years, having saturated the market with millions of images.[9]

PHOTOGRAPHIC SOCIETIES, PUBLICATIONS, AND EXCHANGE CLUBS

The expansion of photographic practice in the mid-nineteenth century promoted the growth of photographic associations. Photographers with divergent interests formed societies in order to promote the medium to the general public, hold exhibitions, trade technical information, and publish newsletters or journals. Some groups, such as the Photographic Exchange Club in Britain, modeled themselves on organizations in the graphic arts, and traded images. In Britain, the Photographic Society of London, founded in 1853, was quickly followed by city-based photographic societies. Its status was enhanced when Queen Victoria and Prince Albert became patrons. The society published the *Journal of the Photographic Society*, which later became the *Photographic Journal*. Other societies and journals helped to disseminate technical information and news of exhibits. The French Heliographic Society, which began in 1851, published the influential journal *La Lumière*. The group was succeeded by the French Photographic Society in 1855. The Photographic Society in Vienna, Austria, founded in 1861, was the first in the German-speaking world. Photographic clubs and publications sprang up throughout Europe, North and South America, and in colonial India and Asia.

In addition, private publishers set up such journals as *The Photographic Art Journal*, which was founded by Henry Hunt Snelling in 1851, and *Anthony's Photographic Journal*, published by E. and H. T. Anthony & Co. from 1870. The rise of the periodical press in the mid-nineteenth century, especially newspapers and journals that began to use photographically derived engravings, opened new markets. Two American weekly papers with readerships that promptly soared into the millions were *Frank Leslie's Illustrated Newspaper*, started in 1855, and *Harper's Weekly*, begun two years later. Each was dedicated to bringing the public visual accounts of current events.[10]

ART AND PHOTOGRAPHY

The idea of photographic representation as acutely accurate permeated the art world. An 1860 issue of the *Art Journal* contended that "the photograph cannot deceive; in nothing can it extenuate; there is no power in this marvellous machine either to add or to take from: we know what we see must be *true*."[11] The emphasis on photographic imagery as rendering what actually took place before the camera helped to suppress the use of a partially photographic technique called the CLICHÉ VERRE. The process, invented in 1839 by British engravers, was renewed by several experimenters, including French image-makers A. Cuvelier (1812–1871) and L. Granguillaume (active 1850s), in 1853. It employed a glass plate covered with a dark coating, like opaque black varnish, something akin to William Henry Fox Talbot's earliest experiments (see p. 18). The artist scratched an image into the coating with a sharp stylus. Since light could pass through the areas scratched away, the plate could be used as a photographic negative. It was placed on sensitized paper, and exposed to light, which cut into the opaque coating; many prints could be made from one plate (Fig. 3.4). Because the *cliché verre* seemed neither sufficiently handmade nor wholly photographic, however, it found only limited success.

To many artists and critics, photographic truth had an undertone of moral truth. Writing in 1859, Francis Frith argued that

We can scarcely avoid moralizing in connection with this subject; since truth is a divine quality, at the very foundation of everything that is lovely in earth and heaven; and it is, we argue, quite impossible that this quality can so obviously and largely pervade a popular art, *without exercising the happiest and most important influence, both upon the tastes and the morals of the people.*

Cuvelier and Granguillaume showed the *cliché verre* process to the artist Camille Corot (1796–1875), who experimented with it, as did other painters, such as Jean-François Millet (1814–1875).[12]

At the same time, Frith wrote, photography was "*too truthful*. It insists upon giving us 'the truth, the whole truth, and nothing but the truth.' Now, we want, in Art, the first and the last of these conditions, but we can dispense very well with the middle term."[13]

The debate over how to make room for imaginative camerawork, while maintaining respect for the utilitarian uses of photography, became a war of words. A British portrait photographer, C. Jabez Hughes (1819–1884), suggested that photography ought to be divided into three classes. The first, mechanical photography, was literal or exact depiction. In the second category, art-photography, the maker, not content with things as they appear, "determines to infuse his mind into them by arranging, modifying, or otherwise disposing them, so they may appear in a more appropriate or beautiful manner." The last category included "certain pictures which aim at higher purposes than the majority of art-photographs, and whose aim is not merely to amuse, but to instruct, purify, and ennoble."[14] The many tensions between depiction and imagination, objective description and moral uplift, education and amusement permeated photographic practice and criticism.

ART REPRODUCTION

On the face of it, the photographic reproduction of art works seems like a simple project. Suggested early in photography's history by François Arago and William Henry Fox Talbot (see pp. 19–20), the reproduction of works of art began as an effort to combine the cataloging capability of photography with the interests of education. In 1852, Roger Fenton was employed to photograph prints, drawings, and sculpture at the British Museum in London, a position he took up again at the end of the Crimean War.[15] The art dealers P. & D. Colnaghi negotiated with the museum to sell the museum's photographs.[16] Similarly, Charles Thurston Thompson, the photographer at the South Kensington Museum who trained Royal Engineers in the medium (see p. 131), photographed items from the museum's collections.

As early as 1851, Francis Wey suggested that the Musée du Louvre in Paris create a gallery of photographs of paintings by French artists not represented in

French museums.[17] In Paris, the Print Room of the Bibliothèque Nationale and the Bibliothèque des Arts Décoratifs collected photographs of architecture and art during the second half of the nineteenth century. At the same time, museums were collecting, however haphazardly and sporadically, works by leading photographers who specialized in picturesque views or architectural photography.

Photographers soon formed firms largely devoted to art reproduction. In 1866, Alsatian photographer Adolphe Braun (1812–1877) began an art reproduction business that quickly became international both in the scope of its reproductions and in its sales. Fratelli Alinari Fotografi Editori, a company that still sells art reproductions, was founded in 1854. *Photographic Art Treasures* (1856), a collection of picturesque views, art reproductions, and morally edifying photographs, appeared in Britain. Throughout the 1860s and 1870s, publishers in Italy, Germany, and France produced *cartes-de-visite* that illustrated art objects. Lantern slides, sometimes called "magic lantern slides," were made of art objects and architecture. The magic lantern was a device for projecting images on to a screen; early lanterns used oil lamps. In the 1870s, when courses on the history of art were slowly introduced into America, Great Britain, Germany, and France, the market for slides increased.[18]

In the later nineteenth century, the rationale for making photographs of art objects available to the public was more democratically phrased than Arago or Talbot had considered, and came to the fore in a more commercial culture than either of them envisaged. American photographer Marcus Aurelius Root (1808–1888) emphasized that images of culture, as well as nature, could benefit "the lowliest of the community." Photographs could bring to "the masses ... abundant and infinitely various stores of knowledge and entertainment," and "no small measure of artistic training."[19] Art education was linked with the process of cultivating taste and temperament in the poor; in an era that stressed self-improvement, art reproduction was touted as a social equalizer. "With a pile of pictures by their sides, which cost almost nothing, they can make the European tour of celebrated places, and not leave the warm precincts of their own firesides," wrote one observer.[20] Reviewing an exhibit of art reproductions, *The Athenaeum* pronounced that "The old selfish aristocratic days of hoarding are gone for ever. Rare Titians, kept in cases to be gloated over at a miserly moment, will be seized and photographed ... Great and true Art is republican, and is for all men, needing no education to appreciate it—no more than we need education when we fall in love."[21]

THE PHOTOGRAPHER AND FINE ART

The notion that photography could replicate art more accurately than other reproductive media arose because of the belief that photography itself was not an art—that is, not a medium open to imagination or subjective response. This belief in photography's objectivity prompted a variety of responses from those who defined art as an expression of human imagination. The American painter Rembrandt Peale (1778–1860) succinctly summed up the complaint when he wrote, "We do not see with the eyes only, but with the *soul*."[22]

French poet and critic Charles Baudelaire (1821–1867) (Fig. 3.5) accepted photography as a means of

3.5
ÉTIENNE CARJAT,
Charles Baudelaire,
c. 1862. Woodburytype.
Metropolitan Museum
of Art, New York.

Although he was friendly with such photographers as Carjat and Nadar, Baudelaire did not believe that photography could be an art. Carjat set up his portrait of Baudelaire against a plain background, and carefully modulated the lighting of the face to bring out the poet's strength of concentration.

record-keeping, yet lamented what he saw as its broad social consequences. He contended that photography's supporters were unwittingly constricting the range of human imagination. Baudelaire wrote that "each day art further diminishes its self-respect by bowing down before external reality; each day the painter becomes more and more given to painting not what he dreams but what he sees."[23] He thought that those who considered that "Photography and Art are the same thing"[24] thinly rationalized soul-deadening matter-of-fact pictures. Similarly, the French painter Eugène Delacroix insisted on a crucial differentiation between the insights that follow on the interaction of eye and mind and what occurs in the process of photography. Although Delacroix commissioned photographic studies of models to be used in his paintings (see Fig. 2.55), he insisted that the camera was a machine that yielded pictures untrue to the complexities of human perception. For him the central activity of art—soul speaking to soul—was foreclosed by photography.[26] While many painters in Europe and America collected, commissioned, and used photographs, they insisted that it was merely a recording instrument. The influence of the photograph on art was seldom discussed positively, even by painters such as Jean-Léon Gérôme (1824–1904), whose highly detailed views of the Middle East resemble contemporary photographs in glossy appearance, fine detail, and subject matter.[27]

Both Baudelaire and Delacroix sat for photographers and socialized in their circles. French photographer Étienne Carjat (1828–1906) was typical of the emergent artist-photographer who led a bohemian life. Trained as a painter and working as a caricaturist and writer, Carjat moved in the world of Paris culture, where he met writers, musicians, artists, and their patrons (see Fig. 3.5).

3.6
NADAR, *Panthéon Nadar,* **1854.**
Lithographic print.
George Eastman House, Rochester, New York.

Nadar's *Panthéon* shows famous people coming to pay homage to a bust of the French writers George Sand, Chateaubriand, and Frédéric Soulié.[25] Making caricatures may have helped him concentrate on facial features that indicate personal temperament.

Comparable portrait work was done by another French caricaturist turned photographer, Nadar (real name Gaspard Félix Tournachon). Nadar drew political cartoons and caricatures of prominent figures, and conceived his *Panthéon Nadar* as a lithograph that would show 1,000 portraits of contemporary celebrities. He managed to complete only one section of the grandiose work, in 1854 (Fig. 3.6). Nadar learned photography late in 1853, at about the same time as his brother Adrien Tournachon, who would go on to aid Duchenne de Boulogne (see p. 148). In a short-lived partnership, the brothers produced a series of photographs of the mime artist Jean-Charles Deburau, posed as Pierrot (Fig. 3.7).[28]

Nadar initially capitalized on the upper-class taste for images of creative people. His quick perception and judgment, learned as a caricaturist, helped him to specialize in making heroic portraits of contemporary cultural figures, especially bohemian artists and writers. Nadar not only sold large, high-priced images, but also marketed his public persona. With photographer Gustave Le Gray (see Figs. 2.69, 2.70), he maintained that he was not a simple operator of photographic equipment but an artist, sensitive to the nuances of personal character as well as rules of composition. "What can't be learned," he wrote, "it's the sense of light, it's the artistic appreciation of the effects produced by different and combined qualities of light."[29]

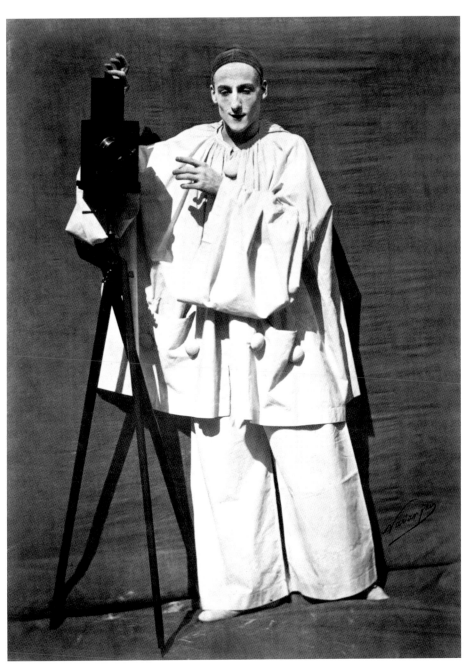

3.7
**NADAR & ADRIEN
TOURNACHON,**
Pierrot the Photographer,
1854–55. **Paper print.
Musée Carnavalet, Paris.**

Cast as a photographer, the Pierrot was understood not as a clown but as a sensitive Romantic artist.

3.8
NADAR, *Théophile Gautier*, 1854–55. Albumen salted paper print, mounted on Bristol board. Musée d'Orsay, Paris.

Gautier proclaimed that anyone who wore a collar on his shirt was too bourgeois. In this image, his disheveled clothes and deep-set eyes cast in dark shadows beneath a well-lit brow portray artistic insight and personal intensity gained by dismissing etiquette.

Nadar's photographic studio became a fashionable intellectual salon.[30] Like Hill (p. 72) and Mathew Brady (see p. 106), he conceptualized photographs, and he posed his sitters, but the image was produced and developed by a staff that grew in numbers with his success. Nadar's portrait of Théophile Gautier (1811–1872), boisterous proponent of art for art's sake and author of the influential novel about Parisian bohemian life *Mademoiselle de Maupin* (1835), visually summarizes the writer's antagonism toward the middle-class values of orderliness and civility (Fig. 3.8).

In addition to photography, Nadar was a fervent advocate of balloon transportation and aerial reconnaissance. He produced the first photographs of Paris from the basket of his balloon *Le Géant* (*The Giant*), and he administered the airmail service during the siege of Paris.[31] Nadar also experimented with artificial light, making the first photographs of the Paris sewers using a carbon arc lamp powered by Bunsen batteries (Fig. 3.9). His interest in science and technology complemented his reputation as a multi-talented originator. Coupled with the artistic and literary circles in which he moved, this helped considerably to elevate the status of the photographer generally.

HIGH ART PHOTOGRAPHY

Other efforts to elevate the public perception of photography included emulating the conventional subjects of painting. The popularity of photographic still lifes, beginning with Daguerre, indicates the success of this course. A different approach, which occurred mostly in Britain, also borrowed from the painterly tradition. It took up the notion of High Art photography outlined by photographer C. Jabez Hughes, "to instruct, purify, and ennoble." In this photography, emphasis was placed on edifying subject matter, such as scenes from the Bible or literary sources, including Shakespeare, Alfred Tennyson, and Walter Scott. *Tableaux vivants*, literally living pictures, were popular subjects for early photographers. The *tableau* required that the actors hold their poses for about twenty seconds, a time well suited to photography.[32] Photography was also influenced by sentimental or moralizing paintings and engravings, as

in a stereograph by British photographer James Elliott (1835–1903) (Fig. 3.10).

William Lake Price (1810–1896), a British painter who adopted photography, made portraits of famous people, scenes from everyday life, still-life

3.9
NADAR, *The Sewers of Paris*, 1864–65. Modern print from a glass negative. Caisse Nationale des Monuments Historiques et des Sites, Paris.

Nadar used a carbon-arc lamp to create an eerie, ghostly apparition of subterranean Paris, etched into immortality by Victor Hugo's book *Les Misérables*.

studies, and *tableaux vivants* from literature. His image of Don Quixote, hero of Miguel de Cervantes's (1547–1616) romance of the same name, drew upon the tradition of inspirational or uplifting painting (Fig. 3.11). It also engaged the interest in historically accurate representation that was flourishing in painting at the time. Lake Price combined his knowledge of art principles and the techniques of photography in his 1858 publication *A Manual of Photographic Manipulation*.

The most famous High Art photograph was constructed by Oscar Rejlander (1813–1875), who worked with Charles Darwin to create studies of human expression (see p. 150). Like many mid-century photographers, Rejlander began as a painter. While studying art in Rome, he made a living by copying Old Master paintings. There he became acquainted with Raphael's famous fresco *The School of Athens*, whose composition and theme of opposing points of view became the basis for a large photographic work, *The Two Ways of Life*, exhibited in 1857 (Fig. 3.12). In the center of the Raphael fresco, Plato points toward the heavens, the realm of the ideal, and Aristotle seems to point to the earth, source of material knowledge. In Rejlander's *The Two Ways of Life*, a sage introduces two youths to life: the one on the left embraces the moral life

of honest industry; on the right, a callow rake is about to venture into a life of dissipation and debauchery. The women who posed were from Madame Warton's (sometimes Wharton) Troupe, a popular theatrical group who performed *tableaux vivants* derived from paintings and, especially, Classical sculpture.[33]

The large print, about 31 inches wide, was made from more than thirty individual negatives in a technique termed COMBINATION PRINTING, which required a great deal of handwork. Rejlander argued that the labor involved, combined with the image's inspiration from a Renaissance source and the morally uplifting theme, distanced the work from ordinary photography and aligned it with painting.[34] Despite its notoriety, however, Rejlander made few more moralizing pictures. Like many photographers, his main means of support was portraiture.

Henry Peach Robinson (1830–1901), another painter–photographer, learned how to combine negatives from Rejlander. A hand-drawn sketch with a photograph inserted shows how Robinson planned his work (Fig. 3.13). The subject of his 1858 combination-print photograph *Fading Away* (Fig. 3.14) disturbed the public with its scene of a dying young girl being attended by her family. Although the space between the girl and the wall beyond the window is

3.11
WILIAM LAKE PRICE,
Don Quixote in His Study, early 1850s.
Albumen print from a wet collodion negative.
Victoria & Albert Museum, London.

Lake Price's image of *Don Quixote in His Study* shows Cervantes's famous character surrounded by items suggested from yet another literary source, Walter Scott's novel *The Antiquary*.[35]

3.12
OSCAR REJLANDER,
The Two Ways of Life, 1857. Albumen print.
George Eastman House, Rochester, New York.

To make this image, Rejlander posed models in small groups, photographed them, then printed the negatives separately on a long, scroll-like piece of paper. The unsubtle story depicts the moral choices available to young lads. Though some viewers were shocked at the image's semi-nude figures, when the photograph was exhibited, Prince Albert ordered a copy for the royal family.

WOMEN BEHIND THE CAMERA

WOMEN AS AMATEURS

On rare occasion, a woman such as Harriet C. Tytler (1828–1907), who was married to a British officer in India, learned photography, traveled extensively, and produced a body of work alone, or as a joint effort with a spouse. Harriet Tytler and Robert Christopher Tytler (1818–1872) made about 300 photographs, some of then as large, two- and three-part panoramas, and exhibited them in India and in the India Office Library in London, where they remain today.[36] But many more women participated in formally arranged and informal exchange clubs for photographers who made non-commercial images. Called "amateurs" for their love of the pursuit, they were not amateurs in the modern sense of being unskilled or beginners. Most amateur photographers were people of means and accomplishment. Their work ranged from scientific pursuits to architectural and landscape views. John Dillwyn Llewelyn (see p. 35) shared his interests in botany, landscape, and still-life photography through exchanges with other amateurs.

unnaturally compressed, the illusion of the image having been taken in one camera shot, not built up from individual pictures, is stronger in *Fading Away* than in Rejlander's *The Two Ways of Life*. Robinson depicted another dying heroine in a combination print titled *The Lady of Shalott* (1861), illustrating a scene in a famous poem by Tennyson. His book *Pictorial Effect in Photography* (1869) was a standard work throughout the nineteenth century.

3.13 (left)
HENRY PEACH ROBINSON, *Group with Recumbent Figure* (Sketch with cut-out), 1860. Albumen print and pastel collage on paper. Gernsheim Collection. Harry Ransom Humanities Research Center, University of Texas, Austin, Texas.

Robinson made a preliminary pencil sketch before shooting segments of his picture, developing them, and gluing them over the rough draft.

3.14 (below)
HENRY PEACH ROBINSON, *Fading Away*, 1858. Albumen composite print. Science Museum, London.

One of Robinson's most successful works, the image shows the all too familiar death of a child in the nineteenth century. Its symbolism is bolstered by the withering fruit arrangement in the center of the picture, and the dramatic, V-shaped cloud that leads the viewer directly to the girl's taut, pale face.

The Sunbeam: Photographs from Nature (1859), an album of photographs and poems edited by Philip Henry Delamotte (1820–1889), distilled a mood of quiet meditation in nature that attracted many amateurs.

A few privileged women such as Lady Augusta Mostyn (1830–1912), an accomplished Welsh landscape photographer, participated in the Photographic Exchange Club in Britain (Fig. 3.15). After her marriage in 1855, she found it difficult to pursue her interests.[37] The photographic work of upper-class women in the nineteenth century is not widely known, because outside of the exchange clubs, their photographs were not exhibited, and many remain in private family collections. One such elusive figure is Lady Mary Filmer (1840–1903), an intimate of Queen Victoria's court, who made portraits, and who cut up photographs and inventively arranged them on sheets of paper upon which she painted watercolors (Fig. 3.16).

Perhaps the most intriguing amateur photographer in the Victorian era was Lady Clementina Hawarden (1822–1865), who took up photography in the late 1850s and in the seven years before her death in 1865 produced about 800 images. Elected to the Photographic Society of London in 1863, she won silver medals for her work in that year and in 1864. Although she made some landscape images, her most intriguing pictures were made of her daughters, mostly in the family's London townhouse, where an upper floor was devoted to her photographic pursuits.[38]

Expert in lighting and composing a scene that seems tantalizingly part of a story, Hawarden often photographed the young women in costumes that probably came from the family's collection. She frequently used a mirror, which not only added depth to the scene, but also employed a favorite Victorian symbol for the tension between reality and appearance, and the line between art and life

3.15
LADY AUGUSTA MOSTYN, *Oak Tree in Eridge Park, Sussex,* 1856. Albumenized print of collodion negative. George Eastman House, Rochester, New York.

Venerable trees and ancient parkland attached to estates were favorite subjects for upper-class British amateur photographers.

3.16
LADY FILMER, *Untitled*, c. 1864. Collaged photographs with watercolor additions. University of New Mexico Art Museum, Albuquerque, New Mexico.

Lady Filmer may have been the first artist to collage photographs—that is, to cut, arrange, and paste photographs on a surface so as to make a statement separate from the individual items included in the work.[39] The figures in the arms of the cross are related to the person in the center. Lady Filmer also added watercolor adornments to her pictures.

PORTRAIT
Julia Margaret Cameron

The Victorian period's most enduringly famous photographer, Julia Margaret Cameron (1815–1879), did not take up photography seriously until she was given a camera in 1863, at the age of forty-eight. Born Julia Margaret Prattle, in India, she was schooled in France, married when she was twenty-three years old, and took up photography only when her children were grown and her domestic duties reduced.

Cameron eagerly experimented with the medium, and during the next decade produced images in order "to ennoble photography and to secure for it the character and uses of High Art by combining the real and ideal and sacrificing nothing of Truth by all possible devotion to Poetry and beauty."[40]

Cameron took portraits of friends, and friends of friends, as well as Victorian cultural figures such as Charles Darwin and Alfred Tennyson. Her likeness of scientist and photography pioneer John Herschel, with whom she had been acquainted since 1836, illustrates her distinctive approach to male portraiture (Fig. 3.17). Herschel's hair, recently washed and, by her request, left uncombed, becomes an outward manifestation of his active mind. In her autobiographical writing, "Annals of my Glass House," Cameron recalled photographing Herschel and another Victorian sage, Thomas Carlyle (1795–1881). "When I have had such men before my camera," she wrote, "my whole soul has endeavoured to do its duty towards them in recording faithfully the greatness of the inner as well as the features of the outer man."[41]

In Cameron's work, friends, family, and servants were changed into characters from the Bible, Greek myth, and Renaissance painting, as well as figures in British lore and literature. By careful draping and delicate lighting, Cameron transformed her parlormaid Mary Hillier into the Virgin Mary. Like many women photographers, she posed more women than men. Because women generally did not have the identity and authority in the cultural and intellectual world enjoyed by men such as Darwin, Herschel, and Tennyson, they were more easily transformed into literary personages. Most of the time, she chose a crucial psychological moment in a story that would be well-known to her audience (Fig. 3.18). She illustrated an edition of Alfred Tennyson's *"Idylls of the King" and Other Poems*, published in two volumes in 1874–75. Cameron appreciated the languidly beautiful women in medieval costume who appeared in paintings by artists of the Pre-Raphaelite Brotherhood, and made several images especially similar to the work of Dante Gabriel Rossetti (1828–1882).

Cameron explained that the slightly blurred focus that became her characteristic style resulted from her early attempts at photography, when she was using a lens with such a short FOCAL LENGTH that only a small region of the sitter's face would be sharp. However accidentally Cameron may have come upon her technique, and no matter how much she was criticized as being technically inexpert for continuing to use it, the style suited her subject matter. A detailed picture of the Virgin Mary would look too much like someone acting out the role, but a cloudy version appears like an imagined vision or a remembered dream. Unlike many women photographers, Cameron publicly displayed her photographs and attempted to sell them, using the well-established print dealers P. & D. Colnaghi in London. Even though her religious and cultural subjects would have been considered appropriate for a pious woman, her attempts to ease family financial difficulties with the sale of prints was frowned on, and provoked criticism of her style as ignorant or slovenly.[42]

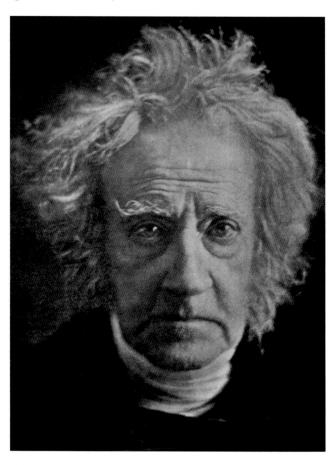

3.17
JULIA MARGARET CAMERON, *Herschel*, 1867. Albumen print. Victoria & Albert Museum, London.

3.18
JULIA MARGARET CAMERON, *Ophelia, Study no. 2*, 1867. Albumen print.
George Eastman House, Rochester, New York.

(Fig. 3.19). Though the photographs resemble *tableaux vivants*, they are mostly untitled, giving no direct clues to their meaning. They remained largely unknown in a family collection, until they were given to the Victoria and Albert Museum in London in 1939.

WOMEN AS PROFESSIONALS

Few women had the resources to set up full-time commercial photographic studios, but women were present in all phases of photographic production. Some, such as Marie Lydie Cabannis Bonfils (1837–1918), wife of the photographer Félix Bonfils (1831–1885), helped in the studio, especially in the making of photographs of women who were culturally uneasy with the camera. Others took over photographic businesses upon the death of a spouse. As albumen paper, which used egg white to give the final photograph a sheen, became more popular, women were employed by the thousands to break and separate eggs.

Women had sometimes been employed to add color to the cold silver tinge of the daguerreotype. When paper photographs supplanted the daguerreotype, women continued as colorists. As the *carte-de-visite* and stereograph industries boomed, women found

employment as laboratory assistants, print cutters, and print mounters.[43] Except for some work with noxious chemicals, C. Jabez Hughes concluded that "in photography there *is* room for a larger amount of female labour, that it *is* a field exactly suited to even the conventional notions of women's capacity, and further, that it is a field unsurrounded with traditional rules, with apprenticeships, with vested rights, and it is one in which there is no sexual hostility to their employment."[44]

Professional training in photography could be more easily obtained than training in painting or sculpture. Women might be excluded or discouraged from art academies, but they could study with photographers who advertised for students, or learn through the many technical manuals. Women could not travel abroad as freely as did John Thomson and Francis Frith, but they did produce landscape work based on local scenery, as well as routine studio portraiture. Tellingly, women did not seem to secure copyright, or to publish their work to the extent that men did, possibly because these activities involved being in the world of business and commerce to a greater degree than was deemed suitable.[45]

3.19
LADY HAWARDEN,
Girl in Fancy Dress,
c. 1860. Collodion print.
Victoria & Albert
Museum, London.

Lady Hawarden is remembered for images of her daughters in poses that suggest they were acting out scenes from literary sources. This image may derive from Alfred Tennyson's *The Lady of Shallot*, in which a woman weaves tapestry alone in a high tower. When she looks into the mirror, she sees the dashing Sir Lancelot, and fatally falls in love with his image.

WAR AND PHOTOGRAPHY

Writing in *The Atlantic Monthly* for July 1859, Oliver Wendell Holmes forecast that "the next European war will send us stereographs of battles."[46] His prediction was darkly realized when the next major war, the American Civil War, erupted in the United States. On the eve of the conflict, there was widespread naiveté about the conduct of war and its effects on camerawork. John Draper (1811–1882), editor of *The American Journal of Photography*, mused that "those who stay at home to take care of the women and children may know almost as much about a battle as the soldiers who see it, or fight it." He fancied that "there will be little danger ... for the photographer [who] must be beyond the smell of gunpowder or his chemicals will not work."[47]

Photographs and photographers' accounts from previous conflicts, such as the Mexican–American War and the Second Burma War (see pp. 46–49), had not been widely circulated, and the possibility that war photographs might be different from heroic war paintings and engravings was consequently not much discussed. Commentators mostly failed to take into account the technical inadequacy of photography to register the swift action of battle, which supplied one of the major visual art themes, or the likelihood that such disruptions as low light or a strong breeze could halt picture-taking at crucial moments. Few mentioned that photographic equipment was still cumbersome, or that plates had to be processed soon after exposure, forcing the photographer to hurry to a makeshift darkroom.

Despite high hopes for photography, sketch artists — often amateurs attached to military units in semi-official positions, or entrepreneurial individuals who sold their works to journals for reproduction as engravings — continued to produce the majority of war images that the public saw. Photographers recorded what they could: fortifications and landscapes, as well as troops and military leaders, before and after battle. What it lacked in spontaneity, photography began to make up for in quantity, both in the number of views taken and in their extensive circulation. Yet this proved to be a mixed blessing: seeing many images eventually reduced the impact of each of them, and considerably hindered the emergence of a single image as a symbol of the conflict and a rallying point. As photographs achieved a new degree of topicality, they were also liable to lose value as their immediate newsworthiness faded. Together with mass-produced stereographic photographs and *cartes-de-visite*, war photographs taught viewers a modern skill: how to ignore or forget images when confronted by an excess of them.

During the nineteenth century, European countries were involved in many so-called "small wars," a term used by Major Charles Callwell to describe the conflicts associated with the expansion of colonial European powers in Asia, North Africa, India, and the Middle East.[48] Callwell saw these conflicts as inevitably "a heritage of extended Empire."[49] Britain was involved in about thirty such wars during the nineteenth century, almost two dozen of which were fought in India between the Indian Mutiny of 1857 and 1900. The presence of photographers at these colonial struggles strengthened the public perception of a link between photography's expansion and territorial conquest.

In February 1856, as peace negotiations after the Crimean War (1853–56) were being conducted, retired statesman and photographer Eugène Durieu (1800–1874) (see Fig. 2.55) reported to the French Photographic Society that photography would conquer unknown territories as the victorious armies of France conquered land.[50] Indeed, photography became a formalized element in military organization: in 1856, a photographic section was formed as part of the Telegraphic School run for the Royal Engineers in Chatham, England; and in 1861, the French Minister of War ordered that one officer in every brigade be trained in photography.[51] By 1870, the camera was commonly used for many tasks, such as copying maps, teaching recruits, and recording experiments with weaponry.

THE CRIMEAN WAR

The conflict in the Crimea, a peninsula at the northern end of the Black Sea, sprang from a tangle of issues relating to European influence in the Ottoman Empire, and pitted Russia against Britain, France, Turkey, and Sardinia.

The war required joint action and cooperation from the allies to plan strategy and to furnish supplies. Newspaper reports by William Howard Russell (1820–1907), published by the London *Times* late in 1854, revealed how mismanagement and disunity among Britain's allies produced severe hardships, food scarcities, and lack of medical care among the troops. In a dispatch written on November 25, 1854, Russell described torrential rains that flooded tents and chilled soldiers who lacked warm, waterproof clothing. The "wretched beggar who wanders the streets of London in the rain," wrote Russell, "leads the life of a prince compared with the British soldiers who are fighting out here for their country." "These are hard truths," Russell warned, "but the people of England must hear them."[52] Political cartoons denounced the situation of the soldiers (Fig. 3.20).

Early in the conflict the War Department ordered two ultimately unsuccessful photographic forays in an attempt to counteract newspaper accounts of the war. The next British efforts to photograph in the Crimea were undertaken separately by Roger Fenton (1819–1869) and James Robertson (1813–1888).

Roger Fenton

A well-known British amateur photographer, Roger Fenton helped to found the Photographic Society in 1853. An artist by inclination and a lawyer by training, he studied painting in France and learned the wax paper photographic process invented by Gustave Le Gray (see p. 78). In the fall of 1852, Fenton was off again, this time to Russia, where he photographed historic architecture, as well as the construction of a bridge across the Dnieper River at Kiev, a structure commissioned by Czar Nicholas I (1796–1855; r. 1825–1855) from Fenton's friend and promoter of photography the British engineer Charles Vignoles (1793–1875).

By the mid-1850s, governments and publishers were speculating about the potential of war photographs. In Manchester, England, the firm of print publishers Thomas Agnew & Sons commissioned Fenton to make images in the Crimea, to which Agnew would retain the reproduction rights. Fenton eventually exhibited his Crimean War photographs in London, and in 1856 Agnew published 160 of Fenton's more than 300 photographs, which could be purchased singly or in handsome volumes. By this time peace negotiations

3.20
ARTIST UNKNOWN,
"Well, Jack! Here's good news from home. We're to have a medal." "That's very kind. Maybe one of these days we'll have a coat to stick it on?" Printed cartoon. *Punch*, February 1855. Victoria & Albert Museum, London.

During the Crimean War (1853–56), journalists and cartoonists made the British public aware of the hardships faced by the troops because of bureaucratic bungling.

64   PUNCH, OR THE LONDON CHARIVARI.

" WELL, JACK! HERE'S GOOD NEWS FROM HOME. WE'RE TO HAVE A MEDAL."
" THAT'S VERY KIND. MAYBE ONE OF THESE DAYS WE'LL HAVE A COAT TO STICK IT ON?"

FOCUS
The Valley of Death

Theirs not to make reply,
Theirs not to reason why
Theirs but to do and die.
Into the valley of Death
  Rode the six hundred.

Alfred, Lord Tennyson, "The Charge of the Light Brigade"

Even before it became immortalized in a famous poem and a famous photograph (Fig. 3.21), the area in the Crimea where so many British troops met their deaths was called "the valley of death."[53] The desolate lowland lived up to its biblical name when, on October 25, 1854, Russian artillery in a strong position fired on a British cavalry brigade whose attack orders had been confused through the chain of command. The Light Brigade incurred heavy losses. Tennyson incorporated the line "Someone had blundered" from newspaper accounts of the incident. When Fenton's photograph was exhibited in 1855, the editor of the *Photographic Journal* in London wrote that the show was the "most remarkable and in certain respects the most interesting exhibition of photographs ever opened." The writer singled out *The Valley of the Shadow of Death* "with its terrible suggestions, not merely those awakened in the memory, but actually brought materially before the eyes, by photographic reproduction of the cannon-balls lying strewd like moraines of a melted glacier through the bottom of the valley."[54]

Fenton did not arrive in the Crimea until months after the event and after Tennyson wrote the first draft of his poem. He was aware of the national sentiments surrounding the "valley of death" when he left Britain. In fact, Fenton made two photographs on the site, the second of which became famous. In the first image, there are hardly any cannon balls in the road; but in the second and better-known photograph, cannon balls have been strewn on and near the road, perhaps by Fenton and his staff, to create the impression that the battle had recently taken place.[55]

The renown of his photograph of the site grew in subsequent years, propelled by the Tennyson poem, the Christian symbolism of death and eternal life, and the complex sentiments felt by the British about the war. The charge of the Light Brigade, not a pivotal battle in the war, became an enduring emblem of devotion to duty during senseless conflicts.

3.21
ROGER FENTON, *The Valley of the Shadow of Death,* **1855. Paper print. Victoria & Albert Museum, London.**

were well under way, and the project proved to be less financially rewarding than the publisher had hoped. Along with some Crimean photographs by James Robertson, Fenton's unsold photographs and negatives of the war were auctioned at a discount in 1856.

One of Fenton's photographs, *The Valley of the Shadow of Death*, aroused strong feelings when it was shown, but most of Fenton's views were inoffensive. Although his letters from the front clearly show that he was frustrated by the war's mismanagement, and, like many others there, suffered from cholera, Fenton's photographs were less explicit (Fig. 3.22). Most did not make direct reference to the war's calamities: he did not depict fallen soldiers, the wreckage of battle, or the results of supply shortages that caused soldiers to loot civilian homes. Like war artists in the past, he made heroic images of military leaders, and his photographs of the soldiers showed them in no danger, often enjoying the same social activities they might at home.

Fenton's tact may have derived from the instructions to the first, failed, government-sponsored photographic party, which was to bring back visual evidence that newspaper accounts of the war exaggerated the disease and starvation endured by the troops. Moreover, Fenton's acquaintance with Queen Victoria (1819–1901; r. 1837–1901) during the first half of 1854, when he created a flattering likeness of the monarch, photographed the royal children (Fig. 3.23), and instructed the royal couple in the rudiments of photography, may have tempered his images.[56] Further, the worst privations occurred during the winter of 1854, when lack of supplies was exacerbated by severe cold and rampant cholera. Fenton visited the Crimea in 1855, when the previous winter's situation had to some extent been alleviated. Aware that the print publishing firm would be marketing the photographs and that there would be a public exhibition, Fenton may have assumed that few people would want to see or to buy images of suffering and carnage. Interestingly, the public and press did not raise issues of content—Fenton's photographs were praised by critics for their factual quality and superiority to words.

James Robertson

James Robertson was a British citizen working as chief engraver of the Imperial Mint in Constantinople, and an accomplished amateur landscape photographer, who made views in the Middle East. Early in the war he traveled to the

3.22
ROGER FENTON,
A Quiet Day at the Mortar Battery, 1855. Salted paper print. The J. Paul Getty Museum, Los Angeles, California.

Fenton's photographs did not depict the hardships faced by the troops in the field, nor did they picture battle scenes. For the most part, his images contradict reports in the British press, by showing that life in the Crimea was dull and uneventful.

sixty images, including the ruins of a redan, or fortification, at Sebastopol, which had been secured only after numerous bombardments (Fig. 3.24). Robertson's photographs were published by Thomas Agnew, who auctioned the unsold photographs and negatives along with Fenton's surplus images. The public does not seem to have remarked on the difference between Robinson's more explicit images and Fenton's tamer ones.

Fenton and Robertson are the best-known photographers of the Crimean War, because their work was published in engraved interpretations in newspapers and issued in multiple photographic prints. But there were other photographers on the scene, including Karl Baptist von Szatmari (1812–1887), an amateur painter and photographer in Bucharest, Romania. He used his social connections to visit the opposing armies of Turkey and Russia early in the conflict that led to the Crimean War. Although all but one of his photographs have perished, the range of subjects, known from a show of his work at the Paris Exposition of 1855, includes group portraits and troop movements. Legend has it that the young Russian novelist Leo Tolstoi, who was in an artillery unit at Sebastopol, made a number of photographs. Like other French photographers, the painter Colonel Jean-Charles Langlois (1789–1870) arrived late in the war. An accomplished war

3.23 (above)
ROGER FENTON,
The Royal Family in Buckingham Palace Garden, **May 22, 1854. Paper print. The Royal Archives © 2002 Her Majesty Queen Elizabeth II.**

Queen Victoria was aware of the power of photography to form her public image. Her more formal portraits are counterbalanced by casual views and family scenes. She also amassed a collection of 100,000 photographs, which she put into ten albums.

area, taking some images about which little is known, before returning to the war zone in 1855. Robertson's trip may have been sponsored by print publishers looking for someone to carry on when Fenton left, or he may have set off on his own initiative. He made approximately

3.24
JAMES ROBERTSON,
Interior of the Redan,
June 1855. Salted paper print. Gernsheim Collection. Harry Ransom Humanities Research Center, University of Texas at Austin.

Unlike Roger Fenton, James Robertson did not shy away from showing scenes of destruction during the Crimean War.

historian, Langlois spent more than two decades depicting France's battles in his large circular painted panorama on the Champs Elysées in Paris. He used his Crimean photographs as a source for a panoramic painting of fighting at the city of Sebastopol and joined fourteen photographs together to form a 360-degree view (Fig. 3.25).[57]

THE AMERICAN CIVIL WAR

For decades, economic and political tensions in the United States between the industrialized northern states and the largely agricultural southern states had been patched over by fragile concessions. One such agreement, the Compromise of 1850, admitted California to the Union as a free, that is, non-slave state, but allowed slavery to continue in the states where it existed, and mandated the return of fugitive slaves from free states. Abolitionist feeling in the North was roused by the provision that runaway slaves had to be returned to the South, and the immediate cause of the war, the secession from the Union by the state of South Carolina, was partly motivated by the dispute over fugitive slaves.

Fighting between North and South began with the shelling of Fort Sumter in South Carolina on April 12, 1861, and ended with the southern surrender at Appomattox, Virginia, on April 9, 1865. During the hostility, war correspondents, artists, and photographers furnished the public with plentiful news and images. Unlike in the Mexican–American War (see p. 47), Americans understood from the beginning that this conflict would be photographed extensively, and that actual photographs, and the engravings taken from them, would create a comprehensive visual chronicle—the first of its kind in American history.[58] The first pictures from the conflict were taken by southern photographers such as George S. Cook (1819–1902) the day after Fort Sumter fell. Born in Connecticut, Cook settled in the South in his twenties, but maintained his contacts with northern photographers, publishers, and suppliers, such as E. and H. T. Anthony & Co.[59]

**3.26 (above)
GEORGE S. COOK,
*Portrait of Major Robert
Anderson*, 1860–65.
Wet plate collodion.
Valentine Museum,
Richmond, Virginia.**

Such was the appetite
to see images of news-
makers, that Cook's
photograph of Major
Robert Anderson,
who commanded the
Federal troops at Fort
Sumter when it fell to
Confederate forces,
was quickly turned into
wood engravings and
circulated throughout
the North.

When the division between North
and South deepened, Cook centered
his work on Confederate subjects. In
February 1861, at the request of the
northern photographer John Jabez
Edwin Mayall (1810–1901) (see p. 28
and Fig. 2.5), Cook made a portrait
of Major Robert Anderson, who commanded the Federal troops at Fort

Sumter, in the mouth of Charleston
Harbor (Fig. 3.26). In the succeeding
months, as the quarrel between the
North and the newly declared southern
Confederacy focused on the continued
presence of Federal troops in the fort,
wood engravings of Cook's photograph
were reproduced in the northern press,
and *cartes-de-visite* made from the
photograph were sold by the thousands.
When Fort Sumter fell to southern
forces, Cook made many photographs,
including the lowering of the American
flag. After the war, Cook amassed
10,000 Civil War photographs, largely
by other photographers, which were
later acquired by the Valentine Museum
in Richmond, Virginia.

The Effect of the War on Photography

While only one photographer, Andrew
J. Russell (1830–1902), was actually
paid by the United States government,
many quasi-official photographers
from the North and South saw the conflict as an opportunity to expand their
markets. Photographic portraits of
such politicians as Abraham Lincoln
were popular, as were images of
military leaders. Families of soldiers
going off to war desired pictures of
their young men, who, in turn, wanted
photographic keepsakes of their
families. Photographers such as the
three Bergstresser brothers from
Pennsylvania set up makeshift studios at
military camps to provide photographs
to soldiers (Fig. 3.27). An article in the

**3.27
BERGSTRESSER
BROTHERS,
*Bergstresser's
Photographic Studio,
3d Div., 5th Corp,
Army of the Potomac*,
c. 1862–64. Albumen
silver print. U.S. Army
Military History
Institute, Carlisle
Barracks, Carlisle,
Pennsylvania.**

Photographers found
ready subjects in mili-
tary camps, where new-
found friendships were
celebrated by having
a photograph made.
In this photographic
studio, the roof opened
to allow the sunlight in.

PORTRAIT
Mathew Brady

Mathew Brady is best remembered for the battlefield photographs that his firm took during the American Civil War. But, as historian Mary Panzer noted, Brady's wartime photographs were dominated by representations of individuals and groups of soldiers.[60] Brady's emphasis on specific people reveals a philosophy that history is shaped by great persons, not abstract historical forces or political controversies.

Brady's interest in portraiture began early in his professional life. Like many enterprising photographers of limited means, the young Brady undertook a number of different tasks that might offer a steady photographic practice. He began his career in New York City during the early 1840s, making cases for painted miniatures and jewelry, as well as daguerreotypes. By 1844, he had opened a daguerreotype studio and was winning awards for his images. He produced a series of portraits of criminals, which were made into wood engravings and published in the American edition of Marmaduke Sampson's *Rationale of Crime*.

By the late 1840s, celebrity photography had become his stock in trade. He produced unflinching portraits, including that of John C. Calhoun, the powerful South Carolina politician who opposed northern abolition movements (Fig. 3.28). This and other daguerreotypes of prominent Americans were transformed by Francis D'Avignon (b. 1813) into lithographs (Fig. 3.29) and published in Brady's *The Gallery of Illustrious Americans* (1850). Produced during the debate that led to the Compromise of 1850, *The Gallery* struck a delicate balance by including images of opposing politicians.

Throughout the 1850s, Brady created portraits of distinguished American figures in law, government, business, society, and the arts, and exhibited them in his photographic studios (Fig. 3.30). Brady's images were sometimes used for personal publicity, being reproduced as inexpensive popular prints. His status rose with the fame of his sitters, whose reputations were strengthened in turn because their images bore his name and were displayed in his gallery. Before the outbreak of the Civil War in 1861, Brady had amassed over 10,000 photographs of celebrities, mostly Americans. Even United States presidents were not immune from the potential of photography.

3.28
PHOTOGRAPHER UNKNOWN, *John C. Calhoun,* c. 1848–49.
Daguerreotype. The Beinecke Rare Book and Manuscript Library,
Yale University, New Haven, Connecticut.

3.29
FRANCIS D'AVIGNON, *John C. Calhoun,* c. 1861. Lithograph.
National Portrait Gallery, Smithsonian Institution, Washington, D.C.

Mathew Brady's famous photograph of Abraham
Lincoln (1809–1865) was taken on the day in 1860 when
he gave an address in New York at the Cooper Union
(Fig. 3.31). Brady sold prints of the photograph, and it was
reproduced in newspapers and magazines. Most people
had never seen Lincoln, but rumors of his physical ugliness
were rife during the presidential campaign. The Democrat
opposition sang a song at rallies that ended "We beg and
pray you—Don't, for God's sake, show his picture."[61] Brady
distracted attention from Lincoln's ganglineness by directing
light to his face. He posed the future president in a states-
manlike attitude and took care that he curled his fingers
(especially of his right hand), so that they would not appear
too long and large. Lincoln credited Brady for part of his
success, remarking that "Brady and the Cooper Institute
made me President."[62] By 1864, Brady and his firm had
created more than thirty photographs of Lincoln, who himself sat for dozens of photographers, one of which was later
used for the "Lincoln head" penny, and another of which
was the source for Lincoln's image on the $5 bill.

Perhaps because of poor eyesight, Brady did not take
most of the photographs that bore his name. Like David
Octavius Hill (see p. 72 and Figs. 2.63, 2.64) in Scotland,
Brady conceptualized images, arranged the sitters, and
oversaw the production of pictures. In his Civil War
work, Brady stressed his conceptual and administrative
capacity by frequently appearing in photographs with
military leaders.

3.30
ALBERT BERGHAUS, *M. B. Brady's New Photographic Gallery, Corner of
Broadway and Tenth Street, New York*, from *Frank Leslie's Illustrated Newspaper*,
1861. Wood engraving. Library of Congress, Washington, D.C.

3.31 (above)
MATHEW BRADY, *Abraham Lincoln*, 1860. Salted paper print (*carte-de-
visite*). Library of Congress, Washington, D.C.

New York Tribune for August 20, 1862, reported that the Bergstresser brothers had "followed the army for more than a year and taken, the Lord only knows how many thousand portraits. In one day, since they came here [to Fredericksburg] they took in one of their galleries, 160 odd pictures at $1.00 each (on which the net profit was probably ninety-five cents)."[63] The recently invented TINTYPE photographs, developed on thin sheets of iron, were particularly popular, cheap, and lightweight (Fig. 3.32). Photographs from the front lines were published in many formats, including the popular *carte-de-visite*. E. and H. T. Anthony & Co. issued more than a thousand pictures per day, sent in by semi-professional photographers and celebrities such as Mathew Brady (1823–1896).

The war was extensively reported by newspaper reporters and magazine journalists. Of the more than 1,400 photographers who made images of troops, military installations, and battle sites, most were from the North.

Southern photographs are more scarce not simply because of the ravages of war, but also because of the severe shortages of photographic materials brought on by economic turmoil and military blockades. Photographers initially processed their work in the field, and then sent the resulting negatives to studios in towns and cities for printing.

There are few differences among the subject categories found in Civil War photographs. Whether of battlefields or individuals, Civil War photographs tend to be stiff and formal. Casual camaraderie among soldiers, such as that pictured in Roger Fenton's work in the Crimea, was seldom recorded. Although African-American troops were photographed and occasional images were made of abused slaves, the Civil War did not engender a far-reaching photographic record of slavery and its aftermath.

The restraints and omissions in subject matter, as well as the carefully balanced compositions, probably owe to the sense prevalent during the war that photography was a type of history writing, dedicated to recording the events, not investigating their tangled causes. The *New York Times* for July 21, 1862, observed:

Mr. Brady deserves honorable recognition as having been the first to make Photography the Clio of war [in Greek myth, Clio is the muse of history] ... His artists have accompanied the army on nearly all its marches, planting their sun batteries by the side of our Generals' more deathful ones, and "taking" towns and cities, forts and redans, with much less noise and vastly more expedition. The result is a series of pictures christened "Incidents of War," and nearly as interesting as the war itself; for they constitute the history of it, and appeal directly to the great throbbing hearts of the North.[64]

Throughout the war, it was customary for major photographers to copyright their images, even though the photographs were frequently published by other firms or individuals. For example, George N. Barnard, who worked for Mathew Brady, copyrighted his work, and later published *Photographic Views with Sherman's Campaigns* (1866), in which he recorded the well-organized destruction of the South's railroads. Northern troops lined up along the tracks, and on a signal simultaneously

**3.32
PHOTOGRAPHER UNKNOWN,** *John and Nicholas Marien of Terre Haute, Indiana,* c. 1862–64. Tintype (original lost). Courtesy the author.

Tintypes were lightweight and more durable than daguerreotypes. An improved postal system could speed the images from the war zone to families at home.

3.33
GEORGE N. BARNARD, *Sherman's Hairpins*, 1864. Stereograph, albumen print. Library of Congress, Washington, D.C.

During his campaign in the south, General Sherman ordered that the tracks of southern railroads be gathered and burned to prevent their being used again. The twisted rails were called "Sherman's hairpins."

picked up one side of the railroad ties and tipped them over. The rails were then burned at high heat so that they twisted themselves into ruin[65] (Fig. 3.33).

Recognition of photographers who worked for other image-makers also became more common during the Civil War. Timothy O'Sullivan (1840–1882), who left Brady's studio in 1862 to work with Alexander Gardner (1831–1882), was given credit for his work in Gardner's publications. He made hundreds of war photographs, including *The Harvest of Death*, his most famous image, taken on the Gettysburg battlefield (Fig. 3.34). It was included in *Gardner's Photographic Sketch Book of the Civil War*, published in two volumes in 1865–66. In the last years of the war, photographs of battles and leading military officers were less sought after. The initial enthusiasm for the vast photographic record that could be made of the war was replaced by a sense of what could not be photographed.

3.34
ALEXANDER GARDNER, *The Harvest of Death, Gettysburg, Pennsylvania*, July 1863, from *Gardner's Photographic Sketchbook of the Civil War*. Stereoscope. Negative by Timothy O'Sullivan. Library of Congress, Washington, D.C.

In his *Photographic Sketch Book of the Civil War*, published after the conflict, Gardner told his readers that this photograph "conveys a useful moral: it shows the blank horror and reality of war, in opposition to the pageantry."[66] This statement may have been a veiled criticism of Mathew Brady, whose photographs favored ceremony and personalities.

PORTRAIT
Alexander Gardner

When Alexander Gardner emigrated from Scotland to the United States in 1856, he was already an accomplished photographer. His association with Mathew Brady, whom he may have met in London when both attended the Crystal Palace Exhibition in 1851 (see p. 29), proved to be beneficial to both photographers. Beginning in 1856, Gardner, an adept accountant and organizer, brought order and a modicum of financial stability to Brady's Washington gallery. With Brady, Gardner foresaw the potential market for photography brought about by the impending Civil War.

Brady's corps of photographers gained access to battlefields and fortifications through the efforts of one Allan Pinkerton (1819–1884), head of the presidential protective organization that became known as the Secret Service. Pinkerton, a Scot, arranged for Gardner and a contingent of photographers who worked with him to be given access to Union encampments, where the photographers carried on covert activities, for example photographing groups of soldiers among whom spies were thought to dwell. These photographers also made copies of maps for the Secret Service, and pictures of feasible battlefields and of structures such as bridges, tunnels and railroad lines for the War Department.

Gardner and his subordinates made many of the photographs associated by the public with Mathew Brady. The battle at Antietam, Maryland, in September 1862 resulted in shocking photographs of the dead (Fig. 3.35), eight of which were engraved and published by *Harper's Weekly* on October 18. On the occasion of their exhibition in New York City, the *New York Times* brooded on their effect: "Mr. Brady has done something to bring home to us the terrible reality and earnestness of war. If he has not brought bodies and laid them in our dooryards and along the streets, he has done something very like it."[67] After seeing the Antietam photographs, Oliver Wendell Holmes, who visited the battlefield soon after the conflict took place, similarly commented:

Let him who wishes to know what war is look at this series of illustrations. These wrecks of manhood thrown together in careless heaps or ranged in ghastly rows for burial were alive but yesterday. … It was so nearly like visiting the battlefield to look over these views, that all the emotions excited by the actual sight of the stained and sordid scene, strewed with rags and wrecks, came back to us, and we buried them in the recesses of our cabinet as we would have buried the mutilated remains of the dead they too vividly represented.[68]

When President Lincoln removed General George McClellan as head of the Union army, Alexander Gardner lost his favored position as "Photographer, Army of the Potomac." He then resigned from Brady's staff, but kept good, if competitive relations with his former employer. Both Gardner and Brady made images at the battle of Gettysburg in Pennsylvania, the Civil War's bloodiest engagement. Most of Gardner's views of Gettysburg feature death and destruction. It was on the Gettysburg battlefield that Gardner reconfigured a scene for the camera, so as to intensify its visual and emotional effects. To make *Home of a Rebel Sharpshooter* (Fig. 3.36), he had the corpse moved to a stone wall, and supported the dead man's head on a knapsack so that it faced the camera.[69] The rifle leaning on the wall is a prop that Gardner carried with him. The fact that Gardner did not keep his arrangement of this scene a secret indicates that the public was willing to allow the photographer to construct a scene that was true in a larger sense

**3.35
MATHEW BRADY,
*Soldiers on the
Battlefield*, 1862.
Albumen silver print
by Alexander Gardner.
Library of Congress,
Washington, D.C.**

3.37
ALEXANDER
GARDNER, *Execution of the Lincoln Conspirators*, 1865. From an original glass negative. George Eastman House, Rochester, New York.

than fidelity to visual fact. Soon after Gettysburg, Gardner was briefly captured by Confederate troops, but released after they had assured themselves that he was not a spy. Like the ability of southern photographer George S. Cook to obtain photographic supplies during the conflict, this suggests that photographers were regarded as neutral observers of war, not partisans.

Gardner's eye for the sensational is evident in the series of photographs he made of the conspirators who plotted the assassination of Lincoln. He photographed several of them after their arrest and published images of their execution (Fig. 3.37). Although the series from which this image comes seems like an innovative precursor of the photo-essays that would appear in twentieth-century magazines such as *Life*, it was probably made primarily for Secret Service records. Images derived from Gardner's photographs were published in *Harper's Weekly* (July 22, 1865), but the actual photographs did not sell well.

The Civil War and Remembrance

After the Civil War, *Frank Leslie's Illustrated Newspaper* published images derived from photographs of prisoners in Southern prisoner of war camps such as that at Andersonville, Georgia (Fig. 3.38). These photographs initiated one of the most lasting debates about the Civil War. While no one doubted the truth of the soldiers' dire condition, its cause has been disputed. About 80,000 prisoners were held by both the North and the South, while prisoner of war exchanges stalled over such issues as whether black northern soldiers would be returned by the South. As the war dragged on, the North's blockades became more punitive, denying food and medical supplies to the South. The editors of *Harper's Weekly* wrote of the Confederates: "they do not [starve their prisoners] intentionally, perhaps, but that does not help the matter. ... We are surely not obligated to tolerate the torture of Union prisoners because we wage the war so strictly that the rebels' supplies fail."[70] In northern newspapers, the poor condition of Union captives was contrasted with what was thought to be the decent and honorable condition of southern prisoners in northern detention centers. Little attention was paid to broadcasting the misery endured by southerners in prisons such as that at Elmira, New York.[71]

After the Civil War, and well into the twentieth century, the photographic books of the war were rumored to have been financial failures. It is true that Brady struggled for a decade to place his Civil War photographs in a public institution; it was not until 1875 that Congress paid him for the title to his prints and negatives. Current research suggests that Gardner's book and Barnard's volume, issued in small numbers, were both moderately profitable.

In 1869, both Brady and Gardner petitioned Congress to purchase, and hence preserve, their negatives. Both proposals were rejected, partly because the government was unsure how to store large numbers of photographs. About 90,000 of Gardner's glass-plate negatives passed to a portrait photographer in Washington, D.C., who, in turn sold them to a scrap glass dealer. The dealer recognized the historic importance of the work and tried unsuccessfully to market the images; finally, the glass and the silver in the emulsion were salvaged, destroying the negatives. Other sources, including the collection of E. and H. T. Anthony & Co., who distributed both Brady and Gardner images, were ultimately obtained by the United States Library of Congress.

THE WAR OF THE TRIPLE ALLIANCE, SOUTH AMERICA

The day after Christmas, 1864, 80,000 troops under the direction of Paraguay's leader, Francisco Solano Lopez (1826?–1870), invaded Brazil. In May 1865, Brazil, Uruguay, and Argentina formed a triple alliance to defeat the Lopez government. The conflict arose over disputes about navigation routes and land claims. Tens of thousands of troops from the four countries were mobilized. The war, which thundered on until 1870, was especially devastating for Paraguay; some estimate that 80 per cent of the country's population died during the hostilities.

3.38
PHOTOGRAPHER UNKNOWN, *Frank Leslie's Illustrated Newspaper,* June 18, 1864. Woodblock print. Library of Congress, Washington, D.C.

ESTEBAN GARCÍA,
First Battalion April 24
in the Trenches of
Tuyuty, 1866. Collodion
print. Biblioteca
Nacional de Uruguay,
Montevideo.

Though constrained by
the technical insuffi-
ciency of photography
to capture action, García
generated the feeling
of front-line activity by
taking a picture above
jostling troops in a
crowded trench. García
did record the horrific
sprawl of Paraguayan
dead, practicing the
unwritten yet universal
custom of picturing far
more enemy corpses
than those of one's
own troops.

As in the American Civil War, photographers were sent to the fronts. One
of the first Latin American war photographers, Esteban García (active 1860s),
from Uruguay, organized their efforts.
Little is known about García, but his
images were published by Bate & Co.,
a Montevideo studio financed by investors in the United States. The North
Americans were hoping to reproduce
what they mistakenly thought was the
substantial financial success of Brady's
American Civil War photographs.[72] Sold
in sets of ten, called *La Guerra Ilustrada*
(*The War, Illustrated*) (1866), the photographs show the troop formations and
battle preparations characteristic of
nineteenth-century war photographs
(Fig. 3.39). Like American Civil War
images, the daily personal experiences
of the combatants are virtually absent.

THE FRANCO-PRUSSIAN WAR AND
THE PARIS COMMUNE

The Franco-Prussian War sprang
from the political and economic rivalry
between France, under Emperor
Napoleon III (1808–1873; r. 1852–70),
and Prussia, led by Otto von Bismarck
(1815–1898), who orchestrated the confrontation. France declared war on July
10, 1870, only to experience repeated
defeats that culminated in the decisive
German victory at the Battle of Sedan
(August 31–September 2, 1870), when

Napoleon III was captured. A provisional government was declared in Paris,
and in the winter of 1870 Prussian
troops laid siege to the city. Passenger
balloons, with such names as *Daguerre*
and *Niépce*, attempted to carry communications from the beleaguered city.
In the lore of war and photography, the
extensive use of carrier pigeons has
become legendary. Packaged in tiny
containers and tied to tails of homing
pigeons, over 100,000 messages of
photographically reduced text passed
between the city and French officials
outside the siege line. Sometimes the
images were projected onto a wall so
that a group of people could view them.
The Prussians used falcons to chase
and kill the French pigeons.[73] Despite
the Parisians' efforts, the city fell after
German bombardment.

Resentment at the royalist leanings
of the postwar French government was
especially keen in Paris. The move to
disarm the National Guard, townsmen
who fought the Germans and who supported an idea of a French republic, further angered Parisians. In mid-March, a
group of anti-royalists and working-class
activists declared themselves the "Paris
Commune." Although the Commune
lasted less than three months, it became
an abiding emblem of a righteous people's revolution, in France and around
the world. During so-called Bloody

3.40
PHOTOGRAPHER
UNKNOWN,
*Communards in their
Coffins*, May 1871.
Albumen print.
Gernsheim Collection.
Harry Ransom
Humanities Research
Center, University of
Texas at Austin.

An unknown photo-
grapher captured the
carnage with an image
of numbered corpses
slumped in their coffins.
This photograph of dead
Communards could be
read by their supporters
as a symbol of tragedy
and by their enemies as
a symbol of triumph.

Week (May 21–May 28, 1871), when the French government repossessed the city, around 25,000 Parisians were killed, more than during the Reign of Terror in the French Revolution or the recent German siege[74] (Fig. 3.40).

During and after the Commune, photography was used to record events as well as to promote, explain, and rationalize political positions. The Communards posed for photographs before and after they tore down the Vendôme Column, erected by Napoleon Bonaparte (1769–1821; r. 1804–14, 1815), whose statue stood on top of it. The decree for the destruction of the

3.41
BRUNO
BRAQUEHAIS,
*The Vendôme Column
after its Destruction*,
1871. Paper print.
Bibliothèque Historique
de la Ville de Paris.

were the subject of a satirical illustration in the *Illustrated London News* for June 24, 1871[76] (Fig. 3.42). It is difficult to gauge completely the meaning of this print. British criticism of French radicalism had run high since the French Revolution of 1789; here, however, the placement of the photographer, and his disregard for the urgent task of the firefighters and the acute suffering of the woman and child in the right foreground, seem to criticize the neutrality and intrusiveness of photography, and the public's hankering for sensational photographs. In other words, the conflict-ridden modern attitude toward the media, which criticizes that which it craves, may have emerged in the late nineteenth century.

After the Commune, the French photographer Eugène Appert (active 1870s) made dramatic, deliberately contrived photographs of the events. In his *Crimes of the Commune* he included nine fabricated prints of events that visually presented the French government's view of the Communards. After obtaining portraits of the leaders of the Commune, Appert hired actors to enact historic scenes from the point of view of the anti-Commune forces. In the studio, he cut out the individual figures, pasted on them the heads of the Communards, then rephotographed the image. These composite photographs vary considerably in quality (Fig. 3.43).

column belittled it as "a monument of barbarianism, a symbol of brute force and of false glory, a confirmation of military rule contrary to the international rights of man."[75] The Communards posed for a number of photographs while it was being pulled down (Fig. 3.41). Bruno Braquehais (1823–1875) took 109 views of the Commune, which were sold in a bound album called *Paris during the Commune*. Ironically, photographs of the Communards were soon used to identify and arrest them, when the French government retook the city.

The activities of photographers in Paris after the fall of the Commune

"SMALL WARS," COLONIAL EXPANSION, AND PHOTOGRAPHY

The Crimean War, the American Civil War, the War of the Triple Alliance, and the Franco-Prussian War were conflicts that, for the most part, engaged national armies against each other. But most conflicts during the nineteenth century pitted troops from the great powers against non-European peoples. Military, commercial, and propagandistic uses of photography were exploited during these small wars and subsequent colonial expansion. The combat-related uses of photography, such as the duplication of maps, description of terrain, and depiction of armaments, became more routine. Photographers increasingly accompanied troops from the major powers, both to record military exploits and to picture foreign countries for audiences back home. In India, China, North Africa, Abyssinia (now Ethiopia), the Middle East, and Asia, photographers were granted the right to photograph troops and the aftermath of battles. They also produced views of foreign lands that stressed the exotic look of the landscape, architecture, and people. In the 1850s and 1860s, dozens of Western photographers without military obligations relocated abroad and set up studios in countries where they hoped to make images for markets back home and for colonial settlers.

The landscape and architectural views produced by photographers attached to military expeditions and those made by commercial photographers are strikingly similar. Both tend to emphasize the unusual aspects of a landscape, an extraordinary temple or public building, or the remoteness of a site. In effect, the photographs, sold singly or in albums, promoted the notion of the photographer as a brave and resourceful explorer, akin to other expatriates, such as military personnel and entrepreneurs, who were living large at the edges of the world.

In the November 1859 edition of *The Photographic News*, an anonymous reviewer noted an exhibition of stereoscopic photographs published by the London firm of Negretti & Zambra. The writer observed that "as ... the camera became more common in Egypt and the Holy Land, the more adventurous photographers turned their steps to more distant and less known countries. Even the jealously-guarded countries of China and Japan cannot shut out the camera."[77] Especially in places where intertwined Western political and economic

3.44
SAMUEL BOURNE,
Valley and Snowy Peaks Seen from the Hamta Pass, Spiti Side,
1863–66. Albumen print from wet collodion negative. Victoria & Albert Museum, London.

In Bourne's view of the Hamta Pass, the mountains rise up in a harmonious half-circle nearly filling the corners of the plate, as loftier, snowier peaks dissolve into the distant sky. Despite his attention to overall symmetry, he did not sacrifice particulars for composition, but managed to integrate myriad details into the picture.

interests expanded, photographers very quickly followed. In Asia, photography was first known primarily in port cities, but from the 1850s photographers began trekking to remote interior regions, photographing the residue of war, the wonders of the natural world, and indigenous art and architecture.

India

After arriving in India in 1863, British photographer Samuel Bourne (1834–1912) made three climbs high in the Himalayan wilds. Despite the physical obstacles and technical problems that beset his treks, Bourne excluded the hardships of the trail from his photographs, restricting difficulties to the long descriptive letters he wrote home to the *British Photographic Journal.* These helped to make him the epitome of the heroic photographer abroad. Bourne wrote that the mountain "scenery was not well adapted for pictures — at least for photography. ... The character of the Himalayan scenery in general is not picturesque."[78] Consequently, he carefully selected scenes and camera angles, in order to depict the Himalayas as a compliant and serene landscape, waiting to be recorded by the camera (Fig. 3.44). One photographic historian credits

Bourne with initiating "an imperial picturesque" — that is, an adaptation of European notions of pictorial organization and subject matter to the look of an exotic locale.[79]

After his journey to photograph the Crimean War, James Robertson traveled with photographer Félice Beato (c.1820s–c.1907) throughout the Middle East. Pictures of India were published under the name of Robertson and Beato or Robertson Beato et Cie, though it is possible that Robertson never actually visited the subcontinent.[80] Beato, however, was certainly in India making photographs, some of them staged, soon after the Indian Mutiny, which began with the 1857 uprising of Indian-born troops in the employ of the British East India Company, the private corporation that controlled trade in India, against the regular British Army (Fig. 3.45). Later called by Indians the First War of Independence, the uprising spurred the British to reorganize the army and restructure colonial rule. For years, the British public feasted on newspaper remembrances and novels based on the Mutiny, which portrayed the British as martyrs and served to justify further colonial expansion and conflicts such as the Boer War. In fact, both sides were guilty of appalling savagery.

3.45
FÉLICE A. BEATO
(attrib.), *The Execution of Mutineers in the Indian Mutiny*, 1857. Victoria & Albert Museum, London.

During the Indian Mutiny, or First War of Independence, Beato photographed from the British perspective, which included severe punishments for the rebels.

Beato was not the first Western photographer in India. John Murray (1809–1898), a medical doctor who had worked for the East India Company, and who taught medicine in Agra, was also a photographer (Fig. 3.46). His images of the Agra area, including, of course, the Taj Mahal, were exhibited in London in November, 1857, and gained large audiences because of the Mutiny. The East India Company itself had employed photographers to document Indian landscape and its antiquities since the mid-1850s.[81] Three brothers—Adolph (1829–1857), Hermann (1826–1882), and Robert (1833–1885) Schlagintweit, natural scientists and Alpine explorers—were commissioned by the company to do biomagnetic measurement in India and the Himalayas. During their four-year stay, Robert made photographic renderings for their report of the scientific mission, and for Hermann's book *Travels in India and High Asia* (1869–80). One measure of the presence of Western photographers in India is the formation of three photographic societies, in Bombay, Madras, and the province of Bengal from 1854 to 1856. Another indication of photography's capacity to replicate the British imperial view of India is found in a monthly publication, *The Indian Amateur's Photographic Album* (1856–58), and in combinations of text and pictures, such as the two-volume *The Oriental Race and Tribes: Residents and Visitors of Bombay* (1863–66), produced by William Johnson of the Bombay Photographic

Society[82] (Fig. 3.47). As in China, Western photographers employed painters trained in the art of the miniature to color photographs.[83]

China

Félice Beato was with Anglo-French troops in China in 1860, during the Second Opium War (1856–60) perhaps in a semi-official capacity. At this period, China had endured a decade of civil war and economic instability, amidst Western pressure to open the country to commerce. The opium trade, hugely profitable to the British, French, Dutch, and Americans, flourished despite being outlawed by the Chinese government. After the First Opium War (1839–42), negotiations with European powers and the United States opened some ports to trade, but hostilities reignited in 1856, when Chinese officials searched a British ship. In 1860, the Western allies took the forts at Taku, near Tientsin, a critical step in the advance on the capital city of Beijing. Beato's sequential documentation of the China campaign may be the first such conscientious series of images. He methodically photographed the aftermath of the allies' efforts to capture the forts at Taku; the interior of one of the strongholds shows the unburied Chinese dead amidst the conquered fort (Fig. 3.48). The bold picturing of carnage predates the grisly photographs taken in the American Civil War (see Figs. 3.34, 3.35).

However vivid the devastation, Beato's photograph by itself did little to explain the condition of China and its relations

3.46
JOHN MURRAY,
Panorama of the West Face of the Taj Mahal,
c. 1850s–1860s.
Albumen print from mixed-type paper negatives. Victoria & Albert Museum, London.

**3.47
PHOTOGRAPHER
UNKNOWN,** *Nagar
Brahmin Women,* from
*The Oriental Races and
Tribes: Residents and
Visitors of Bombay,*
1863. Albumen print.

Many amateur photo-
graphers and ethno-
graphers contributed
material to Johnson's
collection of images
representing ethnic
groups in India.

**3.48
FÉLICE A. BEATO,**
*Interior of the Angle of
North Fort on August 21
1860,* 1860. Albumen
print. **Victoria & Albert
Museum, London.**

There is some evidence
to suggest that Beato
had corpses dragged
into this scene and
artfully arranged, a
staging method he
employed in some of
his photographs of the
Indian Mutiny.

3.49
FÉLICE A. BEATO,
Panorama of Hong Kong, Showing the Fleet for the North China Expedition, March 18–27, 1860. Panorama consisting of six albumen silver prints from five wet collodion glass-plate negatives, each mounted on paper and joined by Japanese tape. Victoria & Albert Museum, London.

Western audiences preferred images of an exotic East, as well as pictures that showed the Western presence in Asia. In this view, Beato included Western mercantile and military ships, photographed from the roof of a British government building.

with the West. After the signing of peace accords between the Chinese government and the Western powers, which Beato tried unsuccessfully to photograph, he managed to photograph Prince Kung, brother of the emperor, who negotiated with representatives of the West. Kung's image, and Beato's views of war and commerce, were sold both in Asia and Britain.[84]

Throughout Asia, the practice of photography directly followed the expansion of Western interests. Expatriates, traveling businessmen, tourists, and viewers in Europe and America provided a ready market for pictures. Photographers and publishers continually speculated about new views and markets, and began traveling abroad, or sending photographers abroad, to seek their fortunes (Fig. 3.0).

In China, for instance, the photographic publishing firm of Negretti & Zambra issued a series of stereographic views which showed scenes in the southern city of Canton after it had been captured by the Western allies, and Beato crafted a panorama of the British Fleet in Hong Kong harbor (Fig. 3.49). Around the globe, photographs of international ports, wharves, and Western commercial buildings were regularly created. Stereotypical images of indigenous peoples and local scenes also became popular. Beginning in the late 1860s, Shanghai photographer L. F. Fisler (active 1866–1887) contrived studio settings of Chinese life for the camera (Fig. 3.50).

The American expatriate photographer Milton M. Miller (active 1850s–

3.50
L. F. FISLER, *Selling Pears (Shanghai, China)*, 1870s. Paper print. Peabody Essex Museum, Salem, Massachusetts.

1870s) set up practice in the thriving city of Hong Kong, which had been deeded to the British in 1842. Miller acquired photographs of Beijing by Beato, which he marketed in addition to his portrait practice. Though active for only a few years in the 1860s, Miller worked in both Hong Kong and Canton, selling photographic prints and producing images of influential Chinese and foreign citizens, as well as occasional city views. The standards for middle-class portraiture, developed in the West, were adapted to the tastes of a new, well-to-do Chinese clientele. Lavish furnishing, placed in an enclosure marked off by a cloth backdrop, formed the setting for people who dressed in fine clothing and displayed artistic treasures. Miller's portraits, mostly of the Chinese upper and middle classes, and persons working for foreign traders, usually show the sitters directly facing the camera (Fig. 3.51). A hint of expression is occasionally evidenced on a sitter's face, but as a rule the camera kept its distance from the sitter.

When traveling around China, the Scottish photographer John Thomson (1837–1921) observed this approach, which he satirized through the words of a fictional photographer, A-hung:

"You foreigners," says A-hung, "always wish to be taken off the straight or perpendicular. It is not so with our men of taste; they must

3.51
MILTON M. MILLER,
Cantonese Mandarin and His Wife, 1861–64.
Paper print. Royal Asiatic Society, London.

Miller adapted his photographic style to the requirements of his Eastern clients. He abstained from the use of dramatic lighting, nor did he take his pictures from unusual angles, as Western portraitists often did of their clients.

look straight at the camera so as to show their friends at a distance that they have two eyes and two ears. They won't have shadows about their faces, because, you see, shadows form no part of the face. It isn't one's nose or any other feature; therefore it should not be there. The camera, you see, is defective ... it won't recognize our laws of art."[85]

Especially in Chinese cities such as Hong Kong, which had established trade with foreigners, artists were employed to copy paintings of Chinese scenes for sale to Western businesspeople and travelers. These images, rendered in a more three-dimensional style than was used in traditional Chinese painting, dwelled on what seemed unusual and exotic to Western eyes. Such elements as rickshaws and sedan chairs, and pictures of workers and tradespeople in typical dress, were also drafted into photographic practice. Chinese costume, particularly the bound feet of women (see Fig. 3.51), and Chinese punishments, such as the cangue (Fig. 3.52), were frequent sub-

jects. With the arrival of photography in China in the 1840s, some Chinese copy-painters turned to reproducing photographs in paint. In time, after training in the studios of foreigners or under the tutelage of Western missionaries, they began making photographs. Hong Kong seems to have been a photographic training center for Chinese, who then set up practice in other cities.

Unlike many Chinese photographers, who used the medium to augment their painting income, the famed Chinese photographer Afong Lai (active 1860s–1880s), probably did camerawork full-time. The quality of his work was noted in 1872 by Thomson, who wrote that "there is one Chinaman in Hong Kong, of the name Afong, who has exquisite taste, and produces work that would enable him to make a living even in London."[86] Lai advertised his up-to-date knowledge of photographic processes, as well as the resources of his well-stocked studio. He also published an

3.52
JOHN THOMSON, *The Cangue*, 1871–72, from *China and its People*, 1874. **Victoria & Albert Museum, London.**

The cangue was a Chinese punishment in which a wooden board was worn around the neck like a portable pillory. Photographs of Asian criminal punishments, especially beheadings, became a persistent theme in Western photography, beginning in the mid-nineteenth century.

album of prints taken after the typhoon that hit Hong Kong on September 22, 1874 (Fig. 3.53).

By the time he became acquainted with Lai's work, Thomson had spent several years traveling around Asia making photographs. His work pattern was to settle in an area for a while, make images, then strike out for new territory. He moved to Singapore in 1863, but made long photographic excursions over the next three years to India, Siam (now Thailand), and Cambodia. His first book, *The Antiquities of Cambodia*, was published in 1867. By 1868, he had resettled in Hong Kong. Thomson's images may stand alone aesthetically (Fig. 3.54), but they were integrated with geographic observation, and ethnographic research in his texts and

3.53
AFONG LAI, *Wreck of the Steamers "Leonor" and "Albay," Praya and Douglas Wharf Destroyed by Typhoon, 22 September 1874,* from *Hong Kong and Macao: The Typhoon of 22 September 1874.* Albumen silver print. Foreign and Commonwealth Office Library, London.

Lai's view of the sunken wreckage of two steamers and ruined docks in Hong Kong harbor was composed to show onlookers in the foreground, and British buildings in the background.

3.54 (below)
JOHN THOMSON, *Island Temple Foochow*, Fukien Province, China, 1870–71. Stereograph. The Wellcome Library, London.

lectures. Like other photographers aware of viewers' tastes, he took photographs of Chinese laborers, punishments (see Fig. 3.52), and street people. Thomson published six books of text and photographs on China, including *Illustrations of China and Its People* (1873–74), a four-volume work of 200 photographs produced in the COLLOTYPE process, an advancement that allowed images to be printed along with text.

Japan

The introduction of commercial photography to Japan coincided with the modernization of the country, and yet it is difficult to discern this momentous change in the images produced during the later nineteenth century. In 1853 and 1854, Commodore Matthew C. Perry used shows of force to establish political and economic relations between the United States and Japan, and helped start the process of modernization in that largely feudal country. On his second mission, Perry brought along a daguerreotypist, Acting Master's Mate

Eliphalet Brown (1816–1886), who made photographs while Perry negotiated with the Japanese for nearly five months. The daguerreotypes were published as wood engravings and lithographs in the official report of Perry's trip.[87]

Given widespread curiosity about Japan, which had been all but closed to foreigners, it was likely that Western and, in time, Japanese photographers would grasp the commercial potential for making views. From the late 1850s, a steady trickle of Western photographers entered Japan; by the early 1860s, Japanese professionals were serving a clientele of wealthy Japanese patrons, as well as foreigners. When Beato arrived in Japan from China, he probably saw the growing economic opportunity. The *London Illustrated News* for July 13, 1863, indicates that he had set up a studio in Yokohama. Despite the political conflict between pro- and anti-modernization supporters, Beato's views imaged a tranquil country, unchanged for centuries (Fig. 3.55). He also made

3.55
FÉLICE A. BEATO,
Mount Fuji, 1868.
Paper print. Old Japan Collection, Surrey, England.

Beato often photographed Mt. Fujiyama, the highest and most sacred mountain in Japan, either highlighting its reach through the clouds or the way in which it dominated the surrounding countryside.

3.56 (opposite)
FÉLICE A. BEATO,
Beato's Artist, c. 1868.
Albumen print. Courtesy Old Japan, Purley, Surrey, England.

The unnamed Japanese artist delicately colored prints for Félice Beato. Japanese experience with art on paper, such as the woodblock prints called *ukiyo-e* and the hand-colored paper stencils called *kata-gama,* may have prompted Japanese artists to begin to tint photographs.

images of what he called "native types," including hand-tinted, somewhat romantic images of the samurai, the Japanese warrior class, whose privileges were repealed as Japan modernized its armaments and built a centrally controlled military.

Many of Beato's images were delicately hand-colored by Japanese artists (Fig. 3.56). Their contact with Western photographers was presumably one of the main ways in which the Japanese learned photography. In 1872, Uchida Kyuichi (1844–1875) made two photographs of Emperor Mutsuhito (1852–1912; r. 1867–1912) and the Empress Haru-Ko, who ruled over Japan as it modernized (Figs. 3.57, 3.58). When offered for sale, these images quickly became popular;[88] they were withdrawn from the market in 1873, however, when the government decided that they represented an inappropriate commercialization of the monarchs. Photographs of the emperor were not officially offered for sale again until 1889.[89]

3.57 (below left)
UCHIDA KYUICHI,
Mutsuhito, the Emperor Meiji, c. 1872. Albumen print. Richard Gadd Collection. Monterey Museum of Art, Monterey, California.

3.58 (below right)
UCHIDA KYUICHI,
Haru-ko, the Empress of Japan, c. 1872. Albumen print. Richard Gadd Collection. Monterey Museum of Art, Monterey, California.

These may be the first photographs of the emperor and empress who oversaw the modernization of the country. The emperor here wears an adaptation of Western dress at the suggestion of advisors who noted that many Europeans liked to exchange *cartes-de-visite*, and would favor seeing him in contemporary clothing.[88] The empress, who also had adopted Western dress, is seen clothed in traditional garb, underscoring, perhaps, the association of women with the continuance of the culture's traditional values.

PHOTOGRAPHY IN THE MIDDLE EAST

During the 1850s and 1860s, the popularity of an extended trip to view ancient sites around the Mediterranean, often called the Grand Tour, stimulated the market for views of Italy, Greece, Palestine, and Egypt. Thomas Cook (1808–1892), founder of the popular Cook's Tours, escorted travelers to Egypt and the Holy Land, where he usually hired photographers to take group pictures. The books, prints, and stereographs produced by British photographer Francis Frith (1822–1898) were extremely popular. They introduced a generation of British viewers to the sights of Egypt and the Holy Land.

Frith's photographs in Egypt encompassed such well-known monuments as the pyramids at Giza, and less familiar works such as the buildings on Philae, an island in the southern reaches of the Nile near Aswan (Fig. 3.59). Frith was also a publisher of photographic books, and arranged his pictures of Egypt in

such volumes as *Egypt and Palestine Photographed and Described by Francis Frith* (1858–60). Like the photographs themselves, Frith's books mix the ancient and the modern; awestruck descriptions of ancient architecture are interspersed with amusing accounts of recent travels. Frith also worked on an 1862 edition of the Bible, which contained fifty-five of his Middle East photographs. Spurred, perhaps, by the popularity of his books on Egypt and the Holy Land, Frith and his assistants set out in 1859 to photograph every city and town in England, Scotland, Ireland, and Wales, including historic monuments and natural sites.[90] This encyclopedic urge, which struck many photographers and publishers, resulted in thousands of images that were sold singly on newsstands and similar venues.

While Frith photographed sites in the Middle East, Egyptian colonel and amateur photographer Muhammad Sadiq (sometimes Sadic Bey) (1832–1902) set out on a military mapping mission to

3.59
FRANCIS FRITH,
First Pylon View of the Great Temple, 1850s. Wet collodion paper print. Victoria & Albert Museum, London.

Frith's view of the deeply incised relief sculpture on the outer gate of Philae's temple of Isis is characteristic of his approach to Egyptian artifacts. He liked to include some local people, not simply to demonstrate the scale of the sculpture, but also to contrast the present with the past, and to let viewers glimpse contemporary Egypt.

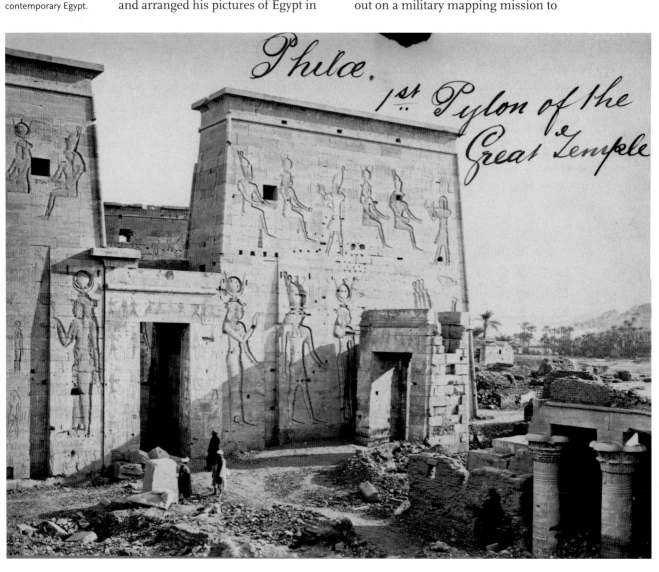

**3.60
MUHAMMAD SADIQ,**
The Holy City, c. 1880.
Albumen print.

While traveling on his official duties, Sadiq made the first known photographs of Islamic holy cities Medina and Mecca. Possibly because Sadiq was a devout Muslim, he encountered no cultural resistance to the making of these photographs.

explore Arabia. Although the exploration did not officially include photography, Sadiq was able to make the first known photographs of the holy city of Medina (Madinah), where the Prophet Muhammad was born. In 1880, Sadiq accompanied a cortege of pilgrims from Egypt to Mecca (Makkah), where he produced a panorama of the Sacred Mosque with the draped Ka'ba, or sacred structure, in the center (Fig. 3.60).

TOPOGRAPHICAL SURVEYS AND PHOTOGRAPHY

In the second half of the nineteenth century, the United States, Canada, and many European countries carried out numerous surveys of their own land, colonies, and foreign territories. Surveys were organized for a variety of purposes, including providing clean water to European settlers, transcribing the geology of an area, scouting routes for railroads, and recording archeological or architectural sites. Often the surveys were carried out by military engineers, who had already recognized the value of photography for determining artillery range and reproducing maps and sketches.

Because the terrain encountered by the foreign surveyors and the photographers who accompanied them was little known, the surveys' sponsors could not thoroughly predetermine what would be photographed. Nevertheless, photographers observed subtle cultural guidelines when selecting, arranging, and framing their shots. For example, Christians associated photographs of the Middle East with the Bible, regardless of the initial intent or context of the image. Photographers were aware of the intellectual and emotional interaction viewers had with such photographs, and they understood its commercial potential. Consequently, they ignored contemporary conditions in places associated with the Bible, and stressed the very timelessness of the setting (Fig. 3.61).

Sergeant James McDonald, assigned by the British Royal Engineers to survey Jerusalem and later the Sinai, photographed early Christian inscriptions and pilgrimage sites. His images of the Sinai Peninsula are composed almost as paintings (Fig. 3.62). As was typical of photographers traveling through the Middle East, McDonald regularly took ethnographic images.

3.61
LOUIS DE CLERCQ,
Eighth Station of the
Cross: Jesus Consoles
the Daughters of
Jerusalem, from *Voyages*
en Orient: Les Stations
de la Voie Douloureuse
à Jerusalem (album 4),
1859–60. Albumen
print. Collection
Centre Canadien
d'Architecture/Canadian
Centre for Architecture,
Montreal.

While photographing
castles built by cru-
saders in Syria and
Palestine, French photo-
grapher Louis de Clercq
(1836–1901) applied his
spare, modernistic style
to a photograph of The
Way of the Cross, that is,
the route of Jesus on the
way to the Crucifixion.[91]
His *Voyages en Orient*
1859–1860 contained
a separate album of
these images.

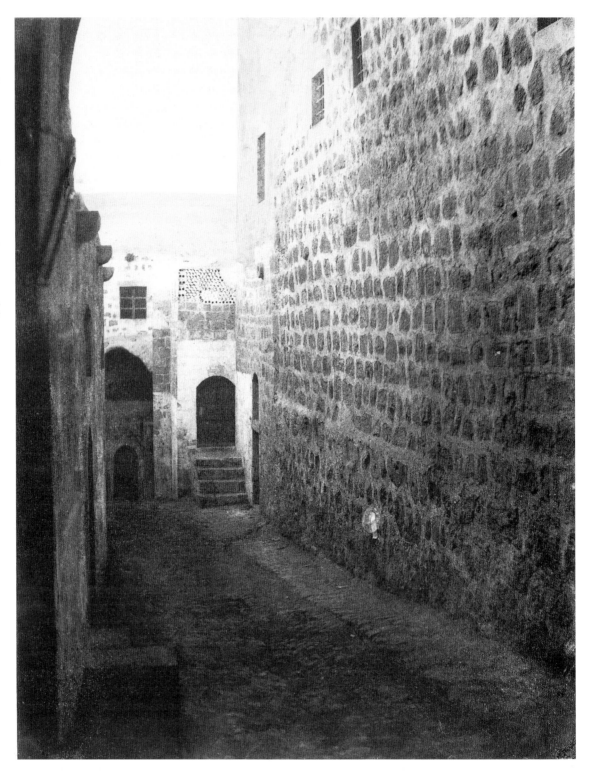

THE ABYSSINIAN CAMPAIGN, OR THE MAGDALA EXPEDITION

It is sometimes difficult to distinguish survey photography from the photography done by major powers during military campaigns. For example, during the Magdala expedition to Ethiopia, launched in 1867 by the British government when Christian missionaries and other Europeans were taken hostage by the emperor, the Royal Engineers furnished Sir Robert Napier's troops with a team of photographers. They reportedly managed to make an astounding 15,000 images, despite the hazards of conflict and the difficulties of terrain.[92] As might be expected, the Magdala expeditionary photographers made routine military photographs of leaders and troop formations. But they also created aesthetically attentive landscapes, including a view of the emperor's mountain fortress (Fig. 3.63), together with images of indigenous houses, and pictures of the Ethiopians in typical clothing or with interesting implements.

3.62
JAMES McDONALD,
*Distant View of Jerbel
Serbal, from the Palm
Grove, Wady Feiran*,
1868–69, from
*Ordnance Survey of
the Peninsula of Sinai*,
part III: *Photographs*,
vol. 2. Albumen print.
Harry Ransom
Humanities Research
Center, University of
Texas at Austin.

3.63
PHOTOGRAPHER
UNKNOWN, *Magdala*
(Emperor Téwodros's
mountain fortress and
capital), 1868. Paper
print. Ogilby Trust
and National Army
Museum, London.

DÉSIRÉ CHARNAY,
Landscape with Tree Planted by Hernán Cortés, Mexico, 1856. Salted paper negative. Musée d'Orsay, Paris.

A tree reputed to have been planted by Cortés would have obvious symbolism for European audiences. Charnay's attitude toward Mexico was typical of the European colonial outlook. In his book *Cités et ruines américaines (American Cities and Ruins)* (1862–63), he wrote that "it was France's duty to rouse Mexico from its numbness. ..."[93]

THE EXPANDING DOMAIN (1854–1880)

3.65 (right)
DÉSIRÉ CHARNAY,
A Mission in Madagasgar: Marou, Malgache, 1863. Albumen print from a wet collodion negative. Private Collection.

Charnay used the rapidly accepted conventions for photographing non-Western peoples by comparing the bodies of three residents of Madagasgar.

DÉSIRÉ CHARNAY AND EXPEDITIONARY PHOTOGRAPHY

French photographer Désiré Charnay (1828–1915) received financial support for his photographs of pre-Columbian sites in Mexico, and locations associated with Spanish conquistador Hernán Cortés, from a branch of the French government (Fig. 3.64). Soon after returning to France, Charnay joined his country's 1863 expedition to Madagascar to extend French political and trade influence[94] (Fig. 3.65). When Charnay returned to Mexico in 1864, he accompanied French troops who were sent to support Emperor Maximilian (1832–1867; r. 1864–67), who had been put on the throne by Napoleon III. After Maximilian was captured and executed by his rival Benito Juárez (1806–1872) in 1867, Charnay stayed in the United States for three years. He later ventured through South America, Java, and Australia, where his interest in writing about and photographing exotic landscapes, ancient ruins, and ethnographic types continued.

THE 49TH PARALLEL SURVEY

Photography of the shared northwestern border of the United States and Canada, running along the 49th parallel, was

begun by an American survey team in 1857, and completed jointly with a British team of Royal Engineers from 1858 to 1861 (Fig. 3.66). Beginning in 1855, some members of the Royal Engineers had been given photographic training. Soon after, Sir John Burgoyne (1782–1871), inspector general of fortifications, originated a program of

**3.66
PHOTOGRAPHER
UNKNOWN (ROYAL
ENGINEERS),** *Cutting
on the Forty-ninth
Parallel, on the Right
Bank of the Mooyie River
Looking West,* **1860–61.
Albumen print from
wet collodion negative.
Victoria & Albert
Museum, London.**

In some of the earliest
photographs of the
Pacific Northwest
region of North America,
British photographers
with an American
survey team recorded
the rough camps, the
making of astronomical
computations, and the
laborious work of cutting
a 20-foot-wide slash
through the forests from
the Rocky Mountains
to the Pacific coast.

systematic training in photography under the direction of one Charles Thurston Thompson (1816–1868), official photographer to the South Kensington Museum (now the Victoria and Albert Museum in London). The photographer–engineers were charged "to send home periodical photographs of all works in progress, and to photograph and transmit to the War Department all drawings of all objects, either valuable in a professional point of view, or interesting as illustrative of history, ethnology, natural history, antiquities, etc."[95] As in most surveys, scientists accompanied engineers to the borderlands. They wrote about the fossils, plants, and animals they encountered. The final map-making and scientific report writing took place in Washington, D.C., though it was never finished because the American Civil War pressed other duties on many of the contributors.[96] The British photographers also joined expeditions in Palestine, the Sinai, China, India, Greece, and Panama.

GOVERNMENT SURVEYS IN THE UNITED STATES

In 1838, the United States Army Corps of Topographical Engineers became a separate branch of the military assigned to explore and map the undeveloped parts of the United States.[97] The Corps remained a military unit, capable of fighting, yet its work was directed toward the advancement of civilian enterprise and public works. After the Civil War, surveys of the American West covered vast regions. As the historian William Goetzmann observed, the Corps could perform scientific exploration, such as mapping unknown terrain, while also serving political and commercial ends, such as scouting roads and railway passages for private entrepreneurs, which would, in turn, displace native peoples.[98] Similarly, photographs of the American West could be simultaneously scientific, commercial, political, and aesthetically pleasing.

In the expansive lands west of the Mississippi River, surveys mixed dispassionate scientific investigation with research on the commercial potential of natural resources. Attempts to map possible routes for a transcontinental railroad line were spurred by pressure from settlers, from business, and by gold and silver finds, such as the discovery of the Comstock lode in 1859, near Virginia City, Nevada. Government surveys often had an encyclopedic mission, attempting to construct orderly records of Native American life, geology, plants, and animals, as well as commercial potential. For instance, the huge *Pacific Railroad Reports* included whole volumes on zoology.[99]

Photography and the Transcontinental Railway

After years of speculation and surveying, the United States Congress in 1862 authorized the construction of a transcontinental railroad. Two years after the end of the Civil War, Alexander Gardner was appointed chief photographer to the eastern division of the Union Pacific Railway. Along with images made by photographers under his supervision, his photographs were published in an album titled *Across the Continent on the*

Kansas Pacific Railway (Route of the 35th Parallel), offered for sale in April, 1869. The album included scenes of small town life, settlers' homes, Native Americans, and military installations, as well as his primary topic, the construction of the railroad. *Westward, the Course of Empire Takes Its Way* shows workers and pioneers laying track at the end of the line (Fig. 3.67). The title alludes to a famous mural painted by Emanuel Leutze for the United States Capitol in Washington, D.C., completed in 1862 (Fig. 3.68). Gardner was working for Mathew Brady in Washington as the painting was being executed, and reports of its progress appeared in newspapers along the east coast. The mural shows pioneers crossing the continent on horseback and in covered wagons; in applying the title to his static, posed photograph, Gardner may have hoped to associate the railroad with the sense of adventure and accomplishment depicted by Leutze.[100]

Andrew J. Russell (1830–1902), who had been the only officially assigned photographer in the American Civil War, was hired by the Union Pacific Railway to photograph the building of a northern route across the American West that

3.67
ALEXANDER GARDNER, *"Westward, the Course of Empire Takes its Way": Laying Track 600 Miles West of St. Louis, outside Hays City, Kansas: End of the Line*, plate 152 from *Across the Continent on the Kansas Pacific Railway*, n.d. Stereograph. Kansas State Historical Society, Kansas, Missouri.

Gardner pictured the construction of the Kansas Pacific Railway, 600 miles west of St. Louis, Missouri. The photograph was published both as a single print and as a stereographic view. Its title was a popular American phrase deriving from a 1729 poem by George Berkeley.

3.68
EMANUEL LEUTZE,
*Westward the Course of
Empire Takes its Way
(Westward Ho!)*, 1861.
Oil on canvas, 33 x 43 in.
(84 x 110 cm). National
Museum of American
Art, Smithsonian
Institution, Washington,
D.C.

The small figure of a
young man at the apex
of the composition is
triumphantly waving
his arm to celebrate the
pioneers' successful
crossing of the Rocky
Mountains.

competed with the proposed track of
the Kansas Pacific, for which Alexander
Gardner photographed. Russell's
album *The Great West Illustrated in a
Series of Photographic Views Across the
Continent; Taken along the Line of the
Union Pacific Railroad* was published
in 1869 (Fig. 3.69).

Timothy O'Sullivan and
Survey Photography

The May 2, 1867, issue of the *New York
Times* noted the departure of a "party
of young men on an important surveying expedition to a section of the Rocky
Mountains and the great basin westward."[101] The journey, sponsored by the

3.69
ANDREW J. RUSSELL,
*Meeting of the Rails,
Promontory Summit,
Utah*, 1869. Albumen
print. Union Pacific
Historical Museum,
Omaha, Nebraska.

Russell's photographs
celebrated the engineer-
ing feats required to
build a railroad across
the rugged terrain of the
western United States.
His images of the meet-
ing of the Union and
Central Pacific railroads
in Promontory Summit,
Utah, on May 10, 1869,
are part of the collective
visual memory of
Americans.

U.S. Congress and carried out by the United States Engineers, was directed by scientist Clarence R. King (1842– 1901). The surveying party was to follow part of the proposed route of the transcontinental railroad, and included Timothy O'Sullivan as the official photographer.

Like his colleague and friend Alexander Gardner, Timothy O'Sullivan journeyed through the American West after the Civil War. With King's survey, he made views of the strangely shaped lava domes that erupted from Pyramid Lake in Nevada (Fig. 3.70). While the survey wintered in Virginia City, Nevada, in 1868, O'Sullivan ventured several hundred feet underground into the Comstock mine, the most famous deposit of gold and silver in America (Fig. 3.71).

O'Sullivan was scarcely back in Washington, D.C., when he joined another survey. The Darién Survey Expedition of 1870 set out to explore the Isthmus of Darién (or Panama), led by Lieutenant-Commander Thomas O. Selfridge under the auspices of the Secretary of the Navy. The group also included sixty Marines, a show of force for the Panamanian people, who suspected that the proposed canal would endanger their way of life.[102] O'Sullivan found photographing in the jungle difficult because of the humidity, the frequent rain, and the thick vegetation, which allowed little light to penetrate. Nevertheless, he produced more than

200 stereo images and 100 glass plates.[103] Some of his pictures adapt the Panamanian landscape to Western tastes (Fig. 3.72), as Bourne had done in India (see Fig. 3.44).

O'Sullivan accompanied two other important American surveys: the 1871 United States Geographical Survey West of the 100th Meridian, commonly called the Wheeler Survey for its leader George Montague Wheeler (1842–1905); and an independent 1873 survey sponsored by Wheeler to photograph Native Americans and the ruins of a cliff-dwelling culture in the Canyon de Chelly, in what is now Arizona (Fig. 3.73). The trip's reputation was tarnished in the press for having allegedly abandoned two white guides, and resulted in the shooting dead of several Native Americans. The photographs taken by O'Sullivan, however, depict none of the ill-feeling or tragedy of the journey, indicating that he, like many nineteenth-century photographers, understood that his documentary work was bound by his assignment and by commercial considerations.

Preservation of the Wilderness: Yellowstone and Yosemite

Westward expansion and development in the United States were driven by political and economic motives, as well as spiritual yearnings for unity, which seemed to compromise the notion of the West as an inviolable wilderness.

3.70
TIMOTHY O'SULLIVAN, *Pyramid and Tufa Domes, Pyramid Lake, Nevada,* **1878. Albumen print. Library of Congress, Washington, D.C.**

O'Sullivan photographed members of the United States Geological Expedition of the 40th parallel clambering on the unusual rock formations in Pyramid Lake. But in this, his best-known image of the area, he showed it undisturbed by the human presence. The far shore is only lightly suggested, while the bold diagonal composition suggests the tremendous volcanic forces that pushed up the domes.

3.71
TIMOTHY O'SULLIVAN, *A Miner at Work in the Comstock Mine*, 1868. Paper print. National Archives, Washington, D.C.

In the Comstock mine, O'Sullivan made pictures with the aid of light created by igniting a magnesium wire. The intense light of the magnesium revealed the close quarters at which the miners worked.

3.72
TIMOTHY O'SULLIVAN, *The Nipsic in Limón Bay, at High Tide*, 1871. Albumen print. George Eastman House, Rochester, New York.

When United States forces entered Panama in 1870, surveying the area for a possible canal, local people were openly suspicious. None of this tension entered O'Sullivan's lyrical picture of the *Nipsic*, the command ship of the survey, framed between two clumps of trees growing on outcroppings in Limón Bay.

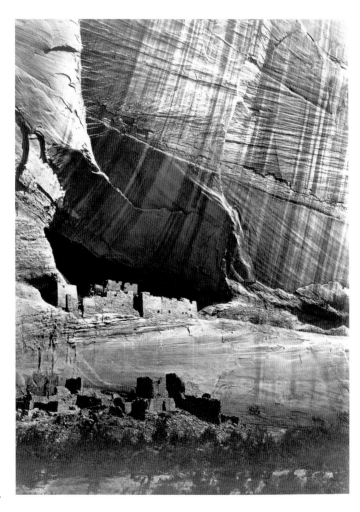

**3.73
TIMOTHY
O'SULLIVAN,**
*Ancient Ruins in the
Cañon de Chelly,* **1873.
Albumen print.
Library of Congress,
Washington, D.C.**

The cliff dwellings in
the Canyon de Chelly
were built by the
Anascizi people in pre-
Columbian times. In
the nineteenth century
popular prints, paint-
ings, and photographs
of ancient Native
American ruins helped
to bolster the notion
that these people were
a dying culture.

There were two Wests in American
perception: the West of such natural
resources as minerals, timber, and
arable land; and the West of ancient
Native American peoples, vast geological wonders, and trackless wilderness.
The Gold Rush era and subsequent
closing of the western frontier threatened to do away with a central psychic
dynamic in American life—the attitude
that, in a pinch, one could head out
west beyond the taint of human society
and live simply. Settlement and enterprise appeared to endanger the unique
American landscape, but the wilderness
seemed hostile to robust economic
development. The history of photographic imaging of the Yosemite Valley
in California and the Yellowstone area
of Wyoming demonstrates how closely
intertwined were the notions of pure
nature and civilized progress.

Carleton E. Watkins (1829–1916)
was not the first person to photograph
the dramatic scenery of the Yosemite
Valley, but he was the best known and
most influential. Another San Francisco
photographer, Charles Leander Weed
(1824–1903), had visited Yosemite in

1859. Watkins's early career brought
him near Yosemite, to the vast Mariposa
estate, where he was commissioned to
photograph the property's mining activities. The photographs were used to
entice foreign investors with the estate's
gold and mineral potential. In his early
commercial photographs, Watkins developed the practice of showing that human
enterprise did not disturb the natural
order (Fig. 3.74). He was one of the first
American artists in any medium to construct a commercial sublime, rendering
nature's grandeur with subtle, unobtru-
sive traces of new economic ventures.

Watkins probably made his initial
1861 trip to Yosemite in the company
of one of the Mariposa estate's entrepreneurs. He returned to Yosemite in
1865 and 1866, under the informal auspices of the California State Geological
Survey, whose members studied the
geology, biology, and mineral potential
of the region, as well as likely sites for
roads. The Gold Rush years had quick-
ened American and foreign interest
in California. Watkins, alert to opportunity, if not always adept in business
matters, began a series of photographs
at Yosemite, whose scenic beauty was
already attracting both a growing curiosity back east and a few intrepid tourists.
Like O'Sullivan at Pyramid Lake,
Watkins preferred to show Yosemite as
an Eden of unsullied awe. The absence
of people accentuated the area as a prime
site in which to witness the processes
of nature.

Watkins's stereograph *From the "Best
General View," Mariposa Trail* (Fig. 3.75)
typifies the soaring sublime that he contrived to express in the expansiveness
of the valley and the height of its crags.
Although more tourists were arriving
in Yosemite by the mid-1860s, Watkins
still took his photograph from a vantage
point that eliminated all traces of the
human presence, and dislocated the
view from contemporary life. Moreover,
the viewer is not situated in a particular
spot, but invited to soar above the valley,
a feeling that would have been made all
the more intense in stereographic viewing. German-American painter Albert
Bierstadt (1830–1902) saw Watkins's
photographs and magnified the conventions, creating sensational tourist-
pleasing images of Yosemite as a pri-
mordial, cotton-candy-swathed Alps.

3.74
CARLETON E.
WATKINS, *Cape Horn,
near Celilo*, 1867.
Albumen silver print
from glass negative.
Gilman Paper Company
Collection, New York.

3.75
CARLETON E.
WATKINS, *From the
"Best General View,"
Mariposa Trail*,
c. 1865–66, from
Watkins' Pacific Coast
stereo series, no. 1134.
Albumen print.
Center for Creative
Photography, University
of Arizona, Tucson,
Arizona.

Watkins's photograph
shows the Yosemite
Valley as it might have
existed at the time of
creation. The dark fore-
ground area and the
tall tree on the right
help to inflate the three-
dimensional effect
of the stereograph by
creating a sense of
deep recessive space.

Eadweard Muybridge (1830–1904),
who would later become renowned for
his photographs of human movement
(see pp. 213, 215; Fig. 4.57), also gained
a national reputation as a photographer
of Yosemite. Born in Britain, Muybridge
settled in San Francisco. Following
the success of Watkins's views of the

valley, Muybridge made his first trip to
Yosemite in 1867. By 1872, he was producing large plate prints that competed
with those of Watkins.

Muybridge's images of Yosemite
frequently fill the sky with dramatic
atmospheric effects. Even when he
chose a point of view that would dangle

the viewer over a precipice (Fig. 3.76), Muybridge did not imitate the hypnotic detail and airless clarity of Watkins's work. Muybridge sometimes printed cloud studies separately in the upper portion of his Yosemite scenes. He also relished moonlight effects, and invented a device that minimized overexposure of the sky, and thereby allowed clouds to appear. In *Spirit of Tutohannula* (1867), he responded to the American association of ancient peoples with wilderness by having an individual enact the ghostly presence of the Native American chief said to have lived on the summit of El Capitán in Yosemite. It was good practice for his staged photographs of the Modoc War (see Fig. 3.80).

William Henry Jackson's (1843–1942) photographs of the Yellowstone area, though not the first, were the images that became enduring visual symbols of this locale. Jackson began his photographic career coloring and retouching portrait photographs. His philosophical outlook on nature was informed by American writers such as

Henry David Thoreau (1817–1862) and Ralph Waldo Emerson (1803–1882), who saw nature as infused by a higher spiritual intelligence. Nevertheless, he was a shrewd businessman, and embellished his photographs with descriptive words such as "castle" and "temple" to describe the sites at Yellowstone. Jackson settled briefly in Omaha, Nebraska, where he made studio pictures and locale shots of the Pawnee, Otoe, and Omaha peoples living in the area. In the *Descriptive Catalogue of Photographs of American Indians by W. H. Jackson, Photographer of the Survey of 1877*, he spoke of Native Americans in terms that were becoming increasingly prevalent. He saw them as dwindling vestiges of a primitive time in America, who could only purchase survival by adopting the values of white Americans (Fig. 3.77).

Like several photographers of the West, Jackson worked for a government-sponsored survey. He joined the first official government and scientific survey of the Yellowstone area, directed by Ferdinand Vandeveer Hayden in 1871.[104]

3.76
EADWEARD MUYBRIDGE, *Valley of the Yosemite from Union Point*, c. 1872. Albumen print. The J. Paul Getty Museum, Los Angeles, California.

Muybridge has chosen a view through Yosemite Valley showing a mass of dark rock in the foreground that contrasts with distant mountains rendered barely visible in the haze. The sheer face of El Capitán rising 3,000 feet can be made out on the right.

3.77
WILLIAM HENRY JACKSON, *(Omaha) Indians Building Houses for the Tribe,* 1877. Albumen print. National Anthropological Archives, Smithsonian Institution, Washington, D.C.

Previous explorations to Yellowstone, which would become the country's first official National Park, aroused public interest in the area's geological wonders, as did the prospect of a rail service for tourists. Aware of public curiosity about the area, Hayden brought with him the landscape painter Thomas Moran (1837–1926), who had made sketches for a recent article in *Scribner's* magazine on "The Wonders of Yellowstone." He also invited sons and protégés of such powerful Washington politicians and lobbyists as Massachusetts Senator Henry L. Dawes, the principal spokesperson in the campaign that resulted in Yellowstone being designated a National Park in 1872.[105] Along the way, Jackson made photographs of gold mining. But for his treatment of the Yellowstone geysers, such as *Mud Geyser in Action* (Fig. 3.78), he turned to retouching, embellishing the steamy emissions.

3.78
WILLIAM HENRY JACKSON, *264. Mud Geyser in Action,* 1871. Paper print. U.S. Geological Service, Denver, Colorado.

Jackson recorded the wonders of the Yellowstone area of Wyoming, much as Watkins recorded the marvels of Yosemite. The images produced by both photographers helped in the effort to make both areas into National Parks.

WAR AND THE PHOTOGRAPHY OF NATIVE AMERICANS

The movement westward brought about regular conflicts with Native Americans, who fought removal from their ancient homelands and consolidation with other, unrelated groups.

The Modoc War

In northern California and Oregon, longstanding tension between the Modoc people and white settlers escalated between 1872 and 1873. Unhappily moved by the U.S. government to the Klamath Reservation in Oregon, many

3.79
LOUIS HELLER,
Frank Leslie's Illustrated Newspaper, June 12, 1873. Woodblock print from a photograph by Louis Heller. Library of Congress, Washington, D.C.

The cover of the newspaper erroneously credited Heller's photographs of Modoc prisoners to Carleton Watkins. The note, in small print at the bottom of the page, tells readers that the images were derived from photographs, an increasingly common announcement that expressed the authenticity of the images.

Modocs returned to their ancestral homelands along the California–Oregon border. In November 1872, cavalry troops arrived to remove the Modocs from settler-claimed land. Eventually the Modocs hid in caverns and depressions found in the rugged lava beds south of Tule Lake, where the remainder of the campaign against them was fought.

The terrain of the lava beds was so unfamiliar to the U.S. military that the Corps of Engineers was called in to make a reconnaissance.[106] The photographer hired to record the topography and, perhaps, copy maps and sketches was Louis Heller (1839–1928). A German-born photographer who worked in California, Heller was the first to reach the war front. His images of Modoc prisoners were used on the cover of *Frank Leslie's Illustrated Newspaper* for July 12, 1873[107] (Fig. 3.79). At the time, Muybridge was a San Francisco photographer in the employ of Bradley and Rulofson, commercial photographers who sold images of California as well as current events. His photographs of the troops and the locale were sent to Washington to show the

difficult circumstances in which the military had been operating against the Modoc (Fig. 3.80). These pictures were also used to illustrate the June 21 issue of *Harper's Weekly*.

The Fort Laramie Treaty

Although dozens of wars such as the Modoc War were fought between 1850 and 1886, the preparation, conduct, and aftermath of battles and skirmishes were seldom reported by the camera. Photographic portraits of Native American leaders were sometimes made, both in their own settlements and in towns where photographers maintained studios. Newspaper articles on the so-called Indian Wars were generally illustrated by artists' conceptions, rather than photographically derived pictures. From time to time, Native American artists rendered the engagements with paintings on animal hide.

A photograph taken by Alexander Gardner in 1868 of the participants in the peace talks and treaty negotiations at Fort Laramie (Fig. 3.81) shows Civil War general William Tecumseh Sherman (third from the right of the

3.80
EADWEARD MUYBRIDGE, *A Modoc Brave on the War Path*, 1872–73. Paper print. National Anthropological Archives, Washington, D.C.

Muybridge posed a Native American scout working for the U.S. Army as an enemy Modoc brave, although he was not a Modoc.

difficult circumstances in which the military had been operating against the Modoc (Fig. 3.80). These pictures were also used to illustrate the June 21 issue of *Harper's Weekly*.

3.81
ALEXANDER
GARDNER, *Untitled*
(Commissioners,
General Sherman
among them, seated
with Indians), May 10,
1868. Paper print.
National Anthropo-
logical Archives,
Washington, D.C.

In this image of the Fort
Laramie negotiations,
the U.S. delegates face
the camera, as if aware
of the historical record
they are making. The
Native Americans
mostly have their backs
to the camera or are
in shadow. Native
Americans would some-
times turn their backs
to the camera and cover
their heads so that the
shadow-catcher would
not capture their
spirits.[108]

U.S. delegation), commander of the
army's Division of the Mississippi, which
included the Great Plains. Sherman took
his Civil War philosophy of "total war"
and applied it to relations with Native
Americans, for whom it meant the annihilation of villages and supplies, as well
as battle.[109] The treaty negotiated at Fort
Laramie in 1868 followed the war for
the contested Bozeman Trail, which
gave white settlers a passage westward.
It came after the most decisive Native
American victory in all of the western
wars.[110] Nevertheless, the May 1868
photograph visually reversed the temporary fortunes of war. It depicted the
beaten white men in a physically superior position, even though the treaty they
were negotiating was highly favorable to
the Native Americans.

Little Big Horn

The provisions of the 1868 Fort Laramie
treaty were violated by both sides, each
of whom entered the other's territories.
Survey parties scouting a route for the
Northern Pacific Railroad entered Native
American territory, where they clashed
with warriors led by Sitting Bull. The
discovery of gold in the Black Hills of
present-day South Dakota motivated
thousands of white miners to invade
the legendary home of the Sioux gods.[111]
In 1874 Colonel George Armstrong

Custer (1839–1876) led a reconnaissance force of over 1,000 heavily armed
troops. There were about 100 wagons in
his train, some carrying equipment to
be used by the engineers, the geologists,
and other scientists who accompanied

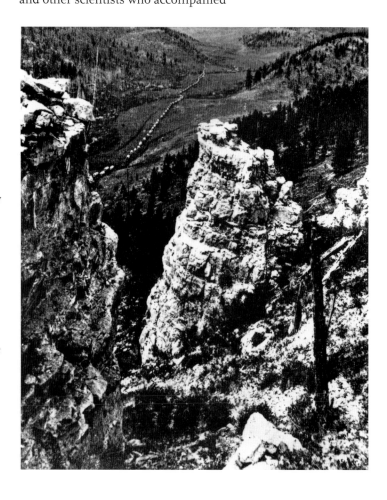

3.82
W. H.
ILLINGSWORTH,
*Indian's Eye view of
Custer Expedition
Entering the Black Hills*,
1874. Paper print.
National Archives,
Washington, D.C.

Thinking that it would
have great public inter-
est, W. H. Illingsworth
accompanied George
Custer's expedition,
making many photo-
graphs along the way,
including what he called
the "Indian's eye view"
of the group.

him. A photographer, W. H. Illingsworth (1842–1893), captured the expedition entering the Black Hills (Fig. 3.82). After several smaller battles, U.S. troops under Custer were thoroughly defeated at Little Big Horn in 1876. Custer's Last Stand, as it came to be called, inflamed the American public, whose support for harsher treatment of the Native Americans gathered strength during the last decades of the nineteenth century.

PHOTOGRAPHY AND SCIENCE

MEDICAL PHOTOGRAPHY

Because the American Civil War was fought near towns and cities, there was acute public awareness of battle injuries and the needs of soldiers. The Sanitary Commission was a charitable organization of private citizens who came together to do whatever the United States government did not do for soldiers during the war. The commission, modeled on the British equivalent that was active during the Crimean War, worked with the government to provide food and medical supplies, ambulance service, rehabilitation, and aid to dependent families. To raise money, the Sanitary Commission held fairs, which included the sale of photographs of

landscapes and famous individuals. Disabled soldiers were the subject of postwar photographs (Fig. 3.83).

Throughout the war, Clara Barton (1821–1912), the first woman clerk in the United States Patent Office, organized relief efforts for wounded soldiers. She managed to secure permission to be on the front lines, where she ministered to northern and southern soldiers. Like many of Brady's sitters, she was a popular figure in American civic life, and gave many public lectures (Fig. 3.84).

The number of amputations suffered by Civil War soldiers shocked both doctors and the general public. In the May 1863 issue of the *Atlantic Monthly*, Oliver Wendell Holmes described how photographs of able-bodied people walking on city streets might be observed in order to devise effective and comfortable artificial limbs.[112] Medical practitioners and hospitals, meanwhile, commissioned photographs of soldiers with wounds (Fig. 3.85). During the war, the Surgeon General founded the Army Medical Museum in Washington, D.C., one of whose purposes was to collect photographs of war injuries.[113] Over 1,000 pictures were collected in compendiums of photographs and engravings based on photographs, including the eight-volume *Photographs of Surgical Cases and Specimens* (1866). Though thwarted by shortages of paper and

3.83
PHOTOGRAPHER UNKNOWN, *Patronize the Disabled Soldier*, from *American Views: New Series*, c. 1866. Stereograph. Bob Zeller Collection, Pleasant Garden, North Carolina.

After the American Civil War, photographs of soldiers continued to be made and circulated, in part for patriotic reasons and in part to show how they fared after government service. Here two veterans with war-related disabilities sell apples and lemonade on Boston Common.

3.84
MATHEW BRADY,
Clara Barton, c. 1866.
Albumen silver print.
Library of Congress,
Washington, D.C.

In addition to his work
during the American
Civil War, Mathew
Brady was known for
a straightforward, yet
intimate portrait style,
which he developed for
pictures of American
celebrities, such as
American Red Cross
founder, Clara Barton.

3.85
PHOTOGRAPHER
UNKNOWN, *Untitled*
(Corporal Samuel
Thummam, wounded at
the battle of Petersberg),
1865. Burns Archive,
New York.

Photographs of
wounded American
Civil War veterans were
made and circulated to
teaching hospitals for
study in an effort to
improve battlefield care,
recovery, and the quality
of prosthetics.

printing supplies, Confederate doctors
also published a journal largely devoted
to battlefield medicine. The *Confederate
States Medical and Surgical Journal*,
issued from January 1864 to February
1865, printed a few photographically
derived woodcuts of injured soldiers.[114]

PHOTOMICROGRAPHY AND ASTRONOMICAL PHOTOGRAPHS

From the first, objects and organisms
made visible by microscopes and telescopes were subjects of photography
(see Figs. 2.0, 2.11, 2.12, 2.13). Indeed,
photomicrography became a photographic specialty beginning in the
1850s.[115] For the French physician and
anatomist Jules-Bernard Luys (1828–
1897), photomicrography was an important aid to scientific objectivity. In his
L'Iconographie photographique des centres

nerveux (*Photographic Iconography of the Nerve Centers*) (1873), which was issued with an atlas of photographs and lithographs of neurological subjects, Luys wrote that photography substituted "the action of light for ... personality, in order to obtain an image both impersonal and accurate"[116] (Fig. 3.86).

From the late 1850s on, proposals to miniaturize and store information in photographs became more frequent. The *American Journal of Photography* for 1858 recommended storing public documents on photographic negatives. With its usual exuberance, *Photographic News* opined that "the whole archives of a nation might be packed away in a snuff-box." Businesses were founded to produce microscopic photographs, either as a means of record-keeping or for novelties, such as penholders fitted with a lens that magnified tiny calendars.[117]

Despite much enthusiasm for its potential, telescopic photography did not proceed as rapidly as photomicrography. Astronomical photography was beset with technical problems resulting from low light, the movement of the earth, and the limitations of photosensitive materials, while the sun's brightness created its own difficulties. Nevertheless, many astronomers, such as John Herschel, saw the potential to create systematic

recording of the sun and its features. Others, in the spirit of François Arago's original conjectures (see pp. 19–20), considered that photochemical reactions might be used to measure light rays.

Photographers continued to have difficulty creating clear images of the moon. Throughout the 1870s, American astronomer and photography advocate Lewis M. Rutherfurd (sometimes spelt Rutherford) (1816–1892) circulated his 1865 photograph of the moon (Fig. 3.87). Working together, engineer James Nasmyth (1808–1890) and astronomer James Carpenter (1840–1899) created a unique series of astronomical pictures. Among the images in their 1874 publication *The Moon, Considered as a Planet, a World, and a Satellite*, were WOOD-BURYTYPE PRINTS of photographs of plaster models of the moon, constructed in accordance with Nasmyth's drawings based on telescope observations. Far from fakery, in their minds, the model was conceived as an instructional tool that provided clear, close-up details not technically possible in actual moon photographs. Nasmyth and Carpenter

**3.88 (above)
JAMES NASMYTH &
JAMES CARPENTER,
*Moon, Crater of
Vesuvius*, 1864. From
*The Moon, Considered
as a Planet, a World,
and a Satellite*, 1874.
Woodburytype.
National Gallery of
Canada, Musée des
Beaux-Arts du Canada,
Ottawa.**

In order to produce
this close-up image,
Nasmyth and Carpenter
built an elaborate
model of the moon,
staged an eruption of
the volcano, which had
not been observed
from Earth, and photo-
graphed the result.

even created events, such as a volcanic
eruption on the moon's surface (Fig.
3.88), and drew parallels between such
natural phenomena as the creases on
the surface of the moon, a human hand,
and an apple[118] (Fig. 3.89).

The largest international effort in
astronomical photography during the
period took place in December 1874,
when scientists from Germany, Britain,
and France entered into a friendly competition to record the passing, or transit,
of the planet Venus across the face of
the sun.[119] The French team included
the scientist and photographer Pierre-
César Jules Janssen (1824–1907), who

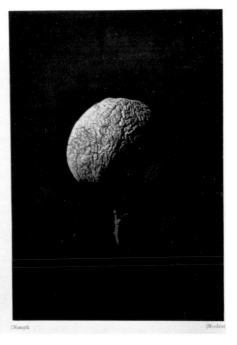

**3.89
JAMES NASMYTH &
JAMES CARPENTER,
*Back of Hand, Wrinkled
Apple*, 1864, from
*The Moon, Considered
as a Planet, a World,
and a Satellite*, 1874.
Woodburytype. National
Gallery of Canada,
Musée des Beaux-Arts
du Canada, Ottawa.**

The search for universal
laws in nature led
Nasmyth and Carpenter
to compare the wrin-
kling of the human
hand to that of an apple,
and, eventually, to the
processes that created
the furrowed surface of
the moon.

**3.90
PIERRE-CÉSAR
JULES JANSSEN,**
Transit of Venus, 1874.
Daguerreotype, partly
colored, full plate.
Société Française de
Photographie, Paris.

Janssen used a gun-like
camera to photograph
the transit of Venus. The
outer ring of the photo-
graph is toothed into
forty-eight segments,
one for each exposure.
Venus appears in each
tooth as a black dot.
The large circle in the
center top of the plate
and the notch in the
lower right were used to
hold and turn the plate
in the gun-camera.

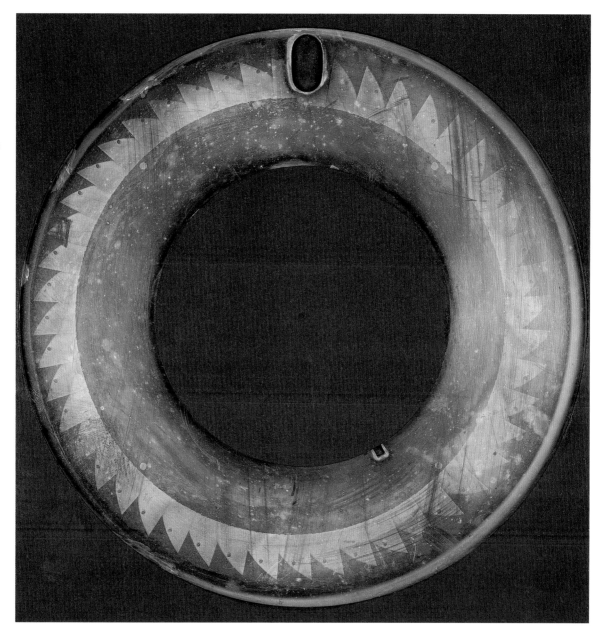

developed a revolver camera, in effect a
gun fitted with a lens, to make sequential
exposures on a daguerreotype plate (Fig.
3.90). Though outmoded for portrait and
landscape photography, the daguerreotype was chosen by the French team, in
part because its metal plates were not
subject to breakage, as were glass plates.

In the second half of the nineteenth
century, the public experience of photographs depicting human society and
the natural world increased. With that
expansion came an intensification of
the visual effects of images. The three-
dimensionality of stereographs is perhaps the most prominent example, but
there are others. Photographers created
panoramic views, some of which mimicked the span of human vision, others
of which attempted to reproduce a
circular, 360-degree view. Throughout

the nineteenth century, painted and
photographed panoramas were used
for popular entertainment and education. Whereas painted panoramas
were rendered on long canvas scrolls,
photographic panoramas were constructed from connected sequences of
camera images.

From 1859 to 1866, French geologist
Aimé Civiale (1821–1893) made a
striking series of twenty-eight large
photographic panoramas in the Italian,
French, Austrian, and Swiss Alps
(Fig. 3.91). Civiale did not conceive his
photographs to show how a human
might perceive the scene, nor to render
the beauty of the Alps. He wanted the
panoramas to illustrate the tremendous
geological uplift that originally formed
the European mountain systems. Civiale
developed a scientific aesthetic for his

CHAINE   DE   L'OBERLAND   LE SIMPLON   LES MISCHABEL HORNER   MONTAGNES DE LA VALLÉE DE ZERMATT

3.91
AIMÉ CIVIALE,
*Circular Panorama
Taken from Bella Tolla
(3030 metres)*, 1866.
Collotype, printed by
Jean-Dominique
Gustave Aroca, 1882
or earlier. Bibliothèque
Centrale du Musée
National d'Histoire
Naturelle, Paris.

purposes, in which the large patterns of the mountains' geological development were emphasized and the myriad surface details were decreased. His work was shown in the exhibitions of the French Photographic Society for a decade, from 1859 to 1869.[120]

PHOTOGRAPHIC STUDIES OF HUMAN EXPRESSION

The notion that inner human character could be interpreted through facial expressions persisted throughout nineteenth-century portraiture in all visual media. In fact, as photographs became more generally available, they made readings of inner character more widespread, either through gallery displays such as Brady's, or through the personal sharing of images. Writing in the July 1863 issue of the *Atlantic Monthly*, Oliver Wendell Holmes envisaged a new human possibility called "photographic intimacy," a friendship established by the exchange of photographs, between two people who have never met. The relationship starts after the exchange of letters and views of scenery. It culminates in an exchange of photographic self-portraits carefully staged among personal objects, and the sharing of photographic pictures of loved ones. In time, Holmes wrote, photography would make the "outer and ... inner life a reality ... but for his voice, which you have never heard, you know ... [the photographic correspondent] better than hundreds who call him by name, as they meet him year after year."[121] The conviction that a clear correspondence existed between inner moods and outward appearances also informed scientific experiments on human gestures and facial expressions, such as the photographs of mental patients taken by Dr. Hugh Welch Diamond in the 1850s (see p. 37).

Duchenne de Boulogne

Outwardly, the explorations undertaken by the French doctor Guillaume Benjamin Duchenne de Boulogne (1806–1875) resemble Diamond's work. Duchenne was a physician at the Paris hospital La Salpêtrière, which treated people suffering from epilepsy, neurological problems, and insanity. Duchenne's *Mécanisme de la physionomie humaine* (*The Mechanism of Human Physiognomy*), published in 1862, was accompanied by an atlas of eighty-four photographs taken between 1852 and 1856 of human subjects whose facial muscles were stimulated by an electric current (Fig. 3.92). With the technical advice of photographer Adrien Tournachon (1825–1903), brother of the famous Parisian photographer Nadar, Duchenne attempted to arouse through electrical stimulation the individual facial muscles that he considered to be involved in human expression. Most of his photographs were of people with mental retardation; forty-five of the eighty-four images are of one older mentally retarded man.

To aid the camera's recording, swift and subtle muscular reactions were ignored in favor of more dramatic and visible ones. Duchenne took his subjects' emotional responses to be typical of all humans; the individual's personality and distinctive range of reactions did not interest him. Unlike Diamond's efforts, Duchenne's work was very specifically related to art as well as science. His *Mécanisme* contained plates in which works of art were compared with his photographic experiments, so as to show how art did not always show physiologically true depictions of human emotional responses. Photographic historian Nancy Roth found that, to his contemporaries, Duchenne's

ICONO-PHOTOGRAPHIQUE

MÉCANISME DE LA PHYSIONOMIE HUMAINE

Pl. 6.

Duchenne (de Boulogne), phot.

**3.92
G. B. DUCHENNE
DE BOULOGNE,**
"Electrical contraction of
the eyelids, the forehead
with voluntary lowering
of the jaw: terror. ..."
plate 63 from *Mécanisme
de la physionomie
humaine: ou analyse
electro-physiologique de
l'expression des passions,*
1876. Paper photograph
tipped in book. Victoria &
Albert Museum, London.

Duchenne used electrical
currents to stimulate
facial expressions. He
seems to have had few
intellectual or scientific
reservations about stim-
ulating the appearance
of emotions artificially,
rather than observing
them as his subjects
responded to people,
things, or thoughts that
provoked a response.

representations seemed too naturalistic for art: one critic wrote that "he's ... to be reproached for stripping art of its every ideal, reducing it to an anatomical realism every bit in keeping with the tenets of a certain modern school of art."[122] The nineteenth-century clash between two approaches to painting, represented by the realism of Gustave Courbet (1819– 1877) and the idealism of Jean-Auguste-Dominique Ingres (1780–1867), was specifically referenced by the commentator in relation to Duchenne's physiological photography.

Darwin

After he published *The Origin of Species* (1859) and *The Descent of Man* (1871), the British scientist Charles Darwin (1809–1882) completed a study that he had begun in 1838. *The Expression of the Emotions in Man and Animals* (1872) argued that the physical signs of emotional states were inherently the same in all humans, and that animals had emotions that they expressed in ways similar to people. The volume underscored Darwin's hypothesis that humans were not a separately created species, but resulted from the processes of natural selection and evolution.

About 9,000 copies of the book sold in the first four months of publication, both because Darwin was a well-known, controversial author, and because the subject of emotional expression was popular at the time.[123] Darwin's introduction acknowledged his debt to the insights and photographs of emotion made by Duchenne de Boulogne. In fact, Duchenne lent Darwin photographs, which he published as part of his study. With some of Duchenne's images, Darwin asked the engraver who worked on the photographs to temper the wrinkles and to remove the instrument that directed an electrical stimulus to the subject's face. Along with illustrations provided by artists, Darwin also included photographs commissioned from the London photographer Oscar Rejlander (see Fig. 3.12), who personally acted out some of the emotional states before the camera. Believing that babies exhibited the purest, least acculturated signs of emotion, Darwin used photographs of babies made by Rejlander and Adolph Diedrich Kindermann (active

1860s–1870s) of Hamburg, Germany (Fig. 3.93). In all, five photographers provided images to Darwin.

Darwin investigated the means by which photographs might be inexpensively included in the text. This had proved difficult because the presses that printed text ran too fast to reproduce photographs and type at the same time, and because most photographs needed to be printed on special paper, not newsprint. But a technique known as HELIOTYPE, invented by the photographer Ernest Edwards (1837–1903), who made a portrait of Darwin in 1868, used printing press plates to reproduce photographs, and thus keep down the price of the book. The resulting images are not sharp and detailed, but they do convey facial gestures adequately.

3.93
G. B. DUCHENNE DE BOULOGNE (1; 2); ANONYMOUS (4; 5); O. G. REJLANDER (6; 7?), *Untitled*, from Charles Darwin's *The Expression of the Emotions*, before 1872. Heliotype.

Oscar Rejlander and Duchenne de Boulougne contributed photographs to Charles Darwin's study of *The Expression of the Emotions*. The fussy baby in figure 1 became a huge hit with the British public. Known as "Ginx Baby," it sold about 300,000 prints.

Charcot

Like his teacher Duchenne de Boulogne, the French physician and neurologist Jean-Martin Charcot (1825–1893) worked at La Salpêtrière, where he drew upon photographs to document his case studies, and was interested in the expression of emotion in art. In one sense, Charcot carried Duchenne's work to an extreme, making weekly public presentations of his patients, many of them female, to an audience of scientists and socialites.[124] Charcot's particular concern with hysteria attracted his most famous admirer, Sigmund Freud (1856–1939).

From 1877 to 1880, Charcot published *L'Iconographie photographique de La Salpêtrière* (*Photographic Iconography of the Salpêtrière Hospital*), a three-volume work that contained photographs of hysterics (Fig. 3.94). Collaborating with the clinician Désiré Magliore Bourneville (active 1870s), and assisted by Paul Régnard (active 1870s), an intern at La Salpêtrière, Charcot sought to photograph the physical expression of mental states. He chose subjects who were known throughout France to be able to respond well to hypnotic suggestion.[125] Like those of Hugh Welch Diamond, Duchenne, and Darwin, Charcot's work and his photographs emphasized facial expression as an infallible indicator of psychological states. And like them, Charcot regarded himself as a neutral observer. Of his visual recording, he stated: "I stand here merely as a photographer, I write down what I see."[126]

PHOTOGRAPHY AND THE SOCIAL SCIENCES

Photography participated in the production of evidence in many fields. Geology, biology, botany, medicine, astronomy, and chemistry used photography to collect and exhibit evidence. European efforts to establish comprehensive and systematic classifications of human beings were enhanced by the intense discussion of Charles Darwin's writings on evolution and the origins of the human species. Theories about the multiple origins of human beings, akin to that which motivated Louis Agassiz to commission photographic studies of slaves (see pp. 40–41) persisted, despite Darwin's insistence on a single human origin. Some commentators interpreted his writings to validate a natural hierarchy of development, from the lower to the higher races, based on visible difference in the anatomy, and on cultural characteristics.

**3.94
PHOTOGRAPHER UNKNOWN,** *Attitudes Passionelles,* plate 21 from Charcot's *L'Iconographie photographique de La Salpêtrière,* 1876. **Paper print. Bibliothèque Interuniversitaire de Médecine, Université René Descartes, Paris.**

Charcot not only photographed sitters acting out various symptoms of mental illness but also invited the public to his sanatorium on Tuesdays to see the performances. His subjects' exaggerated expressions and physical positions resemble poses assumed by actors in the theater, largely because they were called upon to act out their symptoms for the camera, not experience them afresh.

ETHNOGRAPHIC STUDIES AND DISPLAY

Grand schemes to compare and contrast races and to photograph them were launched throughout the later nineteenth century. For instance, it was proposed that the Calcutta exhibition of 1869 should bring together "tribal" peoples from Asia, Polynesia, and Australasia, for purposes of examination and photography.[127] The scheme failed, but ethnographic studies and exhibitions, extensively illustrated by photographs, flourished throughout the 1860s and 1870s. German photographer Carl Dammann (active 1870s) issued an album of 600 small images titled *Ethnological Photographic Gallery of the Various Races of Man* in 1875.

In Russia, more systematic fieldwork aimed at describing physical types and local costumes began to use photography. The Russian Geographical Society issued special instructions for photographers who were attempting to create a scientific study of difference. Full-face, profile, and full-length views of people were considered to be the most scientifically useful.[129] The Moscow Ethnographic Exhibition of 1867

3.95
PHOTOGRAPHER UNKNOWN, *A Croat Couple from the Valley of the Serezan near Zagreb*, exhibited in the Western and Slav section of the *Moscow Ethnographic Exhibition*, 1867. Paper print. **Royal Anthropological Institute, London.**

In an effort to promote pan-Slavic unity, the *Moscow Ethnographic Exhibition* showed models of Slavic people, such as these in a fabricated natural setting, complete with local flowers.[128]

displayed full-scale replicas of architectural interiors showing local implements and regional costume (Fig. 3.95).

The People of India (1868–75) was an eight-volume series of text and photographs. Begun in response to a casual request for a souvenir album by the British Governor General, Charles John Canning, it developed into a huge project involving civilian and military photographers. The 468 tipped-in prints generally show people identified by tribe and caste, holding a tool or weapon denoting their work and social position (Fig. 3.96).

The lack of standardization in anthropological photography led scientists such as Thomas Henry Huxley (1825–1925) and John Lamprey (active 1870s) to create systems by which humans could be photographed for observation and comparison. Huxley's anthropometric poses were cumbersome, but Lamprey's recommendations in his 1869 journal article "On a Method of Measuring the Human Form" became influential (Fig. 3.97). Both Huxley and Lamprey proposed that the scientific study of race should be based on

3.96 (left)
PHOTOGRAPHER UNKNOWN, *Brinjara and Wife*, plate 161 from *The People of India*, 1868. Paper print. Harry Ransom Humanities Research Center, University of Texas, Austin, Texas.

The People of India was part of a large, though informal, British effort to collect statistical data, study the history of Indian civilization, and appropriate the country into "the laboratory of mankind." They believed that Indian society had to develop into a modern one along the same route taken by Britain.[130]

3.97
JOHN LAMPREY, *Front and Profile Views of a Malayan Male*, c. 1868–69. Carbon prints. Royal Anthropological Institute of Great Britain and Ireland, London.

observations of the nude human body, so that differences in skin color, hair texture, physique, and the like would be recorded. This strategy strengthened the belief that there were basic differences among human races, observable through distinctions in physical appearance.

Orientalism

With the global expansion of Western political and economic interests in the mid-nineteenth century, photographers sought to highlight cultural differences. One of the most persistent such types of photograph showed women from the Middle East and Asia in sexually suggestive poses. The term "Orientalism," adopted by cultural critic Edward Said in a 1978 book of the same title, has come to mean the wholesale social labeling of non-Western peoples as passive, rather than active; childlike, rather than mature; feminine, rather than masculine; and timeless, that is, separate from the progress of Western history. More specifically, it describes the phenomenon of titillating sexual interest or intrusive observation of people from non-Western cultures, especially women.[131]

In Western literature, travel accounts, and art before the invention of photography, Middle Eastern women were contradictorily described as closeted in harems, swathed in thick clothing and veils, *and* as sexually aggressive. Images of the odalisque, the drowsily reclining naked or semi-nude female pictured in an intimate or exotic setting, were frequent in Western art. In photography, the mystery and unavailability of Middle Eastern women were enhanced by costume and pose (Fig. 3.98). Not all pictures of Middle Eastern women, however, were made to please foreign fantasies: Marie Lydie Cabannis Bonfils (see p. 98) is reputed to have made the photographs of women who came to the Bonfils family's Beirut studio.[132] In India, legitimate photography of women in *purdah*—that is, in seclusion—was done by British women, such as a certain Mrs. Carrick, who is said to have run a studio in Calcutta. By 1885, Indian women had taken up photography.[133]

Nude and semi-nude images of Eastern women were marketed in many ways. Sensual pictures, in which the model wore traditional clothing to mark her ethnic identity, were issued in *cartes-de-visite*, miniatures, postcards, and albumen prints (Fig. 3.99). The *académies*, or figure studies of women ostensibly sold as aids to painters, sometimes featured Middle Eastern women, whose hairstyle and jewelry signaled their identity and class to the viewers.

Explicit photographs of sexual acts, featuring both Western and non-Western participants, were marketed in the major European capitals and were also available by mail order catalog.[134] Bruno Braquehais, who photographed the French Commune (see Fig. 3.41), also made images of individuals and couples engaged in sexual activities.[135]

"Dying Cultures"

Anthropological photography took on a moral urgency as the notion spread that indigenous peoples did not have the physical and mental strength to survive the encroachment of Western civilization. At the 1866 Intercolonial Exhibition in Melbourne, Australia, a

3.98
PHOTOGRAPHER UNKNOWN, *Arab Woman and Turkish Woman, Zangaki, Port Said*, 1870–80. Albumen print. Victoria & Albert Museum, London.

In this studio photograph, a Turkish woman is masked by a semi-transparent veil, reclining in the manner of an odalisque, suggestively holding a *narghileh* (water pipe). The standing woman grasps a tambourine. By the time this image was made, the harem had been a fixture in Western culture for hundred of years. The image gratifies the fantasy view of the "Orient" as a place where time has stood still.

3.99
KUSAKABE KIMBEI,
Geisha Resting, c. 1885.
Hand-colored albumen
print. Richard W. Gadd
Collection, Monterey
Museum of Art,
California.

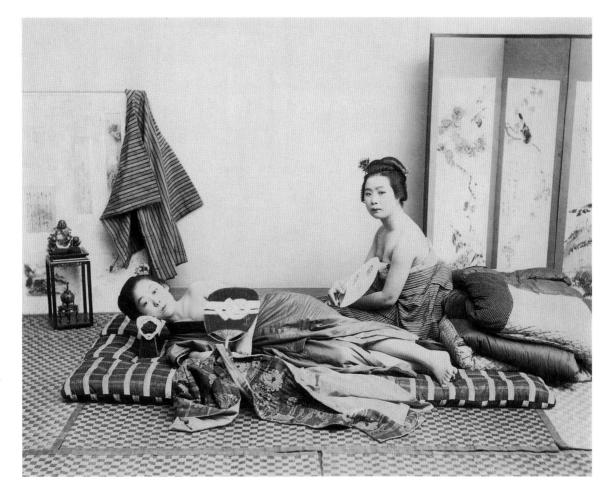

3.100 (below)
C. A. WOOLLEY,
Trucanini, 1866.
Paper print. Royal
Anthropological
Institution of Great
Britain and Ireland,
London.

Trucanini was photo-
graphed in the Western
portrait style, not in the
full-body pose often
adopted for non-
Western people. Yet her
eyes look fierce, and her
mouth suggests both
fear and disdain. When
Trucanini died in 1876,
Woolley marked her
photograph "Last
Tasmanian," as if she
had some sense of her
people's demise.

section was devoted to "The Last of the
Tasmanians."[136] The number of aborigi-
nal Tasmanians was indeed severely
reduced—in 1847, only forty-six individuals had remained. Professional photographer C. A. Woolley (1834–1922)
made a studio study, in the style of
Western portraiture, of a Tasmanian
woman named Trucanini (Fig. 3.100).
The notion of vanishing races was also
applied to Native North Americans (see
pp. 134, 192), though they ultimately
fared better than the Tasmanians.

In 1879, responding to the belief that
the traditional life of Native Americans
was endangered by development, the
United States established the Bureau
of Ethnology.[137] John K. Hillers (1843–
1925) was appointed staff photographer
under John Wesley Powell (1834–1902),
the agency's first director. Hillers had
met Powell while working as a boatman
for Powell's survey of the Colorado
River in 1871. The expedition's photographer E. O. Beaman (1837–1876)
taught Hillers how to use the camera,
and when Beaman left the group,
Hillers took over, making about 3,000
images of the Grand Canyon and of
Native Americans. For the Bureau of

Ethnology, he produced more than 20,000 negatives.[138] After the massacre at Wounded Knee in 1890, when the Indian Wars all but ceased, photographers took up the "grand endeavor" to capture the likeness of Native Americans before they disappeared.

POPULARIZING ETHNIC AND ECONOMIC TYPES

The idea of creating assemblages of thematically related photographs of people was not restricted to scientific pursuits. Studios around the world offered exotic images of people deemed typical of an ethnic group. In Rio de Janeiro, a portraitist advertised "a large collection of black tipos [characters] and their customs, very appropriate for those who are leaving for Europe."[139] The Scottish-born photographer William Carrick (1827–1878) worked in Russia photographing "Rasnoshchiki," the street sellers of St. Petersburg[140] (Fig. 3.101).

In the later nineteenth century, factories and industrial sites were photographed with increasing frequency, and studio shots of laborers, especially craftspeople dressed in work clothes and carrying their tools, became the subjects of many *cartes-de-visite*.[141] Nevertheless, the reality of the urban poverty associated with industrial capitalism was seldom photographed before the end of the nineteenth century. One exception was Henry Mayhew (1812–1887), whose *London Labour and the London Poor* (1851) contained engravings based on

daguerreotypes. It was a financially successful publication, perhaps because government-sponsored welfare programs were beginning to be accepted as a part of modern life. Photographs of strikes, even during the European depression of the 1870s and its labor unrest, are also rare. The poor could not afford photographs, and newspaper images tended to reflect the point of view of private industry. Moreover, reformers in the mid-nineteenth century were generally not stirred to photograph societal problems or remedial programs, because for them the camera was largely associated with the evils of industrialization.

As European cities implemented modernization schemes, the people displaced by renovation were seldom photographed, although the buildings were. An unusual picture was made by Thomas Annan (1829–1887), a photographer in Glasgow, Scotland, who was asked by the Glasgow City Improvement Trust in 1866 to record the vast slums that grew up around mills and factories before the buildings were torn down and rebuilt (Fig. 3.102). Charles Marville (1816–c. 1879), a French artist and photographer, was among the many who produced photographs of old Paris, before the implementation of Baron Haussmann's (1809–1891) improvements (Fig. 3.103).

When John Thomson returned from Asia to Britain, he became a portrait photographer, whose studio was equipped with the usual painted backdrops and fancy posing chairs. He also undertook a photographic survey of London's poor with writer and social activist Adolphe Smith Headingly, who wrote under the name of Adolphe Smith. *Street Life in London* was issued in twelve monthly installments, beginning in February 1877, and was published as a bound book one year later. Thomson and Smith acknowledged Mayhew's efforts on behalf of the poor, presenting their own work as an updated version. Their preface stresses the function of photography to document objectively, without omission or exaggeration. One remarkable picture shows an impoverished homeless widow who made her living minding the children of poor working women (Fig. 3.104).

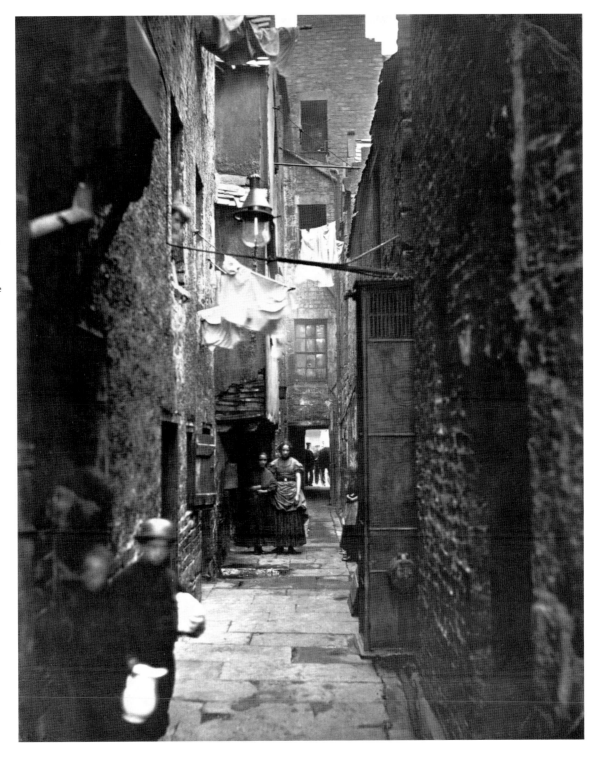

In the last third of the nineteenth century, photographs were used slightly more often in private social reform efforts. Thomas Barnardo (1845–1905), who administered homes and training programs for poor and homeless children, made before-and-after images to advertise his work and to raise funds (Fig. 3.105). In most of the images, Barnardo exaggerated the children's poverty, dressing them in torn clothes and posing them in pitiful positions. The images could be purchased singly or in packets.

PHILOSOPHY AND PRACTICE: "SUPERSEDED BY REALITY"

During the mid-nineteenth century, photography was defined by its makers and users as a complex and contradictory medium. At issue was the notion of realism. For some, such as Oliver Wendell Holmes, realistic photographic images and the development of a commercial network of publishers promised a more democratic diffusion of knowledge in an era when acquired skills and

3.103
CHARLES MARVILLE, *14, Rue des Marmousets* (destroyed): *View from the East. At left, Rue de Glatigny* (destroyed, replaced by the Hôtel-Dieu), n.d. Paper print. Bibliothèque Historique de la Ville de Paris.

Baron Haussmann was entrusted by Napoleon III with the planning of a radical redesign of Paris. Broad boulevards (avenues), railway stations, and new apartment blocks replaced the cramped, winding streets of the old city. Whole districts, such as this eastern section of the Île de la Cité, near Notre-Dame, were torn down in the process.

mechanical invention were effectively eroding the authority of traditional power structures. For governments and the military, as well as topographical surveys, photography became a routine adjunct to operations. In science, specialty photography developed hand-in-hand with geology, biology, astronomy, chemistry, and other empirical pursuits. Photography not only recorded findings, but also made it easier to arrange these findings into taxonomies—that is, broad classifications and categories.

Writing in 1864, Robert Cecil (1830–1903), later British Prime Minister (1885–92, 1895–1902), summed up the general feeling. "It is to science ... that photography, the child of science, renders, and will unceasingly render, the most valuable aid. ... Photography is never imaginative, and is never in any danger of arranging its records by the light of a pre-conceived theory."[142]

The growing acceptance of photography as a reliable representation of the world increased the credibility of photographic evidence. Cecil considered that "the noblest function of photography [is] to remove from the paths of science in some degree the impediments of space and time, and to bring the intellects of civilized lands to bear upon the phenomena of the vast portion of the earth whose civilization has either not begun, or is passing away."[143] Individual photographs thus became building blocks in systems that have

since proved to be more fancifully theoretical than empirically thorough. For example, notions of racial difference were supported by photographs that emphasized some bodily distinctions, while neglect-ing similarities.

In law and police work, photographic evidence of personal identity, clothing, locales, signatures, and the like were increasingly used. In the 1880s these applications developed into internationally

3.104
JOHN THOMSON,
The Crawlers, 1877–78.
Woodburytype. Victoria
& Albert Museum,
London.

Street-dwellers such as the woman pictured here were termed "crawlers," because they would occasionally have enough cash to buy tea leaves, then "crawl" to a pub for hot water. The image of the crawler shows greater emphasis on the individual, in contrast with Thomson's often static presentation of street types.

E. E. J. M.
Home for Working & Destitute Lads.

No. 27.—ONCE A LITTLE VAGRANT.
(*The same lad as on card No. 28.*)

E. E. J. M.
Home for Working & Destitute Lads.

No. 28.—NOW A LITTLE WORKMAN.
(*The same lad as on card No. 27.*)

3.105
PHOTOGRAPHER
UNKNOWN, *Before*
and After Photographs
of Young Boys, c. 1875.
Albumen prints.
Barnardo Photographic
Archive, Ilford, England.

Barnardo was accused
of over-dramatizing
the before-and-after
photographs he took of
children who entered
his homes and training
programs. In response,
he claimed that he was
doing what painters
were allowed to do:
create fictions that
aimed at a higher truth
than the imitation of
appearances. In all, he
took about eighty pairs
of before-and-after
photographs.

accepted systems to organize visual
data. Photographic affidavits (photographs used in legal briefs as sworn evidence) proved to be a potent challenge
to hearsay evidence in the courtroom.[144]
In addition, schemes to prevent crime
by creating national identity cards containing a photographic likeness were
proposed in Britain in the late 1860s.
As one notable advocate of photography
put it in 1869, the expanding domain
of photography made earlier forms of
evidence "superseded by reality."[145]

Because it was accepted as proof,
photography confirmed whatever was
photographed. This sense of authenticity was applied broadly, not only in war,
science, and law, but also in everyday
portraiture and views of foreign lands.
It teased into being a craving for pictures of political, social, and cultural
celebrities. As photography emerged
as evidence, events and personalities
began to be fashioned with an eye for
public circulation.

At the same time, the absence of
photographs effectively denied the significance of a subject or theme that was
not regularly depicted. New bridges
and railroads were photographed; non-
picturesque agricultural and industrial
workers actually toiling in fields and factories were generally not pictured. The
American Civil War military installations and battles were thoroughly photographed; the dismal record of slavery
was not. Foreign wars and landscapes
were programmatically photographed,
as were foreign natural disasters, such
as the Hong Kong typhoon (see Fig.
3.53), when they affected Western commerce. But devastating events and
calamities outside the Western sphere
mostly were not photographed, even
though public faith deepened in photography's ability to confirm events.[146]

Writing from southern India during
the Madras famine, a certain Dr.
Cornish lamented: "I often regret that
I have not a photographer temporarily

FOCUS
Lewis Carroll's Photographs of Children

Charles L. Dodgson (1832–1898) lectured in mathematics and was an ordained clergyman at Oxford University in Britain, but he is better known as the author of *Alice's Adventures in Wonderland* and *Through the Looking-Glass*, written under the pen name Lewis Carroll. He also created about 3,000 negatives during twenty-five years of photographing.[147] His landscape and architectural photographs are unremarkable, and his portraits of adults are mostly conventional, but the photographs he made of the female children of his friends and colleagues have been the subject of much debate. Carroll photographed Alice Liddell, the Alice of his stories, alone and with her sisters. His contrived image of her as a beggar child in artfully ripped clothing and bare feet is perplexing, because it is difficult to reconstruct the Victorian attitude toward children of the upper-middle class, and because Carroll may

have been more than a little enthralled with Alice (Fig. 3.106; see also frontispiece p. ii). Certainly, Alice cannot be mistaken for a pauper: her costume, her grooming, and especially her pose suggest a child playing a role. But is it a sexually charged image?

In recent criticism, Carroll has been accused of instilling private erotic innuendo into his photographs of young girls.[148] The nude and semi-dressed photographs, most of which were destroyed by Carroll before his death, or ordered by him in instructions to his executors to be scrapped, were made with the knowledge of the girls' parents. Amidst the tumultuous changes in the Victorian period, the child became a potent symbol of purity and simplicity. The era insisted on childhood as a time of innocence, and Carroll's pictures pivot on the girls' ignorance of the teasing sexuality of their poses.

3.106
LEWIS CARROLL, *Alice Liddell as "The Beggar Maid,"* c. 1859. Hand-colored albumen print.

3.107
W. W. HOOPER,
Victims of the Madras
Famine, 1876–78.
Albumen print.

Hooper's photographs
of people affected by
the Madras famine of
1876–78 were not taken
as part of a relief effort,
but as part of his gen-
eral photographic survey
of India. At the time,
there was little demand
for images of this sort,
and no government
agencies to collect or
archive them. In fact,
Hooper had the victims
brought to him, and
he arranged them by
age and gender in
preparation for his
photographs. He did
not attempt to relieve
their suffering.

attached to my office while moving
amongst the famine-stricken people. ...
Words at best can but feebly represent
the actual facts, but if members of
Government could see the living skeletons."[149] Moving as they are, images of
human suffering, such as those taken
by British photographer Willoughby
Wallace Hooper (1837–1912) during
the Madras famine in India in the late
1870s, were not routinely or methodically produced (Fig. 3.107).

Generally speaking, it was easier for
photographers to conjecture the opening of the Suez Canal (1869) as an aesthetically challenging and commercially
lucrative subject for photography,[150]
than for cameraworkers to imagine how
to photograph the intangible ways in
which life was swiftly changing in the
developing world. Locomotives could
be photographed; the speed of life could
not. In effect, photography developed
unevenly, omitting or neglecting the
social and psychological responses to
modernization that became the stuff of
fiction and of art movements, such as
Impressionism.

In the face of the societal acceptance
of photography as evidence, those who
pursued the possibilities of photography
as art began to think of ways to counteract the look of photographic testimony.

As early as 1853, the British painter and
photographer William Newton advocated the development of an art photography that consciously worked against
the glut of details produced by "chemical
Photography." Like Julia Margaret
Cameron (see p. 96), he proposed rendering a subject a little out of focus.[151]
For artists and cultural commentators,
the association of photography with
scientific and industrial progress was
not a blessing. British artist and critic
John Ruskin came to consider it a detri-
ment to art and to society. He wrote
that photography could not be an art
because art "expresses the personality,
the activity, and living perception of a
good and great human soul."[152] "Almost
the whole system and hope of modern
life," Ruskin wrote, "are founded on the
notion that you may substitute mechanism for skill, photography for picture,
cast-iron for sculpture."[153] The camera
and the machine both tamped down
human imagination, replacing creativity,
observation, and insight with mediocre
readymade goods. In 1859, French
critic Henri de la Blanchère (1821–1880)
succinctly phrased the complaint:
"The less machine, the more the art."[154]

High Art photography, with its
emphasis on moral values and literary
topics, was no match for the tide of

photographic evidence that defined the wider social understanding of the medium. Julia Margaret Cameron's spiritually infused photographs were popular in her circle, but they did not influence ordinary portraiture. Oddly enough, critics raised few questions about the exactness of photographic realism outside the arts, even when scenes in such photographs as *Home of a Rebel Sharpshooter* (see Fig. 3.36) were openly admitted to be arranged for the camera. Although the difference between an object seen and an object photographed was not much discussed, photographic realism was sometimes the brunt of humor, especially in portraiture, where realism seemed ugly, though truthful (Fig. 3.108). Yet the idea that there could be varieties of photographic realism, ranging from the sublimity of Samuel Bourne's Himalayan photograph (see Fig. 3.44), to the theatrical performance of mental states in the photographs produced for Charcot (see Fig. 3.94), and to the grittiness of John Thomson's views of street life in London (see Fig. 3.104), did not become part of a social dialogue. In sum, artists, photographers, and cultural critics did not offer a serious, sustained debate about the rise and acceptance of photographic realism in society.

As photography emerged as scientific and social evidence, it was also increasingly labeled counterfeit in art. The link between art and science in the popular phrase "the art-science of photography" weakened. In the last decade of the nineteenth century, and the early years of the twentieth century, art and science would be painstakingly disconnected.

3.108
ARTIST UNKNOWN, *Die Kunst der Zukunft (The Art of the Future),* 1859. Lithograph. Museum Ludwig Köln/Agfa Foto-Historama, Germany.

Society's experience of photography sharpened the perception of difference between classical beauty (signified by the figures on the right, who depart sadly, reflecting that "The heart is dead") and the ordinary or the ugly, as typified by the other caricatures.

CHAPTER FOUR

Photography in the Modern Age (1880–1918)

4.0
FRANCES BENJAMIN JOHNSTON,
Self-Portrait (as New Woman), c. 1896. Gelatin silver print. Library of Congress, Washington, D.C.

The New Woman was the subject of serious essays, novels, and poems as well as parodies. Johnston's self-portrait seems like a gentle joke, for despite the "masculine" crossed legs and the cigarette, she is surrounded by souvenirs from her travels and portraits, probably from her successful Washington, D.C., studio.

By 1880, photography had been quietly absorbed into the texture of everyday life. In the late 1880s, there were more than sixty photographic journals and 161 photographic societies around the world,[1] and by the turn of the century, manufacturers of stereographs, such as Underwood & Underwood, were producing 25,000 images a day.[2] The increase in amateur photography prompted newspaper editors to run camera columns, and large photographic firms and news agencies in the developed countries continued to expand sophisticated networks for the accumulation and dissemination of images worldwide.

Nevertheless, there was no particular moment in the vast expansion and societal absorption of photography to mark the point at which it permanently altered the experience of modern life. Instead, the gathering momentum was expressed in multiple, interrelated technological developments during the 1880s, in response to the immense demand for photographs and the voracious information systems in Western society. Experiments in photomechanical processes led to the development of the HALF-TONE PROCESS, which

allowed publications to reproduce photographic images directly, rather than through engravings. During the 1890s, it became cheaper, easier, and faster to use half-tones than to hire artists to make sketches, or to translate photographs into engravings. Spurred by advertising and illustrated periodicals, millions of half-tone images were produced. Along with the stereograph and the postcard, the half-tone invested modern life with visual information to an unprecedented degree.

The speed with which photographs could be reproduced with text, combined with the fast pace of urban life, altered newspapers, which had previously consisted mostly of columns of text with occasional line drawings, engravings, and advertisements. Specialized press photographers, agencies, and networks emerged, and pages were redesigned to include more photographs in place of descriptive text. Rather than wait for news to happen, news photographers were sent around the world to places where incidents were likely to occur. Political figures were regularly photographed, and the pictures rushed to press by land or sea, since, unlike text, they could not yet be cheaply wired to newspapers over telephone lines. Interestingly, a specific date was not appended to many news photographs, perhaps because of the time-lag between taking a picture and publishing it. For example, illustrations derived from photographs of the great flood of May 31, 1889, in Johnstown, Pennsylvania, where more than 2,000 people lost their lives, were published in New York's *The Daily Graphic* on June 6. The delay was longer for international pictures. Photographs from the World War I battles near the Somme in France (June 24–November 13, 1916) ran in *Leslie's* on January 25, 1917.

In the 1880s and 1890s, such periodicals as the *Berliner Illustrirte* [sic] *Zeitung* (*Illustrated Berlin Newspaper*), the *Illustrated London News*, and *The Illustrated American* presented political news together with entertainment listings, social happenings, and society reporting. Non-news, human interest articles, and reports on the doings of celebrities increased and were accompanied by photographs. For news and feature stories, editors sought unusual, candid, or dramatic pictures. American audiences could be counted on to buy papers with scenes of natural and human-induced disasters, such as earthquakes and fires.[3] Although press photography created full-time work for photographers, their output was considered to be the property of the paper. The images were routinely cropped, retouched, and sequenced without the photographer's prior knowledge or permission.

The popularity of illustrated newspapers spawned new daily and weekly newspapers, as well as magazines, all of which engaged in intense rivalry for original pictures (Fig. 4.1). The competition for pictures to sell to the press spurred photographers to invade the privacy of public figures, such as German statesman Otto von Bismarck, who was clandestinely photographed on his deathbed by photographers who climbed in a window.[4] In 1899, the *Penny Pictorial Magazine* started a feature called "Taken Unawares," which contained snapshots of famous people. At the same time, public figures and celebrities often orchestrated events for the cameras that followed them. Theodore Roosevelt

(1858–1919) welcomed the picture and print press on his election campaigns. Photographers Wade Mountford, Jr. (active early twentieth century), and William Warnecke (1881–1939) were with New York City mayor William Jay Gaynor moments after a 1910 assassination attempt, and made pictures showing his startled alarm.

Advertisers began using photographs to sell an ever-increasing number of products. Along with the growth of department stores, catalog shopping, and national advertising campaigns, photography's own association with modernity gave products cachet and fostered a culture of display. In the cities, window shopping became a Sunday afternoon activity.

The invention of DRY PLATES made photography faster and easier. In contrast to the cumbersome wet-plate process, mass-manufactured dry plates did not need to be prepared and processed close to the time of exposure. Writing in 1894, photographer James Lawrence Breese (active 1890s) concisely summed up the impact of the new process: "the photographic artist has ... a wider range at the present time than ever before, for the modern dry plate, so rapid in its action, permits photography from the rigging of a ship in motion, as well as on the busiest thoroughfare of the metropolis."[5] In 1839, exposures could take several minutes; by the end of the nineteenth century, exposure time was reduced to 1/5,000 of a second.

In addition, early photographic chemicals were not sensitive to the full range of colors in the natural world. They rendered some shades of red and blue as dark black. But by 1900, the responsiveness of black-and-white film to the range of colors was perfected and applied to the dry plate, making it better able to reproduce tonal variation in monochromatic prints.

Yielding faster exposure times throughout the 1880s, dry plates worked well with new, smaller, and more portable cameras, called hand cameras. In part, the short exposure time of the dry plate led to the design of camera shutters, which could open and close more quickly than the hand could remove and replace a lens cap. The dry plate allowed photographers

4.1
JOHN D. HOWE,
The front page of
William Randolph
Hearst's *New York
American*, April 24,
1906, with a photo-
graph of San Francisco
in flames. New York
Public Library,
New York.

On April 16, 1906, a
tremendous earthquake
followed by raging fires
demolished the center
of San Francisco. News
of the tragedy was
circulated around the
country long before
photographs could
be transported. The
New York American
bragged that it has
the first photographs—
only eight days after
the event.

New York ✦ American

FIRST PHOTOGRAPHS FROM SAN FRANCISCO!

FIERY DESTRUCTION OF SAN FRANCISCO AS SEEN FROM OAKLAND.

COPYRIGHT, 1906, BY W. R. HEARST, AMERICAN-JOURNAL-EXAMINER.

CALIFORNIA'S GOVERNOR THANKS W. R. HEARST.

to record movement, and permitted
them greater mobility and anonymity.
Because the image registered so
quickly, the photographer did not need
a tripod. In addition, an elaborate
process for making color photographs
called AUTOCHROME was developed
in 1904 by the brothers Louis Lumière
(1864–1948) and Auguste Lumière
(1862–1954), inventors of the motion
picture projector in 1895. Subject to fading, expensive to create, and not capable
of being duplicated, the autochrome
enjoyed a vogue with amateur photographers (see Fig. 4.23).

In 1888, the Eastman Dry Plate
Company in Rochester, New York, began
manufacturing the Kodak camera, the
first of many cameras intended for
casual use by middle-class consumers.

The camera had a fixed focus—that is,
the photographer did not focus the lens,
nor look through a viewfinder. The No. 1
Kodak, introduced in 1888, used what
the company founder, George Eastman
(1854–1932), called American film, a
roll of paper coated with light-sensitive
material. The camera came loaded with
film containing 100 exposures. When all
the pictures had been taken, the entire
camera was sent back to the company
in Rochester, where the prints were
developed and the camera was reloaded.
The company slogan, "You press the
button—We do the rest," enticed people
to carry a camera and make spontaneous shots in a way that had not been
done before. The resulting snapshots—
the word was probably coined by
John Herschel in the mid-nineteenth

century—were 2½-inch diameter circular pictures (Fig. 4.2).

The No. 2 Kodak, which came on the market in 1889, yielded 3½-inch images. In 1900, the company launched the inexpensive "Brownie" camera, which it marketed initially to children. Though snapshots were mostly personal pictures, they did have a significant public impact. Snapshots not only reduced the number of professional portrait photographers; they also deepened the association between informality and photographic truth. Increasingly press photographs emulated the casual look of the snapshot, and the few artists remaining at newspapers made their drawings look more sketchy, as if done quickly on the spot.

Small cameras were not merely intended for amateurs. Manufacturers slimmed down cameras and experimented with roll film to create compact, lightweight hand-held devices such as Hawkeye, P.D.Q. (Photography Done Quickly), and, of course, Kodak, used by professionals and amateurs alike. At the same time, the camera was miniaturized. Tiny cameras fitted into walking-stick handles, pistols, and jewelry were marketed as detective or secret cameras, capable of taking pictures covertly. The SINGLE-LENS REFLEX CAMERA, such as the Graflex, was rigged with an internal

mirror that allowed photographers to examine the scene before the lens. It became the standard news photographer's camera.

The private world exposed by the detective camera contrasted with the public world broadcast by the postcard, which rivaled stereography in popularity and sheer range of subject matter. Picture postcards evolved after changes in nineteenth-century postal regulations in Europe and the United States authorized a simple, undecorated card with a message to be mailed. At the turn of the century, when printing methods such as the half-tone process facilitated reproduction of pictures and text, photographic postcards began to appear in large numbers. Like *cartes-de-visite* and stereograph images, they were both collected and sent to others (Fig. 4.3). Before long-distance telephoning became common, when radio and the movies were infant technologies, people wrote often to each other. Notes jotted on postcards were casual hellos, like e-mailed friendship cards.

Photographic postcards depicted tourist spots as well as ethnic types and news events. Erotic images, such as those displaying partially clad women from colonial Africa, were produced in great numbers. Veiled Islamic women,

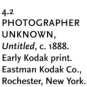

**4.2
PHOTOGRAPHER
UNKNOWN,**
Untitled, c. 1888.
Early Kodak print.
Eastman Kodak Co.,
Rochester, New York.

The earliest snapshots were round, not rectangular as they are today. The ease afforded by snapshot cameras allowed photographers greater spontaneity. They began to take pictures of ordinary events such as picnics and parties. It is impossible to know if the photographer intentionally photographed her shadow in the lower left of the image.

long a subject for ethnographic and erotic photography, were also pictured on postcards.[6] At the end of the nineteenth century, photographer William Henry Jackson (see p. 38) joined with two other entrepreneurs to form the Detroit Publishing Company. Postcards, sometimes in boxed sets, comprised most of the 7 million images issued by the company in an average year. Panoramas, slides, and hand-colored prints, mostly of American farms, factories, cities, natural wonders, and that ubiquitous favorite the cowboy, were marketed worldwide to schools, libraries, and governments, as well as to individuals.[7]

At the height of the craze, Kodak manufactured the Folding Camera 3A, especially for producing picture postcards. The United States Post Office reported that from June 1907 to June 1908 more than 667 million postcards, many of them picture postcards, were sent.[8] The postcard rage originated a type of popular image that would not have seemed humorous in photography's first decade, when trifling with the appearance of reality was considered misplaced. Photographic exaggerations showed grasshoppers the size of turkeys, apples as large as mansions, and geese twice as tall as men (Fig. 4.4). The postcard vogue

4.4
WILLIAM H. MARTIN,
*Taking our Geese to
Market*, 1909. Silver
print postcard. Franklin
County Historical
Society, Kansas.

faded after World War I (1914–18), in part because of new postal regulations that discouraged it.

The overall effect of technological developments in photography around the turn of the twentieth century was to relocate some control of the image from the individual photographer to large manufacturers and the press. This tendency paralleled the development of other major networks and industries, such as the power companies that produced and delivered electricity, and also the large corporations that manufactured and distributed name brands.

THE CHALLENGE FOR ART PHOTOGRAPHY

On the occasion of photography's fiftieth anniversary in 1889, American artist J. Wells Champney (1843–1903) wrote an article surveying the familiar list of its social and technological accomplishments in the fields of science, anthropology, criminology, and military applications. He ended with what would become a frequent refrain: the lack of parallel progress in art photography. "As an aid to science, as a recorder, as a duplicator, photography has helped advance civilization," Champney remarked. Yet "it has failed to occupy the place it may yet hold as a means for expressing original thought of a fine order."[9] At the turn to the twentieth century, more people came to believe that a modern art must evolve at a pace and with an inventiveness similar to those of science and technology.

NATURALISTIC PHOTOGRAPHY

Champney appears not to have known the writings of British photographer Peter Henry Emerson (1856–1936), who a few years earlier had taken up eagerly the perceived challenge of science to art and art photography. Emerson acquired his first camera during his medical training at Cambridge University. By 1885, with the assurance of a private income, he chose to practice photography rather than medicine. He insisted that, in the modern world, science was the only authentic basis for art and photography. Just as the French novelist Émile Zola (1840–1902) had adopted the scientific method and outlook of the doctor Claude Bernard (1813–1878), so Emerson

seized on the ideas of German scientist Hermann von Helmholtz (1821–1894), whose studies of the human eye's range of focus he took as instructive for photography. Both Zola and Emerson attempted to align art with the cutting edge of science, and to make it part of the modern world. In 1880, Zola famously proclaimed that "metaphysical man is dead; with physiological man our position changes."[10] Speaking to the Camera Club of London in March 1886, Emerson likewise declared that "the days of metaphysics are over."[11]

In his most important theoretical work, *Naturalistic Photography* (1889), Emerson expounded his theory of photography. He rejected the idea of art as primarily a vehicle for personal and emotional expression. While maintaining that the artist was a person of special character and ability, he derided works of the imagination as untrue.[12] His own notion of naturalism was based on contemporary science, not art theory, notably on Helmholtz's idea that "perfect artistic painting is only reached when we have succeeded in imitating the action of light upon the eye."[13] At a time when technical improvements enabled photographers to make sharper pictures, Emerson denied that the camera could make art by merely transcribing physical reality. Instead, he argued that the artist should translate exactly how the eye sees, concluding that the photographer should focus on the main subject of a scene, allowing the periphery and the distance to become indistinct. Called differential or selective focus, this approach varied from William Newton's earlier idea of making the entire image slightly out of focus (see p. 162).

Much of Emerson's photography was done on the Norfolk Broads, a marshy area in eastern England where industrialization had not penetrated to the degree that it had in other parts of the country. There Emerson found rural life and traditional occupations; he ignored the beginnings of tourism, which was bringing people to the shallow, navigable waters of the Broads. His first major work, *Life and Landscape on the Norfolk Broads* (1886), was a folio of forty mounted PLATINUM PRINTS (called platinotypes in the period) with accompanying text by Emerson and his friend and traveling companion the artist

**4.5
PETER HENRY
EMERSON,** *Poling the
Marsh-Hay,* **plate 17
from his book** *Life and
Landscape on the
Norfolk Broads,* **1886.
Victoria & Albert
Museum (Library),
London.**

Emerson's photographs
of country life some-
times resemble the
paintings of peasants
by Jean-François Millet,
whom he admired.
Depicting representative
types, rather than
individuals, both often
used a low angle to
monumentalize figures
against the sky.
Photographed in low
November light, *Poling
the Marsh-Hay* focuses
on the sturdy figure
of the woman in the
foreground, allowing
other figures to pass
into shadow.

Thomas Frederick Goodall (1857–1944).
Emerson's pictures emphasized the
unchanged relationship of people to the
land (Fig. 4.5).

Emerson was known as an eccentric
art celebrity, whose ideas and work were
controversial, like those of American
painter James McNeill Whistler (1834–
1903). When he rejected his own theory
in a black-bordered pamphlet titled *The
Death of Naturalistic Photography* (1890),
the public was skeptical. Yet Emerson
maintained that his early theory was
based on a belief that tones in a photograph could be manipulated to a greater
degree than chemists now proved possible. Having promoted art photography
as a cutting-edge application of recent
science, he cast it off because he saw it
as limiting the individuality of the artist.

PICTORIALISM

Although Emerson wrote that he found
much amateur and art photography pre-
tentious, many practitioners ignored

his insults, and based their ideas of art
photography on his photographs, with
their subdued middle-gray tones, soft
focus, and peaceful, agrarian subjects.
Amateurs of art photography creatively
misunderstood Emerson's writings to
authorize moving away from faithful
depiction toward more evocative and
expressive photographs. The resulting
international photographic movement
known as PICTORIALISM gathered
strength in the mid-1880s, peaked in
the 1900s, and persisted into the 1920s.

Pictorialists adopted Emerson's disgust with industrialization and mass-
produced goods, as well as his belief in
photography as a fully-fledged modern
art form. They embraced his choice of
subjects, but jettisoned allegiance to
recent science. In Pictorialist hands,
Emerson's selective or differential focus
became a dislike of the distracting details
associated with vulgar commercial
photography. Pictorialist photographers
often overlaid large parts of a picture
with shadow and fog. In contrast to their
simple subjects, they strove for tonal

complexity, choosing techniques such as platinum printing, which yielded abundant soft, middle-gray tones. They favored procedures that allowed for handworking of both negatives and prints. Their results were in obvious visual opposition to the sharp black-and-white contrasts of the commercial print. Pictorialist photographs were frequently printed on textured paper, unlike the glossy surface of commercial photographs, so that they resembled watercolors, and evoked the earlier Victorian photographs of David Octavius Hill and Julia Margaret Cameron, which they admired and exhibited.

Pictorialists valued the symbolic control over industry, and a sense of superiority over the snapshooters, who did not even develop their own film. One Pictorialist asserted that "the photographer is not helpless before the mechanical means at his disposal. He can master them as he may choose, and he can make the lens see with his eyes, can make the plate receive his impressions."[14] Pictorialist writing encouraged a self-image of cultural heroism, striking back at the worst of the modern world. In his influential 1901 book *Photography as a Fine Art*, critic Charles H. Caffin (1854–1918) described the "men and women who are seeking to lift photography to the level of one of the Fine Arts" as "advanced photographers," and Alfred Stieglitz (1864–1946), who would later emerge as the foremost art photographer, as an "artist, prophet, pathfinder."[15]

As Emerson's justification of selective focus—that is, to match the way the eyes see—faded from currency, the writings of Henry Peach Robinson, which Emerson strongly disliked, were devoured by a new generation. Robinson, best known for his combination prints (see p. 91), was probably even more responsible for popularizing the word "pictorial" than Emerson. His book *Pictorial Effect in Photography*, first published in 1869, was still read at the turn of the century. A few photographers made elaborate *tableaux vivants* of Old Master paintings, extending Robinson's own practice. Serious amateurs, as they were called, sometimes blended contemporary styles and themes in their work. Jane Reece (c. 1869–1961), a commercial portraitist in Dayton, Ohio,

combined turn-of-the-century interest in Japanese prints, with their flattened space, and the principle that one should beautify the experience of everyday life, an idea promoted by the Arts and Crafts movement and the followers of Art Nouveau (Fig. 4.6).

To Emerson's annoyance, another British photographer, George Davison (1854–1930), expanded upon Emerson's theories and promoted an imprecise notion of impressionistic photography.

4.6 (right)
JANE REECE,
The Poinsettia Girl (Self- Portrait), 1907.
Sepia-toned gelatin silver print. Dayton Art Institute, Dayton, Ohio.

Reece lived in New York City for a time in 1909, and exhibited her work with the Photo-Secession.[16] Her mingling of contemporary art styles was typical of Pictorialists, who, like earlier nineteenth-century photographers, allied themselves with art in other media.

4.7
GEORGE DAVISON,
The Onion Field, 1889,
from *Camera Work*,
January 1907.
Photogravure. Library
of Congress,
Washington, D.C.

The blur in Davison's
image was produced
using a PINHOLE
CAMERA, which softened
edges and imparted a
dreamy haze not neces-
sarily present at the time
of exposure. Printed as
a GRAVURE, a technique
favored by Pictorialists
because it suppressed
detail, the image seems
to have flowed into the
fabric of the paper on
which it is printed.

173

4.8 (right)
ROBERT DEMACHY,
Struggle, from
Camera Work, January
1904. Photogravure.
Library of Congress,
Washington, D.C.

Gum printing allowed
Demachy to demon-
strate that a camera's
image was only the
starting point for the
production of an art-
work. Like a painter,
the photographer could
use a brush or other
instruments to alter
and color a scene.

Whereas Impressionism, the French art
movement of the 1870s–1880s, aimed
at capturing a momentary visual imprint
of a scene, impressionistic photography
attempted to render a personal response
to a subject. Soon the words "poetic,"
"art," "naturalistic," and "impressionistic" all came to signal Pictorialist photography, exemplified by Davison's *The
Onion Field* (Fig. 4.7). Unlike Emerson's
work, where the main subject was in
focus, the entire surface of *The Onion
Field* is indistinct. Davison thus shifted
the foundations of art photography from
science to art. Yet the "fuzzygraph," as
Pictorial photographs were mockingly
called, helped foster the photographic
industry, as commercial manufacturers
produced soft-focus lenses and textured
photographic papers for amateur use.

Emerson's renunciation of naturalistic photography did not stop him making pictures or criticizing the growing
popularity of the GUM-BICHROMATE
PROCESS, which made it possible to
add pigment and texture to a print.
French photographer Robert Demachy
(1859–1936) promoted the technique
in influential articles and worked extensively in it himself (Fig. 4.8). Another

4.9
HEINRICH KÜHN,
On the Hillside, 1910.
Gum bichromate print.
Gilman Paper Company
Collection, New York.

Pictorialists' conserva-
tive philosophical
outlook was sometimes
countered by experi-
ments with pictorial
space. In this image,
the background all but
disappears, and the
figure is pushed to the
foreground, as in a
Japanese print.

proponent of so-called gum printing
was German photographer Heinrich
Kühn (1866–1944), whose painterly
photographs using the technique vexed
viewers at the first amateur photographic exhibition held in Berlin in
1896 (Fig. 4.9). Like Emerson, Kühn
was a scientist and a doctor, but his
training did not lead him to a scientifically based theory of art. With photographers Hans Watzek (1848–1903) and
Hugo Henneberg (1863–1918), Kühn
exhibited under the name Das Kleeblatt
(The Trifolium, or Cloverleaf, referring
both to the three-lobed leaf and to the
three-part window of Gothic architecture). Kühn moved easily between
groups of European photographers and
painters. American-born Frank Eugene
(1865–1936) was equally international.
He sometimes combined photography
and printmaking (Fig. 4.10), and favored
dreamy views of leisured women
enjoying nature, a popular theme in
Pictorialist photography. In 1906, he
moved to Germany, where he made
both paintings and photographs.

Like Art Nouveau artists in Europe
and America, the Pictorialists raised
aesthetic experience to a paramount
life goal. From their point of view, what
was needed was aesthetic reform of the
whole society, and they hoped to start
the process by banishing the harsh and
unsightly realm of industry from their
work. Pictorialism created international
networks of artists and amateurs. The
movement was strong in Russia, where
Sergei Lobovikov (1870–1942) adopted it
to render traditional peasant life, not as
ethnographic data, but as an expression

of nostalgia for nature and simpler
times (Fig. 4.11). Like other Pictorialists,
Lobovikov worked with gum bichromate
and made platinum prints; he also
favored the BROMOIL PROCESS, which
allowed him to apply color to the print
with a brush. In Japan, the Pictorialist
look dominated portraits, street scenes,
landscapes, and ethnographic photography until the mid-1930s, when it
finally gave way to the pressures of
Modernism and abstraction.

MOVEMENTS AND MAGAZINES

The first photographic associations
brought together people with diverse
interests and occupations. Their publications covered subjects from art
exhibits and travel to technical instructions and new commercial products.
In the 1890s, however, Pictorialist
photographers felt constrained by the
uncritical commercialism of the older
photographic organizations and the
mediocrity of the images their members
produced. They worried haughtily that

4.10
FRANK EUGENE,
Adam and Eve,
1910, from *Camera
Work*, April 1910.
Photogravure.
Library of Congress,
Washington, D.C.

Eugene scratched his
photographic negative
with obvious etching
needle marks, creating
a hybrid between
photography and print-
making. His method
shocked photographers,
printmakers, and
painters, who objected
to the mixing of tech-
niques and to Eugene's
refusal to make seam-
less illusions.

4.11
SERGEI LOBOVIKOV,
The Widow's Pillow,
c. 1900. Bromoil and
varnish. Mikhail
Golosovskii Collection,
Krasnogorsk, Russia.

Despite the blurry
image, the woman's
raised hand makes clear
that she has endured a
life of manual labor. She
clutches a bundle of
straw gleaned, perhaps,
from the field before her.
As indicated by an intent
gaze at the horizon,
her thoughts seem to
be on times long gone
and faraway places.

snapshot photography was impairing
the aesthetic sensibility of the public.
Believing their medium equal to the
other arts, and a source of spiritual and
aesthetic fulfillment, they wanted to
associate with like-minded people and
to arrange their own exhibits.

Among the first associations formed
solely to advance art photography
was the Wiener Kamera Klub (Vienna
Camera Club), which celebrated its
founding in 1891 with a show of 600

art photographs. Its members included
Watzek, Henneberg, and Kühn. Artists
in other media acknowledged the
aesthetic aspiration of Pictorialist photographers by sitting on juries for photographic exhibitions, and by showing
art photographs at their own shows.
For example, Watzek's gum bichromate
photographs were presented at an
1898 exhibit sponsored by the Munich
Secession, an association of artists
formed in 1892 with interests akin to

4.12
HANS WATZEK,
Sheep, from *Camera
Work*, January 1906.
Photogravure. Library
of Congress,
Washington, D.C.

4.13 (right)
HUGO HENNEBERG,
Villa Falconieri, from
Camera Work, January
1906. Photogravure.
Library of Congress,
Washington, D.C.

As it had for generations
of painters, the Italian
landscape and its
ancient villas attracted
Pictorialist photo-
graphers. Henneberg's
image shows the
Pictorialist concern
with light, water, clouds,
and reflections.

the Pictorialists' (Fig. 4.12). A similar group, the Vienna Secession, showed Henneberg's gum prints in 1902 (Fig. 4.13).

Art photography organizations were typically international in membership: Watzek, Henneberg, and Kühn, for example, were also members of the Photo-Club de Paris, which broke from the more conservative Société Française de Photographie in 1894. Two of the Photo-Club's founders, Robert Demachy and Charles E. J. Constant Puyo (1857–1933), had an international audience for their writings about the gum bichromate process (Fig. 4.14).

Watzek, Henneberg, and Kühn were also elected to the British association called the Linked Ring—formed in 1892 in opposition to the Photographic Society of Great Britain—whose fifteen founders included Henry Peach Robinson and George Davison. The "Links" thought of themselves as members of a spiritual and aesthetic fellowship. Their Photographic Salons were held yearly, exhibiting work they approved, such as that of James Craig Annan (1864–1946), son of photographer Thomas Annan, who had photographed the Glasgow slums before they were demolished (see Fig. 3.102). James Craig Annan admired the work of Hill and Adamson; as a youngster he met Hill, and in the 1890s he began making prints from Hill and Adamson

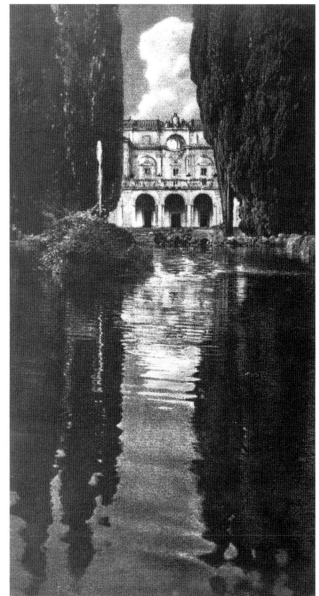

4.14
ÉMILE JOACHIM
CONSTANT PUYO,
*Puyo, Robert Demachy,
and Paul de Singly with
Model*, 1909. Platinum
print. Gilman Paper
Company Collection,
New York.

4.15 (right)
JAMES CRAIG
ANNAN, *Miss Janet
Burnet*, 1893. Vintage
tissue photogravure
from *Camera Work* by
Alfred Stieglitz, 1907.

Annan's photograph of
Janet Burnet shows how
Pictorialists blended
artistic themes and
ideas. He sometimes
printed the photograph
with the subject looking
left and sometimes
to the right. He may
have been influenced by
Whistler's *Arrangement
in Gray and Black
(Whistler's Mother)*.
In the background,
the sitter's name is
rendered as it might be
in a print by German
artist Albrecht Dürer
(1471–1528).[17]

negatives. Having learned the gravure
process in Vienna from its inventor
Karl Klïc (1841–1926), Annan began
working with his father doing fine printing (Fig. 4.15). The GRAVURE process
allowed photographers to translate their
photographs into printer's ink by means
of a copper plate that was etched by
chemicals, then inked, and printed on
a hand-turned printing press.

American photographer Clarence
H. White (1871–1925) was also elected
to the Linked Ring. White's photographs
centered on familiar Pictorialist themes,
rendered with delicate atmospheric
effects (Fig. 4.16). Through his teaching
at Columbia University in New York
City, White became influential in
American photography. Eventually, he
went on to found a photography school
in his own name in 1914. His students
included such luminaries as Dorothea
Lange, Margaret Bourke-White, and
Paul Outerbridge.

White was hired at Columbia by
the painter and theorist Arthur Wesley
Dow (1857–1922), whose understanding
of *notan*, a Japanese concept of graphic
patterning, was widely experimented

with by the Pictorialists. In 2002, when
Dow's large photographic work came
to light, its flat, geometric patterning
suggested that the Pictorialists may have
learned directly from his art, as well as
his theory.

Yet another American, F. Holland
Day (1864–1933), was also elected to the
Linked Ring. Day explored the possibility
of using the camera to depict religious

4.16
CLARENCE H. WHITE,
Morning, 1908.
Photogravure print.
George Eastman House,
Rochester, New York.

The purity of morning
and the idea of a fresh
beginning are indicated
by bright light filtering
through fog. The glass
globe that the model
carries appears in sev-
eral of White's images.

scenes in his Sacred Art series (Fig. 4.17).
These photographs provoked ardent discussions about what constituted a proper
photographic subject. A man of independent means, Day was the co-founder
of the Boston publishing firm Copland
& Day, which published the American
editions of such controversial volumes
as Oscar Wilde's *Salomé* and Aubrey
Beardsley's *The Yellow Book*. His interest
in the erotic human form was expressed

in a number of nude and semi-nude
photographs (Fig. 4.18).

Another Linked Ring member,
British photographer Frederick H. Evans
(1853–1943), rejected the special lenses
and negative manipulations used by
many Pictorialists, in favor of what he
called "pure photography."[18] Writing
about his work, mostly platinum prints,
Evans explained that he found architecture best suited to art photography.

4.17
F. HOLLAND DAY,
Untitled (Crucifix with
Roman soldiers),
1896. Platinum print.
Library of Congress,
Washington, D.C.

4.18
F. HOLLAND DAY,
*Nude Youth with
Laurel Wreath Standing
Against Rocks,* c. 1907.
Platinum print.
Library of Congress,
Washington, D.C.

Day's sensuous images
of the male nude
blend a fondness for
Classical sculpture with
eroticism. Somewhat
obscured by his
Pictorialist technique,
Day's nudes were not
censored for their explicitness but applauded
for their refinement.

His goal was to record an emotional and aesthetic response to space, light, and shadow, especially in the interiors of historic English churches, cathedrals (Fig. 4.19), and French châteaux.

THE PHOTO-SECESSION

Writing in *American Amateur Photographer* in 1904, critic Sadakichi Hartmann (1867–1944) used an exhibition at the Carnegie Institute in Pittsburgh, Pennsylvania, as a springboard for his thoughts on contemporary photography. Not attempting to disguise his distaste, he called the organizers "pictorial extremists, who lay more stress on 'individual expression' than on any other quality." Some works, he scolded, "overstep all legitimate boundaries and deliberately mix up photography with the technical devices of painting and the graphic arts." He wondered whether the Pictorialist photographers were doing an "injustice to a beautiful method of graphic expression"—that is, photography. "Why then," he asked, "should not a photographic print look like a photographic print?" He called for "straightforward depiction" or "straight photography."[19]

One of the organizers of the 1904 Pittsburgh show was the American photographer Alfred Stieglitz, who was well positioned to lead an art movement. Through his work as an editor of *American Amateur Photographer* and *Camera Notes*, the journal of the Camera Club of New York, Stieglitz knew the work of the major Pictorialist photographers in Europe and America. He wanted *Camera Notes* to be international in scope, and to make American photography the equal of European painting, much revered in the United States. By the time Camera Club members objected to his aesthetic agenda, Stieglitz had already built up a following of art photographers who were ready to form their own association. Adopting the word "secession" from the art movements in Vienna and Berlin that were "seceding" from conventional academic work, and in the spirit of the Linked Ring, in February 1902 Stieglitz launched the Photo-Secession. Three weeks later, the Photo-Secession sponsored a large exhibition of "American Pictorial Photography" with the works

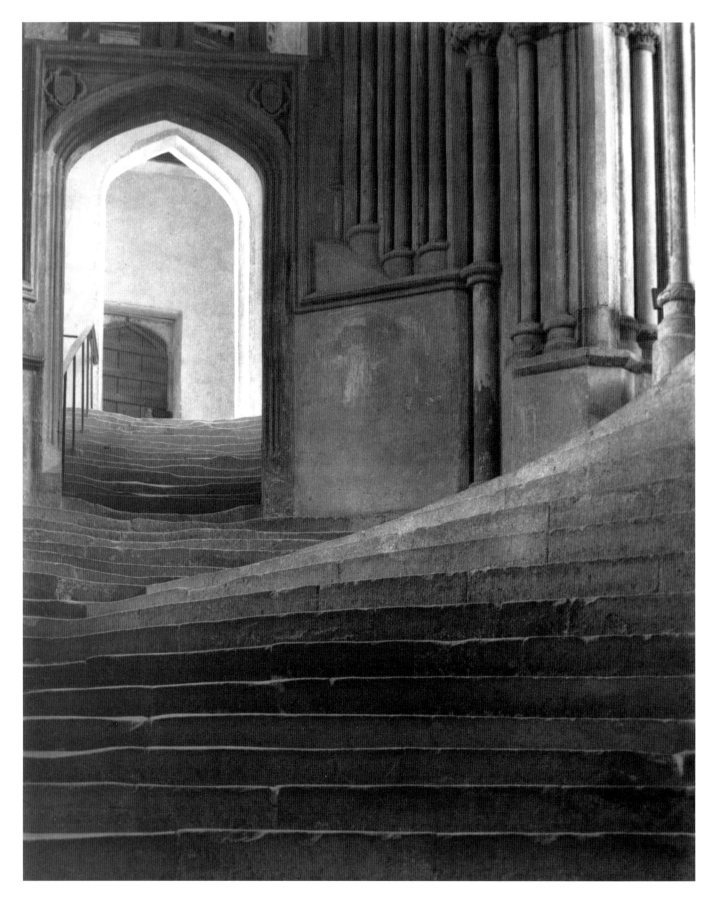

of thirty-two photographers, among them Frank Eugene, F. Holland Day, Gertrude Käsebier, Clarence H. White, and Stieglitz himself. In December, the Photo-Secession then issued a statement of purpose:

The object of the Photo-Secession is:

To advance photography as applied to pictorial expression;

To draw together those Americans practicing or otherwise interested in the art, and

4.19 (opposite)
FREDERICK H. EVANS,
*Steps to Chapter House:
A Sea of Steps, Wells
Cathedral*, 1903.
Platinum print. Museum
of Modern Art, New
York.

The staircase of the
Chapter House at Wells
Cathedral in Britain was
the subject of commer-
cial architectural photo-
graphy before Evans
photographed it. But
the low vantage point
and concern with the
effects of light favored
by Pictorialist photo-
graphers were especially
suited to dramatizing
the sweep of stairs.
Evans chose a point of
view that opposed the
wide lower stairs with
the foot-worn, wave-like
higher stairs on the left.
His photograph was
taken at a time of day
when the individual
steps were fringed with
light, like whitecaps on
the sea.

To hold from time to time, at varying
places, exhibitions not necessarily limited
to the productions of the Photo-Secession
or to American work.[20]

Stieglitz became a major organizer of
the new art photography, but this role
was not unprecedented. Influential
shows had been organized in Berlin
by his mentor Hermann Wilhelm
Vogel (1834–1898), by the Amateur
Photography Club in Vienna, by the
Society for the Advancement of
Amateur Photography in Hamburg,
and, of course, at the annual salon
sponsored by the Linked Ring.[21] In
the United States, too, Clarence White
proved an able advocate for photography with the shows he sponsored
at the Camera Club of Newark, Ohio.
Before the founding of the Photo-
Secession, Day proposed an "American
Association of Pictorial Photographers,"
to be based in Boston. In 1900, he
organized an exhibition of about 300
images, called the "New School of
American Photography," which was
sponsored by the Royal Photographic
Society and shown in London, and the
next year by the Photo-Club de Paris
in the French capital. Though Day's
photographs were shown by the Photo-
Secession, he never formally joined the
group, perhaps because of his rivalry
with Stieglitz.

One advantage Stieglitz possessed
was his periodical *Camera Work*, published from 1903 to 1917. Modeled
on fine art publications, *Camera Work*
was printed in decorative typography
on deluxe paper; abundant samples
of the new photography were mostly
reproduced in gravure. Other journals
advocating art photography included
such lavishly illustrated German magazines as *Photographische Rundschau*
(*Photographic Review*) and *Die Kunst in
der Photographie* (*Art in Photography*).
Stieglitz enlarged the scope of *Camera
Work* to encompass the other arts
and art theory. In July 1912, for example, he published selections from
Russian painter Wassily Kandinsky's
(1866–1944) *Concerning the Spiritual
in Art*.

The covers for *Camera Work* were
designed by Edward Steichen (1879–
1973), a painter-photographer who was
also a founding member of the Photo-
Secession. Outside *Camera Work*,

Stieglitz continued to promote photography in popular magazines and journals. In a 1903 pamphlet, he manifested
the outlook that made him notoriously
difficult to work with. In scarcely veiled
self-praise, he announced that progress
is not achieved by the masses, but
by the "fanatical enthusiasm of the
revolutionist, whose extreme teaching
has saved the mass from utter inertia."
Photo-Secessionists, he announced,
possess a feeling of "rebellion against
the insincere attitude of the unbeliever,
of the Philistine."[22]

Stieglitz also ran the Little Galleries
of the Photo-Secession, which opened
in November 1905 at 291 Fifth Avenue,
New York, in Steichen's former studio.
Steichen organized the first exhibition
at "291," as the gallery became known,
followed by a show of French photography selected by Demachy. Prints by
Hill and Adamson (see Figs. 2.63, 2.64),
greatly admired by Pictorialist photographers, were also shown, and reproduced in *Camera Work*. Working with
Steichen, Stieglitz showed artwork
in other media: drawings by Auguste
Rodin (1840–1917), Henri Matisse
(1869–1954), and Picasso; watercolors by
Paul Cézanne (1839–1906) and Picasso;
sculpture by Constantin Brancusi
(1876–1957) and Elie Nadelman
(1882–1946); lithographs by Henri de
Toulouse-Lautrec (1864–1901); artwork
by Americans such as Marsden Hartley
(1877–1943), John Marin (1870–1953),
and Georgia O'Keeffe; and children's art
and Japanese prints.

The 291 gallery regularly showed
modern art, including the first
American exhibition of Picasso in 1911.
Stieglitz praised Picasso's "antiphotographic" work, meaning that it had
renounced the simple vanishing-point
perspective imposed by the camera.
He advocated that art photography
should be similarly antiphotographic,
not necessarily through abstraction,
but by reaching beyond subject-matter
for personal and spiritual expression.
Stieglitz's own work was shown only
once in a one-person exhibition at 291,
during the so-called Armory Show in
1913, when about 1,300 pieces of modern European art were exhibited in New
York, including Marcel Duchamp's
(1887–1968) *Nude Descending a Staircase*
(see Fig. 4.55).

Alfred Stieglitz

Born in Hoboken, New Jersey, Stieglitz took up photography while he was an engineering student in Berlin, studying photochemistry with Hermann Vogel. Soon his photographs were winning awards, and he was writing essays on the aesthetics and technical obstacles of the field. His early work includes the familiar tranquil scenes and all-over blurriness of Pictorialism, but his depiction of light and textures is clearer than Pictorialist photography. For instance, *Sun's Rays—Paula, Berlin* (1889) delineates the bands of light that pass through the shutter slats outside the room (Fig. 4.20). The technical virtuosity required to create a photograph in this lighting would be understood by photographers, but the personal symbols Stieglitz included would be grasped only by his immediate circle. On the wall behind his companion Paula are photographs of and by Stieglitz. One of them shows the

letter-writer in bed, suggesting their intimate relationship. The Valentine hearts and the caged bird also speak to the private subject-within-a-subject, a favorite visual strategy that Stieglitz would use throughout his life.

When he returned to the United States from Europe in 1890, Stieglitz worked for five years at the Photochrome Engraving Company in New York, and continued to make photographs. His marriage to Emmeline Obermeyer, a woman of financial means, and an allowance from his father, permitted him to leave the business and pursue photography full time. His street photographs in New York City and during extended European trips centered on such everyday scenes as horse-drawn streetcars, rain-slicked avenues, and street children. Foreshadowing the 1904 critique of Sadakichi Hartmann (see p. 179), Stieglitz's images in the 1890s became more straightforward, with

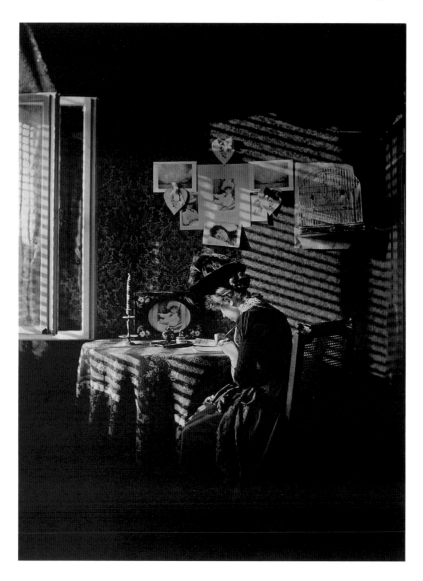

4.20
ALFRED STIEGLITZ, *Sun's Rays—Paula, Berlin*, 1889.
Chloride print. Alfred Stieglitz Collection. Art Institute of Chicago, Chicago, Illinois.

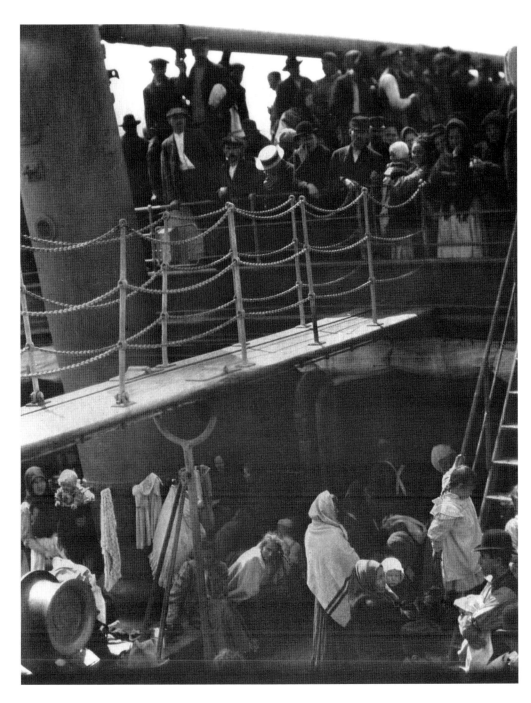

4.21
ALFRED STIEGLITZ,
The Steerage, 1907, from
Camera Work, no. 34.
Photogravure. Museum
of Modern Art, New York.

an increasing emphasis on form, rather than atmosphere. His interests in contemporary art moved toward urban realism, like that of American painter Robert Henri (1865–1929), whom Stieglitz nonetheless accused of making "colored photographs."[23] Stieglitz also responded to the geometric experiments of such European painters as Pablo Picasso (1881–1973).

While sailing on a trip to Europe aboard the *Kaiser Wilhelm II*, Stieglitz experienced what he recalled as a pivotal moment. He was looking over the first-class deck to the steerage below, recognizing there not the disheartened immigrants returning to Europe, but a combination of abstract forms that evoked a profound response:

A round straw hat, the funnel leaning left, the stairway leaning right, the white draw-bridge with its railings made of circular chains—white suspenders crossing on the back of a man in the steerage below, round shapes of iron machinery, a mast cutting into the sky, making a triangular shape ... I saw a picture of shapes and underlying that the feeling I had about life.[24]

The resulting photograph, *The Steerage*, became his favorite image (Fig. 4.21). The instantaneous visual recognition of a personal, not public, symbol informed much of Stieglitz's photography. His numerous photographs of his second wife, painter Georgia O'Keeffe (1887–1986), show how he, like Picasso, used daily life as a basis for art.

PORTRAIT
Edward Steichen

Were it not a gum-print, the self-portrait of Edward Steichen might be mistaken for that of an emotionally intense romantic artist, with his head, hands, and palette brightly highlighted, and his face partially sunk in shade (Fig. 4.22). Early in his career, Steichen took up painting and photography, both of which he pursued until World War I. After two years studying art in Paris, he returned to the United States in 1902 and opened a portrait studio at 291 Fifth Avenue, which later became the Little Galleries of the Photo-Secession. A close friend of Stieglitz (Fig. 4.23), Steichen collaborated with him on *Camera Work* and on exhibitions. Elected to the Linked Ring in 1901,

4.22
EDWARD J. STEICHEN,
Self-Portrait, 1902. Library of
Congress, Washington, D.C.

and a founding member of the Photo-Secession in 1902, Steichen worked on the exhibits that brought modern European art to 291. His Pictorialist work resembles that of Alvin Langdon Coburn (1882–1966) (see Figs. 4.40, 4.41) in its emphasis on design and powerful graphic contrasts (Fig. 4.24). With Stieglitz and other Pictorialist photographers, Steichen experimented with the color photography process known as autochrome (see p. 167), whose muted colors and pebbled surface had a Pictorialist quality.

Unlike Stieglitz, Steichen had no family money. He supplemented his income as an art photographer by doing portrait, advertising, and other commercial work. Born in Luxembourg, he felt he had to show his allegiance by enlisting in the United States Army, where he set up a department of aerial photography. In 1923 he began a career as the chief photographer for Condé Nast publications. During World War II (1939–45), he returned to military service, directing United States naval combat photography. He also organized two patriotic photographic exhibitions at New York's Museum of Modern Art, the *Road to Victory* (1942) and *Power in the Pacific* (1945), which helped him become director of the influential Department of Photography at the museum. In 1955, he organized *The Family of Man* (see Chapter 6).

4.23 (above)
EDWARD J. STEICHEN,
Alfred Stieglitz, 1907. Four-color halftone. Museum of Modern Art, New York.

4.24
EDWARD J. STEICHEN,
Nocturne: Orangerie Staircase, Versailles, c. 1910. Pigment print. Albright-Knox Gallery, Buffalo, New York.

4.25
ALFRED STIEGLITZ,
Equivalent, 1930.
**Gelatin silver print. The
J. Paul Getty Museum,
Los Angeles, California.**

Stieglitz chose the word
Equivalent as a title in a
series of cloud studies.
The images were equiva-
lent to a state of mind or
emotion for which there
are no words.

PHOTOGRAPHY IN THE MODERN AGE (1880–1918)

During the 1920s, Stieglitz continued his photographic experimentation,
creating hundreds of what he called
Equivalents (Fig. 4.25). These cloud
studies show how he never relinquished the assumption of Pictorialist
photography that the ordinary world
abounded with evocative symbols of
emotion.

THE NUDE AND PICTORIALISM

Pictorialism's emphasis on nature
and the natural gave rise to studies of
the male and female nude, created by
White, Steichen, Demachy, Puyo, and
Annie Brigman (1869–1950), among
others. Since boys customarily swam
nude, the beach was a likely place to
photograph them. Alice Boughton
(1886–1943), a member of the Photo-
Secession, published an image that subtly compared the bodies of pubescent
and pre-pubescent girls in a 1909 issue
of *Camera Work* (Fig. 4.26). Those
interested in creating more explicit and
sexually arousing images took advantage
of the acceptance of the Pictorialist
nude, imitating its soft-focus, painterly
surface, or classical references. Wilhelm
von Gloeden (1856–1931) mixed the

exoticism of earlier nineteenth-century sexual photographs with Pictorialist themes. He photographed Italian lads in Sicily, reclining on animal skins and Persian rugs, and surrounded by planters bearing classical motifs (Fig. 4.27). Von Gloeden's less explicit photographs were popular with educated American and European viewers, who sought them out for their evocation of Classical times. His nude photographs were sold as postcards, through they were seldom put in the mail.

WOMEN IN THE PICTORIALIST MOVEMENT

The long-standing association of women with both nature and domesticity made feminine subjects a favorite in Pictorialist practice. Women, too, worked with these themes; in particular, Californian photographer Annie Brigman portrayed women as spirits or souls of trees, rocks, water, and even photography (Fig. 4.28). Portraiture was thought to be done better by women, who were considered to possess a more intuitive grasp of the sitter's personality and a wider range of emotional response than men. With the increased acceptance of women's aptitude, their work was shown in large exhibits and magazines.

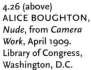

**4.26 (above)
ALICE BOUGHTON,
Nude, from *Camera
Work*, April 1909.
Library of Congress,
Washington, D.C.**

Boughton frequently photographed children. The public's understanding that an intimate natural bond exists between women and children protected her from charges of indecency.

**4.27 (below)
BARON WILHELM
VON GLOEDEN, *Nude
Sicilian Youths*, c. 1885.
Gelatin silver print. The
J. Paul Getty Museum,
Los Angeles, California.**

4.28
ANNIE BRIGMAN,
The Heart of the Storm,
c. 1910. Platinum print.
The J. Paul Getty
Museum, Los Angeles,
California.

The nude figures leaning
into each other emulate
the arc of the storm-
blasted tree trunks in
which they seem to be
taking shelter. Brigman's
photographs often
situated female nudes
in nature to evoke
ideas such as suffering,
endurance, and love.

Frances Benjamin Johnston
(1864–1952) ran a successful business,
branching out from flattering Pictorialist
portraits of prominent people in
Washington, D.C. She photographed
architecture, industrial sites, and documented the activities of the Hampton
Institute in Virginia, where young
African-Americans received training
in the trades. Johnston's Hampton
photographs were among those also
included in the "American Negro
Exhibit," which African-American

W. E. B. Du Bois helped organize for
the international Exposition Universelle
in 1900. Johnston promoted photography as a means of employment and
recreation for women, writing upbeat
essays in such magazines as *Ladies'
Home Journal.* In 1900, she arranged
an exhibit of 142 women's photographs
in Paris, at the same time as the
Exposition Universelle. The show traveled to Moscow, and then back to Paris,
but never found a venue in the United
States. Johnston created a self-portrait

SUFFRAGETTES AT HOME.—(3.) Mrs. How Martyn Makes Jam.

4.30 (above)
PHOTOGRAPHER UNKNOWN,
"Mrs. How Martyn Makes Jam,"
from *Suffragettes at Home*, n.d.
Postcard. Museum of London.

The Suffragists used popular media
such as the postcard to show that
women who crusaded the vote had
no intentions of abandoning their
domestic duties.

4.31 (below)
ARTIST UNKNOWN, *Untitled*
(Advertisement for Kodak cameras),
c. 1910. Poster. George Eastman
House, Rochester, New York.

To persuade more women that
photography was a chic hobby, Kodak
created the Kodak Girl, a fashionable,
independent, yet feminine New
Woman, who took her camera with
her on holiday adventures.

4.29 (above)
PHOTOGRAPHER
UNKNOWN, *Untitled
(Is your wife a
Suffragette?)*, post-
marked 1908. Postcard.

as a caricature of the New Woman,
a figure in revolt against contemporary
standards of feminine behavior
(Fig. 4.0).

In its depiction of women, Pictorialist
photography expressed a deep-seated
conservatism at the historical moment
when more women were working outside the home in schools, factories, and
offices, and when there were focused
international efforts to gain women the
right to vote. In Britain, anti-suffragist
imagery ridiculed women activists
as mannish brutes who neglected their
domestic duties and showed men as
reduced to doing housework (Fig. 4.29).
To counter such propaganda, suffragists
portrayed themselves as tender mothers
and caring homemakers who wanted
to influence government policy on children (Fig. 4.30).

The acceptance of women practicing photography, especially as amateurs,
was expressed in the advertising
image of the Kodak Girl, introduced in
1901, and continued, with fashionable
updates, for decades[25] (Fig. 4.31).

PORTRAIT
Gertrude Käsebier

Gertrude Käsebier (1852–1934) was probably the most successful American portrait photographer in the first decade of the twentieth century. Like Julia Margaret Cameron, Käsebier came to photography later in life, first as a hobbyist, then as an art photographer, and finally as a sought-after portraitist. Her photographs of women sometimes relied on implicit storytelling in the manner of Lady Hawarden. *Blessed Art Thou Among Women* (1899) shows a mother about to send her child into the world (Fig. 4.32). The mother-and-child theme, prominent in Käsebier's photography, was often depicted with the mother helping the child negotiate the passage into life,

4.32
GERTRUDE KÄSEBIER, *Blessed Art Thou Among Women*, 1899. Platinum print on Japanese tissue. Museum of Modern Art, New York.

rather than holding the child close. The photograph, with its religious overtones, is a portrait study of Agnes Rand Lee and her daughter Peggy. A print of the Annunciation (when the Angel Gabriel appears to the Virgin Mary) hangs on the wall behind the figures. Agnes Lee is dressed in loose, flowing robes, as advocated by British artist and reformer William Morris (1834–1896). Soon after the photograph was made, Peggy Lee died. Agnes then posed as the sorrowful mother in Käsebier's 1904 photograph *The Heritage of Motherhood*.

Käsebier's photographs were honored abroad, and she was elected to the Linked Ring in 1900. *Blessed Art Thou Among Women* was included in the first exhibition of the Photo-Secession, and her work was showcased in the first issue of *Camera Work* (January 1903).

Käsebier's sensuous *Portrait—Miss N.* redresses the saccharine charms of motherhood so much associated with her work. It depicts Evelyn Nesbitt, the sixteen-year-old showgirl and mistress of prominent architect Stanford White[26] (Fig. 4.33). Nesbitt figured in a sensational early twentieth-century scandal and murder fictionalized by E.L.Doctorow in the novel *Ragtime* (1975): she married railroad heir Harry K. Thaw, who, spurred by jealousy over her previous relationship with Stanford White, shot him dead in 1906.

4.33
GERTRUDE KÄSEBIER, *Portrait—Miss N. (Evelyn Nesbitt)*, 1902. Platinum print. National Gallery of Canada/Musée des Beaux-Arts du Canada, Ottawa.

Pictorialism's soft focus and association with women, the major purchasers of home products, were particularly persistent in portraiture (Fig. 4.34) and advertising[27] (Fig. 4.35).

ANTHROPOLOGICAL PICTORIALISM

Together with Pictorialism, the international Arts and Crafts movement, with its emphasis on hand-crafted art objects and on home life, provoked an interest

New York Times   Sunday, February 8, 1925

MRS. CONDÉ NAST
wife of the distinguished pub-
lisher of Vogue, Vanity Fair,
and House and Garden, is a
social leader of exceptional
charm. The exquisite taste and
smartness of her clothes are
matched by the intellectual bril-
liancy and the fascinating per-
sonality of their wearer.

"Women are realizing more and
more the necessity of a clear,
smooth youthful skin. The very
clothes they wear — so chic and
simple of line — call for youth in
their faces.
"Pond's Two Creams are the
foundation of a sure and simple
means of caring for the skin, of
keeping the complexion in ex-
quisite condition."

Mrs Condé Nast

MRS. CONDÉ NAST
on the importance of being beautiful

IN Mrs. Condé Nast's apartment that morning I sensed the bustle of arrival. Trunks bulked excit-ingly in the background and Mrs. Nast herself, from the cut of her shoes to her black bengaline frock with its white organdie collar and cuffs—was the chic, the youthfulness of Paris itself. While her line-free, exquisitely cared for skin bespoke youthfulness as eloquently as did her clothes.

"Paris was never so fascinating," Mrs. Nast was saying. "The clothes? Marvelous! So chic and simple of line, so unadorned! But they call for youth in the face as well as in the figure. So the smart woman *must* keep her skin youthful—radiant."

"What did you do for your own skin while you were abroad?" I asked her. "It looks perfect."

"I took plenty of good cold cream along," replied Mrs. Nast. "I posi-tively depended upon it for cleansing —Pond's of course."

Then we talked of both the famous creams Society women are using to keep that youthfulness of skin Mrs. Nast finds essential for harmony with the mode.

This is How to Use Them

Once a day at least, and especially after exposure, smooth Pond's Cold Cream liberally over your face and neck. Let its pure oils bring to the surface the powder and dust with which the pores are clogged.

Repeat this process, and finish with a dash of cold water. Let a little cream stay on all night if your skin is inclined to be dry.

For the delicate finish you want by day, smooth in a light film of Pond's Vanishing Cream. It is instantly absorbed, giving your skin such a soft, lustrous finish that now your powder goes on smoother than ever before and clings longer. And you are perfectly pro-tected against winter cold and wind. So be-fore you go out be sure to use Pond's Vanish-ing Cream. The Pond's Extract Company, 131 Hudson Street, New York City.

Every skin needs these
Two Creams

Mrs. REGINALD VANDERBILT
Mrs. GLORIA GOULD BISHOP
Mrs. O. H. P. BELMONT
Mrs. MARSHALL FIELD, Sr.

are among the women of distin-guished taste who have expressed approval of Pond's Two Creams.

---

in Native American peoples. Idealized as living close to nature, they were also known to be under threat from the incur-sion of Western civilization into their lands.[28] To meet amateurs' interest in Native American life, George Eastman sponsored the photographic expedition of Frederick Monsen (1865–1929). Monsen's *With a Kodak in the Land of the Navajo* (1909) was both a photographic booklet and an advertising device.

Edward S. Curtis (1868–1952) made numerous photographs of Native American life using gravure or platinum printing techniques, lending the pictures a soft, faded quality (Fig. 4.36). Curtis also asked his subjects to enact ritual dances and battles. He carried Native American costumes, which his customers associated with pre-industrial life, using them occasionally to dress his subjects in what his viewers saw as authentic garb.

4.36
EDWARD S. CURTIS,
Photograph and article
"Vanishing Indian
Types," from *Scribner's
Magazine*, June 6, 1906.
Library of Congress,
Washington, D.C.

Curtis's images of
Native Americans
often used a soft focus,
giving expression to
Western culture's
notion that indigenous
people would dwindle
under the pressure of
modern life.

From a photograph, copyright 1905, by E. S. Curtis.

Crow warriors on the edge of a precipice in the Black Canyon.

VANISHING INDIAN TYPES
THE TRIBES OF THE NORTHWEST PLAINS
By E. S. Curtis

ILLUSTRATIONS FROM PHOTOGRAPHS BY THE AUTHOR

THE Northwest Plains Indian is, to the average person, the typical American Indian, the Indian of our school-day books—powerful of physique, statuesque, gorgeous in dress, with the bravery of the firm believer in predestination. The constant, fearless hunting and slaughtering of the buffalo trained him to the greatest physical endurance, and gave an inbred desire for bloodshed. Thousands of peace-loving, agricultural-living Indians might climb down from their cliff-perched homes, till their miniature farms, attend their flocks, and at night-time climb back up the winding stairs to their home in the clouds, and at-

tract no attention. But if a fierce band of Sioux rushed down on a hapless emigrant train the world soon learned of it.

The culture of all primitive peoples is necessarily determined by their environment. This, of course, means that all plains tribes —though speaking a score of languages— were, in life and manner, broadly alike. They were buffalo-hunting Indians, and only in rare cases did they give any attention to agriculture. Buffalo meat was their food, and the by-products their clothing, tools, and implements.

The plains tribes in earlier times were certainly true nomads. For a time, in the

Curtis produced a twenty-volume work, *The North American Indian* (1907–30), which contained more than 1,500 photogravures as well as text. Like Stieglitz's *Camera Work*, the books were produced in limited editions on fine paper.

NON-PICTORIALIST VISIONS
As the invention of dry plates, roll film, and hand cameras encouraged a greater number of hobbyists, it also allowed them to go their own way. Pictorialism did not appeal to everyone. As amateur

photographer Charles L. Mitchell (active 1890s) put it bluntly in 1900: "There are too many 'impressions' and too few clearly conceived, thoroughly expressed realities; too few real pictures, and too much 'trash.'"[29] Non-Pictorialist efforts can be seen in the work of amateurs whose fame in other endeavors preserved their photographic work. For example, the novelist Émile Zola took up photography in the late 1880s, producing unexceptional family portraits and trip mementos. Occasionally, though, he created a bold experiment with composition (Fig. 4.37). French painter Edgar Degas, whose paintings of the ballet inspired some Pictorialist photographers, also found a visual challenge outside of Pictorialist photography. Degas seems to have enjoyed resolving particular formal and aesthetic photographic problems. "Daylight gives me no problem," he commented, "What I want is difficult—the atmosphere of lamps or moonlight"[30] (Fig. 4.38).

Norwegian painter Edvard Munch (1863–1944) used photography throughout his life, not only as a sketching instrument for his paintings, but also to create a series of what he called

"Fatal Destiny Photographs," in which melancholic sitters, including the painter, appear transparent, with the background visible through them. Munch's photographs resemble some of the experiments of Swedish playwright August Strindberg (1849–1912), who took up autobiographical photography, and hoped to make psychological photographs of sitters by intuiting their innermost thoughts. He developed a "Wunderkamera"—a large camera able to take life-size photographs of faces— to increase the sense of psychological presence, and wrote a defense of spirit photography, as photographs purporting to depict the presence of the dead were called.[31] Strindberg also experimented with what he called "celestographs," photographic plates lengthily exposed to starry skies. The results resemble abstract paintings. Irish critic, playwright, and social activist George Bernard Shaw (1856–1950) took more than 10,000 pictures. His self-portraits, pictures of friends, and landscapes typify the varied output of amateurs. Shaw also wrote extensively about photography, defending it as an art and advocating that photographers stick to the inherent

4.37
ÉMILE ZOLA, *Denise Sitting, Doll in her Arms*, c. 1897–1902. Argentic print. Musée d'Orsay, Paris.

4.38 (above)
EDGAR DEGAS, *Berthe Morisot's Salon: Auguste Renoir and Stéphane Mallarmé*, c. 1890. Albumen print.

Degas's portrait of painter Auguste Renoir (1841–1919) and poet Stéphane Mallarmé (1842–1898) reveals Degas in the mirror, operating his camera, while Mallarmé's wife and daughter watch. Degas's face is obscured by the intense light of an oil lamp.

qualities of the camera, which he considered to be sharp focus and no hand-working of the negative and the print. Of George Davison (see Fig. 4.7), Shaw wrote: "if I saw the edges of a house blur as they blur in Mr. Davison's pictures, I should conclude that I was going to faint, and probably do it too."[32]

A whimsical child in an eccentric, privileged French family, Jacques Henri Lartigue (1894–1986) took his first photograph at the age of six. His photography seems to have been guided more by his interest in stopping action than in making art images. He photographed early racing cars, flying machines, and fashionable people parading the boulevards. Although they seem worldly and sophisticated, many of his photographs were taken while he was a child or young adult. While his photographs were mostly taken with a stereographic camera, better able to stop time, they were not meant to be three-dimensional or commercial (Fig. 4.39).

PICTORIALISM: A CONSERVATIVE AVANT-GARDE

By 1909, the Photo-Secession was open to assault by its own revolutionary rhetoric. A vast 1909 international show in Dresden, Germany, arranged by Stieglitz with Steichen's help, was criticized for "doing nothing new,"[33] and many considered the art photography in *Camera Work* to be repetitive. When asked to prepare a large exhibit for the Albright Art Gallery (now the Albright-Knox Art Gallery) in Buffalo, New York, Stieglitz staged what photohistorian Robert Doty called "a finale."[34] The 1910 exhibition of about 600 photographs was organized as a retrospective of Pictorialism, with contributors asked to provide old and new work. The show is often cited as marking the historical moment when photography was accepted as an art form worthy of museums. It was also the point at which the Pictorialist style had become visually sterile, though the "fuzzygraph" vocabulary continued for another decade in commerce and advertising, and was popular in Japan and South Africa into the 1930s.

Was Pictorialism an avant-garde movement? Certainly it introduced a visual fashion dominant for thirty years, and mixed painting and photography in a way that anticipated the hybridization of art media in the late twentieth and early twenty-first centuries. At the same

4.39
J. H. LARTIGUE,
My Cousin Bichonnade,
1905. Association des
Amis de J. H. Lartigue,
Ministry of Culture,
Paris.

Lartigue wittily pictured the life of his fashionable French family. Caught jumping from the middle of the staircase, cousin Bichonnade seems to fly forward, defying gravity.

time, its sentimental subject matter and its rendition of otherworldly women harked back to the nineteenth-century view of women as angels trapped in a domestic environment. Through Stieglitz and 291, art photography did engage with the European avant-garde, such as the FAUVES and CUBISTS, but these painters did not substantially influence art photography in general, which seized upon the notion of an uncomplicated subjectivity. The Pictorialists largely ignored the raw emotionality and anxiety that marked Expressionism, the mainly German art movement much discussed in the 1890s. When Stieglitz and his colleagues took the city as a subject, they did so when atmospheric effects, such as fog, rain, and snow, softened the bleakness.[35]

Like other late nineteenth-century avant-gardists, the Pictorialists and Photo-Secessionists advocated self-expression as soul-preserving in the world of mass production and mass taste. Despite practicing promotional techniques in their magazines akin to those of the newly formed field of advertising, they did not court the praise of critics or the funds of patrons. Rather, they established a network of institutions, publications, and selection strategies to validate their work, while laying claim to unsullied virtue.[36]

As historian Ulrich Keller pointed out, art photography was not primarily concerned with art theory so much as with "spiritual exclusiveness," being "away from 'the Philistine' and 'the masses.'"[37] Stieglitz disparaged those who let money taint their art, though he was in a financial position to take the moral high ground. In 1899, he wrote that "nearly all the greatest work is being, and has always been done by those who are following photography for the love of it, and not merely for financial reasons."[38] In an age of raging labor disputes, Stieglitz praised working for love, not money, but he also emphasized that amateurs were workers too. After the horrors of World War I, the ideology of Pictorialism was in full retreat. Nevertheless, Pictorial-style photographs continued to be made, especially in advertising and amateur work, despite the challenges of Russian CONSTRUCTIVISM, which stressed

design as a way for artists to participate in changing society for the better, and European DADAISM, which questioned the plausibility of beauty and purity after the horrors of trench warfare (see Chapter 5).

Advocates of art photography have viewed Pictorialism as avant-garde on account of its tendency to stress abstract patterns, which became a key visual characteristic of art photography in the 1920s. The work of such photographers as Alvin Langdon Coburn used the visual conventions of Pictorialism, including flattened space and diminished detail, to create abstract patterns on the surface of the photographic print. Coburn corresponded with American painter Arthur Wesley Dow about *notan* (see p. 180) and the Japanese use of perspective (Fig. 4.40). Despite the blurry surface values of Coburn's prints, neither Emerson's differential focus nor Davison's notion of personal impressions are prominent in his work. Instead, drawn to spiritualism and religious symbolism, Coburn sought out patterns in nature as clues to a great spiritual immanence. It is ironic that Coburn, who spurned modernity later in his life and became a Druid, also made the first completely abstract photograph.

Through the influence of poet Ezra Pound (1885–1972), Coburn briefly took up Vorticism, a short-lived English art movement named by Pound in 1913, and promoted by the painter Wyndham Lewis (1882–1957). The movement's magazine, *Blast*, explained that Vorticism would integrate the dynamic movement of FUTURISM with the static geometric analysis of Cubism. The movement hoped to blast away the remnants of the past. Coburn experimented with abstraction, building a Vortescope, a combination of mirrors that produced an image like that of a kaleidoscope, and photographing the result (Fig. 4.41). Coburn's interest in total abstraction lasted only about a month; he never embraced the notion that radical changes in the visual arts could promote change on the social front, an assumption that would guide experimental photography in the 1920s (see Chapter 5).

In the last issue of *Camera Work* (June 1917), Stieglitz featured work by Paul Strand (1890–1976). Strand was younger than Stieglitz and Steichen, and came to photography not through art, but through social concern. As a student of Lewis Hine at the New York Ethical Culture School in 1907, Strand learned photography in an intellectual atmosphere of moral concern for humankind.

He frequented the Little Galleries of the Photo-Secession, where he became acquainted with abstract art, as well as with Pictorialism. Like critic Sadakichi Hartmann, Strand rejected the soft-focused "fuzzygraph" in favor of what he called "absolute unqualified objectivity"

**4.40 (opposite)
ALVIN LANGDON
COBURN,** *Wapping,*
**plate 10 from his
book** *London,* **1909.
Victoria & Albert
Museum, London.**

Coburn's photographs
resemble the tonal paint-
ings of James McNeill
Whistler, because they
were interested in both
the space and pattern
of Japanese prints,
rather than illusionistic
representation.

**4.41 (right)
ALVIN LANGDON
COBURN,** *Vortograph,*
**1917. Coburn Collection.
George Eastman House,
Rochester, New York.**

Coburn created abstract
photographs called
Vortographs that resem-
ble the work of British
painter Wyndham Lewis,
the primary Vorticist
painter. Both borrow
heavily from Cubism and
Futurism. In some of his
Vortographs, like this
one, Coburn used multi-
ple exposure to increase
the abstract effect.

and "straight photographic means."[39]
The 1913 Armory Show of contemporary
European art, especially abstraction,
also influenced him. In 1917, when
Camera Work devoted its last issue to
Strand's photography, Stieglitz wrote
that Strand's work was "brutally direct,"
and "devoid of trickery and any 'ism.'"
"These photographs," Stieglitz concluded, "are the direct expression of
today."[40] Stieglitz included two areas

of Strand's work: close-up, unsentimen-
tal portraits of street people, and near
abstractions made by focusing on
repeated patterns of light and dark
found in the experience of everyday life
(Figs. 4.42, 4.43).

In an essay accompanying his photographs, Strand stated his dislike of
Pictorialism. He called gum-printing,
oil-printing, and handworking of the
negative and the print "the expression

4.42
PAUL STRAND,
Photograph—New York
(Woman with sign
that reads "Blind"),
from *Camera Work*,
June 1917. Photogravure.
Library of Congress,
Washington, D.C.

Strand took his street
photographs with a
trick camera that led
people to believe he was
shooting in another
direction. His portraits
of the poor were not
part of a social reform
program, but intended
to be matter-of-fact
examples of life. His
audience would not
have known about the
trick camera, but they
would have understood
the picture's ironic
slant, namely, the
contrast between the
camera's clear eye and
the woman's blindness.

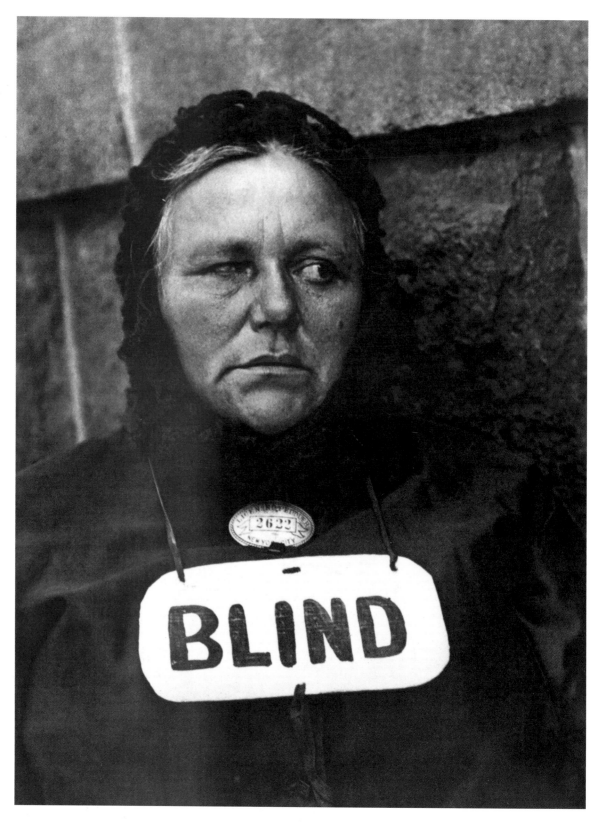

of an impotent desire to paint." Yet
Strand understood the Pictorialist goal
to make photography responsive to the
photographer's intellect and emotion,
which he called the "organization of
objectivity."[41] Strand credited Stieglitz
for creating, through *Camera Work*, a
true American art. "America has really
been expressed in terms of America
without the outside influence of Paris

art schools or their dilute offspring
here," Strand wrote, comparing the
work of White, Steichen, Käsebier, and
Eugene to the unique experimentation
manifested by the builders of skyscrapers.[42] He was wrong, of course, about
the absence of European influence on
American photography, including his
own, but right to sense that Pictorialism
had had its day.

4.43
PAUL STRAND,
Abstractions, Porch
Shadows, Connecticut,
1915. Gelatin silver print
by Richard Benson.
Museum of Modern Art,
New York.

Strand obscured his
subject matter—
shadows cast by a porch
railing and posts—in
a pleasingly balanced
abstraction of comple-
mentary geometric
shapes and tones of
light and dark.

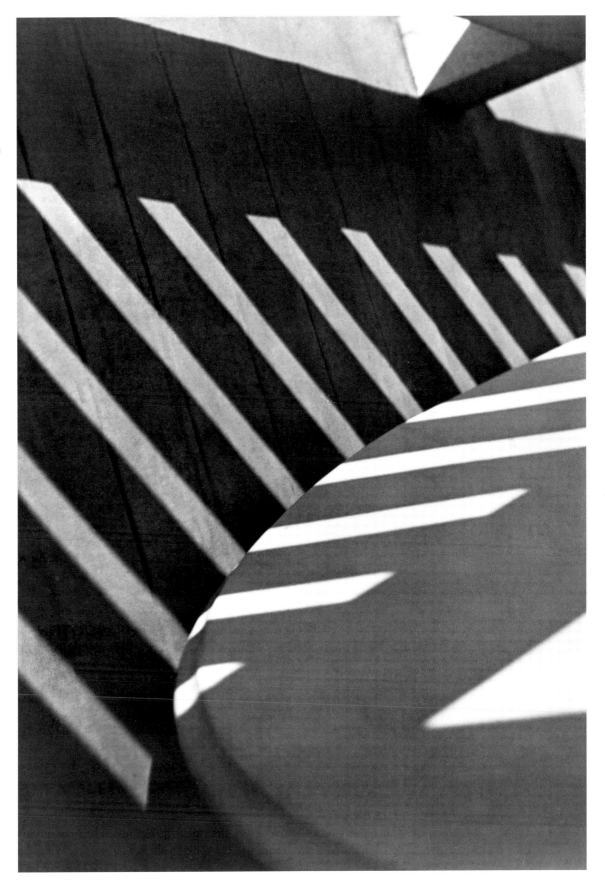

PHOTOGRAPHY AND THE MODERN CITY

Pictorial photographers occasionally
photographed the urban environment,
modifying it with a mantle of color or
cloud. Photographers independent of
Pictorialism also rendered the city and
its inhabitants. British photographer
Paul Martin (1864–1944) recorded
street life and seaside entertainment
in a casual style associated with the

4·44
PAUL MARTIN,
Dancing to the Organ,
Lambeth, c. 1895.
Gelatin dry plate.
Victoria & Albert
Museum, London.

Because of their
spontaneous, snapshot
appearance, Paul
Martin's photographs
seemed unprofessional
to some. The images
gained more public
appreciation in the
twentieth century, when
the snapshot itself came
to stand for unaffected
photography. Martin
also pioneered night
photography, in which a
calm stillness contrasts
with his city pictures.

snapshot (Fig. 4.44). E. Alice Austen
(1866–1952) of Staten Island, New
York, photographed the social life of her
genteel friends, but also ventured into
Manhattan to photograph immigrant
life (Fig. 4.45). Neither photographer's
work was ever aimed at bringing about
social improvements.

New York City, especially after the
opening of Ellis Island in 1892, was
the port through which most of the
immigrants entering the United States
passed. In 1900, over 35 per cent of the
population in big cities such as New
York and Chicago were foreign-born.
Immigrant neighborhoods became the
subject of much public curiosity and
concern. Photographers in expanding
American cities provided the public
with an array of images of the poor.
Firms such as Underwood & Underwood
issued boxed sets of stereographs
depicting immigrants and urban life.
Some pictures, for example the lantern
slides produced by Chicago photographer Sigmund Krausz (active 1890s),

reinforced ethnic stereotypes and
clichés about the urban poor. The rural
poor were not major photographic subjects, outside the idyllic scenes produced
by Pictorialist photographers.

SOCIAL REFORM PHOTOGRAPHY

From the beginning, British suffragists
used photography to record the lives
of poor women and children, arguing
that giving women the vote would draw
more attention to the issue of poverty.
After a slow start, reform organizations
and settlement houses — privately run
charities that did social work among the
poor — began using photography to promote their work.[43] As social work moved
from a voluntary occupation to full-time
professional employment, photographs
were increasingly used in conjunction
with other data. As the public became
more familiar with photographs of the
poor, there were two unexpected consequences: repeated images of people in
squalid conditions bolstered stereotypes
of the poor as inferior; and what is now

called "compassion fatigue" set in, as happened toward the end of the American Civil War when, as photographic coverage increased, public response declined.

Photographs of the poor were still novel and engaging, however, when Jacob Riis (1849–1914) produced his book *How the Other Half Lives* (1890), which contained fifteen half-tone images, and forty-three drawings based on photographs. Riis, a Danish immigrant who became a journalist in New York City, lectured on the condition of the slums, and projected stereopticon lantern slides to illustrate his points. Like many reformers, Riis believed that individuals were formed by their environment. For him the crowded, unsanitary tenements — that is, shoddy apartment houses — were the cause of crime and moral decay. By contemporary standards, Riis was conservative in his suggestions for reform: he did not call for government intervention, but hoped that the wealthy would consider tenement construction as a work of charity and that private investors would take less profit

when building tenements, in order to provide adequate lodgings (Fig. 4.46).

Like many social observers, Riis implicitly divided the poor into two categories: deserving and undeserving. Women and small children often fitted the first category, with unemployed and criminally inclined males in the second. Oddly enough, Riis's photographs have come to stand for late nineteenth- and early twentieth-century social reform, overshadowing other efforts to record the living conditions of the poor in an effort to foster change, such as the photographs taken by the Berlin Housing Enquete in Germany. Also often overlooked are the photographs made by American novelist and avid amateur photographer Jack London (1876–1916) for *The People of the Abyss* (1903), his account of the slums of London's East End. London used photographs, mostly his own, to depict the effects of industrialization on the poor, and to conclude that criminal mismanagement of society was to blame for poverty.

Like Riis, Lewis Hine (1874–1940), did not have a background in art photography.

4.45
E. ALICE AUSTEN,
*An Organ-Grinder
Couple*, New York, 1896.
Library of Congress,
Washington, D.C.

Unlike earlier nineteenth-century street photographers, Alice Austen showed her subjects in the lively context of the city. Near the organ-grinder couple, a street sweeper is at work. In the background, a trolley is approaching, while wagons and carriages move along the street.

Although he visited Stieglitz at 291, and introduced Strand to him, Hine jokingly called the members of the Photo-Secession, the "Seceshes."[47] Hine taught a number of subjects at New York's Ethical Culture School, a progressive institution. He learned photography at the school's request, and went on to work exclusively in the medium. Beginning in 1904, as part of the school's curriculum, Hine made photographs of immigrants arriving at

4.46
JACOB RIIS, *Bandits' Roost, New York*, 1888. Gelatin silver print from the original negative. Museum of the City of New York, New York.

"On either side of the alley are stale beer dives in room after room, where the stuff is sold for two or three cents a quart. After buying a round the customer is entitled to a seat on the floor, otherwise known as a 'lodging' for the night."[44]

PORTRAIT
Jacob Riis

Jacob Riis emigrated from Denmark to the United States in 1870, but endured hardships there while looking for work during the depression years of the 1870s. Riis acquired a job as a police reporter in the Lower East Side of Manhattan, and began writing about the slums, using photography to illustrate his points. Initially he used photographs by others, but eventually took his own. He presented his work in several formats. Lantern-slide lectures were given to mostly middle-class audiences in New York, who had little direct experience of the slums, where they were afraid to venture. He also published his photographs in newspaper and magazines. "Flashes from the Slums: Pictures Taken in Dark Places by the Lightning Process,"an 1888 illustrated newspaper article in the *Sun*, described a foray made by Riis and a group of photographers to research and photograph the life of the "other half."[45] His party toured at night, using the now standard magnesium flash powder to illuminate the darkness and to surprise subjects. The harsh look of the sudden burst of intense white light and the shock registered on the faces of those photographed came to stand for candid and objective photography (Fig. 4.47). Riis's photographs acquired credibility

in part because their compositions resembled the spontaneous look of the newly introduced snapshot. Nevertheless, several of his photographs were posed, such as his images of street children, which show them obviously feigning sleep.

Riis's photographs have been the subject of debate, both because of the photographer's intrusion on the lives of the poor, and because of the interpretations to which they have been subject since Riis's death. The first Jacob Riis exhibit at the Museum of the City of New York in 1947 presented prints that were cropped and enlarged to increase their impact. In grand, artful exhibition prints, the technical defects and spontaneous character of Riis's photographs were suppressed. The show exemplified changes in Riis's reputation following his death in 1914. With the popularity of documentary photography in the 1920s and 1930s, Riis, who photographed only for a short period and downplayed his efforts, was cast as a major recorder of the American experience and a forerunner of the documentary approach. Questions persist about his lack of sympathy with his subjects, and about the transformation of his untidy photography by the museums from its original context in social reform into American art.[46]

4.47
JACOB RIIS, *Police Station Lodgers* (Eldridge Street Station, an old lodger, and the plank on which she slept), c. 1898. Museum of the City of New York, New York.

4.48
LEWIS W. HINE,
A Madonna of the Tenements, c. 1911. Gelatin silver print on glass. George Eastman House, Rochester, New York.

Hine deliberately used religious motifs, such as the Madonna and Child, to create compassion for the newly arrived settlers, who were looked down upon and subject to ethnic slurs.

Ellis Island and living in the poor neighborhoods, so that the students might "have the same regard for contemporary immigrants as they have for the Pilgrims who landed at Plymouth Rock"[48] (Fig. 4.48).

While working at the Ethical Culture School, Hine began freelancing for the National Child Labor Committee (N.C.L.C.), a private agency founded by Dr. Felix Adler, who also established the Ethical Culture Society. The N.C.L.C. attempted to reform child labor by urging legislation to control industrial hiring practices. Hine traveled around the United States between 1907 and 1918, taking about 5,000 photographs of child labor. He often assuming a false identity, to photograph children at work in factories, mines, canneries, and mills (Fig. 4.49). Working for the N.C.L.C. and other social welfare organizations, Hine created what he called the "photo story," a narrative composed of pictures and words to be published in journals and magazines. Hine's layouts were often non-linear, linked more by ideas than a flow of narrative images. In 1937, he criticized the photographs in the new *Life* magazine for "the fetish of having a unified thread."[49]

Hine frequently insisted on receiving a credit line for his images, at a time when photographic reproductions generally did not carry them. He also took

advantage of the possibilities for illustration offered by the half-tone process and the recently created illustrated magazine. He worked extensively on *The Pittsburgh Survey* (1909–14), a multivolume study of working-class life in a city whose mix of immigrants and comfortable professionals, as well as its bitter history of labor conflict, seemed to many to epitomize the industrial metropolis. Hine's images and words aligned with the objective orientation of economic reports and the emergent profession of social work, in contrast to the personal approach favored by Riis. Hine went on to photograph the work of the Red Cross in Europe after World War I, and to publish *Men at Work: Photographic Study of Men and Machines* (1932), which showed the construction of the Empire State Building.

After his years with the N.C.L.C., Hine's attitude toward social photography shifted away from showing abuse to picturing the dignity of the working class. His later photographs, especially what he called "work portraits," put laborers in the center of the picture, celebrating their skill and perseverance. Although he addressed the workers as his audience, most of his photographs appeared in journals read by professional and volunteer social reformers.

Speaking to the National Conference of Charities and Corrections in 1909, Hine suggested that workers be encouraged to photograph their own situations. The idea of worker photography later briefly took hold in Europe, between the world wars. The turn of the twentieth century was an active time for the formation of labor unions in industrialized nations, but there was no systematic network to distribute photographs recording labor grievances, or offering union interpretations of the many labor actions and strikes that took place. As historian Larry Peterson observed: "workers' organizations adopted photography more slowly and haltingly than corporations." He contends that even such militant new unions as the International Workers of the World (I.W.W.) failed to adopt the mass media publicity techniques associated with corporations.[50] Instead, labor groups promoted craft skills and art historical knowledge because they were thought to stimulate the mind and the feelings.

**4.49
LEWIS W. HINE,**
Child in Carolina Cotton Mill, 1908. Gelatin silver print on masonite. Museum of Modern Art, New York.

Lewis Hine photographed youngsters at work in an attempt to instigate legislation against child labor. His photographs show children not being actively abused or neglected, but coping with their situations. Though she is small in relationship to the machine, the young girl in a cotton mill seems self-assured and competent at her job.

**4.50
PHOTOGRAPHER UNKNOWN,**
Female Employees at AEG, 1906. Deutsches Technikmuseum, Berlin.

The AEG company in Germany hired women to assemble electrical appliances. Although women's employment in factories is associated with wartime labor shortages, in 1907 women comprised nearly 36 per cent of the working population in Germany.[51]

During the 1913 textile strike in Paterson, New Jersey, for instance, workers used posters that looked like rough woodcuts, and staged a pageant of their complaints just a few blocks from the Armory Show (see p. 188). There is no extensive photographic protest showing workers trying to keep pace with speeded-up assembly lines, or learning to perform repetitive actions more quickly. More often than not, it was newspaper photographs of labor confrontations, not photographs taken by the unions, that galvanized worker opinions.

Industry, by contrast, used photography to present a positive vision of the company to the workers. The Pullman Company, makers of railroad sleeper cars, was the site in 1894 of a violent labor strike. *The Story of the Pullman Car* (1917) contained thirty-four photographs describing the work of the company, and the company newspaper, the *Pullman Car Works Standard* (1916–19), presented the company as "Pullman's Big Family" to the public and employees.[52] Companies used their financial resources and ready access to the factory floor to make photographs that served their interests; images of admirable working conditions and engineering feats were encouraged in the press (Fig. 4.50). The paternalistic attitude toward workers that developed in some factories was exemplified in the Ford Motor Company's booklet *Helpful Hints and Advice to Employes* [sic] (1915), which contained photographs showing proper living conditions for a Ford worker. The company's Sociological Department took photographs of ideal kitchens and bathrooms as examples to workers.[53] Similarly, General Electric Company began publishing a magazine called *Work News*, which emphasized the notion of community through photographs of workers and company sports teams.[54]

THE IDEAL CITY

The ideal city at the turn of the century was presented at a world's fair held in Chicago during 1893, called the World's Columbian Exposition, which was attended by 28 million people. Dubbed "the White City," for its classically derived, all-white BEAUX-ARTS architecture, the Exposition expressed the notion that American economic success could

renew cities and make them the centers of civilization. Charles Dudley Arnold (1844–1927), director of the Photographic Division of the exposition, made every effort to control photographs of the fair. All newspapers and periodicals had to use photographs issued by him and his office, or approved by them.[55] His view of the exposition is best expressed in the official images he made on mammoth plates and printed on platinum paper (Fig. 4.51). As photographic historian Peter Bacon Hales noted, Arnold's view resonates with the painting of American artist Thomas Cole (1801–1848), in whose work *The Consummation of Empire* (part of *The Course of Empire* series), classical architecture is celebrated as a symbol of American advancement.[56] Night-time photographs of the White City were calculated to demonstrate the union of culture and progress, symbolized by electricity, as the fair's buildings were traced by thousands of incandescent lights. In the photographs overseen by Arnold, the presence of people was minimized, thereby magnifying a vision of order.

The White City featured a Midway or "Midway Plaisance," with the first Ferris Wheel, constructed as an engineering feat meant to rival the Eiffel Tower in Paris, which was built for the 1889 Exposition Universelle. From atop the Ferris Wheel, visitors could look down at living ethnological exhibitions placed along the Midway in a conscious effort to merge information and entertainment. Strollers could enter the most talked about area, a street in Cairo, modeled not after an actual street, but after a similar stretch at the 1899 Paris Exposition. Native villages with ethnic types, including Native Americans, dotted the Midway area, where the daily life of residents was periodically punctuated with ceremonial rituals, some of which had long passed from practice. Anthropologist Franz Boas (see p. 231) recruited Kwakiutl people from British Columbia, whom he asked to execute ritual dances in front of a white sheet, so that their various moves were easier to see and to photograph. One of roughly 600 souvenir photographic albums, titled *Portrait Types of the Midway Plaisance* (1894), which contained ethnic images, announced that "Truly there

4.51
CHARLES DUDLEY ARNOLD, *Basin and the Court of Honor,* 1893. Platinum print. Chicago Historical Society, Chicago, Illinois.

The Chicago World's Fair was conceived as an ideal modern city, combining the past, symbolized in its classical architecture, with the future, denoted in its extensive use of electric lights. Arnold saw the beautiful city as one in which order reigns. Shooting from above and near the middle of the reflecting pool, he exaggerated the length of the water and the surrounding buildings.

was much of instruction as well as joy on the Merry Midway."[57]

African-Americans were discouraged from participating in the exposition. They protested their lack of visibility in letters to newspapers and visits to public officials when they were represented on the Midway by people from Dahomey (now Benin), in West Africa. Abolitionist Frederick Douglass spoke from the Haitian pavilion, asking the crowd to live up to the ideals of the Constitution. Reformer Ida B. Wells (1862–1931) handed out pamphlets that documented the increase in lynching, a subject photographed and circulated in prints and postcards.

SCIENCE AND PHOTOGRAPHY

THE PHOTOGRAPHY OF MOVEMENT

In 1878, French physiologist Étienne-Jules Marey (1830–1904) was reading the science journal *La Nature* when he came across images derived from

photographs taken by Eadweard Muybridge, who had previously photographed at Yosemite in California (see Fig. 3.76). Muybridge's photographs resolved an age-old question for equine experts and painters: do all four legs of the horse leave the ground when the horse moves quickly (Fig. 4.52)? To make the photographs, Muybridge lined a raceway with 15-foot sheeting, upon which lines were drawn at 21-inch intervals. As a horse rushed past, its hooves tripped cotton threads, which in turn tripped shutters on twelve cameras set up opposite the sheeting. Marey, who had been studying human and animal locomotion for a decade, was motivated by the Muybridge images to experiment with photography. In the early 1880s, he invented a gun camera like that used by Pierre-César Jules Janssen (see p. 146), with which he made exposures rapid enough to record the bodily movements of a bird in flight. Marey's work was greatly aided by the speed of dry-plate technology, which made possible the fast exposure time necessary to make instantaneous photographs.

4.52
EADWEARD
MUYBRIDGE, *Untitled*
(Sequence photographs
of the trot and gallop),
from *La Nature*,
December 1878.
Gravures.

The third photograph
in the top row clearly
shows all four hooves
of the galloping horse
in the air, rather than
extended or touching
the ground, as most
painters had rendered
them. Muybridge's work
had begun in the 1870s
at the instigation of
former California gover-
nor Leland Stanford,
who owned race horses.

Another of Marey's inventions used a simple but elegant addition to the camera that let him record the flow of human and animal movement on a single photographic plate. A rotating disk with small slots cut into it at regular intervals was spun in front of an open camera lens. A person walking in front of this apparatus would be in a different position each time the open slot on the disk allowed an image to register. The result showed human movement in time and space. Marey called his work chronophotography—that is, time photography.

Marey's images are visually puzzling and attractive, yet he was primarily interested not in their aesthetic merit, but in the way in which they isolated the imperceptible phases of movement

(Fig. 4.53). He continued to improve his photographic devices so that he could eliminate any overlapping of moving figures. He created a camera in which light-sensitive material moved with each exposure. When continuous photographic film, like that used today, was invented, Marey employed it to produce a short film in July 1889, showing how the human hand works. He published his results in articles and books, notably in *The Flight of Birds* (1890), which influenced early attempts to build airplanes.

The photographer Albert Londe (1858–1917), who worked with Charcot (see p. 151) at La Salpêtrière during the 1880s, extended his medical photography into the creating of X-ray photographs (see p. 214) and the study of movement. A line drawing by Paul

4.53
ÉTIENNE-JULES
MAREY, *Joinville Soldier
Walking*, 1883.

Richer (1849–1933), based on one of Londe's stop-action photographs, may have provided the visual vocabulary for *Nude Descending a Staircase # 2* (1912), the influential painting by Marcel Duchamp (1887–1968). In addition, the dotted lines in the center of the canvas probably derive from Marey's geometric drawings[58] (Figs. 4.54, 4.55). Perhaps the greatest effect in the art world of late nineteenth-century photographs of movement was on the Italian Futurists, who came to prominence in 1909.

As his fame and influence grew, Muybridge became a science celebrity, traveling and giving lectures. He visited France, where he met Marey, and he was invited by the University of Pennsylvania in Philadelphia to carry on his experiments there in a specially built outdoor studio. One of Muybridge's supporters at the university was the American realist painter Thomas Eakins (1844–1916). An accomplished amateur photographer, Eakins used Muybridge's photographs in both his teaching and his art to show how humans and animals actually moved. His 1879 painting *A May Morning in the Park* referred to Muybridge's studies of the horses' gait. By blending scientific accuracy with artistic color and composition, Eakins made his point that modern art had to take the findings of science into account. He helped to bring Muybridge

to the University of Pennsylvania, and worked with the photographer in 1884 (Fig. 4.56). Though he later lost interest in perfecting photographs of human movement, Eakins used outdoor photographs of the nude male for his paintings, both as figure studies and to learn how sunlight illuminates the body. In his own way, he attempted to refresh the classical nude. "Nature," he said, "is just as varied and just as beautiful in our day as she was in the time of [the ancient Greek sculptor] Phidias."[59]

Muybridge's time in Philadelphia proved highly productive. He refined his techniques, creating 100,000 images of movement. He photographed female and male nudes, some in casual poses such as turning to embrace a child or laying bricks, which, if not strictly scientific, may have been influenced by Eakins's location of beauty in everyday modern life. After setting up a studio in the zoological gardens, Muybridge recorded the movements of such animals as elks, camels, and elephants. His eleven-volume work *Animal Locomotion* (1887) offered 781 large plates (19⅛ inches by 24⅜ inches). The studies attracted a varied audience, including prominent scientists such as Louis Agassiz, inventors such as Thomas Edison (1847–1931), and artists including Auguste Rodin.

Muybridge's notes indicate that he always made twelve lateral and twenty-four foreshortened (that is, from the front, or from the back) views of his subjects. But few of his final prints contain

FOCUS
Photography and Futurism

The Italian Futurists were a pre-World War I group of artists thrilled by the prospect of a future filled with motion, activity, and change. They were intrigued by the visual language of stop-action photographs. Giacomo Balla (1871–1958) interpreted photographs of sequential movements in a humorous painting, *Dynamism of a Dog on a Leash* (1912). Balla and his celebrated painting were photographed in the photo-dynamic style developed by Anton (or Antonio) Bragaglia (1890–1960). A photographer and filmmaker associated with the Futurists, Bragaglia accentuated the blur of motion that most action photographers regarded as a fault in their images and tried to remove.

Bragaglia's photodynamic images appeared in a 1913 book, *Fotodinamismo futurista* (Fig. 4.57). In words that approximate the goals of Victorian High Art photography, Bragaglia thought his multiple exposures would help revolutionize photography,

by "purifying[,] ennobling and truly elevating it to art."[60] Unlike other practitioners, who tried to elevate photography by making pictures carry a moral lesson or by copying Old Masters, Bragaglia believed that the photographic artist should render the world's invisible vital energy. He proceeded to dissolve the clear resolution and distinctly segmented pictures of motion studies. He adapted Marey's strictly scientific images to his metaphysical aims, believing that both art and science should seek to reveal the spiritual. The photodynamic photograph, with its obscure and blurry areas, allowed him to record reality "unrealistically."

4.57
ANTON GIULIO BRAGAGLIA, *The Futurist Painter Giacomo Balla*, 1912, from *Fotodinamismo futurista*, Rome, 1913.

thirty-six images (Fig. 4.58).[61] As scholar
Marta Braun discovered, Muybridge
often fabricated his final composite pictures, assembling images that play upon
the willingness of the eye and mind to
see photographs arranged from left to
right as having been taken in that order.
About 40 per cent of Muybridge's photographs of movement are composed of
images that were not taken successively,
as he had claimed.[62] Muybridge's stop-
action pictures contrast with the unaltered scientific investigations of Marey.
Possibly his artistic sensibilities inter-
vened when he encountered a technical
difficulty, or perhaps his willingness to
give the appearance of truth began with
his misleading photographs from the
Modoc War (see pp. 140–41).

Directly or indirectly, chronopho-
tographs influenced art. Most immediately, such artists as the French painter
Jean-Louis-Ernest Meissonier (1815–
1891) and Thomas Eakins made their
paintings of horses accord with what
the photographs showed, rather than
what the eye perceived. Adapting art to
science, however, was seen by some
critics as a capitulation to the machine.
As stop-action photographs became
known outside of scientific circles, they
fueled the discussion about the role of
human perception in modern art.

PHOTOGRAPHY AND THE
INVENTION OF MOVING PICTURES

Although devices creating the illusion
of moving pictures existed before the
development of photography, in the late
nineteenth century there was a burgeoning of parlor-game machines and what
were called "philosophical toys," which
whirled images around a horizontal
cylinder. Viewed through tiny slits in the
cylinder, the sequence of pictures showing running horses and the like created
the impression of movement. Limited by
the size of the cylinder, devices such as
the zoëtrope, the praxinoscope, and the
phenakistoscope operated on the same
general principle of tricking the eye
into seeing motion. Muybridge experimented with a contrivance he called the
zoöpraxiscope, which added the magic
lantern's ability to project an image to
the zoëtrope's simulation of movement.
Muybridge used his own photographs of
movement, heavily outlined or painted
over, to form silhouettes. The device,
first demonstrated in 1879, was again
limited by the size of the turning disks.

About the same time that he was
developing the phonograph to record
and project sound, Thomas Edison took
a hint from the success of Muybridge's
zoöpraxiscope and began work on making pictures move. His kinetoscope,

4.58
EADWEARD
MUYBRIDGE,
*Ascending and
Descending Stairs*, from
Animal Locomotion,
plate 504, 1870s.
Library of Congress,
Washington, D.C.

The progression of
climbing and descend-
ing the stairs is not
sequential, yet in most
cases the eye seems
willing to assume
a continuity where
none exists.

introduced in 1894, made images move in a box-like structure with a viewer. Commonly called a "peep show," after the popular street entertainment begun in the eighteenth century, the kineto-scope used flexible film about 50 feet in length. The film was illuminated behind a magnifying lens, and it sped by the viewer at forty-eight frames per second, generating a show that lasted only thir-teen seconds. In Europe, several inven-tors added public projection to the private peep show. In France, the Lumière broth-ers introduced their film projector to the Parisian public late in 1895.

Although attempts to make pictures move predated the invention of photo-graphy, the concurrent invention of motion pictures by different inventors in the late 1880s and the 1890s seems to have been sparked by stop-action experiments, such as those of Marey and Muybridge. Photographic skills expedited the leap from still to moving pictures: for example, Edison viewed Marey's photographs of movement placed on a moving film strip, and the Lumière brothers manufactured photo-graphic supplies in Lyon, before creating their Cinématograph.

The effect of motion pictures on photography within professional, artistic, amateur, and hobbyist circles is a little-known aspect of photographic history. Some photographers became filmmak-ers, but the wider impact of moving pictures on still photography has yet to be written. Where the first photographs immediately explored artistic, travel, and documentary uses, the first films tended to demonstrate movement itself: the arrival of a train, acrobats prancing and tumbling, workers leaving a factory. Photography's varieties were well estab-lished by the 1890s, and none seems to have been superseded by the emergence of film.

THE X-RAY

The 1895 discovery of the X-ray by Wilhelm Conrad Röntgen (1845–1923), a Dutch-German physicist working in Germany, had profound effects outside science and medicine. Röntgen, who had a practical knowledge of photography, was experimenting with electricity and a cathode ray tube, which beamed an image on a screen, when he chanced to observe a force he would later call the

4.59
WILHELM RÖNTGEN, *Frau Röntgen's Hand*, 1895. X-ray. Deutsches Röntgen Museum, Remscheid, Germany.

Röntgen's X-ray of his wife's hand accompa-nied his initial scientific paper reporting on the phenomenon. He exposed the left hand of his wife, Bertha, to the X-ray for fifteen minutes to create one of the first images of its kind. The large bulge is her wedding ring.

"X" or unknown ray. It emanated from the cathode tube and caused a piece of cardboard coated with a fluorescent material to glow in the dark. He soon learned that the rays could pass through the human body, blackening a photo-graphic plate except where they were absorbed by the calcium in bones (Fig. 4.59). In effect, his X-ray photographs were shadowgraphs like those made by William Henry Fox Talbot decades earlier, though not created by light.

X-ray apparatus, like early photo-graphic gear, could be easily constructed. Moreover, like the initial response to the daguerreotype and calotype, the reception of the X-ray was essentially confident. Earlier scientific uses of photography had not provoked the immense fascination that the X-ray did. An inquisitive public could gawk at X-rays at amusement parks and depart-ment stores—also new phenomena on the urban scene. Department store customers stood in line to look through their own hands at the living bone. Since X-rays did not cause physical pain, people assumed they were safe. Even when Edison created the fluoroscope in 1896, eliminating the use of the photo-graphic plate, people still associated the X-ray with photography. Indeed, before the professionalization of radiology, photographers thought of the X-ray as a branch of their practice; "radiophoto-graphers" were not required to have long medical training. After only a year's preparation, Elizabeth Fleischmann (c. 1865–1905) became the first person

FOCUS
Worker Efficiency: The Gilbreths' Time and Motion Studies

Studies of human movement were not confined to the realm of science. The American engineer Frederick Winslow Taylor (1856–1915) studied the steps laborers use to perform tasks. In 1898 he was hired to reorganize the machine shops at Bethlehem Steel in Pennsylvania. To make the shop operate in a linear, rational way, akin to the machine itself, Taylor renovated the shop floor. His most influential change came from his observation of the most efficient workers and the motions they employed to accomplish a task. After breaking down these actions into the smallest units, Taylor ordered the workers to imitate exactly the motions used by the efficient workers to accomplish tasks. His name became synonymous with what he called scientific management. An idea that had been suggested as early as the 1851 Crystal Palace exhibition's celebration of mass production, "Taylorism" spread through the world, boosting productivity and giving management increased control.

Followers of Taylorism used photography to isolate the individual actions used by workers to perform mechanical acts. As electrification of factories and the use of the assembly line and conveyor belts speeded up production in the early twentieth century, Frank Gilbreth (1868–1924) and Lillian Moller Gilbreth (1878–1972) claimed to demonstrate to industrial laborers the most efficient way to get the job done with a minimum of fatigue. In their essay "The Effect of Motion Study upon the Workers," they contended that the orderly performance of tasks would make the workers happier and more prosperous.[63] To make what was called a chronocyclegraph, or time-cycle image, Frank Gilbreth attached small light bulbs to a worker's hands, and photographed the lights as they traced the worker's actions (Fig. 4.60). The Gilbreths then made models of the light tracings in wire. These wire replicas of the most efficient and speedy actions were used to train workers, who ran their hands over the wires to learn the best pattern for their hands to take.[64] The Gilbreths also filmed "micro-motion" studies of workers' actions. Their work was influenced by the photographs of Muybridge and Marey.

The Gilbreths' time-and-motion studies were seen as modern, scientific management of business, and their work, like Taylor's, was imitated around the world. Labor unions soon protested against intrusive cameras and a philosophy of business that reduced humans to a set of standardized, repetitive actions.

4.60
FRANK B. GILBRETH, *Chronocyclegraph of Woman Staking Buttons*, 1917.
Gelatin silver print. National Museum of American History, Smithsonian Institution, Washington, D.C.

to open an X-ray laboratory in California, and pioneered the use of multiple views of a patient's body.[65]

In the public imagination, the X-ray photograph was sometimes associated with the occult. If the X-ray, a powerful but unseen element, could reveal hidden existence, perhaps it could do other things, such as reviving the dead.[66] Perhaps X-ray glasses would allow ordinary people to see through buildings. The technique was, after all, popularly referred to as "The New Sight." Maybe there were other imperceptible rays that could make ghosts visible and humans invisible, reveal human thoughts, or locate a fourth dimension. The idea of a fourth dimension, simplified from mathematics and philosophy, extended the promise of a break with traditional thinking.[67] Some saw the X-ray photograph as proof that spirit photographs— that is, images purporting to record invisible emanations coming from ghosts—were authentic (Fig. 4.61). What seems today like pseudo-science was taken seriously in certain academic circles. In 1909, at the Sorbonne in Paris, a committee was established to study transcendental photography of invisible beings and forces.[68]

To some viewers, seeing beneath clothing via the X-ray had the erotic shiver of the forbidden. A London store even offered X-ray-proof undergarments. Literature's most famous X-ray photograph may be that in Thomas Mann's famous 1924 novel *The Magic Mountain*, in which the main character, Hans, finds an X-ray of his beloved sexually arousing, but identifies a fluoroscope of his own hand with death.

One of the most enduring science fiction novels, H. G. Wells's *The Invisible Man* (1897), is based on the idea that a man's exposure to "roentgen rays" can make his body invisible.

A few doctors and dentists purchased X-ray machines as soon as they were manufactured. Public acceptance grew gradually, along with medical use during armed conflict, beginning with X-ray-equipped field hospitals set up by the Italians in their 1896 attempt to colonize Abyssinia, and culminating in the routine use of the X-ray during World War I. Soon X-ray photographs were taken from many angles, to pinpoint the location of bullets and shrapnel. As research trickled in about the dangers of X-rays, in an era when the average medical exposure was about one hour long, the public had to adjust to the idea that they could be injured by a substance that could not be seen or tracked, and which took months or years for its effects to develop. California X-ray pioneer Elizabeth Fleischmann died from cancer induced by the new technology.

As historian Bettyann Holtzmann Kevles points out, X-rays were "the first invisible substances generated by scientists to profoundly affect human perception."[69] Several scholars have suggested that the multiple perspectives and monochromatic Cubist palette of Picasso and Georges Braque (1882– 1963) may relate to X-ray photographs. The Italian Futurists embraced the X-ray. One of the movement's founders, Umberto Boccioni (1882–1916), believed that the X-ray would help to wipe away outworn attitudes. "Who can still believe in the opacity of bodies," he wrote. Futurist art, he maintained, was like the X-ray—they both "sharpened and multiplied sensitiveness."[70] A 1913 watercolor by Francis Picabia (1879– 1953), a Paris-born artist who worked in France and the United States, was titled *New York Seen Through the Body*. (In France, the phrase *à travers le corps*—literally, "through the body"— was used by practitioners to advertise X-ray examinations.) Picabia's painting let viewers see through buildings to the structure behind them.

Experiments with X-ray technology by Viennese chemists Eduard Valenta (1857–1937) and Josef Maria Eder (1855–1944) (who would write one of

4.61
W. MOBSBY, *Untitled* **(News photograph of Arthur Conan Doyle), 1921, from Conan Doyle's** *The Wanderings of a Spiritualist***, 1922.**

The author Arthur Conan Doyle (1859–1930) was an amateur photographer. Late in life, he became a spiritualist, and collected spirit or psychic photographs. He included this blurred photograph of himself in *The Wanderings of a Spiritualist* (1922), claiming that it showed the presence of supernatural forces.

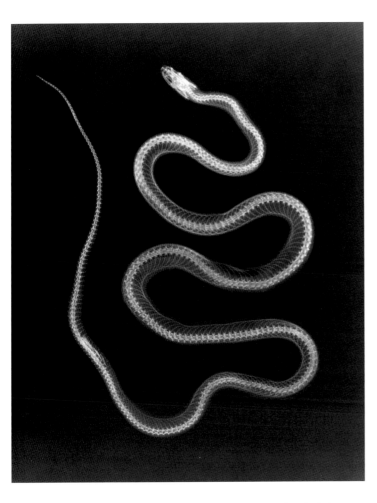

exploration, and it should be recognised as almost the duty of educated travellers in the less known parts of the world to put on permanent record, before it is too late, such of these phases as they may observe."[73] Roland Bonaparte (1858–1924), a relative of Napoleon I, commissioned thousands of photographs around the world, and photographer John Thomson wrote in 1885, "no expedition, indeed, now-a-days, can be considered complete without photography to place on record the geographical and ethnological features of the journey."[74]

Official expeditions set out to clarify national and regional borders, as well as to research roadways, railroads, and resources. As in the mid-nineteenth century, the camera and the gun were accepted equipment for the journey (Fig. 4.63). Likewise, the classification of human types through physical differences continued apace, aspiring to become ever more comprehensive. In short, while the completeness of photography was debated in the realm of art, the medium's objectivity was increasingly central to social science.

4.62 (above)
EDUARD VALENTA &
JOSEF MARIA EDER,
Aesculapian Snake,
1896, from the portfolio
*Versuche über photo-
graphie mittlest der
Röntgenschen Strahlen*.
X-ray. George Eastman
House, Rochester,
New York.

In their arrangement, Valenta and Eder emphasized the delicate bones of the snake by coiling it in repeated curves upon the photographic plate. American critic Christian Brinton wrote that "there is no phase of activity or facet of nature which should be forbidden to the creative artist. The X-ray may quite as legitimately claim his attention as the rainbow."[71]

4.63 (below)
ARTHUR RADCLYFFE
DUGMORE,
*The Author and his
Camera*, from *Camera
Adventures in the
African Wilds*, 1910.
Royal Geographic
Society, London.

Arthur Radclyffe Dugmore's *Camera Adventures in the African Wilds* appeared in 1910. Opposing big-game hunting in Africa, he claimed that hunting with the camera was more exciting than hunting with the gun.[75]

the histories of photography) led them to issue a portfolio of X-ray photographs that expressed aesthetic delight in the revealing images (Fig. 4.62).

PHOTOGRAPHY, SOCIAL SCIENCE, AND EXPLORATION

While art photography was influenced by science and technology, travel, exploration, survey, and social-scientific photography continued patterns set in the mid-nineteenth century. The encyclopedic urge to collect images was newly invigorated by the growing sense that traditional life around the world was disappearing so rapidly that it must be recorded. In the *British Journal of Photography* (1889), Cosmo Burton suggested that a responsible photographic society should "keep a library of great albums containing a record as complete as it can be made, and in *permanent photographs only* of the present state of the world."[72] Similarly, British anthropologist and colonial administrator Everard im Thurn (1852–1932) wrote that "primitive phases of life are fast fading from the world in this age of restless travel and

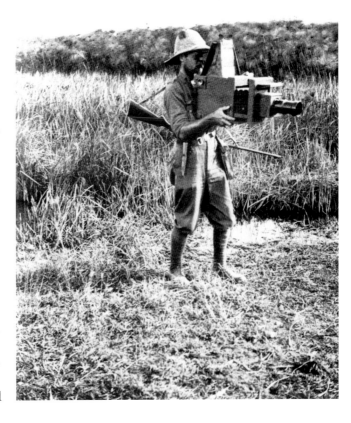

PHOTOGRAPHING AFRICA

In Africa, the Western imagination constructed an alternative to the industrializing world, while simultaneously exploiting its natural wealth. Notions of Africa as the "dark continent," historically cut off from the European Enlightenment and racially inferior, were rekindled in the late nineteenth century. Social Darwinists misinterpreted Darwin's theories to mean that people and societies that had not developed in the manner of Western culture were inherently inferior.

Africa, particularly sub-Saharan Africa, was seen as a prime example of timeless backwardness.

Renowned missionary Dr. David Livingstone (1813–1873), famously assumed lost during one of his attempts to bring Christianity to Africa, took along his brother Charles (1821–1873) as a photographer on an earlier Zambezi expedition (1858–64). Livingstone the missionary also commanded an official British exploration, seeking mineral wealth and agricultural potential. He favored visual aids to his work, referring

4.64
PHOTOGRAPHER UNKNOWN, *Henry Morton Stanley and Kululu* (detail), c. 1872. Albumen *carte-de-visite*. London Stereoscopic Company, National Portrait Gallery, London.

The setting of this *carte-de-visite* was a painted backdrop in a London studio. Stanley is being served tea by Kululu (Ndugu M'hali) (1864–1877), who was given to him by a slave-trader. From the age of eight, Kululu was Stanley's personal servant. He died crossing the Congo River during Stanley's 1874–77 expedition.[76]

MR. STANLEY,

IN THE DRESS HE WORE WHEN HE MET LIVINGSTONE IN AFRICA.

Stereoscopic Co.   *Copyright.*

to the magic lantern he brought with him to show Bible stories as the "oxyhydrogen light of civilization."[77] Charles Livingstone was replaced by John Kirk, who made the first camera images of an official British expedition in Africa.[78] In Kirk's photographs, the dense African foliage indicated fertile land, potentially suitable for Western agriculture. At the same time, the jungle also symbolized to Europeans the triumph of nature over civilization.

While writing for the *New York Herald* in 1871, Henry Morton Stanley (1841–1904) found the ailing missionary, and uttered the now well-known phrase, "Dr. Livingstone, I presume?" There were no photographers on the scene, and Livingstone's death in 1873 in a remote area of Africa precluded photographs being made of him. But public curiosity was served when Stanley was photographed in a London studio, supposedly dressed in the very clothes he wore when he met Livingstone (Fig. 4.64).

By 1880, companies that commissioned and published photographs were established in coastal areas of colonial Africa.[79] Interest in Africa grew after the 1885 Berlin Conference, which authorized European nations with coastal bases to expand their interests into the African interior so long as they did not impinge on other colonial territories. Beginning in the 1880s, large photographically illustrated books

depicting people, land, and riches were published.[80] Trophy animals hunted during safaris were also frequently photographed. Typically, photographs showed Africans as primitive, and European culture and enterprise as progressive. At the turn of the nineteenth century, when the postcard fad flourished, images of Africans were often reproduced in this format (Fig. 4.65). It has been argued that Picasso adapted poses of Africans on postcards made by François-Edmond Fortier (1862–1928), who published more than 8,000 postcards of Africa, for his work during 1906–07, including *Les Demoiselles d'Avignon* (1907).[81]

The spirit of African expansion was expressed in *The Queen's Empire* (1897), a British book celebrating Queen Victoria's Diamond Jubilee. It contained 300 photographic images, including customs, education, and Western engineering feats. The text boasted that "in every part of the Empire we shall find some trace of the work which Britain is doing throughout the world—the work of civilizing, of governing, of protecting life and property, and of extending the benefits of trade and commerce."[82] Armed conflict in Africa was photographed, but was subject to censorship, as in the Boer War (1899–1902), when soldiers and armaments were regularly photographed. Yet, as historian Jorge Lewinski remarked, "there are no pictures of barbed wire, of the results

4.65
PHOTOGRAPHER UNKNOWN, *The Sons of the Cannibals Contemplating the Passion of the Redeemer*, c. 1910. Postcard. Archivio Provinciale dei Padri Cappuccini, Milan, Italy.

Schools were often set up by missionaries in Africa. The exaggerated shadow of the child's head on the print of the Crucifixion was probably added to show symbolically that Christianity was appropriate for Africans.

FOCUS
The *National Geographic*

The National Geographic Society in the United States began in 1888 as a relatively small group of professional geographers and sponsors. When Alexander Graham Bell (1847–1922), the inventor of the telephone, took over the society's leadership, he stressed dissemination of knowledge. Gilbert H. Grosvenor (1875–1966) was employed to build circulation of the society's publication, which he did by studying the content and marketing of widely read magazines, such as *Harper's*. The *National Geographic's* friendly tone and especially its uncomplicated pictures made it a success. While the society's 1915 policy statement underscored "absolute accuracy," it also envisaged an "abundance of beautiful, instructive, and artistic illustrations." Moreover, *National Geographic* promised that "nothing of a partisan or controversial character is printed."[83] The possible conflicts between these goals, such as the clash between accuracy and

aesthetics, were not engaged. In his 1909 book *Scenes from Every Land*, Grosvenor reprinted upbeat, pleasant images from the magazine, offering armchair adventure, while avoiding the worst stereotypes of native people. Still, *National Geographic* often pictured people in the less developed world as primitive, implicitly suggesting that non-industrial societies remain static without Western intervention. Despite early twentieth-century prudery, the magazine did show nudity, especially female nudity (Fig. 4.66). In the United States, a longstanding joke has it that American teenagers have their first look at naked bodies in *National Geographic*. Its policy of accuracy, and its announced educational goal, allowed, even invited, readers to look. In effect, *National Geographic* carried forward the high-minded dual pursuit of information and entertainment beloved by fans of the stereographic photograph.

4.66
UNDERWOOD & UNDERWOOD, *Girls in a Village of East Equatorial Africa*, 1909. Photo and copyright by Underwood & Underwood, New York.

5 4   The dying Bugler's last call—a battlefield incident, Gras Pan, South Africa.
Copyright 1900 by Underwood & Underwood.

4.67
UNDERWOOD &
UNDERWOOD, *The
Dying Bugler's Last
Call—A Battlefield
Incident*, Gras Pan,
South Africa, 1900.
Stereograph, gelatin
silver print. Gernsheim
Collection. Harry
Ransom Humanities
Research Center,
University of Texas
at Austin.

Historian Roy Flukinger
observed that this
photograph was among
the last sentimental
and idealistic images of
war.[85] The harsh realities
of combat and its harm-
ful effects on individual
soldiers would be
pictured throughout
the twentieth century.

of the scorched-earth policy, of Boer
women and children in prison camps
where the mortality rate was nearly
50 per cent and where some 20,000
died."[84] Instead, photographers produced symbolic and sentimental pictures. Underwood & Underwood issued
individual views and boxed sets from
the Boer War for an international market, including a staged stereographic
photograph of a patriotic dying soldier
making a last bugle call (Fig. 4.67).

PHOTOGRAPHING THE PACIFIC
PARADISE: SAMOA

In Western art and literature, the Pacific
islands were long seen as a paradise,
where labor was almost unknown and
physical wants, including sexual ones,
were easily gratified. At the same time,
the inhabitants were seen as exotic
primitives, unable or unwilling to live
according to Western standards. Great
curiosity about the Pacific area was sustained in the eighteenth and nineteenth
centuries by the teasing contradictions
between the Western Puritan work ethic
and a life of reputedly unearned ease
and abundance. In particular, images
of nude or sparsely clad Pacific island
women were taken to indicate a sexual
and moral slackness, owing to the lack
of struggle with nature.

Commercial photographers were
aware of these powerful preconceptions

and were quick to respond. In the
late 1890s, as the Samoan Islands
became trade and naval bases for the
United States and Germany, they
attracted widespread interest. John
Davis (active mid-1870s; d. 1893), the
first commercial photographer in Apia
(then German Samoa; now the capital
of Western Samoa), told a visitor that
"hundreds of native girls and youths
presented themselves at his studio in
hopes that they would make photographs of commercial value for book
illustrations and for selling to tourists."
Yet he chose "only two, or three at the
most, who possessed the thick lips and
sensual features which coincided with
the stock European idea of the South
Sea type."[86]

Photography supported social
stereotypes, even for people who had
been there and bought photographs
as souvenirs. Historian Alison Devine
Nordström suggested that, because
the commercial photographs used for
postcards, stereographs, and half-tones
were stereotypical, once dealers and
distributors collected enough images to
satisfy customers, they did not require
new ones.[87] These images reinforced
the notion that Samoa, like most of
the Pacific islands, was a timeless,
uneventful place. Postcards of Samoa
frequently featured Samoans in scanty
native clothing, as well as beaches,

4.68
JOHN DAVIS,
Samoa Princess Fa'ane,
Apia, c. 1893. Albumen
print on board. Phillips
Library Collection.
Peabody Essex
Museum, Salem,
Massachusetts.

Bare-breasted Samoan
women were often
pictured wearing an
elaborate traditional
headdress and carrying
a large club. Western
photographers favored
the exotic look of
the *taupou,* or village
maiden, a position
of honor in Samoan
society. Thus anthropo-
logical imagery mixed
with tourist visions of
the Pacific.

palm trees, and waterfalls (Fig. 4.68).
The Western presence, in the form of
commercial and governmental buildings, was also pictured. Anthropological
photographs often featured body tattoos,
long associated in visual representations
with the Pacific islands.[88]

CRIMINAL LIKENESSES

During the 1880s, photographs of criminals became routine in police work.
In the past, the camera had been used
occasionally to record the appearance of
suspects and criminals. In the 1850s,
the Swiss government used it to register

indigents and stateless persons, and Alexander Gardner made portraits of President Lincoln's assassins and of their execution (see Fig. 3.37). But in the late nineteenth century, the photography of criminals became as standardized as anthropological photography, largely because of the work of Paris police official Alphonse Bertillon (1853–1914). Son of Louis Adolphe Bertillon, a well-known anthropometrician who used statistics to describe humankind, Alphonse Bertillon developed a verbal and visual system to describe criminals. His main interest was to identify recidivists—that is, repeat offenders. Called "speaking likenesses," Bertillon's invention was what is known today as the mugshot (Fig. 4.69).

4.69
PHOTOGRAPHER UNKNOWN, *Synoptic Table of Facial Expressions for the Purposes of Systematic Identification*, according to Alphonse Bertillon's system, n.d. Musée de la Préfecture de Police, Paris.

Alphonse Bertillon considered that objective photographs of a person's face and profile, together with measurements and typology of specific body parts, such as the ear and the mouth, would produce a unique record of an individual that could be used by the police to identify criminals. To standardize his photographs, he insisted on a consistent focal length, lighting, and distance of the subject from the camera.

As historian Allan Sekula pointed out, Bertillon's system resembled the efficiency systems developed by Frederick Winslow Taylor and Frank and Lillian Gilbreth (see p. 215). Breaking down physical appearance into small, standardized units allowed unskilled clerks to file and retrieve criminal photographs.[89] The creation of large information archives, such as those used in police work, strengthened government control of the populace and, with anthropological photography, came close to fulfilling the abiding nineteenth-century dream of a vast, encyclopedic collection of images.

Bertillon's publications, such as *L'Identité des récidivistes et la loi de régulation* (*The Identity of Recidivists and Legal Regulation*) (1883) and *Identification anthropométrique* (*Anthropometric Identification*) (1893), influenced criminology and police procedures around the world. They fitted into an existing trend that saw criminality as evidence of degeneration—that is, of faulty innate tendencies in the individual brought out by the pressures of modern society.

French statistician Gabriel Tarde published *La Criminalité comparée* (*Comparative Criminality*) (1886), and British science writer Havelock Ellis followed with his own tract *The Criminal* (1890), which contained photographs of American, Russian, and Australian criminals, purporting to show the stigmata, or physical signs, of their moral defects. Ellis's friend the American medical doctor Eugene S. Talbot proclaimed that "criminals form a variety of the human family quite distinct from law-abiding men," and liberally illustrated the 1901 edition of his book *Degeneracy: Its Causes, Signs, and Results* with photographs of criminals and others whom he considered deviant.[90] New York city police inspector Thomas Byrnes glamorized detective work in his 1886 *Professional Criminals of America*, which was also illustrated with photographs. Perhaps the most influential crime tract, Italian Cesare Lombroso's *L'Uomo delinquente* (*The Criminal Man*) (1876), was expanded in the 1890s with added illustrations. Unlike Bertillon, Lombroso thought criminality inherent, the expression of a biological element persisting from primitive times. In the late nineteenth century, fingerprinting, developed under British colonial rule in India and promoted by British scientist Francis Galton (1822–1911), was gradually introduced alongside the mugshot.[91]

Even small, local police departments commissioned mugshots of criminals. In Marysville, California, a small town in the Sacramento Valley, portrait photographer Clara Sheldon Smith (b. 1862) fulfilled a contract with the city from 1900 to 1908, contributing about 500 photographs to the local rogues' gallery (Fig. 4.70). Because prisoners were often brought to her studio unannounced, she sometimes photographed them using the backdrops and lighting set up for her regular customers.[92]

4.70
CLARA SHELDON SMITH, *Claude F. Hankins: Murderer,* 1904. Arne Svenson Collection.

On July 1904, fourteen-year-old Claude F. Hankins shot and killed an older man whom he claimed tried to commit "a crime against nature" with him. He was sentenced to sixteen years in San Quentin State Prison. He received early parole in 1914.

Another systematizing approach to human description and photography was used by British scientist Francis Galton, best known for his studies of heredity and for founding the science of eugenics, which he defined as "science which deals with all influences that improve the inborn qualities of a race."[93] In Galton's words, an improved humankind (presumably British) "should be better fitted to fulfill our vast imperial opportunities."[94] Eugenics suggested a natural social order based on human ability that would surpass social class and wealth; Galton believed that photographs would show human superiority, just as they showed mountains and cathedrals. Photography was touted by reformers such as Galton as superior to painting, which was based on subjectivity, not objective description. Eugenics and photography attracted people in science, industry, academia, and government who had gained success through intellectual achievement rather than birthright. Galton used the mugshot format to photograph prisoners as well as patients, and recommended that the public create family albums with full-face and profile portraits arranged chronologically.[95]

Where Bertillon hoped to use photography to find unique individuals within a vast photographic archive, Galton sought to show general hereditary laws. For his 1883 *Inquiries into Human Faculty*, he invented a form of composite photography to make his points. Relying on the belief in photography's truthfulness, he called such images "real generalization,"[96] of criminals, tuberculosis patients, Jews, and families (Fig. 4.71). Composite images never ceased to interest viewers. They were powerfully invigorated in the late twentieth century by the ease with which images could be melded by computers.

WAR AND PHOTOGRAPHY

The capacity of newspapers and magazines to print photographs, the growth of journals devoted to contemporary events, and increased speed in communications and transportation systems, made it technically possible for the public to see much more of war than in the past. During the American Civil War, topical photographs had to be viewed in a gallery, photographic studio, or bookseller's shop, often weeks after an event. Only engraved interpretations of photographs appeared in journals. But with the success of the half-tone processes for printing photographs with text, photographs could be quickly reproduced and generously displayed in

**4.71
FRANCIS GALTON,
Untitled, from *Inquiries into Human Faculty and its Development*, 1883.**

On a single photographic plate, Galton combined images of the mental and physical types, exposing one negative after another until all had been registered. He computed the exposure time by dividing the exposure time for one plate by the number of photographs he planned to register. Galton used composite photography to obtain what he called "representative faces" and "pictorial statistics" that condense large statistical tables.

the press. As historian Susan D. Moeller argued, the Spanish–American War became the first "living-room" war.[97]

THE SPANISH–AMERICAN WAR

The conflict between Spain, which ruled Cuba, and the United States simmered for several years before American troops were sent into Cuba. Egged on by many inflammatory articles and shocking photographs of atrocities published in newspapers owned by the Hearst and Pulitzer syndicates, Americans empathized with the Cuban guerrilla forces fighting for independence. American newspapers further inflamed the situation by blaming the Spanish for the sinking of the U.S. battleship *Maine*, on February 15, 1898, in the harbor of Havana, Cuba. "Remember the *Maine*" became a popular slogan, and large photographic firms marketed stereographs of the incident. Of all their pictures, Keystone View Company sold more of the wreckage of the *Maine* than any other.[98] The Spanish–American War (April 25–August 12, 1898) was probably the first war filmed by the motion picture camera. Some early filmmakers even faked battle scenes on the roofs of New York City buildings, using toy boats floating in bathtubs, and cigar smoke for the fumes of burning.

On April 25, 1898, the American Congress voted for war, setting off a stream of volunteers to serve in the military. Among them was the then Assistant Secretary of the Navy, Theodore Roosevelt, who formed the First Volunteer Cavalry, known as the Rough Riders. The war's lack of planning, shortages of supplies, and general mismanagement recall the Crimean conflict. Roosevelt's famous cavalry charge up San Juan hill, sung in the press as a valiant and heroic act, was in fact a rash strategy born of desperation. There were no photographs of the actual charge, and the celebrated paintings of the incident by Frederick Remington (1861–1909), who was in Cuba to make illustrations for William Randolph Hearst's New York *Journal*, were made after Remington had returned to the United States. Nevertheless, the favorable publicity generated by the charge ushered Roosevelt into the governorship of New York (1898–1901). In office, Roosevelt acquired a permanent retinue of reporters and photojournalists.

Despite the public interest in the war, few photographers were assigned to it. Frances Benjamin Johnston, who was running a successful portrait studio in Washington, D.C. (see p. 190), worked as a correspondent for the Bain News Service. When Admiral George Dewey was returning from the American victory in the Philippine Islands, a Spanish possession ceded to the United States at

4.72
JAMES "JIMMY" HARE, *Carrying out the Wounded During the Fighting at San Juan,* c. 1914. Gernsheim Collection. Harry Ransom Humanities Research Center, University of Texas at Austin.

During the Spanish–American War, Hare photographed exclusively for *Collier's* magazine. With American writer Stephen Crane, he followed the Rough Riders up Kettle Hill, the major fortress in the San Juan hills. He did not photograph the famous charge, but depicted the removal of the wounded.

the end of the conflict, she got the first interview with him, titled the "Hero of Manila Bay." With Jessie Tarbox Beals (1870–1942), the first American woman to hold a full-time position as a staff photographer on an American newspaper, Johnston was among the earliest women photojournalists.

James Henry Hare (1856–1946) gained a reputation for war photography (Fig. 4.72). Journalists about to sail to cover the Mexican Revolution (1911–14) asked, "Where is Jimmy Hare? This cannot be a war. Jimmy Hare is not here."[99] His notoriety bespeaks the hot competition among magazines and newspapers that sparked the expansion of photojournalism in the early twentieth century. He became part of a team of writers from *Collier's*, which covered both sides of the war between Russia and Japan (1904–05). He also photographed the San Francisco earthquake of April 1906, the First Balkan War (1912–13), and World War I. The magazine boasted that "wherever there is an army in the field, and clash of arms and bullets and the tragedies of war ... there, too, is a man from *Collier's*."[100]

WORLD WAR I

During the Spanish–American War, while news stories could be cabled to newspapers competing for the most topical articles, photographs still had to be transported by sea and land. Nevertheless, the potential existed for civilians to see war in greater detail than ever before. By World War I, it was clear to military officials that both photographs and news stories should be broadly managed to keep clandestine operations secret, and to keep up spirits at home. The assassination of the Archduke Franz Ferdinand (1863–1914), heir to the Austro-Hungarian monarchy, in the Bosnian city of Sarajevo on June 28, 1914, became the trigger for conflict between Germany, Austria-Hungary, and Italy (the Triple Alliance) and Belgium and the Triple Entente, which consisted of France, Russia, and Britain. The United States did not enter the engagement until April 1917. Trench warfare, which characterized the conflict on the Western, or European, Front, caused unprecedented loss of life (see Fig. 4.75). Ten to 13 million people died in hostilities sustained by the mass

production of armaments.[101] On average, troops endured a death and injury rate of 58 per cent.

During the Spanish–American War, newspapers led public opinion in the United States, but during World War I, governments took the lead. Homefront morale proved less of a problem than expected, because the press practiced self-censorship. During the war, photographs were shown in galleries, including the Grafton Galleries in London, which in December 1916 exhibited work done for the Canadian War Records Office. The prints, enlarged to 3 by 3 feet, up to 6 by 10 feet, resembled traditional heroic painting in both size and subject matter.[102] Although the press did not seek to undermine official pronouncements, or to offer the soldier's view of battle, it did critique the photographs of the enemy. In Germany, a regular column in the *Deutsche Photographen Zeitung* (*German Photographic Newspaper*) reported on "the photographic lies our enemies tell."[103] Britain prohibited making photographs of corpses or scenes of conflict. After 1916, soldiers were buried where they were killed, rather than transported home.[104] Horrific tales from battles such as Gallipoli and Verdun were generally not backed up with photographs that the public could see, creating a profound difference between the experience of soldiers and public awareness, especially in Britain, which did not undergo trench warfare on its own soil.[105]

Photographers were eventually banned from the Western Front, causing newspapers and illustrated serials to rely on artists, and photographs already in stock. Another problem troubled photographers and editors alike. *The War Illustrated*, a serial, announced in November 1914 that "from the pictorial point of view modern warfare lacks much which the battlefields of the past provided. Soldiers today are fighting enemies on the continent whom they never see ... For this reason the great mass of photographs which reach us do not show actual hostilities."[106] Others complained that the war, conducted on flat plains, under cover of cloud and darkness, offered uninspired photographs. Occasionally, events such as soldiers "going over the top" of the trenches, were staged for the camera, the presence of which would draw fire during a real charge.[107]

Press photography was not the only kind made during the war. In Britain, the Snapshots from Home League encouraged citizens to send comforting pictures to soldiers (Fig. 4.73). Nurses, ambulance drivers, and soldiers brought small cameras to the war (Fig. 4.74), and newspapers printed photographs found on battlefields, in hopes of identifying the soldiers who might have possessed them. Personal photographs recorded shocking material not considered appropriate for general circulation. The military, meanwhile, experimented with official photographers, whose numbers were limited, but who were given privileged access to troops and events. Britain, Australia, Canada, New Zealand, France, the United States, and Germany all employed official photographers,

often military personnel, whose role was to record, rather than issue photographs to the press. International photographic distributors, such as Underwood & Underwood and Keystone View, sent photographers to the war. Aerial photography for military reconnaissance was perfected; in 1918 Edward Steichen became chief of the newly formed Photographic Service for the United States military.

As in previous wars, gruesome images of the enemy dead were published, but pictures of one's own casualties were mostly limited to the injured receiving speedy humane treatment. A German directive urged photographers to record the "fairness of the German troops and the destructive cruelty of the enemy."[108] Yet as the war went on, greater recognition of its terrible cost began to show up in photographs. Official Canadian photographer William Rider-Rider (1889–1979)

4.73
ARTIST UNKNOWN,
Send them all Snapshots from Home! from *Amateur Photographer*, August 2, 1915.
Birmingham Central Library, Birmingham, England.

Part of the British volunteer effort on the home front was the coordinated effort to send soldiers abroad pictures of their loved ones at home. In a poster made for the YMCA, which sponsored the drive, the woman on the right can be seen taking a photograph of a young child. In the center, a soldier brags about the image he has just received.

**4.74
PHOTOGRAPHER
UNKNOWN,** *Untitled*
(Soldiers in World War I
trenches), n.d.

Although forbidden to
do so, soldiers some-
times brought cameras
with them to the front.
In this haunting image,
a technical flaw caused
the figure on the right
to fade into the muddy
wall of the trench,
inadvertently symboliz-
ing the death of soldiers
trying to gain a small
amount of ground
separating them from
the enemy.

took photographs of the dismal, muddy
trenches at Passchendaele, where the
Germans first used mustard gas (Fig.
4.75). After the war, as the public learned
more of its horrors, images of the
trenches came to epitomize the conflict.

THE RUSSIAN REVOLUTION

The uprising of workers and intellectuals against the Russian monarchy was
facilitated by the government's distraction during World War I. The various
confrontations between March and
November 1917 were not programati-
cally photographed, and, until recently,
most photographs of the revolution
seemed to derive from motion picture
film of such events as the storming
of the Winter Palace. In the post-Cold
War period, images are beginning to
emerge from Russian archives, promising more information about the use
of photographic propaganda by all the
factions. One series of images of the
Russian Revolution was made by the
Bulla photographic agency (Fig. 4.76).
Founded by Karl Bulla (1854–1929),
the agency sent photographs to such
publications as Germany's illustrated
newspapers. Bulla, who also made
photographs of the Russian elite, emigrated to Estonia after the revolution,
leaving his sons to carry on the business.
Viktor Bulla (1883–1944?) became
one of the first to film the news with a
motion picture camera.

PHILOSOPHY AND
PRACTICE: THE REAL THING

In his 1893 short story "The Real
Thing," Henry James tells of a handsome and prominent husband and wife
who have lost their fortune. Once they
were such social celebrities that photographers made their likenesses to sell
in shops. Now financially desperate,
the couple visits an artist who makes
illustrations of contemporary life for
magazines. They hope to earn money by
posing as "the *real* thing; a gentleman,
you know, or a lady."[109] But the artist is
frustrated in attempts to create the illusion of wealth and elegance by using
them as models, and employs instead
a lower-class man and woman who can
more convincingly assume an affluent
attitude. The formerly well-to-do couple
briefly become servants in his home,
then disappear into the city.

The contrast between appearance
and reality was a central issue in the late
nineteenth century and early twentieth.
In both the visual arts and literature,
it appeared in the repeated concern with
masks and identity. In Oscar Wilde's
The Picture of Dorian Gray (1884), the
main character does not age or betray
the effects of his debauched behavior,
but a portrait of him evidences physical
and spiritual decay. The developing
relationship between acceptable public
appearance and the avid consumption

of mass-produced commodities is portrayed in Theodore Dreiser's *Sister Carrie* (1900), a novel whose eponymous heroine is an actor who defines herself in fantasies of material goods, especially as arrayed in a department store.

Photography was increasingly used in the fabrication of biased social evidence. A much reprinted story in legal journals during the late 1880s told of a lawyer who meets a photographer. The attorney accuses the photography profession of making him lose a case. The photographer replies, "you should get some photographs taken on your side also."[111] In effect, the photograph simultaneously confirmed and denied truth, while emphasizing the appearance of accuracy.

In 1893, when Abdulhamid II (1842–1918; r. 1876–1909), ruler of the Ottoman Empire, learned that his dominion was being perceived as "the sick man of Europe," he sent elaborate photographic albums to Britain, France, Germany, and the United States, hoping to change perceptions. Rather than images featuring timeless peasant life, the albums contained photographs of girls' schools, fashionable Western-style shops, a modern military, and factories located in the Empire. Whereas the

Ottoman Empire album comprised actual photographs, the half-tone process enabled localities to produce "booster books," illustrated descriptions of cities emphasizing only those aspects that would encourage commerce.

In a 1909 address to the National Child Labor Committee, Lewis Hine spoke directly to the question of photographic truth. He held that the photograph itself was a symbol of reality, not reality. He warned that an "unbounded faith in the integrity of photographs is often rudely shaken," because "while photographs may not lie, liars may photograph."[112]

The problem of appearances took many forms, sometimes highlighting the limits of ordinary human sense perception. Some photographers, such as Stieglitz, were influenced by the French philosopher Henri Bergson (1859–1941), extracts from whose *Creative Evolution* and *Laughter* appeared in *Camera Work*. Bergson's concern with the limits of intelligence and the need for intuition to perceive beyond appearances was deliciously vague and readily popularized. It blended with notions of the occult and the fourth dimension, and fostered the belief that the spirit

**4.75
WILLIAM RIDER-RIDER,** *Untitled* (Devastation on the battlefield of Passchendaele taken with a panoramic camera), 1917. Imperial War Museum, London.

In June 1917, the poet T. S. Eliot (1888–1965) forwarded a letter written by a soldier to *The Nation*. Eliot's correspondent described the front as "mud like porridge, trenches like shallow and sloping cracks in the porridge, porridge that stinks in the sun."[110]

photograph and the X-ray revealed a world not previously perceptible. For Stieglitz, stretching toward the immaterial meant photographing clouds, not as weather phenomena, nor as pleasing abstract shapes, but as "Equivalents" to ideas that were beyond words (see Fig. 4.25). To art photographers, intuitive insight meant rejecting the appearance of optical reality, and investigating a world of symbols and clues to hidden meanings. In that sense the haze of Pictorialism did not mask reality, but suggested its promise.

In contrast to the static, compartmentalized domain of the archive, Bergson's world was in constant flux. It resembled the experience of the modern, dynamic city, where anonymous people flowed along the streets, an endless current—like the electricity increasingly lighting the metropolis and energizing the factories. While Bergson himself saw camera images as stubbornly mundane, others found just the opposite in scientific photographs of movement, which they argued hinted at a spiritual world beyond physical fact.

For those photographers who eschewed Pictorialism, authenticity was not a simple matter. At the 1904 World's Fair in St. Louis, which presented about 2,000 indigenous peoples in the largest anthropological exhibition ever staged to date, visitors were invited to travel from Africa to Asia, visiting simulated environments and buying photographs and postcards of places that were staged especially for the fair. The effect was far more sophisticated than the painted scrim and gently tinkling cowbells of Daguerre's Diorama (see pp. 11–12), but visitors still accepted the photographs and the environments as simulations, a category between the real and the false that was neither actual nor deceptive. Similarly, while studying the indigenous peoples of the northwest coast of Canada and the northeast coast of Siberia, anthropologist Franz Boas (1858–1942) eliminated traces of the contemporary world, photographing people performing traditional tasks in front of backdrops (Fig. 4.77). Performances before the camera were as old as photography itself, but the practice that would eventually be called documentary photography maintained the myth of objective and unaltered observation.

A split emerged between those who maintained that photography was a channel for intuitive insight and

4.76
PHOTOGRAPHER
UNKNOWN,
*Demonstration by
Revolutionary
Democrats, Petrograd,
June 18, 1917.*
Silver bromide print.
Saltykov-Shchedrin
State Public Library,
St. Petersburg, Russia.

Petrograd (St. Petersburg) was the scene of decisive developments during the Russian Revolution. In February 1917 the Tsar abdicated after demonstrations in Petrograd and Moscow in which troops mutinied and joined the protestors. Press photographers were ready to catch new developments in Petrograd, where workers and soldiers were quick to organize public protests about food shortages and power sharing with Moscow.

self-expression, and those who set up systems relying on the medium's objectivity. It was a split implicit in photographic practice from the first, but it broadened as that practice expanded. The wide division echoed the conflict between positivism—the outlook adopted by science and social science, which asserted that knowledge was derived from the observation of facts—and metaphysics, which suggested that there were important meanings beyond those perceptible in human intellectual systems.

The disagreement was summed up by a commentator for a popular magazine in 1894: "Wherein [photography] presents facts, it is a science. Wherein it presents ideas, it is an art."[113] Science was not without ideas, but it derived its legitimacy from impersonal observation and record keeping. Art, on the other hand, originated in the personal and intuitive experience, and yielded another, even greater sort of truth. Scientific observation rested on a separation between the observed and the observer that did not acknowledge that photographers tinkered with what was observed, as, for example, Muybridge did when he reordered sequences of photographs, or as Hine did when he deliberately eliminated from his picture "non-essential and conflicting interests."[114] Bergson rejected that division, in favor of a fluid interchange between the observer and the observed.

At the turn of the twentieth century, photography was no longer associated with new and sudden social shifts. The quickening of technological and scientific progress, and resultant social change, were symbolized above all by electricity, which was lighting cities, running street cars, and powering large factories. As a machine, the camera was aligned with the First Industrial Revolution. Electricity powered the Second Industrial Revolution, which included: the telephone; the combine, which reaped and threshed grain; automatic looms in the textile industry; the adding machine; the widespread use of typewriters; and the electric light bulb, together with power plants and the network delivering electrical power. Many late nineteenth-century writers saw electricity as a metaphor for rapid and powerful change; the camera gave way to the dynamo. When that tireless boy-inventor Tom Swift improved his camera, in Victor Appleton's 1914 *Tom Swift and His Photo Telephone*, he hitched it to the telephone and electricity.

At the end of World War I (1918), fiercely explicit photographs of the sufferings of the troops began to circulate. The ultimate shocking collection was *War against War!* (1924), gathered by the German pacifist Ernst Friedrich (1894–1967) and published in German, English, French, and Dutch. The experience of the war led some intellectuals and artists to believe that Western civilization itself had lost its authenticity — that is, a claim to cultural and scientific achievement. This perception followed on the declaration of Sigmund Freud (1856–1939) that human nature harbored an unconscious psychic realm that influenced behavior, but which could not be fully known. Alienation, arising from the experience of war and the psychological fragmentation of self, finally did away with Pictorialism's grander assumptions about making life an art, and brought into question the very concept of representation in the post-World War I era.

**4.77
FRANZ BOAS AND GEORGE HUNT,**
Untitled (Anthropologist Franz Boas, left, and photographer George Hunt hold up a backdrop for a photograph of a Kwakiutl woman in the process of cedar-bark weaving), n.d. American Museum of Natural History, New York.

The poses assumed by Boas's subjects were often those that he hoped to recreate in New York's Museum of Natural History, whose president had sponsored his expedition.

CHAPTER FIVE

A New Vision (1918–1945)

5.0
WALKER EVANS, *Allie Mae Burroughs*, 1936, from *Let Us Now Praise Famous Men*, by Walker Evans and James Agee, 1941. Gelatin silver print. Harry Ransom Humanities Research Center, University of Texas, Austin, Texas.

Posed against weathered clapboards, Allie Mae Burroughs's prematurely lined face, with its thin smile and narrowed eyes, corresponds to the horizontal shadows and wood grain behind it, as if the person and the house were close relatives. While the camera's closeness to the subject was calculated to jolt the viewer, its mass of photographic detail connoted honesty and objectivity on the part of the photographer.

A photographer entering the profession in the years between the world wars did so in circumstances vastly different from those prevailing at the turn of the century. The swift proliferation of industry after World War I changed how people worked, the goods they consumed, and thus the images they required. In the 1920s, the industrialization of photography reached a new level, with the expansion of newspapers, general and special-interest magazines, and professional periodicals, all of which employed photomechanical means of reproducing images. In addition, the automatic photo machine, better known as the photo booth, was patented in 1928 and first set up in New York City's theater district, where it became immensely popular.

During the 1920s, mass media grew at an astonishing pace. For instance, the city of Berlin, Germany, boasted forty-five morning and fourteen evening newspapers. In addition, hundreds of illustrated magazines and journals were devoted to special topics, such as fashion, health, and the automobile.[1] As mass-market illustrated journals proliferated, the word "photojournalism" entered common usage. The inescapable presence of photomechanical illustration influenced many of the artistic movements that took root in Berlin, and the city's culture became known throughout Europe and Russia for its visual arts experiments. The popular weekly periodical *Berliner Illustrirte* [sic] *Zeitung* (*Illustrated Berlin Newspaper*), started in 1890, but redesigned to carry many photographs, had a circulation of over 2 million during the 1920s[2] (Fig. 5.1). *BIZ*, as it was popularly called, pioneered the photo-essay, which was rapidly copied at home and abroad. Politically aligned illustrated magazines soon appeared, such as the German left-wing *Arbeiter Illustrierte Zeitung* (*Workers' Illustrated Newspaper; AIZ*), established in 1921 by Willi Münzenberg (1889–1940) specifically to foster liberal and humanitarian causes and critique capitalism.[3] On the political right, the Nazi party founded *Die Illustrierte Beobachter* (*The Illustrated Observer*), which became one of its official papers. In France, *Vu* (*Seen*) was launched in 1928 with the aim of communicating liberal ideas to the working class.

The hardships of postwar Germany and central Europe forced many art photographers to turn to photojournalism for a living, among them Hungarian-

21. Juli 1929
nummer 29
38. Jahrgang

Berliner

Preis
des Heftes
20 Pfennig

Illustrirte Zeitung

Verlag Ullstein

Berlin SW 68

Ferienfreude.

Aufnahme Munkacsi.

A NEW VISION (1918–1945)

**5.1 (above)
MARTIN MUNKACSI,**
Cover of *Berliner
Illustrirte Zeitung*,
July 21, 1929. Bildarchiv
Preussicher
Kulturbestitz, Berlin.

Munkacsi's experience
as a sports reporter
who captured in words
the quick movements
of players helped him
create visually dynamic
photographs for the
illustrated newspapers.
His split-second res-
ponses to action scenes
encouraged a taste
for the fleeting image
among photojournalists,
art photographers, and
the readers of the new
illustrated periodicals.

born Martin Munkacsi (1896–1963),[4]
who photographed for *BIZ* and other
magazines owned by the Berlin firm of
Ullstein Verlag, then the world's largest
publishing house (see Fig. 5.1). A decade
later influential mass-circulation picture
magazines were still being set up. In the

United States, *Life* magazine, founded
in 1936, took its cue from European
models, both in terms of their style and
their use of expert photographers (see
Fig. 5.60). Britain's *Picture Post* began
in 1938, under the direction of Stefan
Lorant (1901–1997), who had previously
made the *Münchner Illustrierte Presse*
(*Munich Illustrated Press*) an outstanding
picture newspaper.

Between the two world wars, the
average person in the industrialized
nations saw more photographs than his
or her late nineteenth-century counterpart, although these images were not
original prints but photomechanical
reproductions in newspapers and magazines. Photographic historians Colin
Osman and Sandra S. Phillips concluded that "taking 1927 as the departure point of the new thinking in picture
journalism, the progress made by 1937
was far greater than in the whole of the
previous history of press photography."[5]
While mass-manufactured images,
in the form of *cartes-de-visite* and stereographs, had been common in the
home in the late nineteenth century,
these were chosen by viewers, arranged
in personal albums or collections,
and could be looked at repeatedly.
Newspaper and magazine images, by
contrast, were selected by photo-editors
or advertising designers, circulated for
a short time, then superseded by more
images. Photographers had many more
outlets for photographs, representing

**5.2
ERICH SALOMON,**
Hague Conference,
January 3–20, 1930.
Gelatin silver print.
Bildarchiv Preussischer
Kulturbesitz, Berlin.

a wide range of political positions. Moreover, the glut of images was producing an increasingly visually sophisticated audience that rapidly came to see printed images as transitory and expendable.

Technological improvements increased the range of pictures that could be taken. The Leica camera, developed before World War I as a device to test movie film, was introduced to a wider audience in 1924. The Leica and its rival, the Contax camera, used 35-mm roll film, whose sensitivity, that is, "fastness," was continually being improved. Also in 1925, magnesium flash power was replaced by the safer flashbulb developed in Germany. Preferring the greater detail rendered by larger negatives, some photographers continued to use big cameras, but there was a universal tendency to mimic the spontaneous look made fashionable by the small-camera users. The public delighted in "candid photography," a phrase first used to describe the work of German photojournalist Erich Salomon (1886–1944), whose social connections gave him access to the corridors of power, where he made photographs that *seemed* beyond artifice (Fig. 5.2). Salomon's work, published in the *Berliner Illustrirte Zeitung*, implied the importance of the public's right to see behind the scenes of important political events.

The inter-war period witnessed the rapid development of journals largely devoted to pictures, especially the TABLOID newspaper, a compact journal featuring eye-catching pictures and far less text than the earlier broadsheet newspapers. Tabloids featured sensational crime and violence pictures, candid celebrity shots, and spectacular disaster photographs—just the thing to pick up while traveling to work on the streetcar, or while downing a quick meal in the factory lunch room. Tabloids told their stories quickly, through large pictures and brief captions.

In London, a women's magazine called the *Daily Mirror* was transformed in 1904 into a picture-driven daily newspaper. In the United States, the *New York Illustrated Daily News*, which became the *New York Daily News*, appeared in June 1919. The masthead of the *New York Daily News* featured a camera with wings, symbolizing the speed with which photographers pursued their stories. By 1930, its circulation had grown to more than 1.5 million. Typical of the audacious spirit of the *Daily News* was photographer Tom Howard's (active 1920s) quest of a picture of murderer Ruth Snyder at the moment of her electrocution. The picture ran with the one-word headline: "DEAD!" (Fig. 5.3). Then, as now, there was highbrow opposition to the prevalence of pictures in tabloids. As journalism historian Michael L. Carlebach observed, "abundant use of pictorial material" was understood "as conclusive proof both of declining literary standards and a nefarious plan to exploit hopelessly naive and illiterate people."[6]

Newspapers aimed at middle-class audiences were also lavishly illustrated. Themed ROTOGRAVURE sections (a process that allowed photographs to print with text) were inserted into Sunday papers. Fashion and high society were all the rage in the inserts, as noted

RUTH SNYDER'S DEATH PICTURED!—This is perhaps the most remarkable exclusive picture in the history of criminology. It shows the actual scene in the Sing Sing death house as the lethal current surged through Ruth Snyder's body at 11:06 last night. Her helmeted head is stiffened in death, her face masked and an electrode strapped to her bare right leg. The autopsy table on which her body was removed is beside her. Judd Gray, mumbling a prayer, followed her down the narrow corridor at 11:14. "Father, forgive them, for they don't know what they are doing," were Ruth's last words. The picture is the first Sing Sing execution picture and the first of a woman's electrocution.—*Story p. 3; other pics. p. 28 and back page.*

5.3
TOM HOWARD, *Dead!* (Execution of Ruth Snyder), front cover of *Daily News*, January 13, 1928. *Daily News*, New York.

The *Daily News* encouraged photographers to get images by whatever means possible. The blurry photograph of murderer Ruth Snyder at the moment of her electrocution was taken by their photographer, Tom Howard, who strapped a hidden camera to his ankle and raised his leg at the appropriate moment.

BLASTS SEND GIANT BALLS OF FLAME SPURTING FROM AIRSHIP

**5.4
PHOTOGRAPHER
UNKNOWN,** *"Zeppelin
Blast Kills Thirty-Five,
from Los Angeles Times,
Friday, May 7, 1937.
Newsprint.*

Many photographers
were present when the
Hindenburg crashed
and burst into flame on
May 6, 1937. A radio
announcer choked and
wept over the airwaves
of his station, and his
grief was broadcast
around the country.
Images of the disaster
were wired to news-
papers across the
United States, which
ran them in next day's
edition—a rapid
response at that time.

in Irving Berlin's popular tune *Easter
Parade* (1933), in which a lad boasts
to his lady that "On the Avenue/Fifth
Avenue/The photographers will snap
us/And you'll find that you're/in the
rotogravure."

The illustrated newspaper was not
the only nineteenth-century innovation
to expand rapidly in the inter-war
period. By 1920, there were about 10
million registered automobiles in the
United States, and automobile production was on the brink of becoming one
of the nation's leading industries. In
1900, the United States had 1 million
telephones; by 1920 there were 7.5
million.[7] Widespread electrification
made possible radio stations and home
radio receivers. During the 1920s, the
radio took its place as a piece of family
furniture, perhaps near the phonograph,
which played popular tunes. As the
historian William Stott has pointed out,
trust in the truth and impartiality of
radio broadcasts surpassed belief in
newspapers.[8]

Newspapers responded to competition from radio by adding more pictures, in particular, dramatic pictures.
Although experiments with wire and
radio transmission of photographs

began before World War I, in the early
1920s publication still depended on
the mails or special couriers to deliver
photographs. Consequently, newspapers
and magazines turned to "evergreen"
features—that is, non-time-linked sin-
gle-topic photo-series and essays about a
person, place, or event. Such features
were so popular that they continued
even after technology allowed instant
transmission of news photographs.
Photographs achieved some of radio's
immediacy when more reliable, though
expensive, image transmission systems
became available in the late 1920s.
The founding of the Associated Press
Wirephoto division in January 1935
marked the start of cheaper transmitting
systems and networks, which remained
technologically similar until replaced
by electronic systems in the 1980s. The
you-are-there feeling of radio and photography was jointly captured in May
1937, when the fashionable transatlantic
airship the *Hindenburg* crashed and
burst into flames in Lakehurst, New
Jersey (Fig. 5.4).

During the 1920s, motion pictures
evolved from an arcade amusement
to a widespread public entertainment.
From 1935 on, stylish newsreels, such
as *The March of Time*, preceded the featured film. The emergence of a technologically driven popular culture in which
a literate, largely urban mass audience
could see the same photographs, go
to the same films, and hear the same
records, affected the way photographers
conceived their images. No longer
was a photograph from a faraway place
thrilling in itself. Kurt Schwitters
(1887–1948), a successful advertising
designer and avant-garde artist,
remarked that "modern man hears and
sees such an enormous amount of
impressions, that already he is accustomed to unconsciously turn off."[9]

In his 1925 article on "The Magazine
as a Sign of the Times," German editor
and radio personality Edlef Köppen
linked the hectic activity of modern
life to the character of the illustrated
magazines. "The mark of our age is
haste, hurry, nervousness," he wrote.
"People have no time, indeed they flee
the calm of contemplation." The public,
Köppen scolded, wanted the pleasure,
variety, and brevity of short acts in a
theatrical review.[10]

The social significance of mass media was quickly perceived by artists. Hungarian-born painter and sculptor László Moholy-Nagy (1895–1946) asserted the unique qualities of sound recording, film, and photography, which he thought were the best media for representing the modern experience. Similarly, in 1921, Vienna-born German artist Raoul Hausmann (1886–1971) asked, "Why don't we paint works today like those of Botticelli, Michelangelo, Leonardo, or Titian? Because our spirits have utterly changed. And not simply because we have the telephone, the airplane, the electric piano, and the escalator. Rather, because above all these experiences have transformed our entire psycho-physiology."[11]

Hausmann was among the first artist-critics to argue that there may be a threshold in human biological capacity at which the proliferation of mediated experiences provided by photography, film, radio, and sound recording alters the individual's perception of the world. That claim is still contested, especially in relation to television, computers, and cyberspace. Nevertheless, the readiness with which people in the 1920s both desired and accepted reproductions of events not directly experienced was remarkable. It was in Germany and Russia, countries in which the legacy of war was particularly far-reaching, that the dream of a utopia achieved through technological means found its most

animated vision. "The mechanization of our planet," as German architect Hannes Meyer (1889–1954) called it in 1926, offered "palpable proof of the victory of human consciousness over amorphous nature." For him, the speed of planes and automobiles broke the bounds of place and tradition. The speed of life made us live faster, and therefore longer. It made us see that things could change: "We learn Esperanto," Meyer wrote; "*We become citizens of the world.*"[12]

REVOLUTIONARY ART: THE SOVIET PHOTOGRAPH

In Russia, the revolution of 1917 (see p. 229), which placed revolutionary socialists in power, had a deep impact on artists, particularly the avant-garde. Even before the overthrow of the czar, abstraction had already become a symbol for a future untainted by the past. After the revolution artists experimenting with Cubism and Futurism responded to the Communist Party's buoyant utopianism, expressed in *The ABC of Communism* (1919), which proclaimed that "within a few decades there will be quite a new world, with new people and new customs."[13] El Lissitzky (1890–1941), an architect who worked in many media, including photography, was one of the most politically committed artists. He renounced self-expression in art, along with easel painting, which he associated with a corrupt past and stagnant aesthetics. With others, Lissitzky insisted that the artist's role was now linked to industry and to reshaping everyday life. In avant-garde circles, the terms "production art" and "production artist" began being used, to indicate that the artist would employ technology in order to mold a new society. Photography was favored precisely because it was the product of a machine that could be mass-produced by other machines.

Lissitzky's *The Constructor* (1924) (Fig. 5.5) shows the artist in his new role as builder or engineer. It features the austere geometric overlays frequently used by Russian avant-garde image-makers, who favored non-realistic, intersecting planes that

5.5
EL LISSITZKY, *The Constructor*, 1924. Photomontage. Getty Research Institute, Los Angeles, California.

Borrowing from two Russian art movements, Suprematism and Constructivism, both of which favored abstract geometric shapes in unshaded colors, Lissitzky superimposed an image of himself on a piece of graph paper, and layered on top a picture of his hand, uniting hand and eye in a symbol of ideal labor. Superimposing one image on another recalled the experiments of Cubism.

flattened Renaissance perspective and thereby condemned the older art of morally bankrupt elites. In Lissitzky's image, the artist's hand fingers a compass, which seems to have drawn a perfect circle around his head. The circle forms a halo, as in a Russian religious painting.[14] The "sainted" new Soviet artist worked with geometric shapes and signs, as well as printers' type, which emerged as primary elements in Soviet poster design and magazine illustrations. Lissitzky also designed trade exhibitions, demonstrating Soviet industrial progress. In these installations, he transformed the shape of the room by having images and text bulge out from the wall or droop from the ceiling.

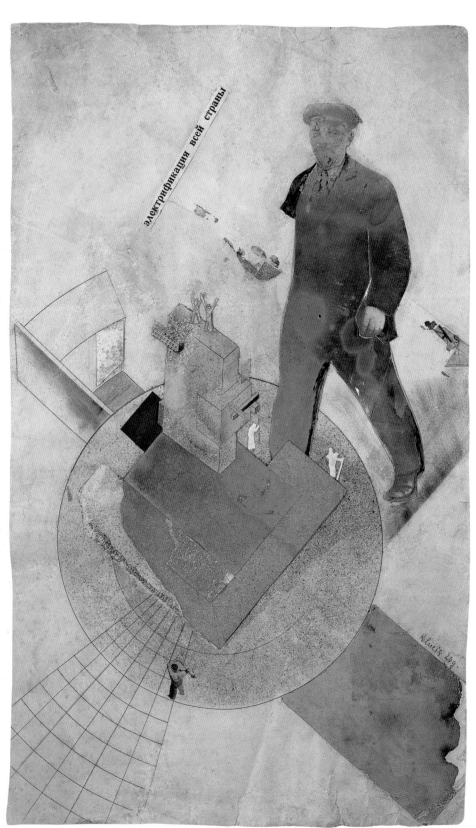

5.6
GUSTAV KLUCSIS,
Electrification of the Entire Country, 1920. Vintage gelatin silver print. Merrill C. Berman Collection, New York.

Klucsis used photomontage to advocate the continued modernization of the Soviet Union, symbolized by electricity and the figure of Lenin striding into, and towering over, the future. Designed as a poster, this propaganda image is combined with abstract shapes that resemble Lissitzky's work (see Fig. 5.5).

Many Soviet artists were also writers and theorists addressing national and international audiences. Latvian-born Gustav Klucsis (sometimes Klutsis) (1895–1938) realized that it was imperative "to construct *iconic* representations for a new mass audience."[15] He used PHOTOMONTAGE (see pp. 242–46), assembling images and text from a variety of mass-media sources, such as newspapers and magazines. The result overturned the expectations of everyday experience and of realistic painting with arresting image collisions. Klucsis, however, insisted that his images should be understood by the illiterate as well as the educated. In *Electrification of the Entire Country* (1920) (Fig. 5.6), a giant-sized Soviet leader, Vladimir Lenin (1870–1924), strides forward confidently into the future as workers on the Modernist building's roof-top cheer him on.

The prospect of a revolutionary art was eagerly taken up by Aleksandr Rodchenko (1891–1956), a Russian painter and sculptor who had absorbed the geometric abstractions of Cubism and who valued the process of COLLAGE, pioneered by the Cubists in the decade before World War I. As his political activity increased in the new arts organizations initiated by the Soviet government in its early years, Rodchenko investigated the role art might play in society. He resolved to make art less theoretical and more practical. With other artists, he went to factories to learn design needs first hand, and he conceived posters, fabrics, and furniture. Rodchenko wholeheartedly embraced photography because he felt it freed artists from inherited aesthetic ideas, especially perspective and the other techniques used to render the world as it is, rather than as it might be. He promoted the notion that new concepts could not be expressed in old media, and was a leading proponent of *faktura*, the idea prominent in Soviet art theory that an artist should discover a medium's distinctive capabilities by experimenting with its inherent qualities.

Looking at the work of photographers who traveled to foreign countries, Rodchenko sneered, "They photograph with museum eyes, the eyes of art history."[16] Rodchenko's hope for new media

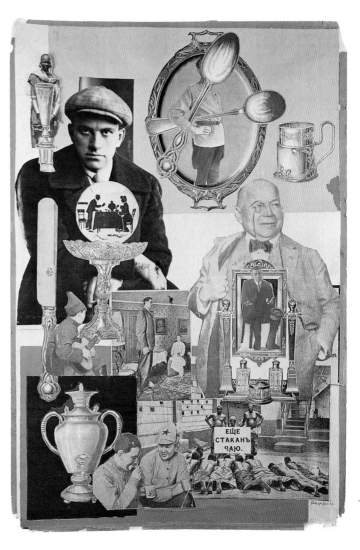

such as film and photography was enhanced by looking at German art and fashion magazines, such as *Die Dame* (*Woman*), *Junge Welt* (*Young World*) and *Moderne Illustrierte Zeitschrift* (*Modern Illustrated Journal*), which featured experimental German photography. In turn, Rodchenko's work appeared in the Russian magazine *LEF* (*Left Front of the Arts*), a left-wing arts magazine founded by poet Vladimir Maiakovskii (1893–1930). In 1923, Rodchenko gathered images from the picture press, and also commissioned a series of photographs from another photographer. He joined these images to make photomontage illustrations for Maiakovskii's poem "Pro Ito" ("About This") (Fig. 5.7). These images are visually arresting, but it is hard to see how uninitiated viewers could have interpreted their symbolic meanings.

The post-revolutionary Russian avant-garde advocated making images in such a way as to obstruct habits of seeing. Odd camera angles, unrecognizable close-ups, multiple exposures, and

5.7
ALEXANDR RODCHENKO, *Untitled*, 1923, to accompany Maiakovskii's poem "Pro Ito" ("About This"). Photomontage. Rodchenko Archives, Moscow.

Rodchenko's photomontages for Maiakovskii's poem rely on an elaborate symbolic programme. Here, telephone lines and a telephone number (67-10) are traced along a tilted skyscraper skyline of what may be New York City. In the top right frame, Maiakovskii listens intently, his passion symbolized by the dinosaur. However, the call is answered not by his sweetheart but her bored housekeeper.

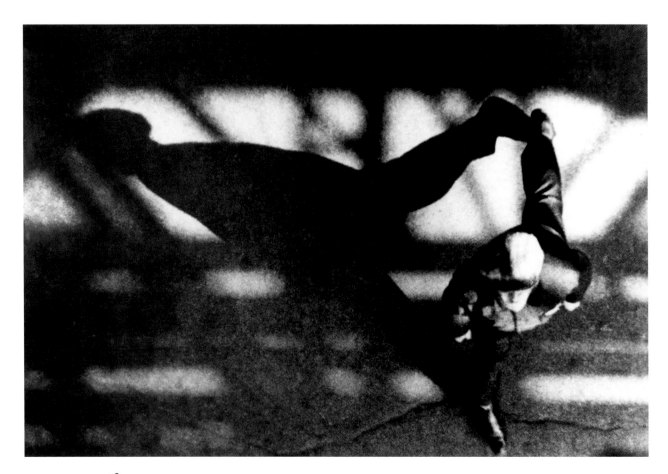

5.8
ALEXANDR RODCHENKO, *Untitled* **(Walking figure), 1928. Gelatin silver print. Rodchenko Archives, Moscow.**

In this disconcerting image Rodchenko discovered an unusual camera angle and haunting shadow effects, which together jolt the viewer into seeing and examining the complex patterns created from an otherwise ordinary scene of a walking man.

confused perspective all served to "make strange" the expected appearance of the world.[17] In the mid-1920s, Rodchenko learned to make his own photographs and moved from photomontage to straight photography (Fig. 5.8). Nevertheless, he continued to disparage "belly button" camerawork—that is, the conventional, balanced picture taken with a camera held near the waistline, while the photographer peered into the viewing screen.

In the years immediately after the revolution, the Soviet government courted experimental artists in its search for innovative methods of mass communication. But by the early 1930s, the romance turned sour. Official policy shifted from avant-garde art—seen as intellectual, bourgeois, and thus part of the capitalist system—and instead promoted Socialist Realism, that is, a conventionally realistic style used as a vehicle for rousing propaganda messages that could be universally understood by the workers.

As the avant-garde was losing official sanction, Rodchenko began the huge official task of photographing the construction of the White Sea Canal or Stalin Canal (1931–33). Using a less startlingly inventive approach than in his earlier work, Rodchenko produced about 3,000 photographs, some of which were published in a special 1933 edition of *USSR in Construction*, a magazine intended to show Soviet progress, especially to audiences abroad. Tellingly, Rodchenko did not record the use of forced labor, nor the deaths of thousands of workers at the site—subjects forbidden by the propaganda controls enforced in the Soviet Union under Stalin's leadership in the 1930s.

DADA AND AFTER

During World War I, a group of writers, artists, and poets met at the Cabaret Voltaire in Zurich, Switzerland, a cultural outpost in a politically neutral country. The group strongly objected to the war and to the bankrupt materialism of the age. They envisioned a new art that expressed their despair, but that would also sweep away tiresome conventions and intellectual barriers. The Romanian-born artist Tristan Tzara (1896–1963), who wrote the *Dada Manifesto* of 1918, saw the task to be done as "a great negative work of destruction."[18] The origins of the name "Dada" are unclear; this nonsensical-sounding word may have been chosen because it has different meanings in several European languages. Through the visual arts and performances, Dada accentuated the disruptiveness of chance collisions of images and sounds.

Christian Schad (1894–1982), a German artist associated with the Zurich Dada group, was influenced by the French artist and poet Jean (or Hans) Arp (1887–1966), who emphasized the need to be unconstrained by traditional notions of composition, and who made low-relief sculptural collages of found objects. Schad, too, created small collages of newspaper clippings and odd bits of paper, and used a similar method to make abstract photographs (Fig. 5.9). Several of Schad's abstract photographs were acquired by Tzara, who dubbed them "schadographs." This sounds like "shadowgraph," a process used by such early photographers as Fox Talbot (see p. 16). Tzara may have been aware of this, but was perhaps also alluding to the meaning of the German word *schaden*, which means "damaged," evoking the Dada sense of things falling apart.

Another group of Dada artists met in Berlin as Germany was disintegrating toward the end of the war. More political than the Zurich Dadaists, they wanted to make social statements. In the words of one their leaders, Richard Hülsenbeck (1892–1974), "the highest art will be that which in its conscious content presents the thousandfold problems of the day, the art which has been visibly shattered by the explosions of last week, which is forever trying to collect its limbs after yesterday's crash."[19] Berlin Dadaists adopted photomontage as a key medium. Often the initial *Klebebild* or "paste picture" was photographed, producing a more

finished look, and preparing the image for reproduction in one of the many avant-garde magazines.

The origins of the photomontage have long been debated, but it seems that Hannah Höch (1889–1978) and Hausmann were two of the earliest Dadaists to make such images. Höch's large photomontage *Cut with the Kitchen Knife Dada through the last Weimar Beer Belly Cultural Epoch of Germany* (*Schnitt mit dem Küchenmesser Dada durch die letzte weimarer Bierbauchkulturepoche Deutschlands*) (1919) made its appearance at the First International Dada Fair in Berlin (1920) (Fig. 5.10). As art historian Maud Lavin observed, the diversity of mass-media sources in Höch's picture testifies to the vast proliferation of newspapers and journals in the years following World War I, and the growing perception that mass-media images were forming a common visual culture.[20] Even though the individual images in early photomontage were generally easy to read, their combination yielded pictures whose meaning was difficult to decipher. In effect, photomontage itself was the message of change. Nevertheless,

5.9
CHRISTIAN SCHAD,
Schadograph 24b,
c. 1920. Gelatin silver print.

Schad placed pieces of randomly collected paper and objects atop photographically sensitive paper, pressing them down with a sheet of clear glass. As the assemblage was exposed to light on a windowsill, Schad observed its development and occasionally moved objects around as they were appearing on the paper.

243

DADA AND AFTER

some parts of *Cut with the Kitchen Knife* can be decoded (they are described in the caption).

Like American photographer Frances Benjamin Johnston, Höch engaged the theme of the New Woman.[21] She juxtaposed images of smartly dressed contemporary women with women in traditional social roles and with such symbols of modernity as automobiles, machinery, and electric lightbulbs. While she criticized contemporary politics and society's hypocrisy toward women as both workers and sexual objects, the jazzy exuberance of her compositions reveals an optimism for avant-garde art and the joy of art-making. During the 1930s, Höch collaged pictures of objects in German ethnographic collections with symbols of Modernism, so as to contrast Western materialism and non-Western traditional practices. Her photomontage series *From an Ethnographic Museum*

5.10
HANNAH HÖCH, *Schnitt mit dem Küchenmesser Dada durch die letzte weimarer Bierbauchkulturepoche Deutschlands (Cut with the Kitchen Knife Dada through the Last Weimar Beer Belly Cultural Epoch of Germany)*, 1919. Photomontage. Nationalgalerie Staatliche Museen, Preussischer Kulturbesitz, Berlin.

In the center a popular dancer of the time pirouettes beneath the head of the artist Käthe Kollwitz (see Fig. 4.35). The head has been speared by a man in front of an elephant. The dancer's right foot rests on a giant ball-bearing. Beneath that is a young revolutionary sailor who is saying "Join Dada" ("Tretet Dada bei"). The word "Dada" is also scattered throughout the work.

FOCUS
Photomontage or Photocollage

Narrowly speaking, photocollage began with the cut-and-paste work of album makers such as Lady Filmer and the combination printing of photographers such as Oscar Rejlander. But the anti-establishment photographic experiments that originated in Soviet and German experimental photography had different social roots and dissimilar social aims from these Victorian forebears.

Photomontage originated in Germany, but was adopted in Russia soon after World War I, through artists' visits and through magazines. The avant-garde Dada movement, initiated by artists who took refuge in Switzerland during the war, spread to Berlin, and from there to Moscow. Experimental artists cut pictures from magazines and newspapers and pasted them together in composite images whose jumbled scale and perspective challenged conventional expectations (Fig. 5.11). These collages (from the French word for "glue") were sometimes photographed so that the unique first image could be printed in multiple versions. Soviet experimental artists called such images not photocollages but photomontages. The word montage has various sources. In silent film, for example,

it specified the rapid succession of images that indicated a change of place or the transition of ideas. The Berlin Dadaist Hausmann wrote that the group agreed on the term "photomontage" because of "our aversion at playing the artist and, thinking of ourselves as engineers (hence our preference for working-men's overalls) we meant to construct, to assemble [*montieren*] our works."[22] Experimental artists used the word photomontage almost exclusively after World War I. Although a photomontage may resemble a Cubist painting, on to which such materials as tickets and menus have been pasted, experimental artists in Germany and Russia aimed to use such materials in a different way. The jumbled appearance of photomontage was more than formal inventiveness; it was a token of the quick changes and disruptions of modern life that seemed, in the period immediately after World War I and the Russian Revolution, to promise progressive social change.

5.11
GEORGE GROSZ & JOHN HEARTFIELD, *Leben und Treiben in Universal City um 12 Uhr 5 Mittages (Life and Activity in the Universal City at Five Past Twelve)*, 1919. Akademie der Künste, Berlin.

5.12
HANNAH HÖCH,
Denkmal I: Aus einem ethnographischen Museum (Monument 1: From an Ethnographic Museum), 1924.
Collage, photomontage. Berlinische Galerie, Landesmuseum für Moderne Kunst, Photographie und Architektur, Berlin.

Höch's ethnographic series contrasted contemporary feminine attire and poses with artifacts from the past and from tribal peoples. Modern eyes peer out of a ritual mask, while an arm and torso become a leg.

produced unsettling effects by juxtaposing snippets of Western and non-Western body parts and artifacts (Fig. 5.12).

Höch's lover for seven years, Raoul Hausmann, was one of the few communists to insist on women's equality in any new society. More subtle than his copious political writing, Hausmann's photomontage images included his contribution to the 1920 Dada Fair, *Tatlin at Home* (Fig. 5.13). This photomontage was more an exercise in freewheeling mental associations and concern for artistic form than a penetrating portrait or social critique. For example, Hausmann explained that he added machinery, including an automobile steering wheel, to the main figure's head because he was interested in portraying a man who had machines for brains. The man with his pockets turned inside out was included because Hausmann fancied that Tatlin could not be rich. Like many photomontagists, Hausmann painted parts of the picture, such as the background.[23]

Another Berlin Dadaist, George Grosz (1893–1959), one of the most politically active artists to emerge from the Berlin Dada group, was also a pioneer of photomontage. Grosz's photomontages have a plainly discernible message, expressed in an apparently spontaneous accumulation of images and texts (see Fig. 5.11).

MOHOLY-NAGY AND THE BAUHAUS

László Moholy-Nagy arrived in Berlin just before the 1920 Dada Fair. He soon met Höch, Hausmann, and other members of the Berlin Dada group. Like them, Moholy-Nagy favored the use of industrial materials and concepts, and he embraced Soviet artists' notion of *faktura*, which he understood to mean that a new vision could be created only when photography was practiced for its own inherent qualities, not as an imitation of painting. While the Dadaists were politically active, many joining the Communist Party, Moholy-Nagy concentrated instead on technology and its relation to art. He insisted that "the first and foremost issue" for photography was to determine "a more or less exact photographic language," independent of the past.[24] His social concern was expressed in his theory that mass production, especially the wide circulation of images, made it possible for an artist to change perceptions of the world, thereby creating a desire for social revolution.

Moholy-Nagy claimed that photography's chief characteristic was light, and that artists should experiment with patterns of light and shade. "This century belongs to light," he argued, and "photography is the first means of giving tangible shape to light, though in a transposed and ... almost abstract form."[25] "Today," he wrote, "everything is concentrated, more powerfully than ever before, on the visual." Moholy-Nagy looked to science

5.13
RAOUL HAUSMANN,
Tatlin at Home, 1920.
Collage (destroyed).
Statens Konstmuseet,
Moderna Museet,
Stockholm.

Despite the title, the
central image of a man's
head is not a portrait
of Vladimir Tatlin
(1885–1953), the highly
esteemed leader of
the new Soviet art,
who was lauded at the
Dada Fair by a sign that
declared: "Art is dead!
Long live the machine
art of Tatlin." Instead,
Hausmann took an
existing image from a
newspaper or magazine
that reminded him
of the Russian artist.

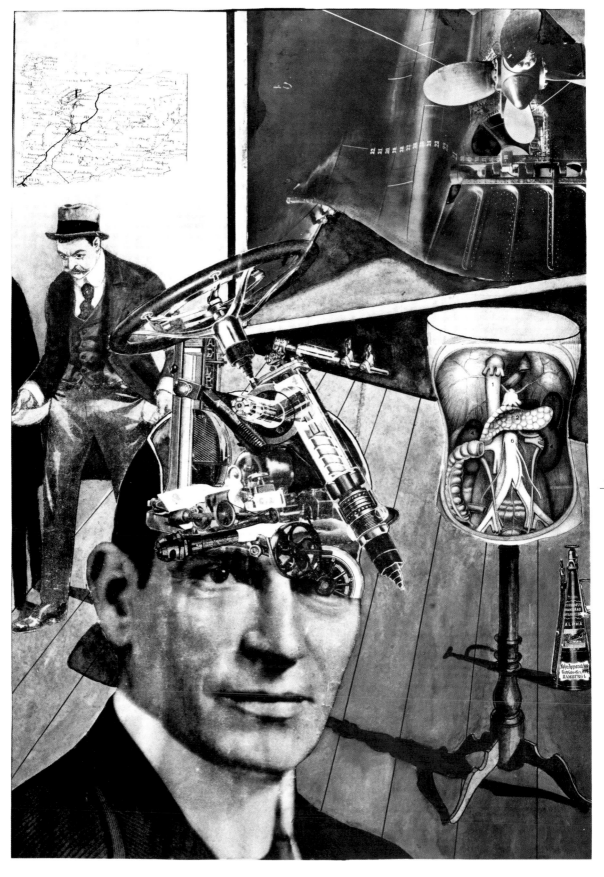

247

DADA AND AFTER

to research the physiological and psychological basis for visual presentations,
which would be as effective as written
language. He announced that "the
illiteracy of the future will be ignorance
of photography."[26]

Like Rodchenko, Moholy-Nagy proposed that photographers should radically change the angle of camera vision.
He advocated such devices as distorting
mirrors that would alter normal views,
and he anticipated the invention of new

**5.14 (above)
LÁSZLÓ MOHOLY-
NAGY & LUCIA
MOHOLY,** *Photogram,*
**1924. Gelatin silver
print. Museum Ludwig,
Cologne, Germany.**

Collaborating with his
first wife, photographer
and critic Lucia Moholy
(1894–1989), Moholy-
Nagy explored the impli-
cations of the argument
that photography should
move beyond repro-
ducing the appearance
of reality and begin to
produce something new.
The photograms they
created depicted not
objects or views, but
abstract shapes, shades,
and forms.

sorts of cameras that would allow the
operator to play with perspective. He
also envisaged photographers adapting
microscopes, telescopes, and X-ray
equipment to their repertoire of image-
making. Among his proposals was
the making of cameraless photographs,
which he called PHOTOGRAMS
(Fig. 5.14).

In 1923, Moholy-Nagy was invited
to join the faculty of the Bauhaus,
the German art school established by
architect Walter Gropius (1883–1969),
whose goal was to integrate the arts
with industry. Moholy-Nagy already
had an international reputation for his
abstract paintings and sculptures, some
of which used industrial materials and
processes, such as porcelain enamel
on steel; he was an energetic member
of a faculty that would later include
artists Wassily Kandinsky (1866–1944)
and Paul Klee (1879–1940). The
Bauhaus curriculum did not include
classes in photography until soon
before it was closed by the Nazis in
1933, but Moholy-Nagy's ideas were
influential. In addition, his 1925 book
Malerei, Photographie, Film (*Painting,
Photography, Film*), published by the

Bauhaus, became an international
reference for the new photography.

The upbeat mood of experimental
photography was captured in the title
of an article by Bauhaus artist Johannes
Molzahn (1892–1965), "Stop Reading!
Look!" (*"Nicht mehr lesen! Sehen!"*).
Molzahn was convinced that formal
education should adapt to the increasingly visually portrayed world rendered
in mass-media newspapers and magazines. He offered "Stop Reading!
Look!" as the guiding motto for teaching and learning.[27] Also at the Bauhaus
was Austrian-born designer and photographer Herbert Bayer (1900–1985),
whose design for the first cover of
the institution's publication, *Bauhaus*,
was a photomontage (Fig. 5.15).
Bayer's post-Bauhaus career included
the design of an infamous photomontage for a Nazi brochure, which
demonstrated the extent to which
photomontage was not a technique
intrinsically wedded to progressive
politics, but a style whose aesthetic
features could serve any political persuasion (see Fig. 5.41).

German-born photographer
Germaine Krull (1897–1985) absorbed

**5.15 (below)
HERBERT BAYER,
Cover of** *Bauhaus 1,*
**1928. From a photo-
montage. Bauhaus-
Archiv, Berlin.**

the techniques promoted by Moholy-Nagy, and grasped the swift interplay of images advocated by Russian filmmaker and writer Sergei Eisenstein (1898–1948), as well as her companion, filmmaker Joris Ivens (1898–1989). Like the French painter Fernand Léger (1881–1955), she celebrated industrialization as a marvelous marriage of the human body and the machine. Her 1928 collection of images, *Métal*, was advertised as "the dance of the metal nudes."[28] The portfolio's cover showed a disconcerting view of the elevator wheels that boosted people to the top of the Eiffel Tower in Paris (Fig. 5.16). Krull's sixty-four unbound prints of French and Dutch

industrial sites in *Métal* were uncaptioned, and sequenced so as to jump from soothing conventional views to slippery superimpositions. Because of her dizzying dynamic angles and other techniques, many of the actual locations were unrecognizable, and had to be taken as symbols of modern life rather than depictions.

DADA AND PARIS

In Paris, Dadaists turned away from the Berlin group's political activism to embrace a wider cultural criticism. It was in Paris that Marcel Duchamp drew a mustache on a photographic reproduction of Leonardo da Vinci's (1452–1519) *Mona Lisa*, and relabeled it

5.16
**GERMAINE KRULL,
Cover of *Métal*, 1928.
Collotype. Museum
Folkwang Fotografische
Sammlung, Essen,
Germany.**

Krull's portfolio of photographs *Métal* celebrated industrialization and modernization. The cover bore Krull's name, superimposed in chunky letters that looked like they had been mechanically stamped out. For decades after its construction in 1889, the Eiffel Tower in Paris was a powerful international symbol for change and innovation.

with a title that sounded lewd when read aloud in French (Fig. 5.17). Before he came to Paris and met with the Dadaists, German painter Max Ernst (1891–1976) was already making psychologically disorienting photographic collages and creating disquieting effects on canvas and paper using such techniques as *frottage* (rubbing a surface so that the texture of an object beneath it shows through). Eerie enigmas pervaded his work (Fig. 5.18). Ernst had little respect for the Berlin Dada's political orientation: "German intellectuals can't even shit or piss without ideology," he snarled.[29]

André Breton (1896–1966), one of the leaders of Paris Dada, praised Ernst and lauded his photography, relating it to the Dada practice of automatic writing. This entailed writing or speaking a haphazard sequence of words to evade the censorship of the rational mind: "Automatic writing," Breton wrote, "is a true photography of thought."[30] Breton's curiosity about psychic states led him toward psychology, especially the theories of Sigmund Freud, which suggested that human behavior is motivated by forces and desires hidden deep within the human psyche, which individuals and society are generally reluctant to acknowledge. Around 1924, Breton rejected the anarchism of Dada, which relied on an ability (difficult to sustain indefinitely) to shock, disturb, or outrage viewers. He sought a more constructive program that would still be based on the power of the unconscious and irrational mind. This led to the founding of the Surrealist movement, of which Breton became one of the major theorists.

DADA AND THE MACHINE AGE IN NEW YORK

In the United States, meanwhile, Dada had had a further manifestation, spurred by contact between exiled European artists and their American counterparts. Man Ray (1890–1976), the American artist born Emmanuel Radnitzky, maintained that there was no such thing as New York Dada,[31] and indeed conditions there were markedly different than in Europe. Involved in World War I in only the final stages, the United States also did not endure years of conflict on its own soil, and was therefore spared the disillusioned anguish that questioned the role of traditional art in an age of trench warfare. Moreover, Americans did not identify non-objective, or abstract, art with political revolt and social change to the degree that many European experimenters did. New Yorkers responded to the visually provocative 1913 Armory Show, the first large-scale exhibition of modern art from Europe and the United States, as a display of art, not as progressive social propaganda. Through the influence of Duchamp and Picabia, both of whom arrived in New York from Europe during 1915 for extended stays, a spirited group of artists came together around the notion that the machine and industrial society formed the fountainhead of a new cultural expression. Duchamp found workspace in the New York home of Walter and Louise Arensberg, wealthy collectors whose residence emerged as the gathering-place for artists including Man Ray, Morton Schamberg (1881–1918), and Charles Sheeler (1883–1965).

5.17
MARCEL DUCHAMP,
***L.H.O.O.Q.*, 1919.**
Color reproduction of
***Mona Lisa* altered with**
a pencil. Private
Collection.

Duchamp's comical addition to a postcard of Leonardo da Vinci's *Mona Lisa*, and his bawdy retitling of the image, expressed his attitude toward unthinking acceptance of tradition.

L.H.O.O.Q.

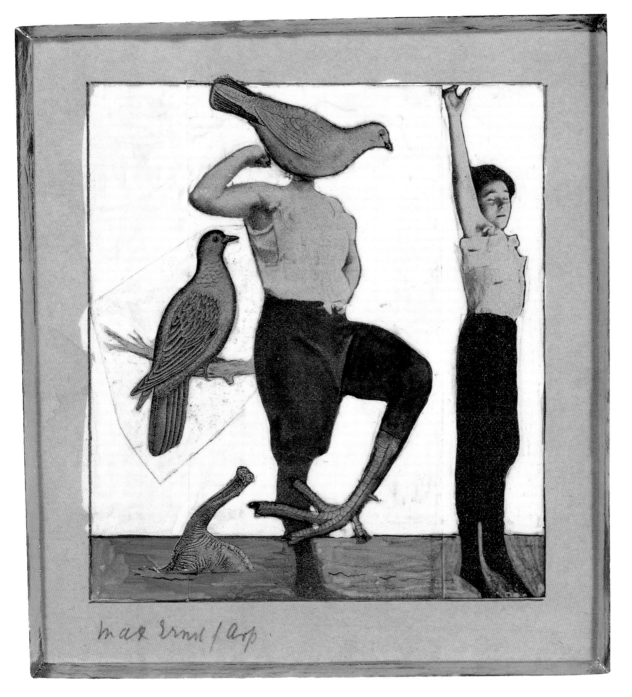

5.18
MAX ERNST & HANS ARP, *Physiomythological Diluvian Picture*, **1920. Collage with fragments of a photograph, gouache, pencil, pen and ink on paper laid on card. Sprengel Museum, Hanover, Germany.**

Combining the optical reality of a photograph (the woman's head) with media suggestive either of flatness or perspective allowed Ernst and Arp to create an image full of puzzling contradictions.

The first and only issue of the magazine *New York Dada* appeared in 1921 with a photograph of Duchamp, disguised as his female alter ego Rrose Sélavy, which had been affixed to a recycled perfume bottle. The issue also carried an experimental photograph by Alfred Stieglitz, whose circle of friends overlapped with those in the Arensberg salon. Stieglitz permitted Picabia and others to use his 291 gallery on Fifth Avenue as the title of a magazine inspired mostly by European Dada experimentation. Despite its liveliness, the New York Dada movement had little enduring impact on photography in the United States.[32]

Schamberg and Sheeler were painters who initially took up photography to make a living, and gradually gained attention for their camerawork. In both his painting and photography, Schamberg moved toward the sharp, flat delineation of geometric forms that was later to influence the group of American abstract realists known as the Precisionists (Fig. 5.19). Sheeler, a founder of Precisionism who specialized in art and architectural photography, made several photographs of Duchamp's *Nude Descending a Staircase* (1912). The term PRECISIONISM has been used to describe paintings depicting specifically American building types, such as skyscrapers and barns, in a near-abstract manner that stresses geometric form. Although Sheeler did much the same thing in his photographs, they are not routinely called Precisionist. With

Paul Strand, Sheeler worked on the 1920 experimental film *Manhatta*, which celebrated the city as a wellspring of progressive modern life, from its newly erected skyscrapers to its smoke-belching chimneys. Geometrically lean and striking shots of the city were interspersed with high-spirited quotations from American poet Walt Whitman (1819–1892). Reflecting on the experience, Strand remarked that "both of us were well along the road of abstract organization of reality."[33]

Sheeler supported his art by working in advertising, producing promotional

**5.20
CHARLES SHEELER,**
Industry, 1932. Gelatin
silver prints (triptych).
Art Institute of Chicago,
Chicago, Illinois.

Sheeler's photographs,
sometimes used as
sources for his paint-
ings, sometimes left
to stand on their own,
included dynamic
images of the Ford
Motor Company's
Rouge River plant, then
the largest and most
complex industrial site
in the world, occupying
1,100 acres.

pictures for spark plugs, tires, and typewriters. In 1927 he received a commission to photograph the Ford Motor
Company's plant near Detroit on the
Rouge River.[34] Sheeler avoided putting
workers in his shots, for fear that viewers would concentrate on them, not the
plant's machinery; and he overlooked
contemporary labor issues by attending
to the massive mechanical elements that
took raw materials and converted them
into automobiles. His large three-part
mural *Industry,* now generally known
only through its much smaller study,
centers on the criss-crossed conveyors
that carried coal and coke (Fig. 5.20).
On either side of the central panel,
Sheeler placed photographs of gigantic
stamping presses. The buildings at the
Rouge River plant thrilled Sheeler, as
much as the French Gothic cathedrals
whose dynamic architecture he later
photographed. For him, industrial architecture marked a stupendous movement
in human progress. "Our factories are
our substitute for religious expression,"
he proclaimed.[35] Many of Sheeler's canvases take up the same subjects as his
photographs, profiting from the simplification of tones and generalization of
forms that he learned through the use
of the camera.

SURREALIST PHOTOGRAPHY

The Surrealist movement was born in
Paris in the mid-1920s. Unlike Dada,
which always remained individualistic,
Surrealism was a self-proclaimed
movement. André Breton's *Surrealist
Manifesto,* published on October 15,
1924, announced the primacy of the
irrational and the belief in a truth above
or beyond realism. Surrealism was
deeply indebted to Freud's theory of the
unconscious, and the methods he proposed for revealing a person's unconscious desires, notably dream analysis
and free association sequences of words
and ideas. Rather than emphasizing
social change on the state level, the
Surrealists advocated the transformation
of human perception and experience
through greater contact with the inner
world of imagination.

Photography was central to Surrealist
practice. In theory, at least, making
photographs could be the visual equivalent of free association, and other methods of side-stepping the monitoring
rational mind. Some Surrealists pointed
their cameras haphazardly, recording
whatever happened to be in front of the
lens. Other efforts were more purpose-
ful, such as Man Ray's experiments with

the photogram or RAYOGRAPH (Fig. 5.21). His untitled rayographs, featuring unlikely conjunctions of mundane, recognizable objects, such as a knife and comb, were published as *Les Champs délicieux* (*The Delicious Fields*) (1922). Tzara contributed a preface cleverly titled "Photography inside out" (*"La photographie à l'envers"*), referring both to the reversal of tones in the rayographs, and to the idea that photographic practice might be turned on its head.

Brassaï (1899–1984), born Gyula Halasz in Brasso, Transylvania, the town from which he adapted his name, was working as a correspondent for both Hungarian and German newspapers when he met the Paris Surrealists. His 1933 series *Involuntary Sculpture* shows Surrealist influence (Fig. 5.22).

Most Surrealist photography alludes to psychological intimations and innuendoes, a scenario in which something has just happened or is about to happen, as in Man Ray's untitled image for the Surrealist publication *Minotaure* (Fig. 5.23). Like several early twentieth-century art groups, the Surrealists believed that "primitive" art and myth bypassed conscious, rational thought to reach into the fertile unconscious. In response to the French government's 1931 international Paris Exposition Coloniale, several Surrealists joined forces to curate a section of the anti-imperialist exhibition *La Verité sur les Colonies* (*The Truth about*

the Colonies), which emphasized the originality and spiritual integrity of art created by indigenous peoples living in Africa and Indochina.

Forbidden sensuality and sexuality were frequent Surrealist topics. Hans Bellmer (1902–1975), born in the German-dominated area of Poland called Silesia, encountered the Berlin Dadaists while studying engineering. Following the well-trodden path to Paris in 1924, he came in touch with the Surrealists. After seeing Jacques Offenbach's (1819–1880) opera *The Tales of Hoffmann*, about a beloved automated doll that is demolished, he was inspired to create his own dolls and photograph them (Fig. 5.24).

5.22
**BRASSAÏ
(GYULA HALASZ),**
*Sculpture involontaire
(Involuntary Sculpture),*
1933. Courtesy Edwynn
Houk Gallery, New York.

Brassaï explored the Surrealist notion that the fantastic could be found in the ordinary. He sequenced close-up photographs of discarded chewing gum, theater tickets, cigarette butts, and paper wads, producing bizarrely monumentalized objects.

5.21
MAN RAY, *Abstract
Composition,* 1921–28.
Rayograph. Victoria &
Albert Museum,
London.

**5.23 (above)
MAN RAY, *Untitled*,
from *Minotaure*, 1936.
Silver print. Michael
Senft Collection, East
Hampton, New York.**

For the Surrealist
publication *Minotaure*,
Man Ray used ominous
shadows to suggest that
a man's upper torso
was transforming itself
into the head of a bull.
In Greek mythology, the
Minotaur was a creature
half-man, half-bull, to
whom the Athenians
periodically sent young
men and women for
sacrifice on the island
of Crete.

**5.24
HANS BELLMER,
Doll (La Poupée),
1935. Gelatin silver
print with applied
color. George Eastman
House, Rochester,
New York.**

In these photographs,
Bellmer mismatched
and twisted man-
nequins body parts.
His grotesque figures
have been scrutinized
for insights into his
personal Oedipal
conflicts, and read
as a sophisticated
retaliatory response to
the fair-haired stereo-
types of the normal,
that is, Aryan body,
celebrated in Nazi
propaganda pictures.[36]

Belgian-born Raoul Ubac (1910–1985) was as technically experimental as his sometime collaborator Man Ray. Both solarized prints, a technique Man Ray originally investigated with Berenice Abbott and Lee Miller, who were his studio assistants at different times (see pp. 290–92, 304–5). SOLAR-IZATION involves briefly exposing a print or negative to light during the development process. The result is a reversal of tones, especially along the edges of objects. Sometimes called edge reversal, solarization is unpredictable, which made it a favorite technique of the Surrealists. Ubac also developed a technique called *brûlage*, or burning, in which film emulsion was melted to produce swirling shapes (Fig. 5.25).

Male Surrealist painters and photographers often used female forms as symbols of the primitive, the mysterious, and the erotic. As recent feminist critics have pointed out, they also pictured women's bodies caged, distorted, or dismembered, as if they were primal forces to be trapped, observed, or punished. The women artists in Surrealist

5.27 (below)
CLAUDE CAHUN,
Self-Portrait, 1928.
Gelatin silver print.
Musée des Beaux-Arts,
Nantes, France.

5.25 (above)
RAOUL UBAC,
La Conciliabule, 1938.
Brulage print. Galerie
Adrien Maeght, Paris.

The prints Ubac produced using *brûlage* depict slippery-looking dissolving forms that signal the transitory quality of human identity. The technique gives the whole print a shimmering, dream-like quality.

5.26
DORA MAAR,
Père Ubu, 1936.
Gelatin silver print.
Metropolitan Museum
of Art, New York.

Maar found an element of something extraordinary—and disturbing—in this close-up shot of an armadillo.

circles did not generally adopt this iconography. Painter Dora Maar (1909–1997), often unjustly remembered only as a lover of Picasso and as a subject in his paintings, was also a member of Man Ray's circle and an experimental photographer with a knack for contriving unsettling images (Fig. 5.26). Claude Cahun (1894–1954), an activist writer and photographer involved with Surrealism in Paris during the 1930s, made self-portraits exploring shifting subjective moments and female gender identity (Fig. 5.27). Born Lucy Renée Mathilde Schwob, Cahun adopted the first name of Claude, which in French can be either a male or a female name.

The Surrealist sensibility persisted well beyond its historical highpoint in the 1920s and 1930s, although shorn of its early radicalism and intense psychologizing. Brassaï's recognition that the extraordinary always prowls close to the ordinary informs his book of photographs *Paris de nuit* (*Paris by Night*) (1933), which teems with people who exist at the twilight of respectable society. To many photographic artists,

257

SURREALIST PHOTOGRAPHY

5.28 (below)
BRASSAÏ (GYULA HALASZ), *"Bijou" of Montmartre*, from *Paris de Nuit (Paris by Night)*, c. 1933. Gelatin silver print. David H. McAlpin Fund. Museum of Modern Art, New York.

Like Toulouse-Lautrec before him, Brassaï introduced viewers to people they might not ordinarily meet, placing viewer and subject in uncomfortably confrontational relationships that exploited the photograph's psychological power.

such outsiders as vagrants and prostitutes represented freedom and non-conformity.[37] Brassaï's *Paris by Night* carried no message of social reform or personal redemption, but showed such people of the night as "Bijou" ("Jewel"), who relished the extremes of life (Fig. 5.28).

For André Kertész (1894–1985), a Hungarian-born photographer and mentor to his Paris friend Brassaï, Surrealist distortion of the human figure was a short-lived, if much discussed, experiment (Fig. 5.29). Nevertheless, the Surrealist feeling for the magic of coincidence and presence of the mysterious in everyday life stayed with him throughout his career, as in *Meudon* (Fig. 5.30). Kertész's joy in seizing a fleeting, yet resonant visual moment influenced many twentieth-century photographers, including Robert Capa (see pp. 302–3) and Henri Cartier-Bresson (1908–2004).

5.29 (above)
ANDRÉ KERTÉSZ, *Distortion # 102*, 1933. Gelatin silver print. Gift of Graham Nash. San Francisco Museum of Modern Art, San Francisco, California.

5.30
ANDRÉ KERTÉSZ,
Meudon, 1928. Gelatin
silver print. Museum of
Modern Art, New York.

In *Meudon*, an old Paris
neighborhood, a man is
seen carrying a package
wrapped in newspaper.
He moves toward the
viewer's right just as a
train advances to the left
on what looks like a high
Roman aqueduct, rather
than a railway trestle.
Kertész dwelled on split-
second coincidences
that seemed to hint at an
uncanny alchemy under-
lying ordinary events.

5.31 (opposite)
HENRI CARTIER-
BRESSON, *Behind the
Gare St. Lazare*, 1932.
Gelatin silver print.

Previously, street photo-
graphers had set up
scenes of this kind to
test the speed of small
cameras.[40] But whereas
other puddle-jumpers
were shown reaching a
dry curbstone, Cartier-
Bresson's plump leaper
is poised forever above
a watery landing. He
both imitates the acrobat
on the fence poster and
seems to defy the solidly
earthbound figure.

A painter and student of art history,
Cartier-Bresson recalled that he was
influenced more by Surrealist theories
of the irrational than by Surrealist art
practice. He fastened on to "the role
of spontaneous expression ... and of
intuition and, above all, the attitude of
revolt."[38] He is legendary for describing
his instantaneous composition of a
scene as "the decisive moment," which
he defined as "the simultaneous recognition, in a fraction of a second, of the
significance of an event as well as of a
precise organization of forms which
gave that event its proper expression."[39]
A famous example is his image of a man
suspended over a rain-drenched area
(Fig. 5.31).

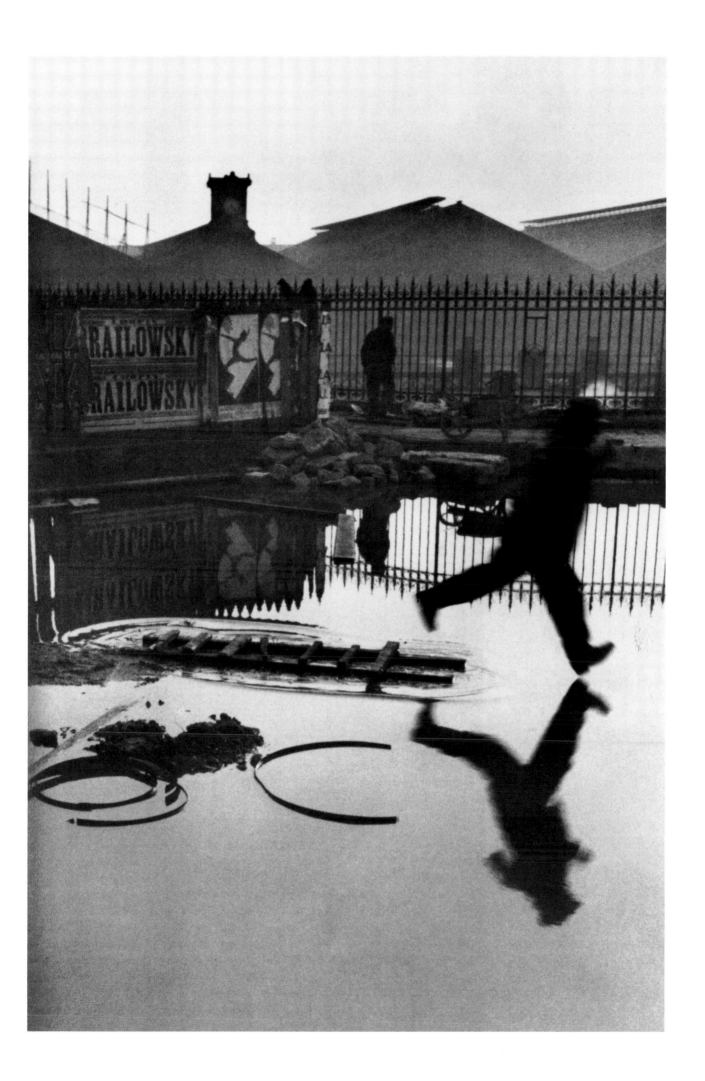

EXPERIMENTAL PHOTOGRAPHY AND ADVERTISING

Experimental photographers in Europe and, to a lesser extent, America applied their graphic techniques and theories to commerce. In the United States, with its lingering affection for the serious amateur Pictorialist who created works of art for love, not money, advertising work was widely seen as a betrayal of artistic talent. Nevertheless, such photographers as Canadian-born Margaret Watkins (1884–1969) (Fig. 5.32) and her protégé American Paul Outerbridge (1896–1958) (Fig. 5.33) both contrived images that translated Modernist visions to advertising.

In Europe, advertising carried less of a stigma, and was even considered a meritorious photographic pursuit. Some Soviet artists saw it as a crucial aspect of modern mass media that could be used to change the public's outlook. Especially in the Soviet Union, theorists were careful to distinguish between capitalist advertising, which they saw as misleading the public, and socialist advertising, which they argued was an educational tool. In 1923, Maiakovskii

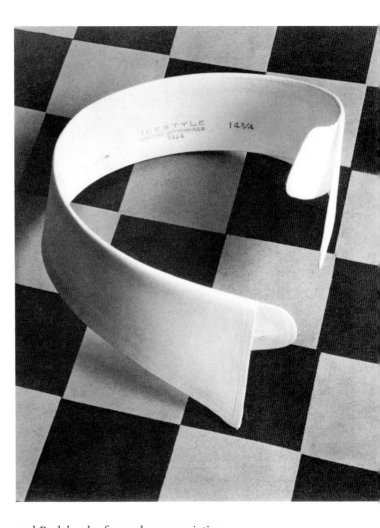

5.33
PAUL OUTERBRIDGE,
Ide Collar, 1922.
Platinum print.
Metropolitan Museum
of Art, New York.

Outerbridge's advertising images stylishly portrayed commodities. His close-up portrait of a disposable shirt collar is gently shaded, as if it were a likeness of the wearer.

5.32
MARGARET WATKINS,
Advertisement for Myer's Gloves, 1920s.
Gelatin silver print. Jok Mulholland Collection, Glasgow, Scotland.

Early advertising used sexually charged images to sell products. Watkins's suggestive style, with its echoes of modern art movements, influenced a generation. She was one of the first women photographers to be employed at a major advertising agency.

and Rodchenko formed an association that they called Maiakovskii–Rodchenko Advertising-Constructor. Maiakovskii's manifesto "Agitation and Advertising" argued that he and Rodchenko "had to put into action all the weapons that the enemy also uses, including advertising."[41] Similar aims guided the formation of the Adbusters Media Foundation in the late twentieth century (see pp. 484–86). Maiakovskii– Rodchenko produced bold graphic designs that occasionally integrated photographs. The firm aimed their advertising at a proletarian audience, and promoted a variety of products including state-manufactured candy, pacifiers, and beer.

In capitalist countries such as Germany, Modernist chic sold upscale products. Moholy-Nagy routinely produced commercial photographs for clients including fashion magazines, publishers, an airline, and an optical company[42] (Fig. 5.34). German photographer August Sander (see p. 289) created an uncharacteristic photomontage for a brand of cologne, and German Krull photographed for automobile companies such as Citroën and Peugeot.

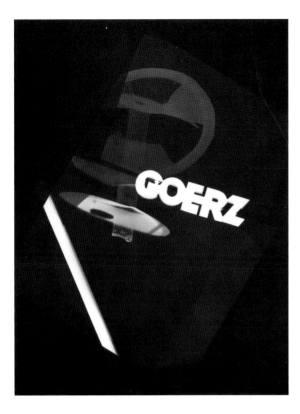

French artist and commercial photographer Maurice Tabard (1897–1984) brought a touch of sophistication and class to a glittering advertisement for a Dunhill cigarette lighter (Fig. 5.35). Speculating on the effectiveness of advertising photography in 1930, German writer Willi Warstat concluded that "the public simply believes without reservation that the *photographic* representation of an object is truer and more real than any artist's graphic representation."[43] Warstat maintained that advertisers must take advantage of that illusion of truth. Advertising photographs in fact presented goods as more than they were, endorsing them with suggestions of sexual allure and financial success. Through advertising, the product became a commodity favored not because it cleaned teeth or provided transportation, but because it pledged to gratify human desires. Swiss-born photographer Hans

5.34 (above)
LÁSZLÓ MOHOLY-NAGY, *Goerz*, 1925. Gelatin silver print. George Eastman House, Rochester, New York.

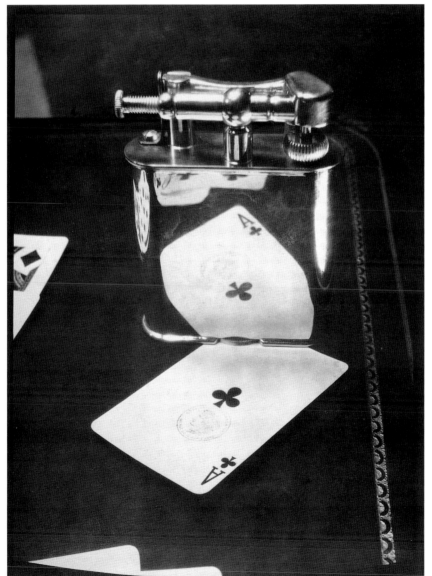

5.35
MAURICE TABARD, *Publicité Dunhill*, 1930. Gelatin silver print. Musée National d'Art Moderne, Centre Beaubourg, Paris.

In order to convey sophistication, the conspicuous ace of clubs is reflected in the gleaming surface of a cigarette lighter. The two edges of playing cards nearest the viewer are reflected near the top of the lighter to suggest a pair of fixated eyes in a face.

FOCUS
Film and Photography

Throughout the 1920s and 1930s, photographers and filmmakers embraced many of the same radical social theories about the visual arts, and used similar techniques to break down preconceptions. For example, Rodchenko interacted with pioneering filmmakers such as Sergei Eisenstein, and even had a small role in one of his films.

In the Soviet Union, cinematographer Dziga Vertov (1896–1954) employed unusual camera angles, super-impositions, and rapidly montaged scenes in such films as the exhilarating *Man with a Movie Camera* (1929), in which a cameraman sweeps through a city recording modern life (Fig. 5.36). Vertov famously announced,

I am kino-eye [film-eye]. I am in constant motion. I draw near, then away from objects, I crawl under, I climb onto them. I move apace with the muzzle of a galloping horse, I plunge full speed into a crowd, I outstrip running soldiers, I fall on my back, I ascend with an airplane, I plunge and soar ...[44]

Much the same could be said for the quick changes of meaning in photomontage, or the surprising angles in Rodchenko's photographs (see Fig. 5.8). Both photographers and filmmakers scorned the laws of gravity, and propelled the viewer on a visual roller-coaster ride. Eisenstein used the new techniques in such patriotic films as *Battleship Potemkin* (1925) and *October* (also known as *Ten Days that Shook the World*) (1927). *October* reenacted the Russian Revolution of 1917, with realistic scenes of the storming of the Winter Palace, a crucial moment in the revolution when the Bolsheviks toppled the czarist regime. The film scenes were later converted into photographs purporting to have been made during the actual assault (see p. 229).

In the years after World War I, before the monopoly of big film studios, artists and photographers were attracted to film as a medium. In his 1922 book *Foto-Kino-Film* (*Photography-Cinema-Film*), Czech artist and writer Karel Teige (1906–1951) wrote enthusiastically about film's potential. Duchamp, Moholy-Nagy, and Man Ray all made non-commercial films. In fact, Man Ray's *Le Retour à la Raison* (*The Return to Reason*) (1923) applied the rayograph process directly to cinema. Among the Surrealist films with visual parallels in photography was *Un Chien Andalou* (*An Andalusian Dog*) (1926), directed by Salvador Dalí (1904–1989) and Luis Buñuel (1900–1983), which deliberately shocked audiences with such scenes as a woman's eyeball being slit by a straight razor. At the exhibition *Film und Foto* held in Stuttgart, Germany, in 1929, the interplay between cinema and photography was manifest (Fig. 5.37). The show of about 1,000 photographic works from Europe, the Soviet Union, and the United States included movie stills, and demonstrated reciprocal uses of camera angles, montages, and superimpositions, which migrated from experimental film and photography to mainstream movies by emulation and the changing employment of cinematographers and writers.

The year 1929 was pivotal in film history. Film speed was standardized at twenty-four frames per second, to accommodate simultaneous sound projection—an indirect indicator of the transformation of filmmaking into

5.36
DZIGA VERTOV,
*Man with a Movie
Camera,* **1929.**

5·37
JAN TSCHICHOLD,
"Film und Foto"
exhibition, Stuttgart,
1929. Poster.
Stadtmuseum,
Stuttgart, Germany.

INTERNATIONALE AUSSTELLUNG
DES DEUTSCHEN WERKBUNDS

FILM

und

FOTO

STUTTGART 1929
FOTO-AUSSTELLUNG VOM 18. MAI BIS 7. JULI
IN DEN NEUEN AUSSTELLUNGSHALLEN AUF DEM INTERIMTHEATERPLATZ
FILM-SONDERVORFÜHRUNGEN VOM 13. BIS 26. JUNI
IN DEN KÖNIGSBAULICHTSPIELEN

OFFSETREPRODUKTION DER FA. G. REISACHER STUTTGART   DRUCK DER UNION STUTTGART

big business, and the subsequent influence of the large studios. Experimental film and photography gave way to documentary film and photography, forms thought to appeal to wider audiences. In Depression-era America, the Resettlement Agency (RA), which evolved into the Farm Security Administration (FSA) (see p. 277), sponsored both photography and film. In 1935, filmmaker Pare Lorentz (1905–1992) was hired to chronicle the Dust Bowl—that is, the dire consequence of soil erosion in the Great Plains that coincided with the economic depression. Working with influential photographers such as Paul Strand, Lorentz made the poignant film *The Plow that Broke the Plains* (1936), employing visual techniques and emotional subjects that FSA photographers would soon emulate.[45] Similarly, members of Film and Photo Leagues included still photographers and motion picture makers. The New York branch made a *Workers' Newsreel*, which they attempted to have shown in theaters.

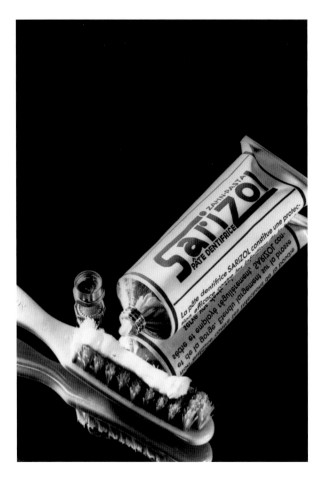

close-ups, and severe angles, were gradually disengaged from utopian aspiration for social change of the sort that followed the Russian Revolution. Nevertheless, the experimental look remained closely associated with dapper newness and swanky modernity. For example, German photographer Albert Renger-Patzsch's (1897–1966) intense close-up advertisements resembled his art photographs (see Fig. 5.40) by zeroing in on the repetitive patterns of rows of commodities, ranging from coffee beans to bathtubs. Former Bauhaus students Ellen Auerbach (1906–2004) and Grete Stern (1904–1999) used their childhood nicknames for their Berlin partnership, foto ringl + pit. They accepted commissions for advertisements and magazine illustrations (Fig. 5.39), as well as fashionable portraits. By 1931, when the New York show called the *Exhibition of Foreign Advertising and Industrial Photography* brought to America the work of European Modernists including Moholy-Nagy, Man Ray, and Bayer, their politics were out of the picture.

EXPERIMENTAL PHOTOGRAPHY AS STYLE

Moholy-Nagy was influential in organizing the international 1929 *Film und Foto* exhibition held in Stuttgart, Germany,

5.38 (above)
HANS FINSLER,
Untitled (Toothpaste and brush), c. 1930. Gelatin silver print. San Francisco Museum of Modern Art, San Francisco, California.

Finsler excelled in glamorizing everyday goods such as toothpaste by cleverly lighted close-ups that hinted at the good life that might be achieved through the use of the product.

Finsler (1891–1972), who taught art history and ran a commercial studio in Germany, was one of the best photographic enchanters (Fig. 5.38).

The techniques of experimental photography, including photomontage,

5.39
Foto ringl + pit,
Petrole Hahn Advertising, Berlin, 1931. Bauhaus-Archiv, Berlin.

Foto ringl + pit counted on viewers being so accustomed to the pose of a glamorous model that they would only gradually detect not a living woman but a mannequin.

to which he contributed ninety-seven photographs, photomontages, and photograms (see Fig. 5.14).[46] At *Fifo*, as the exhibition was called, viewers could see how far photography had changed from the fuzzy look and rural subjects of turn-of-the-century Pictorialism. Collectively, the *Fifo* photographs dwelled on the urban-industrial environment, emphasizing form and texture. Borrowing the name of a contemporary German art movement, observers described such work as exemplifying the *Neue Sachlichkeit*, or New Objectivity. More imprecise terms, such as "New Vision" ("*neue Optik*"), "Modernist Photography," or "New Photography" were also used to denote the emphasis placed on industrial subjects, close-ups, odd angles, and repeated visual patterns.

Some critics decried the commercialization of the Modernist style. Karel Teige angrily observed that *Film und Foto*, as well as the 1930 Munich exhibition *Das Lichtbild* (*The Photograph*, literally "the light picture" in German), propagated a visual fashion emptied of its initial social activism. He noted the tendency in such popular books as *Es kommt der neue Fotograf!* (*Here Comes the New Photographer!*) by writer and filmmaker Werner Graeff (1901–1978),

and the triple-titled *Foto-Auge = Oeil et photo = Photo-eye*, a 1929 compilation of seventy-six contemporary photographs edited by photographer-critic Franz Roh (1890–1965) and proponent of experimental typography Jan Tschichold (1902–1974). In particular, Teige targeted the book *Die Welt ist Schön* (*The World is Beautiful*), by Renger-Patzsch, claiming that its concentration on formal beauty spawned a modish, socially irresponsible version of art for art's sake.[47]

Originally titled *Die Dinge* (*Things*), the book consisted of 100 photographs organized in eight sections, including technology, architecture, and plants. Renger-Patzsch emphasized "thingness" by choosing a view that standardized and regularized the subject (Fig. 5.40). While praising the new photography for tearing the medium "loose from the grip of the petty business machinations of the studios, and from artistic dilettantism," Teige insisted that "photography did not triumph over painting in order to take its place."[48] He appealed for a photography that was grounded in social life, not the art gallery, and invited photographers to recognize that the medium could be successfully practiced by amateurs. Not surprisingly, Teige

5.40
ALBERT RENGER-PATZSCH, *Snake Head*, 1927. Gelatin silver print. The Metropolitan Museum of Art, Gilman Collection, Purchase, Ann Tenenbaum and Thomas H. Lee Gift, 2005.

Der Führer spricht!
Millionen hören ihn.
Das arbeitende Volk,
das Bauerntum,
die wiedergewonnene
Wehrfreiheit
sind die Stützen des
nationalsozialistischen
Deutschland.

The Fuehrer speaks and
millions listen to him.
The working people, the
peasantry and the re-
gained right of self-defence
are the supports of National-
Socialist Germany.

"Le Führer parle!" Des
millions de citoyens
l'écoutent. Le peuple des
travailleurs, la Paysannerie
et la liberté reconquise
de la défense nationale
sont les colonnes de
l'Allemagne nationale-
socialiste.

El "Führer" habla.
Millones le escuchan.
El pueblo trabajador, las
gentes del campo y la
libertad militar recon-
quistada son los sostenes
de la Alemania nacional-
socialista.

5.41
HERBERT BAYER,
Brochure for the
exhibition *Deutschland*,
Berlin, 1936.

Although they deemed
much modern art
degenerate, the Nazis
often took advantage
of the dynamic compo-
sition and iconography
within experimental
photography. Here,
three laudable German
types—a soldier, a
farmer, and a factory
worker—loom over an
admiring throng at a
Nazi rally.

admired Soviet photography, asserting
that it had not lost sight of its ideological
mission. "Service," he concluded, "is the
future of modern photography and its
tasks will be utilitarian: to serve science,
ideas, and social progress." In effect, he
called for a progressive, socially committed documentary photography.

For similar reasons, Renger-Patzsch's
book was also denounced by German
critic Walter Benjamin (1892–1940),
who called its style "the posture of a
photography that can endow any soup-
can with cosmic significance but cannot
grasp a single one of the human connections in which it exists."[49] Benjamin
mocked what he called creative photography, the tendency to look for engaging visual juxtapositions that delighted
the eye, but ignored the mind. He
maintained that taking subjects out of
context, as in severe close-ups, turned
photography "into a sort of art
journalism."[50]

The depoliticizing of experimental
photography at *Fifo* was not an overt,
organized effort. In fact, the show
seemed progressive in its inclusion of
a wide variety of work, ranging beyond
art to X-rays, photomicrographs, press
photographs, and advertising. Yet the
continuous repetition of the style in
newspapers and advertisements dulled

its newness. The art director for Condé
Nast publications, M.F. Agha, shrewdly
remarked, "Modernistic photography is
easily recognized by its subject matter."
He continued:

Eggs (any style), twenty shoes standing in a
row. A skyscraper, taken from a modernistic
angle. Ten tea cups standing in a row. A
factory chimney seen through the ironwork
of a railroad bridge (modernistic angle). The
eye of a fly enlarged 2000 times. The eye
of an elephant (same size). The interior of
a watch. Three different heads of one lady
superimposed. The interior of a garbage can.
More eggs ...[51]

At the same time that the Modernist
style descended into triteness, the
Soviet government shifted its support
away from photographic experimentation (see pp. 239–42), in favor of high-
impact, easily understood propaganda
images.

During the 1930s in Germany,
the rise of the Nazi party, with its love
of nationalistic pictures, and disgust
with what it called cultural Bolshevism,
cooled photographic experimentation
and sent many photographers seeking
asylum abroad. At the same time,
the Nazis recognized the power of
photography, and organized their first
successful propaganda event around
photography in October 1933. The

exhibition *Die Kamera* (*The Camera*) in Berlin took to heart the words of Joseph Goebbels, the chief Nazi propagandist, who declared that "the experience of the individual has become the experience of the people, thanks solely to the camera." Through photography exhibitions such as *The Camera*, the Nazis tried to create a glory-strewn chronology of their rise to power.[52] Ironically, they used the graphic impact of new-vision photography in a brochure designed by Bayer (see p. 248)

to accompany the 1936 Berlin Olympic Games[53] (Fig. 5.41). By the end of the 1930s, the experimental photography developed in the 1920s knew no nationalism or political persuasion. It could be used by Nazis, or against them, as on the cover of *Vu* for April 25, 1934 (Fig. 5.42).

Reflecting on the evolution of photomontage, one of its inventors, Raoul Hausmann, noted that "over time the technique of photomontage has

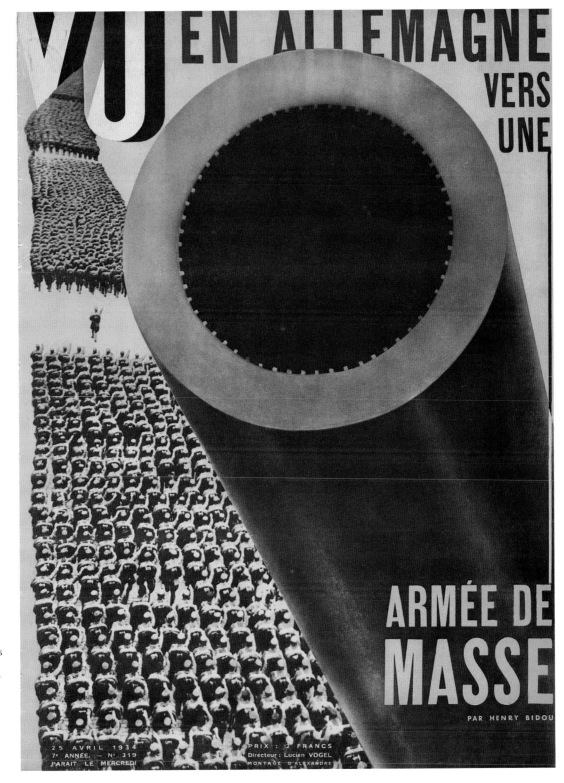

**5.42
ALEXANDER
LIBERMAN,**
"In Germany, toward a mass army," from *Vu*, April 25, 1934. Neogravure. Victoria & Albert Museum (library), London.

The huge gun barrel that looms over the ranks of Nazi soldiers is not merely an emblem of conflict. It also refers to Germany's continuing investment in and development of long-range guns such as "Big Bertha," which during World War I was capable of hurling shells nearly 10 miles.

undergone considerable simplification, forced upon it" by application in "political or commercial propaganda."[54] Commercial propaganda, that is to say, advertising, brought experimental techniques quickly to the mainstream. Packaging and advertising design were coordinated to conflate the newness of the imagery with claims for a commodity's originality and effectiveness. Where earlier forms of product promotion used extensive text, designers now turned to the terse forms in modern art and photography.

The visual techniques of Surrealism were adapted for commercial purposes, most notably in fashion photography. Russian-born George Hoyningen-Huene (1900–1968) worked in Paris, where he moved in the same circles as Man Ray and Salvador Dalí. He photographed such international celebrities as Marlene Dietrich and Charlie Chaplin, as well as the former British monarch Edward VIII, who took the title Duke of Windsor after his abdication in 1936 to marry the American divorcee Wallis Simpson. He quickly moved into the world of *haute couture*, fusing experimental techniques and surreal suggestion in photographs for such magazines as *Vanity Fair* and *Harper's Bazaar* (Fig. 5.43).

A NEW VISION (1918–1945)

**5.43 (below)
GEORGE HOYNINGEN-HUENE,**
Schiaparelli Beachwear,
1930, from *Harper's Bazaar*, 1935. Gelatin silver print. Victoria & Albert Museum, London.

Hoyningen-Huene absorbed the visual vocabularies of twentieth-century art movements, ranging from Cubism to Surrealism, turning them into modish advertisements for upscale goods.

Hoyningen-Huene's friend and student Horst P. Horst (1906–1999) also learned from experimental photography and Surrealist art (Fig. 5.44). The most outlandish advertising photographs in the period were made by Lejaren à Hiller (1880–1969), who revived the *tableau vivant* (see pp. 42, 153–54) for a series of photographs depicting the history of medicine in the 1933 series *Surgery through the Ages*, commissioned by the firm of David and Geck, which made surgical sutures (Fig. 5.45). These photographs were often reprinted and used to decorate doctors' offices.[55]

**5.44 (above)
HORST P. HORST,**
Untitled, 1936. Victoria & Albert Museum, London.

Horst used the slim, overlapping planes of Cubism, as well as the negative–positive look of photograms, in his carefully lit fashion photography. Here he seems to have merged the look of photomontage with the appearance of the rayograph, invented by his friend Man Ray.

CALIFORNIA MODERN

In the United States, advanced technological image-making came to be associated with corporate propaganda, as in Sheeler's images for Ford (see Fig. 5.20). Left-wing political movements mostly rejected such visual effects, favoring instead the look of hand-crafted images to communicate their message. Advertising photography had recourse

5.45
LEJAREN À HILLER, *Étienne Gourmelen*, c. 1933, from *Surgery Through the Ages*, 1933. Gelatin silver print.
George Eastman House, Rochester, New York.

Lejaren à Hiller's advertisements may owe no direct debt to contemporary art, but they exemplify the heightened
sensationalism of advertising imagery in the 1920s and 1930s. In his staged image of Étienne Gourmelen, a
sixteenth-century physician who treated plague victims, the men are clothed, while the slim, nude women disport
themselves in sexually suggestive poses—a little-known symptom of the plague!

**5.46
WILLARD VAN DYKE,**
*Cement Works,
Monolith, California,*
**1931. Gelatin silver print.
Private Collection.**

Van Dyke's angle of
vision made the large
chimney on the right
appear flattened and
tipped inward slightly,
as if it were applied
to the surface of the
picture, similar to a
Cubist collage.

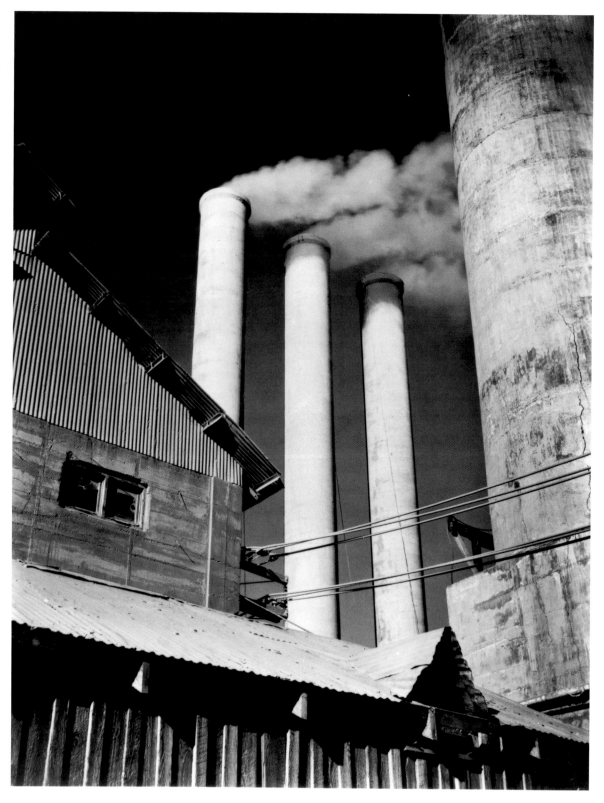

both to the blurry appearance of the
Pictorialist "fuzzygraph" and the lean
lines and crystalline light derived from
European experimental art and photography. Abstraction, which in Europe
had been strongly associated with the
social utopianism of early Modernism,
was valued by American photographers
more for its aura of artistic seriousness.
Surrealism similarly lost its political
content (closely bound with the fight

against fascism in 1930s' Europe) when
it crossed the Atlantic.

The mists of Pictorialist photography
(see pp. 171–201) were still thick in
California in the late 1920s, when a
loose affiliation of friends dubbed themselves Group f.64, and issued a manifesto: "The members of Group f.64
believe that Photography, as an art-form,
must develop along lines defined by
the actualities and limitations of the

photographic medium, and must always remain independent of ideological conventions of art and aesthetics that are reminiscent of a period and culture antedating the growth of the medium itself."[56] In other words, Group f.64 dismissed Pictorialism, despite the fact that several of its members had practiced it, and urged the exploration of camera vision. Their name referred to the small lens opening on their cameras that produced clear detail in the foreground as well as the background, and indicated that they had more in common with regard to the appearance of the photograph than its subject matter.

It is difficult to say exactly how the general strains of Modernism reached the group. Certainly they traveled, and they were familiar with contemporary magazine design and advertising. In addition, the Oakland Art Gallery in California exhibited Bauhaus abstract art, German posters, and works by the Blue Four (*Blauen Vier*), a group of Bauhaus painters, including Kandinsky and Klee, formerly associated with the

German Expressionists collectively called the Blue Rider (*Der Blaue Reiter*), from the title of a picture by Kandinsky. In fact, the Blue Four was not a formal organization, but a term chosen specifically to acquaint American audiences with their work, while alluding to the success of the Blue Rider. The first American Blue Four show was held in Oakland, and led to criticism that Group f.64's notions were drawn from the German artistic invasion of America. Opponents discounted the fact that f.64 did not promote social change, as did the Germans. In West Coast parlance, the Modernist work of Moholy-Nagy was called "pure photography," a term f.64 used at the "First Salon of Pure Photography" (1934), and which their enemies derided as the "carcass" of transatlantic ideas.[57]

The Group's energetic organizer, Willard Van Dyke (1906–1986), photographed a cement works, usually a dusty business, as if it were a sun-drenched Cubist apparition (Fig. 5.46). In the middle of the Depression, Van Dyke began to respond to the growing sentiment that artists should contribute directly to the nation's economic recovery. He did a stint as camera operator for Pare Lorentz (see p. 263) on the shooting of *The Plow that Broke the Plains*, which recorded the plight of Midwestern farmers, and went on to make other documentary films.

As a teenager, Imogen Cunningham (1883–1976) was so impressed with a reproduction of Käsebier's *Blessed Art Thou Among Women* (see Fig. 4.32) that she decided then and there to be a photographer. After college, she went to work in the studio of Edward S. Curtis, where she learned the intricacies of platinum printing. Following photographic study in Germany, in 1910 she opened a portrait studio in Seattle, Washington. When exhibited, her Pictorialist nude interpretation of the Adam and Eve story became the scandal of Seattle. A move to California increased her contact with other photographers, especially Edward Weston (1886–1958). During the 1920s and 1930s her work shifted toward a starkly geometrical style of straight photography. Her female nude studies and close-ups of plants (Fig. 5.47) and flower portraits began to be compared to the simple, sinuous forms favored

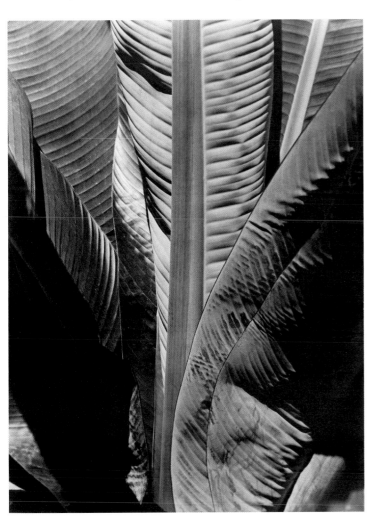

5.47
IMOGEN CUNNINGHAM,
Banana Plant, c. 1929.
Museum purchase,
George Eastman House,
Rochester, NY.

by American painter Georgia O'Keeffe (see Fig. 5.73). Some of her plant studies were exhibited at the 1929 *Film und Foto* show in Stuttgart. Cunningham's strength in this period rested on her ability to find visually arresting pictures in small moments of life. Her later work capitalized on her knowledge of portraiture, as in her informal series picturing older people (Fig. 5.48).

Ansel Adams (1902–1984) and Edward Weston, probably the best-known members of f.64, shared a philosophic regard for natural forms. Adams revealed his belief in the spiritual value of nature to society when he remarked, "I still believe there is a real, social significance in a rock—a more important significance therein than in a line of unemployed."[58] Nevertheless, Adams spoke and showed his prints at the politically involved Photo League in New York. Adams's concentration on dramatic images of natural light effects was fixed well before he became acquainted with f.64. During the 1920s, for example, while working as a guide and custodian in California's Yosemite National

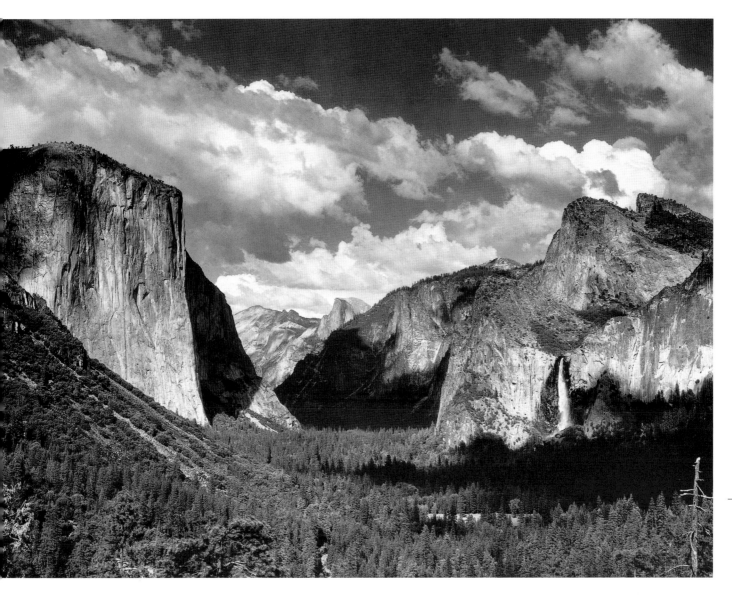

5.49
ANSEL ADAMS,
*Valley View, Yosemite
National Park,
California*, c. 1933.
Gelatin silver print.
Collection Center for
Creative Photography,
University of Arizona,
Tucson, Arizona.

Among Adams's most
famous photographs
are those he took at
Yosemite National
Park. These views
favored startling depth
of field and physical
details, as well as an
attentive eye for light
and weather effects.

Park area, Adams photographed the region (Fig. 5.49).

Meetings with Strand and Stieglitz strengthened Adams's resolve to photograph full-time. At Yosemite, in the midst of the scenery swooningly recorded by Carleton E. Watkins, he worked out the beginnings of what he would call the "zone system" of photography. His method allowed a photographer to previsualize the finished print by comparing light intensities in the scene to be photographed with a chart showing an ascending scale of tones, ranging from black to white. In other words, the main work of picture-making took place not in the darkroom, but before the film was exposed.

After the United States entered World War II, following the Japanese bombing of Pearl Harbor on December 7, 1941, Adams and Dorothea Lange (1895–1965) expressed their sense of outrage at the forced round-up and

confinement of Americans of Japanese descent at the California internment camp called Manzanar Relocation Center in Owens Valley. Though given access to the camp, Adams and Lange were forbidden to photograph guards, guard towers, or barbed wire. Pictures of camp life were also made by Toyo Miyatake (1895–1979), a Modernist Japanese-American photographer interned at Manzanar, who eventually gained permission to photograph around the camp (Fig. 5.50).

Though Edward Weston did not originate an elaborate system of tonal equivalents as Adams did, he, too, believed that "the finished print is previsioned on the ground glass while focusing ... the shutter's release fixes forever these values and forms."[59] Like Adams, Weston joined the f.64 group when he was already established as a photographer, perhaps to underscore his allegiance to Modernism. His first

5.50
TOYO MIYATAKE,
*Three Boys playing near
a barbed-wire fence,
Manzanar Relocation
Camp.*

In recent years,
Miyatake's most repro-
duced photograph has
come to stand for the
unjust incarceration of
Japanese-Americans
during World War II.

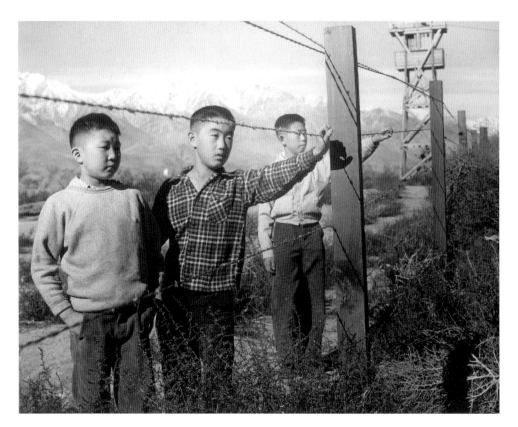

5.50
TOYO MIYATAKE,
*Three Boys playing near
a barbed-wire fence,
Manzanar Relocation
Camp.*

In recent years,
Miyatake's most repro-
duced photograph has
come to stand for the
unjust incarceration of
Japanese-Americans
during World War II.

book of images, *The Art of Edward
Weston*, was available at the group's
inaugural show at San Francisco's
M. H. de Young Memorial Museum in
November 1932. A decade before this

exhibition, Weston had visited Stieglitz
in New York, an event he treasured,
even though the older photographer
dropped one after another of Weston's
prints on the discard pile. In 1923,

5.51
TINA MODOTTI,
Workers, Mexico,
c. 1926–30. Gelatin
silver print. Amon
Carter Museum,
Fort Worth, Texas.

Modotti's political views
and her photographic
practice were stimulated
by her stay in Mexico.
She moved away from
making Modernist
close-ups of natural
forms to photographing
workers, exalting the
dignity and virtue of
manual labor, as in her
image of two workers
managing a load.

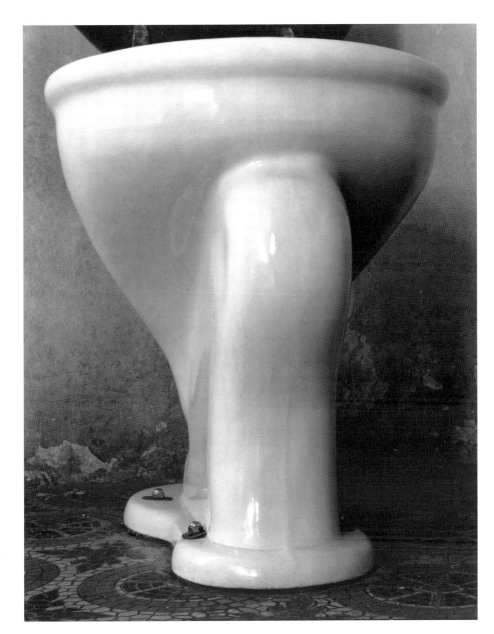

5.52
EDWARD WESTON,
Excusado, Mexico, 1925.
Gelatin silver print.
Center for Creative
Photography, University
of Arizona, Tucson,
Arizona.

Weston compared his
image of a toilet with
the beautiful form of
Greek statues. "Photo-
graphy is realism!" he
announced. "Why make
excuses?" He portrayed
the unpretentious
object as a shape so
captivatingly smooth
that it shed its vulgar
association with mere
bodily functions,
and was transformed
into an instance of
formal grace.

Weston left his struggling portrait business and went to live in Mexico with his companion, the photographer Tina Modotti (1896–1942). Modotti came into her own in Mexico, evolving away from Weston's interest in beautiful patterns to a concern for injustice in society (Fig. 5.51). After 1930, she largely gave up photography in favor of political work. Several of her photographs appeared in *Der Arbeiter-Fotograf* (*The Worker-Photographer*)[60] (see p. 290).

In Mexico, Weston made his most notorious image, *Excusado* (the Spanish word for "toilet") (Fig. 5.52). The toilet exemplifies Weston's close-up, sharply detailed approach to everyday objects such as sea shells and vegetables, especially his celebrated photographs of peppers, which he compared to the sleek sculpture of

Romanian Constantin Brancusi (1876–1957), himself an accomplished photographer. By the time of the inaugural f.64 show, Weston had organized the American contribution to the 1929 *Film und Foto* show, enjoyed a major exhibit of his work at the M. H. de Young Memorial Museum in San Francisco, and had two successful shows in New York City.

Though eagerly involved, Weston's active participation in f.64 activities was only a brief phase in his life. Continuing in style and visual themes he groomed in Mexico, Weston went on to make several series of images involving light, shade, and texture in nature. Oddly enough, his photographs of deeply pleated light and dark patterns of sand dunes, or twisted cypress trees and worn rocks at Point Lobos, California, seem more sensual than

**5.53
EDWARD WESTON,
Nude, 1934. Gelatin
silver print. Center for
Creative Photography,
University of Arizona,
Tucson, Arizona.**

Many of Weston's
images of human nudes
are not erotic, but
arresting glimpses of
the body's contortions.
By contrast, his
photographs of subtle,
textured shadows
originating in nature
are often more sensual.

his images of the human nude (Fig. 5.53). Where Stieglitz is remembered as the photographer who put modern art and photography on the American cultural radar, Weston is revered as a romantic figure, who sacrificed emotional and economic stability to pursue his creative life.

SOCIAL SCIENCE, SOCIAL CHANGE, AND THE CAMERA

While many American photographers of the 1930s had been influenced by f.64's Modernist aesthetic, their subject matter during this decade was more profoundly determined by their varied responses to the social and political realities of the Depression. The emergence of documentary photography as a means of addressing those realities would have a far-reaching legacy for the medium.

The sustained world economic and industrial growth of the 1920s ended abruptly in 1929. In the United States, the stock market crash on October 24, 1929, wiped out over 60 per cent of the value of securities, and set off a chain reaction of bank failures, factory

shut-downs, and mortgage foreclosures. Conditions worsened further in the early 1930s, because of the impact of European financial crises on the United States. Unemployment grew, while foreign trade declined. By the election of 1932, one worker in four was unemployed, at a time when families primarily depended on a single breadwinner, and when relief programs were minimal. Franklin D. Roosevelt (1882–1945) came to the American presidency with a broad series of recovery plans collectively known as the New Deal. As during his governorship of New York, Roosevelt and his associates banned photographs showing him in his wheelchair or wearing the heavy leg braces that he needed as a result of having had polio. Roosevelt was keenly aware of maintaining public faith in his good health. Though there were occasional exceptions, the press largely complied. When he fell flat approaching the speaker's platform at the 1936 Democratic Convention, no written reports noted it and no photographs of it appeared in the press.[61]

In the United States, the Depression was viewed as a challenge to the notion of America as a land of limitless opportunity for those willing to roll up their sleeves and work. As the Depression was gradually perceived as an enduring, not temporary experience, many photographers softened the hard graphics of Modernist photography and adapted them to interpretations of how people now lived. The clear close-ups of troubled faces, angled pictures of ragged breadlines, and angry contrasts between poverty and wealth began to be called documentary photography.

THE ORIGINS OF DOCUMENTARY

In a broad sense, all non-fictional representation, in books or in images, is documentary. But during the 1930s, when the word "documentary" came into wide usage, its meaning was more limited. Writers, filmmakers, and photographers produced a blend of Modernistic style and realistic subject matter, aimed at educating the public about the experience of hardship or injustice. Earlier photographers such as John Thomson and Jacob Riis had pictured misfortune, but they were not interested in visual innovation, and they tended to present people in categories, such as occupation, class status, or ethnic origin. Documentary photographers in the 1930s strove to present their human subjects as ordinary people who were temporarily down on their luck, hoping that viewers would make the imaginative leap to apply the message to themselves. Earlier social documentary photography, with the exception of Lewis Hine's work, was more patronizing toward its subjects.

Filmmaking and film theory helped instigate the beginnings of documentary photography. For example, to make his popular *Man With a Movie Camera*, Dziga Vertov left the studio and roamed the streets recording life as it was lived, before editing it into a fast-paced visual roadshow (see p. 262). In the 1920s, documentary film combined derring-do with exotic stories, as in *Grass* (1923), an account of the hazardous yearly migration of the Bakhtiari people of Iran. *Grass* was shot by Merian C. Cooper (1893–1923) and Ernest B. Schoedsach (1893–1979), who went on to make *King Kong* (1933), a film whose early island scenes demonstrate the active, entertaining qualities of early documentary.

American filmmaker Robert Flaherty (1884–1951) spent sixteen months with the indigenous people near Hudson Bay in Canada chronicling their daily lives in the box-office success *Nanook of the North* (1922). Though acting and scripts were discouraged by documentary filmmakers, they were not purists. For example, during the shooting of *Nanook*, Flaherty restaged a walrus kill. Flaherty's public success helped legitimize the documentary mode, and sent the big film studios in search of "another *Nanook*." The first use of the word "documentary" in its new sense was probably made by influential British filmmaker and theorist John Grierson (1898–1972), in his review of Flaherty's South Sea island film *Moana* (1926).

The documentary current flowed not only through film and photography, but also through social science writing, popular literature, radio programs, and art movements such as the American Ashcan school.[62] Each of these modes reinforced the other, suggesting that the practitioners were neutral observers, boldly recounting facts. Grierson suggested that documentary should be given the power of poetry and prophesy.[63]

He maintained that documentary was "an 'anti-aesthetic' movement" that knew how to use aesthetics.[64] However, photographer Ansel Adams rejected the new fusion of art and observation, complaining wryly that "What you've got are not photographers. They're a bunch of sociologists with cameras."[65]

Over time, as questions about the accuracy and completeness of documentary arose, its primary association with social observation and social advocacy weakened. Today the word is popularly used loosely to describe large visually and thematically related archives or extensive photographic projects, such as novelist Eudora Welty's (1909–2001) far-ranging photographs of three decades of life in the American South (see p. 290), or Carl van Vechten's (1880–1964) 1,400 portrait photographs of famous individuals (see Fig. 5.73). Contemporary documentary photography now frequently navigates between visualizing the personal experience of the photographer and a setting of profuse sociological text.

THE FARM SECURITY ADMINISTRATION

Initiated in 1935, the Resettlement Administration (RA) was among President Roosevelt's efforts to fight the Depression. It was an umbrella agency, charged with coordinating the various rural relief efforts in government departments, including the Agricultural Adjustment Administration and the Federal Emergency Relief Administration. The agency oversaw loans, flood control, migrant camps, and agricultural education. As its name implies, one of the RA's prominent initiatives was to move distressed farmers into more economically viable service and industrial work. The mission of the RA, like many of the New Deal agencies, was regularly questioned by conservatives who felt that direct, planned government intervention into the economy and the daily lives of citizens was un-American, or worse, crypto-socialist.

In 1937, the RA was subsumed into the Department of Agriculture and renamed the Farm Security Administration (FSA). Roy Stryker (1893–1976), who supervised the photographic activity of the RA, continued with the FSA, directing what was officially known as the "Historical Section—Photographic." His job remained much the same: he was to gather photographic evidence of the agency's good works and transmit these images to the press. Stryker's background as a photo-editor consisted solely of his efforts to find illustrations for the textbook *American Economic Life and the Means of Its Improvement* (1925), written by his mentor Columbia University professor Rexford Tugwell. When Tugwell came to Washington to head the RA, Stryker came with him.

Some scholars argue that the orchestration of public opinion through the mass media practiced by the FSA and other New Deal programs parallels the activities of experimental photographers in the early years of the Soviet Union.[66] Certainly the United States and the Soviet Union both envisioned industrial expansion as crucial to future prosperity. But the RA/FSA did not financially support revolutionary departures from visual—or political—conventions, as did the Soviet Union. In fact, the United States government feared socialist connotations, and abstained from calling their efforts propaganda, preferring instead the word "publicity."[67]

The RA/FSA photographers were heir to an understanding of documentary that revolved around emotionally persuasive, stylized depictions of symbolic images. However much they asserted the hard reality of their pictures, they were no more averse to invoking religious imagery than was Hine. Indeed, the photographs that themselves have become part of American history, such as Arthur Rothstein's *Fleeing a Dust Storm* (see Fig. 5.57) or Dorothea Lange's *Migrant Mother* (see Fig. 5.55), elicited biblical associations of wandering in the desert or the Virgin Mary with the baby Jesus.

Early in his tenure, Stryker envisioned a smooth system in which full-time photographers exhaustively covered the agency's good works around the country, and returned the images to the RA for swift nationwide distribution to media outlets. Budget restraints reduced his grandiose vision, yet Stryker still scheduled assignments, drafted shooting scripts, and decided which photographs would be distributed to media outlets ranging from *Time*

magazine to the *Junior Scholastic*.[68] By 1940, the agency claimed to be distributing an average of 1,400 images a month.[69] Stryker's pet idea of focusing on life in small towns may have come from conversations he had with sociologist Robert S. Lynd, who with Helen Lynd wrote the influential 1929 book *Middletown: A Study in Modern America*, a classic in-depth study of an average middle-American small city. Stryker once bragged about his ability to shape views of the Depression that avoided tabloid voyeurism and social strife, saying, "You'll find no record of big people or big events ... There are pictures that say Depression, but there are no pictures of sit-down strikes, no apple salesmen on street corners, not a single shot of Wall Street, and absolutely no celebrities."[70] Roughly twenty photographers,[71] full- and part-time, shot for the agency until 1942, at which time it was subsumed within the Office of War Information. Although some photographs were taken before the RA was renamed the FSA, and after it was engaged to do war work, the images are collectively known as the Farm Security Administration photographs.

Among Stryker's first hires was Walker Evans (1903–1975), who came to the agency in June 1935 with well-established credentials. Through Berenice Abbott (see p. 287), Evans had had the opportunity to view the photographs of Eugène Atget (see Fig. 5.65), which Abbott had amassed in Paris and brought to New York City. Evans responded to Atget's straightforward recording of historic streets and buildings, as well as worn interiors and architectural detail that bespoke the persistence of the past in the present. Unlike the Surrealist photographers, who found Atget's work full of mystery and the uncanny, Evans located there a reserved and courtly melancholy about the transitions of modern life. He spoke of Atget's "lyrical understanding of the street, trained observation of it, special feeling for patina, eye for revealing detail, over all of which is thrown a poetry."[72] Atget's images heartened Evans's aesthetic inclinations, while the commercial and fashion photographs of Steichen ran counter to his sensibilities. Evans wrote that Steichen's "general note is money, understanding advertising

We wonder whether the great American dream

Was the singing of locusts out of the grass to the west and the

West is behind us now:

The west wind's away from us

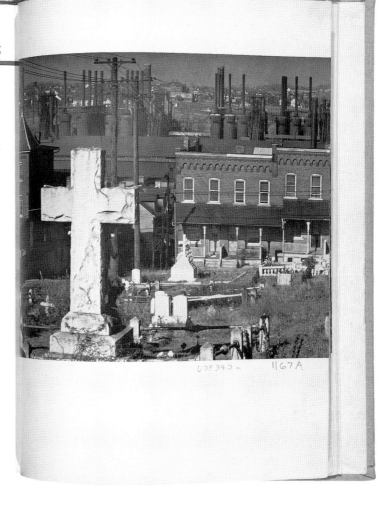

5.54
WALKER EVANS,
Untitled, **from** *Land of the Free,* **by Archibald MacLeish, 1937. Library of Congress, Washington, D.C.**

Evans's photograph symbolically showed the lives of workers in Bethlehem, Pennsylvania. He focused on electrical lines, which extend from the cemetery to the humble housing, and then to the steel mills in the background—the same factories where Frederick Winslow Taylor studied the steps laborers use to perform tasks (see p. 217). In his book *Land of the Free* (1937), Archibald MacLeish used the image, juxtaposing it with his poetry, as shown here.

values, special feeling for parvenu elegance, slick technique, over all of which is thrown a hardness of superficiality that is the hardness and superficiality of America's latter day."[73] In Evans's view, commercialism was not simply Steichen's personal dilemma, but America's national predicament.

Evans believed in finding scenes and objects whose appearance implied a story or acted as a metaphor for an attitude toward life. He felt that his unambiguous, clearly composed images owed a debt to the spare and rhythmic prose style of American author Ernest Hemingway (1899–1961).[74] Evans's image of Bethlehem, Pennsylvania (Fig. 5.54), symbolically guides the viewer from background to foreground through a fatal progression of work, home life, and death. The image shows no people, but used the locale and flattened perspective to indicate the compass of their restricted lives.

Evans secured a leave of absence from the RA to work for *Fortune* magazine on a project with his friend the writer James Agee (1909–1955). Like

other publications in the mid-1930s, *Fortune* contrived human-interest photo-essays on how the Depression affected individuals. For their joint venture, Agee and Evans chronicled the lives of three families of impoverished, cotton-growing tenant farmers in Hale County, Alabama. Agee's procrastination, and *Fortune*'s doubts about the project, eventually prompted the company to cancel the assignment. The project was eventually published as the book *Let Us Now Praise Famous Men* (1941), with a suite of Evans's uncaptioned photographs preceding Agee's text. Agee explained that his prose and Evans's photographs were to be viewed as "coequal, mutually independent, and fully collaborative."[75] Published in the shadow of the commercially successful *You Have Seen Their Faces* (1937), by Margaret Bourke-White and Erskine Caldwell (see p. 284), the Evans–Agee book was a financial failure. Evans's image of twenty-seven-year-old Allie Mae Burroughs, thinly disguised as "Annie Mae Gudger" in the text, exemplified his approach to picture-making (Fig. 5.0).

Evans's disdain for Stryker's assignment guidelines and deadlines made him the legendary bad boy of FSA photography, and he was dismissed in 1937. It is difficult to imagine that the autocratic Stryker could tolerate Evans's desire to record handmade advertising signs or austere domestic interiors as an anonymous folk art. Evans's images tended to lift poverty and the economic effects of the Depression into a timeless picturesque universe. Spare and serene images comprised the bulk of Evans's pictures in *American Photographs*, the title of his 1937 Museum of Modern Art exhibition and his 1938 book. This book influenced a generation of younger American photographers, such as Robert Frank (see pp. 339–40). They admired its dispassionate approach, which for them indicated Evans's caustic alienation from society. His insistence on publishing the images without captions and in no chronological order suggested the sensibilities of an artist who demanded that his work be taken on its own terms.

After the FSA, Evans continued his artful documentary in such series as his subway photographs taken with a concealed camera. But his major source of income was ironically as a writer and

5.55
DOROTHEA LANGE,
Migrant Mother, 1936,
from *Midweek Pictorial*,
October 17, 1936. FSA
Scrapbook, FSA-OWI
Written Records.
Library of Congress,
Washington, D.C.

Lange's photograph recalls religious images of the Madonna and Child, but also expresses Depression era values. The children on either side turn away, symbolically ashamed of their wretchedness. The mother's careworn face, her tattered clothes, and the dirty baby near her breast indicate extreme distress, deserving of compassion. Yet her expression hints at a determination to persevere through hard times.

Look in her Eyes!

THIS WOMAN is watching something happen to America and to herself and her children who are a part of America. You can see in her eyes the horror of what is happening, for she is not looking at it with the objectivity of a statistician or professor. She is making no study of farm tenancy, but is feeling its lashings.

Millions like her do not have to look at the map below to know that the problems of absentee and corporation land ownership are acute and frightening. These problems grow by terrifying strides with each crop disaster, drought and depression.

Once farm tenancy was thought alien to an America where rugged homesteaders needed only to move west from free farm to free farm. Now the ragged tenant-farmer moves from landlord to landlord.

Besides devastating the farming population, the rise of tenancy devastates the soil itself. The nomad farmer is a stranger in the land. He does not plant trees, nurse shrubs, repair gullies nor follow a permanent policy of soil improvement and crop rotation. And worse off than the tenant is the farm-laborer who is subject not only to the will of impoverished tenants, but to the will of the seasons as well.

Revolt in America is brewing faster among the agrarian population than among city workers. Sheriffs are defied in the Corn Belt. Tenant unions and farm labor unions are organized successfully and clashes with owner-vigilantes take place under harvest moons. But the mobilization of sheriffs solves no problems and enlightened landlords now realize that farm tenancy cannot be fought with torch-light raids.

The Resettlement Administration is trying to move tenants off eroded lands and place them where crops actually rise above the surface of

Photo by Dorothea Lange Resettlement Administration

the earth. It is hoped long-term government loans will bring eventual ownership of their new homes to transplanted farmers.

The government can protect the farmer against the institution of the mortgage, just as it can establish mechanisms to protect the farmer against other causes of tenancy—crop disasters, soil erosion, droughts, depressions. An enlightened nation looks to its government, no matter of what political party, to salvage the land and those on it so that by the time these frightened children in this photograph reach maturity, the American farmer once more will stand on his own feet and call the plot of ground he works his own.

PERCENT
Under 40.0
40.0–49.9
50.0–59.9
60.0–69.9
70 and over

APPROXIMATE TREND UNITED STATES
	PERCENT
1890	41
1900	46
1910	50
1920	54
1930	58

Percentage of the Value of Farm Real Estate Not Belonging to the Farm Operator, 1930

October 17, 1936

23

MA BURNHAM

My father was a Confederate soldier. He give his age a year older than what it was to get into the army. After the war he bought 280 acres from the railroad and cleared it. We never had a mortgage on it.

In 19 and 20 the land was sold and the money divided. Now none of the children own their land. It's all done gone, but it raised a family. I've done my duty—I feel like I have. I've raised 12 children—6 dead, 6 alive, and 2 orphans . . .

    *   *   *   *   *

Then all owned their farms. The land was good and there was free range. We made all we ate and wore. We had a loom and wheel. The old settlers had the cream. Now this hill land has washed. And we don't get anything for what we sell. We had two teams when this depression hit us. We sold one team—we had to to get by—and we sold 4 cows.

    *   *   *   *   *

In 19 and 35 we got only 50 and 60 cents a hundred pounds for picking, and in 19 and 36 only 60 and 75 cents, and we hoe for 75 cents a day. Then the government reduced the acreage and where there was enough for two big families now there's just one. Some of the landowners would rather work the cotton land themselves and get all the government money. So they cut down to what they can work themselves, and the farming people are rented out. They go to town on relief—it's a "have to" case. Sharecroppers are just cut out.

Then the Lord taken a hand, and by the time He'd taken a swipe at it there was drought and army worm. I don't know whether that drought was the Devil's work or the Lord's work—in 3 days everything wilted.

Folks from this part has left for California in just the last year or so. My two grandsons—they were renters here and no more—went to California to hunt work. Those who have gone from here . . .

If you see my grandsons in California tell 'em you met up with Ma Burnham of Conroy, Arkansas.

June 28, 1938

photographer for *Fortune*, a periodical devoted to big business.

Unlike Evans, Dorothea Lange came to the RA in 1935 with a sure sense of social justice and of how photography could reveal inequality. As a statement of her belief, in 1923 she tacked lines by English statesman and writer Francis Bacon (1561–1626) to her darkroom door:

The contemplation of things as they are
without substitution or imposture
without error or confusion
is in itself a nobler thing
than a whole harvest of invention.[76]

The seminar she took in New York City on basic photography, given by Pictorialist Clarence White, did not influence the look or the subject matter of her images.

During the early Depression Lange photographed labor demonstrations and breadlines in San Francisco. Her work with activist-economist Paul Taylor, whom she subsequently married, focused her attention on the plight of migrant farmworkers. For the RA, she produced the

photograph that became the national icon of the Depression. *Migrant Mother* is one of several shots Lange took of a thirty-two-year-old woman and her children, who were stranded in a frozen pea field among the crop they had hoped to pick to earn some money (Fig. 5.55). Undoubtedly the most popular image created during the Depression era, the photograph was repeatedly sent out to newspapers and magazines by the Farm Security Administration.

Though powerful, *Migrant Mother* is not typical of Lange's work. She did not readily repeat the mother-and-child theme. With Taylor supplying the text, Lange published captioned photographs in *An American Exodus: A Record of Human Erosion* (1939), a book whose title refers to the destructive southwestern drought of the mid-1930s, and the migration it caused. In the book, photographs were accompanied by quotations from the sitters (Fig. 5.56), unlike the fictionalized statements created by Margaret Bourke-White and Erskine Caldwell for *You Have Seen Their Faces*.

5.56
DOROTHEA LANGE,
Ma Burnham, from *An American Exodus*, by Dorothea Lange and Paul Schuster Taylor, 1939, pp. 150–51. Library of Congress, Washington, D.C.

Lange's photograph of Ma Burnham remains at a respectful distance, and is typically shot from below, monumentalizing the figure. Though she had a fine sense of effective composition, Lange did not emphasize contrasting and harmonizing abstract forms in the manner of Walker Evans.

After her five years with the RA/FSA, Lange continued to make photographs that accorded with her concern for social justice. She and Taylor were adamantly opposed to the 1942 War Relocation Authority (WRA), which forcibly moved Japanese-Americans to internment camps. Like Adams, Lange photographed the internees' life at Manzanar Relocation Center in California. For *Life* magazine, she pro-filed the daily life of a public defender in Alameda County, California, and chronicled the last days of farming com-munities in the Berrysea Valley, north-east of San Francisco, on the brink of being flooded by the construction of a new dam.

Another early recruit to the RA was Arthur Rothstein (1915–1985), who made an enduring image of the Dust Bowl experience (Fig. 5.57). Rothstein's photography has been overshadowed by a notorious set of photographs he made in the barren Badlands of South Dakota during the summer of 1936. Having come across the sun-bleached skull of a steer resting on parched soil, he filmed

it where he found it, but then moved it, and experimented with close-ups and cast shadows. He was accused of fakery for moving the skull; the agency worried that their funds would be cut back, but did not dismiss Rothstein.[77] In fact, sev-eral RA/FSA photographers could have been charged with altering their images; Lange, for example, had a retoucher airbrush out what she considered a flaw in *Migrant Mother*.[78]

Photographers came and went at the RA/FSA, some working only a few months. Although about twenty individ-uals worked for the agency, only a half-dozen or so were employed at any one time.[79] Among the late hires at the FSA, when the agency's focus was changing from small town and rural life to urban enterprise and defense activities, were Gordon Parks (b. 1912) and Esther Bubley (1921–1998). Parks came to Washington, D.C., on a prestigious fellowship, which had been held by other African-Americans, such as Zora Neale Hurston (1891–1960) and James Baldwin (1924–1987), who wrote about the American South and the black

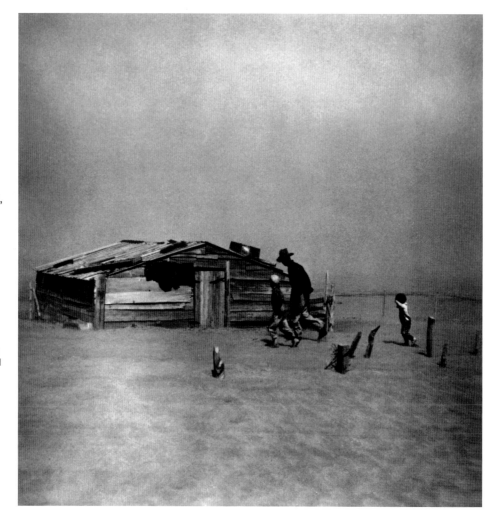

5.57
ARTHUR ROTHSTEIN,
Fleeing a Dust Storm,
Cimarron County,
Oklahoma, April 1936.
Gelatin silver print.
FSA Collection.
Library of Congress,
Washington, D.C.

Influenced by the poignant imagery of Pare Lorentz's film *The Plow that Broke the Plains* (1936), Rothstein traveled to the dustbowl area where it had been filmed to record the ceaseless wind and the sand-drenched atmos-phere. This image shows a farmer and his children leaning into the incessant wind as it scours their land, removing the topsoil and thereby leaving their life in ruins.

As part of a composition that is replete with symbolism and that pointedly echoes Grant Wood's painting, *American Gothic*, Ella Watson stands before the American flag in the office of the Farm Security Administration.

5.59 (below)
ESTHER BUBLEY,
Listening to a Murder Mystery on the Radio in a Boarding House Room, 1943. Gelatin silver print. Library of Congress, Washington, D.C.

experience. Parks began by photographing the life and work of Ella Watson, who cleaned the agency's office (Fig. 5.58).

Esther Bubley was hired in 1942, just as the agency changed its name to the Office of War Information. Her first assignments were in Washington, a city rapidly transforming in response to the United States' entry into World War II. Bubley emphasized women workers, who replaced soldiers. She pictured women at work, driving streetcars and in the new residences for women that were quickly formed in the city and its suburbs (Fig. 5.59). Her images of solitary, pensive women differ greatly from the main visual themes of the FSA. In 1943, she road buses for four weeks, chronicling bus travel, which increased in popularity due to wartime rationing in gasoline and tires. Generally, Bubley's

PORTRAIT
Margaret Bourke-White

By the time she was in her mid-twenties, Margaret Bourke-White (1904–1971) was in the news. Such captions as "This daring camera girl scales skyscrapers for art"[80] show the press's infatuation with a woman who climbed out on to the high steel frame of the Chrysler Building to record its construction, stood on the steel-mill floor amidst flying sparks to photograph a ladle full of molten metal, and shot pictures in remote Canadian logging camps where the

temperature went below minus 20 degrees. Bourke-White loved being a celebrity—she even coordinated her camera clothes to match her designer outfits. At the same time, though, she determinedly moved from assignment to assignment, for *Fortune* magazine, and then for *Life* magazine, often suggesting her own themes and subjects. Her photograph of the Fort Peck Dam in Montana, then the world's largest earth-filled dam, introduced the American

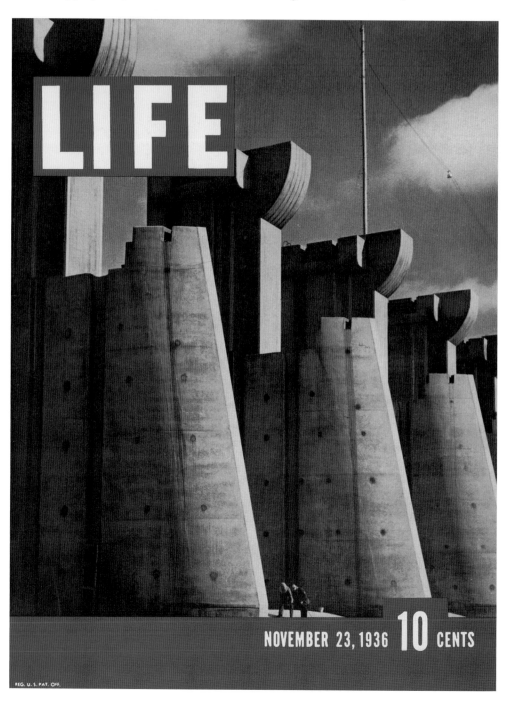

5.60
MARGARET BOURKE-
WHITE, Cover of
Life, vol. 1, no. 1,
November 23, 1936.

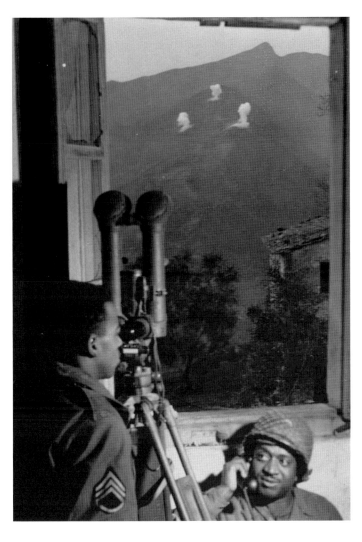

5.61
MARGARET
BOURKE-WHITE,
*Staff Sergeant Robert
Wilson and Private First
Class Wilbur Derrickson
(92nd Buffalo Division)
at an Artillery Outpost,
Italy, winter 1944–45.*
Gelatin silver print.
Syracuse University
Library, Syracuse,
New York.

public to the first issue of *Life* magazine on November 23, 1936 (Fig. 5.60). She not only had the cover; she wrote and illustrated the lead article, demonstrating that her ability to find powerful symbols of industrialization easily converted to revealing how people lived in places like the boom town near the dam. Bourke-White is most frequently remembered for her photographs, but she was also the author or co-author of about a dozen books recounting her adventures and imparting her convictions about social inequality.

In the Soviet Union, she photographed the new industrial town of Magnitogorsk, offering a paean of praise to machines and the people who made them work. With Erskine Caldwell (1903–1987), author of steamy southern poverty stories such as *Tobacco Road* (1932) and *God's Little Acre* (1933), she chronicled the impoverished lives of sharecroppers in *You Have Seen Their Faces* (1937), one of the first books to show this kind of imagery in America.

She and Caldwell frankly contrived dialogue to accompany the images, a deed still debated by those who believe that documentary work must record exactly what people have to say for themselves.

During World War II, Bourke-White photographed German bombs falling on Moscow, was the first woman to fly a combat mission, and sent back raw, painful photographs from the Nazi concentration camp at Buchenwald. Also, she insisted on recording the contributions of the so-called "buffalo soldiers," military units composed of all-black troops (Fig. 5.61). After the war, she photographed Mahatma Gandhi's attempts to gain independence for India, the punishing lives of black gold miners in South Africa, and guerrilla warfare in Korea. At age forty-nine, her career waned, cut short by Parkinson's disease, which she fought for twenty years with the same courage that she deployed in the course of dangerous assignments.

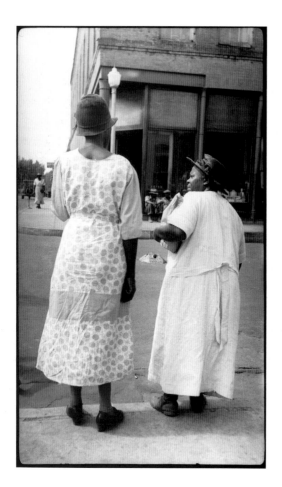

5.62
EUDORA WELTY,
Crossing the Pavement,
Utica, Mississippi,
1930s. Gelatin silver
print. Eudora Welty
Collection. Mississippi
Department of Archives
and History, Jackson,
Mississippi.

Welty was not an official
government photo-
grapher, but traveled
through Mississippi as
a publicist for govern-
ment relief activities.
She brought her camera,
and documented
incidental moments in
small-town life.

was created by writer and poet Archibald MacLeish (1892–1982), who juxtaposed FSA photographs with his verse in *Land of the Free* (see Fig. 5.54). MacLeish placed images next to pages of text, and in a reference to modern storytelling, put a narrow blue line across the top of every text page, alluding to the sound-track that was placed in a thin line along the edge of motion picture film. *The Grapes of Wrath* (1939), John Steinbeck's (1902–1968) stirring account of the lives of poor farmers displaced by the Dust Bowl, was first conceived by Steinbeck as a text with pictures by a *Life* magazine photographer called Horace Bristol (1908–1997).

Richard Wright (1908–1960) was the author of *Native Son*, the bestselling 1940 novel about racism in a northern American city. In the midst of the popu-larity of *Native Son*, Wright was commis-sioned to write another text about black life in America, *Twelve Million Black Voices: A Folk History of the Negro in the*

subjects do not suffer the effects of poverty that might be alleviated by a gov-ernment agency, but are shown coping with the tribulations of war.[81]

The bus-trip series and her boarding-house photographs were among the last assignments Bubley did for Stryker. He left the Office of War Information to work in the photographic section of the Standard Oil Company; Bubley even-tually joined him there, where she was employed to make another sequence of photographs about a cross-country bus trip.[82]

OTHER DOCUMENTS

While the RA/FSA photographs had a lasting effect on America's image of itself, other documentary photography projects were also instigated by govern-ment agencies during the Depression era. Berenice Abbott (1898–1991) photographed for the Works Project Administration (WPA), a controversial New Deal program that found public employment for artists, and Eudora Welty (b. 1909), who was hired as a pub-licity representative for the agency's work in Mississippi, brought her own camera (Fig. 5.62). A bitter look at the Depression and its psychological effects

5.63
CARL MYDANS, *Back
Yard Alley Dwelling,*
from *Twelve Million
Black Voices: A Folk
History of the Negro in
the United States,* by
Richard Wright, 1941.
Library of Congress,
Washington, D.C.

Wright addressed *Twelve
Million Black Voices* to
whites, using the word
"you" from the outset,
and he deliberately
identified with other
African-Americans,
using "we" and "us"
throughout the text.

We answer: "Our problem is being solved. We are crossing the line you dared us to cross, though we pay in the coin of death!"

The seasons of the plantation no longer dictate the lives of many of us; hundreds of thousands of us are moving into the sphere of conscious history.

We are with the new tide. We stand at the crossroads. We watch each new procession. The hot wires carry urgent appeals. Print compels us. Voices are speaking. Men are moving! And we shall be with them. . . .

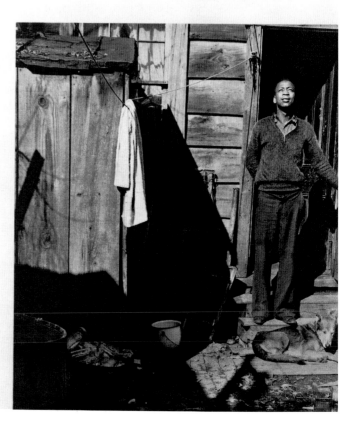

"Daily News" Building, 220 East 42nd Street, Manhattan; November 21, 1935. Completed: February, 1930. Architects: Howells, Hood & Fouilhoux. Owned by News Syndicate Company, Inc.

● Three million circulation Sundays, one and three-quarter million weekdays — more than double that of the next largest American newspaper — this is the DAILY NEWS. Such revenue made possible "The House that Tabloid Built," the DAILY NEWS Building, a 36-story skyscraper, costing $10,000,000.

142

United States (1941), which was illustrated with photographs from the FSA archive (Fig. 5.63). Listed as photo-editor was Edwin Rosskam (1903–1985), a photographer hired as an exhibition designer at the FSA, who also worked with Stryker to promote the use of the agency's images in publications.

The winnowing of the archive for images by different photographers, and the recaptioning of the pictures for *Twelve Million Black Voices*, have been questioned by critics. Foreshadowing reactions to *The Family of Man* show (see pp. 308–10), commentators claimed that reprinting works in a different context turned "what was news into history, what was propaganda into art, or vice versa, altering the relation of the photograph to actuality, confounding hopes for a single, authoritative, stable meaning."[83]

TRANSFORMING THE SOCIAL DOCUMENTARY

Although socially concerned documentary was prominent throughout the 1930s, most photographers were not creating work intended to kindle social change. In fact, like experimental photography, the documentary look became an apolitical visual style. Around the United States, newspapers sent their photographers into the countryside to bring back FSA-like photographs, safely shorn of any social welfare propaganda. The WPA funded American photographer Berenice Abbott to depict the growth of New York City. Her four-year project resulted in the book *Changing New York* (1939) (Fig. 5.64). Abbott typified the New Woman of the 1920s. At twenty years of age, she had moved from Ohio to New York City, where she studied sculpture and met avant-garde artists such as Duchamp and Man Ray. Attracted to the bohemian life of Paris in the 1920s, she worked in the city as a studio assistant to Man Ray from 1924 to 1926, during which time she also co-invented the expressive use of solarization in photography.

While in Paris, Abbott also studied with Eugène Atget (1857–1927), a

5.64
BERENICE ABBOTT,
Daily News Building,
from her book
Changing New York
(text by Elizabeth
McCausland), 1939.
Library of Congress,
Washington, D.C.

5.65
EUGÈNE ATGET,
*Café, Avenue de la
Grande-Armée,* 1924–25.
Silver print from glass
negative. Gilman Paper
Company Collection,
New York.

Atget specialized in
architectural photo-
graphs of old Paris;
he also developed a per-
sonal system to record
other visual subjects,
including street vendors,
storefronts, and gardens.
His unpeopled photo-
graphs of Paris dwell on
older neighborhoods and
established ways of life.

photographer who roamed Paris and
its environs, producing about 10,000
prints in the early twentieth century
(Fig. 5.65). Using a box camera and
glass negatives, Atget resisted the then
fashionable Pictorialist photographic
style, and compiled clear objective
images, which he called "documents."
The Paris Surrealists found Atget's
"documents" unsettling and evocative,
and briefly put the reluctant Atget
forward as an instinctive voice for
their philosophy. By contrast, Abbott
admired his methodical approach. After
his death, she acquired Atget's images,
which in time became part of the
collection at New York's Museum of
Modern Art.

American photographer Doris
Ulmann (1882–1934), who learned
some of her skills from Lewis Hine at
the Ethical Culture School, also took
classes with the Pictorialist Clarence
White. Melding their interests, she used
an old-fashioned glass plate camera and
tripod to put the grainy, slightly out-of-
focus Pictorialist approach in service
of American portrait studies (Fig. 5.66).
Like the pre-World War I photographers
of Native Americans, from time to time
Ulmann asked her subjects to wear old-
time costumes and to pose with home-
stead equipment, such as spinning

wheels, which they did not and could
not operate.[84] Contrary to her intentions,
her Appalachian photographs were
sometimes used by anti-immigration
groups maliciously to contrast images
of early settlers' perseverance and
ingenuity with what they believed to be
the indolence of immigrants.

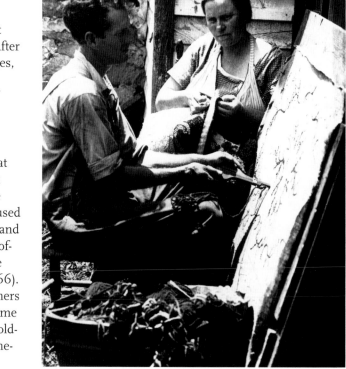

5.66 (right)
DORIS ULMANN,
Mr. and Mrs. Anderson,
Saluda, North Carolina.
Platinum print.

PORTRAIT
August Sander

The detached approach to subject
matter favored by European New
Objectivity (*Neue Sachlichkeit*)
artists and what might be called
"the archival tendency" came
together in the haunting images
produced by German photographer
August Sander (1876–1964).
While running his own commercial studio, Sander began making
portraits of farmers in the rural
Westerwald area of Germany,
which spurred him to plan a systematic portrait gallery of occupa-
tional types, beginning with
farmers, continuing through the
industrial jobs, the professions,
the arts, and ending with unem-
ployed and disabled people. He planned to have
forty-five portfolios, each consisting of twelve related
images that would be collectively called *People of the
20th Century*. Sander was not unique in preparing
a survey of the German people. As a post-World
War I morale booster, perhaps, books containing a
panoply of German portraits came into fashion during
the 1920s.[85] Sander's plan extended the encyclopedic
urge of nineteenth-century photography into the
twentieth century.

During decades of shooting, Sander used a set
formula reminiscent of early photography. His usual
method was to take sharp full-length or half-length
portraits of subjects, posed with props and garments
suggesting their work (Fig. 5.67). Most of his images
show that he arranged his sitters, carefully focusing
so that facial characteristics were distinctive, even
unique. The relationship of the figure to the surroundings in his work is novel—a process of distance and
isolation that unmasks qualities in the subjects, such
as their relationship to others. This was a Modernist
project, at least as it was understood by whole generations of photographers who came afterwards.

Sander's technique—and moments of humor—
sometimes undermined the emotionally detached
scheme he had in mind. He was not interested
in the odd angles and cameraless photographs of
the German experimentalist photographers, and
he renounced both his youthful infatuation with
Pictorialism and the casual spontaneity of the snapshot. Instead, he insisted on three guiding concepts:

5.67
AUGUST SANDER, *Boxers Paul Roderstein
and Hein Heese*, Cologne, 1929. Gelatin
silver print. August Sander Archive, Cologne,
Germany.

"See, observe, and think correctly!"[86] Although the immense
project was never completed,
Sander did publish sixty photographs in *Antlitz der Zeit* (*Face
of the Time*) (1929). He also gave
a pioneering series of radio
lectures in 1931 on the history
of photography.

In 1936, after the Nazi party
came to power, remaining copies
of *Face of the Time*, along with the
printing plates used to produce
them, were destroyed by order of the Government
Bureau of Fine Arts. Sander's images showed how,
in reality, many German people did not have the
"Aryan" facial features and physiques promoted by
the Nazis as the infallible marks of the German race.
Moreover, his series ended with unemployed and disabled people—the very types the Nazis first targeted
for removal to "purify" the Aryan race. After World
War II, Sander added photographs of political prisoners and persecuted Jews to his work *People of the 20th
Century*. He continued to work after the war, although
wartime bombing was responsible for the destruction
of his studio and a postwar fire that destroyed about
30,000 negatives.

Sander did not live to see the enormous influence
his work and ideas would have on late twentieth-
century photography. His detachment from the subject, coupled with his urge to create comprehensive
series, fed the imaginations of Bernd and Hilla Becher
in their ongoing sequences of antiquated technological
structures (see Fig. 6.87). Through the Bechers, many
prominent German contemporary photographers,
such as Andreas Gursky (see p. 388), adopted photographic objectivity as a visual stance in relation to the
built environment. Sander's work has been a touch-
stone of past and present international Conceptual
artists, who have investigated the qualities peculiar
to photography, such as how far a subject is placed
from the camera. Indeed, his images have nourished
the notion that physical distance is an effective visual
metaphor for psychic remove.

5.68 (right)
ERNST THORMANN,
Cover of *Der Arbeiter-Fotograf (The Worker Photographer)*,
November 1929.

Ernst Thormann (1905–1985) focused on street vendors, the unemployed, the poor, and outcasts such as this gypsy child.

WORKER PHOTOGRAPHY

In Europe and Russia during the 1920s, left-wing groups calling themselves worker-photographers organized to combat what they identified as "bourgeois picture-lies" about working conditions and attempts to organize protest movements.[87] Their concern to combat deceptive press images attests to the power of the illustrated newspapers and magazines as display cases for political ideas.

Like the sports and hiking clubs organized by the Communist Party to motivate workers, photography groups aimed to raise consciousness through picture-taking. Willi Münzenberg, the German publisher who founded *AIZ* (see p. 239), had his periodical carry photo-reports by workers, as well as being read by them. He also issued *Der Arbeiter-Fotograf* (*The Worker-Photographer*), the journal of the German worker-photography association, which sought to instruct its readers how to make images with a "class eye,"[88] and to break down the customary distinction between the producer and consumer of mass-media images (Fig. 5.68). Often anonymously, camera-carrying workers captured protest rallies and strike actions. They photographed workers' families, but were rarely successful in infiltrating factories to make images of hazardous conditions.[89] The worker-photographers brought their class eye

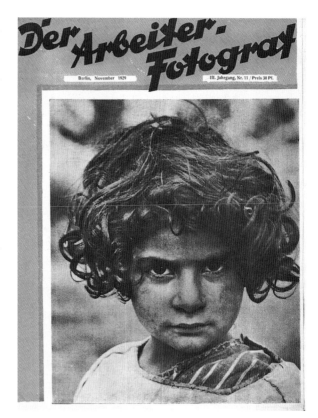

to bear on Renger-Patzsch's book *The World is Beautiful*, claiming that the world was ugly and evil, and in need of change.[90] At the same time, artists such as Grosz and Köllwitz were criticized for making the condition of the workers seem too hopeless.[91]

Worker-photographer groups were also started in the Netherlands,

5.69
HUMPHREY SPENDER, *Midway Clowns*, Blackpool, 1937. Gelatin silver print. Bolton Museum and Art Gallery, England.

Spender made a documentary series of images in the north of England, showing life among the working class. He mixed the sharp, angular style of the picture press with a Surrealist's sense of the uncanny, as in this image of a fairground stall.

Belgium, and Britain.[92] A popular theme was a day in the life of an individual or a city. This was taken up in Britain by Mass-Observation, or M-O, a group that simultaneously targeted false mass-media images of workers and the middle class, and images promulgated by out-of-touch academic sociologists and self-interested government officials. They published *May the Twelfth*, containing written accounts of a day in the life of over 200 observers. On this day—May 12, 1937—King George VI (1894–1952; r. 1936–52) was crowned, ending the crisis that arose when Edward VIII abdicated the throne the previous December. M-O's intent in *May the Twelfth* was far from the simplistic "where-were-you-then?" motif. The group hoped to undermine faith in government, by showing that it did not communicate with the people about the impending abdication. At the same time, M-O wanted to skewer British psychological reliance on the monarchy, exposing the operation of a modern

myth. M-O gathered full and part-time writers, painters, poets, and local people to produce an "anthropology of ourselves."[93] Humphrey Spender (1901–2005), a photographer for the *Daily Mirror*, also shot for M-O. He traveled to the gritty towns of England's northern industrial areas, building a trove of about 900 images, most of which were not published because of the expense involved (Fig. 5.69).

Although he did not work for M-O, German-born and -educated Bill Brandt (1904–1983) took up a similarly anthropological form of documentary when he settled in London in 1932, after studying with Man Ray in Paris. Two books of photographs, *The English at Home* (1936) and *A Night in London* (1938), examined British life, particularly its class system and behavior. Brandt's point of view is evident in the interpretive strategies he used in these books. His *Parlourmaid and Underparlourmaid Ready to Serve Dinner* (1932–35) (Fig. 5.70) is full of astute social observation.

**5.70
BILL BRANDT,**
Parlormaid and Under-Parlormaid Ready to Serve Dinner, 1932–35. Gelatin silver print. Bill Brandt Archive, London.

The two servants here are ready to attend at a lavishly set table. Their starched aprons and stiff poses resemble the folded napkins in the foreground. The taller woman's stern expression is set off by the anxious expression of the underling. The scene's implicit drama—the sense that something is about to happen—may owe to Brandt's infatuation with Surrealism.

Despite its name, the Workers' Film and Photo League, founded in New York in 1930, was not a working-class organization but a group of film-makers and photographers committed to depicting urban life, especially in poorer neighborhoods, and to keep a supply of class-conscious images available for left-wing publications. The film-makers and photographers soon split into two groups, and the word "worker" was dropped from their titles. Members of the Photo League included W. Eugene Smith (1918–1978), who once served as its president, and Jerome Liebling (b. 1924), whose two years spent with the league anticipated his lifelong career in humanistic documentary work

(see p. 420). The Photo League offered lectures, classes, and cooperative ventures. While working for *Fortune* magazine, Margaret Bourke-White and Berenice Abbott attended meetings of the New York branch.[94]

Among the league's undertakings were "production groups," like-minded photographers interested in experimentation, or in such themes as contemporary youth and neighborhood life. Under the direction of Aaron Siskind (1903–1991), the so-called Feature Group worked on the Photo League's most widely recognized project, the *Harlem Document*, containing pictures of the area's poor and a text composed by African-American sociologist Michael

**5.71
AARON SISKIND,
Reflection of a Man in a Dresser Mirror, from *Harlem Document*,
c. 1938. Gelatin silver print. George Eastman House, Rochester, New York.**

From 1938 to 1940, the Features Group was the most publicly visible of the various project-oriented teams at the Photo League. Originally planned as a book, some of the pictures from the *Harlem Document* appeared in *Fortune* magazine, and were exhibited at the 1939 San Francisco World's Fair.

5.72
JAMES VAN DER ZEE, *Couple in Raccoon Coats*, 1932. Gelatin silver print.

Van der Zee made portraits and photographed the social activities and aspirations of the black middle class. Here a prosperous couple wearing fashionable raccoon coats display their late-model Cadillac.

Carter[95] (Fig. 5.71). The Photo League was harassed by the FBI for seven years, beginning in 1940; it finally disbanded in 1951, after its listing as a subversive communist front organization in 1947 made it difficult to continue.

While the Photo League was working on its *Harlem Document*, a different, generally more upbeat, Harlem document was being informally created by other image-makers. The work of James Van der Zee (1886–1983), a popular portraitist and street photographer, was steeped in nineteenth- and early twentieth-century devices, including extensive props and elaborately painted backgrounds. As historian Deborah

Willis observed, his photographs of middle-class African-American life often suggest that the postwar mass movement of blacks from the South to take factory jobs in northern cities was a success (Fig. 5.72). Like Van der Zee, Marvin Smith (1910–2003) and Morgan Smith (1910–1993), twin brothers who ran a popular Harlem portrait studio, recorded social affairs and political events, and captured the beginnings of the Civil Rights movement in their pictures of the campaign "Don't Buy Where You Can't Work." At the same time, Carl van Vechten, the first American critic of modern dance, wrote for the *New York Times* in the era when Isadora Duncan

5.73
CARL VAN VECHTEN,
Georgia O'Keeffe,
June 5, 1936. Library
of Congress,
Washington, D.C.

Carl van Vechten was
a writer and critic
whose serious hobby
was photography. He
amassed an archive of
about 1,500 celebrity
photographs, including
this striking image
of the American artist
Georgia O'Keeffe,
whose portrait he clev-
erly composed using
angular shadows remi-
niscent of her paintings.

5.74 (below)
LAURE ALBIN-
GUILLOT, *Diatom,*
from *Micrographie*
Décorative, pl. xviii,
by Laure Albin-Guillot,
1931. Photogravure.
George Eastman House,
Rochester, New York.

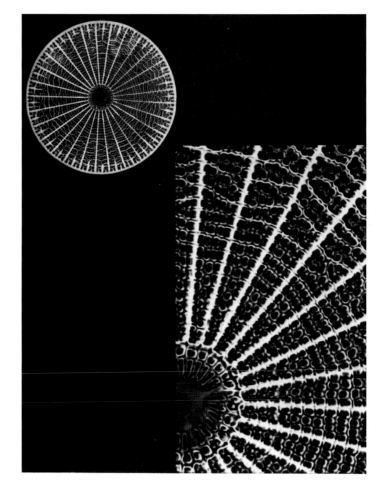

was choreographing creative rebellion
in that field. He promoted black artists
and writers, and photographed his
large circle of acquaintances, ranging
from poet-playwright Langston Hughes
(1902–1967) to publisher Alfred A.
Knopf (1892–1984) and the painter
Georgia O'Keeffe (Fig. 5.73).

POPULAR SCIENCE

At the 1937 Museum of Modern Art
exhibition of photographic history, the
first such comprehensive show in the
United States, curator and historian
Beaumont Newhall (1908–1993) presented samples of photojournalism,
sports photography, film stills, and aerial photography, as well as an array of
art photography, organized historically.
He also included scientific photography,
not simply to record technical advances
in that area, but also to display the
aesthetic appeal of forms and processes
revealed through scientific procedures.
From *Micrographie décorative,* a 1931
portfolio of photogravures by French

5.75
DESIGNER UNKNOWN, "Zwei Welten ..." (Two Worlds). Advertisement for Eukotol Skin Cream in *Münchner Illustrierte Presse*, no. 5, January 31, 1932, p. 105. Institut für Zeitungsforschung, Dortmund, Germany.

★ **Makrokosmos,** griech »große Welt«, d. i. der Riesenorganismus des Weltalls.

● **Mikrokosmos,** griech »kleine Welt«, d. i. die winzig kleine Zellwelt unseres Organismus.

Zwei Welten ...

● Die Haut verbindet den Makrokosmos mit dem Mikrokosmos. Sie ist die Berührungsfläche beider Welten.

Von der Verhaltungsweise der Haut hängt weitgehend ab, ob die Gewalten des Makrokosmos sich nützlich oder schädlich auf den Mikrokosmos auswirken. Die Haut muß also stets gesund und voll lebendiger Spannkraft sein. Der beste Weg, diese Spannkraft zu erhalten und zu stärken, ist die äußerliche Zufuhr von Aufbaustoffen, wie sie in Eukutol 3 enthalten sind.
Denn **Eukutol 3** liefert der Haut:
● den Aufbaustoff Cholesterin,
● das hauterneuernde Regenerationshormon,
● die hautschützenden sauren Mineralstoffe. ●

Grüngoldene Dose RM 2.15, große Tube RM 0.90, halbe Tube RM 0.45

scientist Laure Albin-Guillot (1879–1962), Newhall chose a microscopically enlarged view of a diatom (a form of single-celled alga), showing its ornate symmetrical design (Fig. 5.74). Newhall did not, as later Postmodern critics have suggested, wrench a scientific image from its original context and force it into an aesthetic category so that it could function as a museum display. Albin-Guillot had already enlarged the meaning of this type of photography with her choice of title and her selection of pictures.

The artistic and popular appreciation of scientific images owed much to the spread of illustrated magazines and journals aimed at a general audience, as well as the development of textbooks with photographically derived images. Even advertising utilized images drawn from science (Fig. 5.75). Theorists such as Moholy-Nagy encouraged viewers to look at X-rays, which were also included in the Newhall show, not as medical information but as a remedial kind of new vision. At the 1929 *Film und Foto* exhibit, influenced by Moholy-Nagy's

ideas, scientific photography was divided into three sections: documentation; research in photographic process; and expansion of the senses, a category more about seeing than about scientific knowledge.[96]

In the late 1930s, Berenice Abbott began experiments with scientific photography. By the early 1940s, she saw the need to invent a visual recording system, called "Projection Photography" or "Supersight," which allowed the user to project and enlarge subjects on a 16 by 20 inch piece of film or paper.[97] When she became photography editor of *Science Illustrated*, she carefully selected views that explained scientific principles to lay readers. Her interest in scientific education continued throughout the 1950s, when she worked with a commission of scientists and teachers to improve the illustrations of science textbooks (Fig. 5.76).

After he escaped the Nazi campaign of terror against the Jews, Roman Vishniac (1897–1990) emigrated to the United States in 1940. The Russian-born Vishniac, who was a physician, microbiologist, and Ph.D. art historian as well as a photographer, added photomicrography to his skills, primarily to make a living. He specialized in depicting small living organisms, and wrote and lectured on the hidden beauty revealed by the microscope.

But in the public's mind, it was Harold Edgerton (1903–1990) who was most closely associated with demonstrating the beauty of scientific photography. His early work in the 1930s, taken with the STROBE lighting system he helped to invent, was a fixture in *Life* magazine, and appeared in books marketed to lay readers, such as *Flash! Seeing the Unseen by Ultra High-Speed Photography* (1939), and in short movies such as *Quicker than a Wink* (1940), which won an Oscar. The 1937 Museum of Modern Art display exhibited Edgerton's crowd-pleasing stop-action image of the crown-shaped splash made by a milk drop as it hit the surface of the liquid (Fig. 5.77). Edgerton perfected strobe lighting throughout the 1930s by synchronizing intense but short bursts of light with turning engine rotors. In 1939 he began working with the military,

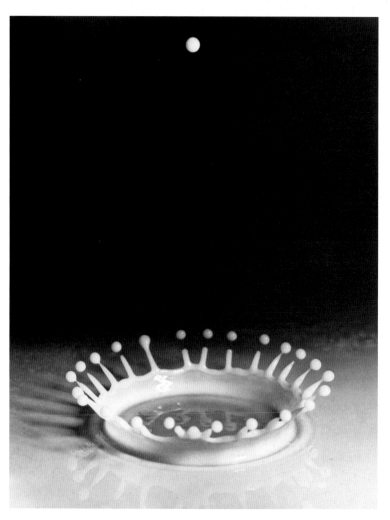

developing the lighting necessary for
night-time aerial photography, a technology that won him the Medal of Freedom
in 1946.

WORLD WAR II

While German photographer Alfred
Eisenstaedt (1898–1995) was working
for the Associated Press, he photographed Joseph Goebbels, the Nazi
party's chief propagandist who became
the National Minister of Propaganda, at
the 1933 League of Nations Assembly in
Geneva, Switzerland (Fig. 5.78). In that
year, the Nazis required that all German
photographers register with the government, a move that broke the worker-
photography movement and sent *AIZ*
into exile in Prague, Czechoslovakia.
From the mid-1920s, Hitler's rise to
power was orchestrated by the German
illustrated press, which was increasingly
controlled by Berlin's Ministry of
Propaganda. Heroizing photographs of
Hitler, montaged over pictures of the
vast political gatherings the Nazi party
staged, carefully portrayed him as a
powerful, popular leader. Two volumes

of photographs taken by Hitler's favorite photographer, Heinrich Hoffmann (1885–1957), showed him not only as a political figure, but also as a simple man of the people, reading the newspaper, talking with farmers, and pondering the wonders of nature.[98]

From 1933 on, as the Nazis fomented an atmosphere of race hatred and scapegoating, Jewish people were character-ized as lazy and slovenly in print and in press photographs. Boycotts of Jewish shops were encouraged by notices pro-claiming, "Jewish business! Anyone shopping here will be photographed."[99] From 1935 to 1938, Roman Vishniac, then living in Berlin, frequently worked with a concealed camera picturing Eastern European Jewish life. He trav-eled to Poland, Russia, Hungary, and

**5.78
ALFRED
EISENSTAEDT,**
Joseph Goebbels, 1933.
Gelatin silver print.

Eisenstaedt's riveting image of the Nazi Propaganda Minister, Joseph Goebbels, shows him with a menacing expression and claw-like hands. As Eisenstaedt recalled later, "He looked at me with hateful eyes and waited for me to wither. But I didn't wither. If I have a camera in my hand, I don't know fear."

5.79
ROMAN VISHNIAC,
Boy with Earlocks, 1937.
Gelatin silver print.

1933, after *AIZ* was banned, Heartfield moved to Prague, and then to Britain in 1938. Moholy-Nagy came to the United States, where he founded a new Bauhaus (1937), soon renamed the Institute of Design, in Chicago. Vishniac also came to America, where insufficient English kept him from practicing medicine, so he went on to do photomicrography. Erich Salomon got as far as the Netherlands, where a Dutch Nazi betrayed him. He and his whole family died in Auschwitz.

When the war broke out in Europe in 1939, correspondents and photographers were sent there, sponsored by publications and photoagencies. As in World War I, war photography was censored. For example, Bourke-White's images were often printed as contact sheets (rows of small, negative-size images on photographic paper) and reviewed by military censors before being sent to *Life* magazine. Some photographs were sent by radio transmission, but most, with captions written by the photographer, were physically transported by the

5.80 (below)
JOHN HEARTFIELD,
Durch Licht zur Nacht
(*Through Light to Night*), May 19 1933.
Photographic collage.
Akademie der Kunst, Berlin.

In his photomontages for *AIZ*, Heartfield criticized Nazi practices. In this image, he shows Propaganda Minister Joseph Goebbels ordering a book-burning. In the background is the former German parliament building, the Reichstag.

Romania on behalf of the American Jewish Joint Distribution Committee, making pictures that could assist their money-raising efforts to aid poverty-stricken Jewish communities (Fig. 5.79).

By the time war was imminent, Goebbels determined that there should be no independent media in Germany. Journalists, photographers, writers, film and radio producers, publishers, printers, painters, and poets were conscripted into the Propaganda Division of the Army.[100] The twisted logic of Goebbels's schemes was a favorite target of the photomontages created by John Heartfield's (anglicized name of Helmut Herzfeld; 1891–1968) for *AIZ*. Heartfield, who had been one of the Berlin Dadaists, turned his talents to satirizing growing Nazi power (Fig. 5.80). A skilled designer of books and posters, he did not make his own photographs, but selected them from mass-media illustrations, or commissioned them from other photographers. His searing photomontages, which exposed the real effects of Nazi social policies on the ordinary citizen, appeared in *AIZ*. Rumblings of war, official censorship and persecution, and anti-Semitism sent many illustrious photographers in Germany into exile. In military. Photographers often had to form pools, meaning that photographs by any one of them could be used by all of them. The practice reduced the number of photographers in the field and eased the work of censors. The huge improvement in cameras and film since World War I allowed soldiers from all sides to make snapshots and send them back home, although these, too, were supposed to pass through the censors' hands. By using handmade pinhole cameras and smuggled film, secret photographs were made by wily American prisoners of war in German camps.

For the Allied troops, motion picture studios issued millions of free celebrity images, including so-called pin-ups of popular stars such as Rita Hayworth and Betty Grable. The military trained photographers to accompany units, and aerial photography, some done by the naval aviation unit under the command of Captain Edward Steichen, accounted for about 85 per cent of the Allied information on the enemy.[101]

To avoid disclosing information the enemy could use, and because the 1930s' documentary emphasis on individuals and typical days persisted, newspapers and magazines stressed the personal encounter with war far more than in World War I. Stationed in the Pacific, American photographer W. Eugene Smith managed to get so close to the action that he was seriously wounded on the island of Okinawa in 1945. His pictures centered on the physical and emotional experiences of soldiers at the front line (Fig. 5.81).

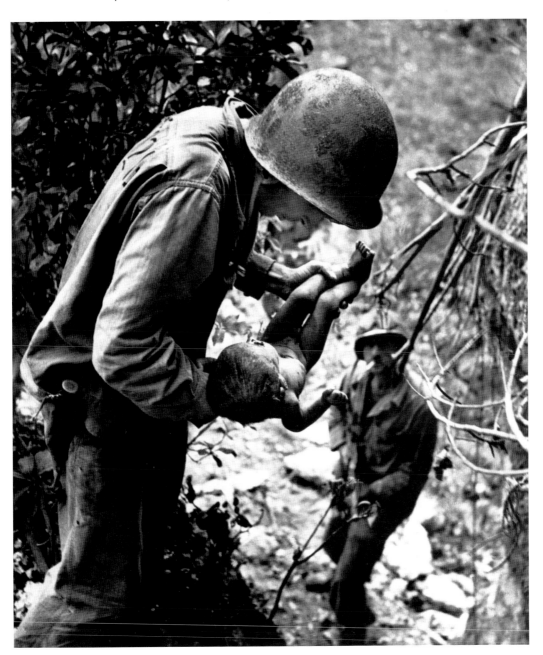

5.81
W. EUGENE SMITH,
U.S. Marines with a Wounded and Dying Infant, June 1944.
Gelatin silver print.

Smith's photographs emphasized the individual soldier's experience of conflict, helping the viewer relate to being in a foxhole or under fire. This image shows a wounded Japanese infant found by marines during bitter fighting on the island of Saipan. Smith's point of view influenced the photography of the Korean and Vietnam wars.

5.82
LEE MILLER,
Buchenwald, April 1945.
Gelatin silver print.
Lee Miller Archives,
Chiddingly, East Sussex,
England.

During World War II,
Miller, who had turned
her talent in fashion
photography to record-
ing the effects of the
Blitz, or air war, in
London, was among
the first photographers
to depict the horrors
of Nazi concentration
camps at Dachau and
Buchenwald.

Life magazine fought the government
to show the American wounded and
dead, though not with the explicit horror
accorded the enemy dead, especially the
Japanese, who were also frequently the
subject of racial caricature in print and
in cartoons. The United States kept a
secret file of ghastly war photographs,
called "The Chamber of Horrors," in
the Pentagon.[102]

The Museum of Modern Art staged
large photographic exhibits to support
the war effort. Two such shows, both
curated by Steichen, were immensely
successful with the public. *Road to
Victory* (1942) used many RA/FSA
photographs, updated and recaptioned
from Depression themes to such
patriotic slogans as "War—they asked
for it—now, by the living God, they'll

get it."[103] Designed by Herbert Bayer,
who emigrated to the United States in
1938, *Road to Victory* used the exciting
shaped-space concepts of European
experimental photography installations.
The visual strategies that Bayer had
used to promote the Nazi party were
thus turned against them. Steichen's
second show, *Power in the Pacific* (1945),
utilized images from the United States
Navy, whose photographic unit he had
himself directed.[104]

At the end of the war, when troops
entered the concentration camps where
Jewish and other prisoners worked and
died, photographers recorded the grim
scenes. At Buchenwald, Bourke-White
pictured the charred remains of victims
and the shrunken bodies of living
skeletons. Lee Miller (1907–1997), the

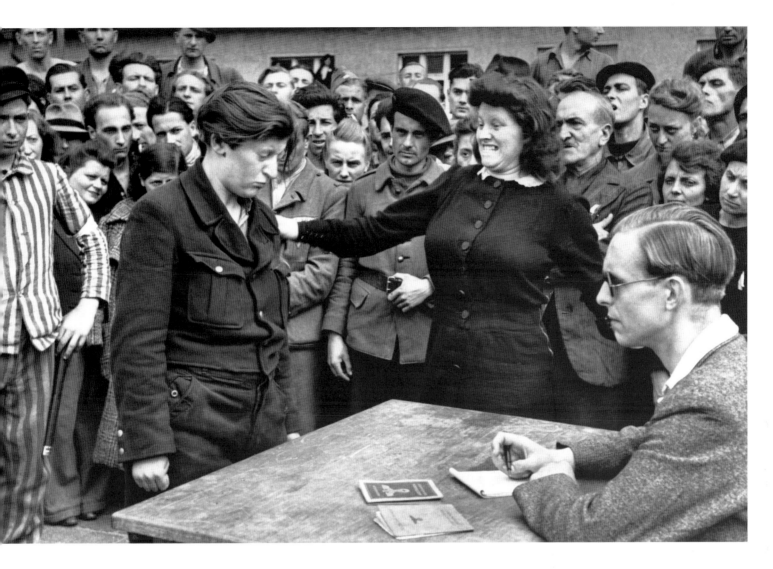

photographer who had developed solarization with Man Ray, was a member
of the London War Correspondents
Corps, and later an accredited correspondent with the U.S. Forces. She,
too, defied the prevailing notion that
women were too emotionally delicate
to face the horrors of extermination
camps. Her unsparing photographs
at Buchenwald catalog the means of
annihilation, and the lives of those
who survived (Fig. 5.82). When she
sent her equally shocking photographs
of Dachau, she cabled her editor:
"I implore you to believe this is true."

Henri Cartier-Bresson was captured
by the Germans during the war and
imprisoned. He escaped and joined the
French Resistance. After the war, he
recorded the reaction of French people
to those among them who had aided
the Nazis. In this image he sought the
decisive moment that told the story of
the denunciation of a French Gestapo
informer (Fig. 5.83).

PHILOSOPHY AND PRACTICE: THE "COMMON MAN" AND THE END OF MEDIA UTOPIA

In his much-cited 1936 essay "The
Work of Art in the Age of Mechanical
Reproduction," critic Walter Benjamin
argued that the proliferation of photomechanical reproduction marked
one of history's watershed moments.
For the masses, he forecast that reproducibility would be truly revolutionary.
In the end, it would "pry an object
from its shell ... [and] destroy its
aura."[105] Thus removed from "the
fabric of tradition," photographically
reproduced and widely distributed
pictures of once class-bound objects
would become strategic elements
in fomenting social change among
the masses, who could witness at
first hand the decline of privilege in
their new access to art reproduction.
Benjamin's hopes for the mass media

5.83
HENRI CARTIER-
BRESSON, *Gestapo
Informer*, Dessau,
Germany, 1945.
Gelatin silver print.

Cartier-Bresson chose
the precise moment in
which a French Gestapo
informer is denounced.
The apparent glee of the
accuser is matched by
the emotions of anger,
scorn, or disbelief
etched on the faces of
the assembled crowd.

**5.84
ROBERT CAPA,
*Death of a Loyalist
Soldier*, Spain, 1936.
Gelatinsilver print.**

In Capa's image, a
lone anti-fascist soldier
pitches backwards
at the instant bullets
seem to rip through
him. Published in *Vu* in
September 1936 and
Life in July 1937, it
propelled its maker into
international celebrity.
The circumstances
in which he took the
picture, however,
have been disputed for
fifty years.

were echoed throughout European
experimental photography, especially
in Germany.

As historian Maud Lavin summed
up, "the burning issue for the German
avant-garde from 1922 until Hitler's
seizure of power in 1933 was not at all
a rebellion against art institutions, but
rather a serious and prolonged engagement with mass culture."[106] Similarly,
American documentary photographers
thought their images were self-
validating, needing only wide exposure
in the press to change the hearts and
minds of the people.

Benjamin was wrong about the special aura that unique objects have. Far
from destroying the aura, art reproductions served to increase it. Photographs
of Leonardo da Vinci's *Mona Lisa* roused
people to want to see the original. Oddly,
photographic reproducibility sometimes
destroyed the aura of the original photograph. For example, the many thousands of people who cut out and saved
press pictures of Dorothea Lange's
Migrant Mother thought they had the

original, because it was the very one that
affected them.

Written from a left-wing perspective,
Benjamin's essay is typical of international writing in the 1930s in its concern
for what was alternately called "the people," "the masses," "ordinary humanity,"
and "the common man." Notions of
progressive social change aimed at the
common man sustained photographs
in such divergent styles as those done
by the Russian experimental photographers and those published by the
FSA. The immense brutality and
destruction of World War II, and the
advent of the atomic bomb, eroded a
great deal of faith in the future of the
human race. At the same time, the dissolution of experimental photography
into commercially viable styles, and the
control of visual media by large corporations and news agencies, dampened
belief in the inherently revolutionary
nature of camerawork.

One mark of the waning faith in
photography, which became widespread
after World War II and continues today,

is the repeated inquiry into the authenticity of the documentary photographs that emerged as icons of the war experience. The twentieth century's most famous war photograph, *Death of a Loyalist Soldier* (Fig. 5.84), was taken by the Hungarian-born photographer Robert Capa (1913–1954). This moment-of-death image purportedly shows an incident during the Spanish Civil War (1936–39), a conflict between a coalition of leftists called loyalists, and the fascists, led by General Francisco Franco. The war inflamed much debate in Europe and America. However, stories that the image was not made by Capa, or that the death was staged, were rumored immediately after World War II, and came to wide public inspection in Phillip Knightley's 1975 book *The First Casualty*.[107] The issue and its evidence have been passionately discussed ever since, with no clear resolution.

Part of the controversy has to do with Capa's professional and popular reputation. His statement that "if your pictures aren't good enough, you're not close enough" became the dictum for subsequent generations of war and adventure photographers. Less well known, but still a guideline for photographers, photo-editors, and the public, was his observation on the slight blur in *Death of a Loyalist Soldier*: "if you want to get good action shots, they mustn't be in true focus. If your hand trembles a little, then you get a fine action shot." Ironically, another of Capa's celebrated images was also blurred—but by accident (Fig. 5.85).

Other famous World War II photographs have been similarly scrutinized. Joe Rosenthal's (b. 1911) picture of the raising of the Stars and Stripes on the Pacific island of Iwo Jima, another American icon, has been long rumored to be questionable[108] (Fig. 5.86). Indeed, the picture seemed staged to the editors at *Life* magazine, and they initially rejected it for publication. Perhaps the most widely reproduced war photograph, Rosenthal's *Iwo Jima* influenced Russian photojournalist Yevgeny Khaldei (b. 1917), who tried to

emulate its composition and attract some of its renown when Berlin fell to the Soviet army (Fig. 5.87). In Europe and Russia, this image, thought not to be contrived in any way, was one of the strongest visual mementos of that conflict. Also often accused of being staged is Eisenstaedt's much-loved photograph of a sailor kissing a nurse in New York City's Times Square on V.J. day, when Japan surrendered and the war ended.

In the postwar phase of our age of mechanical reproduction, iconic images have often been greeted with suspicion. Almost a century earlier, Alexander

Gardner could openly describe his staging of *Home of a Rebel Sharpshooter* (see Fig. 3.21). By contrast, war photographers such as Capa and Rosenthal were unable to deflect doubts that anyone can be lucky enough to be at the right place at the right time to make such powerful and well-composed symbols. At the same time, the war years had seen photography exploited to an unprecedented extent by government and the military on both sides to control public opinion. Prized for its contribution to uniting nations during the war, photography was far less certain of its role in the postwar world.

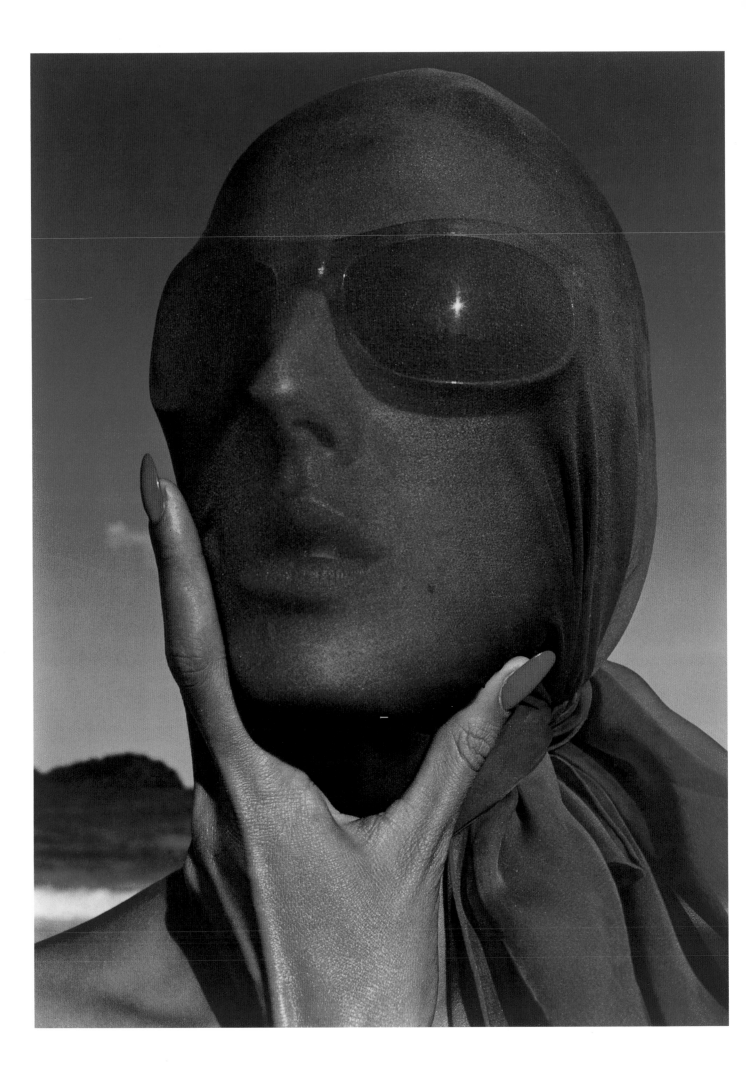

Through the Lens of Culture (1945–1975)

6.0
HIRO, *Tilly Tizzani with a Blue Scarf*, **Antigua, 1963, from cover of** *Harper's Bazaar*, **May 1963. Victoria & Albert Museum, London.**

Post-World War II magazine advertising quickly embraced color reproduction. In her fashion photography, Hiro tended to isolate figures and accentuate deeply saturated colors, all of which served to remove models from the real world.

While postwar Europe and Asia staggered under the loss of millions of people, coupled with economic devastation, the United States, which did not suffer physical damage on its mainland, emerged as the world's leading industrial and military power. By 1947, the relief and unity felt by the Allies after their victory in World War II had given way to a world polarized by what the American presidential advisor Bernard Baruch called the Cold War. Beginning in 1945, the Soviet Union established its influence among eastern European nations in the territories previously occupied by Nazi Germany. In addition, the Soviets administered eastern Germany, one of the four zones into which Germany was partitioned at the end of the war.

When the Soviet Union and the eastern European nations in its sphere of influence refused rebuilding funds under the Marshall Plan, initiated by U.S. Secretary of State George C. Marshall, suspicion of Soviet long-term expansionist intentions rapidly spread in the West. Fired by the fear that its wartime ally wanted to spread communism throughout the world, and that the human misery of the immediate postwar period would make such a message attractive, the United States redoubled its economic aid to Europe and some Middle Eastern countries.

The ravaged condition of the European nations, and the surprisingly deep economic downturn of the postwar British economy, helped make the United States a superpower. America's exclusive possession of atomic weapons confirmed that position. In addition, the United States was the only postwar nation sufficiently prosperous to consider direct military and economic confrontation with communist countries. Fear of communism increased with the 1949 victory of Mao Zedong (1893–1976) in China, and mixed with nuclear fear when the Soviets exploded their first atomic bomb in 1949. In a 1946 speech, former British Prime Minister Winston Churchill (1874–1965) described an "iron curtain" dividing Europe: this seemed to come true in 1948, when the city of Berlin was cut off from the West by Soviet occupation forces, and supplies had to be airlifted to the city. Later, the Berlin Wall, built in August 1961, effectively isolated East Germany and the eastern European nations from the West.

THE FAMILY OF MAN

In 1955, a large photography exhibition titled *The Family of Man* was mounted at New York's Museum of Modern Art. The show proposed photography as a means through which the alarming tensions and uncertainties of the Cold War era could be seen in a wider context of human values, emphasizing the theme of common humanity against the destructive effects of political polarization and other forms of divisiveness. The exhibit reaffirmed a faith in humanity for an audience shaken by gruesome images of Japanese atomic injuries in *Life* magazine and troubled by the new specter of global nuclear war. It pleased the general public more than any previous photographic exhibition, and the book derived from it became the best-selling photographic book of all time.

Edward Steichen, who returned from his wartime duties to head the museum's photography department, selected and organized the images according to universal themes, such as birth, work, and love. To generate the impression of global unison, Steichen homogenized the look of the individual photographs: cropped and shorn of their original titles, the exhibition prints were processed in a commercial lab, where their tonal values were harmonized. The prints were also transformed into poster-size images.

Steichen hoped that *The Family of Man* would illustrate "the essential oneness of mankind throughout the world." Aiming to highlight "human consciousness rather than social consciousness," he discarded images that demonstrated strong political and cultural differences.[1] The unity of humankind was stressed even during the planning stages of the show, and the Museum of Modern Art announced that it would open simultaneously in New York, Europe, Asia, and Latin America—a proposal that was never realized.[2] Steichen's utopian aspiration, in which supposed enemies and outcasts are revealed to share a common humanity, and national boundaries are ignored, should be seen against the background of hysterical anti-communism in early 1950s, America and the equally shrill optimism of postwar consumer culture. The United Nations, founded in 1945, and its Universal Declaration of Human Rights, proclaimed in 1948, had offered a vision of the good society rising from the ashes of battle; Steichen's show underlined both the nobility and fragility of this vision.

To choose from among the 2.5 million photographs submitted, Steichen looked for "swiftness of seeing," the visual summing up of an idea in a single moment that formed the kernel of Modernist photographic practice familiar to audiences from nearly three decades of illustrated magazines and newspapers.[3] In the end, he selected about 500 images from sixty-eight countries. As Jacob Deschin, camera editor of the *New York Times*, observed, *The Family of Man* was an "editorial achievement rather than an exhibition of photographs."[4] Steichen clustered untitled photographs around concise sayings drawn from cultures around the world. For motherhood, he chose the biblical phrase, "She is a tree of life to them ..." (Proverbs 3: 18); images of laborers carried a quotation of the ancient Hindu religious poem, the *Bhagavad-Gita*: "If I did not work, these worlds would perish ..."

Overall, his installation design owed its dynamic programming of ideas and emotions to the exhibition spaces created by Russian and German artists between the world wars (see pp. 239–49), but critics generally did not acknowledge these European precedents. Indeed, photographer Barbara Morgan (1900–1992) thought that the show was so original that it needed a new term, perhaps "photographic mosaic," "three-dimensional editorializing," or words that related it to rapidly shifting images, such as movies or television.[5]

The concept of a photography based on universal human experiences also underpinned the first group project by Magnum Photos, a photographic agency founded in the penthouse restaurant of the Museum of Modern Art in 1947 by Robert Capa, Henri Cartier-Bresson, and other photojournalists seeking greater editorial control over their pictures. "People are People the World Over," a series of monthly photo-essays showing common activities in rural families around the globe, such as laundering clothes, shopping, and cooking, was published in the *Ladies' Home Journal*.[6]

At *The Family of Man*, viewers walked though themed areas (Fig. 6.1). They came across familiar images, such as

**6.1
PHOTOGRAPHER
UNKNOWN,** *The
Family of Man* exhibi-
tion, January 24–May 8,
1955. Museum of
Modern Art, New York.

The Family of Man
benefited from earlier
experimental European
installations, in which
the viewer's route
was directed. Walking
through the show was
like leafing through an
issue of *Life* magazine.
Indeed, Steichen
modeled many aspects
of the show on picture
magazines—from
the relative scale of the
images, to the use of
picture agencies, and
the anonymity of the
images' authorship.

Lange's *Migrant Mother* (see Fig. 5.55),
and met unfamiliar ones as well. At the
end of the show, however, the seemingly
open-ended themes became more directive. A display of photographs depicted
three women, three men, and three children; next to these was placed a stark
warning by British philosopher Bertrand
Russell (1872–1970) about the capacity
of the hydrogen bomb to destroy all
human life. Just beyond was a panel
showing a dead soldier and a question
posed by Sophocles: "Who is the slayer?
Who the victim? Speak." Lastly, the
viewer passed under an overhead lamp
into a darkened area where a 6 by 8 foot
back-lighted TRANSPARENCY revealed
a red-orange image of the 1954 U.S.
hydrogen bomb test explosion on Bikini
Atoll in the Pacific Ocean. The glowing
picture erupted into the viewers' space,
startling them after they had become
accustomed to so many black-and-white
images. The exhibition plan then directed
viewers to a huge photograph of the
United Nations General Assembly, and
to a final series of images showing
children at play.[7]

Although public response to the
show was overwhelmingly positive,
some photographers objected to

Steichen's transformation of their
work into tonally harmonized, standard-
format prints. Further, they charged that
the show denigrated the skill involved in
making photographs, and lessened the
value of the medium just at the moment
when it was struggling for acceptance in
art museums and galleries. A few critics
also felt manipulated by Steichen's
agenda, and questioned his underlying
ideological message. Phoebe Lou Adams
complained:

If Mr. Steichen's well-intentioned spell
doesn't work, it can only be because he has
been so intent on the physical similarities
that unite 'The Family of Man' that he has
neglected to conjure the intangible beliefs
and preferences that divide men into countries and parties and clans. And he has
utterly forgotten that a family quarrel can
be as fierce as any other kind.[8]

In his zeal to find international common
ground from which to work against
the widely feared nuclear cataclysm,
Steichen had obliterated the specific cultural settings of the images. For example,
Farm Security Administration photographs such as *Migrant Mother* were
blended with other images of unspeci-
fied calamities. Images of workers from

the Belgian Congo, Bolivia, Denmark, Germany, and the United States were thematically linked, without regard for the drastically unequal circumstances of labor in those countries. Nathan Farbman's (1907–1988) photograph of an African storyteller in Bechuanaland (now Botswana) became part of a cluster of images on education, twisting its meaning to relate it to Western educational practices. In addition, Steichen ignored most popular forms of photography. He included a few snapshots, but did not show photographs of everyday family life taken by non-professionals with unsophisticated equipment.

In a sense, *The Family of Man* was the last expression of the documentary SOCIAL REALISM that had characterized American photography during the 1930s' Depression era. Around the world, photographers were focusing on the cultural values that differentiate, not unite, societies and groups of people. The particular struggles, histories, and contexts that Steichen removed from the images were fast becoming major subjects. A major theme in photography outside the United States was resentment against the perceived Americanization of other cultures. When *The Family of Man* reached Paris, French critic Roland Barthes (1915–1980) identified its "ambiguous myth of the human 'community,'" which suppressed "the determining weight of History."[9] Barthes equated the exhibition's theme of universal oneness with American imperial aspirations.

CULTURAL RELATIVISM AND CULTURAL RESISTANCE

Steichen's focus on common humanity reflected a larger movement to affirm the basic rights of all peoples. The 1948 Universal Declaration of Human Rights defined those rights as the "common standard of achievement for all peoples and all nations," and listed thirty articles, first among them the idea that "all human beings are born free and equal in dignity and rights." Each of the articles expressed human rights in terms of individual rights. Group, ethnic, racial, or national rights were pointedly absent from the list.[10] As the historian Eric Sandeen concisely pointed out, the

United Nations, like *The Family of Man*, represented a Western view of universal community: "By using the rhetoric of international goals and principles, [the United Nations] bound the members together with one view of what was admirable and what was unacceptable in all human culture."[11] Even as the United Nations announced its Universal Declaration, mainstream cultural outlets from *Life* to *National Geographic* were giving renewed attention to the very different proposals found in the theory of cultural relativism.

The concept of cultural relativism was developed by anthropologists in the 1920s and 1930s, and encompassed several interrelated ideas. It asserted that human values are not universally the same, but emerge from dissimilar cultural experiences. In an era when modernization seemed to mean the loss or diminution of diversity, cultural relativism accented the value of tradition. American anthropologist Melville J. Herskovits (1895–1963) clearly articulated one of its core values: "Our civilization may indeed be recognized as in no way inherently superior to another ... and this is why the imposition of a foreign body of custom, backed by power is so distressing an experience."[12] Around the world, notions of cultural relativism fueled resistance to outside interference, be it military intervention, economic takeover, or the promotion of ideas that might erode cultural identity.

Within the United States and Europe, as well as in other parts of the world, those who disagreed with measuring material wealth as a standard of well-being turned to non-Western and unassimilated indigenous cultures as sources of alternative values. In the United States, photographers again journeyed to Native American groups, not to picture them as vanishing peoples, as had happened in the early twentieth century (see pp. 192–94), but to venerate spiritual wisdom and ethical values, which they thought were more in tune with the rhythms of nature than were the artificial demands of modern society. *Through Navajo Eyes* (1972), a report of the 1966 project of Sol Worth (1922–1977) and John Adair (b. 1913) to teach members of the Navajo community to use motion picture cameras to assert their identity, enlivened many discussions about

FOCUS
Making an Icon of Revolution

In 1960, Cuban photographer Alberto Díaz (1929–2001), more popularly known as "Korda," photographed Ernesto "Che" Guevara (1928–1967), who was then serving in Fidel Castro's government. Korda was so impressed by his image of Guevara that he cropped out all extraneous visual information in order to emphasize Guevara's revolutionary zeal (Fig. 6.2). Undoubtedly, Korda's background as a portrait, advertising, and fashion photographer guided him in the process of making what would become a popular symbol of revolution. This image of Guevara, gazing

into the future, beneath a beret bearing the revolutionary star, was not published when it was made, but became an international emblem of political resistance after Guevara was killed seven years later in Bolivia. On the evening of the announcement of Guevara's death, a ten-story portrait based on Korda's photograph was hung on the exterior of Havana's Ministry of the Interior building, which fronts on the plaza where Castro revealed the revolutionary's death to Cubans gathered there. The image was quickly disseminated throughout Latin America, where it became an icon of martyrdom. It was also adopted by American students and antiwar protesters during the Vietnam War era (1964–75). In the 1990s, Korda contested the photo's commercial exploitation in ways he said "dishonored" his subject; in 2000 he won a $50,000 settlement from a British advertising agency over the use of the photo in a campaign to market a brand of vodka. He donated the money to buy medicine for children.

UPI (United Press International, a news and photography agency) inadvertently promoted Guevara's fame, when it circulated a photograph of Guevara's corpse posed in a way reminiscent of religious paintings of the dead Christ, and thereby strengthened Guevara's identity as a self-sacrificing fallen martyr in largely Christian Latin America[13] (Fig. 6.3).

6.2 (above)
LIBORIO NOVAL,
Alberto Korda Holding Photos of Che Guevara, March 5, 1960.

6.3 (left)
PHOTOGRAPHER UNKNOWN, *Death Picture of Che Guevara,* 1967.

the potential of the camera to record non-Western experience.

Cold War tension between the United States and the Soviet Union politicized the arts. Both superpowers used artists and exhibitions to promote themselves around the world. Among the major cultural programs of the United States Information Agency (USIA) was the tour of *The Family of Man*, which traveled abroad from 1955 to 1962, appearing in thirty-eight countries to a total audience of 9 million people. With additional materials commemorating Hiroshima, the exhibition was mounted in Tokyo and at Ground Zero, the spot in Hiroshima where the atomic bomb exploded. The Soviet authorities even let the exhibit run in Moscow. Publicity framed the show as evidence of the individual freedom that fostered American prosperity, much as the art movement Abstract Expressionism, with its gestural handling of paint and absence of realistic subject matter, was cast as an example of American intellectual freedom, in contrast to Soviet Socialist Realism.[14]

The "American Way of Life," as it was called, derived from postwar economic prosperity, manifest in a housing boom, the growth of suburbs and shopping malls, and increased automobile use. It fostered the notion of material abundance as a universal gauge of societal achievement. The propaganda slogan implicitly disparaged "un-American" and "anti-American" societies, such as the Soviet Union, which offered fewer material comforts, but where all citizens were (at least in theory) seen as equal beneficiaries of centralized state-run programs, rather than lone competitors in a world governed by free-market capitalism.

Propaganda use of cultural objects during the Cold War set off the rapid politicization of artists and photographers. In Latin America, Africa, and Asia, where American art symbolized American political power and economic clout, photography came to be understood as a means to create and communicate a defiant, or at least oppositional, cultural identity.

CENTRAL AND SOUTH AMERICA

In the postwar period, many people living in Central and South America resented the extensive cultural, political, and economic influence of the United States. They attempted to forge a distinctive Latin American identity in the arts and in photography. These efforts were strengthened by reaction to U.S. interventions in South America and the Caribbean, beginning with the invasion of Cuba at the Bay of Pigs in 1961, and including U.S. support of Augusto Pinochet (b. 1915), who overthrew the elected Chilean government of Salvador Allende (1908–1973) in 1973, and of the dictatorial regime of Anastasio Somoza (1925–1980) in Nicaragua throughout the 1970s. As photographer and critic Fernando Castro (b. 1952) recounts, "Latin American photographers busied themselves exposing every trace of U.S. penetration they could find. Those who did not participate in this ideological purge, ridding themselves of any taste for U.S. art, dress, or speech, were branded *alienados*—alienated from their own people and culture."[15]

In the years before World War II, Latin American photographers had responded positively to European experiments in photographic form, such as Surrealism (see Chapter 5). In the decades after 1945, a wide range of photographic practice persisted, from local photographers using nineteenth-century studio styles to those who were thoroughly conversant with contemporary international styles and techniques. This layering of practices could be found throughout the post-colonial world in the postwar period of modernization and nation-building. As in North America and Europe, photographers increasingly found work creating advertising and other commercial images. Throughout Latin America, photojournalism was carried out by press photographers attached to illustrated newspapers, or by freelancers, who sometimes sold their work through regional photographic agencies. Yet, despite the many professional photographers in Latin America, it was mostly foreign practitioners who were sent in when the area was portrayed in magazines abroad.

During the 1959 Cuban Revolution, local photographers such as Raúl Corrales (b. 1925) documented the progress of the struggle, along with foreign correspondents and photographers. Nevertheless, Cuban images were not purchased by international agencies, and most of the pictures of Cuba seen around the world were taken by foreign photographers. A significant exception was Alberto Díaz (1928–2000), who created a defining image of the revolution (see Fig. 6.2). In the early years of the Fidel Castro (b. 1927) government, photojournalism played an important role in communicating ideas visually to a largely illiterate public. Castro reputedly waved a copy of *Life* magazine in front of one of his associates, saying "I want something like this"; *Revolución*, a picture magazine, was soon founded.[16]

In post-World War II Latin America, photography took many forms, ranging from the work of itinerants to fashionable portraits such as those made by Grete Stern, one of the partners in studio ringl + pit (see p. 264), who emigrated from Germany to Argentina. Especially before the spread of the Polaroid photograph (see p. 357) in the late 1960s, roving rural photographers used old-fashioned paper negatives, created in large wooden cameras constructed from parts of broken, older cameras. These itinerants used painted backdrops showing religious scenes or cityscapes, which they set up in designated spots for photographers near marketplaces and rural fairs. "Los Ambulantes," or the traveling ones, offered inexpensive portrait images[17] (Fig. 6.4).

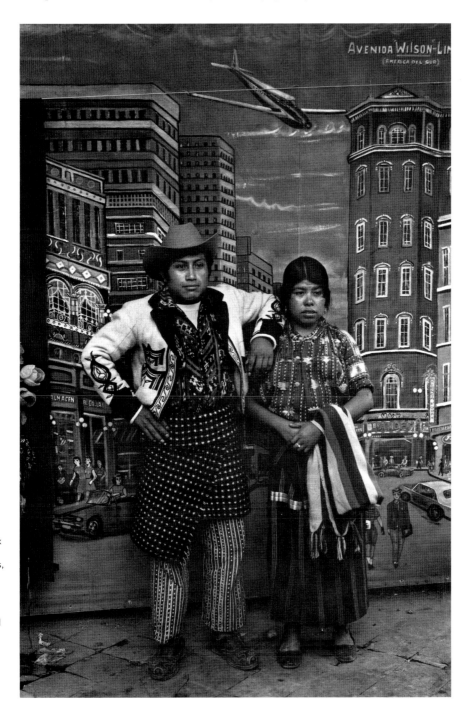

6.4
ANN PARKER,
Young Indian Couple with Cityscape, Sololá, Guatemala, 1973.

While in rural Guatemala, Parker was struck by the lively practice of itinerant photographers, who traveled with elaborate painted backdrops against which peasants chose to be photographed. Dressed in traditional finery, the man and woman are pictured before a busy city street scene, complete with an airplane flying overhead.

During the 1970s, Latin American documentarians, photojournalists, and art photographers sought to counteract simplistic or derogatory depiction by foreigners, while still affirming the multicultural character of the region. The First Colloquium of Latin American Photographers, held in Mexico City in 1978, was accompanied by the influential exhibition *Hecho en Latinoamérica* (*Made in Latin America*). The title built ironically on the once common label "Made in America," which identified imported goods from the United States, not the other Americas. In an

introduction to the catalog, organizer Raquel Tibol emphasized the growing desire to view Latin American photography as "an artistic family." "The narrow confinement within our borders was becoming unbearable," she wrote.[18] According to Tibol, Latin American photographers shared several outlooks, including "the rejection of an alienating and unjust society; the denunciation of exploitation, marginalization and colonization; a rupture with conventional aesthetic models, [and] an impulse toward a reaffirmation."[19] In other words, she hoped that photographers

6.5
PEDRO MEYER,
Untitled (Wealthy
woman with two maids
and a male servant
behind her), 1978, from
Hecho en Latinoamérica
exhibition, 1978. Gelatin
silver print.

In this image from
Hecho en Latinoamérica,
Meyer uses visual
devices to convey the
contrasting attitudes of
a wealthy woman and
her domestic staff. She
is seated and decked
out in finery; they are
standing, uniformed,
and carrying serving
trays. She occupies the
foreground, while the
servants form a strong
wedge behind her back.
Viewers can see the
servants' peeved smiles,
which are hidden from
the seated woman.

could unite a political vanguard with an artistic avant-garde. The socio-economic contrasts throughout the book underscored the disparities between rich and poor (Fig. 6.5).

Two more conferences and exhibitions were held in 1981 (Mexico City) and 1984 (Havana, Cuba). These efforts led to international group shows abroad, and a system of awards for outstanding work.[20] One result of the heightened regional identity was the increased activity of Latin American photographers working in Bolivia, Brazil, Chile, Cuba, Guatemala, Venezuela, and elsewhere, who chronicled the daily existence of the indigenous peoples threatened by modern development and ecological devastation.[21] Pre-Columbian peoples living traditionally came to symbolize a pure Latin American experience before colonization, and represented resistance to external political and cultural interference.

Brazil and Argentina

Claudia Andujar (b. 1931), a Swiss-born photographer who arrived in Brazil in 1955, embraced the outlook proclaimed at the First Colloquium of Latin American Photographers, and she exhibited her work in *Hecho en Latinoamérica*. During her treks in the 1970s and 1980s to photograph the Yanomami people of northern Brazil, she witnessed their deaths as a result of epidemics in the wake of a gold rush that brought 40,000 miners to the Amazon basin, and the dislocation of villages when the jungle was leveled to make way for roads. For a time, she gave up photography to set up health clinics among the Yanomami and to lobby the Brazilian government for the creation of a reserve the size of Portugal for them, a feat accomplished in 1992.

Andujar did not adopt the straight-forward documentary style of the Farm Security Administration photographers (see pp. 281–87). Rather than rendering her subjects in simple compositions and lighting schemes, she used extreme contrasts of dark and light, to add complexity to the image's surface (Fig. 6.6). Unlike the early twentieth-century photographers who showed Native North American people as physically and mentally exhausted, and therefore

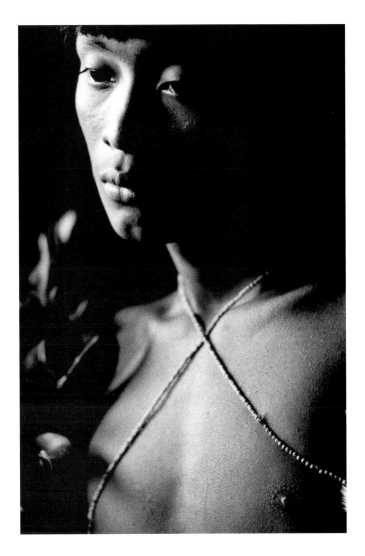

unable to cope with modern life, Andujar manipulated the graphic contrasts of her work to create sensuous surfaces that suggest vitality. Her book *Yanomami* (1978) conveyed the message that these people were endangered not by their inadequate cultural achievement, but by the moral deficiency of the major culture. She underscored the idea of an impending holocaust by dedicating the book to the people who perished at the Nazi concentration camp at Dachau. For her photographic and humanitarian efforts, Andujar was awarded the Lannan Foundation Cultural Freedom Prize in 2000.

Image-making among indigenous peoples became the hallmark of the photographers interested in portraying Latin American identity, but photographers also looked closer to home for instances of injustice and abuse. Civil unrest, revolutionary activity, and repressive government measures were routinely photographed. Argentinean photographers Sara Facio (b. 1932) and Alicia D'Amico (1933–2001) began

**6.6
CLAUDIA ANDUJAR,**
Yanomami Youth During a Traditional Reahu Festival, 1978.

Andujar's portraits of Yanomami life are often permeated by dark shadows, from which a figure slowly emerges. Her lighting is like that of the jungle, where bright sunshine occasionally penetrates the darkness created by the thick rainforest canopy. This strong stylistic interpretation stands in marked contrast to the conventions of nineteenth-century anthropological imaging (see Fig. 3.97).

**6.7
SARA FACIO AND
ALICIA D'AMICO,
Untitled, from their
book *Humanario*, 1976.**

Inmates lie or sit in the
sun-drenched courtyard
of a mental institution,
as if recently touched
by a terrible disaster.
The slack, isolated
bodies, stuck in a deep,
drug-induced stupor,
evince the disregard of
the asylum.

collaborating in the late 1960s on a
series depicting life in a state-run
mental institution, published in 1976
as *Humanario* (Fig. 6.7).

Mexico

In Mexico, photographers had already
avidly turned to local subject matter
before the First Colloquium. They
recorded the lives of ordinary urban
dwellers as well as the persistence of
ancient religious practices among rural
peoples. In a series of influential photographic essays published in popular
Mexican illustrated magazines such
as *Hoy* (*Today*) and *Siempre!* (*Always!*),
Mexican photojournalist Nacho López

(1923–1986) depicted everyday life in
Mexico City, sometimes posing his subjects to create a humorous or poignant
effect. His photo-essays present the
poor as animated, capable actors in
their own realm, not as victims awaiting
misfortune's next call (Fig. 6.8).[22] López
believed that photography found its
finest expression in photojournalism,
which thrust the image-maker into the
midst of life's theater. He came to detest
what he and other Latin American
photographers called "folkloric" photography, the pursuit of picturesque
subjects rather than social contexts.[23]
Another Mexican photographer, Héctor
García (b. 1923), traveled the country

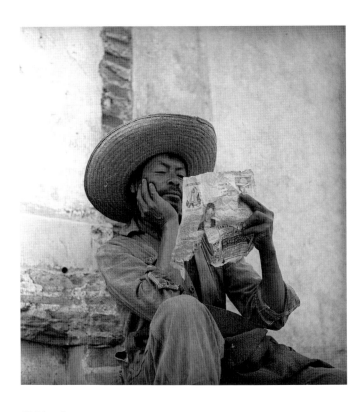

seeking out the survival of ancient, pre-colonial rituals. He concentrated on laborers, producing pictures that emphasize their individual imagination (Fig. 6.9).

Foto Hermanos Mayo, or the Brothers Mayo Photography, an anonymous collective originally from Spain, enthusiastically supplied Mexican and foreign illustrated magazines and newspapers with pictures that examined issues from the working-class point of view. The Mayo archive of about 5 million negatives is probably the largest of its kind in Latin America.[24]

During the 1970s, former painter Lourdes Grobet (b. 1940) used photography as an element in "environments," that is, multimedia precursors of INSTALLATION ART. She also made a series of bogus referendum ballots, to make her point about the deficiencies

6.8 (above)
NACHO LÓPEZ,
Campesino, 1949. Nacho López Foundation. Fototeca del Instituto Nacional de Antropología e Historia, Mexico City.

One of López's most celebrated images, this photograph of a peasant reading a newspaper has been widely reproduced for over half a century. The man's hat hints at his rural background, but his overalls indicate that he has migrated to the city.

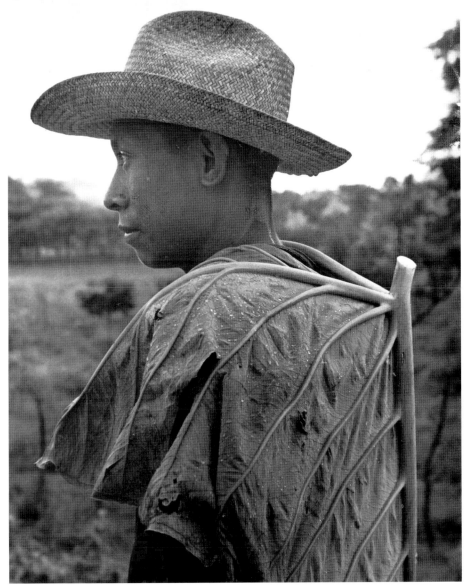

6.9
HÉCTOR GARCÍA,
Campesino Covered with a Leaf, 1965.

PROPOSICIONES

☐ Verdadero
☐ Falso

☐ Verdadero
☐ Falso

M. L Grobet 1978

**6.10 (above)
LOURDES GROBET,
Proposiciones, 1978.
Mixed media.**

Grobet's counterfeit
ballots required the
viewer to check boxes
"true" (*verdadero*) or
"false" (*falso*). But the
information was aligned
in such a way that it
was impossible for the
viewer to make such a
coherent response.

of the voting process (Fig. 6.10).
Another Mexican photographer,
Graciela Iturbide (b. 1942), began her
career photographing indigenous and
rural people in the 1970s. Her work
often focuses on the adaptation of
traditional life to the modern world,

a prominent motif in Mexican cultural
expression (Fig. 6.11). During the
1990s, her work centered on Mexicans
living in east Los Angeles, the largest
Mexican population outside the country,
and along the United States–Mexican
border. She does not mourn the loss of

**6.11
GRACIELA ITURBIDE,
*Woman Angel, Sonara
Desert, Mexico*, 1979.**

A Seri Indian woman
literally balances
between modernity,
symbolized by the
portable radio, and the
earth, an emblem of
traditional life, which
she reaches for with
her left hand. Iturbide
suggests the abiding
spiritual life of her subjects, especially women.

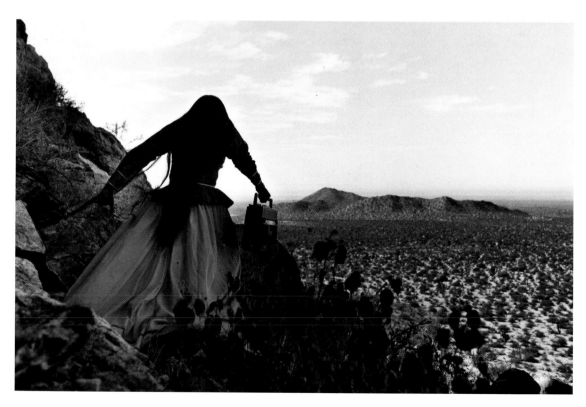

PORTRAIT
Manuel Álvarez Bravo

Nacho López, Héctor García, and Graciela Iturbide all studied with photographer Manuel Álvarez Bravo (1902–2002), the most influential photographer in Mexico during the last half of the twentieth century. Although Álvarez Bravo's uncanny compositions recall the eerie and mysterious visual spectacles favored by Surrealism,[25] he maintains that Surrealism has been a minimal influence.[26] More important, he claims, was his friendship with Tina Modotti during the 1920s, which led him to view the Modernist photographs of her companion, Edward Weston.[27] In addition, he and Henri Cartier-Bresson interacted and mutually influenced each other. Álvarez Bravo also confronted Modernist simplification of forms when he photographed the work of the Mexican muralists José Clemente Orozco (1883–1949), David Alfaro Siqueiros (1896–1974), and Diego Rivera (1886–1957) for the magazine *Mexican Folkways*.[28] "My work is more related to Mexican art and Mexican life than to photographic traditions," he asserted.[29]

Beginning in the 1940s, Álvarez Bravo's photographs were increasingly seen outside Mexico. Three of his images were included under sweeping categories such as "birth" and "death" in Steichen's *The Family of Man* exhibition in 1955. In these non-Mexican contexts, viewers could overlook Álvarez Bravo's many allusions to ancient myth, folklore, and ritual, with their multiple, intertwined inflections on fecundity and death. For example, *La Buena Fama Durmiendo* (*Good Reputation Sleeping*) (1938–39) shows a young woman slumbering in the sun (Fig. 6.12). She rests on a blanket or rug, and her ankles and thighs are wrapped with what look like bandages. Her pubic area is emphasized against the white fabric. The seductive, sexually charged nude intimates Surrealism's concern with eroticism and altered states of consciousness; the image was shown at an exhibition organized by Surrealist leader André Breton.

The photograph is strongly imbued with particular Mexican themes that owe nothing to Surrealism. Within Mexican folklore, the thorny cactus pieces lying beside the figure are signs of danger. They warn about the perils of sleep, while protecting the sleeper. The bandages, which owe to an incident in which Álvarez Bravo observed dancers binding their feet, suggests an associative link between the sleeping figure and dancers portrayed in the sculptural reliefs of ancient Mexican civilizations. In one interpretation derived from Mexican cultural experience, the image simultaneously alludes to both the Virgin Mary and the ancient earth goddess Coatlicue, both of whom conceived sons without sexual intercourse.[30]

In Álvarez Bravo's work, some of which is especially staged for the camera, the past is alive in the present in a way different from Western history, which firmly situates events in chronological time and keeps the past at bay. It is interesting to note that Álvarez Bravo never offered extensive interpretations of his work, possibly because their poetic nuances might be sapped in prose. Consequently, he did not respond to the charge that his images promote an internal Mexican exoticism of the sort nineteenth-century travelers sought in photographs of colonial subjects.

6.12
MANUEL ÁLVAREZ BRAVO, *La Buena Fama Durmiendo (Good Reputation Sleeping)*, 1938–39. Gelatin silver print. Museum of Photographic Arts, San Diego, California.

6.13
SEYDOU KEÏTA,
Two Women, 1959.

cultural identity or romanticize the severe poverty that confines people in traditional cultures. Instead, she shows indigenous Mexican people as constantly in flux, accommodating to change that began half a millennium ago with the Spanish conquest.

AFRICA

Like most photographers living in colonial areas, Africans learned camerawork and business procedures in European-run establishments, or as part of service in colonial military units. Consequently, portrait photography by Africans of Africans adapted many attributes of colonial photography, such as the portrayal of worldly accomplishments, and the display of tokens indicating social class or personal interests. Photography was brought to villages by traveling photographers, who, like those in Latin America, made portraits against the cloth backgrounds they took with them.

Within the constraints of received traditions, photographers such as Mali resident Seydou Keïta (1921–2001) infused the Western portrait with

African qualities. The urbanization of Bamako, a city where the railroad meets the Niger River, is evident in his portraits of government officials, shopkeepers, politicians, and socialites. Unlike anthropological photographs, which stress the primitivism of Africans, the participants and photographer in Keïta's work collaborate to create an image of lively, confident town life (Fig. 6.13). Accordingly, his advertisements promised "The Image You Want."

Though most post-World War II portraiture in Africa, as in Europe, did not employ experimental techniques, a few photographers, such as Kenyan Omar Said Bakor (1932–1993), made composite portraits that sprang from the client's desire to add people to an extant photograph. Unlike European photomontage, however, Bakor's work was not strongly illusionistic. He used the technique in a way that let the process show, as a means of portraying people's inner desires and aspirations, and also perhaps as a visual equivalent to the non-linear nature of African storytelling (Fig. 6.14).

The "Africanization" of portrait photography received fresh impetus in the 1960s, as many countries began to achieve political independence from colonial European powers. African backdrop scenes showed specific African scenes, and sitters increasingly chose to wear traditional African attire.[31] Independence also brought the establishment of official photography agencies, such as AMAP in Mali and A Foto in Angola, tasked with communicating government-approved points of view.[32] Inspired, possibly, by the achievement of independence in other countries, Mozambique photographer Ricardo Rangel (b. 1924) reoriented his own

6.14
OMAR SAID BAKOR,
Untitled, 1975.
Photomontage.

When Bakor placed the photograph of two young women on the speaker of a radio, indicating their desire to be known as celebrities, he let the rough edges show.

Using available light,
rather than a flash,
unpremeditated compo-
sition, and intentional
blurring of forms,
Rangel focused on inter-
personal relations as
observed in the night-
spots of the Mozam-
bique port of Maputo.
His work repudiates
sunny mainstream press
photographs of life in
wartime Mozambique.

camerawork in the service of social
change. During the 1960s, when guerrilla warfare was being waged against
Portuguese colonial authority, Rangel
shot a series called *Our Nightly Bread*,
capturing the night life in the port city
of Maputo (Fig. 6.15). Rangel founded
a photographic training center, which
continues to instruct most students of
photography in Mozambique.

By South African custom and law,
press photography was reserved for
white practitioners. Nevertheless,
the medium was enlisted in the fight
for social justice during the 1950s.
In Johannesburg, the Progressive
Photographic Society was formed, and
Drum magazine, founded in 1951 as
an entertainment magazine for urban
blacks, was reformulated as a showcase
for young writers and photographers
who wanted to portray contemporary
culture. *Drum* contrived ways to
show the work of South African photographers, whether black, white, or
of Asian extraction, including Cloete
Breytenbach (b. 1933), Ernest Cole
(1940–1990), Bob Gosani (1934–1972),
and Ranjith Kally (b. 1925). They resolutely pictured life under apartheid, the
policy of racial separation formalized
in 1948 and regulated with increasingly
severe laws throughout the 1950s.
Drum magazine expanded to several
other African countries; at its height,
its circulation was about 450,000.

Since publications could be banned
at any moment, the writers, editors, and
photographers at *Drum* were not openly
hostile to apartheid. Nevertheless,
during the 1950s, the magazine pushed
the limits of resistance, publishing Alan
Paton's novel *Cry, the Beloved Country*,
a best-seller about the conflict between
a black minister and a white suprema-
cist farmer. Occasionally *Drum*'s photographers got themselves arrested in
order to record the effects of the harsh
criminal justice system, or such practices as convict labor.

Peter Magubane (b. 1932), who
ultimately became chief photographer
at *Drum*, once shrewdly turned the
prevalence of black stereotypes to his
advantage, in order to make a series of
photographs of the 1956 trial of some
apartheid protesters. Magubane hid his
camera in a loaf of bread and lounged
outside the courthouse pretending to
eat it, all the while secretly photographing people as they arrived. At considerable risk, Magubane resolved to record
abuse of black workers (Fig. 6.16) and
anti-apartheid demonstrations, whose
activities were distorted in the newspapers that backed government policy.
Similarly, when detained by the police,
Ernest Cole cleverly played on his cap-
tors' biases, claiming that he was doing
a report on black juvenile delinquency.
Cole's *House of Bondage* (1967) is one
of the most comprehensive indictments
of South African racial policy produced
by a photographer (Fig. 6.17).

Drum photographers also contributed
to political resistance by making pictures in such places as jazz clubs, where
they showed black social life unfettered

African township is bulldozed out of existence to make way for white expansion. Government trucks will move residents and their few possessions to matchbox houses in new locations, usually in remote areas, perhaps not even named on map. Even to live there, families must qualify. People at right did not, and thus have not only had their homes razed, but have nowhere to go.

56

by apartheid policy. After 1960, when the ruling government reacted to anti-apartheid activities by declaring a state of emergency, black photographers faced jail or exile. Magubane was held in solitary confinement for a year and a half, and then was banned from taking pictures for five years. Undeterred, during the 1980s, Magubane and other photographers, many of them trained in their craft at *Drum*, used photography to record the oppression and resistance that led to the end of apartheid. Not all anti-apartheid photographs directly pictured incidents of injustice and racial domination. For forty years, David Goldblatt (b. 1930), a white man who left his family's menswear business in 1962 in order to make photographs, shot scenes of ordinary daily activities. His views of shanty towns, billboards, shacks, and public monuments subtly alluded to the condition of racial inequity. In *The Transported: A South African Odyssey* (1989), Goldblatt collected photographs he made during the early morning, two-and-a-half-hour one-way bus ride endured daily by black workers from the segregated "homeland" of Kwandebele to the city of Pretoria, where they labored but were not allowed to live (Fig. 6.18). After the end of apartheid in South Africa, Goldblatt continued his strategy of contrasting visually the environments of the rich and the poor.

The West began to take notice of Afrocentric photography in the decades after World War II. Stephen F. Sprague's pioneering 1975 study of the use of photography among the Yoruba people of West Africa made the case that they had been integrating photography into their art practice since the 1930s.[33] At the core of Yoruba photography were cultural guidelines about how to render likenesses; these were based not on art conventions, but on broader rules for human interaction. The notion of *jijora* indicated that an image, including a photograph, should be made at the mid-point between generalization and resemblance; individualizing specificity should be avoided in favor of a modest idealization. At the same time, the concept of *ifarahon*, or visibility, suggested clarity and order. In practical terms, *ifarahon* meant that both the sitter's eyes should be visible, so the sitter

had to look directly into the camera. Moreover, the photographer should not employ such poses as the profile view nor introduce dramatic lighting or unusual angles. Sprague's work is an example of the shift in anthropological and cultural studies toward a consideration of indigenous and post-colonial uses of the medium. Yet it remains true that, as anthropologist Joanna C. Scherer observed, "the serious analysis of non-Western or native photographers is a relatively untouched field."[34]

ASIA
India

Photographic practice in India took off quickly within months of the medium's official disclosure to the world in 1839, and grew rapidly among colonial and Indian practitioners (see pp. 117–18). In the years immediately preceding and following World War II, India constituted a large market for photographic supplies, manufactured by international companies such as Kodak and the German company Agfa. Illustrated publications such as the *Illustrated Weekly of India* provided outlets for Indian-made images. The pre-World War II period saw the start of specialty magazines for photographers, including *Indian Photography and Cinematography*, launched by S. Lakshiminarasu in 1937, and the Kodak-sponsored *Kodak Indian Magazine* (later *Tropical Photography*), founded in 1940. Camera clubs consisting largely of Indian members were well established in the bigger cities and towns. However, as historian G. Thomas reports, "no deliberate attempt was being made by Indians to establish an Indian idiom in photographic communications."[35] The British Royal Photographic Society's programs and its operations were widely admired. As in nineteenth-century Britain, various groups in India exchanged photographs by mail in what was called the "Postal Portfolio" movement.

Although Margaret Bourke-White photographed in postwar India, publishing a book called *Halfway to Freedom: A Report on the New India* (1949), and Henri Cartier-Bresson worked there several times, the pictures they produced were mostly not for the Indian market. After India achieved independence from Britain in 1947, a new proposal for photography "of Indians, by Indians, for Indians" was eagerly heard, and a national society, the Federation of Indian Photography, was established in 1953.[36] The call for Indian photography followed on the success of the Independence movement's wide distribution among the populace of photographic postcard images picturing organizer Mahatma Gandhi (1869–1948). Beginning in the

1930s, the postcards were used as a rallying device that could bypass British-controlled media. After Independence, cameras made exclusively for the Indian market were manufactured by New India Industries, in conjunction with Agfa, and Kodak changed its name from Kodak Limited to the Indian Photographic Company. By 1965, film was also being manufactured by Indians for Indians.

Homai Vyarawalla (b. 1913), a self-taught photojournalist who covered World War II for the *Illustrated Weekly of India*, recorded the jubilant crowds celebrating Independence and followed the political life of the new country during the 1950s. She worked for the *Times of India*, and as a contributor to *Time* and *Life* magazines. Another photojournalist to emerge during the Independence movement was Sunil Janah (b. 1918). His pictures of the 1942 famine, the Independence struggle, and Gandhi's assassination in 1948 gave him an international reputation (Fig. 6.19). When Margaret Bourke-White began her work in India, she sought him out for advice

During his long career, Janah recorded major events in Indian life, such as Gandhi's assassination in 1948. In this image, most of the people who have rushed into the streets to hear the news are unaware of the photographer's presence.

**6.20 (above)
RAGHUBIR SINGH,
Shiva Temple, Jahngira,
1983.**

The Ganges: Sacred River resulted from Singh's six-year chronicle of life along the river. He was accused of prettifying social problems to create a representation of India as a timeless land, particularly through his decorative use of color. "I realized fairly early," Singh countered, "that there was no contradiction between sadness or poverty, and color."[37]

**6.21 (right)
PHOTOGRAPHER
UNKNOWN,** *Untitled*
(Manakal's son), c. 1965.
Photomontage. Bombay
Photo Studio, India.

A dead child is remembered in a photomontage placing his image inside one of a rose, linking scent with memory. As anthropologist Christopher Phinney reported, commemorative photography can "make traces of persons endure, and ... construct the world in a more perfect form ...".[38]

and contacts. Janah's Calcutta studio became a meeting place for artists and intellectuals, including the filmmaker Satyajit Ray (1921–1992).

India's best-known photographer at home and abroad was Ray's friend Raghubir Singh (1942–1999). Singh credited his interest in photography to his teenage viewing of Cartier-Bresson's 1949 book *Beautiful Jaipur*. Unlike many non-Western photographers, for whom the new reliable color film (see p. 354) was too expensive, Singh started his career in color photojournalism, supplying images for international publications such as *National Geographic* and the *New York Times*. During the 1970s, he began creating photographic books on Indian regions, including Kerala in the south,

**6.22 (above)
SHINZO FUKUHARA,
*Light With Its Harmony
8: Pond*, c. 1910. Gelatin
silver print. Shiseido
Corporation, Japan.**

Shinzo and Roso Fukuhara's work alluded to the spatially compressed vistas of Japanese painting and the look of traditional brush and ink work—a look that continues to intrigue contemporary Asian photographers.[39]

Kashmir in the north, the Ganges River (Fig. 6.20), and cities such as Bombay (Mumbai) and Calcutta. His books were sold internationally and marketed to tourists in India.

Post-colonial Indian photography took another turn in the industrial city of Nagda and the village of Bhatisuda in the central subcontinent. In this area photographic practices developed out of custom and religion, and disregarded Western notions of realism.[40] Like the Yoruba people of Africa, the residents of Nagda and Bhatisuda created an aesthetic form and meaning for their works that ignored the usual studio conventions. Before the advent of widespread color photography, they freely requested that the photographic image be painted over with color. In addition, photographs of family members were then montaged, sometimes bringing together relatives who could not attend a baptism, wedding, or funeral, in order to create an image of the whole extended family. A distinctive genre of montaged photographs emerged as memorials of the dead (Fig. 6.21). It has been suggested that the development of a moderately independent representational system such as that at Nagda and Bhatisuda may have sprung from classic Indian narratives, notably the story-within-a-story structure of the *Mahabharata*.[41] What might be called non-Western photographic folk practice exists side by side in rural and urban settings with Western-derived photojournalism.

Japan

Taking its cue from Western examples, Pictorialism dominated Japanese still-life, landscape, and portrait photography into the 1930s. It was followed by other Western-inspired styles, such as Modernism, whose sharp angles and severe close-ups affected art photography, advertising, and portraiture. Likewise, Surrealism and European experimental photography were investigated in Japan, and their disjointed and collaged effects were adapted to create visually exciting commercial art. As in other countries, the pre-World War II period saw the flourishing of illustrated publications, specialty magazines for photographers, and the manufacture of Japanese cameras for the home market. While international styles flourished

in prewar Japan, some photographers, such as Shinzo Fukuhara (1883–1948) and his brother Roso Fukuhara (1892–1946), sought to counteract both the fuzzy look of art photography and the deep perspective offered by the camera (Figs. 6.22, 6.23).

Shinzo and Roso Fukuhara were the sons of Arinobu Fukuhara, founder of the cosmetics firm Shiseido. Like their father, who modeled his merchandise on European products, they judiciously borrowed Western visual styles for their photography. Shinzo, who studied pharmacology in the United States, took over the company presidency in 1915, and streamlined the firm's advertising and window displays in the manner of Western Modernist art and photography, but his and his brother's photography was resolutely otherworldly. Much of Shinzo's work was destroyed in a 1923 earthquake.

During World War II, Japanese propaganda and war photographs dwelled on injured or dead enemy bodies and ruined buildings, the same subjects pictured in other war-torn countries. Japanese photographers arrived on the scene soon after the atomic bombings of Hiroshima and Nagasaki. At the epicenter in Hiroshima they found a ghastly photograph-like silhouette of a man's shadow scorched into a wall by the heat and light of the bomb. Sent to Nagasaki by the Japanese military, photographer Yosuke Yamahata (1917–1966) spent August 10, 1945, making images of the city's ruins. His 119 pictures are the largest archive of photographs made of an atomic bomb site, gained at the cost

6.23
ROSO FUKUHARA, *Sangaatsudo*, c. 1915. Gelatin silver print. Shiseido Corporation, Japan.

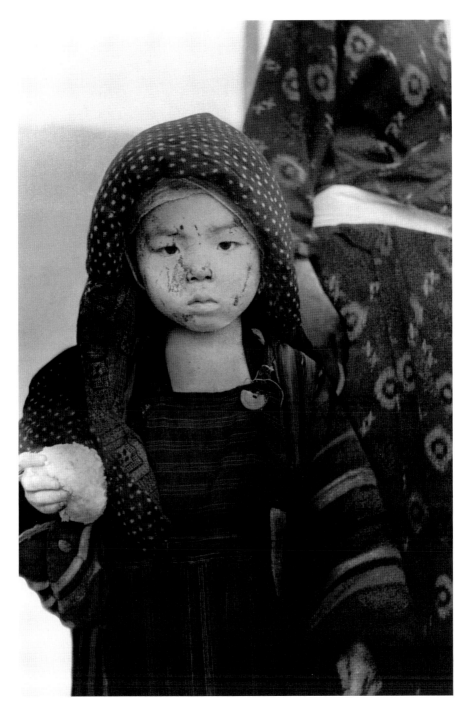

6.24
YOSUKE YAMAHATA,
A Boy with a Rice Ball,
from his book *Atomized
Nagasaki*, 1952.
Gelatin silver print.

The cover image from
Yamahata's 1952 book,
Atomized Nagasaki,
shows a dazed child,
clothed in a headdress
thought to protect the
wearer from radiation,
and looking directly
into the camera. Unlike
the other photographs
hung near it in *The
Family of Man* show,
which were labeled only
with their country of
origin, Yamahata's
image was specifically
labeled "Nagasaki."

of severe radiation exposure that probably contributed to his early death from
cancer. Some of his pictures were published in Japanese newspapers immediately after the country surrendered, but
the army of occupation under American
General Douglas MacArthur soon
banned all atomic-related information
and pictures for seven years.[42] When
Edward Steichen traveled to Japan to
gather images for *The Family of Man*
exhibition, he met Yamahata and was
moved by his book *Atomized Nagasaki*
(1952). For the anti-nuclear war section
of the show, Steichen used a Yamahata
photograph of a small injured boy
clutching a rice ball (Fig. 6.24).

Defeat in World War II raised questions about postwar national identity for
Japanese artists working in such media
as dance and film, as well as photography. As Mark Holborn observed, "it is
impossible to look at postwar Japanese
photography without recognizing the
effect of the almost inconceivable events
of 1945 on the collective imagination
of the nation."[43] The war experience
reverberates through Japanese postwar
artwork, in themes linking death, devastation, and defeat. After the atomic
bombings, the anatomy of the human
body, not a major subject in traditional
Japanese art, was thrust forward as
a contradictory symbol of ruin and

endurance. The countervailing desire for normalcy also coursed through postwar Japanese photography. Because Japan's museums did not take a major interest in exhibiting and collecting photography, books became the primary way to circulate photographs. Consequently, Japanese photographers conceived their work in terms of visual properties that would reproduce effectively in the dull, grainy palette of printer's ink, and which would be viewed consecutively on book pages. The delicacies of fine photographic prints, best appreciated in a portfolio or in a gallery, became secondary.[44]

After a prohibition by the U.S. authorities on atomic-bomb related images was lifted in the early 1950s, several photographers began to shape meanings from the experience of Hiroshima and Nagasaki. Indeed, the havoc wrought by the bomb on human beings and on civic life became a central symbol for life and death in the iconography of postwar Japan. Ken Domon (1909–1990), a photographer with wide-ranging interests including the photography of Japanese art, published *Hiroshima* (1958), an unsparing look at the survivors of the blast. For the Japanese, this book became the best-known account of the bombing. Wanting to underscore the perseverance of Hiroshima's people, Domon issued *Living Hiroshima*, twenty years after his first study (Fig. 6.25).

In 1950, Domon co-founded the Shudan Photo Group, which renounced prewar Pictorialist prettiness as well as modes of extreme self-expression. The group exhibited in Japan with Western photographers they admired, including Margaret Bourke-White, W. Eugene

6.26
SHISEI KUWABARA,
Untitled (People affected by "Minamata Disease"), from his book *Minamata Disease,* 1972.

Kuwabara's use of heavy shadows to portray people physically affected by mercury poisoning helps to hinder voyeurism, while expressing the seriousness of the situation.

Smith, Henri Cartier-Bresson, and Bill Brandt.[45] Their philosophy was soon superseded by that of another group, Junin-no-Me ("The Eyes of Ten"), which favored stylized interpretations of physical existence. After viewing the work of Junin-no-Me, Domon remarked that the period of objective documentary was over and that a period of subjective documentary had begun.[46]

In the early 1960s, industrial pollution introduced poisonous mercury into the waters near the fishing village of Minamata, causing profound birth defects. Shisei Kuwabara (b. 1936) photographed the tragic results in images whose grainy dark surfaces parallel the visual language used by photographers to chronicle the physical effects of atomic devastation (Fig. 6.26). Influenced by these pictures and Kuwabara's book on Minamata, American photographer W. Eugene Smith similarly recorded the calamity, producing a large series of photographs that trace the introduction of mercury waste into the water, its effects on a generation of children, and the attempts of citizens to seek justice through the court system.

Some photographers shunned subjectivity and sought other means to chronicle postwar Japan. Eikoh Hosoe (b. 1933), who was a child during World War II, fused ancient Japanese myth and contemporary experimental dance in his series of thirty-five prints called

6.25
KEN DOMON,
Hiroshima: The Marriage of A-Bomb Victims, 1957. Gelatin silver print. Ken Domon Museum of Photography, Yamagata, Japan.

The longing to return to normalcy after exposure to atomic radiation was frequently expressed in pictures of domestic life and the happiness born of daily existence.

PORTRAIT
Shomei Tomatsu

Introducing his photographs about the effects of the atomic bomb blast at Nagasaki, Shomei Tomatsu (b. 1930) wrote: "Nagasaki has two times. There is 11:02, August 9, 1945. And there is all the time since then."[47] The pivotal influence of the explosion on postwar Japanese experience was summarized in the introductory photograph of Tomatsu's book *Nagasaki: 11:02* (1966), which shows a scorched wristwatch stopped at the time of the detonation. The text accompanying Tomatsu's pictures begins with impersonal scientific data on the heat and energy of the blast, as well as the symptoms of radiation exposure, but the photographs are far from objective. For instance, when Tomatsu photographed a beer bottle melted in the infernal heat, he lighted it in such a way that it suggests a skinned animal carcass (Fig. 6.27). In another image, a man's head appears out of black shadows into a spotlight where dark and light abstract shapes reveal themselves to be skeins of scar tissue moving up his neck. The man's face is dramatically lighted to indicate the skull beneath the skin. With Ken Domon, Tomatsu also worked on an extensive project, the *Hiroshima–Nagasaki Document* (1961).

Tomatsu's work was at the forefront of the trend in postwar Japan toward subjective documentary, in which the presence and the world-view of the photographer fuse with the subject matter. He forcefully argued that merely reporting a scene does not help to illuminate situations.[48] In many of his photographs, the subject is off-center, or lies at the edge of the work, or is masked with dark shadows. In a hospital just for atomic bomb victims, the face of an obviously ill man addresses the viewer from the extreme upper left of the picture; the disfigured face of a child injured in the womb by radiation is all but lost in a welter of tree leaves that discreetly obscure the face while offering the comforts of nature. Tomatsu was also concerned to show the period of recovery. In his work, immutable human scars and bomb-induced changes in the landscape are balanced by photographs that show the restoration of work and family life in Nagasaki.

The devastation of the atomic bombings caused Tomatsu to think that Japan had to begin afresh, not by trying to revive the past, as some, such as the writer and actor Yukio Mishima (1925–1970), urged. Consequently, Tomatsu's work examined the emergence of postwar Japanese identity. His willingness to make images of contemporary, often urban life helped sever the allegiance of many photographers to the notion of a purely Japanese aesthetic based on older visual arts traditions. The pensive, personal character of his images, with their deliberate shaping of a subject through exaggerated contrasts of black and white, has been a major force in Japanese photography.

329

SHOMEI TOMATSU

6.27
SHOMEI TOMATSU, *A Bottle Melted and Deformed by Atomic Bomb Heat, Radiation and Fire, Nagasaki,* 1961.

6.28
EIKOH HOSOE,
Kamaitachi 31, 1968,
from his book
Kamaitachi, 1969.

For Hosoe, photography
is a component of a
multimedia artistic
expression. Created for
his *Kamaitachi* exhibi-
tion, a hunched dancer
posed on the edge of a
rural fence beneath an
ominous sky. Founder
of the Black Dance
Theater (*Ankoku Buto-
Ha*), Tatsumi Hijikata
plunged his palms into
gold ink and stamped
each print in a ritual act
of authorization.

Kamaitachi (1969), which visually narrate the lot of villagers fatally enchanted
and wounded by a dancer taking the
part of an evil wind, representing the
nuclear blast. Throughout the book,
the lowering sky threatens the ever-
darkening earth, and fear of the vicious
wind becomes panic about the atomic
explosion. The narrative ends with
a picture of total darkness. Presented
as a book and an exhibition in 1969,
Kamaitachi (Fig. 6.28) expresses both a
dangerous innocence and the persistent
anxiety the Japanese felt about continued American influence.

The war between Japan and the
Allied forces lasted three years and
eight months; the postwar occupation
of Japan, largely administered by
Americans, was about twice as long
(August 1945–August 1952), and the
United States maintained large military
bases in the country after the official
end of occupation. During the 1960s,
anti-American student demonstrations
sparked by indignation at the Vietnam
War heightened national interest
in elements of traditional Japanese
culture and religion thought to have
been erased by Americanization.

Where *Kamaitachi* spoke to a Japanese
audience about these concerns in a
mythic structure, Hosoe's most famous
book *Barakei* (*Killed by Roses*) (1963; 2nd,
revised edition 1971) established the
photographer's international reputation.

In *Barakei*, Hosoe collaborated
with Mishima, whose themes revolved
around Japan's humiliation by occupying forces. Their presence compelled
the emperor to renounce his divinity
and to align himself with modernization
and rapid reconstruction. No doubt
Hosoe and Mishima were among
the millions of Japanese who reeled
when what became known as "The
Photograph" appeared in the press
(Fig. 6.29). Depicting the first meeting
of the Emperor Hirohito (1901–1989;
r. 1926–89) and General Douglas
MacArthur, designated Supreme
Commander for the Allied Powers in
Japan, "The Photograph" showed an
informally posed and somewhat
casually dressed MacArthur standing
beside the self-conscious, formally
outfitted emperor.

Hosoe and Mishima both attempted
to blend experimental art with ancestral
Japanese art forms, and to infuse the

postwar Westernizing present with the strength of ancient Asian tradition. Hosoe's portraits of Mishima in *Killed by Roses* dwell on Mishima's fascination with samurai swords and physical pain, an uncanny anticipation of the writer's famous act of ritual suicide. Rehearsed and performed like a theater piece, Mishima's *hara-kiri* was enacted on November 25, 1970, after he and a band of his supporters took over a military office and demanded to address soldiers about the loss of traditional Japanese values, and the erosion of the emperor's power in modern, democratic Japan.

Despite growing anti-American sentiment, the Modernist photograph was not neglected in Japan. It found a staunch advocate in the work of American-born Yasuhiro Ishimoto (b. 1921), who learned photography in the Colorado relocation camp where he was interned during World War II. He also studied at the Chicago Institute of Design, founded by László Moholy-Nagy as the New Bauhaus in 1937. Under Moholy-Nagy, who brought Aaron Siskind and Harry Callahan (see below) to the school's faculty, the Institute of Design acquired an international reputation for its dedication to experimental techniques and formal innovation in graphic design and photographic practice. Ishimoto traveled to postwar Japan, where he applied the lessons of Moholy-Nagy's new vision photography (see pp. 246–49). Although he continued to spend time in the United States, Ishimoto became a Japanese citizen in 1969. Responding to a comment by photographer Minor White, Ishimoto stated: "I studied at the New Bauhaus in Chicago, so I agree that my work can be said to contain American and German influences, but I do not agree that I have any Japanese traits."[51]

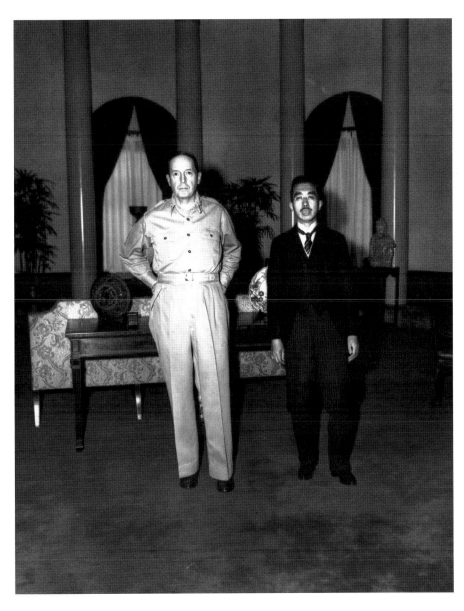

**6.29
PHOTOGRAPHER UNKNOWN,** *Untitled* **("The Photograph"—the first meeting of General MacArthur and Emperor Hirohito, September 27, 1945), 1945. National Archives, Washington, D.C.**

The seemingly simple news photograph upset Japanese viewers, who thought that General MacArthur insulted the emperor by dressing too casually. The picture reputedly marked the moment when the Japanese recognized that they had been defeated and that the Americans were in charge.[49] Yet the picture also showed that the Americans would support some form of continuing monarchy.[50]

FOCUS
Photographing the Atomic Bomb

Photographs from the atomic bombings of Hiroshima and Nagasaki did not run in U.S. newspapers on the days these cities were bombed (August 7 and August 9, 1945, respectively, United States time). The pictures that were released on August 11, 1945, were taken from the air by George R. Caron, a tailgunner aboard the *Enola Gay*, the airplane that delivered the bomb to Hiroshima. They were published widely in subsequent weeks, appearing, for example, in the August 20, 1945, issue of *Life*. Though they gave many people their first look at the tall, dome-topped cloud rising 20,000 feet over the city, the Hiroshima images scarcely approximated the mushroom-shaped cloud that emerged as the emblem of the atomic age. A photograph of the Nagasaki explosion that accompanied it in the same issue of *Life* came closer.

Comparisons of the soaring column of dirt and debris that follows an atomic fireball explosion to a mushroom first occurred in military descriptions of the tests preceding the Japanese bombings. In fact, the resemblance began to enter the language vocabulary before the 1946 atomic test on Bikini Atoll that produced a distinctive mushroom shape. The public repeatedly viewed the Bikini blast in photographs as well as through newsreels and television (Fig. 6.30). In a bizarre twist, the Pacific island later gave the famous bathing suit its name.

Aerial views of the destruction at Hiroshima and Nagasaki appeared in the United States within weeks of the bombings, but close-up images of the damage to people and property shot by the Japanese were confiscated by the United States War Department before they could be disseminated. Bits of movie footage, cut from film made by the Japanese shortly after the Hiroshima explosion, were included in an August 1946 newsreel about the Bikini Atoll tests. The *New York Times* reported that one of the images showed victims who appeared "as though they had been seared by an acetylene torch."[52] In that same month, the *New Yorker* published writer John Hersey's vivid chronicle of what he saw in Hiroshima. Pictures made by Japanese photographers were not widely seen by the American public until a 1952 issue of *Life*. When the magazine ran pictures of the first hydrogen bomb explosion in 1954, it also published an editorial tinged with fear and relieved with deathbed humor, reflecting increased public apprehension about the specter of nuclear warfare.[53] The initial public feelings of awe and patriotism following Hiroshima and Nagasaki eroded throughout the 1950s, allowing the anxiety about the atomic bomb gradually to spread. Nevertheless, atomic energy remained a strong, yet contradictory, prospect for the future. To some, harnessing the atom foretold a utopian tomorrow, in which nuclear power freed humans from work and nuclear medicine cured diseases. To others, experiments with the atom launched a growing pessimism about the dark side of human nature.

6.30
PHOTOGRAPHER UNKNOWN, *Atomic Cloud During Baker Day Blast at Bikini*, 1946. Gelatin silver print. National Archives, Washington, D.C.

6.31
YASUHIRO
ISHIMOTO,
Chicago, 1962.
Gelatin silver print.

Indeed, Ishimoto's work in Chicago strongly resembles that of other street photographers in the postwar period. Waiting for the exact moments of alignment when, for example, shadows appear to be following the people who make them, Ishimoto's work recalls that of European photographers such as Cartier-Bresson and the work of Ishimoto's American teacher, Harry Callahan. Never sentimental, Ishimoto grasped the feelings of alienation, self-delusion, and futility expressed in American photography during the 1950s (Fig. 6.31). Misunderstanding Ishimoto's disheartened perception of human relationships, Edward Steichen put two of his photographs in the exhibition *The Family of Man*.

Ishimoto's international reputation was sealed when he published the result of his six-year-long study of Katsura Rikyu, the so-called Detached Palace in Kyoto, Japan. In these images, the palace from the early 1600s resembles the spare geometry of modern architecture. Published in 1971, *Katsura: Tradition and Creation in Japanese Architecture* was a collaboration with Modernist architect Kenzo Tange (1913–2005), as well as Bauhaus artists Walter Gropius, who wrote an introductory essay, and Herbert Bayer, who designed the book.

Despite the recovery of the Japanese postwar economy and the efforts of several prominent Japanese photographers

to recuperate postwar culture, Daido Moriyama (b. 1938) lingered on the notion of social decline, beginning with defeat in World War II and the subsequent "Americanization" of the nation.[54] His most famous image is a gravelly picture of a dirty, exhausted, snarling stray dog (Fig. 6.32). Like his mentors, Shomei Tomatsu (see p. 000) and Hosoe, Moriyama exploits photography's graphic properties to express fierce emotion. His images are, as photographer Leo Rubinfien observed, "the visual equivalent of nausea, vertigo or horror."[55] Their tilted, slightly out-of-focus quality shows Moriyama's acknowledged debt to the idiosyncratic work of American photographer William Klein (see Fig. 6.43).

Where Tomatsu's expressionistic images ultimately rely on the factual credibility of what was before the lens,

6.32
DAIDO MORIYAMA,
Stray Dog, Misawa Aimori, 1971.
Gelatin silver print.
Gift of Van Deren Coke.
San Francisco Museum of Modern Art, San Francisco, California.

Moriyama's stray dog, an unwanted and dangerous animal, is an outcast and a loner and blends the photographer's sense of himself as an angry outsider with the perception that his country is irretrievably conquered. The figure appears elsewhere in Japanese postwar photography and film as a frightening symbol for social isolation, as in Akira Kurosawa's 1949 film *Stray Dog*.

Moriyama's work is radically personal: "My photographs have always been ... private letters that I write and send to myself," he explained.[56] He once renounced all hope by rejecting photography in a 1972 collection called *Sashin yo sayonara* (*Farewell to Photography* or *Photography, Good Riddance!*), in which pictures were "blurred, too dark, too light, or otherwise hard to read."[57]

THE WEST AND THE COLD WAR

Fear of communism and the threat of nuclear warfare hung over the war in Korea (1950–53), which was the outcome of festering economic and political discontent in North Korea about the Allies' postwar decision to divide the country in two along the 38th parallel. Soviet- and Chinese-supported North Korean troopers battled South Korean and United Nations forces, composed of fifteen nations, including the United States. In contrast to their patriotic photographic coverage of World War II (see Fig. 5.86), newspapers and magazines heightened public fear of nuclear warfare and stirred doubt about the war's goals, using anti-heroic images of ordinary soldiers enduring danger far from home. Battle-toughened photographers such as Larry Burrows (1926–1971), Carl Mydans (1907–2004), and David Douglas Duncan (b. 1916) sent back close-up photographs of ordinary soldiers suffering cold, privation, and the death of friends. Duncan's photo-essay for *Life*'s 1950 Christmas issue undermined cozy assumptions about what a Christmas essay should contain. Entitled "There Was a Christmas," it showed an image of a young Marine more as victim than victor (Fig. 6.33). Reflecting on his Korean images, Duncan concluded that "war is in the eyes."

The Korean War ended in 1953, but international tensions continued to rise. In 1955, the Soviet Union and the eastern European nations of Poland, Czechoslovakia, Hungary, Romania, Bulgaria, Albania, and East Germany signed the Warsaw Pact, a mutual defense agreement. In November 1956, a Hungarian revolt against Soviet occupation was suppressed, and in October 1957 the Soviets launched the space satellite Sputnik 1, proving the superiority of its long-range rockets. In the United States, anti-communist hysteria led to fear that "reds" were infiltrating the nation's institutions. Federal employees were asked to sign loyalty oaths. Senator Joseph McCarthy still zealously headed the powerful House Committee on Un-American Activities (HUAC), which had subpoenaed prominent entertainers as suspected communists in 1947 and 1951.

The livelihood of many within the arts community was seriously threatened by these investigations. In 1954, McCarthy set out to locate communists in the U.S. Army, a campaign that led to his downfall. After more than a decade of highly visible political photography during the New Deal and World War II, artists and photographers left the fray, having been harassed by the government or discouraged by the slowness of social change. Recalling the 1950s, photographer Lisette Model (see p. 347) exclaimed, "It was terrible. You didn't know *what* to photograph."[58] Disgusted with politics and angered by the shallow materialism of what economist John Kenneth Galbraith famously called "the affluent society" in his 1958 book of the same name, many artists, writers, and photographers turned to the inner world of private contemplation.

ANNIHILATION, ALIENATION, ABSTRACTION: AMERICA

As writer Tom Englehardt observed, "from 1945 to 1975 victory culture ended in America."[59] The "heroic war ethos" of 1945 gave way to fear, insecurity, and societal disillusionment. America's inability to end the nightmarish spiral of the arms race slowly undermined the logic of mutually assured atomic destruction and confidence in the nation's place in the world. The national mood was captured in a best-selling book by the sociologist David Riesman. First published in 1950, *The Lonely Crowd* leapt to prominence in a paperback edition of 1953 that sold 1.4 million copies.[60] It warned of a major shift in the American character, a turning away from guidance by an inner compass, toward seeking direction from others. Reisman substantiated readers' worries about the American postwar future. Artist and photographer Ben Shahn (1898–1969), who had

6.33 (opposite)
DAVID DOUGLAS DUNCAN, *Untitled*, cover of *Life* magazine, 25 December, 1950.

The text accompanying David Douglas Duncan's photo-essay noted that the holiday celebration took place in "the valley of the shadow of death," recalling the disastrous charge of the Light Brigade during the Crimean War (see Fig. 3.21). The image was captioned, "This is the face of a man who eats frozen rations in the snow and who may be interrupted at any moment to run, to fight, or to die."

made images for the Farm Security Administration, summed up the parallel changes in photographic practice: "during the thirties art had been swept by mass ideas, so during the forties there took place a mass movement toward abstraction. Not only was the social dream rejected, but any dream at all."[61]

Perhaps the best example of the shift from social documentary to abstraction is provided by Aaron Siskind's work. An active member of the Photo League, and

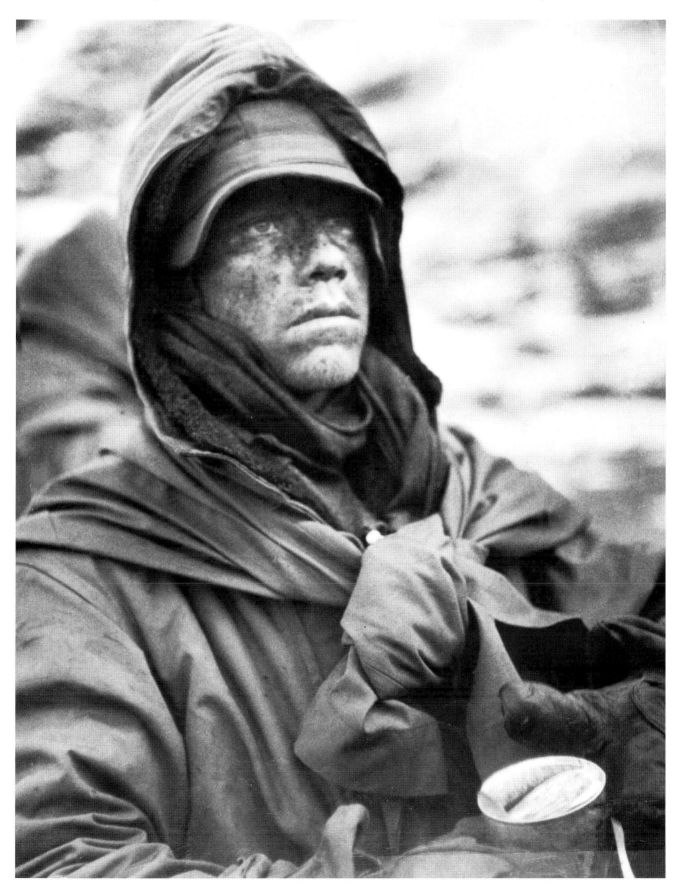

promoter of its famous *Harlem Document* (see Fig. 5.71), Siskind began experimenting in the 1940s with abstract qualities in nature and the built environment. He photographed sites where humans had left their marks, but not the human figure, unless isolated and contorted into an unusual shape. At the same time, he eliminated any hint of narrative content, and worked against the camera's construction of deep perspective, flattening the photographic image as if it were an Abstract Expressionist canvas by an American painter such as Franz Kline (1910–1962), Mark Rothko (1903–1970), or Willem de Kooning (1904–1997), whom he knew and whose artwork he photographed. One of his images was hung at the Ninth Street Show (1951) in New York City, an exhibit that was instrumental in bringing ABSTRACT EXPRESSIONISM to a wider audience.

As Siskind put it, "the so-called documentary picture left me wanting something." However much close-ups of peeling paint might look like an abstract painting (Fig. 6.34), Siskind insisted that this sort of work was not "a compromise with reality. The objects are rendered sharp, fully textured, and undistorted (my documentary training!)." Siskind described the instant of finding his subjects in the world of visual experience as "emotional," "psychological," and "utterly personal." He concluded that "the inner drama is the meaning of the exterior event." Like many artists in the 1950s, he sought to

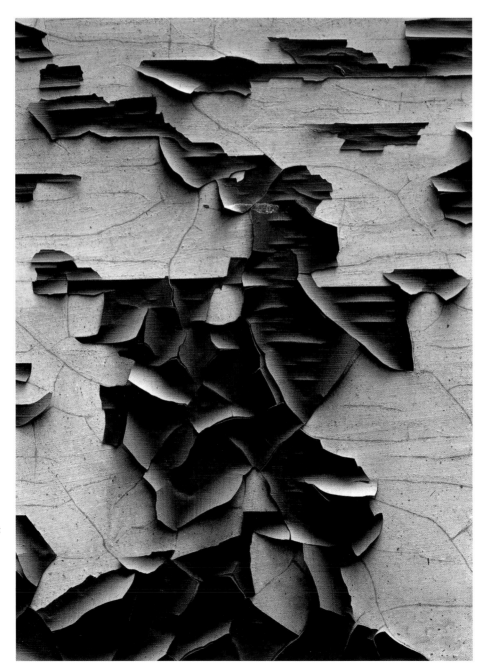

**6.34
AARON SISKIND,** *Jerome, Arizona*, 1949. **Gelatin silver print. Aaron Siskind Foundation. Hallmark Cards Inc., Kansas City, Missouri.**

By coming in close to what appears to be peeling paint, Siskind isolated a composition with a central, if abstract figure, balanced by an array of shapes in the upper and lower parts of the picture. The photograph may owe to Siskind's close relationship with Abstract Expressionist painters, who employed thick slashes of paint on their canvases.

6.35
LOTTE JACOBI,
Photogenic, c. 1950.
Vintage gelatin silver
print. Lotte Jacobi
Archives, Dimond
Library, University of
New Hampshire,
Durham, New Hamp-
shire. Courtesy
Hallmark Cards Inc.,
Kansas City, Missouri.

While never a major
trend, abstract photo-
graphs, such as those
produced in Jacobi's
Photogenic series,
repeatedly appeared
in post-World War II
image-making, challeng-
ing the notion that
photography's role is to
record the appearance
of reality. In this image,
Jacobi sketched forms
and created a sense
of depth by moving a
light source over photo-
sensitive paper.

begin anew in primal experience or, as he put it, to unlearn socially educated responses so as "to see the world clean and fresh and alive, as primitive things are clean and fresh and alive."[62]

While Siskind turned to exploring the inner world, other artists and writers looked to indigenous peoples for lessons on living outside the tainted modern world. John Collier, Sr., who served from 1934 to 1945 as President Franklin Roosevelt's Commissioner of Indian Affairs, helped arrange the landmark exhibit *Indian Art of the United States* at the Museum of Modern Art in New York (1941). The tone for postwar appre-ciation of Native Americans was set at that exhibit, when its organizer René d'Harnoncourt dismissed the notion of primitivism as a backward stage of early civilization, and underscored the moral weight of Indian culture.[63] John Collier, Jr. (1913–1992), the commissioner's son, made extensive and generally unro-manticized photographs among the Navajo people and among Peru's indige-nous peoples. Similarly, Laura Gilpin (1891–1979), who spent the greater part of her career photographing among Native Americans in the Southwest, ardently studied Navajo history and life for her 1968 book *The Enduring Navajo.*

Detached from their origins in Europe between the world wars, Surrealism and abstraction became international visual languages, not only in advertising but also for a younger generation of artists. To escape persecu-tion in Nazi Germany, Lotte Jacobi (1896–1990) had to leave 90 per cent of her work behind. After arriving in the United States in 1935, Jacobi set about combining a career in portrait photo-graphy with the production of abstrac-tions she called "photogenics." These resulted from drawing with a light source, such as a pen light, on photo-graphically sensitive paper (Fig. 6.35). Working in Arizona for more than fifty years, Italian-born Frederick Sommer (1905–1999) blended Surrealism and abstraction in psychologically disturb-ing images. He photographed still lifes made from the desiccated corpses of desert animals, fusing formal beauty with frightening decay. Like his friend the Surrealist Max Ernst, Sommer experimented with de-forming the photograph's realism. He superimposed images, created *clichés verres,* and con-structed negatives from oil paint sand-wiched between sheets of cellophane. Even his straight photographs look like altered images (Fig. 6.36). Like Siskind, with whom he photographed in 1949, Sommer favored blocking out the horizon line and focusing on surface texture and flatness.[64] Just as Abstract Expressionists such as Jackson Pollock (1912–1956) brought to center stage the physical process of making art, so Sommer emphasized technique at the expense of realistic description.

6.36
FREDERICK SOMMER,
Arizona Landscape,
1943. Gelatin silver
print. Center for Creative
Photography, Tucson,
Arizona.

As happened in Europe, American Surrealist photography gradually lost its sense of outrage and estrangement, becoming more a means of psychic inquiry and fanciful imaginings. Even though American Jerry Uelsmann (b. 1934) claims that his seamless separate realities draw on what he calls "the darker side of myself,"[65] there are no horrific scenes in his work. A student of Minor White (1908–1976), Uelsmann creates illusionistic images that seem to capture a parallel world, where elements recombine in unexpected, but not repugnant ways (Fig. 6.37). In one print he showed himself in the bathtub as Oscar Rejlander and as Henry Peach Robinson, a reference to the nineteenth-century combination-print makers and their efforts to insert visual information into the photograph that the camera was incapable of recording.

Surrealism and abstraction were among a number of strategies for contesting the notions that photography must record the external world, or that it was obliged to support the humanitarian task of social betterment. Minor White, a photographer who sought spiritual insights in poetry, psychological theory, myth, and religion, did not so much reject the material realm as reconfigure it. White thought of photography as a process wherein the visual world was rediscovered as a font of spiritual illumination for those willing to look. Widely seen as a mystic, White nonetheless stressed that the poet-photographer must move beyond self-discovery to communication. Writing to a person seeking his advice, White counseled: "Your photographs are still mirrors of yourself. In other words your images are raw, the emotions naked. These are private images not public ones. They are 'expressive' meaning a direct mirror of yourself rather than 'creative' meaning so converted as to affect others as mirrors of themselves."[66]

White much admired Stieglitz's photographs, especially the series known as *Equivalents* (see Fig. 4.25),

6.37
JERRY UELSMANN,
Untitled (Landscape with a floating tree), 1969. Victoria & Albert Museum, London.

Uelsmann's precise combination-printing techniques allow him to invent alternative worlds in which nature operates in ways contrary to its habits on earth.

White's assimilation of Eastern religions allowed him to bring a contemplative quality to his photography. The *Empty Head* is more than a wondrous shape made up of ice crystals. It refers to the emptying out of the noisy self during the practice of meditation.

in which he used cloud shots to intimate inner states. Like Stieglitz, White insisted that photographs could be much more than literal transcriptions of optical reality, and he preferred to work in series of images arranged to form complex poetic meanings. He began making "sequences" soon after returning from service in World War II, and this "cinema of stills" became his basic unit.[67] Wanting a more interactive interpretation of his work, White often spoke of "reading" photographs, not merely glimpsing them. In the 1940s, he was already numbering his sequences, some of which were personal explorations of homoerotic desire that were never publicly exhibited during his lifetime. The order of individual photographs within a sequence was not fixed, but changed from time to time. Certain themes recur in his work, such as the fleeting performances of natural light. Ordinary doors and windows open on to unanticipated glimpses of fantastic yet momentary illumination (Fig. 6.38).

At the end of the nineteenth century, White might have been a Pictorialist, locating spirituality in suggestive haziness. Instead, he looked to the intensely detailed views and vigilant printing methods of Ansel Adams and Edward Weston, and to their use of the straight photograph to convey metaphysical meaning. In the postwar period, when social reform efforts were too often misconstrued as communist ventures, White became a spiritual activist. His teaching at institutions on the East and West coasts, and curatorial position at George Eastman House in Rochester, New York, allowed him to encourage personal insight and spirituality among photographers, and to promote the use of photography as metaphor or symbol. In 1952, White became editor of *Aperture*, a magazine devoted to art photography, which he founded along with others, including Dorothea Lange and Ansel Adams. Although his work was criticized by Postmodernists in the late twentieth century as "mystical trivia,"[68] White's influence on photography endures in the meditative fine printing of his students, such as Paul Caponigro (b. 1932) and Jerry Uelsmann, as well as the independence of Eugene Richards (see p. 413).

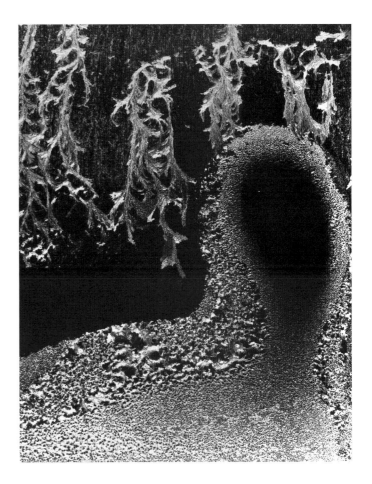

The Americans

Minor White's spiritualism was not the only personal approach to photography to have a lasting impact on the medium. The photographs of Swiss-born photographer Robert Frank (b. 1924) induced many young photographers to cruise the streets and highways of America looking for pictures. A commercial and fashion photographer when he came to the United States, Frank also made his own work, which came to Steichen's attention while he was selecting images for *The Family of Man* exhibition.

Encouraged by his friend and mentor Walker Evans, Frank began the first of several road trips around the United States, where he made pictures that would unravel the certitude of documentary photography as practiced by the F.S.A. photographers and the picture press. Where Depression-era documentarians witnessed a troubled yet resilient America, summed up in such images as Lange's *Migrant Mother* (see Fig. 5.55), Frank saw a soul-damaged population, fluctuating between violence, ignorance, and despair. In the collection of these images called *The Americans* (French edition, 1958; American edition, 1959), first published in France because no

American publishing house would issue it, Frank transformed tokens of American postwar prosperity, such as automobiles and television sets, casting them as conduits of an insidious commercialism that was profoundly alienating individuals from each other and from the wider society. In this way, he can be seen as part of a wider artistic resistance movement, which included the Beat poets and novelists, engaged in the struggle to find alternatives to the power of consensus-based art forms. Despite Frank's recurrent images of motion and communication, such as highways or telephones, the people in *The Americans* seem stuck in one place: the loneliness of their own psyches. As Peter C. Mazio observed, "The only mobile person in Robert Frank's *The Americans* is the artist himself."[69] In his book, American flags sometimes fly in the faces of observers, obscuring their vision, and people seldom find eye-contact with each other (Fig. 6.39).

Rather than the clear, detailed pictures of photojournalism and the documentary tradition, Frank's prints are often gritty, tilted, and blurred. Shot with a 35mm camera, which allowed him to take pictures quickly and secretly, they have an unpremeditated look that—like the action paintings of Jackson Pollock—combines great intensity with a free, risky handling. *The Americans* does not progress through a legible visual narrative, but consists of fragmented "indecisive" moments experienced by the photographer. For some viewers, Frank's concentration on ragtag Americans and his apathetic attitude toward the craft of photography were tantamount to "un-American" behavior of the kind persecuted by McCarthy's committee.

With the wider circulation of a 1960s' American edition, and subsequent republications that kept the book in print, Frank's photographs gained a wide intellectual presence as a protest against numbing mass culture, materialism, and social conformity. The preface to this United States printing was written by Beat generation writer Jack Kerouac (1922–1969), whose jittery romantic novel of the American highways *On the Road* was published in 1957 and featured Frank as one of its characters. Kerouac's hipster language, reeled off in streams of association, like a poem by Allen Ginsberg (1926–1997), located the authenticity of the pictures in their apparently impromptu nature, reminiscent of jazz improvisation.

Kerouac also drew Frank—and photography—into the sphere of American existentialism and Beat generation hauteur, with its emphasis on cool, self-absorbed rebelliousness in the face of narrow social conformity. In effect, Kerouac suggested that Frank's photographs could be savored like serious avant-garde literature, which assailed the deeply rooted American tradition of rural innocence and integrity, and prophesied the coming of shabby morality and self-delusion to the American heartland. Like Walker Evans, whose *American Photographs* (1938) pictured automobiles, graveyards, and luncheonettes as signposts of American feeling, Frank became a photographer-hero, both for his vision and for his lifestyle, which reflected personal discoveries. Evans had, in fact, helped to obtain for Frank the Guggenheim Fellowship that allowed him to make the trips on which *The Americans* was based.

In 1962, Frank remarked that "photography is a solitary journey. That is the only course open to the creative photographer. There is no compromise: only a few photographers accept this fact."[70] Taking a cue from the New York Abstract Expressionist painters and Beat generation poets, among whom he lived and worked in the 1940s and 1950s, Frank believed that anti-authoritarianism was a basic form of political resistance. How one lived was far more consequential than overt political action. In the 1960s, he moved away from photography to filmmaking. Ultimately he left the United States for a remote area of Nova Scotia, Canada, where he continues to make photographs and films.

On the Streets

Street photography is as old as the medium itself; one of Daguerre's early images shows a Paris Boulevard (see Fig. 1.13). But in the postwar period, street photography was increasingly practiced by art photographers who discovered in the shifting crowds on America's city streets countless images that expressed the photographer's inner feelings or evinced the seedy materialism of postwar American culture.

6.39 (opposite)
ROBERT FRANK, *Drug Store, Detroit*, 1955, pl. 147 from his book *The Americans*, 1959. Gelatin silver print. Courtesy Pace McGill Gallery, New York. © the artist.

The Americans captures the sense of unfulfilled lives and spiritually vacant environments of the post-World War II period. Whether by accident or design, contemporary issues sometimes intrude on Frank's work, as in this view of a lunch counter where white men are served by African-American women, who would not be welcome to eat at the counter they serve.

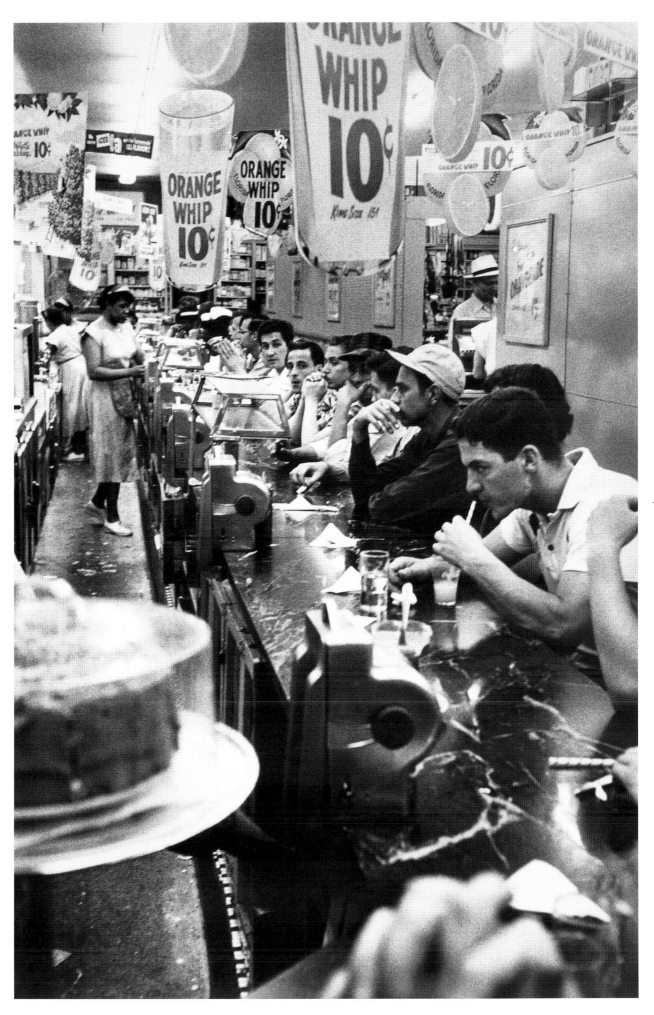

Harry Callahan (1912–1999), Siskind's colleague at the Chicago Institute of Design, found fresh material on the streets through what he called "seeing photographically."[71] Callahan's brooding street photographs are crammed with stark contrasts of black and white, allowing few middle gray tones (Fig. 6.40). While he viewed the city as tense and inhospitable, he could shift outlooks to savor lyrical flashes of beauty in humble tufts of grass, elegant lines drawn by

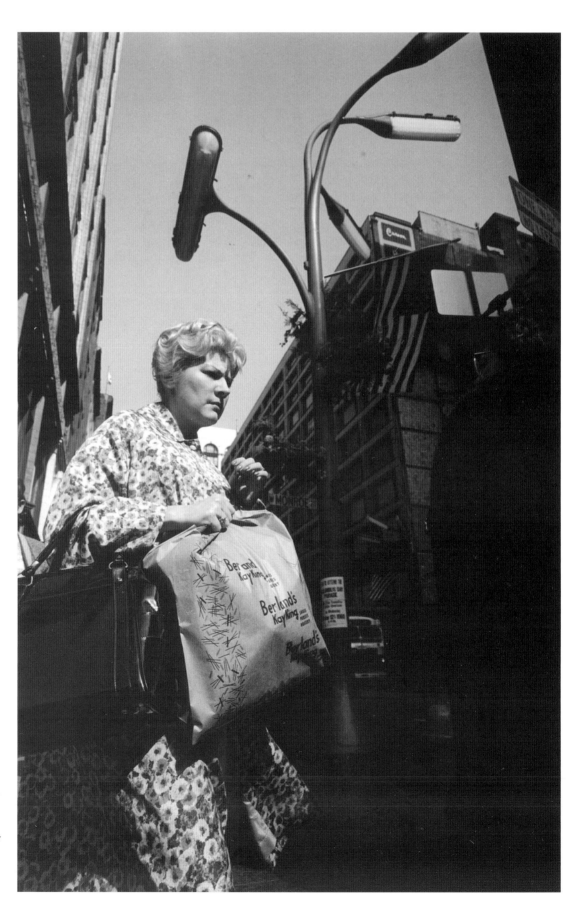

6.40
HARRY CALLAHAN,
Chicago, 1961.
Gelatin silver print.

Shooting from below, so as to accentuate the jumble of lines created by the tall buildings and splaying streetlight, Callahan focused on the determined facial features of the shopper. The floral pattern on her dress contrasts with an environment that has rebelled against nature.

utility wires against the sky, or the graceful features of his wife's form (Fig. 6.41).

Although Callahan's influence was felt throughout American photography, street photographers were generally more enchanted with what became known as the "snapshot aesthetic," an apparently uncomposed everyday subject, illuminated only with available light, and taken in a way that mimics instantaneous sight. Although the trend toward making these seemingly casual and unprepared, sometimes blurry, and often deliberately imperfect pictures owes to the influence of Frank's *The Americans*, several photographers had earlier explored the snapshot aesthetic.

For example, when Roy DeCarava (b. 1919) worked on the photographs for the book *The Sweet Flypaper of Life* (1955), with a text by poet and writer Langston Hughes, he balanced posed portraits with unrehearsed scenes on Harlem's streets and in people's homes. Neither Hughes nor DeCarava attempted to make a sociological report or to advocate reform measures. Each insisted on rendering Harlem artistically.[72] Thickly shadowed or blurred images alternate with studies of sharply delineated light and shade. In DeCarava's work, the snapshot aesthetic merged with Cartier-Bresson's "decisive moment." The mixture is apparent in a shot showing an elegantly dressed young woman on her way to her graduation (Fig. 6.42).

The former painter William Klein (b. 1928), who spent most of his career abroad, had begun to snatch cheerless images along New York City's streets before Frank published *The Americans*. Klein conceived his early work in book form, where he would have greater control over the printing and arrangement of his images, as in his self-published *Life is Good and Good for You in New York: William Klein Trance Witness Revels* (1956). Less well known than Frank, Klein was even more experimental in his camerawork. He distorted the image, overexposing with a flash, or deliberately using wide-angle lenses for close-ups, in order to blur or stretch shapes (Fig. 6.43). Self-taught, Klein bypassed prescribed methods of taking pictures and looked to the tabloids. "My aesthetics was the New York *Daily News*," he wrote. "I saw the book I wanted to do as a tabloid gone berserk, gross, grainy, over-inked, with a brutal layout, bull-horn headlines."[73]

The impertinent tabloid photographs Klein enjoyed may have been made by Weegee—the nickname of Austrian-born Arthur Fellig (1899–1968)—who sold his specialty, raw crime-scene photography to many New York newspapers. His well-deserved moniker derived either from the squeegee he used in one of his first jobs as a darkroom assistant, or from the ouija board, a device used at séances to contact the dead. With a short-wave radio in his car and home, Weegee monitored police broadcasts and arrived so quickly on the scene that he seemed able to anticipate the crime. Weegee's New York is a place of barely submerged brutality, fear, and

6.41
HARRY CALLAHAN,
Eleanor, 1947.
Gelatin silver print.

6.42
ROY DeCARAVA,
Graduation, 1949, from
his book *The Sweet
Flypaper of Life*, 1955.
George Eastman House,
Rochester, New York.

Some of DeCarava's
photographs are so
thick with shadow that
forms are barely visible.
In this image, however,
the girl's pleasure on
the way to a graduation
is highlighted in a
wedge of light that
pierces the desolation
of the empty lot. The
billboard does double
duty, as a caption for the
girl's achievement, and
as an ironic contrast
with its surroundings.

confusion (Fig. 6.44). Weegee became
an art-world celebrity, who exhibited and
lectured at the Museum of Modern Art
in New York. His sensational images of
crime and violent death, rendered in the
harsh light of the exploding flash, were
not unique, however. The ubiquitous
tabloid newspapers established a stylish
visual vocabulary and cast of urban
characters (corpse, cop, and criminal)
that encouraged *films noirs* such as
Murder, My Sweet and *Double Indemnity*,

both released in 1944, and *The Naked
City*, adapted from Weegee's 1945 collection of photographs with the same title.[74]

The Social Landscape

The appearance of a new photographic
trend, indifferent to social reform but
acutely focused on the qualities of
camera vision, was recognized in 1966,
at the Brandeis University exhibition
*Twelve Photographers of the American
Social Landscape*. The show gave the
style its name, and was quickly followed
by another compendium at George
Eastman House, Rochester, New York
where curator Nathan Lyons opened
Toward a Social Landscape (1966).
Soon after, the Museum of Modern Art
mounted its exhibition *New Documents*
(1967). In these presentations, Lee
Friedlander (b. 1934) emerged as a
major figure. Friedlander was impressed
by Frank's *The Americans*, and made his
own road trip around the United States,
shooting cemetery stones and memorial
statues for an elegiac project called *The
American Monument* (1976). Friedlander
admired Weegee's hardheaded urban
dramas and André Kertész's grasp of
visual coincidence. He balked at supplying viewers with clear visual clues with
which to decipher his work. Whether

6.43
WILLIAM KLEIN,
*Swing and Boy and
Girl*, New York, 1954.
© William Klein. Gelatin
silver print. Howard
Greenberg Gallery,
New York.

6.44
WEEGEE (ARTHUR FELLIG), *Their First Murder*, October 9, 1941. Gelatin silver print.

Weegee photographed murder and mayhem for tabloid newspapers. His signature style often included an array of human reactions, from shock and grief, to excitement about the chance of getting one's picture in the news-paper. He liked to include bystanders, who, in their ability to ignore death and human suffering, and become ghoul-ish voyeurs, acted as surrogates for newspaper readers.

picturing the jumble of signs and traffic on the street, or layers of reflections in the glass of storefronts, Friedlander obscurely hinted at a story, only to fall back on an exercise in camera vision. He saw photography as a picture-making system with rules as peculiar to itself as painting. Just as the painter's brush leaves marks on the canvas, so the camera leaves marks of its rectangular framing device, the kind of lens used, and the chemistry of the film and processing. In *New Orleans* (1968), Friedlander toyed with the photographic tradition of deep perspective (Fig. 6.45). He frequently includes his reflection or shadow in his work, not to indicate that the image is a personal metaphor for a state of mind or emotion, but to demonstrate that it is a picture made with the camera whose outlines often show in the print.

6.45
LEE FRIEDLANDER, *New Orleans*, 1968. Gelatin silver print.

Friedlander never lets the viewer forget that the photograph is a con-scious construction of reality. In this image, the photographer stands in front of a plate-glass window taking a picture of the man and the street behind him, as well as of a small picture inside the shop. The viewer's eyes move back and forth trying to establish a point of view.

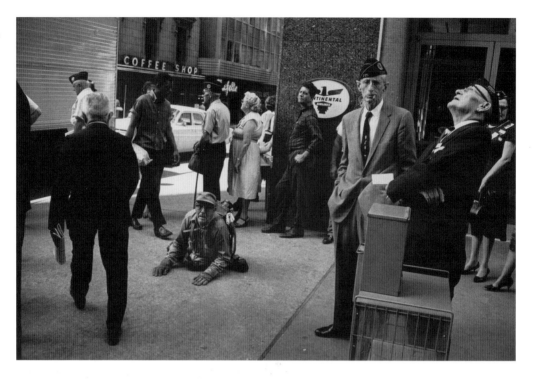

6.46
GARRY WINOGRAND,
*American Legion
Convention, Dallas,
Texas, 1964.* Gelatin
silver print. Museum of
Modern Art, New York.

6.47 (right)
LISETTE MODEL,
*Albert-Alberta, Hubert's
Forty-Second Street
Flea Circus, New York,*
c. 1945. Gelatin silver
print. National Gallery
of Canada/Musée des
Beaux-Arts du Canada,
Ottawa.

Model was unsparing in
her portraits, focusing
on departures from the
norm, as in this photo-
graph of a freakish
character who was an
attraction at a 42nd
Street dime museum.

More blunt than Friedlander, Garry
Winogrand (1928–1984) was also
among the new social landscape image-
makers. Like Friedlander, he did a stint
as a photojournalist for the picture press.
One of his images, an uncomplicated
view of a couple frisking in the water at
a bathing beach, was included in *The
Family of Man*. It did not give an inkling
of the psychologically complex and tense
series of street photographs that he
would begin in the 1960s. With funding
from a Guggenheim grant, Winogrand
set out in 1964 to tour America, as
Walker Evans and Robert Frank had
done before him. But Winogrand had
a particular agenda; he wanted to photograph the United States in the wake
of the 1963 assassination of President
John F. Kennedy.

Winogrand is often quoted as
saying "I photograph to find out what
the world looks like photographed."[75]
Where Friedlander's work resembles
fortuitously found collages, Winogrand's
pictures homed in on human gestures
and body stances that indicate interpersonal tension and inner turmoil.
Sometimes his caustic view of human
nature is echoed in abrupt cropping of
the image, or in shots where the camera
has been tilted.

Winogrand asserted that the photograph was not simply a window on the
world but a new fact. His fear that the
subject matter of the street might over-
whelm his investigation of photography's

unique picture-making qualities was
well founded.[76] In his image of a man
with multiple amputations (Fig. 6.46),
the chance arrangement of figures,
oddly reminiscent of a *tableau vivant*, is
not so compelling as to blunt the tense
human implications of the scene.

Comparing the work of Friedlander and Winogrand to European street photographers such as Kertész, one can see that the American work tips the balance between form and narrative toward form, and tilts the scales between individual expression and neutrality toward neutral vision, or disinterested irony. What remains personal in much social landscape photography is the selection of the picture, especially because Friedlander and Winogrand both exposed many rolls of film and picked the picture from contact sheets.

The influence of the social landscape photographers was felt throughout the 1960s, but it did not completely obliterate the work of street photographers with a greater interest in content and personal point of view. For example, when Austrian-born photographer Lisette Model (1901–1983) emigrated to the United States in 1938, she had already polished her observation of human foibles and vanities. In France, where she had lived since 1926, Model's lens recorded the self-delusions of the rich and fashionable as they lounged in the fancy resort area of Nice. In New York, she showed her work at the Photo League, and continued to be fascinated by those who are infatuated by glamor, including people on the margins of society (Fig. 6.47). Because she

was not able to make a living from her art and freelance fashion work, Model turned to teaching in 1949, eventually becoming one of New York City's leading photo-educators.

Among her students was Diane Arbus (1923–1971), who took private lessons from Model, and also studied with her at the New School for Social Research. Arbus responded to what she saw as Model's hard-boiled audacity and courage to confront extremes in human situations. In addition, Arbus sharpened her nerve when she accompanied famed New York tabloid ace Weegee on his assignments to photograph murders. Included with Friedlander and Winogrand in the 1967 *New Documents* exhibition at the Museum of Modern Art, Arbus's work was more personal, transforming the social world into a visual terrain to be mined for metaphors resonating with her inner feelings.

Arbus turned normalcy on its head, making the ordinary bizarre and naturalizing the unusual. In her photographs of people, many of them made while she roamed the streets of New York, clothes and cosmetics are futile efforts to camouflage psychic emptiness or damage. When Arbus photographed children, she revealed them as little versions of bad-tempered, mean-spirited adults (Fig. 6.48). On the other hand,

6.48
STEPHEN FRANK,
Untitled (Diane Arbus with her photo of a boy holding a toy grenade in Central Park, New York), 1970.

When Diane Arbus lectured at the Rhode Island School of Design in 1970, she showed several of her photographs to the assembled students. One of them, Stephen Frank (b. 1947), took this picture of Arbus with her print of a grimacing boy holding a toy grenade in Central Park. His threatening appearance is made all the more chilling when juxtaposed with the young family approaching in the distance, the very semblance of normality.

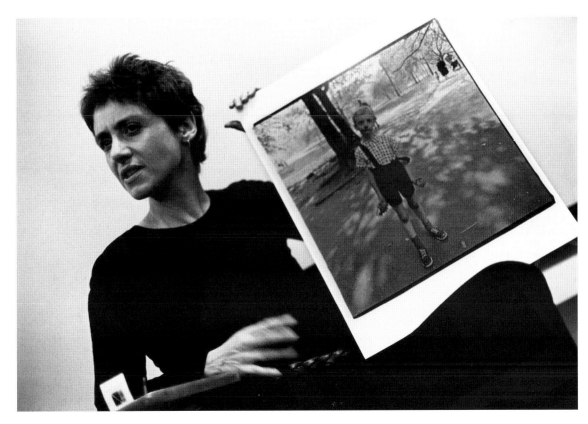

her photographs of people at the margins of society, such as female impersonators, show them to be more virtuous for having unmasked their subjective inclinations. For Arbus, marginal people were symbols of her own psychological fragility and trauma.

During the postwar period in American photography, Arbus was not alone in undermining sentimental ideas of the innocence of childhood. Ralph Eugene Meatyard (1925–1972) coaxed children to wear weird masks that did not so much conceal their innocence as reveal their strangeness (Fig. 6.49). Teenage life became a regular subject in the work of many street photographers, including Bruce Davidson (b. 1933). Davidson spent two years chronicling the lives of a Brooklyn gang called the Jokers, and two years photographing the homes of families living on New York

6.49 (above)
RALPH EUGENE MEATYARD, *Romance (N) from Ambrose Bierce, No. 3*, 1962. Gelatin silver print. George Eastman House, Rochester, New York.

6.50
BRUCE DAVIDSON, *Untitled*, from his book *East 100th Street*, New York, 1966–68.

Davidson was one of the few photographers adept at blending the dark outlook of postwar photography with the attentive humanism of the Depression era. Using a large-format view camera and a flash, he spent two years photographing life on East 100th Street in New York City, where he balanced scenes of hardship with those of hope and endurance.

City's East 100th Street (Fig. 6.50). Like many photographers of his generation, Davidson was inspired by Frank's *The Americans*: "in it I saw an America that diminished the dream and replaced it with piercing truth. It was hard for me to endure those bitter, beautiful photographs, for I had still within me the dream of hope and sympathy that I had found in the widow, the dwarf, and the gang."[77]

Davidson's resilient empathy reveals itself in his New York City photographs, which fix on the strong community and family relationships that persist in the face of deprivation. His approach stands in sharp contrast to that of other photographers who prowled American streets to expose living symbols of alienation and despair. As historian Jonathan Green observed, "the icons of the sixties have few redeeming features: the dwarf, the freak, the prostitute, the disenfranchised, the outlaw motorcyclists, the drug addict, the insane, the retarded, the prisoner, the napalmed child, the brutal cop, the assassin's assassin."[78] Danny Lyon (b. 1942), who assisted Robert Frank with filmmaking, chronicled

motorcycle gangs in his own work. He presented these young people as rebels whose choice to live outside middle-class social values paid off in strong bonds of companionship (Fig. 6.51).

Perhaps the most disturbing images of teenagers were rendered by Larry Clark (b. 1943), who gained fresh notoriety for his 1995 film *Kids*, which features explicit scenes of underage drug use and sex. His 1971 book *Tulsa* covered similar territory: it is a first-hand account of the time he spent among drug-users, some of whom were his friends (Fig. 6.52). While postwar photographers, such as Lyon, spent extensive time among their subjects, Clark personally sampled the drug culture he imaged. His candid photographs provoked negative reactions, in part, as critic Joseph Marshall observed, because "Clark implied what [Robert] Frank didn't say ... that getting high, despite its social costs and its dangers, is an appropriate response to the banal meaninglessness of American life."[79] Compared to this abrasive nihilism, Helen Levitt's (b. 1913) sometimes whimsical, always compassionate, street photographs of

6.51
DANNY LYON,
Cal, Eikhorn, Wisconsin,
1966. Gelatin silver
print.

6.52 (right)
LARRY CLARK,
Tulsa Portfolio, 1972.
Gelatin silver print.

Clark's photographs of
the deteriorating lives
lived by drug dealers
and users in Tulsa,
Oklahoma, assailed the
bright humanism of
Depression-era docu-
mentary photography.
In this image, in which
a man lies in pain from
an accidental gunshot
wound, the viewer's
sympathies are pulled
in different directions.

6.53 (below)
HELEN LEVITT,
New York, c. 1940.

In her photographs of
poor and ethnic neigh-
borhoods in New York
City, Levitt focused on
street life, and, espe-
cially, the interactions
of children. Her debt to
Henri Cartier-Bresson,
who was living in New
York when Levitt began
photographing, shows
in the contrast between
the obviously pregnant
young woman, and the
insouciant smile of the
girl carrying milk bottles
at breast height.

children (Fig. 6.53) are exceptional in
their amiable, bemused observations,
an attitude more familiar in the work of
European photographers.

Many postwar photographers worked
in extensive series based on life experiences, be they road trips or observations
gained through insight and meditation.
The scope of these series, dramatized by
the photographer's unique perspective

on how to order the images, propelled
the photographic book into prominence. The rhythm, connections, and
contradictions of form and subject
generated by sequenced images had a
lasting impact on contemporary photographic practice. In the work of Duane
Michals (b. 1932), the photographic
sequence blended with two other postwar trends, the deliberate staging of
scenes to be photographed, and the
addition of text, not as an explanatory
caption but as an integral part of the
work. A successful advertising photographer, Michals developed a signature
blend of photography and the film
frame during the late 1960s. His book
Sequences (1970) contains arrangements
of images that narrate appearances
of spirits and passages between life
and death. Like many postwar photographers, Michals favored a palette
of dense black, hazy grays, and form-
dissolving light (Fig. 6.54).

Suburbia

Postwar prosperity fueled the migration
of Americans from the cities to the
suburbs, where the prospect of green
space and domestic comforts was under-
written by the larger hope of rising to a
higher social class. As historian David
Halberstam wrote, many in the freshly
minted middle class "were children of
people who never owned a home and
who had rented cold-water flats in the
years before the war."[80] In the American
West, long a symbol-laden landscape
in art and photography, the spectacular

6.54 (opposite)
DUANE MICHALS,
The Bogeyman, 1973.

Michals staged events
to be photographed,
so as to produce a nar-
rative series of images
telling about psycho-
logical fears and obses-
sions. In this sequence,
the child reading, per-
haps about monsters,
is carried away by a
coat transformed into
a phantom.

banality of regularized suburban houses suddenly springing up in formerly open expanses caught the critical eye of photographers such as Lewis Baltz (b. 1945) (Fig. 6.55) and Robert Adams (b. 1937), who preferred the distanced view and a

seemingly neutral style, the visual analog of their prosaic subjects (Fig. 6.56).

This approach to landscape photography was reported in an influential 1975 exhibition, *New Topographics: Photographs of a Man-Altered Landscape,*

6.56
ROBERT ADAMS,
Newly Occupied Tract Houses, Colorado Springs, Colorado, 1969.

Many American suburbs were built in the decade following World War II. Their rapid appearance in isolated clumps surrounded by open landscape attracted photographers, who implicitly contrasted the open and vacant suburban terrain with the congested urban environment.

at Eastman House in Rochester. The drab, dispassionate images in this show rebutted the sometimes lush, sometimes sublime attitude toward the land expressed in a photographic tradition derived from nineteenth-century images of the American West. In addition, the neutral vision that framed *New Topographics* linked photography with the international art movement called Conceptualism (see p. 370), and helped accelerate the acceptance of camerawork in academia and the art world.

In a series of photographs published in the book *Suburbia* (1972, 1999), Bill Owens (b. 1938), a photographer for a small newspaper in Livermore, near the Bay Area of California, portrayed not only the look of the suburbs but also the dreams, longings, and discontents of the residents. Owens admired the visual sociology of the F.S.A. photographs, and his work is replete with small, telling details.[81] Ungroomed nature is threatening: one photograph shows a teenager straddling the branches of a small tree, shaking off all the leaves to be raked by a second lad below.

In another picture, a couple sits in a garage crammed with motorcycles and other vehicles. In the quotation accompanying the photograph they mellowly remark, "We enjoy having these things." When Owens moved inside suburban homes, he found the focus of the modern living-room to be the television set, mostly left on and disgorging advertisements, football, old movies, space launches, and occasional glimpses of a grimly determined President Richard Nixon (1913–1994). Owens captured not only the tackiness of furnishing and ubiquitous polyester clothing but also the dissent and dislocation of suburbanites, whom he does not patronize or stereotype. An African-American woman notes that her children are growing up without an anchor in black culture; a Chinese-American family cannot find Asian groceries nearby. Teenagers grumble that there is nothing to do in the suburbs. The impact of the national mood is caught in women's complaints about staying home and taking care of children (Fig. 6.57).

6.57
BILL OWENS, *Untitled*, from his book *Suburbia*, 1972, 1999.

Owens's suburban images balance between parody and commiseration. He was alert to the range of feelings brought forth in the new surroundings, and to the intrusion of public events into private lives. Holding a baby in the midst of a messy kitchen, this woman argues, "How can I worry about the damned dishes when there are children dying in Vietnam?"

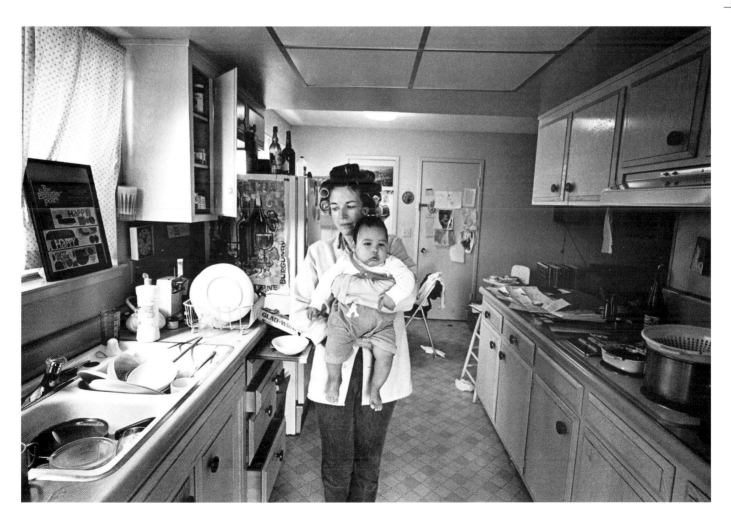

TECHNOLOGY AND MEDIA IN POSTWAR AMERICA

Color Photography and the Polaroid Process

The concluding segment of Steichen's *The Family of Man* exhibition disrupted the long chain of black-and-white photographs with a large color transparency of a hydrogen bomb explosion. Before the war, and in the decade after it, magazines such as *National Geographic* used color transparencies. Magazine advertising occasionally appeared in color, and fashion photographers leapt at the chance to use color to depict clothing and to glamorize settings. Horst P. Horst, Paul Outerbridge, Richard Avedon (1923–2004) (Fig. 6.58), and Avedon's student Japanese-born photographer Hiro (b. 1930) (Fig. 6.0) electrified the pages of large-format fashion magazines with strong color accents. Soon color slipped the bonds of description and was used by image-makers such as photographer and art

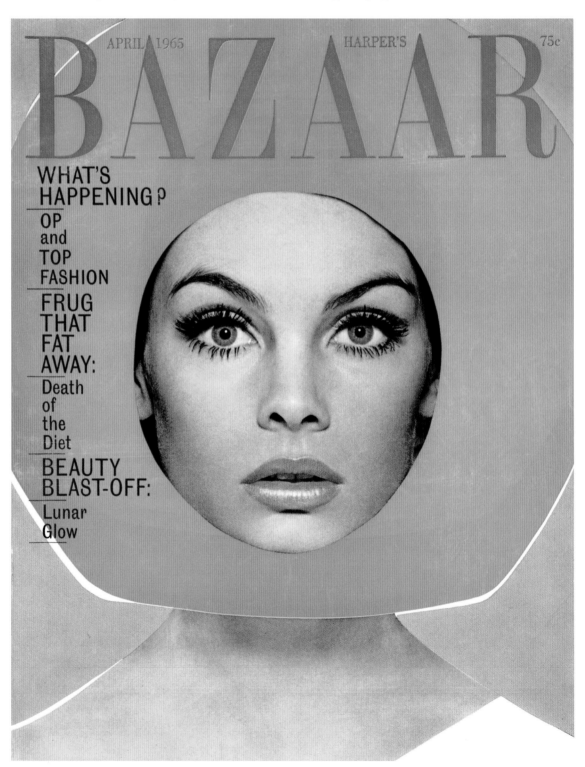

**6.58
RICHARD AVEDON,
Cover of *Harper's Bazaar*, April 1965.**

Avedon's long relationship with the fashion magazine *Harper's Bazaar* allowed him to try out color as much as—or more than—any experimental photographer of the period. His palette derived from trendy colors of the time, including hot pink, which he helped spread through the clothing and cosmetics industries.

Necessity was the mother of Stern's inventive treatment of a cocktail made with Russian vodka. During the Cold War, Russian products seemed un-American. Stern's solution was to make the vodka seem un-Russian, by photographing chic, exotic settings.

director Bert Stern (b. 1929) to contrive seductive advertisements in which bright color saturates the whole environment (Fig. 6.59). Similarly, Deborah Turbeville (b. 1937) created her own distinctive cool-toned colors and dusky atmosphere for fashion shoots, and contrived scenarios for the models to perform (Fig. 6.60).

Natural light and hues seemed particularly suited to color work. Radiant pops of chromatic light were rendered in transparencies by Minor White, who even planned programs of dual-screen projection for his work. Eliot Porter (1901–1990), who used color transparencies and the cumbersome but more permanent DYE-TRANSFER system, collected his nature views in the book *In Wildness Is the Preservation of the World* (1962) (Fig. 6.61), and in

large-sized or "exhibition format" prints, both of which were sponsored by the Sierra Club.

Despite color's intermittent successes, in the 1950s and early 1960s most magazines continued to run black-and-white images, which were less expensive and less time-consuming to produce. In 1955, the year of *The Family of Man,* color film that a photographer could process had been available for less than a decade. To promote the use of color film, the Kodak company then attempted to persuade leading photographers such as Ansel Adams, Paul Strand, Charles Sheeler, and Edward Weston to try it by commissioning images from them. When the firm wrote to photographer Weston, asking if he would make an 8 by 10 inch Kodachrome print, Weston reluctantly

**6.60 (right)
DEBORAH
TURBEVILLE,
The Bath House, 1975.**

Set in a public bath,
Turbeville's vision
of active and passive
women seen through
a haze of steam
created a sensation
when it first appeared
in American *Vogue*.

**6.61 (below)
ELIOT PORTER,
October 3, 1858, from
Henry David Thoreau's
book *In Wildness Is
the Preservation of the
World*. Sierra Club Books,
San Francisco, California,
© 1962.**

The title of Porter's book,
taken from the writing
of nineteenth-century
American essayist and
poet Henry David
Thoreau (1817–1862),
praised nature as both
a spiritual and material
resource. Throughout
his book, he juxtaposed
quotations from Thoreau
with intensely colored
images of nature.

October 3, 1858

Standing on the railroad I look across the pond to Pine Hill,
where the outside trees and the shrubs scattered generally through the
wood glow through the green, yellow, and scarlet, like fires
just kindled at the base of the trees, — a general conflagration just fairly
under way, soon to envelop every tree. The hillside forest is all aglow
along its edge and in all its cracks and fissures, and soon the
flames will leap upwards to the tops of the tallest trees.

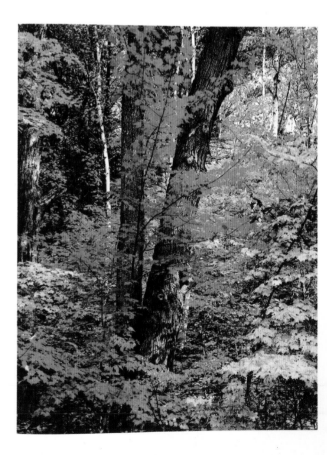

agreed, saying that he loved the landscape around Point Lobos in California so much that he would have abhorred seeing "it murdered in color by an 'outsider.'"[82] Weston accepted an offer from Kodak to revisit some of his favorite spots, where he rendered images that showed a visible tension between the descriptive powers of color and the expressive qualities of line (Fig. 6.62). Weston's anxiety about color film was grounded in what he perceived as its greater realism—that is, its more comprehensive resemblance to the world of experience.

Walker Evans remained resistant to the process throughout the 1960s. He railed against "screeching hues," and the "bebop of electric blues, furious reds, and poison greens," and asserted that "there are four simple words which must be whispered: color photography is vulgar."[83] Like other art photographers, Evans thought that color was too

embedded in commercial culture to be used by serious artists.

Despite these reservations, Evans did experiment with color. During his postwar years as a photographer with *Fortune* magazine, he issued portfolios of photographs that he hand-tinted so as to control the selection and strength of the color. In the early 1970s, Evans began to try Polaroid film and cameras. Invented in 1947 by Edwin H. Land (1909–1991), the Polaroid process originally generated monochromatic prints. By the 1970s, the method had improved to yield so-called instantaneous color prints, that is, pictures developed on the spot. Evans worked with the Polaroid SX-70 system, a fully automatic method that timed the film's development inside the camera and expelled a final print for which the photographer made no contribution to the color scheme. Using the somewhat subdued colors of Polaroid's SX-70 system, Evans returned to making

6.62
EDWARD WESTON,
Waterfront, Monterey,
1946. Silver dye bleach print (Cibachrome). Center for Creative Photography, University of Arizona, Tucson, Arizona.

The black-and-white linear elements of this image, like the masts and lines, set off the color of the boat and the water. Nevertheless, Weston was skeptical about color photography, holding that, "as a creative medium, black and white photography has, at the start, an advantage over color in that it is already a step removed from a factual rendition of the scene."[84]

6.63 (above)
WALKER EVANS,
Untitled (Crushed beer
can), 1973–74. Polaroid
print. Metropolitan
Museum of Art,
New York.

pictures of American signs and letter-
ing, themes he began in his youth and
which he carried out in his work for
the Farm Security Administration.
He praised the Polaroid quick payback
process, saying that it encouraged sudden inspiration. As he had in his earlier
work, Evans conceived Polaroid images
in series. Importantly, he challenged
the tenacious complaint that color need-
lessly prettified photographs. In such
prints as the one depicting a crushed
beer can (Fig. 6.63), Evans integrated
color and form; despite the small (3⅛ by
3⅛ inch) format of the print, the scene
has a puzzling monumentality.

In spite of the efforts of Kodak and
Polaroid to convince artists to work with
the new techniques, the biases against
color photography expressed by Weston

and Evans permeated the world of serious art photography. Notwithstanding
the occasional museum exhibition of
color work, art photography persisted
mostly as a black-and-white medium.
This attitude put it at odds with commercial photography and photojournalism,
both of which adapted more quickly
to the possibilities of color to promote
products or to interest readers. The art
photographers' preference for black-
and-white sharply contrasted with the
adoption of color film by amateurs,
who happily moved from black-and-
white snapshots to color pictures. The
proliferation of color in commercial
photography transformed the experience of the average person. The reality
effect—the sense of authenticity and
honesty—passed from black-and-white
film to color. Millions of people gazed
up at the Kodak-sponsored 18 by 60 foot
color transparencies called *Colorama*
hung on the east balcony of the Grand
Central Terminal in New York City[85]
(Fig. 6.64). Ansel Adams, who occasionally worked on the Kodak projects, nevertheless calculated that these displays
were "aesthetically inconsequential but
technically remarkable."

Curiously Adams, a consummate
technician, did not seem to realize that
technically remarkable images, such
as pictures from space, have their own
aesthetic of the marvelous. In fact, the
public came to expect that photography
would keep up with other kinds of

6.64
RALPH AMDURSKY,
Colorama (Blue
"Woody" Stationwagon
in Front of Summer
Cottage) n.d. Kodak
print. Eastman Kodak,
Rochester, New York.

Kodak designers fash-
ioned the perfect home
and ideal domestic life
for a large transparency
that hung above Grand
Central Terminal in New
York City. The house has
traditional elements,
such as columns and
shutters. The family's
leisure time activities
are indicated by garden-
ing tools and recreation
equipment. The scene
of comfortable middle-
class life was designed
by Norman Rockwell
(1894–1978), the
American designer
known for patriotic
pictures and sentimen-
tal views of life's little
incidents.

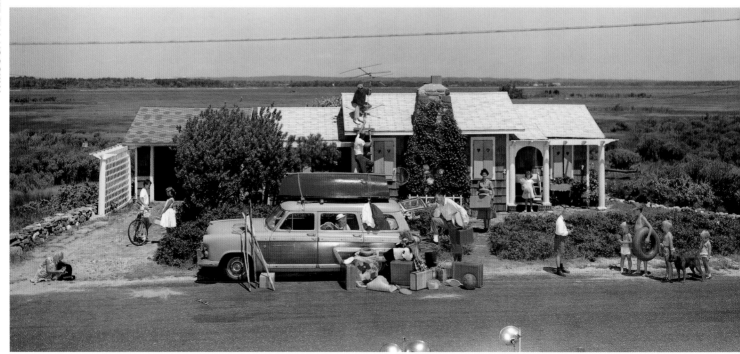

technological advances. In 1969, Apollo 11's pictures of the far side of the moon needed to be as accomplished as the mission was successful (Fig. 6.65). As space exploration continued, audiences took it for granted that the picture magazines would render views of the earth from space in color. Similarly, advances in science have been accompanied by parallel accomplishments in scientific imaging. Pictures of a human fetus's development in the womb, patterns observed by particle physicists, and the hypnotic beauty of small viruses were issued in color for audiences to enjoy as scientific and aesthetic wonders (Fig. 6.66).

Color motion pictures, costly to produce before World War II, became less expensive and more common after the 1950s period of *film noir*, with its deeply shadowed, highly stylized ambience. Television, too, began the transformation from black-and-white to color. The first all-color children's television show, *Howdy Doody*, began in 1955, following the appearance of color television sets on the market in 1953. By the mid-1960s, color television sets became more affordable and so their sales increased.

Television, Photojournalism, and National Events

Despite increased sales of television sets by the mid-1960s, national television news did not surpass newspapers and

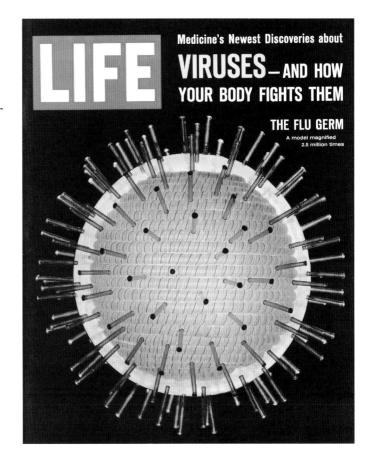

picture magazines as the public's major source of current events information until the early 1970s. By that time, television news programs progressed from fifteen-minute readings of the news, accompanied by a few still photographs, to nightly half-hour broadcasts, with reports from news bureaus around the world, supplemented by film, videotape, and occasional live coverage. In effect, television seized the market for instantaneous images, the previous domain of newspapers, and, to some extent, news magazines. The public's shift from print media to television was signaled by the demise of *Life* magazine's weekly publication in 1972, owing to declining advertising revenues, as clients switched to purchasing television commercials.

Public events, such as the assassination of President John F. Kennedy (1917–1963) and its aftermath, entered the public memory through a blend of photography, radio, film, and television broadcasts. Pictures obtained from the space exploration, which began in the late 1950s, were all photographs, until astronauts sent back a live television broadcast from the moon in 1969. Arresting in themselves, photographs of the earth from space graphically

**6.66
PHOTOGRAPHER UNKNOWN, Cover of *Life Magazine*, February 18, 1966.**

Just as the public thrilled to photographs taken in the vastness of space, images of minute entities such as viruses delighted the readership of popular magazines such as *Life* and underscored the power of science.

**6.65
APOLLO II, *Untitled* (The far side of the moon), Apollo II mission, July 1969.**

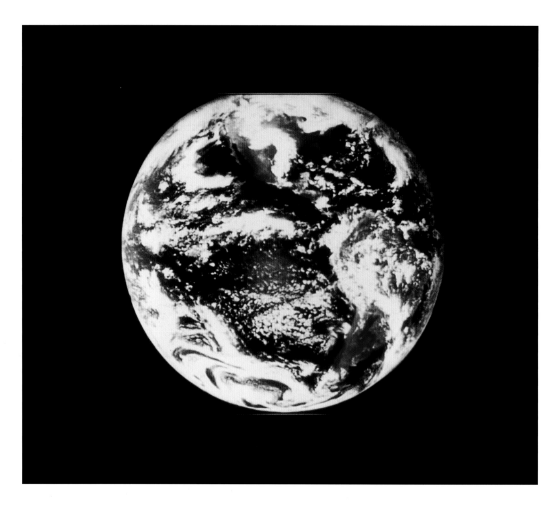

demonstrated the interdependence of earth's natural systems (Fig. 6.67).[86]

Americans also learned about the Civil Rights movement, which started in the late 1950s to protest racial segregation in the South and to secure voting rights for African-Americans, from a mix of photography and other media. Photographers such as Davidson and Lyon were on the scene, picturing events and confrontations. In fact, Lyon joined the Student Nonviolent Coordinating Committee (SNCC), where he helped to produce posters and other organizational materials. Civil Rights organizers knew how to use the media to gain publicity, and how to craft events with visual appeal for the nightly television news shots. Ernest Withers (b. 1922), the first African-American police officer hired in Memphis, Tennessee, also worked as a photographer, and expressed his support with a memorable image of the famous march on Memphis by sanitation workers (Fig. 6.68). Photographer Charles Moore (b. 1931) caught members of the Birmingham, Alabama, Fire Department as they turned high-pressure hoses on protesters (Fig. 6.69). Historian David Halberstam characterized the lynching

of Emmett Till in Mississippi during the summer of 1955 as the first powerful media event of the Civil Rights Movement. Photographs taken by David Jackson (1922–1966) were published in the African-American press, but not in mainstream media. They showed Till in an open coffin, on to which his mother had taped pictures of him as a vibrant youngster. The contrast between his youthful image and his abused corpse galvanized African-Americans across the United States and the photographs remain indelible symbols of racial strife.

From 1955 to 1975, television and photography combined to disseminate images of the Vietnam War. While *Life* magazine's photographs never approached the patriotic fervor expressed in Joe Rosenthal's images of the flag-raising on Iwo Jima during World War II (see Fig. 5.86), they did repeatedly communicate the average person's experience of the war, an approach pioneered by W. Eugene Smith. That theme was prominent in the June 27, 1969, issue of *Life*, which displayed "The Faces of the American Dead in Vietnam," in what resembled a high-school yearbook of the perished.[87] Feature stories concentrated

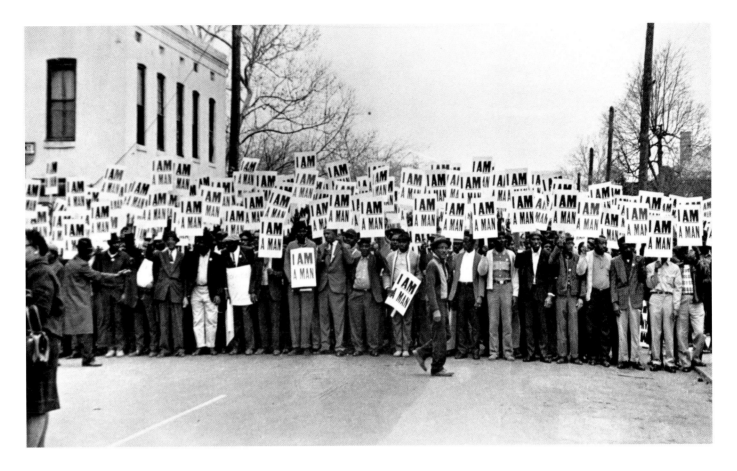

6.68 (above)
ERNEST WITHERS,
Workers Assembling
for a Solidarity March,
Memphis, Tennessee,
1968.

Withers took his picture
from a spot in which
the individual identities
of the marchers were
somewhat obscured, in
effect, replacing faces
with the repeating signs
declaring, "I *am* a man."
This strike by Memphis
sanitation workers
brought Civil Rights
leader Martin Luther
King (1929–1968) to
the city, where he was
assassinated.

on the experience of individual soldiers,
as Smith had done in World War II.

For example, the April 16, 1965,
edition of *Life* published twenty-two
black-and-white pictures by British
photographer Larry Burrows, who chronicled the war experiences of a twenty-

one-year-old soldier. Burrows, who later
died in a helicopter crash, mounted a
camera on the airborne machine gun the
soldier used during battle so as to record
the gunner's facial expressions. But it
was the pungency of his color work that
transformed the battlefield's ankle-deep

6.69
CHARLES MOORE,
Birmingham, 1963.

Moore effectively places
the viewer close to the
firefighters who are
buffeting non-violent
Civil Rights protesters
with water from high-
pressure hoses. The
eye urgently follows the
stream from left to right,
where the force of the
water explodes on the
body of a protester.

6.70
LARRY BURROWS,
At a First-Aid Center During Operation Prairie, 1966.
Dye-transfer print.
Spencer Museum of Art, University of Kansas, Missouri.

6.71 (right)
PHILIP JONES GRIFFITHS, *Napalm Victim*, Vietnam, 1967.
Gelatin silver print.

mud into an emblem for America's futile involvement in Vietnam (Fig. 6.70). David Douglas Duncan, who saw the ordinary soldier in Korea as a reluctant aggressor (see Fig. 6.33), was soured by the wanton violence of Vietnam. The pictures he shot there were gathered in his book *War without Heroes* (1970). Philip Jones Griffiths (b. 1936), who would later write and illustrate *Vietnam, Inc.*, a scalding indictment of the war as big business, photographed the conflict for three years, mostly as it was experienced by the Vietnamese peasants (Fig. 6.71). The image of a South Vietnamese general executing a handcuffed Vietcong suspect was captured by photographer Eddie Adams (1933–2004) (Fig. 6.72). During his more than twenty-five trips to Vietnam after the war, Griffiths photographed a widow holding a copy of the newspaper photograph of her husband, who was killed in Adams's famous photograph.

Some lasting images of the war experience were created only in photography. For example, when President Richard Nixon ordered the bombing of enemy camps in Cambodia, student protests arose around the country. Photography student John Paul Filo (b. 1948) caught the outcry of a young woman as she

knelt beside the body of a Kent State University student shot dead by a member of the Ohio National Guard (Fig. 6.73). Vietnamese photographer Huynh Cong ("Nick") Ut (b. 1951) provided the lasting document of terrified and injured children running from an accidental napalm attack on a building where

**6.72
EDDIE ADAMS,
*General Loan Executing
a Vietcong Suspect*,
February 1, 1968.
Gelatin silver print.**

This image, recording
the execution of a
suspected communist
sympathizer, roused
national anger in the
United States against
the summary street
justice administered by
a Vietnamese general.

**6.73
JOHN PAUL FILO,
Untitled (Kent State:
girl screaming over dead
body), May 4, 1970.**

Filo created an enduring
image of anger fused
with grief, when student
Mary Ann Vecchio
reacted after National
Guard troops killed the
first of four students
during an anti-war rally.

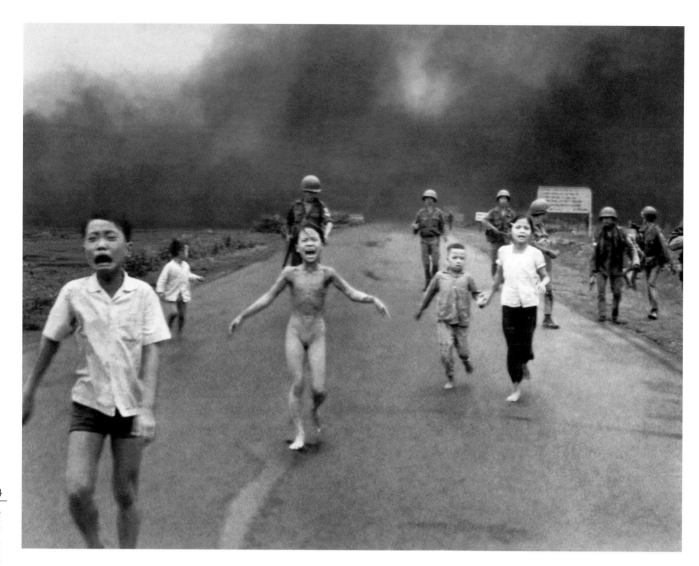

**6.74
HUYNH CONG
(NICK) UT,** *Children
Fleeing a Napalm
Strike,* June 8, 1972.

non-combatants had taken cover (Fig. 6.74). Motion-picture and video equipment were absent when Ron Haeberle (b. 1941), an army photographer, recorded the massacre of civilians in the Vietnamese village of My Lai by a United States Army company. Haeberle submitted the black-and-white pictures he took to the army, but kept the color film, which he began showing in the United States when he was demobilized. An image published in the Cleveland (Ohio) *Plain Dealer* soon traveled around the world. Working together, staff from the Museum of Modern Art, New York, and members of the Art Workers' Coalition used the image to create a gripping anti-war poster, which the museum later refused to sanction. With the question and answer, "Q: And babies? A: And babies," derived from a television interview with a soldier who had witnessed the massacre, the poster became a rallying point against the war (Fig. 6.75).

Yet it was Adams's still image (see Fig. 6.72) that became an acclaimed

symbol of the war's injustice and its cold-blooded attitude toward the loss of life. More than twenty-five years after the war ended in 1975, photographs taken by North Vietnamese civilian and military photographers were published through the efforts of British photographer Tim Page (b. 1944), who had photographed the war in the south. Page discovered that North Vietnamese photographers such as Vo Anh Khanh (b. 1939) (Fig. 6.76) used mostly inexpensive black-and-white film and relied on the jungle night to create an outdoor darkroom. They seldom photographed the dead, but set out to inspire their embattled viewers with scenes of endurance and patriotism.

PHOTOGRAPHY IN ART

During the postwar decades, while photography gained a greater presence in international art movements, photojournalism emerged as a new source for artists interested in topical issues.

6.75
**RON HAEBERLE &
PETER BRANT,**
*Q. And Babies? A. And
Babies*, 1970. Offset
lithograph, printed in
color. Museum of
Modern Art, New York.

The photograph taken
by Haeberle, then a U.S.
Army photographer,
showing the result of
deliberate killing of
civilians, became the
most famous anti-
Vietnam poster in the
United States and
around the world.

6.76
VO ANH KHANH,
U Minh Forest, Ca Mau,
September 15, 1970.

During what they called
"The American War,"
civilian and military
photographers from
North Vietnam rode
bicycles to the front to
capture scenes of suffer-
ing and courage. Vo's
image of a mosquito-
netted operating room
located in a swamp
to avoid detection is
all the more startling
because its subjects
seem so unruffled in
their improbable setting.
The victim was a
guerrilla wounded by
American bombing.

Sculptor Duane Hanson (b. 1940) modeled his *Vietnam Scene* on published war photographs, and George Segal (1924–2000) created sculptures based on Civil Rights Movement images, as well as on the shooting of students at Kent State University during the Vietnam War protests.

The wider use of photography also owed to the fact that artists in many media increasingly employed the camera to record their work. Meanwhile, the growth of mass media, especially in service of advertising, roused artists and critics to attend more closely to the effects of photography. The European avant-garde movement called the Situationist International, which emerged in the late 1950s, based its critique of consumer culture on what French critic Guy Debord (1931–1994) called in a 1967 book of the same title "the society of the spectacle." Inspired by Dadaist debunking, the Situationists attempted to subvert the profusion of mass media by appropriating its images and re-presenting them in ways that demonstrated the superficiality and hypocrisy of advertising and newspaper illustrations. At times, they freely rearranged appropriated images; in

other instances, they let captions interpret the image (Fig. 6.77). The Situationists' examination of the mass media's impact on everyday life prefigured the critiques of consumer culture and gender stereotyping in the late 1970s and 1980s (see pp. 432–35).

The Situationist movement was generally secretive, its members largely anonymous, and much of its work was intentionally ephemeral; consequently, it was not a primary influence on later movements such as Pop art. Begun in Britain during the 1950s, Pop art derived from the word "popular," as in "popular culture." The seminal Independent Group (IG) included artist Richard Hamilton (1924–2005), whose 1956 collage *Just What Is It That Makes Today's Homes So Different, So Appealing?* combined advertising images for products such as television sets and vacuum cleaners (Fig. 6.78). In the context of postwar Britain's severe economic recession, Hamilton's collage is a bittersweet parody that simultaneously critiques and celebrates the prospect of long-denied consumer items, symbolized by American products and attitudes toward conspicuous consumption.

**6.77
PHOTOGRAPHER
UNKNOWN,**
*Roles Reserved for the
Negro in the Spectacle,*
**1963, from *The World
of Which We Speak*,
1970. Situationist
International.**

Situationists took photographs intended for one purpose, changing their captions to reveal other meanings. In this case, what appears to be a newspaper or travel industry shot has been recaptioned to highlight the condition of black South Africans.

Des rôles réservés au nègre dans le spectacle. — I. Bon nègre, en République Sud-Africaine, 1963.

« Le président Johnson inaugurera mercredi la foire internationale de New-York... un spectacle de 1 milliard de dollars... D'autre part le Congrès pour l'égalité raciale... a fait part de son intention

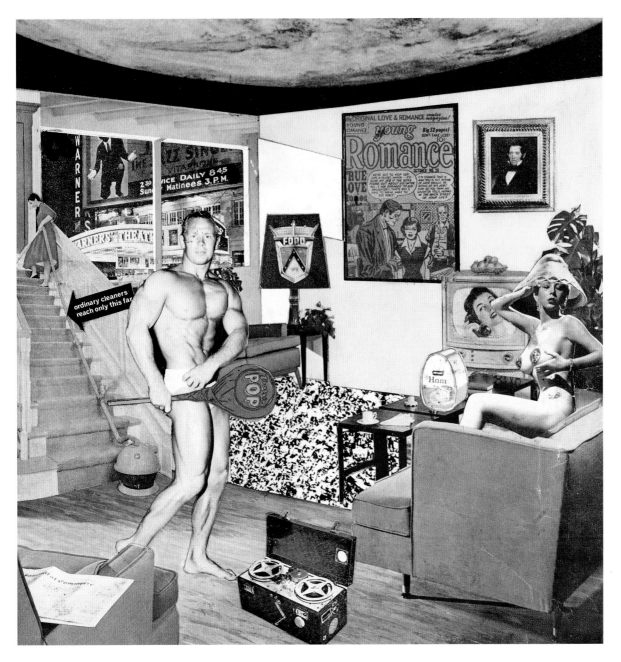

6.78
RICHARD HAMILTON,
Just what is it that
makes today's homes so
different, so appealing?,
1956. Collage on paper.
Kunsthalle, Tübingen,
Germany.

Hamilton combined
American mass-
produced consumer
images. For the ceiling
of the room, he used
an image of the earth
from space taken by a
rocket and published
in a 1956 issue of the
picture magazine *Look*.

British Pop art was anti-academic, rejecting the traditional themes and subjects taught in art school. Members of the Independent Group took inspiration from Moholy-Nagy's 1947 book *Vision in Motion*, and from his belief in the vigor of advertising, and the need to express the modern world through collage and the reuse of scientific photographs such as X-rays.[88] But they reversed Moholy-Nagy's complaints about the throwaway design of American goods, finding them entirely appropriate for an art that they insisted must be of its time. Hamilton analyzed the admirable elements of popular art as "transient, expendable, inexpensive, witty, sexy, gimmicky, glamorous, and 'big business'."[89] Hamilton's collage has been canonized in the history of art, surpassing works

by other members of the Independent Group, for whom photography played a major role, including Nigel Henderson (1917–1985) and Eduardo Paolozzi (1924–2005), who together assembled collages that incorporated mass-media images of movie stars, household products, and hot cars (Figs. 6.79, 6.80).

In the United States during the 1960s, Pop artists were nonchalant about "the society of the spectacle," accepting mass-produced commodities and images as the inescapable norm of modern life. Artists Larry Rivers (b. 1923) and Andy Warhol (1928–1987) appropriated sensational tabloid images, such as car crashes, enlarging their scale and deepening their tonality to accentuate the omnipresence of photographic reproduction. Warhol was a dedicated

6.79 (left)
NIGEL HENDERSON,
Head of a Man, 1956.
Photograph on board.
Tate, London.

6.80 (right)
EDUARDO
PAOLOZZI, *Meet the
People*, 1948. Collage
mounted on card.
Tate, London.

fan of film stars, beginning a collection of their publicity photographs when he was a child. He carried a camera with him to social events, and snapped flattering pictures of people that he felt were always on camera, always performing a public identity. He also concentrated on the paparazzi, or celebrity photographers, who stalked their prey, embodying the public's delirious curiosity about such figures, as in the character of Paparazzo in Federico Fellini's 1961 film *La Dolce Vita*. During the late 1960s, Ron Galella (b. 1931), whom Warhol called his favorite photographer, epitomized the paparazzi. He pursued celebrities such as actress Elizabeth Taylor, singer Elvis Presley, and First Lady Jacqueline Kennedy, who found

6.81
ANDY WARHOL,
Marilyn Diptych, 1962.
Acrylic on canvas.
Tate, London.

Warhol used the silk-screen technique to create repeating rows and columns of Marilyn Monroe's portrait. He altered each of the pictures, letting the colors bleed into each other, smudge, and overlap in an echo of the cheap color printing methods of celebrity magazines. The exaggerated result was a counterpart to the frantic public appetite for celebrity likenesses.

their tabloid images recycled into Warhol's art. Warhol exploited the thrill of illicit looking at the same time that he critiqued it in his repetitive images of the famous. Likewise, celebrity photographs were central to *Interview*, the tell-all magazine he founded in 1969.

Warhol urged portrait clients to visit photo booths, then called Photomats, the four-for-a-dollar automatic photograph machines common in amusement arcades and some malls. Before the lens they could self-dramatize for images that Warhol later turned mostly into SILKSCREEN prints. Some of his most famous work was based on publicity shots of such luminaries as Elvis Presley and Marilyn Monroe (Fig. 6.81). The repetition of the portrait image in such works registered the fan's longing for more glimpses of the celebrity, and anticipated the extraordinary public appetite for photographs of Diana, Princess of Wales (1961–1997), in the 1980s and 1990s.

Warhol's friend, the artist Robert Rauschenberg (b. 1925) had been creating photograms, or cameraless photographs, on blueprint paper since the 1950s. In his "combines," Rauschenberg incorporated mundane objects found along the street, such as pieces of cardboard, bits of signs, magazine photographs, and old postcards, as well as paint (Fig. 6.82). More than Warhol, Rauschenberg wanted to puncture the pretensions of "high art" in traditional media, especially the work of the Abstract Expressionists, by making art that was not conceived as a mirror of life, but contained bits of life itself. He, too, adapted the silkscreen process, blending images from newspapers and magazines.

At about the same time, some painters adopted a style known as photo-realism to respond to the look of color photographs, in particular their flatness and illusion of depth. To render these qualities, they projected photographic slides on to a canvas, then precisely copied details, using an airbrush, which sprays a thin stream of diluted paint that leaves no trace of handwork. Like street photographers, the Photo-realists chose mostly urban scenes, and concentrated on highly polished surfaces such as glass and chrome (Fig. 6.83). American Chuck Close (b. 1940)

employed the Photo-realist vocabulary in portraiture (Fig. 6.84). His eerily airless large-scale, close-up portraits anticipate the approach of late twentieth-century photographers such as Thomas Ruff (see Fig. 7.45), whose big pictures show abundant physical details of sitters, yet are silent about the subjects' personal characters. The photographic source of Photo-realism became a favorite theme in the work of Audrey Flack (b. 1931), who arranged snapshots like elements of a still life, and who

**6.82
ROBERT RAUSCHENBERG,**
Untitled Combine (Man with White Shoes), 1955. Panza Collection. Museum of Contemporary Art, Los Angeles, California.

Based on a mysterious image of a man in a white suit, Rauschenberg's combination of collaged photographs and a chicken does not so much tell a story as argue that art can be made from the detritus of life.

6.83
RICHARD ESTES,
Woolworth's, 1974.
Oil on canvas, 38 × 55 in
(96.5 × 139.7 cm). San
Antonio Museum of Art,
San Antonio, Texas.

6.84
CHUCK CLOSE,
Self-Portrait, 1968.
Acrylic on canvas,
8 ft 11½ in × 6 ft 11½ in
(2.73 × 2.12 m). Walker
Art Center Collection,
Minneapolis,
Minnesota.

mimicked the way the camera can exaggerate highlights. The garish colors of her work may also derive from photographic sources, particularly the deeply saturated shades employed in advertising (Fig. 6.85).

For Conceptual artists, active internationally in the 1960s and 1970s, photography became important because its record-keeping function favored their focus on making and communicating ideas or concepts, rather than producing material objects. In addition, photography was used by artists who found no irony in making lasting images of ephemeral projects, such as installations, performance art, and the so-called Happenings of the late 1950s and early 1960s, in which impromptu public events or situations were presented to onlookers.

Celebrated for his earthworks, such as *Spiral Jetty*, which became familiar mostly through photographic reproduction, Robert Smithson (1938–1973) was

6.85 (below)
AUDREY FLACK,
*World War II (Vanitas),
Incorporating Part of
Margaret Bourke-White's
Photograph "Buchen-
wald, April 1945,"*
1976–77. Oil over
acrylic on canvas,
8 × 8 ft (2.43 × 2.43 m).

In this work, Flack gathered such objects as a Star of David, and copied part of a photograph by Margaret Bourke-White, showing Jewish survivors of Nazi concentration camps to create a tribute to those lost during World War II.

one of the many postwar artists who may have come to photography to record their work, but who soon began to investigate the medium on its own terms. He dwelled on photography's relationship to time, through what he called "mirror displacements," produced while traveling in the Yucatán area of Mexico (Fig. 6.86). In his writings, Smithson imagined an "Infinite Camera," a voracious yet indifferent perpetual machine that would gobble up the visual stream and produce unlimited reproductions.[90] His thoughts parallel those of other artists, such as Warhol, who exalted the impersonal camera.

Similarly, the British pair of artists known as Gilbert and George (Gilbert Proesch, b. 1943; George Passmore, b. 1942) moved from performances, in which they presented themselves as living sculpture, to making "photo-pieces." Unlike Smithson, who continued to work in sculpture and earthworks, Gilbert and George turned primarily to the large photoworks. In their living sculpture art works from the late 1960s, they collapsed the distinction between art and life. In similar fashion, their personal lives and interests became the subjects of their photo-pieces.[91]

Photography's boundless potential for mimicking appearances prompted American Douglas Huebler (1924–1997) to propose his *Variable Piece # 70 (In Progress)*, in which he set out to do the impossible: photograph everyone living on the planet. Huebler was adroit at mining the vein of deadpan ridicule that ran through Conceptual art. By contrast, German photographers Bernd (b. 1931) and Hilla Becher (b. 1934) soberly began elevating the photograph's ability to archive the appearance of specifically so-called "dead-tech" objects, namely, antiquated industrial

**6.86
ROBERT SMITHSON,**
Seventh Mirror Displacement, 1969.
Guggenheim Museum, New York.

Arranging a dozen mirrors in the ordinary landscape, rather than near the often photographed monuments of ancient Mexican cultures, Smithson brought the sky down to earth. He used a small, inexpensive Instamatic camera to record his construction. After the picture was taken, he packed up the mirrors, leaving the landscape as he found it. The brief insertion of mirrors then existed only as a photographic record.

constructions such as blast furnaces and gas towers (Fig. 6.87). Because of their dispassionate style, these images were included in the 1975 show *New Topographics* (see pp. 352–53). Yet the rich gray tonalities of their work, along with the public nostalgia aroused by the disappearance of mechanical technologies, prompted audiences to respond with a sentimentality that was alien to Conceptual philosophy.

The photographic interests of Conceptual artists bypassed the fine arts tradition of Alfred Stieglitz, the spiritualism of Minor White, and even the formalism of Lee Friedlander and Garry Winogrand. Instead Conceptualists plunged into an examination of publicly accepted notions of photographic truth. American painter Mel Bochner (b. 1940) and British artist Victor Burgin (b. 1941) formulated work that probed photography's ability to create an aura of authenticity. Bochner's *Misunderstandings (A Theory of Photography)* from 1967–70 consisted of an index-card sized negative of a photograph of his arm. Because it is a direct product of the camera, the negative is putatively closer to the original scene, more truthful than the positive. In London, Burgin also alluded to photography's relationship to reality when he created what he called a *Photopath* (1967). Photographing sections of a gallery floor, Burgin then printed images the exact size and tonality of the wood

372

THROUGH THE LENS OF CULTURE (1945–1975)

6.87
BERND & HILLA BECHER, *Gas Tower (Telescoping Type), off Pulaski Bridge, Jersey City, New Jersey, U.S.A,* **1981.**

Although they focus on structures associated with outdated technology, the Bechers' images carry on the notion of neutral vision popularized by the New Objectivity artists in Germany during the 1930s.

and stapled them to the boards, creating a system in which "images are perfectly congruent with the objects."[92] One of the most famous photographs to emerge in the postwar era—an image that found its way on to public kiosks and studio walls—also toyed with the notion of photographic truth. Idiosyncratic French artist Yves Klein (1928–1962) produced a picture showing himself springing off a wall into space (Fig. 6.88).

Conceptual art's attempts to dematerialize the art object not only put an emphasis on less expensive materials, such as photographic film, but also stressed language, which was used to describe works that were conceived, but never intended to be made. Conceptualists maintained that words, like photographs, function in a web of social meanings. The interaction between image and caption, ever-present in magazines, advertising—and textbooks—had been shunned in art photography, which expected the image to carry the full burden of meaning.

But the captioned photograph became a wellspring for Conceptual artists. Bruce Nauman (b. 1941) made a photograph called *Self-Portrait as a Fountain* (1966), in which he spurted water from his mouth (Fig. 6.89). The photographic work of Belgian artist Marcel Broodthaers

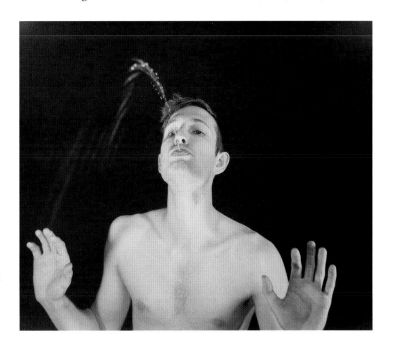

(1924–1976) often turned on the contradiction between image and words. He amusingly wrote that "the idea of inventing something insincere finally crossed my mind and I set to work straightway."[93] His *La Soupe de Daguerre* (*Daguerre's Soup*) (1976) is a collage of photographs, including photographs of other media, all referring to food (Fig. 6.90).

Not all Conceptual artists used photography to critique the medium and its myths. Dutch painter Jan Dibbets (b. 1941) turned from mono-chrome painting to abstract photo-graphy to explore time and manipulate the elements of perspective. As its title

implied, Dibbets's series of photographs *The Shortest Day of 1970 Photographed in my House Every Six Minutes* recorded the passage of daylight before the camera. Similarly, Japanese photographer Nobuo Yamanaka (1948–1982) used the camera to suggest the flow of human sight. In the early 1970s, he helped organize installations that relied on slides pro-jected on to the surface of a river or through suspended sheets of transparent material. He also constructed a large, walk-in camera obscura, not for purposes of tracing a drawing, but to experience a fugitive image hovering on a wall.[94]

Likewise, Hitoshi Nomura (b. 1945) combined an interest in human sight

6.91
HITOSHI NOMURA,
'Moon' Score, 1977–80.
National Museum of
Modern Art, Tokyo.

Nomura bluntly stated
that "My artmaking
begins precisely with a
desire not to talk about
it."[95] His work gently
parodies scientific
records. For the 'Moon'
Score series, he shot a
full roll of film (thirty-six
exposures) each night
for more than a decade.

AN ARTIST IS NOT MERELY THE SLAVISH
ANNOUNCER OF A SERIES OF FACTS.
WHICH IN THIS CASE THE CAMERA HAS
HAD TO ACCEPT AND MECHANICALLY
RECORD.

with an inquiry into what he called
"afterimages," meditations on duration
and phenomena, such as decay and
evaporation, which must be seen over
time. Reminiscent of time-lapse photography, like that of Étienne-Jules Marey,
Nomura employed the look of scientific
photography to tease out an awareness
of duration and perception (Fig. 6.91).

The biggest change in the relationship between photography and art was
the developing interest of artists in the
medium. While recording their work,
exploring the possibilities of demateral-
izing art, or critiquing mass media,
artists who had little or no training in
photography discovered fresh visual
possibilities in it. As they adopted the
camera, they did not take up the burden
of prejudices and received ideas that
weighed down photographic practice
throughout the nineteenth and early
twentieth centuries. The appeal of what
seemed to be an under-utilized, non-
traditional medium set American artist
John Baldessari (b. 1931) on a one-way
street away from painting. He burned
his easel works and turned to reproducible media, such as photography and
video (Fig. 6.92). For most artists, the

6.92
JOHN BALDESSARI,
Untitled, 1967. Acrylic
and photoemulsion
on canvas.

Baldessari, who aban-
doned painting for newer
media such as photo-
graphy, challenges the
"how-to" books that
suggest a photographer
should be careful not
to create implausible or
comic effects. Here he
contrasts a bold state-
ment about individuality
with a banal photograph
of a parking lot.

discovery of photography was not so drastic, but was quietly revolutionary. In the postwar decades, photography gradually emerged as another medium, like paint, wood, or stone, in which artists routinely worked.

PHILOSOPHY AND PRACTICE: PHOTOGRAPHY "BORN WHOLE"

Reviewing the importance of Bill Brandt's photographs, John Szarkowski (b. 1925), the influential director of the Photography Department at New York's Museum of Modern Art, wrote in 1973 that "for purposes of approximate truth, it might be said that photographic tradition in England died sometime around 1905." In the 1930s, he continued, "England had forgotten its rich photographic past, and showed no signs of seeking a photographic present."[96] These ideas offended British photographers, who quickly pointed to the work of fashion photographer David Bailey (b. 1938), whose images of such cultural celebrities as the Beatles and Andy Warhol helped shape the notion of the Swinging Sixties (Fig. 6.93). A star in his own right, Bailey's carefree lifestyle became the basis for the internationally popular movie *Blow-Up* (1966), which scrutinized the limits of a photo-grapher's societal observations. Bailey's meteoric rise at *Vogue* magazine owed to his insistence on bringing fresh faces, such as models Jean Shrimpton and Penelope Tree, to fashion shoots. His emerging fame also owed to his large black-and-white portraits of hip celebrities such as Andy Warhol, or those whose humble class background matched his own, such as the actor Michael Caine. Szarkowski also completely overlooked British Worker Photography (see pp. 290–94), perhaps because of its ties with socialism.

Szarkowksi's central theme, particularly as expressed in the influential *The Photographer's Eye* (1966), was exactly the reverse of the nineteenth-century notion that photography should emulate the other arts, especially painting. Szarkowski insisted that photography needed to abandon its "allegiance to traditional pictorial standards" and be inventive in terms of inherent qualities

with which "photography was born whole."[97] In other words, he articulated the excitement about the medium that postwar artists such as John Baldessari had discovered.

Szarkowski repeatedly asserted that the images by little-known photographers, or commercial photographers operating in areas such as photojournalism, could as successfully explore the medium's potential as the work of art photographers.[98] To prove his point, he built a 1973 exhibition called *From the Picture Press* from the archives of the tabloid newspaper, the New York *Daily News*. In the show's catalog he wrote that "as images, the photographs are shockingly direct, and at the same time mysterious, elliptical, and fragmentary, reproducing the texture and flavor of experience without its meaning."[99]

Improvising on a seasoned theme in art history, expressed specifically in the work of architectural historian George Kubler, Szarkowski proposed that the history of an art form should be traced through apparent changes in its formal characteristics such as line, not through changes in its subject matter.[100] Simply put, as media evolve, they elaborate and explore their formal potential. In his popular book *Looking at Photographs* (1973), Szarkowski envisioned a kind of historical check-value in which formal innovations could only go forward. "The chief arbiter of the game is Tradition," he wrote, "which records in a haphazard fashion the results of all previous games, in order to make sure that no play that won before will be allowed to win again."[101] In other words, progress in photography centered on novelty—not new subjects, but fresh formal approaches.

Szarkowski listed five interdependent characteristics unique to photography. The first, "the thing itself," declared that the photograph was a picture, not the equivalent of reality. The second feature, "the detail," referred to photography's "compelling clarity," and also to the fact that photography can only "isolate a fragment" of reality. He emphasized the importance of "the frame," or the "central act of choosing and eliminating," and he noted the "vantage point," which allows photographers to present the subject from unexpected points of view. On a more philosophical note,

6.93 (opposite)
DAVID BAILEY, *Mick Jagger,* **1964.**

David Bailey emerged as the photographer of "cool" in the London of the Swinging Sixties. Although there were three inspirational models for Michelangelo Antonioni's 1966 film *Blow-Up*, it is David Bailey whom the public identified with the raffish, whippet-thin, womanizing fashion photographer in the film. A poorly educated lad from London's East End, Bailey absorbed the rudiments of picture making from the movies, and taught himself photography; he counts Cartier-Bresson and Bill Brandt among his influences.

Szarkowski insisted that "all photographs are time exposures, of shorter or longer duration."[102] Each of the five characteristics of photography was illustrated by the work of historic and contemporary photographers. Whether distance shots or close-ups, virtually all the images in *The Photographer's Eye* are sharply focused and readily accessible.

Among the trends Szarkowski held up as definitive examples of photography's progressive investigation of its inherent characteristics were "the decisive moment" developed by Henri Cartier-Bresson, the "straight photograph" exemplified by Paul Strand and Walker Evans, and the humanistic Depression-era documentary, as embodied in the work of Dorothea Lange and Authur Rothstein. The next in line in the chronological discovery of formal properties were the efforts of contemporary American photographers such as Robert Frank, Lee Friedlander, Garry Winogrand, Harry Callahan, and Danny Lyon.

Szarkowski also extended his standards to color photography, praising the work of William Eggleston (b. 1939) as no less than the "discovery of color photography."[103] Beginning in 1965, Eggleston began to experiment with color film, and centered on vernacular color found on a tricycle, a backyard barbeque, or a cracked ceiling (Fig. 6.94). In the 1976 catalog of Eggleston's work, Szarkowski noted that the photographer was true to the landscape of the Memphis, Tennessee, area where he worked, and also faithful to "photography as a system of visual editing." The goal of photography, Szarkowski continued, "is not to make something factually impeccable, but seamlessly persuasive." The photographer's work is to discover "new patterns of facts that will serve as metaphors for their intentions." Color, in Szarkowski's view, challenged the photographer's ability to resist its simple prettiness and devious nullification of form.[104] He argued that in Eggleston's photographs color and subject matter were faultlessly blended into a formally exciting private view of the world.

By 1978, when Szarkowski mounted the extensive exhibition *Mirrors and Windows: American Photography since 1960*, it was evident to him that a lot more had been taking place in photographic practice than he had envisioned twelve years earlier in *The Photographer's Eye*. He tried to organize the *Mirrors and Windows* exhibition along a continuum ranging from the idea of the mirror, or artist's concern with self, typified by the introspective photography and writing of Minor White, and the notion of window, typified by Robert Frank's book *The Americans*, with its emphasis on the appearance of the world. But the variety of photographs he selected quickly eluded that terminology and became more of a postwar survey. He included work done mostly in the 1960s through the mid-1970s, including images by Eggleston and Eliot Porter, as well as such artists as Sol LeWitt (b. 1938) and Robert Smithson. Along with the photographers such as Friedlander and Winogrand, who exemplified the quest for what Szarkowski called photography's inherent characteristics, there were new imaging technologies, including John Mott-Smith's (b. 1930) 1966 series of pictures arising from computer analysis, and the Polaroid pictures of Lucas Samaras (b. 1936), in which the photographer manipulated the soft,

6.94
WILLIAM EGGLESTON, *Greenwood, Mississippi*, 1970. The J. Paul Getty Museum, Los Angeles, California.

William Eggleston's photographs resemble Photo-realist paintings, in that they often dwell on qualities of light, and reflections on different surface textures, such as metal and concrete.

While experimenting
with the Polaroid
process, Samaras
discovered that he
could move the gooey
chemicals around while
the picture was being
developed between
two pieces of paper.
The result is often a
frightening distortion
of the human figure.

freshly exposed chemical emulsion with his fingers or other mechanical aids (Fig. 6.95).

Mirrors and Windows recognized the growing significance of appropriated mass-media images in the work of such artists as Rauschenberg and Warhol. Also included was work by West Coast artist Ed Ruscha (b. 1937), who saw the camera as essentially a bland, inexpressive device with which to record dispassionately a banal human environment (Fig. 6.96). Similarly, the scoffing humor of Conceptual artist Robert Cumming (b. 1943) was evident in two prints, one a positive and the other a negative, showing blackboard exercises for students learning how to shade shapes such as rectangles and cones to create the illusion of depth. Of course, the negative print reversed the black and white values, turning the lesson inside out (Figs. 6.97, 6.98). Cumming was one of the earliest American photographers to construct scenes of this

kind solely to be photographed. His work also anticipated the fabricated-to-be-photographed style of the 1980s. *Mirrors and Windows* also contained the work of Robert Heinecken (b. 1931), who transformed advertising and pornographic images, and experimented with collage, printing processes, and even the shape of the work (Fig. 6.99).

Szarkowski also chose images by Ray K. Metzker (b. 1931), and praised his "photomosaic," in which a dimly perceptible human figure appears in forty-nine different poses within a large grid, a successful attempt to find beauty in scientifically-derived systems. Metzker's figure is reduced to the significance of a slim squiggle of paint (Fig. 6.100). Likewise, body parts in the Heinecken photomosaic have all but lost their identity. From a standard viewing distance on the gallery wall, both the Heinecken work and the Metzker image rely on the visual rhythm of overall abstract patterns rather than subject matter.

6.96
ED RUSCHA, From
Nine Swimming Pools
and a Broken Glass,
1968.

Ruscha not only made
neutral photographs of
ordinary subjects such
as gas stations, parking
lots, and swimming
pools, he also gathered
them in books without
any explanatory text.
Nine Swimming Pools
is just that—nine
photographs of
swimming pools.

Missing from the *Mirrors and
Windows* catalog and show was work
by video-maker and photographer
William Wegman (b. 1943), whom the
general public was coming to appreciate
for humorous portraits of his dog Man
Ray, named for the Surrealist artist.
Costumed and posed for black-and-
white, as well as color Polaroid photographs and videotape, the dog patiently
modeled for Wegman, whose pictures
were meant to underscore the theoretical point that representation is the product of a photographer's interpretation
and creation, not an objective view
of the world. Moderately successful in
the art world, the images were a hit
on calendars sold around the world to
people with little or no knowledge of
Conceptual art (Fig. 6.101).

Increasingly in the 1960s and 1970s,
artists working in other media, as well
as photographers not committed to
notions of the medium's uniqueness
and purity, began to exploit mass-media
images. Szarkowski included an array
of these kinds of pictures in *Mirrors
and Windows*, but he does not seem to
have understood the extent or direction
of this change in American art. He

mainly argued that in the quarter
century before *Mirrors and Windows*,
photography had moved from "public
to private concerns."[105] Recalling the
serious, broadly based social concern
of Farm Security Administration and
Depression-era American photography,
Szarkowski stated that *The Family of
Man* exhibition marked the end of the
period in which photographers willingly
submerged their personal interests to
a larger goal. For him, the two major
tendencies of new photography could
be found in the realistic yet personal
pictures of such photographers as
Robert Frank and the romantic and spiritual approach typified by Minor White.
As he wrote, "neither pretended to offer
a comprehensive or authoritative view
of the world, or a program for its
improvement."[106]

For Szarkowski, the shift away from
the public realm reflected larger social
conditions. The picture magazines
were failing in the 1960s—even before
Life magazine suspended publication
in 1972. Their grand ambitions, seen in
photo-essays such as Margaret Bourke-
White's attempt to explain the effects
of World War II in the Soviet Union,

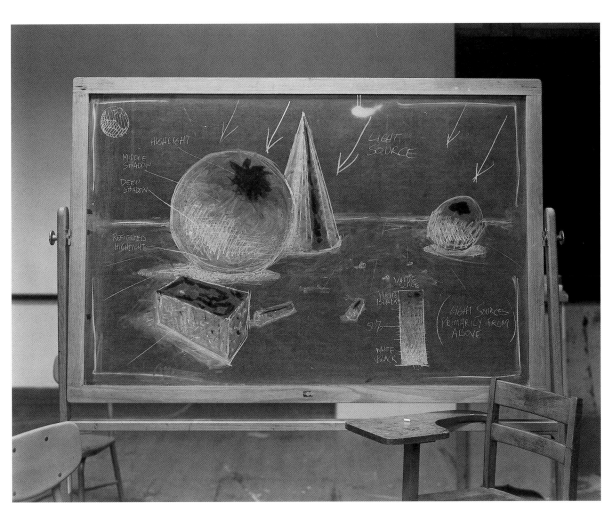

6.97
ROBERT CUMMING,
*Academic Shading
Exercise*, 1974.
Positive contact print.

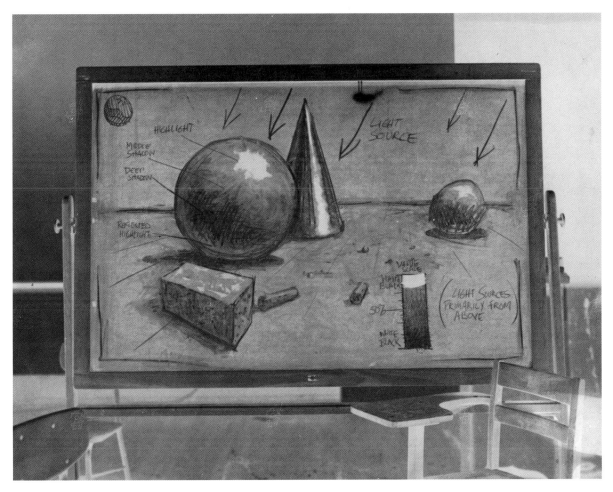

6.98
ROBERT CUMMING,
*Academic Shading
Exercise*, 1974. Paper
negative print.

**6.99
ROBERT HEINECKEN,**
Refractive Hexagon,
**1965. Twenty-four
moveable photographic
pieces on wood. Gelatin
silver prints. Center for
Creative Photography,
University of Arizona,
Tucson.**

The abstract shapes
suggestive of the
human body may be
rearranged to form
other shapes or series
than the six-sided object
into which the twenty-
four pieces have been
shaped. Acknowledging
Heinecken's efforts to
dissolve the residue of
fact in his work, John
Szarkowski recognized
that a joyless sexuality
managed to seep
through the abstraction.

or Eugene Smith's efforts to define the ancient culture of a Spanish village in a mere seventeen images, were strained beyond the capacity of the medium. In particular, Szarkowski pointed to "photography's failure to explain large public issues" such as the Vietnam War. He claimed that neither the images of British war photographer Don McCullin (b. 1936) (Fig. 6.102) nor those of Larry Burrows (see Fig. 6.70) could even "begin to serve either as explication or symbol for that enormity." Instead, he proposed that the shock of the war was best communicated by the psycho-logically expressive photographs of Diane Arbus.[107]

For Szarkowski, photography's shrinking authority was due in part to the success of television and to air travel, which made the world seem less exotic. But the basic conundrum was what he perceived to be the limitations of

photography. "Most issues of impor-tance," Szarkowski concluded, "cannot be photographed." The world-renowned photograph showing the moment when Jack Ruby shot President John F. Kennedy's alleged assassin, Lee Harvey Oswald, showed a man in pain, but did not—and could not—explain the political and emotional significance of the event[108] (Fig. 6.103).

Szarkowski did not fathom that photographers, artists, and viewers tended to experience the mass media as one medium—a blend of pictures originating in advertising, television, radio, film, and magazine journalism. The era's media guru, Marshall McLuhan (1911–1980), understood the media melange, which prompted him to revive a confident faith in the direct educational powers of media not seen since the 1858 issue of *The Athenaeum* envisioned young lower-class British

6.100
RAY K. METZKER,
Composites:
Philadelphia, 1964.
Gelatin silver print.
Purchase. Contemporary
Exhibition Fund, Alfred
Stieglitz Restricted
Fund, Alice Newton
Osborn Fund.
Philadelphia Museum
of Art, Philadelphia,
Pennsylvania.

At first, Metzker's
sequences of images
resemble the motion
studies done by
Étienne-Jules Marey and
Eadweard Muybridge.
But a close look reveals
that many of the figures
repeat, with different
shadings, and that no
progressive flow of
motion is achieved in
any direction.

6.101
WILLIAM WEGMAN,
Man Ray Portfolio—
Man Ray Contemplating
the Bust of Man Ray,
1978. Silver gelatin print.
Collection of the artist.

**6.102 (opposite)
DON MCCULLIN,
*Corpse of North
Vietnamese Soldier*,
1968. Copy-negative
print.**

McCullin juxtaposed
the grisly corpse of a
fallen North Vietnamese
soldier with his personal
effects, including photo-
graphs and letters,
scattered on the ground
by plundering American
soldiers who did not
find them valuable.
McCullin admitted this
was the only time in
his career that he
composed a picture,
by gathering the objects
strewn about and
moving them close to
the corpse.

lads imaginatively rambling around Egypt
by way of the stereograph (see p. 83).
McLuhan got it wrong when he argued
that the medium was the message,
meaning that the subject of a work was
inextricably linked to its means of broadcast, and that the means was more
important than the subject. The so-called
"cool," disjointed style of television was
easily adapted into what McLuhan had
thought to be the "hot," or linear character of photography. Indeed, Frank's *The
Americans* had the loose, jumpy quality
McLuhan felt typified television.

On the other hand, McLuhan's
enthusiasm for a coming-together of
societies around the world, and a fusion
of the arts, brought about through the
widespread use of electronic media,
was far more attuned to the heightened
attractiveness of pluralist approaches
and multimedia techniques in the arts,
especially those that emerged in the
late 1960s and early 1970s. While the
arts were actively looking into what was
then called intermedia, combinations
of older media such as photography
and paint with sound, theater, dance,
and newer media such as film and video,
Szarkowski promoted photography as
a unique and pure picture-making
process.

Szarkowski's emphasis on the unique
formal properties of photography helped

to promote the institutional life of
photography in museums and universities. Founded in 1937, the Department
of Photography at the Museum of
Modern Art, New York, became the
major arbiter of trends in the United
States during the postwar period.

In 1947, George Eastman House
in Rochester, New York (now the International Museum of Photography at
George Eastman House, IMP/GEH),
named for the Kodak Corporation's
founder, began collecting and archiving
historic film and photography under
the guiding hand of historian Beaumont
Newhall. Especially in the 1960s, departments of photography were established
at numerous American colleges and
universities to teach what was regarded
then as an independent medium with
its distinctive history and methods.

The Society for Photographic
Education, an organization of photographers, writers, historians, and curators
that came together in 1963, was originally formed on similar assumptions. In
other words, just as many image-makers
were starting to explore the persuasive-
ness of mass-media photography, which
made the world seem "already seen,"
the leading photographic institutions
were grounding the medium's existence
as an academic and museum subject in
the notion of its uniqueness.

**6.103
BOB JACKSON,
*Lee Harvey Oswald
Shot*, 1963. Gelatin
silver print.**

On live television,
on film, and in photo-
graphs, Americans saw
the accused assassin
of President John F.
Kennedy shot in a
Dallas, Texas police
station. By the mid-
1970s, critics such as
John Szarkowski would
ask just what photo-
graphy could reveal
about this or any
other event.

CHAPTER SEVEN

Convergences (1975–2000)

7.0
THOMAS STRUTH,
Musée d'Orsay, Paris,
1989.

A student of Bernd
and Hilla Becher, as
well as of Gerhard
Richter, Struth adapted
their cool, objective
style to conveying the
air-conditioned atmos-
phere of art museums,
in which spectators
often seem small in
relation to the works.

The worldwide convergence of political systems, economic networks, and cultural creations has been escalating for about 500 years. In the mid-nineteenth century, when Félice Beato photographed in the Middle East, and then moved on to India, China, and Japan, he recognized the growth of new markets among Europeans anxious for views of the countries in which their nations had political, military, and commercial involvements. In contemporary terms, Beato was reacting to globalization, the dynamic outreach of the developed nations, which wove together worldwide trade and political coalitions, assisted by far-reaching communications and transportation networks, as well as military strength.

People living in the last decades of the twentieth century experienced a globalization so rapid that Beato would barely have recognized the phenomenon. Advances in communications expedited commercial and cultural exchanges to the speed of computers. The integration of world financial markets and trade agreements, such as the European Union, stimulated the production and sale of consumer goods, and made globalization a key marketing

term. Record numbers of skilled workers and manual laborers migrated around the world in search of employment. This unprecedented international mobility of people, money, and materials was a key function of globalization, which also encouraged a transnational perspective on such issues as the phenomenon of global warming, the potentially disastrous shift in climate that is seen by many scientists to be the result of human activity in the form of industrial pollution and vehicle emissions.

Culturally, globalization saw some national and ethnic cultural practices being amalgamated into internationally appreciated forms. World music, a blending of Caribbean, African, and other local musical styles with rock and roll, was heard all over the planet. Conceptual art, a movement that originated in North America and Europe during the 1960s (see p. 371), had been disseminated around the world by the 1980s. Conceptualism's emphasis on art as idea continued to be expressed in photography, film, and video, and was adapted to specific political circumstances. As Cuban photography curator Cristina Vives Gutiérrez observed,

Conceptualism is an attitude about the function of art, not a clearly identifiable visual style. Its manifestations can be remarkably diverse.[1]

The promises and threats held out by globalization were frequently voiced together in the late twentieth century. Vast global systems seemed to endanger the significance of individual human lives. The architectural manifestations of globalization and their impact on people were rendered by German photographer Andreas Gursky (b. 1955) in huge photographs of large, contemporary public buildings, such as the Hong Kong Stock Exchange and the German Bundestag, or parliament building (Fig. 7.1). Gursky, who studied with Bernd and Hilla Becher, makes images that are simultaneously glamorous and ominous. He favors architectural subjects such as big hotels, office buildings, and stock exchanges that cater to global capitalism. His large photographs, sometimes 10 feet wide, approach the size of historical paintings, and shine with intense color, like that used in William Eggleston's work, which influenced Gursky. Despite their loud colors, these large prints have a neutral quality, owing to the physical distance of the camera from the subject, and to their high finish, like commercial work, which sometimes makes them look like large pieces of colored plastic. Gursky's images are frequently computer-modified and printed with the aid of a computer, making use of the vast array of new tools for picture-making available to photographers in the digital age. During the last years of the twentieth century, it was often remarked that large photographs like Gursky's put color photography on the physical scale of nineteenth-century history paintings. In that sense, Gursky may be seen to be a painter of pixels.

To date, globalization has not meant the total homogenization of cultural values and expression. Despite the proliferation of American popular culture, economic globalization is not yet synonymous with cultural identity. Corporate logos and consumer goods reach into every corner of the world, yet some aspects of cultural experience remain local, regional, and national. Indigenous ways of life have been cruelly disrupted, even destroyed, by the invasion of Western media, yet others have found satellite broadcasts and the Internet to be potent countervailing forces. Globalization has been accompanied by an ongoing negotiation of cultural difference, and in that sense cultural globalism is different from economic domination. The extinction of many of the world's languages through the historical process of colonization, and the rise of global media outlets that promote English, now either the first or second language of much of the commercial and scientific worlds, have been met with resistance in areas where language signifies cultural attainment to its speakers. Thus Catalans in Spain use television to maintain the vigor of their language, and Inuits in northern Canada keep the Inuktituk language alive through satellite broadcasts to far-flung settlements. The notion that global capitalism can be tailored to specific cultural settings is clearly problematic—but it has remained popular nonetheless. Russians repeatedly voiced a desire for global ties shaped by a distinctly Russian capitalism that would protect the singularity of the indigenous culture. Similarly, social thinkers in India called for a uniquely Indian modernization that would reject certain industrial and technological pathways as inappropriately Western.[2]

Ironically, the compression of time and space made possible by jet travel and instant electronic communication has enabled transient workers to maintain active ties with political, cultural, and religious practices in their home countries or ethnic groups. By contrast, the European immigrants photographed by Lewis Hine (see Fig. 4.48) shortly after their passage through New York's customs station on Ellis Island might have to wait months for a letter from family and friends back home. Whereas, in the past, moving to a new country often meant severing ties, an immigrant traveling to the United States today can (money permitting) phone home from the plane, or send photographs by e-mail from a laptop computer. Free e-mail accounts and access to the Internet through public libraries and other agencies let immigrants stay in touch with their homelands, and read electronic newspapers in their native languages.

7.1 (opposite)
ANDREAS GURSKY,
Bundestag, Bonn, 1998.
Mixed media.

In his rendition of the Bundestag, built in Berlin after the reunification of Germany in 1990, Gursky shows individuals stunted by the huge gleaming structure, and, symbolically, by the mega-systems that they have built.

As never before, hybrid cultural identities can be maintained through generations. An Italian-American immigrant during Hine's time probably did not become fully assimilated into American culture, but the children and grand-children of immigrants did.

In the late twentieth century, however, immigrants and their descendants could choose to hover between the cultural and ethnic identity of their families, and the culture of their new country.

Migrations of people from place to place, whether to seek work, escape famine, or to flee political tumult and repression, became frequent photographic subjects, both for photojournalists and for those photographers who experienced cultural dislocation firsthand. Writing about her sense of displacement, Korean-born image-maker Young Kim (b. 1955) noted, "My work reflects the continuous process of negotiating between two cultures. It is based on my experience of immigration and of locating myself in relation to ever-changing definitions of home in personal, social, and cultural contexts."[3] Kim depicts psychological distance

through physical distance, placing small family pictures in large frames (Fig. 7.2).

Crossing borders was a characteristic of photographic practice itself in the late twentieth century. By the mid-1970s, photography had moved squarely into the art world, and artists active in other media integrated photography into their work, either through the direct use of the medium or by making reference to the ubiquitous presence of camera-generated pictures in the contemporary world. As it had been for sculptor Robert Smithson,

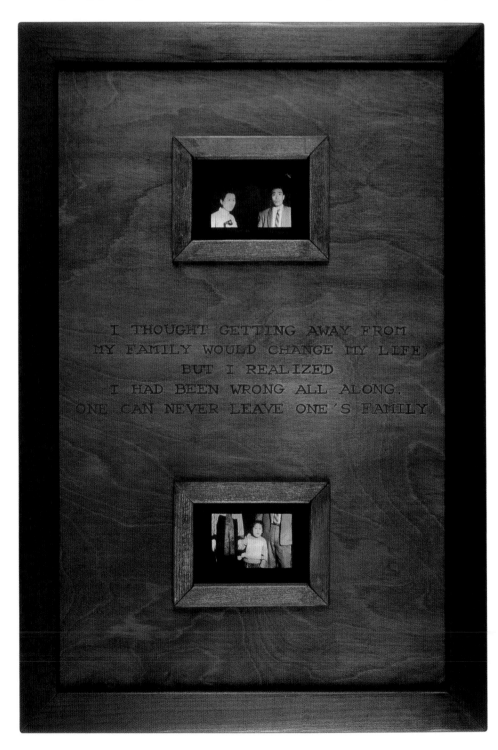

7.2
YOUNG KIM,
Distances, no. 3, 1992.
Gelatin silver prints,
plywood, ink, acrylic.

To express growing psychological remove from her Korean heritage, Young Kim framed small family photographs on larger panels, with inscriptions. The difficulty in making out the images suggests the struggle to stay connected and the sense of absence.

7.3
ADRIAN PIPER,
Pretend no. 3, 1990.
Four black-and-white
photographs, one pencil
drawing on graph paper,
silkscreened texts.

To suggest that the
public regularly denied
the violence against
protesters during the
American Civil Rights
movement, Piper super-
imposed red-lettered
captions on news
photographs, and
included a line drawing
of the monkeys who,
in the popular saying,
"see no evil, hear no
evil, and speak no evil."

photography continued to be an
adjunct to late twentieth-century artists
working primarily in other media, such
as sculptors Kiki Smith (b. 1954) and
Damien Hirst (b. 1964). Similarly
multimedia artists such as Sophie Calle
(b. 1953) regularly depended on the camera to record her performance pieces
and installations. Video-maker Matthew
Barney (b. 1964) recorded ephemeral
work and printed stills from his videos,
while Adrian Piper (b. 1948), easily
moves among performance, installation,
video, and photography (Fig. 7.3).
Sigmar Polke (b. 1941) made reference
to the ominous overhead lights and the
barbed-wire enclosure of concentration
camps as shown in postwar news
photographs (Fig. 7.4). Likely enough,
photographers sensed this openness,
and some, such as Yinka Shonibare
(see p. 454) moved into sculpture and
installation work.

Throughout the Western world,
artists who came of age after the skirmishes to confirm photography as an
art medium found the camera to be an
exciting picture-making process, whose
full potential had not been explored.
German artists Anselm Kiefer (b. 1945)
(Fig. 7.6) and Gerhard Richter (b. 1932)

(see p. 438) employed photography
in their image-making, largely without
reference to the celebrated masterworks of photographic history, or the
reigning technical standards of photographic image production. British
artist David Hockney (b. 1937) collaged
sequences of snapshots or Polaroid
prints, creating a total picture that contains myriad alterations of the angle of
view and distance from the subject, in
conscious reference to early twentieth-
century Cubist painting and collage
(Fig. 7.6). Sliced, crumbled, over-
printed, underexposed, blurred, and
even cameraless photography was
welcome in the art world.

Once a simple means to record
performance art, photography gradually
became integral to the initial conception of performance pieces. For French
performance artist Orlan (b. 1947),
photographs are indispensable traces
of the repeated surgical remodeling
done on her face to make it resemble
famous art-historical versions of
feminine beauty. Submitting to the
surgeon's knife in cumulative stages,
rather than in a single operation, Orlan
targets the incessant, intense longing
for perfection some feel about their

7.4
SIGMAR POLKE,
Lager, 1982. Acrylic
and various pigments
on fabric, 158 × 98 in
(401.4 × 250 cm).

Polke worked on
unprimed canvas
so that his pigments
would seep through
the fibers like a stain.
In this image, the
stain courses through
an image of a German
concentration camp.

7.5 (opposite)
ANSELM KIEFER,
*Siegfried's Difficult Way
to Brünhilde,* 1988.
Lead and photo in a
glazed steel frame.

Photography allows
Kiefer to relate
Germany's modern
history to familiar
elements of mythology.
Siegfried, the hero of a
medieval German saga,
rode through flames
to rescue Brünhilde.
In this image, the path
seems to be a rotting
railway, recalling the
trains that took Jews to
the death camps.

physical appearance. She has used
video, photography, and most recently
digital imaging to record and investigate
the surgical transformation of her face
(Fig. 7.7).

    The continuing assimilation of photo-
graphy into the art world was only one
of the many camerawork convergences
during the period. Photojournalism
and documentary work blended with
each other, and with art photography.

Fashion and celebrity photography
adopted techniques from art photography, and art photographers mined
the methods of fashion and celebrity
images for the sake of social commentary. In addition, advertising photography sometimes took up social issues
and the visual language of documentary
photography. The effects of these new
hybrids are still unfolding, but the
preliminary outlines of the changes

7.6 (opposite)
DAVID HOCKNEY,
*Christopher Isherwood
Talking to Bob Holman,
Santa Monica,
California, 14 March
1983,* 1983.
Photographic collage.

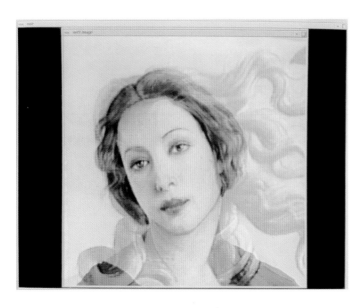

wrought by these convergences are apparent in a number of new configurations, including the new alignment of photography and science, and, of course, the digital revolution.

7.7 (left)
ORLAN, *Omniprésence Vénus,* **2001. Composite photograph.**

Orlan melded her features with those of Venus in Renaissance artist Sandro Botticelli's *Birth of Venus* (c. 1480). Wavering between the real and the ideal, the photograph grotesquely epitomizes ceaseless desire.

PHOTOGRAPHY, NATURE, AND SCIENCE

The relationship between photography, a technologically based medium, and advancements in science has long been a matter of concern. More than a century ago, Peter Henry Emerson asserted that photography had to reject the canons of established art and follow the cutting edge of science for up-to-the-minute instructions on how a photograph should look. Today, the human relationship to nature and to science is examined from a point of view far from Emerson's understanding. Some contemporary observers, such as Jungian psychologist James Hillman, see science not as an ever-unfolding source of aesthetic options, but as an immense force that demystifies nature and thereby stifles human perception of beauty in nature.[4]

As we learn more about the depletion of the rain forests, global warming, and the extinction of species, and take an expanded custodial attitude toward the planet, the wonder born of innocence and detachment from nature is likely to change (Fig. 7.8). Where people are unable to experience feelings of a we in their regular surroundings, they tend to seek amplified experiences. In the United States, national parks such as Yosemite that offer extremes of natural magnitude in sheer cliff walls and waterfalls have become overcrowded. Another response is conveyed in Derek Johnston's image of Havisu Falls, near the Grand Canyon in Arizona. In the image, wild nature is bottled and displayed as a specimen contained in a plain gallon jug (Fig. 7.9).

Where nineteenth-century scientific inquiry focused on the visible manifestations of nature, such as geological transformation and biological evolution, in the twentieth and twenty-first

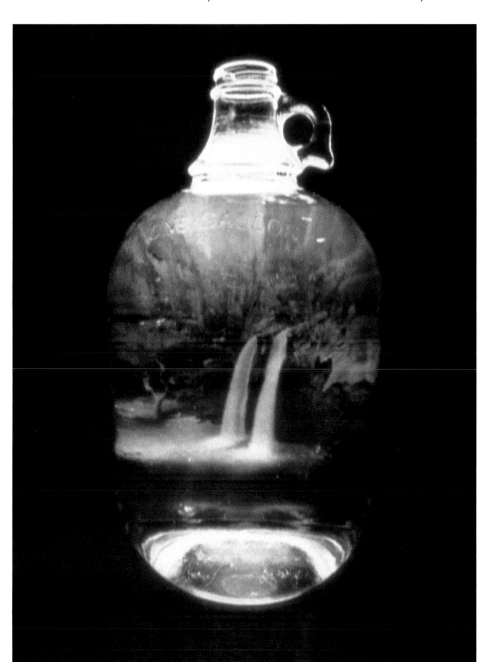

7.8 (opposite)
NASA, *View of Venus*,
May 26, 1993.

This image was produced by the Magellan science team at the Jet Propulsion Laboratory in Pasadena. Simulated color was used to enhance small-scale details. The bright area near the center is Ovda Regio, a mountainous area of Venus. The dark areas reveal the results of meteorite collisions.

7.9
DEREK JOHNSTON,
Landscape Specimen
004 (Havisu Falls),
1996. Hand-coated
platinum/palladium
print. Museum
of Contemporary
Photography, Chicago,
Illinois.

Johnston pictures Havisu Falls, on the sacred land of the Havisu (Native American people living in Arizona), confined within a manufactured container. The image alludes both to the late twentieth century's notion of nature as an invalid in need of human care, and to the artificial boundaries of the Indian reservation where the waterfall is located.

centuries attention turned to the invisible yet crucial building-blocks of nature, from sub-atomic particles to the human genome. For South-African-born New York City resident Gary Schneider (b. 1954), science and technology have permanently altered the portrait, shifting it away from external appearances—a traditional source of beauty—to the irreducible kernel of identity lodged in the human chromosome.[5] As historian and curator Ann Thomas observed, Schneider's series of photographs *Genetic Self-portrait* is simultaneously a depiction of his uniqueness and a portrait of our time, which tries to square cultural conditioning with the strength and scope of biological determinism, implied by the fact that, across the human spectrum, individual differences reside in only 1 per cent of our genetic make-up.[6] Despite its title, Schneider's series extends beyond nuggets of genetic information to personal interpretation. Simply prepared photograms of Schneider's hands and ears accompany chromosome sequences (Fig. 7.10). The medium he uses—the platinum print—was a favorite of the Pictorialists.

High-resolution, sometimes computer-aided microscopic imaging allows the eye to look through the body at its smallest particles. The increasingly common experience of viewing

DNA, in both the scientific community and the public realm, marks another crucial stage in the historical process of seeing inside the body, which began with the X-ray and now includes such techniques as magnetic resonance imaging (MRI), positron emission tomography (PET), and ultrasound scanning. Each of these techniques employs non-photographic means that are translated into computer-enhanced images, which are informally called pictures or photographs. TOMOGRAPHY, an advanced X-ray process, produces thin cross-sections of the body, not just from one point of view, like a photograph, but from 360 degrees. The ongoing *Visible Human Project* combines photography with the latest imaging devices to draw together an exhaustive archive of cross-sections of the human body to be used for medical research (Fig. 7.11).

The dual response of fascination and revulsion that such investigations into the natural world can inspire has been taken up by American Catherine Chalmers (b. 1957). She poses home-raised insects, such as cockroaches and praying mantises, in front of shiny white backgrounds, as if they were fashion models (Fig. 7.12). In her series of images called *Food Chain*, Chalmers adapted fashion photography to the diminutive realm of rapacious insects, who reduce each other to scattered limbs.

7.10 (left and right)
GARY SCHNEIDER,
Pair of Tumor Suppressor Genes on Chromosome 11, 1997. **Platinum print.**

Schneider used sophisticated scientific imaging processes to obtain pictures of his chromosomes, which he then reclaimed as art by printing them in the platinum process.

By contrast, Suzanne Bloom (b. 1943) and Ed Hill (b. 1935), both pioneers in DIGITAL IMAGING who work under the name MANUAL, see an encouraging watershed moment in humankind's relationship to nature presaged by digital information and imagery. Using image-manipulation software, they made combination-pictures of forests and abstract shapes (Fig. 7.13). Their installation of these photographs titled *The Constructed Forest* was subtitled *("This is the End—Let's Go On"—El Lissitzky)*. It seized the Russian artist's idea that a new society must renounce the old Romantic art of self-expression

7.11 STANFORD UNIVERSITY, *The Stanford Visible Male,* from *The Visible Human Project™,* **National Library of Medicine, 1990s. Stanford University, California.**

The Visible Human Project began as a project to aid anatomy study and hone surgical skills. It has evolved into an enormous, ongoing program to create exact multi-dimensional pictures of the human body.

7.12 CATHERINE CHALMERS, *Bug* from *Food Chain,* **1994–96. Massachusetts Museum of Contemporary Art, North Adams, Massachusetts.**

Greatly magnified and presented in large, carefully lit color prints, Chalmers's images of the cycle of insect life have all the fascination of food photography in a trendy magazine. Because she has translated scientific photography into glamor photography, which prizes looking for its own sake, she has been accused of aestheticizing death.

7.13
**SUZANNE BLOOM &
ED HILL (MANUAL),**
**From *The Constructed
Forest*, 1993. Digital
color print.**

The team that formed
MANUAL helped
pioneer art applications
of digital imagery.
This image combines
conventional views of
nature, represented
by growing trees, with
images that look like
wood, but are, in fact,
computer inventions.
It suggests that the
next social transforma-
tion will be achieved
by embracing digital
technology.

and embrace industry and machine art,
including photography, as the new wave
of the future.

For MANUAL, photography is
now an impotent Romantic art, and the
computer a means through which social
progress might be made. Nature and
culture—the forest and a new, digital
art—come together in MANUAL's work,
pointing away from the old promise
of industrialization toward the positive
potential of cyberspace.

No other technological innovation
in the history of photography, a medium
regularly jolted by inventions and their
commercialization, brought on such
drastic conjectures about the future
as did electronic or digital imaging.
Computer-assisted picture-making made
a largely unremarked-upon appearance
in a 1966 work by American John
Mott-Smith (b. 1930), shown in John
Szarkowski's 1978 book *Mirrors and
Windows*. Extensive discussion about
the social consequences of computer-
manipulated images sprang not directly
from art practice, but from the public's
reaction to stunning special effects
in such movies as the *Star Wars* series,
which began in 1977, and through
the rapid spread of computers in the
late twentieth century, which supplied

the print and broadcast media with
enhanced capacity to alter photographs
easily and expertly.

When the cover picture of the
February 1982 issue of *National
Geographic* showed two of the famous
pyramids at Giza in Egypt somewhat
closer together than they actually are,
digital imaging overstepped a previously
inconspicuous line between socially
accepted fiction, such as *Star Wars*,
and unacceptable tampering with the
appearance of optical reality. *National
Geographic* gave the public the jitters
about the capacity for computer-assisted
pictures to lie.

POST-PHOTOGRAPHY

THE END

In 1839, when photography was
disclosed to the world, painter Paul
Delaroche, a supporter of photography,
is rumored to have declared, "From
today, painting is dead." The attribution
is probably apocryphal,[7] and in any
event painting is still a very living art.
Nevertheless, the remark became part
of photographic folklore and has been
repeatedly enlisted to insinuate that an
ironic, cosmic cadence is at work in the

history of the medium. If painting was killed by photography, then photography may be destined to die by means of a new medium. For example, while lauding the success of color photography in a 1985 issue of *Creative Camera*, Susan Butler claimed that "From today black-and-white is dead." Before long, all of photography would be declared vanquished at the hands of an even more robust and welcome reformer.

In the 1990s, the critic Nicholas Mirzoeff looked back and identified traditional camerawork's time of demise, announcing that "photography met its own death some time in the 1980s at the hands of computer imaging."[8] Likewise, William J. Mitchell, an early advocate of digital manipulation at the Massachusetts Institute of Technology in Cambridge, paraphrased Delaroche, announcing in 1992 that "from this moment on, photography is dead — or more precisely, radically and permanently redefined as was painting one hundred and fifty years before."[9]

A more measured yet minority view was expressed by Spanish photographer and critic Joan Fontcuberta (see p. 442), who noted that, because the computer has become "a sophisticated technological prosthesis we cannot do without," it is not surprising that artists would use it as an accessory to their work, like a filter or a telephoto lens.[10] Fontcuberta pointed out that previous technological improvements did not fundamentally alter the medium, and that "the metamorphosis from silver grains to pixels is not itself that significant." After all, he cautioned, "the silver-grained structure of actual photographs has already been replaced in the print media by the photomechanical dot."[11] Moreover, he reasoned, from its inception, all photography has been "altered" in the sense that the camera frames and focuses on a chosen subject, thus eliminating other topics. Manipulation, Fontcuberta argued, "is exempt of moral value." What should be judged is the intent of the manipulation, not the process itself.[12]

Deceitful photographs, perhaps the most prominent concern from the mid-1980s to the early 1990s, did not start with the computer. In the 1870s, photographer Eugène Appert staged scenes with actors and used old-fashioned cut-and-paste methods on the resultant photographs to contrive subtle political propaganda for the forces opposing the French Commune. Comparable attempts to alter recorded history were made on behalf of Joseph Stalin during his dictatorial rule in the U.S.S.R. from 1929 to 1953. Officials such as Leon Trotsky (1879–1940) who fell from favor were physically eliminated and their portraits were airbrushed out of group photographs.[13] Still, the availability of the means to falsify photographs does not mean that photographs will be routinely adulterated.

Anxiety about the effects of digital technology was the latest appearance of photography's oldest ghost, technological determinism, which continued to evoke illusory beliefs that, in its relative simplicity, past photography was more innocent than contemporary modes, and that "straight" photography is the norm of camerawork. During the 1980s and 1990s, concern for the possibly malevolent effects of computer-manipulated photographs overshadowed other powerful ways in which photographs have been and will continue to be deceptive. Omitting images, such as the scenes of forced labor that Aleksandr Rodchenko excluded from his series on the building of the White Canal (see p. 242), can be as deceitful as reshaping pictures. Moreover, in a medium that thrives in multiples, a potential taken further by computer replication, important subjects can be hidden in plain sight in the midst of a plethora of distracting pictures.

Analyses of photographs of the Gulf War (1990–91) reveal that news magazines such as *Time, Newsweek*, and *U.S. News and World Report* ran pictures of military hardware more than any other subject. Virtually no pictures of actual combat were shown, and the few photographs of American casualties that found their way into print followed the iconography established during the Korean War, as in David Turnley's (b. 1955) image of a grieving, wounded soldier accompanying the body of a dead comrade on an evacuation helicopter. Most television coverage was of military briefings and interviews with politicians and experts.[14] Nevertheless, the public perception persists that Operation Desert Storm was witnessed up close on television screens across the world.

Delaying the publication of pictures is yet another form of concealment.

During the Gulf War, *Time* magazine and the Associated Press wire service (AP) both refused to publish or distribute grisly photographs of the charred bodies of Iraqi troops killed along the so-called "highway of death." Eventually *Time* published one of these pictures, in a year-end round-up issue, about nine months after the war. Potentially, computer-assisted and disseminated images may fall into any or all of these modes of misrepresentation. Indeed, computer-assisted photographs have largely followed paths already well trodden by past photographic practice.

Nevertheless, in their work *The Dystopian Series* Aziz & Cucher (American Anthony Aziz [b. 1961] and Venezuelan Sammy Cucher [b. 1958]) capture the persistent fear that digital technologies pose a threat that is muffled by enthusiasm for technological advancement. In their large prints, sitters pose thoughtfully, while computer-generated skin closes their eyes, mouths, and ears (Fig. 7.14). These "desensitized" humans, whose minds are cut off from direct perception of the world, stand for the pair's suspicion of blind faith in digital futures, which they perceive as similar to the naive confidence that people in the second half of the twentieth century had with regard to the promise of nuclear power and the rewards of space travel. Recognizing that cyberspace brings with it the potential "democratization of the artistic impulse,"[15] they still counsel that uncritical attitudes toward the cyberworld will only deepen the individual self-centeredness promoted by an on-line life, while diminishing the collective experience they deem crucial to society's welfare. Aziz & Cucher accuse technophiles of hymning a new romanticism, drawn from the jargon of biogenetics, computer science, and popular psychology, to exalt "a smooth universe of interfaces, amazing speed, multilocality, and superconductivity, populated by friendly cyborgs, artificially intelligent machines and the shallow creations of our transpersonal selves." "No one seems to care," they admonish, "that this idealized world functions on the basis of extreme human isolation, mediated experience, and global consumerism."[16]

Even commentators wary of inflated digital enthusiasm are convinced, with Joan Fontcuberta, that "the true computer-photography fusion gives rise to a powerful electronic laboratory, which introduces factors too decisive for us to sustain our conventional views of image

7.14
AZIZ & CUCHER,
Dystopia, 1994.
Installation at the Jack Shainman Gallery, New York. Digital prints.

Through digital means, Aziz & Cucher create portraits in which one can see the freckles and wrinkles on the faces of sitters whose senses have been blocked by computer-generated tissue, so as to make the sitters seem cut off from direct experience of the world.

making."[17] From the vantage point of 1995, he predicted that the widespread use of digital-imaging by amateurs would vanquish the notion of photographic objectivity while permitting a faster and larger dialogue among artists and the public. Ironically, both digital ardor and digital angst owe to earlier Postmodern attitudes, which questioned the truth-value of traditional photography while simultaneously hailing the social power of mass media. By the nature of its production techniques, digital imaging seems to have undermined the authority of the traditional photograph as an index of the material world. At the same time, the union of the photograph, the computer, and high-speed, broadband transmission chimes with cultural dreams about a democratic art. Unfortunately, picture theory and philosophy, while helpful, are not adequate to the job of assessing the domain of digital imaging, because this realm is extending at such a high speed into all areas of commerce, government, and private life.

EVERYTHING OLD IS NEW AGAIN

Describing the work of Mexican artist and photojournalist Pedro Meyer (b. 1935), Joan Fontcuberta observed that Meyer's pictures run the gamut from snapshots to digitally altered images that obviously stray far from the appearance of optical reality. In general, that range describes the great extent to which computer-assisted imaging is used in newspapers, books, art, advertising, propaganda, and even pornography. A few photographs benefit from being unretouched, while most are adjusted to differing degrees on the computer screen. Computer manipulation has largely replaced and upgraded darkroom techniques for retouching photographs.

Although it is possible for computers to compile data and create pictures that mimic the appearance of the world without ever using visual bits of information captured from optical reality, at the present time that practice is largely confined to entertainment vehicles, such as animated films and computer games. Most digitally modified pictures are processed so as to make them look more "real," and thereby convey notions of truth that have freighted the medium from the first. To denote this state of looking real by being made through digital means, Joan Fontcuberta invented the term, the *vrai-faux* (the true-false) and applied it to Pedro Meyer's particular use of the illusion of three-dimensional, photographic space in his magical, digitally altered photographs (Fig. 7.15).

7.15
PEDRO MEYER, *The Temptation of the Angel,* **1991. Digital color print. California Museum of Photography, Riverside, California.**

Meyer considers himself a documentarist who interprets reality, rather than a fabricator of alternative worlds. Here, a woman carrying a torch to light the *temescal* (traditional Mexican steambath) approaches a young woman portraying an angel. Meyer said he wanted the angel to be unaware of the older woman approaching her. Just what the angel might be tempted by remains unclear.

Critic Katy Siegel observed that Andreas Gursky's photographs "look loud," because Gursky "digitally tweaked the colors for maximum saturation, to almost hallucinatory effect."[18] Gursky's "tweaking" also extends to transporting or removing forms and figures, but not to the point that it is evident to the casual viewer. For him and many other digital technology users, the computer facilitates the production of clearly detailed enlargements. Perhaps the best example of the persistence of photography as an idea issues from the millions of cyberspace-dwelling vernacular images of births, parties, and vacation trips, taken with digital cameras or made chemically, printed, and then scanned into computers. These images are widely understood by their makers and viewers to be historically continuous with chemically based photographs, regardless of their electronic means of recording and dissemination.

Just as the notion of photography as optical truth has lived on in the digital era, so past themes, concepts, and styles carried through into the present. Canadian Dyan Marie (b. 1954) employs digital techniques to soften and swirl forms (Fig. 7.16), in the manner of Surrealists such as Salvador Dalí, in whose best-known work, *The Persistence of Memory* (1931), pocket watches melt like warm cheese. The ease with which computer software can appropriate, intermingle, and also dissolve images ensures the perpetuation of Surrealism's taste for the incongruous, what the French poet the Comte de Lautréamont (Isidore Ducasse) (1846–1870) famously called the beautiful "chance encounter of a sewing machine and an umbrella on an operating table" (*Les Chants de Maldoror*, 1868).

Digital processes have also been used by social campaigners and critics such as Hulleah Tsinhnahjinnie (see p. 418), for whom they facilitate copy-ing old photographs and collaging them with bits of appropriated imagery, to create pointed yet humorous indictments of Eurocentric points of view (Fig. 7.17). In his work, Taiwanese artist Chen Chieh-Jen (b. 1960) has moved from performance art to digital photographs, in which he inserts his own image into disturbing historical images of Chinese history (Fig. 7.18). Like many users of computer-assisted software,

7.16
DYAN MARIE,
Learning to Count THREE: Whirlwind,
1993. Digital color print.

Marie's image is an improvisation on the lines of her hand. She uses digital means to deepen crevices into tiny spirals of pliant flesh.

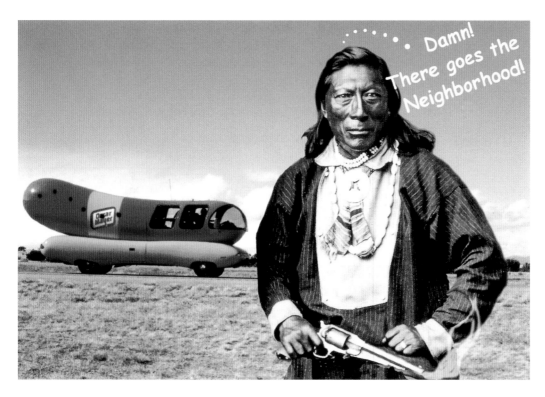

7.17
HULLEAH
TSINHNAHJINNIE,
*Damn! There goes
the Neighborhood!*,
1998. Digital print.

Tsinhnahjinnie trans-
poses white worries
about the prospect of
land values declining
when non-whites move
into the area.

Chen paints and draws using a pen attached to a digital touchpad. Some electronic processes rely on a computer mouse to select and merge images, where others depend on traditional manual dexterity. In other words, computer-assisted image production has not completely superseded traditional drafting skills. Perhaps that is why critics lauded Canadian Jeff Wall (b. 1946) for reinventing painting in the 1990s.

Wall continues to work in the pre-digital format he developed two decades ago. He stages episodes for the camera,

7.18
CHEN CHIEH-JEN,
Self-Destruction, 1996.
Digital print.

Chen digitally inserted
his body and face sev-
eral times into an old
photograph of commu-
nist sympathizers being
beheaded in Shanghai.
He toys with the
viewer's perceptions of
how and why material
comes to be understood
as fiction.

and displays the resulting images as large transparencies placed in front of light boxes, like those used to illuminate advertisements. Sometimes he has concocted scenes of contemporary life, making visual reference to famous paintings by Édouard Manet (1832–1883) or Paul Cézanne (1839–1906); in other instances, he updated the genre of history painting, transposing it to views of current events. His use of computer assistance is not usually evident in his final images, except in their large size, whose overall clarity is more readily attained with the assistance of software. For *Dead Troops Talk (A Vision after an Ambush of a Red Army Patrol, Near Moqor, Afghanistan, Winter 1986)* (Fig. 7.19), actors depicted an incident reminiscent of epic history paintings such as Antoine-Jean Gros's (1771–1835) *Napoleon on the Battlefield at Eylau* (1808), which filled a large canvas with a harsh winter battlefield, sensational gore, implausible heroism, and an incidental character who looked accusingly at the viewer.

Where Wall adapted Postmodern ideas to the present, Japanese photographer Yasumasa Morimura (b. 1951) pursued the movement's uneasiness with fixed notions of gender and ethnic identity. Before and since digital assistance became very widely available,

7.19
JEFF WALL, *Dead Troops Talk (A Vision after an Ambush of a Red Army Patrol, near Moqor, Afghanistan, Winter 1986)*, 1991–92. Cibachrome transparency, fluorescent light, aluminum display case.

By comparison with nineteenth-century history painting, Wall's scene is a domesticated spectacle. Like many artists who came of age in the Postmodern moment, he sometimes leaves clues to the image's artificiality, such as the obviously fake blood that stains the clothing of troops in *Dead Troops Talk*.

Morimura made self-portraits in the guise of famous pictures. Using traditional and digital means, he inserted himself into the self-portrait by Dutch artist Vincent van Gogh (1853–1890), which showed the artist with a bandaged ear. In his more recent work, Morimura enacted celebrated photographs of Western movie actresses, including Marilyn Monroe, in her famous pin-up pose published in *Playboy* (Fig. 7.20). Since the computer could have been used to conjure a more convincing imitation, one assumes that he intended to show the artificial breast-bra, polyester wig, lipstick-enlarged lips, and whitish make-up. Especially for a Japanese audience, these accoutrements are reminiscent of Japanese kabuki, a traditional form of theater in which men play all the women's roles.

Mariko Mori (b. 1976) similarly stared in and produced her own work, employing cutting-edge digital devices. In *Pure Land* (Fig. 7.21), her candy-colored galaxy is inhabited by futuristic images culled and combined from postwar monster movies, popular toys, and even artificial, bubble-gum flavors, such as blueberry. *Pure Land* also recalls the Japanese concept of the "floating world." Once a Buddhist notion for transcendence of the material world, the floating world was appropriated in

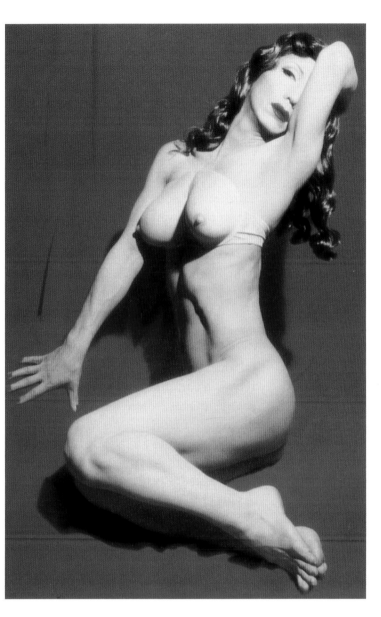

the seventeenth century to characterize transient pleasures, and eventually applied to the elaborate erotic etiquette of the geisha, whose robes Mori seems to be wearing. Like Morimura, Mori jumbled references to tradition, commerce, fashion, and Japan's infatuation with the West into pictures that play on the persistent bearing of the past on the present. In the early twentieth century Mori moved away from her trademark staged digital photography, because she thought it was too judgmental. Instead, she now creates big-budget, high-tech environments that combine light shows, video installations, and some photographs.

Unexpectedly, the time saved by digital means allows some image-makers to make wider use of older, more time-consuming media. For example, Keith Cottingham (b. 1965) electronically hybridizes photographs of his soft-clay sculpture and anatomical drawing with appropriated images of race, gender, and age (Fig. 7.22). The resultant image, as in his *Fictitious Portraits* series, recalls the cool light and sensuous skin tones of late Italian Renaissance artist Michelangelo Merisi da Caravaggio (1573–1610). Electronic reproduction permits Cottingham to "use and abuse photography's myth, its privileged claim to the real." Like Andres Serrano's images of bodily fluids (see Figs. 7.70, 7.71),

**7.20 (left)
YASUMASA
MORIMURA,**
*Self-Portrait (Actress),
Red Marilyn,* **1996.
Ektachrome print.**

Through digital means, Morimura tries to combine his image with that of Marilyn Monroe. However, Morimura's incomplete transition from male to female, and from Asian to Caucasian, involves contemporary doubt about the mutability of personal identity.

**7.21
MARIKO MORI,**
Pure Land, **1997–98.
Glass photo interlayer
(1 of 5 panels).**

Androgynous space-traveling Smurfs sit like Buddhas and play musical instruments, while hovering with a traditionally garbed Mori over what looks like a post-apocalyptic Japan. The image alludes to atomic-age cinema monsters such as Godzilla and Mothra, who required traditional maidens as sacrifices or as servants. In addition to photographs, Mori has also experimented with three-dimensional photographs and videos.

7.22
KEITH COTTINGHAM,
Untitled (Triple), 1993.
Digitally constructed
color photograph.

Digital triplets pose
like the Three Graces
of Greek mythology.
The too perfect shadow
on the standing figure's
abdomen, the breadth
of his collarbone, which
seems to sweep over
his shoulders like the
ribbons on a cape, and
the highlights in his
hair that resemble
brushstrokes, remind
the viewer that these
figures are fabricated.

Cottingham's pictures, are, in his words, "both beautiful and horrific," playing on the psychological longing to substitute the picture for the real thing.[19]

Perhaps in response to a world in which humans increasingly interact with machines, some image-makers have adapted the photograph to electronic environments that reciprocate the movements of visitors. In Polish-American artist Miroslaw Rogala's (b. 1954) *Lover's Leap*, computers track a viewer throughout the installation (Fig. 7.23). *Lover's Leap* is far removed from Edward Steichen's *Family of Man* exhibition, in which the viewer's path through the exhibit was as carefully determined as the images that could be seen there. Describing Rogala's installation, curator Lynne Warren voiced an increasingly familiar declaration: "This is the post-photographic image. The image-maker is no longer the godlike determinant of perspective and viewpoint."[20]

Rogala's work is physically based in a gallery, but long-time critic of American foreign policy photographer Esther Parada (1938–2005) has taken advantage of digital montage for almost twenty years, and for a while made work that was entirely web-based. She orchestrated interactive sites, such as *Transplant: A Tale of Three Continents (Wherein a Victorian love story between a Chicago heiress and an English aristocrat reveals a web of colonial maneuvers connecting the United States, England, and India)* (Fig. 7.24). Viewers were invited to follow their own path among photographs that are plainly or enigmatically labeled. A story about a young bride "transported" from her family home and then to India unfolded in an indirect, non-linear way, with clickable asides about such topics as British imperialist conduct in India during the nineteenth century. The essence of this phase of Parada's work—extensive

Rogala's installations
interact with participant-
observers, whose
entrances and move-
ments into the structure
and around the exhibit
set off the projection of
different pictures—a
procedure the viewer
quickly learns to exploit.

series of photographs, framed by suggestive text, and made available on the
World Wide Web—captured the imagination of those who long for inexpensive
means of disseminating images and text
beyond established institutions such as
newspapers and galleries.

While websites may eventually offer
more users a global reach into visual
information, a strong countervailing
trend developed at the beginning of
the third millennium. Image-makers,
museums, galleries, news organizations,
and image archives have responded to
the commercial possibilities of the web
by commodifying more and more pictures in extensive pay-per-view-or-use
operations. For example, Corbis.com,

an image-bank holding over 70 million
pictures, was established by Microsoft
founder Bill Gates in 1989. It resembles
a nineteenth-century photographic studio from which users could get images
in many sizes and qualities, ranging
from postcards to archival prints. In
image-banks, the name of the photographer is often omitted in favor of subject matter. Mark Getty, founder of Getty
Images and descendant of the family
that founded the Getty petroleum firm,
also owns about 70 million photographs.
He succinctly summed up the economic
potential of images when he remarked
that "intellectual property is the oil of
the 21st century."[21] Together, Gates and
Getty control almost 50 per cent of the

7.24 (below)
ESTHER PARADA,
*Transplant: A Tale of
Three Continents
(Wherein a Victorian
love story between a
Chicago heiress and an
English aristocrat reveals
a web of colonial
maneuvers connecting
the United States,
England, and India),*
1996. **Website.**

Parada turned to elec-
tronic media in the mid-
1980s. She now exhibits
her photographs in
interactive series on the
web, such as *Transplant*,
which withholds all the
details of a love story
until the viewer has
explored all the photo-
graphs and text available
on the site.

407

POST-PHOTOGRAPHY

As you examine some of these connections, I encourage you to question the misleading polarities (such as natural vs. artificial, pure vs. corrupt, spiritual vs. commercial, real vs. virtual) which often inform our perception of historical events; or color our understanding of the shift from traditional (idyllic/pastoral) to modern (corrupt/technological) times.

nearly $2-billion imagery business. Armchair travel on the web, through photographs of historic events, as well as the world's vistas and its art, may eventually acquire a price tag. Recently, both Corbis and Getty Images have moved into news and sports photography, taking them into the market for photographs of the present.

FACE VALUE

The Fall 1993 cover of a special issue of *Time* magazine used computer software to create a female image of multiethnic America, combining physical attributes of Anglo-Saxons, Asians, Africans, and Hispanics with those of people from South Europe and from the Middle East[22] (Fig. 7.25). To keep her from

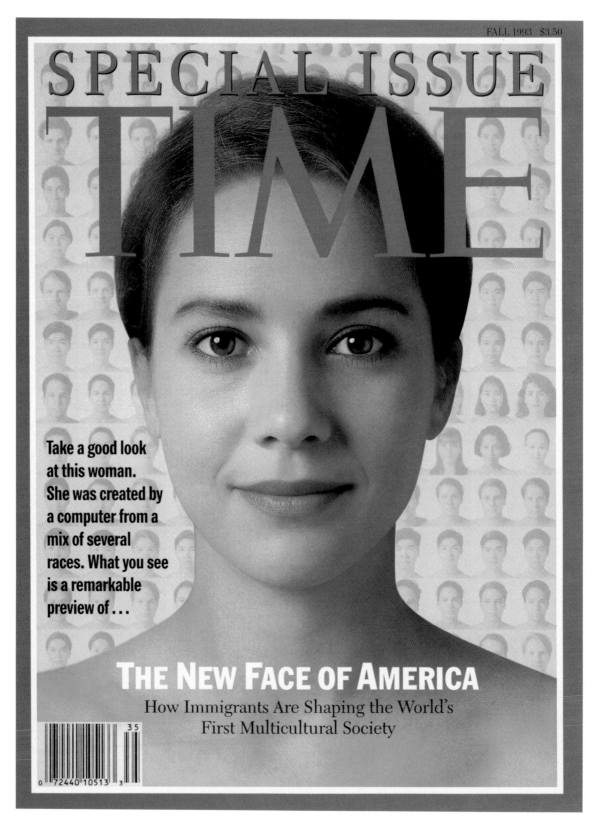

7.25
Time cover, special issue, Fall 1993.

Digital combination prints, layering physical aspects of different ethnic groups, proved to be one of the most enticing visual motifs in the last decades of the twentieth century. Fashion photographers such as Hiro did it, photo-editors on news magazines called for it, and artists such as Nancy Burson (see Fig. 7.26) explored the overlaid look.

SPECIAL ISSUE
TIME
FALL 1993 $3.50

Take a good look at this woman. She was created by a computer from a mix of several races. What you see is a remarkable preview of . . .

THE NEW FACE OF AMERICA
How Immigrants Are Shaping the World's
First Multicultural Society

looking like the fabricated product she was, designers gave her an engaging semi-smile, and used shadows to imply the slightly asymmetrical face of real humans. The concept of merging portrait photographs has a long history, going back to the late nineteenth-century combination portraits of English scientist Francis Galton. During the 1980s, American Nancy Burson (b. 1948) achieved notoriety for her eerie computer-generated composite pictures, which blended the facial features of politicians including Stalin, Mussolini, Mao, Hitler, and Khomeni, or film stars such as Bette Davis, Audrey Hepburn, Grace Kelly, Sophia Loren, and Marilyn Monroe. Her blend of Black, Asian, and Caucasian features into an ominous

mugshot (Fig. 7.26) struck some critics, such as Allan Sekula, as a pointless use of the computer's skills.

Today, Burson's smudgy black-and-white computer-assisted prints look dated, because more recent digital equipment and software, pioneered in television and advertising production, offer crisp, ultra-naturalistic, and seamless production values. Contemporary computer imaging in art, journalism, and commerce tends toward sharp realizations, oddly reminiscent of the daguerreotype, whose mirror-like surface simultaneously gripped foreground and background visual detail, challenging how the human eye sees. With a little know-how and user-friendly software, the average personal computer

7.26
NANCY BURSON, *Mankind (an Asian, a Caucasian, and a Black blended, weighted according to current population statistics)*, 1983–84. Gelatin silver print.

Burson's work walks a fine line between art and science. For twenty years she has developed computer programs that combine portraits in order to demonstrate the transparency of appearances. She has also helped law-enforcement agencies find missing children by "aging" them with the help of computer software.

user can achieve a professional-looking image. Insofar as image-makers are attracted to changing high-tech systems, they are involved in an incessant and expensive game of catch-up brought about by the vast proliferation of image-enhancing techniques and the rapid obsolescence of software and computers. Digital devices age rapidly: today's state-of-the-art gear will soon show up at the recycling center.

THE PREDICAMENTS OF SOCIAL CONCERN

The decline of the picture magazine after World War II, and the concomitant rise of television news, shrank the number of outlets available for documentary and photojournalistic images. Newspaper and magazine photo-editors increasingly prescribed the exact subject and style they wanted from photographs, thereby cramping the individual initiative of photojournalists. To a greater degree than in the past, editors rather than photographers chose which, if any, of the images submitted would be published. As a consequence, though documentary photographers and photojournalists continued to work for newspapers and magazines, they also published books, and exhibited in museums and galleries, where they were able to exercise greater control over the selection and presentation of their work, and where they did not have to contend with tight deadlines.

The presence of documentary and photojournalistic photographs in museums and galleries was not new. From the beginning, reportage images, such as those taken by Roger Fenton of the Crimean War, were presented in art spaces. Images made for the Farm Security Administration also found their way into the art world. Nevertheless, in the past, image-makers, audiences, curators, and scholars had considered art photography, documentary photography, and photojournalism as having their own separate lines of development and different social agendas. By the late twentieth century, however, these distinct photographic genres were increasingly coming to resemble each other in style and subject. No single term emerged to express this hybridization, but the need for a label to describe

the new phenomenon is evident in the attempt of Weston Naef, curator of photographs at the J. Paul Getty Museum in Los Angeles, California, to characterize the work of Brazilian photographer Sebastião Salgado (see pp. 420–21). Although Naef described him as "an artist, using photojournalism as the vehicle for his art," Salgado has repeatedly maintained that he is not an artist, but a documentarian.[23]

As critic and historian Vicki Goldberg observed in 1988, "some of the most arresting documentary work now leans heavily, even self-consciously, on art and art photography."[24] Contemplating the origins of what he considers is a shift away from documentary, cultural historian Stuart Hall suggested that no approach can isolate itself from being weakened or co-opted. He speculated that during the last decades of the twentieth century, some artists and photographers lost confidence in the idea that documentary embodied the essential truth of photography.[25] The current blending of documentary work, photojournalism, and art photography, as well as the popularity of constructed and staged photographs (see p. 450) seems to bear out his conjecture.

The merger of art, journalism, and documentary is apparent in the images of Americans Mary Ellen Mark (b. 1940) and Eugene Richards (b. 1944). Affiliated with the Magnum Agency, both sought employment where their ideas would be subject to the least interference by editors. Their work centers on the plight of unfortunate people, yet their images are seldom sentimental. Mark and Richards did not venerate the poor in the manner of the confidently humanistic pictures made by photographers working for the Farm Security Administration. Although Mark's images are frequently seen as having been influenced by Diane Arbus's work, she does not deliberately belittle subjects, as Arbus sometimes did, nor are they primarily symbols for her own psychological outlook. Mark's photographic series on homeless children and teenagers in Seattle, Washington, is compassionate yet unflinching (Fig. 7.27).

While photographs showing unfortunate people as victims of political injustice and catastrophic circumstance continued to be made and shown, in the new hybrid of art, documentary, and

In the past, a photographer such as Dorothea Lange (see pp. 281–82) might have elected to photograph a homeless child as the casualty of social neglect, rather than as a willful runaway with a gun. Mark, by contrast, suggests these children's quick passions and uncertain judgments. She constructed the image so that a long tunnel of receding space seems to push the children forward for our attention, while simultaneously signaling their estrangement from society.

photojournalism, the romantic humanism of the popular 1955 *The Family of Man* book and exhibit (see pp. 312–14) was overturned. It was replaced by the idea that human nature is a convoluted and unpredictable blend of dignity and imperfection.

To be sure, this chastened estimate of human nature is not simply a photographic phenomenon. The twentieth century's grim record of millions of deaths caused by large and small wars, as well as by many disregarded famines, does not inspire faith in the inherent goodness of humankind. The end of the Cold War, and of the tendency to see the world in terms of sharply competing ideologies, may also have contributed to a diminution of human expectations. From Lewis Hine to the Photo League, social documentary photography was animated by the idea that images could precipitate social change. During the late 1950s and the 1960s, social documentarians began to lose faith in the capacity of pictures to do this.[26] Robert Frank and Diane Arbus used the camera to denote their dissatisfaction with society's shallowness, not the need for social change. Their mood of dark resignation was sustained in the documentary photography of the next generation. For instance, in his book *Interior America* (1978), Chauncey Hare (b. 1934) laid waste to whatever hopefulness Bill Owens had found in suburbia,

and cast his camera on the bleak settings that framed the experience of even bleaker Americans.

The work of British photographer Chris Killip (b. 1946) is typical of the ongoing turn away from directly promoting social change towards personal observation and interpretation of the social scene. Killip's book *In Flagrante* (1988) pictured the effects of deindustrialization on downtrodden residents in and around the northeastern city of Newcastle upon Tyne. *Britain in 1984,* the powerful concept and title of an exhibition at London's The Photographers' Gallery, encouraged photographers to pursue personal documentary projects, especially those that revealed the effects on the poor and working class of Prime Minister Margaret Thatcher's social policies. Among the work shown was that of Paul Graham (b. 1956), who had already jettisoned the documentary tradition of black-and-white photography. With the example of William Eggleston's rambling tour of the American South in mind, Graham set out to show how color could add to the documentary record. His uncompromising 1986 book *Beyond Caring,* an ironically titled look at the frustrations and failures of Britain's social welfare system, was illustrated by views of people seated on day-glo orange benches below the abrasive sheen of fluorescent lights installed in the waiting rooms of the Department of Health and Social Security (DHSS) (Fig. 7.28). For this series of pictures, Graham frequently used signage as chance titles for his pictures, just as many photographers for the Farm Security Administration had done in the late 1930s. Yet unlike them, he took pictures on the sly, and deliberately distanced himself from his subjects, sometimes even placing a physical barrier, such as a table or a bench, between the camera and his subjects. Often the most emotionally affecting person is farthest from the camera. Graham continues to work experimentally. In the images produced during a recent tour of the United States, he intentionally whited-out pictures in which people of color appear, as if to indicate that they are invisible. Another British photographer, Martin Parr (b. 1952), achieved an international reputation for his images of self-centered British middle-class suburban life. Unlike Killip's sullen introspective views and Graham's subtle symbolism, Parr's *The Cost of Living* (1989) is punctuated with wry, satirical perceptions of human behavior (Fig. 7.29).

Photography's blighted vision of human nature was accompanied by a change in the formal appearance of documentary and photojournalism. In a hurried era, with round-the-clock television news, ubiquitous video cameras, and small, concealable digital cameras that could quickly transmit still photographs around the world, the static, balanced, easily discernible images promoted in the past by the Farm Security Administration and picture magazines such as *Life* blurred and shattered. Audiences exposed to television images for many hours a day adjusted to rapid, highly condensed picture sequences, such as thirty-second advertisements and rapid-cutting music videos. Largely through exposure to television and film, viewers became accustomed to quick transitions, such as jump-cuts, and shaky hand-held camera motions. Typically, photojournalism and documentary work also picked up on the look of speed and chance.

For example, Eugene Richards's pictures are stylized, and regularly use dim light, surprising angles, and disjointed sequences to remind the viewer

7.28
PAUL GRAHAM,
Waiting Room,
Southwark DHSS,
South London, **1984.**

Graham's work is filled with visual contradictions—here, the perky orange color of the chairs is at odds with the drowsy frustration of the people waiting for assistance.

7.29
MARTIN PARR,
Tupperware Party, 1985,
from his book *The Cost
of Living*, 1989.

While listening to a
Tupperware demon-
strator, the women in
the audience display
contrasting expressions
of polite boredom.
Unlike many other
photographers of his
generation, Parr
admires these visual
anecdotes and seeks
them out.

of the photographer's presence and interpretive role. Like Mary Ellen Mark, he spends long periods with his subjects, returning time and again to keep up with their progress, and his photographs are accompanied by text that reads like a personal diary. *Exploding into Life* (1986), Richards's paradoxically titled chronicle of the medical experiences he and his companion Dorothea Lynch endured during her losing battle with breast cancer, is a searingly frank presentation of what was then a largely unphotographed theme, the individual experience of cancer in the milieu of modern medical technology. *Cocaine True, Cocaine Blue* (1994), a controversial collection of pictures and intimate personal stories about drug use, brought viewers into a world of day-to-day self-deception and ruin (Fig. 7.30). Viewing the exhaustion and despair in so much of Richards's work, Cornell Capa, brother of Robert Capa and former director of the International Center of Photography in New York City, noted that "He is too strongly attuned to misery."[27] Others have declared that Richards's intimate pictures encourage voyeurism.[28]

Another characteristic of recent photojournalism and documentary work is an increased reliance on words to contextualize photographs. In the past, large books by socially concerned photographers such as Dorothea Lange relied on extensive text written by someone else. Sociologist Paul Taylor furnished the data and arguments that accompanied Lange's pictures in *An American Exodus: A Record of Human Erosion* (1939). American Susan Meiselas (b. 1948), who combines history, social science, and photography in her work, emerged as one of the main photographers of the protracted small-scale wars that characterized the last decades of the twentieth century. Her books *Nicaragua* (1981) and the much larger *Kurdistan* (1997) contain not only photographs but also substantial data, orchestrated by Meiselas. In Nicaragua, where she photographed life under the late 1970s' regime of dictator Anastasio Somoza, rebels had taken up arms

7.30
EUGENE RICHARDS,
*Crack Plague in Red
Hook, Brooklyn*, 1994.
Gelatin silver print.

"Composed shots lie,"
Eugene Richards
believes, because they
turn "people into arche-
types—The Hungry
Child, The Drug Addict.
I feel more comfortable
taking fragmentary
photographs, so you
know that this is not the
final, correct answer."[29]

against a brutal right-wing government that was receiving U.S. aid. The hostilities eventually left about 50,000 dead and one-fifth of the population homeless. Meiselas's images captured the spasmodic flurry of street fighting (Fig. 7.31) and the evidence of atrocities. Her most recent work, the result of many trips to the West Papuan highlands, is a multipart study of how the region's local people, who call themselves the Dani, interacted with outsiders, including colonial administrators, Cold Warriors—and photographers.

Akin to Meiselas, French photographer Gilles Peress (b. 1946) prepares extensive historical chronologies to accompany his books and gallery exhibitions. With fragmented foreground close-ups, slanted horizon lines, and visual components that enter the frame at all angles, Peress's images often resemble the work of American street photographers Garry Winogrand or Lee Friedlander (Fig. 7.32). Like them, Peress embraces disunity as a condition of the world, and tries to find its visual

equivalent for his work, most recently during the genocide in Rwanda and in the Iraq War.

Despite a growing acceptance of visual ambiguity and jumpiness in photojournalism and documentary work, this approach has not pleased the public in times of crisis. In American photo-journalism, for example, abiding social conditions, such as poverty, may be rendered with harsh shadows or despondent graininess. Nevertheless, traumatic events such as the April 1995 terrorist bombing of the federal building in Oklahoma City, Oklahoma, seem to call for a clear, uncomplicated composition and explicit visual narrative that connote sincerity and truthfulness. Except for its startling use of color, the image that became a national symbol of the event, that of a firefighter holding a dead child (Fig. 7.33), could have been made in the 1930s. Similarly, as critic and historian David Perlmutter found, photographs used in social science textbooks are chosen for compositions that do not call attention to themselves or to their makers.[30]

7.31
SUSAN MEISELAS,
Street Fighter in Managua, from her book *Nicaragua*, 1981. Gelatin silver print.

7.32
GILLES PERESS,
*Demonstration in
Favor of the Ayatollah
Shariatmadari, Iran*,
1980. Gelatin silver
print. Courtesy the
artist.

Peress disowned the
notion of neutral, com-
prehensive reporting
in his book *Telex Iran*,
which integrates images
with copies of the
telegrams sent to and
from his photoagency,
Magnum. He warned
readers that "these
photographs, made dur-
ing a five-week period
from December 1979
to January 1980, do not
represent a complete
picture of Iran, or a final
record of that time."[31]

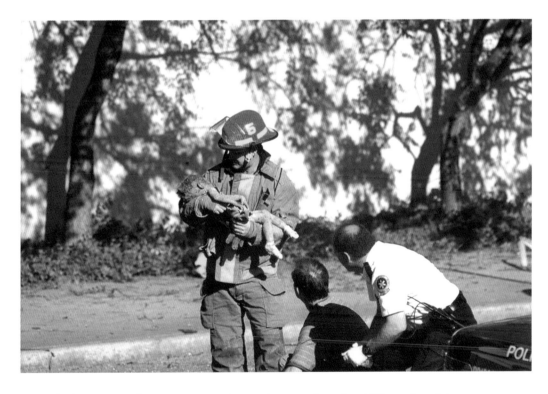

In the late twentieth century, extensive textual descriptions of the sitters' social or personal circumstances were regularly added to documentary photography and concerned photojournalism. Photographs were not expected to stand on their own, presumably communicating to viewers in a universal visual language. In *Living with the Enemy* (1991), for instance, a book recording incidents of domestic violence and their aftermath, American photographer Donna Ferrato (b. 1949) did not linger solely on battered women (Fig. 7.34). In abundant text and many

pictures, she related life stories of the battered and the batterers, and she laid bare the circuit of violence, from home, to hospital, to court, to shelters, to prisons, or to therapy sessions. Ferrato's consciousness of domestic violence's large province earned her commenda-tions by critics who otherwise questioned the effectiveness of documentary work.

THE COLOR OF CONCERN

Concerned photojournalists and docu-mentarians, such as Susan Meiselas and American James Nachtwey (b. 1948),

7.33
**CHARLES H. PORTER
IV,** *Fireman and Child
in Oklahoma City*, 1995.

The public fastened
on the photograph of
mortally wounded one-
year-old Baylee Almon
in the arms of a fire-
fighter who responded
to the terrorist bombing
of the Alfred P. Murrah
Federal Building in
Oklahoma City.

**7.34
DONNA FERRATO,
Cover photograph of
her book *Living with
the Enemy*, 1991.**

In 1991, the same year
that *Living with the
Enemy* was published,
Ferrato started a
non-profit organization
called the Domestic
Abuse Awareness
Project (DAAP) to raise
funds for women's shel-
ters. She recalled that
"I felt it was important
to find ways to show
as many aspects of the
problem as I could."[32]

author of the 1989 *Deeds of War* (Fig.
7.35), were sometimes reproved for
using sensational high-key colors that
so startled the viewer that they hampered contemplation of the image.
Black-and-white work continued to be
associated with seriousness of purpose,
and with a dedication to craft, even
though one could argue that color film
more accurately equates to the way we
see the world. Philip Jones Griffiths
(b. 1936), the British war photographer
who produced the penetrating indictment *Vietnam, Inc.* (1971), denounced
color as "the biggest single hindrance
to photojournalism the world has ever
seen."[33] Decades of amateur photography, and the broad use of color in
advertising, made it seem too facile and
too emotionally arousing for somber
subjects such as war and human suffering. Moreover, increased use of color
film in art photography prompted the
association of color with fabrication,
fantasy, and self-expression.

Documentarians and photojournalists working in color were accused of
adulterating the medium by making the

photograph look too much like a painting. Some did indeed mine the history
of art and magazine advertising, which
they scrutinized for clues to effective
color usage. Larry Burrows, for instance
(see Fig. 6.70), rummaged through Old
Master paintings for ideas, and occasionally did sketches to precast the kind of
battle photographs he wanted to make.
The increasing custom of photojournalists and documentarians to publish
beautifully crafted books and mount art
gallery exhibitions added to the unease
about blurring the line between personal
expression and reporting. Lastly, to photographers who came of age in the first
half of the twentieth century, color documentary and color photojournalism repudiated the venerable heritage of socially
concerned black-and-white photography,
such as the work of Lewis Hine.

The profusion of color photography
signaled for many the loss of ethical
gravity, and with it the abandonment
of the idea that photography could play
a role in social change. Even in black-
and-white work, raw emotionalism, the
equivalent of color's supposed excess,
was suspect. Thus, the monochrome
images created by Brazilian-born photographer Sabastião Salgado (b. 1944)
were reproved for what critic and historian Vicki Goldberg called "too much
humanism"[34] (see pp. 420–21).

The proliferation of color photography
in Western advertising, commerce, and
art highlighted the economic inequities
that divide photographers practicing
in developing countries from those in
the developed world. The color process
is more expensive than the black-and-
white method, and it requires a greater
infrastructure, including costly printers,
or digital cameras, computers, and connections to the Internet. Black-and-white
film can be developed and printed in a
simple darkroom. Often Third-World
newspapers and magazines, especially
those aligned with poorly funded opposition causes, do not have the capacity to
print color photographs.

During the last decades of the twentieth century, Western photographers were
typically college graduates, with specialized education in photography or related
subjects that stressed continual innovation
and offered exposure to a wide range of
historic and contemporary image-making.
By contrast, the primary Third-World

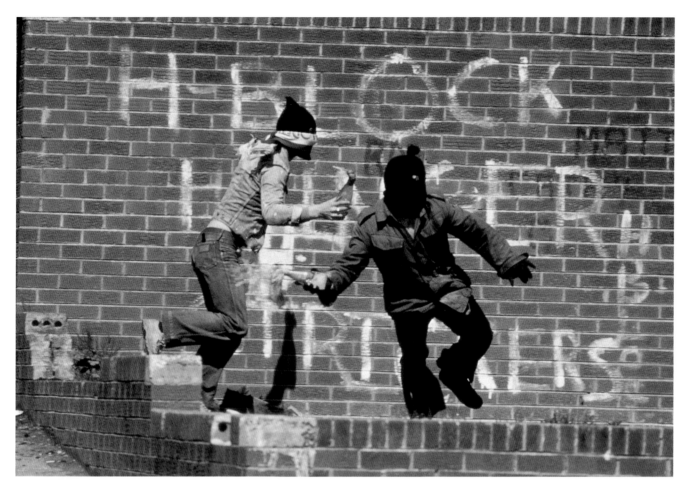

7.35
JAMES NACHTWEY,
Rioters in Belfast,
Northern Ireland, 1981,
from his book *Deeds*
of War, 1989. Gelatin
silver print.

In many of Nachtwey's
photographs, human
figures are seen in
incongruous poses, as
if they were participating
in modern dance, not
modern mayhem. The
tension between absur-
dity and tragedy ener-
gizes his signature style.

route to learning camerawork remained
self-instruction or informal apprenticeships on newspapers and in photographic studios. For example, Héctor
García (see pp. 316–17), who was an
orphaned street child and manual
worker, learned photography while serving as an office boy at several Mexican
publishing firms. An education like
García's does not acquaint learners with
many permutations of style, nor does it
offer much expensive, technologically-
based image-making. Therefore, while
photography produced in and for people
in developing regions may have ample
meaning and consequence for viewers,
its conventional approaches, lack of
color, and want of means by which to
circulate the images to the wider world,
make Third-World photography and
its history largely ignored outside its
immediate domain.

NEUTRAL VISION

During the 1980s and 1990s, the notion
of neutral vision was repeatedly examined by cultural critics and by artists. *The*
Predicament of Culture (1987), a much

discussed book by American anthropologist James Clifford, investigated
twentieth-century ethnology and literature, to conclude that photographers
had relinquished the idea of objectivity
for subjective exploration. The British
anthropologist Elizabeth Edwards and
British critic David Green looked back
at earlier, purportedly impartial anthropological photography, such as that
initiated by T. H. Huxley (see p. 152),
and revealed the means by which these
methods were used to demonstrate
implicitly the superiority of Western
civilization.[35] In a sweeping indictment,
photographer-critic Allan Sekula (b. 1951)
pointed out that Modernist photographic
practice is "shielded by a bogus ideology
of neutrality."[36]

One reason for the decline of the
neutral-record photograph in the social
sciences is that non-Western peoples,
the former subjects of the record-keeping procedure, have themselves taken
up photography as a way of counteract-
ing stereotypes propagated by it. Native
American photographer Jolene Rickard
(b. 1956) put it clearly: "Working in
photography, one is forced to deal with
issues of representation or risk promoting

7.36
JOLENE RICKARD,
Untitled, adapted from
the series *Scientifically
Unnatural*, 1993.
Ektachrome and silver
gelatin print with
rubbings.

Rickard is a member
of the Turtle clan from
the Tuscarora Nation.
On the left of this
combination picture
are two costumed
Native American dolls,
teasingly anonymous
owing to their lack of
facial features; on the
right is an international
group of women in
traditional dress.

visually the ideals other people have placed in your head"[37] (Fig. 7.36). In the United States, the Native American Journalists Association sponsors "shoot out" contests in which Native American photographers vie to present scenes of contemporary everyday life that specifically counterbalance many stereotypes. Globalism and localism operate simultaneously within Native American photographic theory. Theresa Harlan, who teaches Native American Studies and curates photography exhibits, maintained that in her scholarship she uses "the term 'international' in place of 'intertribal' to stress the diversity of indigenous nations within and outside the borders of the United States."[38]

Some photographers, such as Hulleah Tsinhnahjinnie (b. 1954), concentrated on fracturing stereotypes of Native Americans by focusing on intertribal issues, or by investigating the laws that determine who is and who is not considered an Indian. Recently, Tsinhnahjinnie has begun working with computer-enhanced techniques and has linked up with indigenous people on other continents to share experiences, especially of what it's like to be the subject of tourist cameras (see Fig. 7.17).

Another factor in the transformation of identity photography, both in the popular press and in social science, has been the ongoing domestication of the exotic. Once a source of titillating cultural difference existing at the margins of Western societies, the exotic can now be experienced in almost any large world city. Dutch photographer Bettina

WitteVeen found it while visiting New York and San Francisco. In a series she called *Hybrid Identities*, she extended the traditional anthropological close-up view to contemporary white men and women whose bodies display a mix of modern Western and traditional South Pacific body art (Fig. 7.37).

Despite the mounting condemnation of neutral vision, it remained a strong component of late twentieth-century imaging. Standardized poses, uniform backgrounds, and fixed distance were used routinely for millions of national identity cards, medical illustrations, passports, drivers' licenses, employee badges, and the like. Mug shots of prisoners

7.37 (below)
BETTINA WITTEVEEN,
Jon, from the series
*Hybrid Identities, New
York City*, 1997–98.

**7.38 (above, top)
TOSHIHIRO
YASHIRO,** *Yanaginoya
Fukushima,* **1994, from
his series** *Time-Space
(Ji-kukan),* **1994.**

Time-Space (Ji-kukan)
series coolly imaged
the gender-segregated
Japanese public baths,
an architectural form
and social activity
that has been falling
from favor.

**7.39 (above)
ZHUANG HUI,**
*Commemorative
Picture of Teachers and
Students of Loyang
Police School,
Hunan Province,
May 13 1997,* **1997.
Gelatin silver print.**

The long, unvaried
rows of police cadets
and instructors extend
beyond the frame,
helping to homogenize
the figures as indistinct
integers in a sequence of
interchangeable figures.

looked much as they had in the nineteenth century (see Fig. 4.70). After the
defeat of the Khmer Rouge regime in
Cambodia in 1979, the public was able
to see the conventions of photographic
objectivity used to produce more than
5,000 standardized images of people
who were about to be killed (see p. 426).

The broad utilitarian use of
would-be neutral photographs sparked
many political and artistic responses.
Internationally, Conceptualism's take
on objectivity persisted in the work of
such artists as Ed Ruscha, Bernd and
Hilla Becher, and a younger generation
of photographers, such as Toshihiro
Yashiro (b. 1970) (Fig. 7.38). Chinese
photographer Zhuang Hui (b. 1963)
parodied neutral vision's uniformity by
making rigorously unvaried, single-shot
panoramas of large groups, such as
factory workers or the population of a
whole town (Fig. 7.39).

Russian Vladimir Kuprejanov
(sometimes Kuprijanov) (b. 1954) energized monotonous ID cards when he
photographed sixteen women telephone
operators in Moscow, and then placed
a line of verse written by Russian poet
Aleksandr Pushkin (1799–1837) below
the portraits, where one normally would
find names and numbers (Fig. 7.40).
Kuprejanov orchestrated an oblique

political commentary in this sequence,
called *In Memory of Pushkin.* The first
few pictures in the series show weary,
morose middle-aged faces, but the final
images present younger, more contented-
looking women. At the bottom of the
images, the lines from Pushkin's poem
"Farewell to the Sea" metaphorically
advance from the present darkness to an
inviting view of a distant shore. Created
in 1985, the year that Mikhail Gorbachev
(b. 1931) assumed the office of General
Secretary of the U.S.S.R., *In Memory of*

**7.40 (below)
VLADIMIR
KUPREJANOV,**
*"The lights of the day
extinguished,"* **from his
series** *In Memory of
Pushkin,* **1985.**

Kuprejanov's close-ups
imitate the visual tech-
niques used in modern
television news programs
to indicate authenticity.
The photographer brings
the viewer uncomfortably
close to the sitter's
face in this series of
sixteen photographs.

PORTRAIT
Sebastião Salgado

Although he was in the right place to make the well-known images showing the 1981 shooting of President Ronald Reagan (1911–2004), Sebastião Salgado is not a news photographer. An economist who never finished his Ph.D., Salgado has photographed in more than sixty countries, focusing mainly on people who survive day-to-day: physical laborers, refugees, victims of famines, and, most recently, groups who migrate because of natural disasters or civil unrest.

Through magazine and newspaper illustration, Salgado's work attracted an appreciative public that is mostly unfamiliar with debates about the efficacy of documentary work. His popularity permitted him to pick his projects and to schedule his own time. Salgado rejects the use of color film, calling it a distraction. He prefers to use available light and highly sensitive black-and-white film, because he finds flash illumination artificial. Salgado pointedly differentiates his image-selection process from the "decisive moment" popularized by Cartier-Bresson (see Fig. 5.30). Where Cartier-Bresson perfected the technique of waiting for the one instant in which compositional elements and the subject of a photograph come together, Salgado attunes himself to the extended rhythms of a particular site.

Salgado's approach can be seen in his best-known series, *An Uncertain Grace* of 1990, which records the bone-wearying toil of laborers excavating pyramid-sized pits in the wilds of northern Brazil in order to extract gold deposits. The series begins with a panoramic establishing shot showing hundreds of tiny, mud-swathed figures straining under loads of earth, and struggling up long ladders to the top of the pit. Salgado, who often packs his pictures with visual references to religious art, makes the workers look like souls trying to climb out of purgatory (Fig. 7.41). The next several pictures move in closer, allowing viewers to see the armed guards who overlook the scene, and to make out individual faces among the throng. Later shots come in closer still, to study the perseverance expressed on sweaty faces, or the grace of a hand holding a heavy burlap bag of earth. The final shot is again a wide expanse of the excavation and its denizens.

Salgado's style harkens back to the Depression era, when press and advocacy photography confidently presented humans as pure of heart, despite their suffering and hardships. Seen primarily in magazine articles, but also through books and exhibitions, Salgado's affecting pictures of human suffering during a famine in northern Africa helped to raise money for the humanitarian aid group Médecins sans Frontières (Doctors without Borders). His photographs of Cambodian children who lost legs to land mines helped to raise funds for a factory to manufacture artificial limbs.

Despite his good works, Salgado has been the subject of two recurring questions—one concerning the implicit politics of his images, the other having to do with the formal qualities of his prints. He has been chastised for neglecting to record local struggles to organize and change conditions. Although Salgado has depicted worker protests, as in his pictures of Brazilian peasants marching for agrarian reform, it is not the dominant theme of his imagery. While showing human suffering at its most wretched, Salgado's images are elegant poems of composition and luminosity. Viewers understand the symbolism of harsh black-and-white pictures used to describe misery in photographs such as those by W. Eugene Smith or Shomei Tomatsu. But Salgado enhances shimmering light so that it transforms burlap sacks of earth into treasure pouches, and warms the gaunt faces of the starving so that they look like tranquil martyrs.

Salgado's own books, *Workers, An Archeology* (1993), *Migrations* (2000), and *The Children* (2000), generally disappointed the literati, who labeled his work "sentimental voyeurism," and who are uneasy in the presence of Salgado's signature mixture of beauty and affliction.[39] While no one openly accused Salgado of building his reputation on the backs of the unfortunate, his signature mixture of beauty and affliction not only made some viewers uneasy but also seemed to frustrate criticism, for fear of being thought to be insensitive to the plight of the unfortunate. Other observers judged Salgado's radiant prints offensive, because they seemed to suggest that misery is the immutable way of the world, or that a divine presence will ennoble those who suffer.

Salgado's defenders point out that formal beauty has suffused panoramas of suffering throughout Christian art, and that, in an age when news photographs of misery are broadcast around the clock, beauty grips the viewer's attention and is a counterweight to the ubiquitous violence of television and film. In an era that that refined remoteness into an art language, Salgado boldly wore his heart on his sleeve. His constant concern for the relief of poverty and disease in Africa helped spur the early twenty-first-century efforts to obtain debt relief for poor countries on that continent.

7.41
SEBASTIÃO SALGADO, *Serra Pelada, Brazil*, from his book
An Uncertain Grace, 1990.

Pushkin conveys the Russians' cautious hopes for economic reform and political liberalization. Like Kuprejanov, Ukrainian photographer Boris Mikhailov (b. 1938) found it necessary to tip-toe around the Soviet bureaucratic rules by using literary references as indirect allusions to social and psychological conditions. His series *By the Ground*, begun in 1991 as Soviet control of Ukraine began to diminish, deliberately makes reference to Maxim Gorky's (1868–1936) celebrated Russian play *The Lower Depths* (1902), which poignantly describes the lives of social outcasts. For this series, Mikhailov literally shot his pictures at belly level, to emphasize degradation. In 1997, Mikhailov began the *Case Studies* series, in which he sarcastically criticized the beginnings of capitalism and its effects by paying hungry, homeless people to pose for him (Fig 7.42). The pictures remain controversial because of what some perceive as the camera's cynical, cold-eyed stare at helpless people. One critic cited them as an example of the pornography of power.[40]

In Chile, during the repressive regime of Augusto Pinochet, neutral vision's purportedly nonpartisan stance was turned in on itself to create images for the political opposition. Photographer Eugenio Dittborn mocked the regime's oppression by making an accusatory hybrid of the identity card and the mugshot (Fig. 7.43). Similarly, Korean Conceptual artist Park Bul-dong (b. 1956) satirized the appearance and purpose of election campaign posters (Fig. 7.44).

No words inform the large, richly detailed, yet uninformative portraits taken by Thomas Ruff (b. 1958), a German photographer who studied with Bernd and Hilla Becher (Fig. 7.45). Ruff adapted the uniform picture-making techniques used by the Bechers to explore the extent to which viewers contribute interpretations to portrait photographs. In contrast to the dramatically lighted portraits of the past, such as those of Carjat (see Fig. 3.5), where posture, lighting, and facial expressions cued a viewer's response, Ruff's work is resolutely uninflected.

The scientific method, neutral vision's mainspring, figures in the work of American-born Canadian photographer Lynne Cohen (b. 1944). No people appear in the icy interiors of lecture halls, laboratories, military installations, and corporate headquarters she photographs. Cohen's sterile interiors evoke a claustrophobia that seems to seep through the antiseptic air. Working primarily in black-and-white, her images share the thin humor of pictures by Conceptual artists such as Ed Ruscha. As writer and cultural critic David Byrne commented, in Cohen's pictures "coolness is being flipped back on itself to look ridiculous."[41] In the scientific observation room, one of Cohen's repeating subjects, it is never clear what activity is being viewed or why (Fig. 7.46). Cohen focuses on the stale sameness of the observers' world, not on the people, animals, or things they scrutinize.

The public's continuing faith in photographic impartiality is an ongoing motif in the work of French artist

7.42
BORIS MIKHAILOV,
Untitled from the *Case History* series, 1997–98.

Mikhailov created more than 500 photographic "case studies" of homeless people in Kharkov, Ukraine, where he watched the steady post-Soviet decline of social services.

7.43
EUGENIO DITTBORN,
Commonplaces, 1984.
Airmail painting no. 8,
rubber stamp and
photosilkscreen on
wrapping paper.

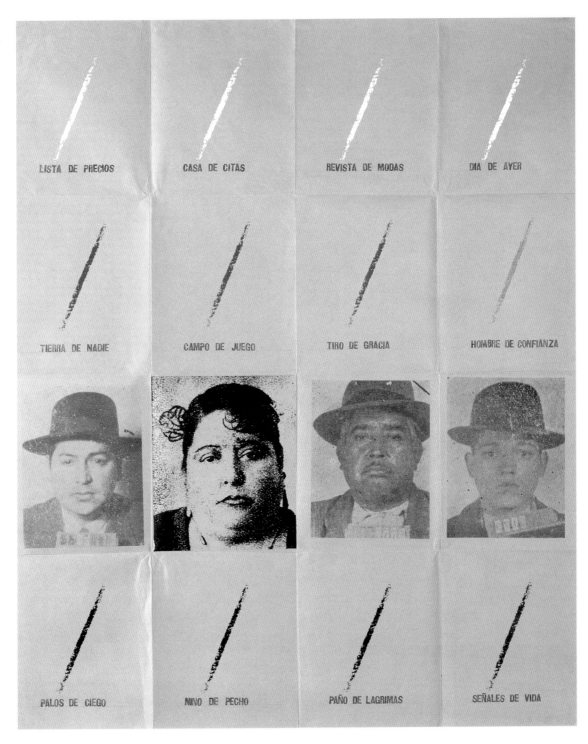

LISTA DE PRECIOS   CASA DE CITAS   REVISTA DE MODAS   DIA DE AYER

TIERRA DE NADIE   CAMPO DE JUEGO   TIRO DE GRACIA   HOMBRE DE CONFIANZA

PALOS DE CIEGO   NIÑO DE PECHO   PAÑO DE LAGRIMAS   SEÑALES DE VIDA

Christian Boltanski (b. 1944). He suggests the public importance of his photo-based installations by setting them in civic spaces, such as Grand Central Terminal in New York, or by inventing the look of public places such as hospitals and churches in his museum installations. Boltanski conjures up the darkened interiors of shrines and churches by using miniature lights that glow like candles. He evokes the past by placing old objects, such as letters and clothing, next to portrait photographs. The dim illumination and religious objects of his *Monuments* (*Les Enfants de Dijon*) (*The Children of Dijon*) hint at a memorial chapel (Fig. 7.47). Black electrical cords, like old cobwebs, power the tiny lights and link the images in an implicit web of meaning.

In France, where Boltanski is considered to be a Conceptual artist who manipulates ideas, his work is understood as a critique of adults' persistent yearning to reclaim the golden days of their youth. Elsewhere, Boltanski's *Monuments* are taken to be poignant mementos filled with emotionally charged references to the Jewish Holocaust. He has resolutely declared

7.45 (above)
THOMAS RUFF, *Portrait,* **1987. Chromogenic color print.**

Ruff's portraits are close-up and impersonal. All the facial details captured by the camera provide physical identity, but offer no clues from which the viewer can ascertain the sitter's mental attitudes or interests. He deliberately attempts to overturn the deeply ingrained notion that one can read personal character from a photograph.

7.44 (above)
PARK BUL-DONG,
Nightmare no. 3 **(Electoral campaign poster), 1985. Collage of photograph and text on paper. Collection of the artist.**

In a series of election posters promoting outlandish fictional candidates, political activist Park Bul-dong taunted the South Korean authorities with sarcastic humor that got him arrested and his work confiscated. His photo-based pieces relate insulting political ideas guaranteed to offend a staid voting public.

7.46 (right)
LYNNE COHEN,
Observation Room, **n.d. Gelatin silver print.**

Cohen's interior shots are frequently undated, adding to their eerie timelessness and banality. The past presence of never seen workers, indicated by forgotten briefcases, soiled coffee cups, or, in this case, a sketch mounted on the table, poses questions about the emotional state of people who inhabit these rooms.

7.47 (right)
CHRISTIAN BOLTANSKI, *Monuments (Les Enfants de Dijon),* (*The Children of Dijon*) 1985. Installation. Black-and-white and color photographs, metal frames, glass, light bulbs, wire.

7.48 (below)
LORNA SIMPSON, *Five-Day Forecast,* 1988. Five black-and-white prints in one frame and ten engraved plaques.

Although the text and pictures in Simpson's work are clear, their combined meaning is not. The bottom row of words listing mistakes is not aligned with the top row listing the days of the week. Simpson places the burden of interpretation on the viewer, whose habits of linking words with pictures serve as a frustrating lesson in the complexity of meaning.

neutrality, stating that his art means whatever it means to individual viewers.

The presence of text accompanying pictures that play on the conventions of neutral vision is no guarantee of additional or clearer meaning. American photographer Lorna Simpson (b. 1960) appended words to her neutral photographs, yet the resulting combinations are puzzling (Fig. 7.48). The faces of the African-Americans in these life-size or over-life-size photographs are deliberately cropped, and their individuality

disguised by plain backgrounds and simple clothing. Simpson uses standardized observational techniques, such as fixed distance, to disguise the differences among her subjects, which can only be observed by carefully looking beyond the visual structures that suggest sameness. The sitter's arm positions and the folds of her simple gown are not identical in each image. When Simpson began to work in film recently, she created comparably enigmatic pictures.

The Cambodian Genocide Photographic Database

When Cambodian Communist leader Pol Pot (c. 1925–1998) assumed leadership in 1975, he directed his troops and supporters, known as the Khmer Rouge, to move urban populations to the countryside to work as farm laborers. Many died by succumbing to starvation, disease, and murder. Ultimately, Pol Pot oversaw the deaths of nearly 2 million of the country's 7 million people. While private possession of a camera was viewed as an emblem of privilege and a tool of political defiance during the Pol Pot era, government-sponsored photographs were produced, among them mugshots of the people who were jailed (Fig. 7.49).

Large-scale rural genocide sites, called the "killing fields," were discovered after Pol Pot's government was defeated by the Vietnamese. Prison records were also uncovered, including those for Phnom Penh's Tuol Sleng prison, known as "S-21," where as many as 20,000 people were imprisoned, tortured, and murdered. More than 5,000 of the Tuol Sleng mugshots have been found. Prisoners in these pictures have official-looking numbers pinned to their clothing,

but the function of the images is not clear. The photographs do not identify specific individuals, nor do they reference remaining records of forced confessions. It may prove true that the pictures catalog batches of prisoners.

At Yale University in New Haven, Connecticut, the Cambodian Genocide Database has made more than 10,000 photographic images and thousands of documents related to the Cambodian holocaust available on the World Wide Web, in the Khmer language as well as English, in hopes that the mostly anonymous victims may be identified. Preserved and restored, the original photographs are part of the collection of the Tuol Sleng Museum of Genocide in Cambodia.[42]

7.49
PHOTOGRAPHER UNKNOWN, *Untitled*
(Cambodian prisoners), 1975–79. Gelatin silver print.

THE LOOK OF POLITICS

During the 1980s in South Africa, photographic agencies such as Dynamic Images, The Brotherhood, Vakalisa, The Black Society of Photographers, and Afrapix were founded to lend support to image-makers such as Peter Magubane and David Goldblatt, who were committed to using photography in the struggle for social change. These collectives furnished images to alternative and underground newspapers, as well as to the world press.

Afrapix, which ceased activity in 1990, included younger members such

7.50
SANTU MOFOKENG,
Shebeen in White City, Soweto, c. 1987. Gelatin silver print. © Santu Mofokeng/South Photographs.

7.51
ZWELETHU MTHETHWA, *Untitled,* 2002. Chromogenic color print.

An emphasis on individual creativity characterizes Mthewtha's extensive study of the private spaces people create in their homes. Mthewtha was rigorous in obtaining the approval of the sitters who feature prominently in his images.

as Johannesburg-born Santu Mofokeng (b. 1956), who moved from street photography to a more stylized and autobiographical approach to his work. As Mofokeng wrote, "I was unhappy with the propaganda images which reduced life in the townships into one of perpetual struggle, because I felt this representation to be incomplete."[43] In the politically charged atmosphere of apartheid in South Africa, when photographers were greeted with suspicion by many factions, the desire to move away from overtly political photography was taken by anti-apartheid partisans as a token of irresponsibility. Still, Mofokeng persisted in showing aspects of "unvictimized" life in the neighborhoods, as well as moments of camaraderie and enjoyment (Fig. 7.50). Within the context of South African photography, he invented a new social documentary approach.

In his recent work, Mofokeng has been collecting urban family albums made by middle- and working-class African blacks, and presenting the images in slide shows that recall the days before racial policy split South Africa. Like his scenes of everyday life, which were so long excluded from public view, the old family portraits and other scenes had not been accumulated by libraries or museums. Zwelethu Mthethwa (b. 1960), who lives in Cape Town, is equally concerned to underscore the strength and pride of people, who, despite the end of apartheid in 1994, still endure unemployment and live in shantytowns. Since 2000, he has been photographing people in the unique interior settings they have made for themselves (Fig. 7.51). With a host of artists, writers, and photographers, Mofokeng, Mthethwa, and Goldblatt emerged from the isolation that apartheid brought with it and quickly achieved wide recognition in international exhibits.

THE NEW SOCIAL DOCUMENTARY

In the United States, a new social documentary also followed from specific political and social circumstances. A mix of anti-Vietnam War activism and Conceptual art ideas helped shape a new philosophy and practice that differed from the work done by Eugene Richards and Mary Ellen Mark. The ideas and interests of an informal study group that formed during the mid-1970s in California proved important to a generation looking for direction about photographic practice in general, and documentary projects in particular. Members of this group, including Martha Rosler (b. 1943), Allan Sekula, and Fred Lonidier (b. 1942), emerged as intellectual and visual leaders of a new social documentary.

Among the most widely influential writings read by the group, and by others seeking a fresh direction in photography, was a 1936 essay penned by German historian and critic Walter Benjamin, called "The Work of Art in the Age of Mechanical Reproduction." Benjamin held that mechanical reproduction, principally based in film and photographic techniques, was capable of breaking down what he called the "aura" of the original work of art—that is, our sense of an art work's uniqueness based on its having been made at a particular time and occupying a singular physical space. Simply put, he reasoned that, when multiple cheap reproductions of a work of art such as Leonardo da Vinci's *Mona Lisa* were readily available, many people could own it, and, therefore, would not feel a need to visit the original. In effect, there would be no original, because the actual painting would come to be understood as just another copy. Benjamin held that this ongoing democratization was the forerunner of a sweeping historical change that would break down tradition, making way for revolutionary social and cultural change.

It hardly mattered that Benjamin, writing decades before the glut of mass media, including television, was wrong about the popular effect of mechanical reproduction. In truth, the vast manufacture and marketing of copies, be they of art or music, only increased people's desire to see the original in a museum or to hear it played at a concert. What attracted most of his readers was not Benjamin's historical foresight, nor his vision of a profoundly different socialist future, but his notion that the original could vanish in a welter of facsimiles. Benjamin's essay confirmed the existence of an image-world that molded people's perception of themselves, forged their desires, and fashioned their political beliefs. Importantly, the essay implied that political action consisted not only of protests, like those during the Vietnam War, but also of an ongoing, vigorous questioning of conventions and stereotypes promulgated by the mass media.

The study group also encountered the thoughts of Benjamin's close friend the German critic and playwright Bertolt Brecht (1898–1956). The new social documentarians and their supporters favored analysis of the social and political context of photographs, and often vindicated their view with Benjamin's approving reference to Brecht's notion that "less than ever does a simple *reproduction of reality* express something about reality."[44] Among the other Brechtian ideas that found favor was his understanding of how to affect an audience with a story. Brecht believed in constructing obviously artificial situations and disrupting the anticipated narrative with the unexpected.

The study group also looked at contemporary art and film, especially the experimental work of French filmmaker Jean-Luc Godard (b. 1930), from whom they took the idea of recasting older themes and of thwarting the illusion of reality by letting the means of picture-making show. They debated articles appearing in *Screen*, a British journal whose theoretical inquiries into film realism could be broadly applied to other visual media.[45] In an interview with Benjamin Buchloh, himself an influential historian and critic of photographic practice, Rosler commented, "we wanted to be documentarians in a way that documentarians hadn't been. As readers of Brecht, we wanted to use obviously theatrical or dramatized sequences or performance elements together with more traditional documentary strategies, to use text, irony, absurdity, mixed forms of all types."[46]

Even before the study-group sessions, Rosler made political art in the form of three photomontage series called *Bringing Home the War* (1967–72) that combined mass-media images of the Vietnam conflict with pictures taken from design and architectural magazines (Fig. 7.52). Similarly, Lonidier integrated his political activities with his black-and-white photography, as in his *Twenty-nine Arrests: Headquarters of the 12th Naval District, May 2, 1972*, and Sekula was working on what he called

a photonovel, titled *This Ain't China* (1974), a fabricated tale about rebellion by food-service workers. Soon, Rosler, Lonidier, and Sekula were at the core of what, by the mid-1980s, was being called the "new documentary," or the "new social documentary," created by sophisticated, college-educated, politically active intellectuals who wanted to use photography as an important element of social critique.

Historian and critic Abigail Solomon-Godeau observed at the time that "it seems increasingly justified to speak of a new generation of photographers committed to rethinking documentary in a rigorous and serious way."[47] These thinkers did not want to make photographs so much as integrate image-making into political analyses of poverty and injustice. They vigorously studied historical documentary photography, such as that of Jacob Riis, Lewis Hine, and the Farm Security Administration photographers (see Figs. 4.47–4.50), and attempted to find ways in which they could comment on social oppression without generating what they called "victim photographs" that only evoked self-satisfying sympathy or excited voyeurism among viewers. Wary of fashioning such

7.52
MARTHA ROSLER,
House Beautiful,
c. 1967–72, from the
series *Bringing Home
the War.* **Collage.**

Using collage, political artists such as Rosler created up-to-date commentary by ripping pictures from newspapers and magazines. The juxtaposition of terror-stricken Vietnamese peasants and chic modern domestic interiors highlighted the disparities among Western and non-Western nations engaged in the Vietnam War.

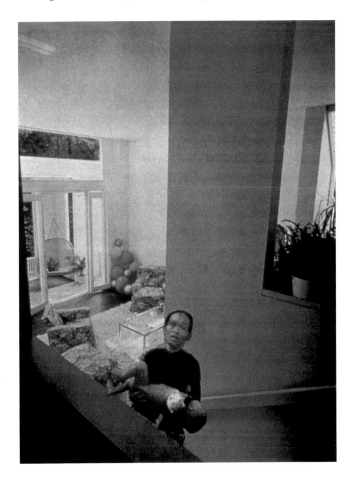

images, the new social documentarians surrounded their photographs with copious text that illuminated wider issues of corporate greed and government neglect, and expressed the experiences of manual workers and the poor. With limited success, they struggled to find venues beyond the art world for their work.

Lonidier went on to make investigative series, such as *The Health and Safety Game* (1976), in which he juxtaposed photographs of workers' injuries and appended statements by them.[48] Aware of the social and economic distance between himself and the subjects of his photographs, Lonidier wrote that artists who pursue oppositional cultural practice must continually search for non-elitist ways of practicing.[49] Starting with his early photographs, Lonidier worked closely with labor unions. The effect of his continuing political agitation was witnessed during his 1999 exhibit in Tijuana, Mexico, which was critical of the North American Free Trade Agreement (NAFTA) and the establishment of *maquiladoras* (internationally run factories in Mexico, near the United States border, that employ Mexicans at a fraction of American wages). The show was shut down by the concerted efforts of the manufacturers, who put pressure on the Mexican government.

Lonidier's work received less academic attention than the images and ideas circulated by Rosler and Sekula, whose writings were widely read and debated in colleges, universities, and art journals. In particular, Rosler's image-and-text series *The Bowery in Two Inadequate Descriptive Systems* (1974–75) condensed notions of documentary that held sway throughout the 1980s. Explaining the series, Rosler wrote that it is "a work of refusal. It is not defiant antihumanism. It is meant as an act of criticism."[50] In her *Bowery* series, Rosler demonstrated how both language and images are insufficient to a full description of a poor area of New York City where homeless persons gather to drink alcoholic beverages (Fig. 7.53). She did not set out to provoke concern for the plight of those living in the Bowery; instead, she tried to examine the weakness of words and pictures to encompass social realities, and to puncture humanist assumptions about documentary photography's ability to contribute to human progress.[51]

Beginning in the late 1970s, critical essays on the history and theory of photography by Rosler and Sekula, along with Douglas Crimp, Christopher Phillips, Rosalind Krauss, Abigail Solomon-Godeau, and Sally Stein, hit the field of photographic studies like a sharp wind. Some readers resentfully closed their windows and turned away from what they identified as a damaging storm; others let the gust into the increasingly interdependent realms of the museum, gallery, and art school, where it unsettled received ideas. By 1983, when *New York Times* photography critic Andy Grundberg wrote his essay "Two Camps Battle over the Nature of the Medium," it had become obvious that "lines are drawn between those who think of photography as a relatively new and largely virgin branch of art history, and those who rebel at the very notion of photography being 'estheticized.'" "The split is real," Grundberg commented, "and the rhetoric is fierce."[52]

**7.53
MARTHA ROSLER,**
The Bowery in Two Inadequate Descriptive Systems, **1974–75. Text and gelatin silver prints.**

In this series, Rosler paired photographs and slang words for drunkenness. None of the images shows people, just empty liquor containers. Similarly, the words offer only shorthand stereotypes, not lives as they are lived. The two parallel representational systems do not add up to a thorough description of the area.

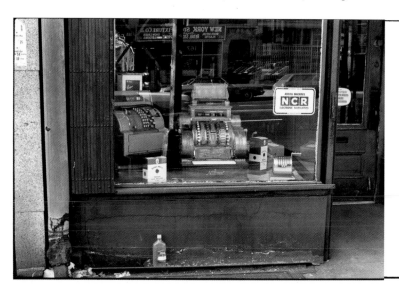

stewed

boiled

potted

corned

pickled

preserved

canned

fried to the hat

Among the most forceful new writers was artist-critic Allan Sekula, who combined political theory, social commentary, and photographic criticism in a way reminiscent of the politically engaged European artists and photographers between the world wars. Like Martha Rosler, Sekula insisted that photography was not simply an autonomous picture-making system, but was knit into the broad patterns of global history. He reproached Edward Steichen's *The Family of Man* exhibition for its influential attempts to construct photography as a universal language, and for its covert promotion of the family "as the exclusive arena of all desire and pleasure."[53] With others, including British writers David Green and John Tagg, Sekula examined the history of photography within the development of fact-finding and cataloging systems, such as prison photographs and anthropometric images, that is, pictures made to show measurement of the human body, and thereby substantiate racial stereotypes.[54]

Sekula's essay "On the Invention of Photographic Meaning" (1975) became one of the most read, discussed, and anthologized articles within art and photography circles. Its basic premise, that the photograph is not a clear window on reality, but defined by the culture and setting in which it is found, became a commonplace in the field, especially among image-makers and historians looking for new ways to reinsert photography into the social world. Like Rosler, Sekula bluntly announced that "the ills of photography are the ills of aestheticism."[55]

In his writing and photography, Sekula proved to be less pessimistic than other critics about the ability of photography to document social experience and to effect change. He insisted that he did not want to "ignore or suppress the creative, affective, and expressive aspects of cultural activity, [because] to do so would be to play into the hands of the ongoing technocratic obliteration of human creativity."[56] Sekula praised the photographic collages of John Heartfield for deconstructing Nazi propaganda, and cited Rosler's *The Bowery in Two Inadequate Descriptive Systems* as coming "the closest to having an unrelenting *metacritical* relation to the documentary genre."[57] He maintained that the window-on-the-world style of concerned documentary and photojournalism had to give way to "a hybridized, pictorially disrespectful narrative approach to the photographic medium."[58] He commended Lonidier's images, and his aim to show his case-studies outside the art world. Significantly, Sekula was also one of the few critics to extend his perspective to other than Western settings. While discussing the photography of Ernest Cole, who worked for *Drum* magazine in South Africa (see pp. 321–23), Sekula recognized that distinct social situations, such as racial apartheid, called for approaches particular to the situation. Moreover, he cautioned critics and photographers that it "would be wise to avoid an overly monolithic conception of realism, [because] not all realisms necessarily play into the hands of the police."[59]

In discussing Cole's work, Sekula noted that the South African preferred to construct narratives using photography and text in situations such as unemployment or workplace struggles, where "ideology fails to provide a 'rational' and consoling interpretation of the world."[60] Indeed, Sekula's series, from the early *This Ain't China* (1974), through *Fish Story* (1987–1995; exhibition 2000), a seven-year-long multimedia investigation of the maritime trades, to *Geography Lesson* (1997), which links changes in the Canadian landscape to the mining industry and wealth-seeking, Sekula remained constant in his efforts to relate the lives of working people to the expansion and changes of global capitalism. For example, he collaborated with the writer-activists Alexander Cockburn and Jeffrey St. Clair, to photograph the 1999 protests against World Trade Organization labor policy in Seattle, Washington.

Speculating in 1986, Abigail Solomon-Godeau worried that the political philosophy of the new documentarians would be marginalized within the art and photographic communities. In fact, the opposite occurred. The new documentarians found ample support within the art world, whose practices and supporters were the subject of their critiques, and at universities, where they gained influential faculty positions. New social documentary joined the panoply of late twentieth-century photographic practice. It did not dislodge the continuing popularity of earlier documentary approaches, such as the alienated vision advanced by Robert Frank (see pp. 339–41), the personal interaction model used by Eugene Richards, or the universal humanism exhibited at the *Family of Man* show.

Interestingly, the new social documentarians did not make the distribution of cameras and instruction a central part of their political work, which, to be fair, was intentionally aimed a elites in an effort to reform elite knowledge. With the exception of Lonidier, who spent more than twenty-five years working with unions and other labor organizations, the new documentarians wrote in language that required familiarity with history and philosophical distinctions, an obvious obstacle to non-intellectual audiences. Nevertheless, two photographers pioneered the use of photography to improve the ability of children to read and write. For more than twenty-five years, American Wendy Ewald (b. 1951) has helped children value themselves and their photographs in a career that affected both rich and poor. In 2005, London-born, Montreal-raised photographer Zana Briski (b. 1966 won an Academy Award (with Ross Kaufmann) for the film *Born into Brothels*, based on her many years of working in India

with the unfortunate children whose circumstances are starkly revealed in the film's title.

In Britain, however, various activist organizations used photography to communicate with the public at large. Beginning in the mid-1970s, the Hackney Flashers, of which Jo Spence (see below) was a member, produced photographic exhibitions and slide sets on women and inequity in the workplace, which traveled beyond the art gallery to community centers and libraries. Similarly, from the late 1970s to the early 1990s, Lorraine Leeson (b. 1951) and Peter Dunn (b. 1946) collaborated with community groups to conceive visual responses to cutbacks and facility closures in a largely working-class neighborhood. Through such projects as the Bethnal Green Hospital Campaign (Fig. 7.54), the East London Health Project, and the Docklands Community Poster Project, they circumvented government-influenced mainstream media outlets, distributing eye-catching billboards and street posters as well as postcards. These were sent to other cities where neighborhoods situated in former industrial areas were being threatened by unsympathetic redevelopment.

**7.54
LORRAINE LEESON
AND PETER DUNN,**
Health Cuts Can Kill,
one of a series for the
**Bethnal Green Hospital
Campaign, 1978. Street
posters.**

Leeson and Dunn
created posters and
billboards to show how
closing public health
facilities would affect
people in the working-
class East London
neighborhood. The
signs told their own
story, but also countered
proposed plans to turn
the neighborhood into
a gentrified area.

Where American theorists tended to be overwhelmed by what they perceived as the mighty tide of mass-media images crushing all efforts at societal change, social documentarians and activists such as the Hackney Flashers held that political and personal transitions were possible, and could be achieved through photographs that exposed injustice. Similarly, as Nelly Richards reported on the use of the medium under the Pinochet regime in Chile (see p. 312), the opposition to the right-wing dictator believed photography to be a means of exposing the conditions that the military regime sought to hide, including the so-called torture and "disappearances" of protestors. Although Chilean image-makers associated with the opposition, such as Eugenio Dittborn, acknowledged the sway of mass media, they chose not to accept the nihilistic view that change was unattainable.

THINKING PHOTOGRAPHY

Attempts to conceive a new social documentary were based on a thoughtful rejection of documentary traditions, as well as the incorporation of ideas from outside the area of photographic practice. Just as nineteenth-century photographer Peter Henry Emerson investigated contemporary philosophical and scientific ideas for ways to reform photography, so late twentieth-century photographers looked to concepts outside the discipline to inform their philosophy. The 1982 book *Thinking Photography*, edited by artist-critic Victor Burgin, introduced a new audience to the debates within the field of photographic studies, through an anthology of Burgin's own writing, and that of others, including Benjamin and Sekula.

One of the most influential thinkers in the period was French philosopher Roland Barthes, who coined two terms that were much discussed in photographic criticism. The first, *studium*, designated photographic content that interests the intellect; the second, *punctum*, taken from the Latin word for "to puncture," referred to the sudden arresting effect that a photographic image can have on the viewer. The terms were introduced in Barthes's 1980 book *Camera Lucida*, which, despite its title,

referred not to the pre-photographic tool used to make images, but to a philosophical light (*lucida*) thrown on photographic practice. Reviewing family photographs, Barthes found himself reacting only to the *studium*, or factual basis of the images, until he encountered a picture of his mother as a five-year-old child standing with her seven-year-old brother on a little wooden bridge in the family's Winter Garden, or greenhouse. "Something like an essence of the Photograph floated in this particular picture," Barthes wrote. Because the experience was so personal, Barthes refused to illustrate the photograph. "It exists only for me," he observed: "For you, it would be nothing but an indifferent picture, one of the thousand manifestations of the 'ordinary.'"[61]

While contributing *studium* and *punctum* to contemporary critical discourse, *Camera Lucida*'s personal, unsystematic, and mystical essay disappointed some critics, who were hoping that Barthes would (uncharacteristically) use the book as an opportunity to bring together his earlier thoughts on photography. *Camera Lucida* followed other influential writing on photography. In "The Photographic Message" (1961), Barthes wrote that the newspaper photograph has two messages, one brimming with socially inscribed "denoted" and "connoted" meanings, which ride on a second perception that photography is "a message *without a code*." In other words, he recognized that photography itself is an idea or mental concept, grounded in the notion of neutral vision. Another seminal question, articulated in such books as *S/Z* (1970; English translation 1974) and such essays as "The Rhetoric of the Image" (1964), and "The Death of the Author" (1968), repeatedly queried the notion of originality. Barthes suggested that, for a visual or verbal text to be understood, its meanings must already exist in the social world. Consequently, the text, and, for that matter, perception of the world, cannot be entirely new, but result from a combination of already extant meanings that the reader/viewer brings to the text or image. When images and text exist together, as in photojournalism and advertising, the interplay between the bundles of meaning becomes even more complex, though not original.

Similar ideas were advanced by the French philosopher and historian Michel Foucault, who wrote persuasive books and essays on the furtive nature of power and pondered the originality of authors. Like Barthes, Foucault politicized photography without linking it to any particular social movement or cause.

For photographers and critics, the writings of Barthes and Foucault opened the way to a philosophical and historical reconsideration of photographic practice and discredited pictures of the kind deemed original by virtue of individual expression. Their ideas suggested a new image-making, cognizant of the social re-production of meaning, especially in mass media. Such ideas were close to those discussed and acted upon by Rosler, Sekula, and Lonidier, who tried to find new ways to integrate political action and camerawork. The photographers who admired both Barthes and Foucault, however, were frequently less politically active than the new social documentarians. They sought new insights and incentives for picture-making, not for directions on how to change society.

One of the most powerful ideas taken from Barthes and other thinkers concerned the futility of originality. Since mass-media photography was replete with messages, new pictures were not needed. In part or in full, existing images could be appropriated and re-exhibited. These "ready-mades" differed from the everyday objects earlier proposed as art by Marcel Duchamp (see Fig. 5.17), in that they were not things but pictures of things frequently marketed to arouse consumer desire. Some photographers argued that these acts of appropriation were inherently subversive, because the effect of seeing mass-media images framed in a new context would enlighten and politicize beholders. The recognition that images pilfered from magazines and newspapers had visual forebears in Dada photography, as well as in experimental camerawork between the world wars, sparked a renewed interest in what had hitherto been a neglected area of historical scholarship.

Beginning in the late 1970s, American critics such as Rosalind Krauss, Craig Owens, Hal Foster, and Douglas Crimp focused on the demise of the original as a vastly important sign that Modernism, with its enthronement of artistic expression and originality, was also dying. Two widely read essays by Crimp, "Pictures" (1977) and "The Photographic Activity of Postmodernism" (1980), linked photography to French theory and to Benjamin's notions of aura and originality. Crimp was also among the earliest observers to see the fulfillment of contemporary theory in new approaches to photography, such as those employed by Cindy Sherman (b. 1954) (see Fig. 7.35) and Sherrie Levine (b. 1947), whom he included in the 1977 New York exhibition *Pictures*, from which the essay was derived. By the late 1970s, photography was rapidly emerging as the vogue art, not simply because of its growing acceptance in the art world, but because of the way it dovetailed in practical terms with contemporary concerns about representation and originality. Simultaneously, the term "Postmodern" became current, to characterize what was increasingly perceived as a new period following Modernism.

THE POSTMODERN ERA

The concept of the Postmodern or Postmodernity predated what has become known as the Postmodern era. Historian Arnold Toynbee employed the term in *A Study of History* (written before World War II, but not published until 1947) to speculate on a vast historical period that began in the late nineteenth century, and which would culminate with the decline of Western power and the rise of non-Western societies. Toynbee's sweeping hypothesis was largely forgotten in the late twentieth century when Jean-François Lyotard's dense, short 1979 book *The Postmodern Condition* (English translation, 1984) posited Postmodernism as the next phase of Modernism. Lyotard maintained that Modernism's successor was already at work, disintegrating "metanarratives," or grand, longstanding social rationales about the improvability of the human condition made possible by the progress of knowledge, especially science. As these overarching visions declined, Lyotard argued that they would be replaced not by other unifying ideas but by a welter of competing notions, whose fertile chaos would feed a new freedom from the oppression and authority of scientific knowledge.

Lyotard's analysis was fanciful, underestimating the predominance of science and the prodigious ability of capitalism to adapt with the times. Nevertheless, from his book, philosophers, social commentators, critics, and artists construed a broad theory that explained and justified the present moment as a state of flux, propelled by instantaneous information churned out by mass media, and shaped by global finance and business networks, whose prevalence lessened the importance of the nation state in the world order.

In art circles, Postmodernism came to mean a rejection of themes and subjects that interested Modernist artists, such as abstraction and the subjective expression of unique intellects. Artists in many media reintroduced the human figure, or turned to mass-produced kitsch for image sources. Photographers, too, dwelled on the body, often deriving or appropriating images from commerce, advertising, and film. Some explored the potentials of the blurred image, in which forms were suggested but not clearly delineated.

In his essay for the catalog accompanying the *Pictures* exhibit, Crimp acknowledged how the experience of media created a generation gap between those raised on television, movies, and ubiquitous magazines, and those brought up in the less image-saturated culture of the period prior to World War II. "To an ever greater extent," he wrote, "our experience is governed by pictures, pictures in newspapers and magazines, on television and in the cinema. Next to these pictures, firsthand experience begins to retreat, to seem more and more trivial. While it once seemed that pictures had the function of interpreting reality, it now seems that they have usurped it."[62] Soon after, in response to another exhibit ominously called "Last Exit: Painting," critic Thomas Lawson argued that "the camera, in all its manifestations, is our god, dispensing what we mistakenly take to be truth."[63]

Although her writing was seldom cited by commentators on Postmodernism and photography, cultural critic Susan Sontag (1933–2004) built her widely read book *On Photography* (1977) upon the notion of a similar, even more noxious "Image-World," in which photographs injured human memory and drained away the instinct to know the world at first hand. This remove from reality, in Sontag's view, left us passive viewers at a spectacle of recycled pictures.[64] Sontag did not, however, put forward the consummate Postmodern conviction that, because of its omnipresence, the image world provided a new source of realism for artists. She maintained that an authentic, valuable, first-hand reality had been plundered and debased. In sum, a chilly, sobering down-draft in the intellectual climate whirled away any remnants of Marshall McLuhan's rapturous 1960s' praise for the mass media's educational and peace-making powers (see p. 382).

POSTMODERNIST PHOTOGRAPHY

Among the artists included in Douglas Crimp's *Pictures*, and discussed in his "The Photographic Activity of Postmodernism," was Sherrie Levine, who confronted the art world with her re-photographed well-known images made by famous photographers such as Edward Weston, Walker Evans, and Eliot Porter. Called "APPROPRIATION," Levine's reuse of images such as Walker Evans's image of Allie Mae Burroughs (see Fig. 5.0), highlighted the ubiquity of the copy and the insignificance of the original. To make her point, she photographed art and photography examples reproduced in books so as to contrast copying a copy with original archival images and printing original negatives. By taking an image, rather than making an image, Levine repressed the notion of her art as original and unique. By the late twentieth-century, Levine's appropriations were themselves being appropriated by other artists, including Dylan Stone (b. 1967), who took her black-and-white copies of Eugène Atget's Paris interiors and exhibited them as small three-dimensional, full-color set into shoe boxes.

More frequently, appropriationists procured mass-media images. Artist and writer Richard Prince (b. 1949) found his source images in magazines, cutting, cropping, rearranging, and reprinting them to isolate the devices used in advertising to summon up desire

(Fig. 7.55). Levine and Prince are typical examples of the powerful convergence of image-making and social analysis that occurred during the last decades of the twentieth century. Social-science observation by artists, expressed primarily in art, became known as critical practice.

In *Pictures*, Douglas Crimp noted the work of Cindy Sherman, who would become one of the most celebrated image-makers of the 1980s and 1990s. Her series of black-and-white photographs called *Untitled Film Stills* seemed to be derived from 1950s B-movie melodramas and from film stills — that is, the photographs displayed in theater lobbies. The film still exaggerated movie-born gender stereotypes, especially that of the beleaguered, fretful, or frightened heroine. While Sherman found suggestions in film-still poses, she did not make reference to any particular movie. Photographing herself in make-up, wigs, and costumes, she imitated or evoked a culturally prevalent image (Fig. 7.56). Viewers could recognize the source of her images, not

because she actually clipped them from old movies, but because the poses she assumed condensed the much-repeated portrayal of women in films.

Crimp pointed out that Sherman's self-portraits do not ever reveal Cindy Sherman. Her *faux* film fragments played up the notion of the Postmodern copy and its opposition to the ideas of invention and genius. Sherman's later work shifted to larger, deeply saturated color pictures, in which she performed appearances based on pin-ups, fairy tales, and Old Master paintings. Eventually, she took herself out of the picture, substituting prostheses or plastic body parts used in medical education, and combining them to form grotesque bodies in the manner of Surrealist photographer Hans Bellmer (see Fig. 5.24). Despite these changes, Sherman's interest remained constant throughout the last decades of the twentieth century, as she continued to expose not only the shallowness of gender stereotyping but also the titillating pleasure of looking.

7.55
RICHARD PRINCE,
Untitled (Cowboys), 1993. Ektacolor print. Barbara Gladstone Gallery, New York.

Through the 1980s, during the presidency of Ronald Reagan, Prince worked on a series of cowboy images derived from ads for Marlboro cigarettes. Usually more grainy and blurry than the originals, the appropriated images ironically maintain much of the glamor that was used to sell cigarettes. In addition, they becloud the American West as a heroic terrain.

436

CONVERGENCES (1975–2000)

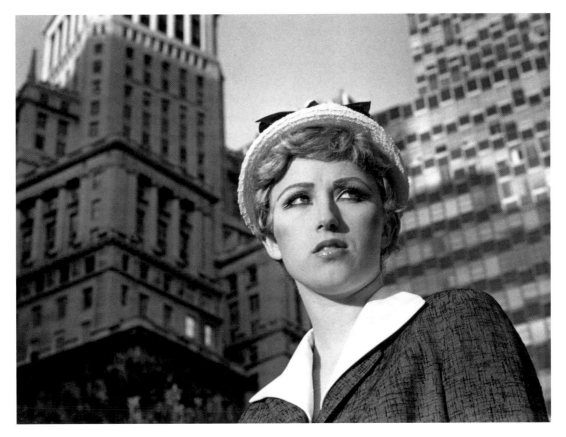

**7.56
CINDY SHERMAN,
Untitled Film Still, 1978.**

Sherman costumed
and coiffed herself to
look like troubled and
anxious women from
B-movies of the 1950s.
She enacted the stereo-
typical role of the
woman in jeopardy, not
taken from a specific
film, but improvised
from an array of them.

ART PHOTOGRAPHY AND PHOTOGRAPHY-BY-ARTISTS

The mid-1970s witnessed the increased use of photography by artists who usually worked in other media, and the retreat from conventional art photo-graphy by image-makers such as Cindy Sherman. Noting the development, critic Abigail Solomon-Godeau commented that "although the attempt to draw a distinction between art photography and photography done by artists might initially be taken for a semantic quibble, or worse, as informed by the desire to privilege the photographic work of artists over that of photographers, there remain significant differences in the two forms of practice."[65]

Art photography, of course, had a history going back to the beginnings of the medium. One of Daguerre's first success-ful photographs rendered a traditional art subject, the still life (see Fig. 1.12). The quintessential art photographer was Alfred Stieglitz, an unashamed elitist who positioned art photography as the moral opposite of crass commercial imaging. As Solomon-Godeau pointed out, art photographers continued to trea-sure subjective and intuitive expression, the intricacies of craft, and the sharp dividing line between fine art and commercial imagery. Briefly put, art

photography aspired to the condition of painting, which meant recognition as a fully-fledged art, and access to the inter-twined realms of gallery and museum.

In contrast, photography-by-artists owed little to the traditional aspirations and values of art photography. It critiqued the notion of personal expression, hold-ing up to public view the way in which the mass media spewed out copies of copies of copies of stereotypes. For those who praised and those who disparaged her work, Cindy Sherman became the exemplar of the photography-by-artists movement. In fact, she was one of the first image-makers who worked exclusively in the medium to be called an artist rather than a photographer.[66] Of course, the renunciation of personal expression was central to the philosophy of Conceptual artists and photographers, such as Edward Ruscha, who dispassion-ately itemized and compiled ready-made images of ordinary locations and build-ings, such as gas stations and motel swimming pools (see Fig. 6.96).

Ideally, photography-by-artists was intended as part of a broad social inter-vention, aimed at exposing the so-called illusions of individuality and originality that formed the bulwark of the art mar-ket. In fact, the boundary between art photography and photography-by-artists broke down almost as soon as it was conceived. By the mid-1980s, photography-by-artists had not shattered or reformed the art market, but had refreshed and recommercialized the notion of the avant-garde artist, whose attacks on mainstream society and consumerism had become an expected and marketable model of artistic behavior. Photography-by-artists was represented in chic galleries and showcased in prominent exhibitions and books. Because of its links to contemporary theories of language, notions of representation, and gender identity, photography-by-artists received an international academic welcome. It was the recurrent subject of lectures and discussions, not only in art and photography departments but also in literature, philosophy, and sociology classes.

For its part, the art photography exemplified by Stieglitz did not lose its appeal for the public but considerably increased in monetary value, as evidenced by the high auction prices recorded during the late twentieth-century economic boom. During the late 1970s and 1980s, the uncertain distinctions between art photography and photography-by-artists helped break down the compartmentalization of museum departments according to media, a configuration that was already taxed by hard-to-categorize activities such as installation and performance art. Heads of museum painting departments and photography departments vied with each other to collect work by such artists as Cindy Sherman. Sometimes museum photography departments broadened their acquisition goals; at other times new positions were created to embrace what were, and are, called "new media."

By the end of the century, the terms "photo-based artist" and "photo-based work" replaced "photography-by-artists," and with that substitution also vanished the association of photography-by-artists with a tough, ongoing social or media criticism. At century's end, photo-based work was normal fare. Surveying the New York gallery scene during the year 2000, critic David Rimanelli observed a "narrowing of that time-honored (if rarely acknowledged) distinction between those spaces devoted to contemporary art (including that which is photographically based) and venues catering to photography." "Given its absolute and tiresome omnipresence," he opined, photography "looks like the academic painting of our time."[67]

BLURRING THE SUBJECT

The Postmodern notion of indeterminate, circular meaning gave the blurred image a new lease on life as a multivalent symbol, alluding to transient and fragmentary moments, fuzzy or disfigured identities, or indistinct and ambiguous knowledge. Interestingly, blur has had many uses in the history of photography, the best-known of which was the Pictorialist image, with its pretensions to high art. More recently, photographers such as Duane Michals blurred the actions of human figures to add mystery and wonder to a scene. Likewise, Tunisian photographer Kamel Dridi (b. 1951) revealed Muslim religious life in North Africa and Saudi Arabia in photographs published in the leading French newspaper *Le Monde*. He uniquely employed blurred images to evoke, for people brought up in the Muslim faith, early memories of ceremonial movements and gestures (Fig. 7.57).

Since the mid-1960s, German painter Gerhard Richter has reworked photographic sources, often his own snapshots, creating paintings that maintain photography's deep perspective, but blurring the surface almost to the point of unrecognizability. Some of his so-called "photo paintings" glow with suffused Romantic light, but others have a sinister dreaminess to them, as if the subject, hovering between painting and photography, cannot or will not allow itself to be fully grasped (Fig. 7.58). Produced a decade after the events, Richter's paintings refer to a specific incident of the deaths in prison of political activists, only to obscure it like a memory that is ten years old. Through blur, which indicates an eye dimmed with tears and a mind clouded with opinions, he transformed simple archival photographs into symbols for the tangled issue of German historical memory in and of the twentieth century. The smudged surfaces of the canvases erased the sharpness of their newspaper sources, imitating not only hazy recall but also the sense of lost idealism, felt especially by Germans who lived through the tensions and moral compromises of the Cold War.

Blur also found a place in staged photographs. While they were students at Yale University, photographer David Levinthal (b. 1949) and Garry Trudeau (b. 1948), the cartoonist who draws the political comic strip *Doonesbury*, collaborated on a book called *Hitler Moves East: A Graphic Chronicle, 1941–43* (1977). Levinthal leads viewers to believe that they are looking at old, blurred action shots of World War II taken by an intrepid photojournalist. In fact, he fabricated table-top scenes with toy soldiers and then obscured the resulting photograph sufficiently so that its miniature source was not immediately apparent. Viewers fill in missing visual information from their memories of war portrayed in photojournalism and film.

The work of James Welling (b. 1951) is also purposefully misleading. He photographs what appear to be black-and-white renditions of abstract paintings, or deeply shadowed abstract photographs in the manner of Aaron Siskind and Frederick Sommer (see Figs. 6.34, 6.36). Welling relies on the viewer's recollection of abstract art, especially as seen for years in black-and-white photography, to accept the absence of recognizable subject matter in *August 16a* (Fig. 7.59). In fact, the picture is no more than a shadowy close-up of aluminum foil.

German-born photographer Uta Barth (b. 1958) creates fragmentary,

7.58
GERHARD RICHTER, *Shot Down (1)*, 1988, from his series *18 Oktober 1977*. Oil on canvas, 39 1/4 × 55 in (99.7 × 139.7 cm).

For *18 Oktober 1977*, a series of gray-toned paintings centering on the prison deaths of several left-wing activists, Richter blurred lurid newspaper photographs. Claiming not to be political, he maintained that he wanted to portray ideological commitment, not a particular point of view.[68] Nothing is certain about the deaths; the activists may have taken their own lives, or been murdered.

7.57 (above)
KAMEL DRIDI, *Mosque, Fes*, 1987. Société Française de la Photographie, Paris.

The bare lightbulb contrasts with the soft, suffused light emanating from the mosque's interior. Dridi records moments of daily prayer in which the faithful make gestures signaling submission to the will of Allah.

7.59
JAMES WELLING,
August 16a, 1980.
Gelatin silver print.

CONVERGENCES (1975–2000)

7.60
UTA BARTH, *Ground #42*, 1994. Color photograph on panel.

The rooms Barth photographs are usually almost empty, so as to emphasize their existence as containers for light. She focuses here on the unoccupied foreground space so as to blur the depth of field out of which dimly emerge two reproductions of paintings by Johannes Vermeer, *The Milkmaid* (Rijksmuseum, Amsterdam) on the left and *The Lacemaker* (Louvre, Paris) on the right. Barth's technique recalls Julia Margaret Cameron, for whom the avoidance of focus could suit the mood of her subject matter (see Fig. 3.18).

fuzzy pictures that depict light and color punctuated by wisps of identifiable subject matter (Fig. 7.60). In Barth's work, any trace of narrative seems to dissolve, an effect hastened by her off-kilter, seemingly out-of-focus approach. In fact, she does focus her work, but on an imaginary plane of space, rather than recognizable objects. She seeks to present the peripheral and marginal—the things that stand on the edge of our attention. To stress her interest in perception, she sometimes hangs her work at eye-level. Her photographs express the impossibility of intelligible experience or certain definition, as well as the desire, however repressed, to seek pleasure in simply looking. Her technique recalls the attitude of Victorian photographer Julia Margaret Cameron, for whom photographic focus had to fit the mood of the subject matter, not necessarily mimic the clarity of normal optical vision.

The black-and-white series by New York-based Japanese photographer

Hiroshi Sugimoto (b. 1948) shares with Barth a regard for the fragile beauty of uncertainty, expressed in grainy atmospheric effects. Sugimoto often works in series, beginning with his eerie photographs of wildlife dioramas at the American Museum of Natural History in New York, and including his lush black-and-white images of early twentieth-century movie theaters across the United States. For more than two decades, he has traveled the world seeking high vantage points from which to aim his camera at the point where the sky and ocean come together at the horizon (Fig. 7.61). The boundless vistas he portrays are reminiscent of Pictorialism's thronging gray tones. Sugimoto's work manifests the dichotomy between the rapture of visual pleasure and the cold comfort of human systems of measurement.

The pinhole camera, favored by Pictorialists such as George Davison (see Fig. 4.7) because its wide angle stretched and fogged photography's typically deep

7.61
HIROSHI SUGIMOTO,
Aegean Sea, Pilion 1,
1990.

With all references to land eliminated, Sugimoto's delicate evocations of gray water, light, and mist seem as though they might have been taken anywhere near the sea. Nevertheless, he is punctilious in specifying the place he photographed and keeping records. Nineteenth-century photographers of the American West similarly anchored their delight in nature with specific geographic labels.

441

THE POSTMODERN ERA

7.62
BARBARA ESS,
Untitled, from her series
Food for the Moon,
**1986–87. Monochrome
color photograph
mounted on fiberboard.
National Museum
of American Art,
Smithsonian Institution,
Washington, D.C.**

Ess is less interested
in subject matter than
in camera effects. In
this image, the distor-
tions of perspective
and loss of clarity at the
edges transform the
commonplace into an
otherworldly vista, at
once attractive and
threatening. Ess usually
works in large-format
prints that approach the
size of paintings.

pictorial space, was reinvestigated by
late twentieth-century artists such as
Barbara Ess (b. 1946) (Fig. 7.62). Along
with Japanese photographer Nobuo
Yamanaka (see p. 380), Ess was one of
the first image-makers in the period to
withdraw from the high-tech possibilities
of advanced cameras and film, as well as
computer enhancement, in favor of the
simpler pinhole camera.

London-born Adam Fuss (b. 1961)
is likewise disposed toward older, ele-
mentary forms of photography. He
extensively employs cameraless image-
making in the form of the photogram
or what William Henry Fox Talbot called
"photogenic drawing." Using a technique that also fueled experimental
photography between the world wars,
Fuss sometimes records only the action
of light on sensitive film, or the concen-
tric circles made by falling droplets of
water. For the enigmatically titled *Wish*
(1992), he arranged two rabbits as if they
were heraldic animals on a medieval
shield (Fig. 7.63). Fuss identifies more

with painters than photographers, stating
that he is less interested in Postmodern
theory than in the expressive qualities of
photographic techniques.

By contrast, Spanish photographer
Joan Fontcuberta was a postmodernist
before the movement began! From his
precocious teenage years, he approached
photography as the art of fabrication—
in every sense of the word. His very first
photographs were staged, and he quickly
moved into montage. His use of the
photogram is rooted in his axiom that a
photograph best conveys that fact that
it is a photograph, an idea that neatly
reinforces Postmodern notions of media
and representation. Even though a photogram is a trace of the objects set on or
near the light-sensitive paper, Fontculbert
toys with the viewer by not visually disclosing which of the flower images that
impressed themselves on the final photograph were actual flowers and which
were from mass-manufactured wallpaper
(Fig. 7.64). In other words, the copy of
the real is no more real than a stereotype.

7.63 (above)
ADAM FUSS, *Wish*,
1992. Color photogram.

In Fuss's photogram,
the entrails of two
rabbits mix and flow
into irregular shapes
that look like thick paint.
They form an enclosure
for the suggestion of
a human figure in the
lower center of the
image. The unsettling
effect is like viewing
the residue of a secret
magic rite that left
its remains on photo-
graphic paper.

7.64 (above)
JOAN FONTCUBERTA,
*Ich danke Ihnen für
die Rosen*, from his
series *Paper Gardens*,
1990. Photogram on
foil wrapping paper.

7.65 (left)
CARLOS SOMONTE,
*Woman with
Rattlesnake Skin,
San Luis Potosí, Mexico
(Señora con piel de
serpiente, San Luis
Potosí, Mexico)*, 1990,
from the series *The
Last Poets (Los ultimos
poetas)*.

Somonte deliberately
used an inexpensive
camera to create a print
looking deteriorated
with age, perhaps to
make his subjects look
as though they have
endured hardship for
long periods of time,
or as a visual metaphor
for continuity between
past and present.

7.66
BARBARA POLLACK,
Installation view of
The Family of Men,
Thread- waxing Space,
New York, 1999.

Pollack used out-of-date
film and old Polaroid
cameras to create *The
Family of Men*. After
exposure, she smeared
and smudged the emul-
sion while it was devel-
oping. In contrast to
Steichen's 1955 exhibi-
tion, *The Family of Man*,
Pollack's show displays
not universal harmony,
but interpersonal
tension embodied
in strained visual
distortions.

During the last decades of the twentieth century, the DIANA camera and other
inexpensive instruments found favor
with photographers, who were attracted
to its foggy, unevenly lit image. By shooting with a cheap plastic camera, Mexican
photographer Carlos Somonte (b. 1956)
rejected documentary realism in his
series *The Last Poets*, which was based
on images of the poor inhabitants of
Mexico's northern and central desert
areas (Fig. 7.65). Easy to achieve with a
Diana camera, Barbara Pollack's blurry
photographs require considerable
planning. Her *The Family of Men* (1999)
installation, which invoked the design
of the 1955 exhibit at the Museum of
Modern Art by suspending large-scale
pictures at different heights (see Fig. 6.1)
showed indistinct color photographs
of her husband and son (Fig. 7.66).
Pollack's main focus is voyeurism—that
is, the desire to look—and what it feels
like to be looked at. To that end, she
intentionally blurs the image to frustrate
the viewer's gaze, and make the viewer
more aware of efforts to look.

FEMINISM AND POSTMODERN PHOTOGRAPHY

In an influential article titled "The
Discourse of Others: Feminists and
Postmodernism," critic Craig Owens
pointed out a convergence of "the
postmodernism critique of representation," and "the feminist critique of
patriarchy."[69] He looked back at Martha
Rosler's series *The Bowery in Two
Inadequate Descriptive Systems* (see
Fig. 7.53), retroactively casting it as a
Postmodern work because of Rosler's
attempt to undermine the truth value
of visual and verbal texts. He reasoned
that her "refusal of mastery"—that is,
a deliberate effort not to resolve meaning in an image—was a critique of
representation that also related to
contemporary feminist rejections of
imposed gender identity.[70] Owens also
enlisted Cindy Sherman's film stills to
point out how the artist assumed roles
so as to reveal them as gender stereotypes. Applying the psychoanalytic
theory of French thinker Jacques Lacan
(1901–1981), Owens was one of the first

to fix on the notion that, if gender is not innate but culturally acquired, it can also be culturally rejected and redirected. The initial bridge Owens built between Postmodernism and feminism supported many subsequent accounts, and encouraged comparable investigations of received ideas on race and sexual preference.

The intense focus on gender as a kind of performance, rather than the expression of an inherent feminine or masculine temperament, followed a period in which some feminist photographers and photographic historians had begun to rehabilitate the reputations of nineteenth- and early twentieth-century women photographers such as Julia Margaret Cameron and Frances Benjamin Johnston. After producing the book *The Feminine Eye in Photography* (1973), at a time when the work of many women photographers was largely unknown, Californian photographer Judy Dater (b. 1941) created portraits showing women comfortable with their own bodies (Fig. 7.67). Several other studies and exhibitions attempted to show the breadth of women's photographic work. Anne Tucker's *The Woman's Eye* (1973), Val Williams's *Women Photographers:*

The Other Observers, 1900 to the Present (1986), and Naomi Rosenblum's *A History of Women Photographers* (1994) helped gather initial data, and gave impetus to the ongoing study of the social factors that have excluded women from histories of photography.

The restoration of women's past photographic pursuits and the presentation of female sexuality began to be berated by critics, who attacked the uncomplicated notion that there was something distinctive about images by women. They believed that it promoted the idea of an inherent feminine essence. For example, British writers Griselda Pollock and Janet Wolff asserted that there is no intrinsic feminine or masculine essence, only complex networks of culturally conditioned markers that construct what superficially appears to be coherent gender identity.[71] They questioned the experimental writings of French theorists Hélène Cixous and Julia Kristeva, both of whom put forward the concept of "writing from the body," or "feminine writing" — that is, the possibility of creative expression that eludes through indirection the dominant male point of view.

The French theorists' ideas were becoming widely persuasive in academic settings, including art schools, where it had already become important to visualize an alternative feminine condition, one sufficiently protean and anti-authoritarian to evade the pervasive gender stereotype of the nurturing, yet emotionally ruled woman. Conceptual artists such as the French image-maker Annette Messager (b. 1943) responded to this vein of feminist theory. Messager created her fragmented photo-pieces as an embodiment of Cixous's idea that the feminine was not fixed but was, instead, an aggregate of unstructured perspectives that thwarted summarization. In *Mes Voeux* (*My Vows*), Messager suspended from strings of different lengths several hundred photographs of women's body parts (Fig. 7.68).

Efforts to undermine the fixity of feminine identity discouraged the retrieval of information on women photographers simply because they were women. Throughout the 1980s and 1990s, essentialist feminists — that is, people who believed that femininity is a real inborn trait — vied with culturalists,

7.67
JUDY DATER, *Maureen with Fan*, **1972, from the book** *Women and Other Visions*, **1972.**

Dater's career as a portraitist led her to chronicle women as they would pose and costume themselves before the camera. Several sitters chose to allude to their ease and acceptance of sexuality.

7.68
ANNETTE MESSAGER,
My Vows (Mes Voeux),
1990. Black-and-white
photographs and string.

Messager's collection of
images could have been
collaged photographic-
ally, but she suspended
each to accentuate
their separateness and
movement. They are
held in suspension, just
as, in feminist theory,
gender identity is frag-
mented and transitory.
In outline, the piece
forms a circle, a symbol
of wholeness and the
mothering earth. Yet the
pictures do not add up
to one woman, or even
several women.

who held that gender roles were culturally determined. In photography, this
argument ignited competing exhibition
rationales and vigorous critical reviews.
For instance, the 1987 show *Reclaiming
Paradise: American Women Photograph
the Land* was conceived to show a basic
sameness underlying women's photography from different eras, a resemblance
that stood in very opposition to landscape views taken by men. The exhibition hoped to show that women used
visual strategies that indicate a caring
attitude toward the earth, whereas, by
contrast, men frame the land in ways
that indicate a desire to possess and own
it. Critic and photographer Deborah
Bright (b. 1950) was among those who

objected to the premise of a woman's landscape photography. She pointed out that aligning women with nature and natural functions had long been used historically to "devalue women and their cultural production." For Bright, the claim that women are "naturally" creative also suggested that men must create "artificially," through cultural and technological means alien to women.[72]

While scholars debated the desired direction of photographic history and practice, American graphic designer Barbara Kruger (b. 1945) culled photographically derived mass-media images for use in an extensive series of confrontational poster-like pictures based on Postmodern assumptions about women in society. Like experimental German photographers between the world wars, she inserted bold, blocky type derived from advertising into her compositions, both as design elements and for their meaning (Fig. 7.69). The art museum was only one location in which Kruger's work appeared; she also sought out public venues and commercial formats, putting her images and slogans on billboards and even department store shopping bags.

Despite the oppositional messages in her images, Barbara Kruger was well incorporated into the art world, the sales gallery, and even advertising, where her

**7.69
BARBARA KRUGER,
"We won't play nature
to your culture," 1983.**

Kruger pointedly aimed her work at the audience, using personal pronouns such as "we," "you," and "yours"—in the manner of product advertisements. The tauntingly titled "We won't play nature to your culture" strenuously pointed out the exclusion of women from cultural work because of their association with the natural world.

FOCUS
Culture Wars

A fabricated-to-be-photographed image was at the center of a national debate in the United States about public funding for the arts. On May 18, 1989, New York Senator Alphonse D'Amato demonstrated his hostility to public funding of the arts in the United States by ripping up a photograph of a work by the then little-known artist Andres Serrano (b. 1950). The offending image showed a crucifix suspended in an illuminated bubbly, reddish-yellow liquid. The radiant glow around the crucifix made it seem like a work of devout religious fervor. Were it not for the title, *Piss Christ*, viewers could not tell that the liquid was urine (Fig. 7.70).

The piece had been exhibited at a show of fellow-ship winners held by the Southeastern Center for Contemporary Art in Winston-Salem, North Carolina. The program was sponsored by private foundations, including The Rockefeller Foundation and The Equitable Foundation, as well as the government-funded National

7.70
ANDRES SERRANO,
Piss Christ, 1987.
Cibachrome, silicone,
plexiglass, wood frame,
edition of 4.

Endowment for the Arts.[73] Only the last organization, which channeled public money, was criticized for its support.

Serrano devised and labeled his work to bring about a collision of extremes: intense aesthetic pleasure and strong physical revulsion. Another piece, *Semen and Blood III*, for example, shows these bodily fluids swirling in a dynamic abstraction (Fig. 7.49). But Serrano undercut the enjoyment of shapes and colors with a title that unambiguously declares its unorthodox materials, and put viewers in mind of the connection of sexuality with disease, particularly AIDS. Some observers complained that they were repelled by Serrano's pictures, just as if they were in the physical presence of the substances. Others felt fooled into experiencing visual pleasure from elements repugnant to them.

The dispute ignited by Senator D'Amato raged on, fueled by people of faith who felt that Serrano had desecrated a cherished religious symbol at public expense. Critic Steven C. Dublin observed that the public

controversy over *Piss Christ* was prompted by a national sense of uncertainty about the future, which also kindled a longing for traditional values of home and church during the Reagan administration. These feelings found a target in Serrano's picture. In the end, government funding to the arts was placed under the scrutiny of the so-called "Helms amendment," named for its sponsor, North Carolina Senator Jesse Helms. It barred public moneys from underwriting so-called "obscene" work, unless it had "serious literary, artistic, political, or scientific value."[74]

7.71
ANDRES SERRANO, *Semen and Blood III*, 1990.
Cibachrome, silicone, plexiglass, wood frame, edition of 4.

work was considered stylish. Indeed, by the mid-1990s, appropriation itself was mocked as a worn-out visual device, as when Amy Adler (b. 1967) photographed her own drawing of Sherrie Levine's appropriation of a photograph by Edward Weston.

CONSTRUCTED REALITIES

In a period of multiple convergences, one of the most fruitful for photographic practice was the hybridization of Conceptual art's interest in ideas, Postmodernism's investigation into visual and verbal signs, and the increased presence of installation art beginning in the late 1970s. The mixture was evident in the widespread practice sometimes referred to as the "staged photograph." Interestingly, attempts to create fictions for the camera never acquired an accepted label. Especially in its early years, staging was awkwardly called the "fabricated-to-be-photographed" approach, meaning that a scene was composed mostly, but not always totally, of inanimate objects. Equally ambiguous terms were also tried, such as "the constructed photograph," which did not indicate the collage technique, but referred to any scenes assembled for the camera. As early as 1976, American critic A. D. Coleman outlined an extensive history for what he called the "directorial mode," in which he made the case that contemporary staged photographs had precedents, such as Civil War photographer Alexander Gardner's deliberate moving of a dead Confederate soldier so as to compose a more richly symbolic image (see Fig. 3.36), or the nineteenth-century stereograph, in which many narrative scenes were enacted as a matter of course (see pp. 82–83).[75]

Of course, the *tableaux vivants* orchestrated by nineteenth-century photographers Oscar Rejlander and Henry Peach Robinson (see Figs. 3.11, 3.14) were assembled to be photographed, but the artists' motives could hardly be more different from those of contemporary picture-makers. Sometimes Rejlander and Robinson could not make the stubborn paper negatives and imprecise lens clearly capture the image they had mentally conceived. Rejlander and Robinson welcomed the hands-on, directorial aspects of composite

photography as a way to negate the criticism that photography was witlessly automatic and therefore not an art.

But when fabricated-to-be-photographed approaches became widespread in the 1980s, former technical difficulties had long been overcome, and the issue of whether a photograph could be art was not raucously contested. Photographers and critics began to adopt the long view, noting that from its beginnings, mundane photographic studio work normally demanded staging, rehearsal, and lighting strategies. In particular, the history of advertising photography is filled by a steady stream of sophisticated fabricating techniques, such as intricate artificial lighting and suggestive, unnatural color, used to enhance the appeal of products. In addition, the omnipresence of movies and television, in which a director orchestrates scenes, may have amplified photographers' desire to direct for the still camera. Though the movement seems to have arisen within photographic practice, it was abetted by the success in the early 1980s of the edgy narrative paintings created by artists such as Eric Fischl (b. 1948) and, more recently, the suburban Surrealism of German painter Neo Rauch (b. 1960).

The lack of an overarching "-ism" for staged photographs may owe to the fact that it was not an art movement driven by a core of beliefs, but an approach that interested image-makers with different artistic perspectives and ideological positions. What the fabricators had in common was not a philosophy but a methodology, and, perhaps, a boredom or anger with the limitations of Modernist idioms. Where Modernist photographers combed the visual field for delightful coincidence, poignant metaphors, or abstract patterns, none of which was (or should have been) contrived, the photographers working in the directorial mode conceived and fabricated subjects, disregarding photography's traditional assignment of finding meaning from the look of the world. In addition, the Postmodern dismantling of photographic truth indirectly encouraged the creation of photographic fictions.

The making of scenes, rather than the taking of scenes, was epitomized in the work of American sculptor-photographer Sandy Skoglund (b. 1946),

Skoglund unified the area in her room-sized installations by applying the same color paint to the walls, floors, and furnishings. The bright orange goldfish who fly in the air and wriggle on the floorboards make the picture both fanciful and menacing—a balance often achieved in her work.

**7.73 (right)
PETER FISCHLI &
DAVID WEISS,**
Untitled, from the
series *Stiller
Nachmittag*, 1985.
Kunsthaus, Zurich.

The balancing act of
vegetables and a cheese
grater may be a sly par-
ody of Cartier-Bresson's
"decisive moment."
Instead of finding an
instantaneous visual
anecdote on the streets,
the photographers
painstakingly made one
and photographed it.
The work demonstates
twentieth-century
artists' fascination
with everyday life and
common materials.

who created room-size installations
to be viewed in their own right as three-
dimensional sculptures, as well as
photographs. In her work, exaggerated
objects, such as cobalt-blue leaves or
safety-orange fish, invade spaces occupied by sense-dulled people stranded
in monochrome settings (Fig. 7.72).
Skoglund's work anticipated the partnership between sculpture and photography
that pervaded art in the last decades of
the twentieth century, ranging from the
tongue-in-cheek balancing acts pictured
by Swiss artists Peter Fischli (b. 1952)
and David Weiss (b. 1946) (Fig. 7.73) to
the cool, cerebral black-and-white world
pictured by James Casebere (b. 1953)
(Fig. 7.74). Large, richly colored and
fabricated-to-be-photographed scenes
were also made by German artist
Thomas Demand (see Fig. 8.4). By
constructing scenes and objects forthe
camera's eye, the photographer can
control every detail of the image.

JAMES CASEBERE,
Chuck Wagon with Yucca, 1988. Gelatinsilver print, edition of 7.

Casebere, who began his career in sculpture, works with both larger-than-life pieces and dollhouse-sized objects, all derived from the world of experience but presented in a flat monotone, with the distinguishing edges and textures smoothed away, as in memory or a dream. In this image, the wheels of the chuck wagon are too polished to seem authentic, and the canvas covering lacks roughness.

By contrast, Mexican artist Gabriel Orozco (b. 1962), prizes fleeting perceptions of art, especially the unintentional presence of sculpture in everyday life. Orozco points to the gracefulness of a melting popsicle, chronicles the brief life of a human breath exhaled on to the polished surface of a piano, and fabricates makeshift scenes to be photographed (Fig. 7.75). American Laurie Simmons (b. 1949) works with doll-house-like settings in which plastic figures, almost exclusively women, robotically act out routine incidents of domestic life (Fig. 7.76). When Simmons began making images of

7.75
GABRIEL OROZCO,
Cats and Watermelons (Gatos y sandías), 1992. C-type print.

Orozco's work accentuates the temporary and the ephemeral. He makes fanciful, impromptu sculpture in public spaces, whose momentary existence is recorded with the camera, such as his whimsical grocery-store arrangement of cat food cans on a heap of watermelons.

7.76
LAURIE SIMMONS,
Blonde/Red Dress/Kitchen, **1978.**

Simmons's doll-actors and deadpan enactments of women's roles in society seemed to find a response from a generation that grew up play-acting with Barbie™ dolls. Her work from the mid-1970s to mid-1980s was largely concerned with female behavior, enacted by the dolls, whose poses, gestures, and facial appearances were saturated with clichés drawn from mass media.

males, she continued her concern with authenticity and originality by manipulating ventriloquists' dummies. With many other late twentieth-century artists who use the camera, Skoglund, Fischli and Weiss, Casebere, Demand, Simmons, and Orozco want to be principally known not as photographers but as artists who work with photography, as well as other media.

The success of performance art before a live audience during the late twentieth century influenced the conception of staged photographs. For example, starting in the mid-1980s, Japanese photographer Tokihiro Satoh (b. 1957) initiated what might be called ephemeral sculpture or light performance pieces, not conceived for a live audience but intended solely to be viewed as a photograph (Fig. 7.77). In interior settings, Satoh used projected light, such as a flashlight, and in exterior locations he captured and reflected sunlight with a mirror, all the while moving so quickly that his camera, adjusted for long, slow exposure, could record only twinkles and trails of bright light, not his body. Like Robert Smithson before him, Satoh created transient environments that exist only for the camera. Yet where Smithson tried to stop the flow of time, Satoh wanted his so-called "breath-graphs" to suggest time's

progress; he imagined that his pictures intimated the accumulated streams of human energy that had been expended in the settings he photographed.

7.77
TOKIHIRO SATOH,
Photo-Respiration (Breath-graph no. 22), **1988.**

After making his large prints, Satoh presents them in Plexiglas boxes that serve as frames, or he suspends the images from the ceiling, as here. In effect, the photograph of a fleeting light sculpture becomes three-dimensional photo-sculpture.

Crewdson's melodra-
matic stagings suggest
an undercurrent of
abnormal events. His
creations were among
the most influential on
young photographers
working in the late
twentieth and early
twenty-first centuries.

CONVERGENCES (1975–2000)

The directorial mode was instigated by artists and photographers for whom video constituted an absorbing initial experience of directing, rather than physically making, a work of art. It also benefited from the allure of film and, especially the cultic admiration of film directors such as Alfred Hitchcock, whose exceedingly planned scripts often revolved around the innocence of an ordinary individual who must cope with an extraordinary happening. Gregory Crewdson's (b.1962) disquieting and shadowy scenes are produced with big budgets and the assistance of a crew whose jobs are same as they would be on a film project. Like a film director, Crewdson does extensive post-production additions and alterations, using cutting-edge digital editing tools. Working in series, he crafts enigmatic scenes that often take place in small towns or suburban tracts. These locales, standard settings for the American dream of the good life, are seen in many films by Steven Spielberg, whom Crewdson admires, but in Crewdson's work subur-ban life is on the brink of being splin-tered by nail-biting anxiety. He invokes the uncanny and the edgy supernatural

effects that made the television series *X-Files* popular. Crewdson wants to explore "the American psyche through the American vernacular landscape, much as [the painter, Edward] Hopper did."[76] For example, in Crewdson's *Ophelia* (Fig. 7.78) a scene from the *Twilight* series that he began in 1998, a woman seems to float on water that has mysteriously filled her living-room. The subject, drawn from William Shakespeare's play *Hamlet,* is about a sensitive young woman who becomes mentally unbalanced and drowns her-self. Many painters and photographers, such as Henry Peach Robinson and Julia Margaret Cameron (see Fig. 3.18) also took up the subject.

Famous paintings from the canon of Western art also served as sources for fabricated images. The Life of Christ, as seen in the history of art, inspired sev-eral photographers to stage such scenes as the Last Supper and the Crucifixion. In one of his series the London-born, Nigeria-raised artist Yinka Shonibare (b. 1962), who works in many media, posed himself incongruously in the midst of figures enacting a scene whose setting, gestures, costumes, and colors resemble late eighteenth- and nineteenth-century painting (Fig. 7.79). American photographer Joel-Peter Witkin (b. 1939) also mined art history for ideas, occasionally improvising elaborate tableaux recalling familiar paintings in the Western tradition, and then aging the resultant image by scratching the negative and antiquing the print's tone. The aging appearance adds an unsettling, dreamlike effect to his fantastic visions, which are often charged with an unsettling eroticism (Fig. 7.80).

As image-makers began to "make" and then "take" their pictures, they also increased the size and intensity of their pictures. For example, Satoh's *Breath-graph # 22* is 95¼ inches by 77½ inches. This development was showcased in a 1983 exhibit at New York's Museum of Modern Art, called *Big Pictures*. Not only did photographs come to emulate the size of large paintings in museums and galleries; they

also acquired deeply saturated, tropically hot colors, more obviously associated with paint than with photographic materials. Sandy Skoglund's installations and photographs erupt in the piercing colors of acrylic paint. Similarly, the collages of waste materials gathered together and photographed by British artist Tim Head (b. 1946) concentrate on the eye-catching density of the color used in packaging consumer goods. During the 1980s, Head began gathering discarded mass-produced materials to serve as the basis for his photographs. At once luridly attractive and repugnant, Head's images of ecological casualty imitate the push-pull of desire and guilt (Fig. 7.81). In the 1990s, the art gallery and the photograph came together in yet another way, in the large photographs of Thomas Struth (b. 1954)—finely detailed yet huge studies of people contemplating art in a museum (Fig. 7.0). The odd, quasi-religious convention of maintaining silence or talking in

**7.79
YINKA SHONIBARE,**
Diary of a Victorian Dandy (21:00 hours),
1998. C-type print.

Shonibare poses amidst well-to-do party-goers in a fabricated scene. Despite its nineteenth-century title, the image ironically recalls the eighteenth-century satirical paintings by William Hogarth (1697–1764), in which the black figure would be not an admired and socially prominent individual, but a servant. The photograph may reflect Shonibare's experience of his high-profile rise to prominence in London art circles during the 1990s.

7.80
JOEL-PETER WITKIN, *Eve Knighting Daguerre,* 2004. Toned gelatin silver print.

In a setting that suggests the props closet of a nineteenth-century photographic studio, Eve seems to have simultaneously knighted and seduced a new Adam, in the form of Daguerre, one of photography's earliest inventors

7.81 (below)
TIM HEAD, *Toxic Lagoon,* 1987. Cibachrome print.

British curator and art historian David Mellor pointed out that Tim Head's *Toxic Lagoon* typified the "sublime catastrophe" mode of British art, in which the lovely countryside is transformed into a damaged and polluted space, indicative of the boom-to-bust movement of the British economy and the break-up of the social safety net during the 1980s.[77]

hushed tones while visiting the art gallery finds a visual correspondence in the poses and expressions of people attempting to deliberate images considered to be masterworks in Western art. Unlike Andreas Gursky, Struth does not uses digital means, but achieves his prints employing a large-format camera similar to those used by nineteenth-century photographers.

FAMILY PICTURES

Although staged photographs did not arise as part of a consistent art movement, several motifs recurred, among them the subject of the family, a topic taken up around the world during the late twentieth century. Focus on domestic life intensified, in part because the concept of the ideal family had been rocked by a high divorce rate, picked over in family therapy, and mangled in the popular media, from *Roseanne* through *The Simpsons*. During the Reagan administration (1981–88) in the United States, and the years that Margaret Thatcher was Prime Minister of Britain (1979–90), traditional values, in particular the glorified norm of the white, middle-class family, were enlisted as remedies for a tattered social morality thought to reveal itself in the increase of single-parent families, the rising demand for abortion and birth control, and in the growth of gay and lesbian activism.

Of course, many early photographers made images of their family members, chiefly because they were near at hand. William Henry Fox Talbot photographed his wife, Constance, who also made her own photographs. From the beginning, amateurs and professionals practiced lighting techniques and rehearsed stances using members of the family. Nevertheless, few nineteenth-century photographers operated like Lady Clementina Hawarden and Julia Margaret Cameron, purposefully posing family members in evocative attitudes suggestive of characters in literature and myth. In the postwar period, Edward Steichen's *The Family of Man* exhibition and the best-selling book that accompanied it became conceptual markers to which most photographers had to attend, whether they were inspired by the emphasis on the universal bonds of family life, or distressed by the omission of personal, social, and economic circumstances that differentiate people from each other.

In addition, throughout the twentieth century, families accumulated extensive collections of images, the majority taken with simple cameras and increasingly reliable film. The content of family photographs was dominated by celebratory occasions, such as weddings, birthdays, and vacations. Few families resolutely set out to record the look of everyday life, such as messy kitchens and unmade beds. Fewer still made visual records of emotionally trying times, or used the camera for psychological self-study or therapy. Interestingly, the very themes and subjects omitted in family pictures were explored by a wide variety of photographers, and studied by artists and scholars. British critic and photographer Jo Spence (1934–1992) was one of the first image-makers to use her own baby pictures, family snapshots, and early studio portraits to investigate her socialization into gender and class roles. Out of this experience she and actor Rosy Martin developed what was called "the reconstructive process," a psychological therapy in which new photographic portraits were made in order "to disrupt, replace or rework" an aspect of personality (Fig. 7.82). Artists came to view the casual snapshot, with its innocence of technique and composition, and the cheap camera, with its lack of sophisticated metering or fine lenses, as exciting means with which to extricate photography from its longstanding infatuation with "artistry." Canadian photographer Jeff Wall dubbed this far-reaching, self-imposed, de-skilling of photographers as like "amateurization."[78]

Toward the end of the Cold War in Russia, Soviet photographers "amateurized" their photographs, creasing and spotting the print in experiments with what they called "the aesthetics of defect."[79] Ignoring the fact that the humble and crumpled snapshot could be as riddled with conventions as the refined studio portrait or the news photograph, some photographers looked to it as a means to escape the pervasive influence of Henri Cartier-Bresson's "decisive moment." German writer Ulf Erdmann

**7.82
JO SPENCE,**
Transformations, from
her book *Putting Myself
in the Picture,* 1986.

In the phototherapy
developed by Jo Spence,
with the help of actor
Rosy Martin, the sitter
and the photographer
work together to enact
images of psychological
traumas and visions
of their remediation.
Spence managed to
infuse humor through-
out the project.

**7.83
UTE MAHLER,**
Untitled, from *Living
Together,* c. 1981.

Mahler's photographic
series *Living Together*
focused on the family,
an approved subject
for East German photo-
graphy. But she moved
beyond the idealized,
happy household to
show the variety of peo-
ple who live together,
and their idiosyncrasies.

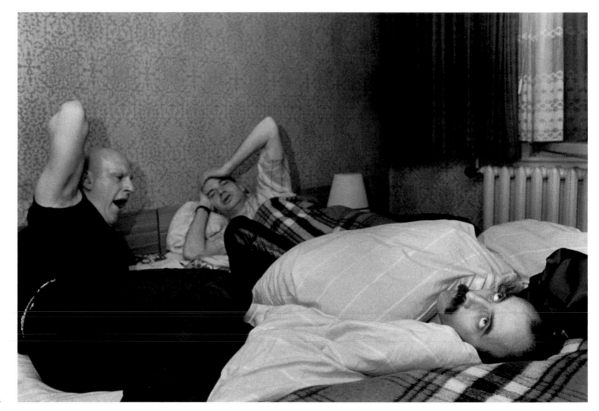

Wang shows middle-aged to older couples, who increasingly live by themselves, since the government policy of one-child families has fractured the traditional multi-generational family group. Rather than being known through their children, these couples display their possessions. In the last picture, photographs of family members have become peripheral to the electronic family presented on the television.

Ziegler accused the "decisive moment" of being an intellectually and visually reductive technique that diminished photography to a mere anecdote.[80] Family photographs not only refreshed art; they also energized social commentary. In East Germany during the 1980s, Ute Mahler (b. 1949) pictured an array of households that repudiated the official state-sponsored view of the normal family (Fig. 7.83). The Chinese photographer Wang Jinsong (b. 1963) focused on the family as an act of political resistance. His *Standard Family* series illustrates the effects of China's policy of one-child families in images of middle-aged and older couples that would be immediately understood by Chinese viewers (Fig. 7.84). Yet, as Wang explained, the image can be appreciated negatively, by those who object to China's rule, and positively, by those who favor population control.[81]

The fall of the Berlin Wall in 1989 and the reunification of the eastern and western halves of Germany the following year marked a change in German photographers' attitude toward the medium's social role. Arguing that the post-1989 period lacked vitality and ideological coherence, they became engrossed by lengthy, non-narrative depictions showing the tedium of daily life. However, the hold of the "decisive moment" was evident, even in the work of image-makers who emphatically tried to escape it. For example, Andre Zelck's (b. 1962) pictures of a marginally employed working-class family in the heavily industrialized Ruhr area of Germany vacillate between precise, telling moments, and rambling pictures of miscellaneous scenes (Fig. 7.85).

The notion that home life had eclipsed street life in American art and documentary photography was the theme of a much discussed 1991 exhibition at New York's Museum of Modern Art called *Pleasures and Terrors of Domestic Comfort*. Curator Peter Galassi

7.85
ANDRE ZELCK,
Untitled, from his series
*Familienbande (Family
Group),* 1992–96.

Zelck's family scene
seems to show a
moment beneath the
notice of most snapshot
makers. Despite its
apparent casualness,
the image is composed
of interlocking triangular
shapes, starting in the
lower right-hand corner
with the wedge of table
that enters the picture.
It reveals the difficulties
of breaking away from
the angular designs of
Modernist photography.

7.86
PHILIP-LORCA DI
CORCIA, *Brian,* 1988,
on the cover of the book
accompanying the show
*Pleasures and Terrors of
Domestic Comfort,* 1991.
Offset, printed in color.
Museum of Modern Art,
New York.

An edgy foreboding
seeps through Philip-
Lorca di Corcia's images
of ordinary domestic
life. In this picture, the
boy's thoughts seem
far removed from the
simple task of making
a snack.

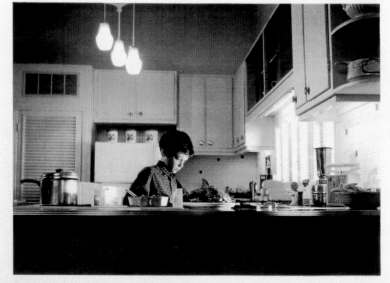

Pleasures
and Terrors
of Domestic Comfort

The Museum
of Modern
Art, New York

Peter Galassi

Faucon frequently mixes
posed mannequins and
living humans in fantas-
tic scenes that emerge
out of mundane acts
and often concern
children. Yet not all the
figures in a Faucon
image are counterfeit.

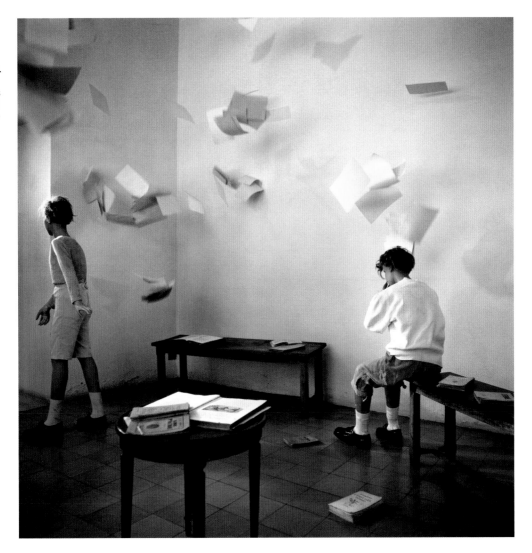

sampled family photographs ranging
from the disconcerting staged tableaux
of Philip-Lorca di Corcia (b. 1953) (Fig.
7.86), through Tina Barney's representations of affluence (see Fig. 7.95),
Sally Mann's controversial images of
her immediate family (see Fig. 7.102),
and Larry Sultan's views of his parents'
daily routine (see Fig. 7.94). In the last
decades of the twentieth century, when
photographers increasingly created sets
and scenarios, family life and interaction with friends were increasingly
pictured. Larry Sultan used his parents'
home as the setting for the photographs
directed by him, but other photographers, such as French image-maker
Bernard Faucon (b. 1950), contrived
elaborate backdrops and tableaux for
tense, enigmatic domestic dramas
(Fig. 7.87).

EXTENDED FAMILY

Photographers of daily life frequently
expanded the definition of family from
blood relatives to groups with which
they associated. In particular, the ever-
expanding domain of youth culture
became a fertile terrain for photographic
description. German Göran Gnaudschun
(b. 1971) assembled his photo-book
project *Longe–44 Leningrad* as a chronicle of his life with a folk-punk band
called 44 Leningrad. In Gnaudschun's
words, *Longe,* or daily life, "does not
aspire to relate a story, but the everyday
cycle of constantly changing yet always
recurring basic feelings."[82]

Similarly, Wolfgang Tillmans
(b. 1968), a German who currently lives
in London, began his career photographing the London club scene and
street life for unconventional British
fashion magazines such as *The Face,*
but achieved an international reputation
for informal photographs of his coterie
of friends (Fig. 7.88). Like Charles
Baudelaire (see pp. 87–88), Tillmans
believes that an artist must render the
ever-changing look of the contemporary
world and not pursue timeless beauty—
a rationale, perhaps, for his continued

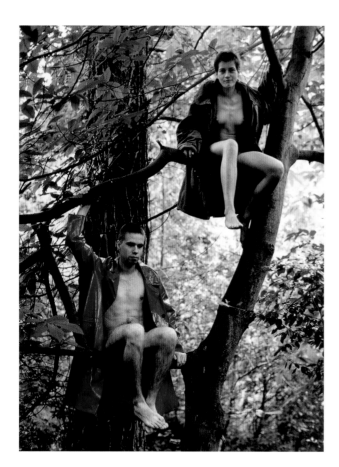

**7.88 (above)
WOLFGANG
TILLMANS,** *Lutz and
Alex Sitting in the Trees,*
1992. C-type print.

work in fashion photography. He won
the prestigious Turner Prize in Britain
in 2000. American artist Jack Pierson
(b. 1960) created clusters of disjointed,
blurry, or overexposed shots of his life
and companions (Fig. 7.89). An air of

listless "hanging around" is relieved by
scenes of frantic sexual melodrama.

Although Tillmans and Pierson
bear little resemblance to the politically
inspired Postmodern photographers of
the late 1970s and 1980s, their outlook
on truth as an unrealizable goal for
photography is similar. By insisting on
portraying the private self, both photographers testify to the modest limits
of the medium. At the same time, they
further glamorized the mass-media-
induced fantasy that it is pleasurable to
be incessantly photographed in private
life, as well as in public.

During the 1980s, Pierson was a
member of an informal network of
photographers that has since been called
the Boston School. Also in the group
were Philip-Lorca di Corcia and Nan
Goldin (b. 1953), whose work during
the last decades of the twentieth century
exemplified the trend toward books
and exhibitions that mingled private
and public views of family and friends.
By far the best-known and most influential of her efforts was the sound and
slide show titled *The Ballad of Sexual
Dependency* (1981–86). The show consisted of about 700–800 transparencies
(slides) detailing the intimate lives of
Goldin and her friends, her "re-created
family"[83] (Fig. 7.90). Her 1996 book

**7.89
JACK PIERSON,**
Untitled, from his book
*Jack Pierson: The Lonely
Life.* **Edition Stemmle,
Zürich, 1997.**

Although he photo-
graphs friends and sur-
roundings, Pierson is
anxious not to narrate
his photographs.
Instead, he wants
people to escape into
the picture, completing
"the story themselves,"
because, as he says,
"there is a collective
knowledge of common
clichés and stereotypes
that is very effective."[84]

7.90
NAN GOLDIN,
*Nan and Brian in Bed,
New York City*, 1983,
from *The Ballad of
Sexual Dependency*,
1981–86.

I'll Be Your Mirror included personal interviews as well as pictures of friends who were HIV-positive. Goldin has traveled extensively, and her sexually charged work, characterized by a revealing flash and a palette of strong colors, has been internationally influential in validating the use of photography as a diary of daily life. Her approach was widely influential in fashion photography (see p. 482). *Heartbeat*, Goldin's 2002 slide show, with music composed by John Tavener (b. 1944) and sung by Bjork (b. 1965), moved away from the portrayal of personal pain evident in *The Ballad of Sexual Dependency* to reveal the domestic routines of couples.

The sexual subjects and shock-value of Goldin's images from the 1980s paralleled some of those produced by the Japanese photographer Nobuyoshi Araki (b. 1940), whom Goldin met in the early 1990s. Araki roams the streets of Tokyo collecting photographs with an array of cameras ranging from the latest technological advances to inexpensive devices. Frequently tilted, these views glimpse the friction between traditional and ultramodern Japanese life. But Araki's most notorious images show women in sexually submissive or suggestive poses derived from pornography (Fig. 7.91). In both his street scenes and his photographs of women, Araki attempts to

7.91
NOBUYOSKI ARAKI,
Untitled, from his series
Desire and the Void,
1996–97.

At first glance, Araki's street views and his sexually charged pictures of women would seem to have little in common, even though they are part of a series called *Desire and the Void*. Yet both types of images contrast traditional Japanese ways of life with the present, and the temptations of modern existence.

show what he believes is an obsessive-ness lurking in the Japanese character.[85]

In Japan, Araki's casual, snapshot-like photographs and Nan Goldin's diaries of friends and life experience had an unpredictable impact on young Japanese women photographers.[86] Until the 1980s, when formal training in photography became available through art schools, women in Japan found it difficult to learn the medium. Apprenticeships with master photographers were routinely given to men. A woman who succeeded in learning and practicing the craft was called a "*Joryu* photographer," meaning one who works in a woman's style.[87] The popularity of the diary-like photographs by Araki and Goldin served to validate women's lives and image-making. Indeed, Yurie Nagashima (b. 1973) became a celebrity for her images of family and friends (Fig. 7.92).

The extent and availability of family photograph collections, some tracing back several generations, spearheaded the late twentieth-century image-makers' reuse of old images, from daguerreo-types to snapshots. Korean photographer Young Kim (see Fig. 7.2) searched through her family's albums for materials with which to express her anxiety at living between two worlds. Californian artist Doug Muir (b. 1940) reprinted images he took with an inexpensive, fixed-focus camera during his childhood.

His pictures center on gestures and facial expressions that reveal interpersonal relationships that were probably unrecognized by the participants at the time (Fig. 7.93).

While Muir does not fundamentally alter the snapshots that form the basis of his work, another Californian, Larry Sultan (b. 1946), plainly demonstrates that his pictures are his interpretations, by bleaching, blurring, and enlarging family snapshots and home movie stills. For *Pictures From Home* (1996), an exhibition and book, Sultan directed his

7.93
DOUG MUIR, *My
Brother Gary and his
Girlfriend Joanie*, Otisco
Lake, Amber, New York,
1959. Gelatin silver print
of a snapshot.

102

7.94
LARRY SULTAN,
Untitled, **from his book**
Pictures from Home,
1992.

Reviewing his son's
photographs, Sultan's
father remarked to his
son, "Whose truth is it?
It's your picture but
my image."[88]

parents in poses for new photographs
(Fig. 7.94). Sultan's work went beyond
the affections and tensions of his family,
to offer a public statement about the
erroneous exaltation of American family
life promoted by the political right wing
during the Reagan era.

At first glance, the photographs by
Tina Barney (b. 1945) of her relatives
offer an inside look at the private lives
of the wealthy, who actively work to prevent themselves from being seen can-
didly. Barney's images feature informal
and secluded domestic moments, such
as preparations for a party (Fig. 7.95).
At the other end of the socio-economic
scale, Richard Billingham (b. 1970)
reveals people with a seeming indifference to the lens. Employing an inexpensive auto-exposure camera and budget
film-processing, Billingham logged his
British family's strained existence, much
of which turned on his father's alco-
holism (Fig. 7.96). The dirt, disorder,
and dishevelment pictured in his work
have long been associated with truthful
photographic documentation, for example in the images made by Jacob Riis
(see Figs. 4.46, 4.47). It is intriguing to
compare the grime and raw passion in
Billingham's pictures with the cleanli-
ness and order transcribed in Barney's
work. Despite the apparent artlessness
of their images, Barney and Billingham
do not break free from the prevailing
stereotype that the rich and poor

are the way they are because of their
inherent temperaments.

Family pictures provided an important source for authenticating forgotten
social history. During the late twentieth
century, museums began to exhibit and
create histories for so-called OUTSIDER
ART, which drew on non-traditional
forms of folk art and shed new light on
family photographs. Sociologists such
as Pierre Bourdieu scrutinized family
picture-making with the belief that its
social significance surpassed the stated
intentions of the photographer. He and
others deduced that family pictures
consecrated social identity, within and
beyond the family. Interestingly, lower-
class families seldom had family-
produced photographs of past generations, owing, perhaps, to an unease about
the visual signs of their social identity, as
well as to practical economics. Groups
for whom political powerlessness was
accompanied by the lack of public visibility sought out family albums with
which to reclaim their ancestors' stories
and place in society's collective memory.

In addition to his own photographs
of daily life, Santu Mofokeng concocted
an ongoing broad historical research
project called *Black Photo Album: Look
at Me, 1890–1950,* which attempts to
locate and preserve family photographs
of black South Africans, including the
seldom acknowledged middle class.
The big mixed-media works by Radcliffe

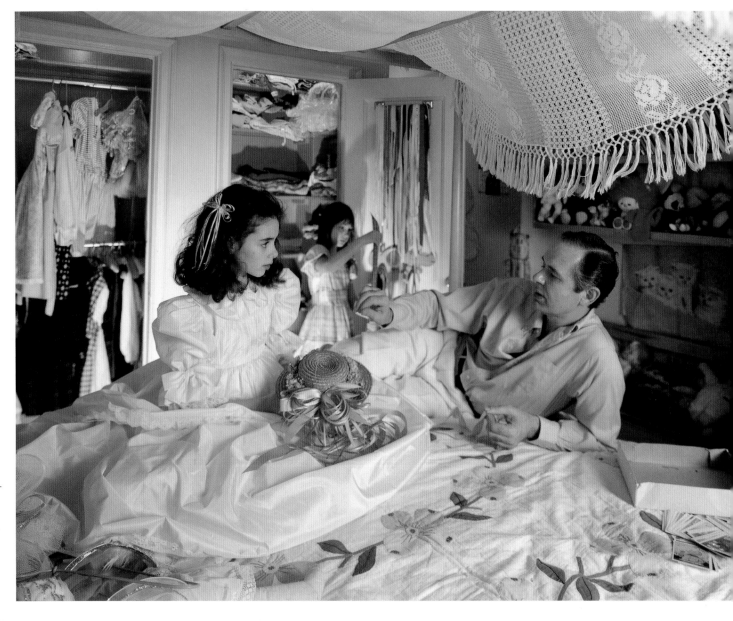

7.95 (above)
TINA BARNEY,
Marina's Room, 1987.

Barney's works have the look of informal snapshots. Nevertheless, though her pictures cut through the glamor of formal portraits, it would be naive to think that her subjects are completely unaware that they are performing in front of the large camera she uses. They have become expert in creating informal poses.

Bailey (b. 1968), who is based in Atlanta, Georgia, incorporate real tintypes and other old photographs handed down in his family. Much like Mofokeng, Bailey wants to indicate the existence of a flourishing black middle class, and authenticates his research into late nineteenth-century African-American life by using actual photographs as evidence (Fig. 7.97).

On a large scale, historian and curator Deborah Willis brought together the first comprehensive view of African-American photographers in her *Reflections in Black: A History of Black Photographers, 1940 to the Present* (2000). Willis's earlier work *Picturing Us: African American Identity in Photographs* (1994) gathered reflections penned by black writers, historians, and image-makers on the impact that a special

photograph had on them. Clarissa Sligh (b. 1939), one of the contributors to *Picturing Us*, recalled the lasting influence of a 1956 newspaper photograph of her taken when she was the plaintiff in a lawsuit aiming to integrate the segregated schools of Arlington, Virginia. Today, Sligh is an image-maker who regularly mines her family albums to reveal the ways in which the lives of her ancestors reflect African-American history (Fig. 7.98). The pictures that American Darrel Ellis (1958–1992) worked with during his short lifetime were taken by his father, who died one month before Ellis was born. Ellis altered the shapes in his father's images, creating fleeting light sculptures by projecting photographs onto irregular plaster surfaces and foam molds. He further distorted the pictures by photographing them

7.96 (right)
RICHARD BILLINGHAM, *Untitled*, 1994. Color print on aluminum.

Made while he was an art student, Billingham's candid photographs of his unsettled family life resemble the intrusive images captured with video cameras for reality television, which got its start about the same time.

7.97 (below)
RADCLIFFE BAILEY, *Untitled*, 1999. Acrylic, photograph, and mixed media on wood. Clarice M. Laubenheimer Collection.

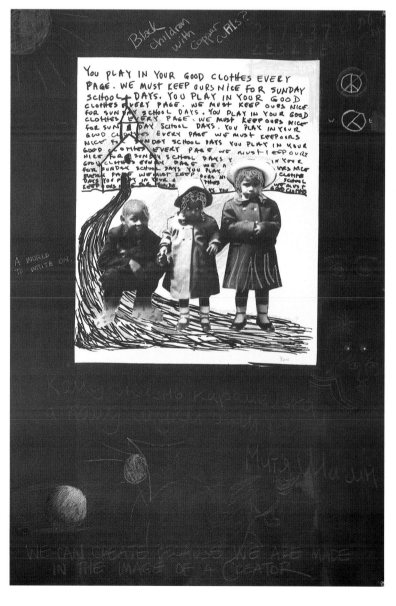

7.98 (right)
CLARISSA SLIGH, *Untitled*, from the series *Reading Dick and Jane with Me*, 1990. Cyanotype with crayon added while on exhibit at Art Awareness, Lexington, New York.

In her series *Reading Dick and Jane with Me*, which elicits the racial assumptions of an old reading primer, Sligh altered family pictures with text and applied color, in an effort to show that memory is constructed, and never simple.

7.101 (opposite)
ADOLFO PATIÑO,
*Constant Navigation
(Navegación constante)*,
1991–92, from the series
*Elements for Navigation
(Elementos para una
navegación)*, from the
larger series *Relics of
the Artist (Reliquias de
artista)*. Family photo-
graphs, Polaroid 669
photographs, negatives,
Canon laser copies,
Polaroid SX-70 photo-
graphs, old postcards,
prints on paper sewn
with cotton thread on
felt, satin, and amate.
Enriquez Schneider
Family Collection,
Mexico.

A stiff snapshot of the
artist and his brother
becomes, in the second
picture, a silhouette
framing repeated
images of Christ as the
Sacred Heart. In the
third image, the boys
have been replaced by
outlines. In the final
image, they are restored
to their original setting,
but a medical illustra-
tion of a human heart
has been superimposed
on them, and below it
is an actual tin votive
figure of human eyes,
used by worshippers
to ask for miraculous
recovery of the body
part represented.

Surrounded by purple
flowers (the color of
mourning), Chong's
tribute to his aged and
infirm aunt evokes what
amounted to a tragic
romantic life. "These old
studio portraits," says
Chong, "are poignant
signatures of individuals
who peopled an age
that now through the
prism of time seems
so different."

from extreme angles that flatten and
stretch the pictures' space. For Ellis,
these mutations expressed a yearning
for memories of his father (Fig. 7.99).

In a similar manner, Albert Chong
(b. 1958), a Caribbean photographer
of African and Asian descent, uses the
medium to create a personal dialogue
with his ancestors, and to encourage
viewers to acknowledge the mixing
of cultures. His self-portraits, called
"I-traits," usually involve his moving so
quickly in front of the camera that his
identity is a blur. Other works incorporate old photographs in assemblages
put together as part of a ritual to connect with the past. In *Aunt Winnie*, for
instance, Chong constructed a homage
to his mother's sister from a studio
portrait made in the 1940s (Fig. 7.100).
Similarly, Mexican image-maker Adolfo
Patiño (b. 1954) accentuates the personal
and homemade quality of family photographs by sewing them to handmade
bark paper. He works in series, frequently repeating whole images or miscellaneous snippets, sometimes using
a simple family photograph to elicit the
feeling of memory and loss[89] (Fig. 7.101).

The rescue and reuse of family
photographs further encouraged the
growing interest of historians, curators,
and artists in past photographic
processes, such as cyanotype (which
Clarissa Sligh employed). A personal
investigation of alternatives to silver-
based photographic processing led
American photographer Bea Nettles
(b. 1946) to concoct an enduringly
popular 1977 volume called *Breaking
the Rules: A Photo Media Cookbook*. Sally
Mann (see pp. 470) spent the 1990s
learning the tricky visual language of
the wet-plate collodion process, and

FOCUS
Looking at Children

During the 1980s and 1990s in the United States, some family photographs provoked boisterous debate about the right of both amateur and professional photographers to show children in poses that revealed genitalia, or to suggest that children possess adult sexual knowledge.[90] Photo-processing laboratories and drugstore photo-developing machine operators were put on notice to report pictures of nude children on the rolls of film brought to them. Laws prohibiting child sexual abuse and the sale of child pornography occasionally punished innocent snapshooters who pictured their naked children romping in a backyard wading pool. In the worst cases, children were temporarily taken away from parents and put in foster care until the legalities were cleared up, and homes were subjected to search and seizure of prints and personal records.

American art photographer Sally Mann (b. 1951) was surprised to find her work at the center of angry criticism from religious and conservative critics, as well as from those who deplored what they felt to be the vulgarization of the American family. Only 20 per cent of the photo-graphs that Mann published in the book *Immediate Family* (1992) showed her children topless or nude, yet for many the volume came to symbolize disturbing changes in American life, including how early it was that children were now becoming acquainted with the demeanor of adult sexual behavior. In addition, some of Mann's pictures, such as *Naptime* (Fig. 7.102), angered viewers who were repulsed by their own identification of erotic

7.102
SALLY MANN, *Naptime*, **1989, from her book**
Immediate Family, **1992.**

nnuendo in the image of a young girl with tousled hair and pouting lips who is awaking from sleep.

Unlike the response to Mann's photographs, the explicit prepubescent frontal nudity pictured during the Pictorialist era by photographers such as Alice Boughton (see Fig. 4.26) seems to have gone unremarked. This was perhaps because in the years before the immense use of sexuality in mass-market advertisements, the poses and expressions of children did not so readily suggest sexual awareness or pleasure.

Those who defended Mann's pictures asserted her right to make the images, and maintained that these were truthful portrayals of children's expressions of sexuality. Her advocates were quick to note that male photographers such as Harry Callahan (see Fig. 6.41) were not rebuked for photographing nudity in intimate family pictures. Mann's detractors held that, as an adult, she could comprehend the sexually expressive qualities of the photographs in a way that the children could not. Therefore, they accused her of abdicating her parental responsibility to protect her children from lewd gazes of strangers.

The display of child sexuality became an issue that cut across political divisions, uniting some feminists and some conservative activists in censorship efforts. Within photographic circles, the topic initiated new inquiries into the motivations of nineteenth-century photographers Julia Margaret Cameron and Lewis Carroll (see Fig. 3.106), both of whom showed nude or nearly nude children.[91] Critic Anne Higonnet helped to frame the discussion by contrasting representations of the innocent child, pictured in photographs and paintings as not understanding sexuality, with the knowing child who is sexually precocious. In her study and others, social history and psychological theory directed attention to the photographer, the viewers of such pictures, and the condition of women in the societies that provided a market for such images.

Regardless of circumstance, the fact that a child stood before the lens in a state of undress became the salient point in a number of legal actions. Across the United States, some photographers and arts publications were scorned or punished for presenting images of childhood sexuality. For example, in New York City, the publication *Nueva Luz* (*New Light*), issued by En Foco (In Focus), an organization dedicated to promoting photography by people of color, was criticized by the *New York Post* for publishing photographs by Ricardo T. Barros (b. 1953) that showed his nude wife and children.[92] The newspaper was outraged that the organization received public money with which it supported *Nueva Luz*.

The most notorious incident involving public hostility to sexual images took place in 1989. The threat of losing public funding drove the Corcoran Gallery of Art in Washington, D.C., to cancel an exhibit of Robert Mapplethorpe's (1946–1989) photographs, some of which were explicitly homoerotic prints, and a few others of which showed glimpses of children's genitalia. The parents of the children in the Mapplethorpe pictures knew the pictures and gave their permission for the prints to be exhibited. One of those pictures, titled *Rosie*, shows a little girl innocently raising her skirt while adjusting her pose (Fig. 7.103). Eventually the same Mapplethorpe exhibition was exhibited in Cincinnati, Ohio, where it gave rise to a much publicized trial, which, though won by the defendants, raised public ire at the use to which tax dollars were being put. Along with the uproar about Andres Serrano's pictures (see Figs. 7.70, 7.71), the publicity surrounding the Mapplethorpe show culminated in reduced national and local spending on the arts.

7.103
ROBERT MAPPLETHORPE, *Rosie,* **1976.**

Cuban-American photographer Abelardo Morell (b. 1948) has revitalized the use of room-size camera obscuras. Brazilian-born Vik Muniz (b. 1961), who is known for his humorous and irreverent use of art media, revived the look of the *cliché verre* in a series of images based on Rembrandt's etchings. To produce the work, Muniz photographed a composition made of nails, pins, and paperclips, after carefully arranging them to give the illusion of etched lines. Some nineteenth-century processes now even have their own websites. During the late 1990s, as film-based black-and white photography was being replaced by digital means, interest in the medium sparked a renewed interest in the darkroom with its sinks, trays, and chemical mixes.

Even the tedious and physically hazardous daguerreotype method made a return during the late twentieth century. One enterprising photographer, Robert Shlaer (b. 1943), employed the technique during a four-year project retracing John C. Frémont's 1848 trip through the American West, deducing from engravings the actual scenes of now lost daguerreotypes made by the expedition's photographer.[93] In 2001, a Boston exhibit invented a name for the use of nineteenth-century techniques in contemporary photography, calling such work "crafted" images.

Artists' reuse of ordinary photography supplemented scholarly attention to vernacular photographic practice, such as the heavily overpainted photographs studied by Christopher Phinney in his investigation of camerawork in India, and Mexican *foto-esculturas* or photo-sculptures. This hybrid between the flat photograph and the spherical sculpture was invented in the 1920s and became popular through the 1950s. It was customary for the sitter to direct the session, or to suggest flattering

**7.104 (below)
ARTIST UNKNOWN,**
Hombre (Man),
c. 1950. Hand-painted photograph over wood, plaster, woodframe, glass. Private collection.

Foto-escultura, or photo-sculpture, usually used existing formal portraits, which provided the basis for a three-dimensional wood form on which they were eventually molded. Elaborately framed, they were often displayed on home altars.

modifications to the photograph that would be used to make the *foto-escultura*. The practice of photo-sculpture evolved from the public's longing to magnify the vivid sense of personal presence. Not surprisingly, photo-sculptures became meaningful additions to funeral ceremonies (Fig. 7.104).

NATURE AND THE BODY POLITIC

Of the millions of images of nature made by amateur and professional photographers, most operated within the enduring nineteenth-century visual vocabulary of awe and magnificence. Photographs from space followed the tradition of the sublime landscape, accentuating the distance of other galaxies and the breadth of celestial bodies (see Figs. 6.65, 6.67, and Fig. 8.15). As a matter of fact, the hold of the nineteenth-century sublime upon wilderness imagery remained so strong that a few contemporary landscape photographers preferred to operate primarily with cumbersome old equipment, like that used by Carleton Watkins and other nineteenth-century photographers of the American West.

In the late twentieth century, images of nature did not receive as much critical scrutiny as did the concepts of gender and ethnic identity. Occasionally a voice was raised to protest the intrusion of cameras in precincts where endangered species might be disturbed by the presence of the photographer and equipment.[94] A few critics pointed out that photographs and films of animals were not objective, but modeled on an idealized view of Western family life. Some artists, such as Scottish-born sculptor Andy Goldsworthy (b. 1956), created on-site and gallery installations of natural materials, which were either returned to nature or allowed to decay, their only record being a photograph.

Invocations of magic and ritual, which regularly infomed installation and performance art in the late twentieth century, were sometimes felt in photographic practice. Adam Fuss's photograms (see Fig. 7.63) sometimes seem like traces of ceremonial acts, and Robert ParkeHarrison's (b. 1968) *Earth Elegies* (1999–2000) portray him dressed in a priest-like black suit, while he tries to mend a simulated rupture in the earth. Equally sacramental is *Patching the Sky* (1997), in which the formally dressed artist-shaman stands

473

NATURE AND THE BODY POLITIC

**7.105
ROBERT
PARKEHARRISON,**
Patching the Sky, 1997.
**Photogravure with
beeswax.**

Performance art was one of the forces that helped shape photography in the late twentieth century. It is a short step from photographing a performance to make a record of it, to performing for the camera. ParkeHarrison's rituals exist for the moment, and for the record.

on a makeshift platform attempting to suture a spot in the unmistakably artificial heavens (Fig. 7.105).

More often, nature was a distant presence with which humans could not convincingly connect, but for whose fate they were implicitly responsible. In photography, this feeling of alienation had been foreshadowed by *New Topographics* photographers, such as Robert Adams (see pp. 352–53), who declared that "Scenic grandeur is today sometimes painful."[95] Where nineteenth-century artists sought spiritual sustenance through sublime and beautiful displays in the natural world, contemporary artists tended to express the loss of transcendence.

American Joel Sternfeld (b. 1944) mastered the distanced landscape photograph, as in his view of dead and dying whales (Fig. 7.106). In his early twenty-first century work, he has begun to use digital manipulation to reprint these images. The resulting increase in the overall sharpness of these pictures tends to befuddle the eye and increase the sense of detachment. Since the 1970s, American John Pfahl (b. 1939) has been cleverly undermining landscape views with additions that prevented viewers from easily comprehending the spatial relationships before their eyes (Fig. 7.107). Where Pfahl constructs physical impediments to seeing in a landscape view, some photographers exploit obstructions that were already there, especially the automobile. To contrast with postcard and travel-magazine idealization of an uninhabited wilderness, they focus on the inevitable cluster of tourists' automobiles parked near the scenic outlook. Putting the human subject before nature, not being able to discern what is happening in nature, or being at a fixed, dream-like remove from the landscape has characterized the human separation from the natural world.

**7.106
JOEL STERNFELD,
*Approximately 17 of 41
whales which beached
(and subsequently died),
Florence, Oregon,
18 June, 1979.* Dye transfer print. Hallmark
Photography Collection.
Hallmark Cards Inc.,
Kansas City, Missouri.**

Sternfeld uses physical distance to symbolize emotional detachment. The tragic death of the whales takes place in a space remote from the viewer, as if it were impossible to care about their plight.

7.107
JOHN PFAHL,
Australian Pines, **1977.**

Pfahl placed bands
around the tree trunks
so that the top seems
to be at the horizon line
and bottom where the
sand slopes down to
the sea. Consequently,
the sea looks like flat
blue ribbons stretched
across the trees.

As Andres Serrano's work showed
(see Figs. 7.70, 7.71), beauty and repug-
nance can be effectively mingled in the
same work. A similar effect sometimes
occurs in photographs of nature as a
wounded victim. Pictures of strip mines,
clear-cut forests, and oil spills flaunted
intense coloration and spectral glamor.
In Richard Misrach's (b. 1949) pictures
of *Bravo 20,* a bombing range in northwestern Nevada, the crater and rusting
convoy teeter on the edge of abstraction
and apocalypse (Fig. 7.108). When the
work of Canadian Edward Burtynsky
(b.1955) made its appearance in a 2004
show and book covering his twenty-
year career, it revealed a similar tact.
Burtynsky exposes the paradoxical relationship between beauty and destruction. He concentrates on landscapes
made spectacular through pollution,
mining, and industrial decay. Underlying
his work is the worldwide reach of
industrial development driven by the

relatively cheap cost of oil. For example,
his 2002 series *Shipbreaking* features
the beauty of the Chittagong Delta of
Bangladesh, inflected by the rusting
orange hulks of oil freighters that have
been strewn on the beach, awaiting
disassembly for their metal scraps
(Fig. 7.109).

In art, documentary, and advocacy
photography, the human body emerged
as nature's chief representative. Within
Postmodern theories of representation,
the body was repeatedly theorized as
the point at which society's values shape
human personality. Cindy Sherman's
multiple self-portraits, in which she is
always and never herself (see Fig. 7.56),
and Annette Messager's fragmented
body parts (see Fig. 7.68) epitomized the
Postmodern attitude that personality is
ever-changing. Similarly, the disjunction
between words and pictures in Lorna
Simpson's pictures of the human body
(see Fig. 7.48) showed the force of

7.108
RICHARD MISRACH,
Bomb Crater and
Destroyed Convoy, 1986.
Chromogenic color
print.

In a lengthy plan
accompanying his
photographs, Misrach
proposed that the exper-
imental and practice
bombing site in Nevada
called *Bravo 20* by the
military be transformed
into a United States
national park to memo-
rialize an environmental
disaster.

476

7.109
EDWARD BURTYNSKY,
Nickel Tailings No. 34,
Sudbury, Ontario, 1996.

7.110
CARRIE MAE WEEMS,
Diana Portraits, from
the *Sea Island* series,
1992. Ektacolor prints,
three panels.

societal labeling. History, the body, appropriation, and issues of ethnic identity met in Carrie Mae Weems's (b. 1950) reuse of nineteenth-century daguerreotypes made by J. T. Zealy to support Louis Agassiz's racial theories (see pp. 40–41). By rephotographing, reshaping, and framing the images, as well as adding a somber blue tone to the circular outer pictures, Weems transformed scientific photographs that made a spectacle of the body into an affecting memorial (Fig. 7.110).

Other sorts of personal identity also focused on the body. Sunil Gupta (b. 1953), an Indian-born Canadian citizen who lives in London, produced the photographic series *Exiles* (1987), depicting gatherings of gay Indian men. His work continues to contrast his daily life with that of ideals (Fig. 7.111). While Gupta appreciates experimental techniques such as photomontage and digital representation, he nonetheless chose a straightforward view of the plight of those who are seldom represented except in pornographic pictures. In his choice of visual presentation, Gupta, who is gay and HIV positive, is typical of people seeking greater social visibility. As video-maker and writer Marusia Bociurkiw aptly pointed out,

7.111
SUNIL GUPTA, *Untitled* from *Trespass II*, 1993

To confront South Asian values and heritage, Gupta compares modes of contemporary life by contrasting his own nude body with a depiction of a robust figure who has a gun tucked into his bullet belt.

Adamantly anti-digital, Pierre et Gilles insist on the craft of hand-painting their photographs, which they assert show the beauty inherent in popular culture items such as pulp comics. Their work appears on posters and postcards, as well as in gallery prints.

"the absence of photographic representations amid a larger culture so heavily saturated by media images can make the act of production seem transgressive."[96] In that spirit, perhaps, the French collaborators Pierre et Gilles have been creating sensuous, color-laden, often

homoerotic photographs since the mid-1970s (Fig. 7.112).

American photographer Linn Underhill (b. 1936) undermined the conventions for women's portraits by deliberately avoiding the association of the female body with nature. She refused

7.113
LINN
UNDERHILL,
Untitled, from
*Returning the
Gaze*, 1995.

to fragment the body or to deflect the sitter's gaze from the camera, and hence the viewer. Printed life-size, and hung inches from the gallery floor, Underhill's images unsettled viewers who were accustomed to the hint of submission and seduction that characterized formal studio portraits of women (Fig. 7.113). Underhill's women present themselves as uncomplicated everyday people, but Catherine Opie's (b. 1961) sitters in the 1991 series *Being and Having* manifested obviously fake accessories, as if gender clues were something they put on or took off at will (Fig. 7.114). *Chicken* sports a false mustache and even a phony tear. In a later series showing lesbian couples, Opie, like Underhill, reverted to a less experimental format and conventional studio techniques, validating the sitters' frankness with photography's styleless style.

During the period, homoerotic desire was depicted by artists in direct images of sexual arousal, and in pictures that critique received ideas about gays and lesbians. Following the lead of advocates and artists, scholars took renewed interest in the history of homosexuality and its images. The then largely unknown work of French Surrealist photographer

7.114
CATHERINE OPIE,
Chicken, 1991,
from her series *Being
and Having*, 1991.
Chromogenic print.
Patrick Breen Collection.

Opie's images often fuse stereotypes of outward physical appearances, in an attempt to make the viewer struggle to interpret ethnic and gender identity. In this image, the obviously false facial hair and artificial tear do not effectively change the appearance of the person wearing them — a lesson, perhaps, in the futility of gender pretense.

479

NATURE AND THE BODY POLITIC

**7.115
GARTH AMUNDSON,**
Detail from the
installation *Dr. Kempf's
Nightmare,* 1995.
Muslin, embroidery,
and transfer, queen-
sized bed.

Amundson hand-
stitched the pictures to
muslin sheets that were
also embroidered with
derogatory labels for
homosexuals. Putting
the pictures and words
on a bed, Amundson
not only made reference
to erotic desire, but
used the display as a
ceremonial wedding
or acceptance of his
homosexuality.

Claude Cahun (see Fig. 5.27) was studied
and widely exhibited. Indeed, Cahun's
self-portraits were recast as a forebear
of Cindy Sherman's investigation of
feminine roles.

Because pictures of homosexuals
in the mainstream media emphasized
stereotypical looks and behaviors, the
body became the locus of politically
oppositional gay photography. Still, in
Garth Amundson's (b. 1963) pictures,
the body is implicitly rendered. For
his 1995 piece *Dr. Kempf's Nightmare,*
Amundson recast medical photographs
gathered by psychiatrist Edward J.
Kempf at the turn of the nineteenth
century as part of his attempt to prove
homosexuality an illness (Fig. 7.115).

The AIDS crisis of the mid-1980s
sparked a variety of artistic responses,
the best-known of which is probably the
Names Project Quilt, with panels sometimes adorned with photographs commemorating individuals who died of the
disease. Pictures of emaciated people suffering with AIDS, taken by photographers
such as Nicholas Nixon (b. 1947), or
those used in advertisements sponsored
by the international clothing company
Benetton (see p. 484) were subject to
debates about what was considered to
be an indulgent and counterproductive
voyeurism. Activist groups, such as

ACT UP, argued for "the visibility of
PWAs [People With AIDS] who are
vibrant, angry, loving, sexy, beautiful, acting up and fighting back."[97] In response,
media-savvy photographers created photographs of healthy-looking AIDS patients,
and showed the pictures not only in
galleries but also in poster form in the
streets. Photography was also the back-
bone of the safe-sex campaigns around
the world, most notably in the internationally traveling exhibition *Visual Aids.*

As happened in South Africa under
apartheid, people whom society has
marginalized have been concerned not
only to critique disparaging imagery,
but also to originate depictions that had
been absent or censored. For instance,
when Burmese-American Chan Chao
(b. 1966) photographed students and
ethnic members of the Burmese resistance, he created large, direct portrait
studies, concentrating less on the sitters'
military exploits, which were played up
in the press, than on their routine daily
lives in the encampments along the
border between Thailand and Burma
(Fig. 7.116). A comparable approach
has been taken worldwide by people
with disabilities, who attempt to redress
photographs that show them as victims.
British photographer, writer, and activist
David Hevey (b. 1959) has tried to devise

**7.116 (opposite)
CHAN CHAO,** *Member
of KNLA,* from his series
Something Went Wrong,
1999. C-PRINT.

Chao's highly detailed
portrait photographs of
students who organized
guerrilla attacks against
the repressive govern-
ment of Burma aim to
distinguish their individuality and thus frustrate
propaganda attempts
to classify them as
anonymous outlaws.

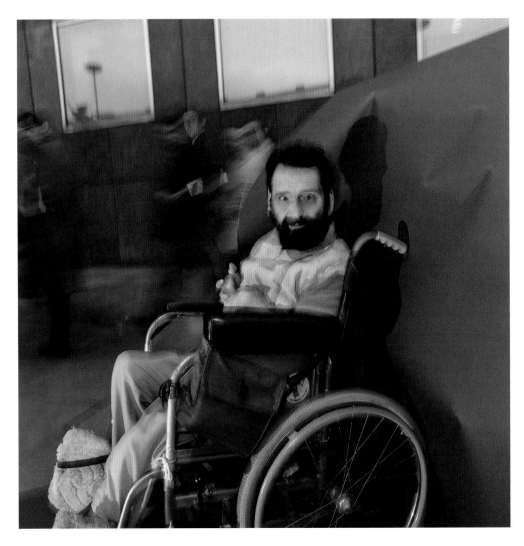

**7.117
DAVID HEVEY,
Untitled, from *Beyond
the Barriers: Disability,
Sexuality, and Personal
Relationships*, 1992.**

In Hevey's photographs,
people with disabilities
refuse to pose as vic-
tims of their conditions.
Instead of presenting
themselves as helpless
and needy people, he
shows them as active
participants in the pub-
lic realm. With such
images, the disabilities
movement attempted to
reform advocacy photo-
graphy, moving it away
from the sentimental
and the lurid.

what he calls a "post-tragedy form of
disability representation" (Fig. 7.117).
Hevey faults Postmodern theory for not
taking into full account the "distribution,
audience and production" of images.[98]
Like Jo Spence, whom he greatly
admired, Hevey distrusts academic
nit-picking and bickering, which he
believes obliterates the larger issues of
class with psychoanalytic analysis.

ENTER FASHION

In an era of exceptional hybridization
among photographic genres, none was
more surprising than that of fashion
photography, art, and social concern.
The merger was somewhat precedented
in the experimental photography of the
1930s, but the vast growth of goods and
media since that time produced a much
larger, more dynamic consumer economy in which styles and images changed
rapidly and ideas had a short shelf-life.

Many art photographers, such as
Nobuyoshi Araki, Nan Goldin, Jack

Pierson, Cindy Sherman, and Larry
Sultan, created fashion advertisements
that strongly resembled the implicit
narratives of gallery work. In fact, Goldin
was able to move some of the lingerie
advertisement photographs that she took
in the run-down Russian Baths in New
York City into her open-ended slide show
The Ballad of Sexual Dependency.

Of course, mainstream fashion magazines continued to feature models whose
engaging cuteness or chill beauty reliably
sold conventional clothing and cosmetics. But during the last decades of the
twentieth century, the urban music and
club scene bred an anti-fashion industry
and, with it, progressive magazines such
as *i-D* and *Dazed and Confused*, which
featured clothing and settings that would
never have been published in more commercially oriented publications. At the
same time, the rapid expansion of the
youth market and youth culture, which
began accelerating after World War II,
fostered the increasing development of
clothing, jewelry, and cosmetics just for
teenagers and young persons.

Late twentieth-century
cutting-edge fashion
photography favored
a gritty realism. In
Day's image, a littered
room sets the scene
for a model with dirty
feet who is wearing
designer lingerie.

Fashion-forward clothing advertisements also abandoned the idealized, pristine locales of high fashion for the grime and disarray of the real world. Likewise, tall, slim, carefully coifed and rigidly posed models were replaced by everyday people who did their own make-up and had "bad hair days."

Former model Corinne Day (b. 1965) frequently set her fashion shoots in actual lofts and apartments, where dirty coffee cups, old newspapers, littered rugs, and grungy furniture created an ambiance far from the glamorous, squeaky clean settings of high-fashion photography (Fig. 7.118). Fashion photographers tended to picture evocative interpersonal relationships, putting the product second. For example, in one of Day's pictures, a model's face is blotchy and red from crying because of an off-camera event; in another, a naked young man sprawls across a bed while looking questioningly into the camera's lens.

Another British photographer, Nick Knight, frequently conceived his photographs as demimondaine night-time scenes. Like Corinne Day, Knight photographed some internationally known models, but he also favored ordinary people inhabiting favorite hang-outs. His pictures for "One in Ten," an anti-breast cancer campaign, broke from the topic's sentimentality to show women who had been treated for the disease wearing heavy make-up and posed in sexually

alluring postures (Fig. 7.119). The term "heroin chic" arose to describe unkempt settings and models shown with bruises and red-rimmed unfocused eyes.

Because of its world-weary appearance, the photography of underground or fashion-forward clothing was sometimes labeled Postmodern, though it mostly lacked the theoretical intricacy of art theory. Alternative fashion photography continues to hasten the breakdown of barriers that have separated the medium's genres. It is not unusual or shameful for a documentary photographer, such as Mary Ellen Mark, to do fashion work. The ungainly yet descriptive moniker "fashion-plus-culture" has emerged to describe this continuing trend.

Fashion and social trends met in a different way when Wolfgang Tillmans guest-edited *Big Issue*, a magazine sold on the streets of London by the homeless. He made the weekly periodical desirable by exhibiting in its pages a mix of photographs from different genres similar to those appearing in upscale galleries (Fig. 7.120). The most notorious combination of fashion and politics was made by the Benetton Group, an international clothing retailer. In the mid-1980s, Benetton began to market multiculturalism by attiring models from different ethnic groups in its clothing. By the 1990s, the "United Colors of Benetton" ads turned away from displaying the company's products and toward showing

7.119
NICK KNIGHT, *One in Ten*. Photo Nick Knight; styling Katy England. Show Studio and Dazed and Confused, 2001.

Rather than portraying women who have survived breast-cancer operations as maimed victims, Knight chose to create erotic scenes to suggest that their sexuality could prosper after surgery.

people in distress, such as Haitian refugees, prisoners on death row, or persons with AIDS (Fig. 7.121). The fact that these images were widely criticized for reinforcing class, ethnic, and gender stereotypes did not deter the company from expanding its efforts.

During the 1990s, Benetton revived a strategy used by corporations in the 1950s, such as Pepsi-Cola, which hired accomplished photographers such as Esther Bubley (see p. 282) to create "documentary advertising" for a multilingual magazine. Called *Panorama,* Pepsi's bi-monthly aimed to lessen the hold of Coca-Cola on the Latin American market by featuring international friendship and understanding.[99] Under the leadership of designer Tibor Kalman (1949–1999), Benetton created the magazine *Colors.* In the most famous issue, public figures were made to look like people of color, while people of color turned white. The ad campaign and magazine sparked consumer protest, and provoked Benetton dealers in Europe and the United States

to sue the company on the grounds that the advertisements had a negative effect on sales. Benetton advertisements prompted the international use of new composite words, such as advertorial (advertising + editorial) and infotainment (information + entertainment). In the early twenty-first century, just as the promise of linking advertising and social concerns was being reconsidered, *Colors* was revamped, turning away from iconoclastic images, while dwelling on less disquieting social movements.

After the Benetton furor, it seemed unlikely that another manufacturer would attempt to join advertising and political action. However, the Adbusters Media Foundation, a countercultural enterprise based in Vancouver, Canada, launched the glossy magazine titled *Adbusters* (vol. 1, no. 1, Summer 1989), aimed at unraveling marketing strategies and critical of consumerism. Using the high-tech tools of advertising photography, *Adbusters* deconstructed visual clichés, such as the appearance of the cover girl (Fig. 7.122).

Victoria Line

Martha Osamor. "She has devoted her life to campaigning for human rights across the world, nurturing small-scale pressure groups. She is totally committed to other people"

**7.120 (above)
WOLFGANG
TILLMANS,** *Victoria
Line* **and** *Martha
Osamor,* **from** *The Big
Issue,* **special edition
"The View from Here,"
August 28–September 3,
2000, no. 401.**

**7.121 (right)
THÉRÈSE FRARE,** *Pietà*
(AIDS patient), 1992.

The Benetton company
linked themes of social
awareness to the drive
to create consumer
loyalty by incorporating
photographs of people
afflicted by poverty
and disease.

UNITED COLORS
OF BENETTON.

7.122
**Cover of *Adbusters*,
Winter 2000, no. 28.**

At first glance, the
pouty blonde looks like
the standard cover-girl
using sexuality to sell
magazines. On closer
inspection, one sees the
heavy make-up which
is unable to disguise
her scarred cheek and
large pores, flaws that
would have been eradi-
cated in conventional
advertising images.

Adbusters

JOURNAL OF THE MENTAL ENVIRONMENT
WINTER 2000 $5.75
№ 28

MANUFACTURING DESIRE

PHILOSOPHY AND PRACTICE: THE PASSING OF THE POSTMODERN

In a 1993 interview, photographer-critic
Barbara Pollack spoke for many when
she announced her frustration with
Postmodernism:

It's the nineties. I don't have to discuss Lacan
any more. The phrase "postmodernism"
presumed that everyone had already shared
in the modernist expedition. But I consider
myself a prime example of people who are
saying, "Hey, before you say that modernism
is over, let me share in that adventure."
There are myths inherent in modernism
that may romanticize the role of the artist or
may be sexist but have certainly influenced
my life. I am ambivalent about giving up
those myths.[100]

The major ideas of Postmodern photography were played out by the mid-1980s.
Looking back in 1987, Abigail Solomon-
Godeau was convinced that critical practice itself was in a critical condition.
Within a decade of Douglas Crimp's
1977 article "Pictures," which allied then
little-known photographers such as
Cindy Sherman with oppositional writing
on the nature of language, power, and
representation, Postmodern photography had been incorporated into what
Solomon-Godeau called the "emporium
of photography." Major postmodern
shows in galleries dedicated to presenting art photography signaled what she
aptly called "deconstruction in reverse."
Instead of analyzing the art market, with
its emphasis on originality and genius,
postmodern photography itself began

to be marketed as original and inspired, thereby vitiating its critical stance.

How did the passing of the Postmodern happen? Douglas Crimp, one of the first to announce the arrival of Postmodern photography, was also the critic who noticed its slide into an accepted and marketable commodity. In the wittily titled article "Appropriating Appropriation," written for the 1982 catalog accompanying the show called *Image Scavengers*, he observed that Postmodern photography was being diluted by the artists who first fashioned it, such as Richard Prince and Cindy Sherman, while simultaneously being subsumed into the art institutions as just another category of art. In that vein, Solomon-Godeau asserted that the conventions of art history and museum practice easily historicized Postmodern photography as the photography after Modernism, just as Post-Impressionist painting followed Impressionism. Thus categorized, Postmodern photography became what it so desperately attempted not to be, another art-historical style/period. In addition, the roaring art market of the 1980s latched on to Postmodern photography, by then predigested in popular arts magazines and newspapers, and found it a profitable investment.[101]

In an important sense, there were several Postmodern moments in recent photographic history. The first, starting with the 1977 *Pictures* exhibit in New York, ended in the mid-1980s, when some of the movement's most persuasive proponents, such as Crimp and Solomon-Godeau, began to question Postmodernist photography's increasingly cozy relationship with the art market. The second period persisted until the mid-1990s, during which time, Postmodern theory and photography found a central place in many college art departments, as well as in literary studies, art history, and cultural studies. Future historians may be tempted to date the conclusive demise of Postmodern photographic practice to a particular place and time: New York City, Monday evening, November 8, 2004, when Barbara Kruger's iconic photograph, *Untitled (I Shop Therefore I Am)*, a once heretical and divisive indictment of consumer culture, was sold at auction for $601,600.

Nevertheless, the end of postmodern photography was less dramatic. By the mid-1990s, Postmodernism was about twenty years old, and of decreasing interest to young artists, for whom the issues it raised about Eurocentrism and colonialism, the construction of social truth, the sources and misuses of gender and ethnicity identity, the conundrums of representing the past and the present, had been absorbed into the majority culture and were part of their education since childhood. As critic Jeff Rian observed, "From the younger perspective, social consciousness is a given."[102] In that sense, Postmodernism was — and is — a highly successful intellectual movement, which reshaped a broad spectrum of high-school and university curricula. Many prior intellectual movements, such as existentialism, cannot make that claim. There is no clear marker for the end of Postmodernism, because many of its most admirable principles are now commonly held.

Postmodernism changed the art and academic worlds in several ways. It shifted emphasis away from traditional art to reproducible media, such as film, photography, and video. Because Postmodernism questioned the tacit assumptions of Western art, it helped to refocus attention on marginal and non-Western art practices. In that sense, Postmodernism was not only a cultural phase, but also an unwitting collaborator in the expansion of Western culture's global reach (see p. 496).

In 2000, Adam Lamminan wrote in *Adbusters* about what he dubbed "the hidden potential of the post-postmodern crisis" of uncertainty. He summed up what he believed to be the popular effect of the movement on the young: "Everything is relative and nothing is sacred … Many of us are either desperately clinging to a sinking ship of fixed ideals or floundering in a sea of ideas." But the "upside," as Lammiman called it, is that "it is no longer possible to ignore the existence of viewpoints different from your own. Seeing so many points of view, each with its weaknesses, makes it difficult to believe that your own ideas are flawless."[103] While less rigorously philosophical and more idealistic than the ideas of Postmodern photographers and theorists, this attitude is central to the legacy of the Postmodern era.

CHAPTER EIGHT

Into the New Millennium

At midnight on December 31, 1999, people around the world, including many who never observe this version of the New Year, stared at timepieces and wondered if they had stockpiled enough food and water to get them through the crisis that loomed as the clock struck twelve. They feared the so-called Millennium Bug, an elegantly simple glitch in the settings of countless computers that were running factories, municipal water supplies, nuclear power plants, banking systems, hospital equipment, airplanes, and thousands of other crucial applications. Beginning in the 1960s, and continuing into the later decades of the twentieth century, computers were not programmed to turn from 12/31/99 to 1/1/00. Billions of dollars were spent globally to repair computer equipment or replace it entirely. When the clock did strike twelve, the lights stayed on, traffic systems continued to run, and lots of pundits had some explaining to do.

Bug or no bug, the problems and possibilities that existed in 1999 were those of the new century and the new millennium. There were no world-changing technologies born in the dawn of 2000, and simmering social crises of the late twentieth century, such as the calamitous toll of AIDS in Africa, were unaffected. The new millennium's first day may have been uneventful, but the new century was soon be punctuated by horrific happenings: the events of September 11, 2001, the displacement of more than 2 million people through war and famine in the Darfur region of Sudan in Africa, beginning in 2003, the bombing of civilians in Bali (October 11, 2001), Madrid (March 11, 2004), and London (July 7, 2005), the tsunami in South Asia (December 26, 2004), and the deaths and destruction caused by hurricanes in the southern United States and by a massive earthquake in South Asia late 2005 (Fig. 8.1).

As happened after World War I, years may pass before one can glimpse the sure outlines of a reorientation in visual practice precipitated by the early twenty-first century calamities. Moreover, while artists and writers immediately reacted to the tumult in the century's first five years, history teaches that it often takes a decade or more for a society to settle on the communally resonant symbolism with which to depict and memorialize catastrophes. It is rare for an art work, such as Picasso's *Guernica*, which was made in 1937, months after the little

8.0 ANDREAS SERRANO, *Torture*, 2005. Cibachrome.

8.1
JOHN MCCUSKER,
Canal Street,
New Orleans,
September 2005.

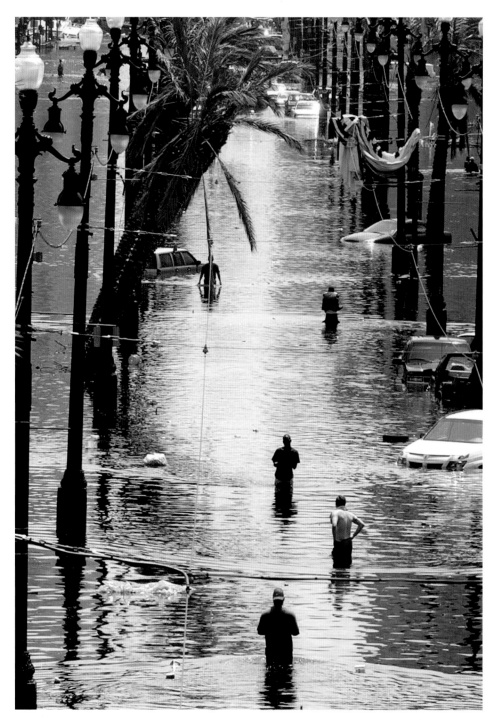

8.2
Heroes, 2001.
Postage stamp.

Heroes is one of the few so-called "semipostal" stamps issued by the United States Postal Service. The monetary difference between the cost of producing the stamp and first-class postage was given to the families of emergency relief workers killed or disabled during the events of September 11, 2001. *Heroes* raised more than 10 million dollars.

Basque village of the same name was used for bombing practice by the Nazis, to succeed in speaking to many generations. Societies find it difficult and painful to reach consensus about visual symbols, as shown by the prolonged debate about the plans for new buildings and memorials on the New York City site of the September 11 attacks. Recognizing the difficulty of creating memorials that are meaning to people living in the present and the future, the United States Postal Service modestly restricted the scope of the postage stamp based on the famous photograph of firefighters raising the U.S. flag over the smoldering ruins of the World

Trade Center. Called "Heroes," the stamp functioned as a tribute to those who served at the catastrophe, and as a fundraiser for those who were bereaved (Fig. 8.2).

PAST AND PRESENT

One reason why it is too soon to pronounce on how the calamitous events of the early twentieth century will play out, is that the forward motion of late twentieth-century culture is still very strong. In photographic practice, many trends, subjects, and ideas also made an easy transition to the new century. The convergences of photographic genres and content continued to strengthen. The relationship of ephemeral art, performance art, and sculpture with photography seems to have expanded, as more artists closely incorporate the photography of short-lived or fragile works into their original concepts.

The use of historical photographic materials and cameras continues to swell. Sally Mann depicts landscapes using the nineteenth-century glass-plate-based collodion process, and incorporates the medium's particular flaws as expressive effects in her work. Many photographers choose to use "found" or "orphaned" vernacular photographs in their work. The use of digital cameras and computer programs that make and shape images has great momentum, yet black-and-white photography has seen a resurgence in high school and college classes. Nevertheless, the Kodak Corporation announced in 2004 that it would no longer make paper for black-and-white photography, prompting some commentators to suggest that black-and-white photography has become a redundant process, along with daguerreotype, cyanotype, and photogravure. Moreover, artists who were not trained in photography are attracted to the visual language of historical photographic processes. Among the unanticipated adaptation of former photographic practices in the developed world is renewed interest in posthumous photography both as a memento for the dead person's family and as an image shown in a gallery. In developing countries, posthumous photography has been more regularly practiced.

SLIDE SHOW

Slides and slide projectors were used for education and entertainment before photography was invented. Drawings or paintings on glass were projected by means of lenses and oil lamps. Today, the humble slide commands surprising attention. New research has revealed that Thomas Eakins, the late nineteenth-century champion of American realist painting and draughtsmanship, not only traced projected images on to several of his well-known canvases, but also beamed figures from disparate photographs onto the picture plane building up his image in a way that anticipated how digital artists now use Photoshop. In response, a writer in the *New York Times* resurrected one of the earliest accusations against the use of photography by artists, and accused Eakins of cheating.[1]

When the Kodak Corporation announced in 2003 that it would stop manufacturing slide projectors in the following year, a shiver ran through the various photographic communities. Was this a watershed moment? What would it mean to teaching and to photographic practice if the era of slide projection was about to end?

Other manufacturers of slide projectors did not follow Kodak's decision, perhaps because they were not struggling under huge financial losses — as was Kodak, which saw its future in the production of digital goods and services. Indeed, the slide projector's technology, so simple that it predates electricity, will continue to be used in classrooms worldwide, because government-funded schools around the world, unlike colleges and businesses, still have insufficient classroom access to computers, on-line connections, and digital projectors. Moreover, slide libraries and collections hold millions of images whose transfer to electronic media remains time-consuming. It is more likely that digital image resources will grow on their own, not through the protracted process of slide scanning. In addition, artists and photographers whose art, public presentations, and personal records consist primarily of slides, have a complex intellectual relationship with the projected still images, a connection explored in a wide-ranging exhibition that began at the Baltimore Museum of Art in 2005, and which traveled the United States in 2006.

The work on *SlideShow* was nearly complete when Kodak made its decision to stop manufacturing their popular slide projectors. Consequently, the show's intention, to demonstrate the extent to which the artists and photographers conceive their images as a variety of light work, was prematurely overwhelmed with eulogies for the technology. Nevertheless, the exhibition confirmed that, beginning in the 1960s, artists and photographers found much to love in the slide machine. Slides allowed photographers such as Nan

Goldin continually to vary their presentations. Goldin's *The Ballad of Sexual Dependency* expanded to include her fashion photography, and was tailored to a specific subject, such as the AIDS crisis. In addition to Goldin, photographers such as Helen Levitt, Robert Smithson, Jan Dibbets, and, more recently, the team of Fischli and Weiss created works specifically for the slide projector, either dramatically engaging the pause between images, or, conversely, by using a dissolve mechanism to melt one image into another.

The intense light that pours through the slide as it is projected is similar not

**8.3
ALFREDO JAAR,**
Lament of the Images,
2002. Installation including three texts on Plexiglas panels, each approximately 29.5 x 23.5 in (75 x 60 cm), in the first room, and a light wall in the second room. Photograph by Laurent Lecat. Page from *Art in America,* September 2002, page 86.

Jaar's background in architectural design and theater enables him to devise spatial settings in which, typically, he shapes the experience of light to reveal the shifting border between art and contemporary political and social issues.

Alfredo Jaar: Lament of the Images, 2002, installation including (above) light wall in second room and (below) three texts on Plexiglas panels, each approx. 29½ by 23⅝ inches, in first room. All photos this article, unless otherwise noted, © Laurent Lecat.

Cape Town, South Africa, February 11, 1990.

Nelson Mandela is released from prison, after 28 years of brutal treatment by the apartheid regime. The images of his release, broadcast live around the world, show a man squinting into the light as if blinded.

More than half of Mandela's sentence was spent on Robben Island, a windswept rock surrounded by the treacherous seas of the Cape of Good Hope. Only seven miles off Cape Town, the island had been used as a maximum security prison for "non-white" men since 1959. Mandela's fellow inmates there included Walter Sisulu, Ahmed Kathrada, and Govan Mbeki, the father of current South African President Thabo Mbeki. Mandela later said that Robben Island was "intended to cripple us so that we should never again have the strength and courage to pursue our ideals."

In the summer of 1964, Mandela and his fellow inmates in the isolation block were chained together and taken to a limestone quarry in the center of the island, where they were put to work breaking rocks and digging lime. The lime was used to turn the island's roads white. At the end of each day, the black men had themselves turned white with limedust. As they worked, the lime reflected the glare of the sun, blinding the prisoners. Their repeated requests for sunglasses to protect their eyes were denied.

There are no photographs that show Nelson Mandela weeping on the day he was released from prison. It is said that the blinding light from the lime had taken away his ability to cry.

Kabul, Afghanistan, October 7, 2001.

As darkness falls over Kabul, the U.S. launches its first airstrikes against Afghanistan, including carpet bombing from B-52s flying at 40,000 feet, and more than 50 cruise missiles. President Bush describes the attacks as "carefully targeted" to avoid civilian casualties.

Just before launching the airstrikes, the U.S. Defense Department purchased exclusive rights to all available satellite images of Afghanistan and neighboring countries. The National Imagery and Mapping Agency, a top-secret Defense Department intelligence unit, entered into an exclusive contract with the private company Space Imaging Inc. to purchase images from their Ikonos satellite.

Although it has its own spy satellites that are ten times as powerful as any commercial ones, the Pentagon defended its purchase of the Ikonos images as a business decision that "provided it with excess capacity."

The agreement also produced an effective white-out of the operation, preventing western media from seeing the effects of the bombing, and eliminating the possibility of independent verification or refutation of government claims. News organizations in the U.S. and Europe were reduced to using archive images to accompany their reports.

The CEO of Space Imaging Inc. said, "They are buying all the imagery that is available." There is nothing left to see.

Pennsylvania, U.S.A., April 15, 2001.

It is reported that one of the largest collections of historical photographs in the world is about to be buried in an old limestone mine forever. The mine, located in a remote area of western Pennsylvania, was turned into a corporate bomb shelter in the 1950s and is now known as the Iron Mountain National Underground Storage site.

The Bettmann and United Press International archive, comprising an estimated 17 million images, was purchased in 1995 by Microsoft chairman Bill Gates. Now Gates' private company Corbis will move the images from New York City to the mine and bury them 220 feet below the surface in a subzero, low-humidity storage vault.

It is thought that the move will preserve the images, but also make them totally inaccessible. In their place, Gates plans to sell digital scans of the images. In the past six years, 225,000 images, or less than 2 percent of them, have been scanned. At that rate, it would take 453 years to digitize the entire archive.

The collection includes images of the Wright Brothers in flight, JFK Jr. saluting his father's coffin, important images from the Vietnam War, and Nelson Mandela in prison.

Gates also owns two other photo agencies and has secured the digital reproduction rights to works in many of the world's art museums. At present, Gates owns the rights to show (or bury) an estimated 65 million images.

only to that of a film projector, but also to the concentrated, strong light of television, which became the dominant mass medium in the 1960s, and which, in turn, encouraged video artists. Light, the "photo," in "photography," emerged in the late twentieth century as an ephemeral medium that served the interests of Conceptual and Minimalist artists, as well as the growing number of twenty-first-century artists in all media who want to investigate perception.

One of the powerful linkages between the late twentieth century and the early twenty-first was the continuing swift convergence of various screen- and projected-image forms. As the world learned from the photographs taken in the Abu Ghraib prison (see below), a digital-camera image can be stored in a computer, which links to e-mail, which links to the Internet, which links to other computers, to photo-phones, and to the international news agencies and television networks. The day after the 2004 election in the United States, college student James Zeitlin thought up a joke. He bought a web domain name and created a website he called sorryeverybody.com, which featured one photograph: an image of Zeitlin holding a sign that read, "Sorry, world we tried!" By means of rapid electronic world-of-mouth, the site received 26,000 pictures and 75 million hits over the next few weeks. The speed with which digital images can be transmitted may have more social consequences than the transition from analog to digital camera.

Digital technology also facilitates big photographs, such as those by Andreas Gursky, which emulate the edge-to-edge clarity of daguerreotypes, as well as the size and luminosity of screens. Today, large screens are used not only for film and video, but also as flatscreen billboard advertisement in public places. Conceivably, the transition from analog devices, such as the slide projector, to digital devices, was made easier because of the consumer's familiarity with lighted screens.

So ubiquitous is the radiant screen in contemporary life, that the screen itself has become the subject of art. Chilean-born Alfredo Jaar (b. 1956) constructed his 2002 installation *Lament of the Images* by placing three illuminated wall texts on Plexiglas panels in a darkened room. The text explained three historical moments when, for widely varying reasons, crucial photographs were not available: the first, Nelson Mandela's February 11, 1990, release from prison, when he was unable to weep for joy, because after years of breaking rocks, the powdery lime that covered his body and turned it white also impaired his ability to cry; secondly, the media black-out during the October 7, 2001, bombing of Kabul, Afghanistan, by U.S. forces, during which Western news agencies were prevented from obtaining live pictures; lastly, Corbis's reported withdrawal from public view of million of news and historical photographs. After reading the texts, visitors to Jaar's installation pass into another room where they are momentarily blinded by a large, brightly lit screen that symbolizes the eradication of public information in the age of mass media (Fig. 8.3).

THE MEDIUM OF THE MOMENT

Reflecting on the current fame of photography, Peter Galassi, chief photography curator at the Museum of Modern Art, New York, noted that "it is *the* medium of the moment."[2] Similarly, a 2002 *Art in America* article by critic Phyllis Tuchman announced that "photography rules right now." Just as those born after 1970 subliminally absorbed the Postmodern concern with ethnicity and gender long before they attended college, so they also never knew a time when photography was not broadly accepted in museums, galleries, and universities. Reporting on the ten-year segment of the "Photography in Britain since 1968" conference, held in November 2004, Richard West, an editor of *Source: The Photographic Review*, titled his remarks, "When Dinosaurs Ruled the Earth," and illustrated it with a drawing that showed a tyrannosaurus doing battle with a triceratops.[3] For the young, the financial sacrifices and intellectual ordeals routinely faced by many photographers until the last two decades of the twentieth century are ancient history, as are the heated debates about media and photography that grew directly out of feminist and Postmodern criticism.

8.4.
THOMAS DEMAND,
The Clearing, 2003.
Museum of Modern
Art, New York. C-print.

Demand used about
270,000 pieces of
paper to simulate the
leaves in the life-size
model for his photo-
graph *The Clearing*.
Despite the many
hours of work required
for the scene building,
he destroyed the
model, whose only
record is the
photography.

The career of Dutch photographer-
sculptor Thomas Demand (b. 1964)
tracks the public understanding of the
rise and current state of photography.
Demand attended the Düsseldorf Art
Academy (where, later, Andreas Gursky
and Thomas Struth were enrolled)
when the highly influential Bernd and
Hilla Becher taught there. Demand,
who studied sculpture, not photography,
creates life-size models, mostly out
of cut paper, based on photographs of
notorious settings, such as the passage-
way to serial killer Jeffrey Dahmer's
apartment, the legendary staircase that
survived the bombing of Dresden during
World War II, and the office used for
the recount of the Florida vote during
the U.S. presidential election of 2000.
He photographs these models and then
destroys them. In effect, Demand makes
photographs of paper replications of
news photographs. Thrice removed
from the original, which itself was a
reproduction, and devoid of people or
little signs of wear and tear, Demand's
scenes are as chilly and airless as a plane
at 35,000 feet. While his photographs
circle the questions about mass media
and photography that the Postmodern
era raised, their preparation demands
a level of craft that was generally not
central to the movement.

Occasionally, Demand painstakingly
constructs a scene with no obvious

paper trail in the media. *The Clearing*
(2003) was purchased by the Museum
of Modern Art, New York, and shown
in the museum's 2005 retrospective of
Demand's work (Fig. 8.4). It was given
pride of place in the museum's dining
area, during the reopening of the
refurbished museum, recognizing the
medium's elevated status in the art
world. In the past, such a spot would
have been awarded to a masterwork
of modern painting by Picasso or
Matisse. The image, which is about 16
feet wide and 6 feet tall, has a particular
resonance in New York City, site of the
attack on the World Trade Center. Its
unstated subject, a startling daybreak
moment Demand experienced in the
Public Gardens of Venice, shows mist
rising in response to the first rays of
the sun, which strike the leaves in the
upper left and the tree trunks on the
right. The curators left it to viewers in
New York to decide if the ambiguous
title of *The Clearing* signaled a new
beginning, or, as the photograph's flecks
of brash orange might suggest, the
beginning of an apocalyptic finale.

Like Demand, artists in other
media increasingly use photography
and base their work on photographic
icons. A recent critic for *The New
Yorker* magazine suggested that today
"painting owes as much to photography
as the other way around."[4] For instance,

painter Dotty Attie (b. 1938) approximates the look of particular nineteenth-century photographs by Thomas Eakins and others. Painters working in the early twenty-first century, such as Eric Fischl, have increased their investigation of photography's formal language, particularly its light and it framing effects, in relation to the conventions of painting. Of course, painting and photography have intersected before, in the paintings of Eakins, Degas, and more recently in the work of David Hockney and Gerhard Richter.

Today, the range of photographic sources turned to by artists from other media is much wider than in the past, ranging from adaptations of vernacular photographs, such as family snapshots, to news photographs and masterworks of the Western canon. At the same time, painters' tactics vary, including the reproduction of a photograph on canvas, application of paint directly onto a photograph, and digitally collaging materials. More and more, photographers create installations and videos, borrowing freely from photojournalism and art-historical images and styles. Just as

artists frequently adapt photographs to their purposes, so too photographers increasingly make overt references to familiar paintings, mimicking an artist's typical style and subject matter. British-born Tom Hunter (b. 1965) created a series called *Persons Unknown*, in which he ennobled homeless people in poses and backgrounds closely based on the famous woman-at-the-window paintings by the Dutch painter Jan Vermeer. His recent work, focusing on youth in London, enlists Pre-Raphaelite painting as the basis for contemporary interpretations, such as the death of a young woman, whom he posed as a jeans-wearing Ophelia, Hamlet's beloved, envisioned in a painting by John Everett Millais (1829–1896).

The notion that photography can now successfully emulate masterworks of the Western tradition stems in part from the medium's recent increased status in the art world. Advertising photography, too, has been quick to take advantage of great works, sometimes to instigate publicity through shock and scandal. Just as Lejaren à Hiller produced a sensational interpretation

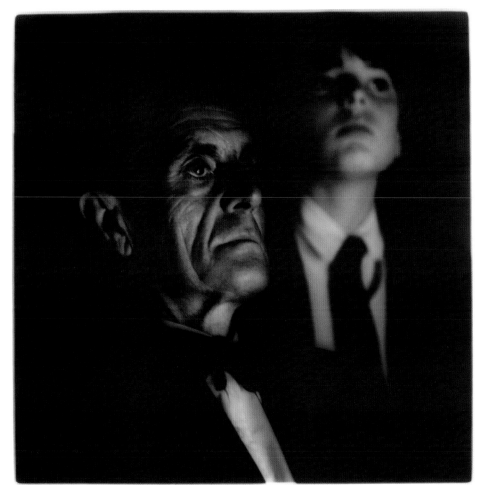

8.5
BILL HENSON,
Untitled, 28/77, 1990–1,
from the *Paris Opera Project* series. C-print.

Conflicts that enliven Western art and literature, such as the friction between youth and age, ignite the edgy intensity of Henson's images. By situating realistic depictions in the midst of unnatural or theatrical lighting he also deploys visual discord.

of medical history (see p. 269), so too the Paris fashion house of Marithé and François Girbaud produced a 2005 billboard advertisement mimicking the poses in Leonardo da Vinci's *Last Supper*. It featured a female Jesus with other models, all wearing designer clothing. The public display brought on a lawsuit from the Catholic Church for abuse of a sacred image.

Undoubtedly, the strongest inheritance from the twentieth century is the directorial mode, popular not only in photography, but also in film and video. A speculative article by Elizabeth Van Ness in the *New York Times* recently pointed out that film directing has become a popular advanced degree among those who do not plan to take up movie making. She suggested that consequently cinema studies might become the new M.B.A.[5] The association of directing with the power to command groups of people is sufficiently strong that students who want to go into business choose to learn film and video. Photographs in the directorial mode remain plentiful worldwide. Indeed, work carried out by photographers not expressly involved in the technique has been pulled into its orbit. Notable among those caught up in the gravitational pull of directorial photography is Australian Bill Henson (b. 1955), among whose greatly varied work are large photographs overflowing with broody dark shadows that form the site of evocative narratives about youth and decay. Although Henson obviously has made selections in these scenes, they are not directed in the manner of photographs like those of Gregory Crewdson, which require big budgets and a large crew (Fig. 8.5). Nevertheless, they are pulled into the force field of the directorial mode because they share some of its dark, edgy anxiety.

Not only has the directorial mode gained an international panoply of adherents and a firm market, but its look—intense detail and deeply saturated color—has been taken into consideration when processing prints that were not produced by photographer-directors and a large crew of assistants. A look back at the photographs used on the front pages of leading world newspapers, or a glance at mainstream fashion magazines from the late 1990s and those of 2005, will demonstrate a shift toward vivid and portentous renderings in which dark patches of shadow set the tone.

PHOTOGRAPHIC PRACTICE AND GLOBALIZATION

No doubt, the early third millennium's calamities tarnished some of globalization's promise. Nevertheless, many of the questions that came to the fore were foreshadowed in the late twentieth century, and probably would have emerged regardless of events.

In the arts and in photographic practice today, globalization is being differentiated from globalism, defined as a mischievous return to utopian Modernism, with its yearning for universal cultural and social values. Looking back at the decade of the late 1980s to the late 1990s, curator Francesco Bonami observed that the West had been confronted with new art from countries whose creative resources were largely hidden before the dissolution of the Soviet bloc. In response, the West "melted under the warmth of the multicultural electric heater." But after an initial fascination, the West reflexively looked inward at its own roots and, finding them insular, had to face the fact that life experience outside Western culture could nurture vital art.[6] For photography, as for the arts, many of the newly seeded questions about globalization have revolved around identity issues. For example, installation artist and photographer Yinka Shonibare believes that the time has come "to resist the temptation of defining artists by the narrow confines of nationality." He considers that the aesthetic and political concerns found in art should be understood to spring from an artist's judgment, not national origin.[7] In an era of highly integrated art information, photographers such as Shonibare can achieve an international reputation. Likely enough, globalization fostered questions about cultural territory, national identity, and social roots. But these queries do not have the same emphasis of those raised during the Postmodern period, where identity issues were frequently associated with an underclass, or with indigenous people who struggle to maintain their languages and custom.

In short, as some artists and photographers seek to move away from national and ethnic identification, others are making commitments to create art and photography that is directly and deliberately tied to the contemporary conditions of regions and nations. As Jean-Hubert Martin pointed out about the 2005–06 exhibition *Africa Remix*, "Being the same and different seems to be the paradoxical condition in which contemporary art evolves."[8]

For example, while Shonibare rejects being tagged as a Nigerian-British photographer, several Mexican photographers and critics insist the image-making should be for and about regional Mexican issues. They take exception to what they understand to be the international view of Gabriel Orozco (see p. 452), which casts off his origins or "de-localizes" his work from the region to the world.[9] In contemporary Mexican art and photography, the explicit Mexican combination of economic hardship, political corruption, migrant-worker exploitation, and drug trafficking has produced a milieu that Mexicans call the "aesthetics of corruption."[10]

In this harsh climate, art and documentary photographers judge that the art most needed is that which identifies and interprets social conditions for a wide audience. Perhaps the most famous instance of this strategy is the photography of Mexico City photographer Daniela Rossell (b. 1973), who documents the extravagant and conspicuous consumption of Mexico's rich in her ongoing series *Ricas y Famosas* (*Rich and Famous*). The women who sit for Rossell's portraits are like rare hothouse plants, nurtured in an overheated environment from which they can seldom leave because of the constant threat of kidnapping (Fig. 8.6). While Rossell's work has been shown internationally, its greatest impact and meaning are found in Mexico. Her photographs are free from the interest in folklore and tradition that engaged Mexican art and photography in the past and fixed the

8.6
DANIELA ROSSELL,
Paulina with Lion from
Rics Y Famosas (Rich and Famous), 1999.
Color photograph.

A theme of conspicuous consumption runs through Rossell's often gold-toned photographs of Mexico's rich and famous residents. Here the subject, clothed in tennis garments, places a foot on the head of a stuffed lion, symbolizing her social clout.

country's international cultural identity. Moreover, they were not conceived as a visual example of an abstract theory, but formulated out of actual social conditions.

In Mexico, the dedication to making images about the present means focusing on the poverty and unemployment caused by the virtual collapse of Mexican industry, which was brought on by the spread of global capitalism and by the North American Free Trade Agreement (NAFTA), which came into effect in 1994. What might be called critical nationalism is also abundantly apparent in the photographs that document the installations of Teresa Margolies (b. 1963). Like Gabriel Orozco, Margolies favors transient works of art that depend on photography to record them. For more than a decade, Margolies has given aesthetic expression to her country's high violent-death rate. Working in the morgue to which unidentified gunshot victims are often brought, she collected the soap and water used to wash corpses, and created a lyrical installation of floating bubbles to memorialize the dead. Both Rossell and Margolies reject the elitism of Postmodern theory and stress that their work should be accessible to and understandable by a wide cultural swath of people. Their work does not depend on critical theory to be understood. In addition, the beginning of another shift, from social protest to social programs, is apparent in the work of some Mexican artists, who run programs, like employment agencies, for the indigent.

In India, Ravi Agarwal (b. 1958) makes related photographs that give a glimpse of the inequities of economic globalization. He often configures his pictures of large cities, such as New Delhi, to show homeless workers living in the shadow of shiny new hotels and skyscrapers. Agarwal shares another pursuit that has become apparent in contemporary Mexico. Like the Mexican artists who set up organizations to help the poor find employment and food, he is an activist who founded Toxics Link, an environmental exchange service for grassroots organizations, and he is the head of Srishti, a citizens group that devises strategies to manage urban medical and municipal waste in India. In the United States, photographer

Lonnie Graham (b.1953) not only makes images but also uses his financial resources to create human-betterment projects. For instance, he began the African-American Garden Project, which brought farmers from Africa to the United States to teach African agricultural techniques. He believes that "as artists we must not limit ourselves to our imaginations."[11]

In the past, photographers concerned with social change, such as Jacob Riis and Margaret Bourke-White, hoped to stimulate reform directly through their images; photographers in the newly independent India proposed that photography should be "of Indians, by Indians, and for Indians" (see p. 324). By contrast, some contemporary photographers and artists consider it necessary to reach beyond their image-making into direct social action.

The re-accentuation of the worth and distinctiveness of regions, coupled with the continuing interrogation of abstract, unifying systems, such as globalization and Modernism, has kindled further reflection on colonialism, not just as it was practiced in the past, but as it currently takes place. For example, Croatian critic Andreja Kuluncic (b. 1968), whose photo-based posters confront contemporary social problems, links Croatia's application to join the European Union with the tendency of the country's artists to seek more international attention. In turn, international curators arrived, seeking new art works. "We don't want to be colonized," Kuluncic declared, adding that curators have a fixed idea or stereotype about what Croatian art and photography are, an attitude that stifles change and original thinking.[12]

Many issues that inflect contemporary discussion of globalization have been the subject of articles and exhibitions created by Okwui Enwezor. In shows such as *Documenta* XI (2002) and *The Short Century* (2001), art and photography from developing countries were extensively displayed. Enwezor is concerned that that other curators tend to reject images and objects that refers to topical subject matter, or which are grounded in particular geographic locations and conditions.[13] To those who find documentary and even contemporary images without aesthetic appeal, Enwezor replies that today "boundaries between art, journalism, and sociology are essentially nonexistent."[14]

GLOBAL/LOCAL

Globalization's shrinking of time and distance has created a cultural moment in which photographers and artists can more easily cut themselves loose from geography and local culture, or have their work decontextualized by curators. Contradictions abound, as it becomes increasingly possible to think globally and act locally, and vice versa. For example, the exhibition *Ultra-Baroque: Aspects of Post-Latin American Art*, which toured the United States and Canada in 2002–03, readily stretched the term "baroque" from its conventional dates and meaning to include nineteenth and twentieth-century acts of resistance to colonialism and economic repression on the part of indigenous or mestizo people. "Latin America" still refers to the geographic area of Central and South America, but with a decided new emphasis on both regional and transnational interactions.

In Dubrovnik, Croatia, during the spring of 2004, photographs from the war that gripped the former Yugoslavia for a decade were selected by ten photographers and exhibited at a new gallery called War Photo Limited, whose aim

was to show people what happened in the nearby area during the war. Among the images were some by Ron Haviv (b. 1965), including a 1992 image from Bijeljina that shows a young Serb militiaman about to kick a prostrate woman in the head (Fig. 8.7). Haviv's photograph is untitled, but residents certainly would be able to deduce who was a Muslim and who was a Serb. While the exhibition was free to locals, its aim was to educate international visitors from the cruise ships that dock in Dubrovnik. Conversely, in 2003, when Peru's Truth Commission issued a 5,000-page report on the history and social effects of the radical group called Shining Path, they decided that they could reach far more Peruvians if they created a photography exhibition out of the image-bank of about 1,700 photographs. The high Andes city of Chorrillos, located in an area that saw much violence, was chosen as the site of a temporary museum called Yuyanapaq, a Quechua word meaning "to remember." Peruvians by the thousands flocked to see photographs that were documentary as well as interpretive art. Since then, the exhibit has continued to be mounted in other areas of the country, including Lima, the capital. Although the photographs have worldwide interest,

8.7
RON HAVIV, *Untitled* from *Blood and Honey: A Balkan War Journal*, Bijeljina, Bosnia, March 31, 1992.

The soldier's graceful balletic stance belies the cruelty of this scene as the viewer realizes that he is about to kick the prostrate and helpless woman at his feet.

Yuyanapaq was mainly an exhibit by and for Peruvians. Similarly, *Why Are We the Way We Are?*, a Guatemalan exhibition composed largely of photographs, started in Guatemala City during 2004 and continued circulating through 2005. Like the Peruvian show, the Guatemalan exposition was composed of image calculated to communicate the history of the country, including is recent armed conflicts. It used life-size photographs to create what was for some the first experience of looking into the eyes of an indigenous person. As Jim Vokert, associate director of the Smithsonian's National Museum of the American Indian, observed, the show was not about art, but "its significance is that it has the ability to affect the culture of a country, and is rare in a museum context."[15] In one of the photo-installations, the viewer's face was reflected in a mirror placed in the center of multiple rows of head-shots that emphasized the facial differences among Guatemalans.

During the early twenty-first century, the craving to break free from imposed ethnic and national identities is at odds with the desire to make photography for and about specific locales. In the present moment, there are also inklings that the "Us and the Other" approach to art and photography is being challenged by the notion that there is no non-Western art or photographic practice that has been uninflected by Western ideas and economics. The idea of the exotic, morally superior Other seems to be giving way to the observation that there is no outside intellectual space from which one can fashion a high-minded

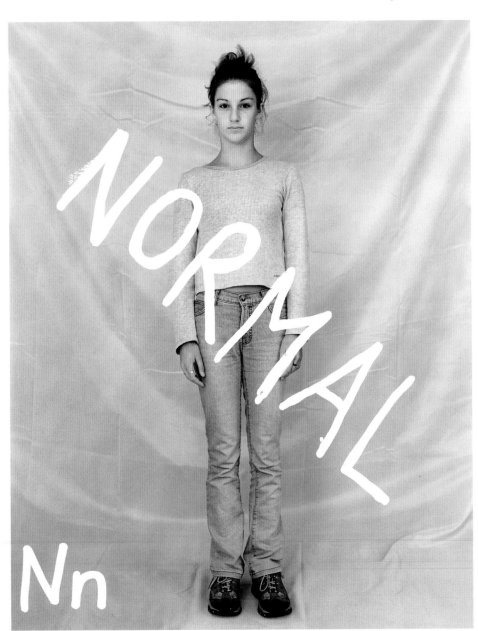

8.8
WENDY EWALD,
White Girl's Alphabet,
2002. Chromogenic print.

A student shows that the letter N stands for "normal," which is to say that whiteness connotes being or feeling normal. Standing against a simple background, she demonstrates her knack for wearing the right clothes and shoes while the word NORMAL traverses the image diagonally.

objective critique. That point of view was taken up at a controversial 2005 show organized at the International Center of Photography in New York City.

As its title implies, *White: Whiteness and Race in Contemporary Art* shifted the focus away from other identities and on to the one that is often assumed but seldom discussed. To grasp the cultural understanding of whiteness, Nancy Burson placed an advertisement for men who thought they looked like Jesus. She photographed them and then employed her composite technique to show how much skin color influences people's mental image of Christ. In 2002, as part of her ongoing engagement with young people and their ideas, Wendy Ewald collaborated with high-school students at the Phillips Academy in Andover, Massachusetts, to create *White Girl's Alphabet* (Fig .8.8). The students linked alphabet letters to the concepts they explored, contrived costumes that exemplified the ideas, and were photographed by Ewald. Ultimately, they created a photograph for each alphabet letter and concept.

Hints of a more holistic interpretation of globalization were noted in a much discussed, theory-thick book titled *Empire*, by Michael Hardt and Antonio Negri, published in 2000. The authors insist that globalization is not just another phase of capitalism, but a new form of power that is circulating throughout the world. There is no place beyond its reach. In this "Empire," as they call it, revolution is more possible than in the past because the very instant communications systems that make Empire possible also empower its opposition, whom they call "the multitude."[16] Hardt and Negri are no friends of Postmodernism, whose emphasis on ethnic identities they see as obscuring a global view. Instead, they see the multitude coming together physically and digitally to defend global rights, such as fair wages. The book was quickly picked up by historians, critics, artists, and photographers. Whatever its flaws, *Empire* is a book like Marshall McLuhan's *Understanding Media* (1964) (see page 383), which people do not always read critically, but from which they find passages that suggest hope and excitement in the future.

The Arab World

Not surprisingly, after September 11, 2001, studies and exhibitions of photography having to do with Islam or with Arab identity multiplied. At the 2003 Venice Bienniale, curator Catherine David organized a section called "Contemporary Arab Representations." She maintained that the word "representations" was far better than the word "art" to describe the various media presented in the show, including photography. Curators of photography and art exhibitions have had to confront the dilemma of defining the so-called Arab world, a phrase that is often used to imply cultural homogeneity where it does not exist. Wisely, Catherine David has designated one country, Lebanon, as a laboratory in which to consider photographic practice. Other shows, such as *Nazar: Photographs from the Arab World*, held during 2004 in the Netherlands, defined the Arab world as comprising places where Arabic is the predominant language. They also included images of what might be termed the Arab diaspora to Europe and North America. Palestine represents the most acute case of Arab dispersion, and at the Venice Bienniale of 2003, Sandi Hilal (b. 1973) and Alessandro Petti (b. 1973) created billboard-sized enlargements of identity photographs and passports belonging to Palestinians, but issued by the countries in which they were currently living in exile, such as Italy, Israel, and Jordan.

Many exhibitions of Arab photography include many regional, national, or religious identities, which intentionally makes them difficult to generalize an Arab stereotype. That effort to differentiate Arabs was taken up by Walid Raad (b.1967), who combed the rich files of the Arab Image Foundation (AIF) in Beirut, Lebanon, for ordinary photographs that would visually chronicle Arab diversity. Ironically he found them among hundreds of commercial portraits made for ID cards and other public uses. Despite efforts to standardize the image, these conventional photographs show a great variety of physical features, an aspect of identity photographs also emphasized in the Guatemalan exhibition *Why Are We the Way We Are?*.

FOCUS
China

After the death of Mao Zedong in 1976 and the dissolution of the Cultural Revolution (1966–76), which forcibly attempted to bring the arts and photography into line with Chinese Communist social objectives, Chinese photographers cautiously began to explore the limits of their freedom. While their exhibitions were sometimes shut down or denounced, the work that they were able to send abroad often received accolades, prompting the Chinese government to recognize that artistic freedom at home could help the country's image abroad.[17] Although impassioned debates about the social responsibilities of photography still affect them, photographers have increasing control over their own work.

From 2004 to 2006, the exhibition *Between Past and Future: New Photography and Video from China*, organized by Wu Hung and Christopher Phillips, traveled North America and Europe, after having been launched at the International Center of Photography in New York. The comprehensive show tracked the major developments in Chinese photography since 1976, but its major emphasis was on work created in the late 1990s and the early twenty-first century.

The efflorescence of Chinese photography accompanied the escalation of experimental art and access to visual technology, which began in the 1990s.[18]

Thus, many artists who work in other media became familiar with photographic practice and some even took it up exclusively. As happened in the West, the directorial mode attracted many Chinese photographers. Hong Lei (b.1960), a painter turned photographer, not only sets up the scenes he photographs, but also scratches and paints on the print's surface. One of his images uses the Forbidden City, China's ancient capital, as a backdrop. It features a bejeweled dead pheasant which was likely brought down to earth by the beads wound in its wings (Fig. 8.9). Hong's photographic work often derives its settings and motifs from traditional Chinese painting, where, for instance, pheasants and other birds adorn ideal landscapes. Hong fears the effects of globalization on Chinese tradition, and openly longs for the past glories of Chinese art. Nevertheless, his photographs are often glazed with blood-red color, an indication that he can also be critical of the past.

Chinese photographers sometimes associate photographic realism with Socialist Realism and the repressive period of the Cultural Revolution. Consequently, they temper the camera's ability to make imprints of the observable world. For example, Wang Jinsong (see p. 458), whose work seems documentary, usually uses a grid to organize his many disparate pictures, and to

8.9
HONG LEI, *Autumn in the*
Forbidden City, **1997. C-print.**

break up the viewer's easy assumption of photographic realism. Similarly, the breadth of Zhuang Hui's images (see p. 419), and the great number of individuals packed into them, constitute a work that is simultaneously a document and a critique of the realist photography's shortcomings. Liu Zheng (b. 1969), sometimes referred to as China's August Sander, teasingly photographs realist sculpture as if the figures were alive. His seven-year project *The Chinese* is stylistically more adventuresome than Sander was, yet it shares the encyclopedic urge to record the panoply of people and activities within a nation (Fig. 8.10).

As photographers in China continue to experiment with the limits of public expression, the human body has become increasingly central in their work. Performance art flourishes, and artists such as Chen Lingyang (b. 1975) have fused fantasy and feminism in a visual rumination on women in art. Chen's *25:00* shows a figure she calls the giantess, who is waiting for what Chen notes is the impossible twenty-fifth hour in the day when she will shake off her languor, realize her social worth, reflected in her physical size, and become "large" in the world. The sleeping giantess, digitally perched on the recently constructed buildings of modern urban China, seems equally decipherable as Chen and as the contemporary Chinese woman (Fig. 8.11).

While contemporary photographic practice flourishes, historic work created and preserved by official and unofficial photographers is slowly making its way into the public realm in China and elsewhere, hinting at the possibility that the most populous country on earth may eventually be able to construct its own photographic history.

8.10 (left)
LIU ZHENG, *Buddha in Cage,*
Wutai Mountain, Shanxi Province.
Gelatin silver print, 1998.

8.11 (below)
CHEN LINGYANG, *25:00*, 2002.
Digitally combined photographs.

YOUTH AND BEAUTY

Throughout the last quarter of the twentieth century, beauty was held accountable for photography's lapses and misdeeds, especially in the area of social concern. In his enduringly influential essay, "On the Invention of Photographic Meaning" (1975), photographer-critic Allan Sekula savaged art for art's sake, writing that "the ills of photography are the ills of aestheticism," and that "aestheticism must be superseded, in its entirety, for a meaningful art, of any sort, to emerge."[19] Critic Hal Foster concurred in his popular anthology *The Anti-Aesthetic* (1983), whose title was drawn from a phrase fashioned in Walter Benjamin's authoritative essay "The Work of Art in the Age of Mechanical Reproduction."[20] Foster questioned whether the aesthetic was now a threadbare illusion.[21] Time and again, beauty has been sent packing to the cobwebbed attic of outmoded ideas. The anti-aesthetic persisted into the twenty-first century. For example, in 2003 Martha Rosler opined that in the United States, "the debate over beauty has been deeply reactionary, a cry for 'art for art's sake' to return us to the grand old days when the critics were in control, patrons knew what to buy and artists didn't mess with politics."[22]

Mindful of the lessons from the recent past, a few photographers modestly began to explore what might constitute a fragile post-Postmodern beauty. For German photographer Rineke Dijkstra (b. 1959), beauty is as tentative as the hesitant step being taken by the adolescent boy she photographed in Berlin's Tiergarten (Fig. 8.12). In her pictures of young men and women, some of whom she has photographed for years, Dijkstra secures both fact and symbol. Measured against the stark, blank faces of Thomas Ruff's photographs (see Fig. 7.45), Dijkstra's portraits are lush, informative, and loving. She is, in her own words, a believer in observing rather than in asking questions, a conviction that would have cast her as a reactionary in the postmodern era, but which has special resonance in the post September 11 period.[23] Because she focuses on the vulnerable yet inevitable time of life when the innocence of childhood visibly and

spiritually grows into experience, she has fashioned widely understood elegiac visual metaphors for lost innocence, coupled with a consolation that radiates from the calm surrender of her young subjects to the path of physical and mental maturity.

A similar melancholic tone informs Bill Henson's photographs (see p. 496), especially his recent work, in which nude adolescent bodies populate a post-apocalyptic suburban night. Similarly, the predominantly female subjects photographed by American Justine Kurland (b. 1969) frequently inhabit actual natural settings, whose dead tree branches and rutted terrain, though enclosed in a conventional landscape composition, fall short of the painterly ideal (Fig. 8.13). In these post-Paradise settings, such as that portrayed in *Ochre Anointment*, strange and often erotic rituals seem to be taking place.

Kurland is one of a group of women, including Dana Hoey, Katy Grannan, Malerie Marder, and Jenny Gage, who studied with Gregory Crewdson at Yale University in New Haven, Connecticut, and whom Crewdson grouped together in *Another Girl, Another Planet*, a New

8.12
RINEKE DIJKSTRA,
Tiergarten, Berlin,
August 13, 2000.
C-print.

Dijkstra tentatively reintroduced the human form as a source of visual pleasure by choosing to photograph the awkward grace of teenagers in a Berlin park. Her large color portraits of young people teetering between the free rein of childhood and adulthood's equipoise dwell on the casual, utterly unclassical and temporary beauty of transient states of being.

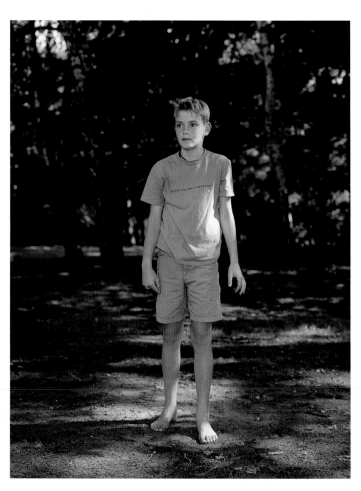

In Kurland's vision of paradise, young women do not compete for good grades and highly paid jobs, but run away from civilization to pursue a vaguely mythological existence in a new nature from which men are absent.

York exhibition Crewdson helped organize in March 1999. The show led to years of back-handed praise and reference to the women as "girl photographers," although they do not claim to be a group. Another Yale graduate from Crewdson's photography program, Anna Gaskell (b. 1969), was missing from that show, but seems closest to Crewdson in her interest in the supernatural and the uncanny. Like the other "girl photographers," she constructs edgy pictures, mostly of young women. In her series *resemblance*, she presented a series of images in which young women (actually students at Phillips Academy in Andover, Massachusetts) seem to be creating an ideal human. Based on her musings on works by Lewis Carroll, as well as by French author Villers de l'Isle Adam (1838–1889) and German author E. T. A. Hoffman (1776–1832), Gaskell concocts dramatic moments filled with foreboding and hints of secret ritual (Fig. 8.14).

Gaskell's literary sources pinpoint a divergence within the late twentieth-century directorial mode; where television and the movies once acted as sources, now myth and fairytale have begun to play a large part. Both, of course, contain sinister elements, but the latter are probably more rich and flexible, and they open into a territory of imagination and psychological probing. The early twenty-first century popularity of photography by young women of young women was triggered in part by the response of young women — and men — to these photographs. Not only did this unexpected surge of interest set off speculation that the young might constitute a new market for art; it also influenced advertising. Eighteen- to twenty-five-year-olds constitute the demographic, as it is called, to which most media advertisements are aimed. Consequently, upscale photographic advertisement for companies such as Prada included sulky women lounging together or anxious single figures in lonely settings.

The American "girl photographers" were part of a larger and global refocusing on young women. For example, the internationally successful film *Whale Rider* (2002) showed a New Zealand Maori girl coming of age by making a new place for herself in traditional

**8.14
ANNA GASKELL,
*Untitled no. 74
(Resemblance)*, 2001.
C-print.**

An unsettling ambiguity
often dominates
Gaskell's work. Here,
it is not clear whether
the figures in white
robes are performing
a laying-on-of-hands to
help or to thwart the
person whose legs they
are touching.

culture; in *Bend It Like Beckham* (2002),
an Asian-British teenager struggles
not only with gender roles, but also
with the tug of her family's heritage.
Confident young women appear in *The
Adventures of Guille and Belinda and the
Enigmantic Meaning of their Dreams*, a
series of photographs begun in 1999 by
American-born Alessandra Sanguinetti
(b. 1968), who divides her time between
New York and Argentina. She palled
around with two rural girls on and off
for five years, and photographed them
as they acted out their fantasies.

Since she was a teenager in the
1990s, Japanese photographer Hiromix
(b. 1971, as Toshikawa Hiromi) has
recorded and circulated photographs
of her everyday life. Known as the quintessential *onna no ko no shashinka*—that
is, girl photographer—she became
an example to many young women.
Today's girl photographer in Japan is
more likely to direct eerie scenes involving teenagers and young women. For
example, throughout the last decade,

Japanese performance artist and photo
grapher Miwa Yanagi (b. 1967) perfected menace-tinged digital fantasies
about department store "elevator girls,"
who welcome and give directions in
upscale Japanese department stores.
Her work was showcased in the 2002
PhotoEspaña (*Photo/Spain*), titled
Femeninos (*Femininities*). Another exhibition based on the notion of girlhood
as an eccentric and absorbing phase
of life was the internationally drawn
exhibition *Girl's Night Out*, which was
shown across the United States in
2004–06. It featured photographers
such as Daniela Rossell and Rineke
Dijkstra. Perhaps the most interesting
aspect of the show was its sponsor,
the Neutrogena company, which
makes skin-care products aimed at
young women.

SNAPSHOT DIARISTS

The early twenty-first century witnessed
an increase in personal photography
among the young, which has its historical

precedents in such popular work as Nan Goldin's *The Ballad of Sexual Dependency* and in the snapshot style introduced during the 1990s by influential contemporary photographers such Corinne Day and Wolfgang Tillmans. The success of *Look-Look* magazine, which was founded in 2003, rests on its active solicitation of informal and art photographs by young people, many of whom are in high school. *Look-Look* has given digital cameras to teenagers around the world and hired them to make pictures. The results seem less like staid photo-album images of birthdays and weddings and more like the tilted angles and odd coincidences of street photography in the 1960s and 1970s.

While digital cameras, cameraphones (see below), and photoblogs have encouraged people to create visual diaries of themselves and their own activities, these efforts tend to render an uncomplicated view of reality. Diaristic photography, on the other hand, sets out clues to subjective feelings in pictures with indefinite and implied narratives. Moreover, diaristic photographers do not insist on a particular interpretation. As Craig Garrett observed, diarists avoid contemporary political issues by turning inward. They seem to say, "this is my life, my observation, my reality."[24] The diarists' procedures may seem akin to the literary or cinematic use of metaphor to suggest inner feelings, but the diaristic photograph is even more open-ended. It does not stand for states of mind that elude description; rather, it invites the viewer to engage the image and construct a narrative from his or her experience. Where photobloggers and cameraphone users expect to communicate through their pictures, diaristic photographers hope to spark a reaction or an independent narrative in the mind of the viewer. Noting a comparable mindset underlying Anna Gaskell's photographs, art historian Claire Daigle detected a diaristic mode of narration, but one that is "distinctly impersonal," signaling "a shift away from the subjective to the demonstrative."[25] So-called reality television, which features ordinary people doing or saying mundane and extraordinary things, may have encouraged diaristic photography, but it cannot account for its cool tone and "whatever" attitude.

SCIENCE AND SOCIETY

In the early twenty-first century, the public had unprecedented access to space photographs generated by cameras onboard unmanned vessels, such as the Hubble Space Telescope, the Mars Global Surveyor Orbiter, NASA's Mars

8.15
MARS ROVER,
"Spirit" approaches "Methuselah" Outcrop on Mars, April 13th, 2005.

"Spirit" and "Opportunity" are the small robotic devices called rovers that are directed from Earth to inspect and photograph the surface of Mars. Each image is automatically time-stamped with the number of seconds since January 1, 2000.

rovers, the Cassini spacecraft and its lander, named Huygens, created by NASA and the European Space Agency, and Great Britain's Mars Express, which was launched by the European Space Agency (Fig. 8.15). Pictures of vast cone nebulas, where stars are created, and gauzy remnants of supernovas, the remains of exploded stars, competed with images of Saturn's largest moon, Titan, cloaked in tangerine skies. The colors of outer space reminded art critics and photographers of abstract art, and at a conference held in 2003, they debated whether a photograph taken by a robot could be considered art.

Less debated was the way in which the photographs transmitted from distant space crafts obtain the color. The cameras on the Mars rovers only take black-and-white pictures. Filters and computer manipulation do the rest. Nevertheless, black-and-white images do not easily translate into color.[26] Just as colorized black-and-white films from the early twentieth century do not have the rich depth that color film produces, so the Mars rover pictures look more like they were dunked in orange Kool-Aid.

Black-and-white photographs of supernovas taken by the Hubble Space Telescope resemble blurry pictures of what look like white jellyfish in a dark sea. However, when colorized, they take on the appearance of bursting fireworks. The color of space photographs is mostly created on this planet, both to intensify indications of color as they are rendered in black-and-white, and to please human eyes. So-called "raw images" are usually available on project websites, but they are generally not published in newspapers and magazines.

Ray Villard, long-time public relations director for the Hubble project, was candid in his assessment of colorization. "It's hard to tell the story if you don't have a stunning image to back it up," he said. In an attempt to convince the public that unmanned journeys to the cosmos are worth their exorbitant cost, space photographs more and more resemble digitally drenched color of art photographs or stills from action-adventure movies. Then again, critics point out that color is a subjective capability limited to some inhabitants of earth, not an objective quality. Scientists in other disciplines routinely tint their work. For example, at the Oak Ridge National Laboratory in Tennessee, the sharpest picture ever made of atoms was tinted red, not because it appeared red, but to make it more attractive.

High-tech photographic imaging has become an ever-increasing meeting ground for artists and scientists. Their works compete in an international contest for the best photography taken through a microscope sponsored by the camera company Nikon. ANGIOGRAMS, a type of X-ray that employs a sharp contrast material to highlight blood vessels in the human body and brain, are found on hospital light boxes and in art books. Artist Catherine Wagner uses the medical diagnostic tool called magnetic resonance imaging (MRI) coupled with a scanning electron microscope to create photographs that peer inside objects, like an ear of corn, to disclose its rough symmetry. The increased fidelity of body-imaging has come home to many in the form of an ultrasound photograph—that is, a sound pattern turned into a visual image. Prenatal portraits are now available commercially, as traditional glossy prints or on CDs, from which they can be transmitted on the Internet.

THE ANIMAL KINGDOM

While surveillance cameras are becoming more common in urban areas, they are also entering the jungle. The World Wildlife Fund placed thirty "camera traps" in the tropical forests of Indonesia, where they gather photographs of the rare Sumatran tiger. Camera traps also record tigers in Africa and jaguars in Central America. But as the human genome project reveals the genetic similarity of humans and apes, it is primates who have most captured the public imagination. In 2003, Sebastião Salgado photographed the game preserves of the Democratic Republic of the Congo, Rwanda, and Uganda, home to the endangered mountain gorillas, whom he called the animals most like humans. Salgado perceived that mental concentration in gorillas looks like that of humans.[27] For Kenya-born James Mollison (b. 1973), the capacity of the great apes to look thoughtful creates their individuality.

(above left) Millie,
orangutan, three-years
old, born in the United
States.

(above right) Kola,
gorilla, 14-years old,
Republic of Congo.

(below left) La Vieille,
chimpanzee, Republic
of Congo.

(below right) Joji,
orangutan, six-years old,
Indonesia.

Two hundred years
ago, apes were mostly
thought to possess the
least desirable human
qualities, such as
violence and aggression.
By contrast, Mollison
emphasizes their
individuality and com-
passionate attention.

His close-up portraits show none of the familiar circus-act cuteness for which they are best known. He deliberately did not correct the effect of the flash bouncing off the ape's retinas, but left it as a sign of his presence (Fig. 8.16).

PLATFORMS

If the late twentieth century was the time of the computer revolution, then the last ten years have been the era of a quieter change, the development of "platforms," which allow operating systems in digital devices to communicate with each other, often wirelessly. In effect, that means that digital cameras and cameraphones can download their pictures onto the Internet, or that people can link these devices to self-service printing machines that are available in malls and camera shops. Phones can send pictures to other cameraphones or to moblogs—that is, mobile phone blogs. Interestingly, while people still want to print out their photographs, they increasingly do not want to do so at home, but choose to take advantage of the frequent technological upgrades at public photo kiosks and on-line services. Consequently, Adobe, the company that make the Photoshop software with which to alter photographs, now advertises its product as enabling creativity. Hewlett Packard enjoins users to get inventive and make black-and-white photographs with their printers.

Photoblogs have multiplied rapidly since 2000. While the blogsphere presents Internet users with a huge number of choices, those choices are, as critic David Brittain pointed out, modeled on the global marketplace, where ideas co-exist alongside commercial activities.[28] Bloggers do not consider the presence of commerce to be a drawback, and frequently point out that taste-makers should not narrow the photoblog's content. Many photographs are increasingly transmitted to blogs from cameraphones, whose sales are projected to reach 1 billion by 2010.

The cameraphone is the slimmer, more democratic descendant of the simple Kodak camera that was first marketed in 1888. Because of its size, the cameraphone can be used stealthily in the public sphere, sometimes to the annoyance of people on the street whose actions have been fashioned into recorded dramas, edited by the cameraphone owner. Some public places, such as courtrooms, have banned the cameraphones and use detectors to ferret them out. Nevertheless, so-called "cellphone paparazzi" take full advantage of this device to capture the likeness of celebrities.

The escalating use of cameraphones has breathed new life into the simple snapshot and created many new photographers, especially among the young. It has encouraged the practice of citizen photojournalism, and extended the photographic diary, like that created by Nan Goldin, to millions who find it a creative outlet. The current question for both digital camera and cameraphone pictures is how long they will last. There are no conclusive tests for the longevity of CDs, nor can one assume that the file formats used today will be readable in thirty years.

Yet these might be the wrong questions to ask about images whose owners may never have made them material by printing them. The millions of digital images now on hard drives and memory chips may be changing the definition of the snapshot and family photography as a palpable, lasting record, the stuff of albums. In the era with so much fleeting imagery, the photograph may come to be understood like television broadcasts, which can be stored for future viewing, but generally are not.

WAR AND PHOTOGRAPHY

The merger of photographic fields was further confirmed by images of and about the Iraq War. Martha Rosler, who made photomontages about the Vietnam War in the 1970s, used the technique to relate extravagant American domestic interiors and views of Saddam Hussein's palace to war casualties. James Nachtwey, whose images of prior conflicts were shown in galleries as well as magazines and newspapers, was injured in 2003 while photographing in Iraq. Gilles Peress, whose work also bestrides art and photography, took photographs in Iraq in 2005, when the war had clearly changed into a struggle with urban bombers and insurgents. In addition, painter-photographer Gerhard Richter created the book *War Cut* (2004), which contains reproductions of his abstract paintings juxtaposed with news accounts of the war.

The 2004 revelation of U.S. soldiers' amateur photographs showing prisoner abuse in Iraq's Abu Ghraib prison kindled what is perhaps the largest worldwide public interpretation of photographs. Of course, other photographs, such as Dorothea Lange's *Migrant Mother* were influential and much discussed, but what they depicted was seldom questioned. By contrast, the Abu Ghraib debate centered on what the images represented, with different views ranging from the notion that they showed little more than a fraternity prank to the idea that they pictured a repulsive spectacle of torture. On May 6, 2004, President George W. Bush apologized publicly for the way in which the photographs humiliated the prisoners and their families, while adding his take on the interpretation quandary. He remarked that he was "equally sorry that people seeing these pictures didn't understand the true nature and heart of America."[29]

The Abu Ghraib photographs were unknowingly made in the directorial mode that dominated late twentieth- and early twenty-first century photographic practice. In many of these photographs, prisoners were forced to act out scenes of humiliation for the camera. For example, the striking scene of a roughly hooded and cloaked figure from whose outstretched hands dangle electrical wires associated with painful interrogation techniques, does not show torture, but has been fabricated both to trick the subject and the viewer into thinking that torture is about to begin. Initially, the soldier-photographers e-mailed the images to friends, apparently in a spirit of amusement and camaraderie.

The image of the hooded figure instantly embarked on a new and full life in the other arts. Andres Serrano directed a reenactment of it for the front cover of the *New York Times Magazine* (Fig. 8.0), and Richard Serra (b. 1939) created two lithographic interpretations. In Iraq, the artists' union quickly prepared paintings and sculptures that emphasized the prisoners as victims. In the United States and Europe, graphic designers converted it into election campaign posters and magazine covers. Its instantly recognizable silhouette was transmogrified into a global symbol of menace.

PHILOSOPHY AND PRACTICE: SEEING AND BEING SEEN

Photographs such as the notorious one purporting to show Presidential candidate Senator John Kerry, a Vietnam War medal-winner, sitting near Jane Fonda at an anti-Vietnam War rally, were circulated during the 2004 United States presidential election campaign, renewing a uneasiness about photographic deception. Of course, misleading political photographs did not start with digital imaging or the Internet. In the 1870s, photographer Eugène Appert staged scenes with actors and used old-fashioned cut-and-paste methods on the resultant photographs to contrive political propaganda for the forces opposing the French Commune (see pp. 113–5).

Concern for the possible malevolent effects of computer-manipulated photographs overshadows other powerful ways in which photographs have been and will continue to be deceptive. Omitting images, such as the scenes of forced labor that Aleksandr Rodchenko excluded from his series on the building of the Russia's White Canal (see p. 242), can be as deceiving as reshaping pictures. In 2004, the U.S. military ban on

news agencies photographing the flag-draped coffins of soldiers killed in the Iraq conflict was tested when an employee of a military subcontractor took such a photograph. Spokespersons for the U.S. government stated that the ban was devised to protect the emotional sensitivity of families who have lost soldiers. *The Memory Hole*, a website devoted to preserving records of all kinds, soon received allegedly mistaken permission to post photographs of the dead soldiers. Although the ban still stands, it has been subject to many successful challenges.

The vulnerability of viewers continues to serve as a rationale for newspapers and television companies not to present photographs, or to preface their presentations with a warning. Interestingly, there was nearly complete public and news agency consensus not to show photographs of the bodies falling or jumping from the World Trade Center on September 11, 2001.

The settings in which viewers see shocking photographs can set the tone for their reception. Those who viewed the Abu Ghraib photographs on-line or on television did not voice many objections. But when the Abu Ghraib photographs were shown at the International Center of Photography in New York City and at the Andy Warhol Museum in Pittsburgh, some people found the display unpatriotic and inappropriate in an art setting.

What is the proper setting for such photographs? Although photography was disclosed to the world in 1839, there never developed special civic venues where photographs can be seen, other than in art galleries and museums. Perhaps in the current era of multiple convergences, it will prove less problematic to recognize that historical practice has designated museums and galleries as sites for viewing photographic prints of all kinds.

Yet the question remains: does the public have the stamina to see horrific photographs? Is this a legal or an ethical issue? In her final book, *Regarding the Pain of Others* (2003), philosopher-critic Susan Sontag rethought the impact of horrific photographs, such as war photographs, which she had concluded in her earlier and influential work *On Photography*, desensitized and, literally, de-moralized the public. But in her revised view, she proposed that the vast repository of war photographs that has accumulated since photography was invented does have a moral purpose. She pointed out that individual photographs, such as that by Ron Haviv (see Fig. 8.7), may tell us very little about the specific causes and motives of war. Nevertheless the collective social archive of war photographs serves as a constant reminder of human suffering and wickedness. "Let the atrocious images haunt us," Sontag declared. "Even if they are only tokens, and cannot possibly encompass most of the reality to which they refer, they still perform a vital function." She forcefully concluded that "remembering *is* an ethical act."[30]

Democratic access to images and to information developed as a permanent ideal in Western culture during the Enlightenment. It became attached to photography by the mid-nineteenth century, as in the enthusiasm expressed by an anonymous writer in an 1858 issue of the British journal *The Athenaeum*, who foresaw an educational revolution caused by stereographic photography, such that "perhaps in ten years or so the question will be seriously discussed ... whether it will be of any use to travel now that you can send out your artist to bring home Egypt in his carpetbag to amuse the drawing room with" (see p. 83, note 7). Of course, international travel is a common event in the West these days, but it remains beyond the economic means of most of the world's people. While estimates project that the number of personal computers sold will reach 2 billion by 2008, most of this growth is in the West, although China, Latin America, Eastern Europe, and India are making important gains. The economic imbalances continue to produce inequities in knowledge.

More than ten years ago, photographer-critic Joan Fontcuberta predicted that the widespread use of digital imaging by amateurs would vanquish the notion of photographic objectivity, while permitting a faster and larger dialogue among artists and the public. Ironically, both digital ardor and digital angst carry the lingering Postmodern questions about the truth-value of traditional photography, while simultaneously hailing the transformative power of the mass media. The union of the photograph, the computer, and high-speed, broadband transmission chimes with cultural dreams about a democratic art in a democratic society.

At photography's inception, when thinkers such as François Arago and William Henry Fox Talbot speculated about the medium's future, they saw it integrated into art, science, and industry, without a peep of protest on the part of those affected by the changes it might bring. The way that photography faithfully indexed the world made the medium seem objective, like a faithful, aloof scribe, rather than an excitable, rabble-rousing partisan. Their scientific training disposed Arago and Talbot to predict that the medium's accepted neutral vision would become attached to the ideal of free and open information systems. They could not have foreseen that their medium would largely be responsible for generating the notion that mediated experience was to be dreaded, because it brought with it alienation from other humans and the shriveling of existence into an obsession with material pursuits.

A positive, even lyrical perception of the mass media was constructed by the Cuban-born artist-photographer Felix Gonzalez-Torres, who while waiting tables mused about how to rephrase the medium's contradictions. Improvising on Alfred Stieglitz's renowned series of *Equivalents*, a set of cloud photographs made to demonstrate that symbols of transcendence were freely available to those who looked for them in nature (see Fig. 4.25), Gonzalez-Torres stacked in a gallery hundreds of inexpensively produced pictures of clouds to be taken away by visitors (see Fig. 2). Whereas Stieglitz's *Equivalents* eventually sold for hundreds of thousands of dollars, Gonzalez-Torres's mass-produced pictures were free.

Photography's future is not a leaden certainty because people such as Gonzalez-Torres view the inconsistencies in its network of history, ideas, and practices as chafing faultlines whose energy can be routed to spark new insight and promise. However much we must be on our guard for the negative social effects of new media, we can also stay alert for and encourage new visions.

GLOSSARY

Abstract Expressionism A mid-twentieth-century art movement, principally in the United States, whose artists promoted the use of color and form to suggest mental states and emotions.

Albumen paper Light-sensitive paper used in conjunction with the collodion negative (*see* COLLODION PROCESS). Printing paper was coated with a mixture of egg white and salt allowed to dry, and then sensitized with a silver nitrate solution. The sensitized paper was placed under a negative and exposed. Albumen paper offered a rich tonal range and a stability greater than the paper treated with salt and silver nitrate that was used to create the salt print. The print had a glossy surface, different from earlier processes in which the image seemed to have sunk into the paper, like a watercolor. Albumen paper was perfected by Louis-Désiré Blanquart-Evrard, and quickly commercialized.

Angiogram An X-ray technique that highlights blood vessels.

Appropriation Literally, to take possession of. Appropriation also refers to an art strategy used in the late 1970s and the 1980s in which an artist took advertising, historical, or popular imagery and incorporated it in a new work of art, so as to alter its meaning.

Aquatint An etching process added to engravings that produces light tones, resembling watercolor washes. Powdered resins are applied to the plate, which is then heated. As it melts, the resins create grains, which, when etched, produce tonal areas in the final print.

Autochrome Invented by Auguste and Louis Lumière in 1904 and marketed in 1907, the autochrome was the first practical method of making color photographs. Like the daguerreotype, the autochrome was a unique image, but developed on a glass plate, not metal or film. The process involved exposing a glass plate that had been covered with tiny granules of sub-stances sensitive to colored light. In the darkroom, a positive was developed on the original glass plate, creating a transparency that could be seen by means of a hand-viewer, or through projection by a magic lantern device, precursor of the slide projector. The autochrome usually had a pebbly surface quality, which resulted from the little light-sensitive pellets used in the manufacturing process.

Beaux-Arts A term derived from the French for "fine arts." When applied to architecture, it denotes the academic classical style that was taught at the Ecole des Beaux Arts in Paris. American architecture was particularly influenced by this style in the period 1885–1920.

Bromoil process A variety of the OIL-PIGMENT PROCESS introduced in 1907 that was easier than the oil-pigment process and could be used for enlarge-ments. Bromo-gelatine paper was exposed to a negative, then bleached to eliminate the silver image. The remaining gelatine formed a relief print upon which color could be applied with a brush.

Calotype Also called the Talbotype, after its British inventor, William Henry Fox Talbot, who patented the process in 1841. As with Daguerre's generous donation of the DAGUERREOTYPE to the world (which did not include England), there were legal restrictions on its use. Photographers had to apply for a license, although Talbot gave the calotype process free to science and amateur photographers.

To create a calotype negative, from which a positive print is made, good-quality writing paper or drawing paper was saturated with a solution of silver nitrate. After the paper dried, it was dipped in a solution of potassium iodide. A light-sensitive layer of silver iodide resulted. This paper could be prepared ahead of time. Before use, it had to be coated with a mixture of silver nitrate and gallic acid to sensitize it. When the light-sensitive paper was exposed in the camera, it produced a LATENT IMAGE, that is, one that could not be seen by the eye. To bring out the latent image, the paper was washed in a mixture of silver nitrate and gallic acid, fixed with HYPO, and flushed with water.

The negative was then placed over sensitized paper called salted paper, which had been brushed or dipped into a solution of sodium chloride or ammonium chloride or a mixture of the two. Both were sandwiched in a printing frame and exposed to sunlight until a positive print was registered. The print was then rinsed in water to decrease its light sensitivity.

Camera lucida From the Latin for "light room." The camera lucida was neither a light, nor a room, but a prism, mounted on a slim rod attached to a drawing board. By adjusting the prism, an artist could create the illusion that a scene was projected onto the drawing board.

Camera obscura From the Latin for "dark room." The camera obscura was originally a darkened chamber with a hole or lens in one wall that allowed an image of the outside world to be projected onto the opposite wall. Small, portable versions were later constructed, which made it possible to copy images reflected on to a panel of translucent glass. The camera obscura ultimately became the box of the photographic camera.

Carte-de-visite Called a card photograph in the United States, the *carte-de-visite* was a small photographic portrait mounted on a cardboard backing that was about the size of a visiting card.

Chiaroscuro Chiaroscuro, from the Italian for "dark and light," refers to the contrasts between light and shade in a painting or a photograph. Chiaroscuro is often used to highlight an important subject and to create dramatic effects.

Cliché verre A coated glass photographic plate into which an artist scratches an image with a sharp stylus. Since light can move through the areas scratched away, the plate can be used as a photographic negative. It is placed on sensitized paper, and exposed to light, which passes through the lines cut into the opaque coating. Many prints can be made from one plate.

Collage The combination of different materials, such as paper, paint, fabrics, photographs, newspaper clippings. Usually pasted on a board or an artist's canvas.

Collodion process Also known as the wet-plate process. A technique developed by Frederick Scott Archer in 1851, in which glass plates were sensitized to light with a sticky substance called collodion mixed with light-sensitive silver salts. Unlike the CALOTYPE process developed by William Henry Fox Talbot, the collodion process was patent-free, which increased its popularity with photographers. By the 1860s, the technique replaced both the daguerreotype and the calotype. Glass plates were covered with a solu-tion of collodion, a sticky mixture of ether, guncotton, and alcohol, to which light-sensitive silver iodide and iodide of iron were added. The plate was then sensitized with a coating of distilled water and silver nitrate. While the plate was still damp, it was placed inside the camera and exposed. The method was dubbed the wet-plate process, because exposure time was diminished when the plate was damp. After exposure, the plate needed to be developed quickly. In the field, photographers set up traveling dark-tents, complete with chemicals.

The process required relatively strong light and long exposure times—sometimes minutes. Moreover, the process was especially sensitive to blue, yielding dull, blank white skies. Yet since the light-sensitive materials were caught up in the film of collodion, they did not leave the kind of paper fiber imprint that paper negatives did. The collodion process was used with albumen paper.

Collotype An adaptation of lithography used to make multiple prints derived from photographic negatives. Photosensitized gelatin was applied to a glass plate, and then exposed to a negative. After careful processing, the resulting plate could be inked and printed on paper.

Combination printing A technique that uses two or more negatives to make a final print. Parts of the sensitive paper are masked so that they will not develop, while a negative is printed where desired. The technique was used by early photographers, such as Gustave Le Gray, to compensate for over-exposed skies, which did not register cloud formations.

Constructivism An early twentieth-century art and design movement originating in the young Soviet Union during the 1920s. Its emphasis on rejecting traditional materials and subjects, and its stress on the union of art and utilitarianism, soon became international.

C-print A c-print (color print) is a term used when referring to any enlargement from a color negative.

Cubism An early twentieth-century art movement that began in Europe but which quickly generated an international following. In Cubist art, aspects of an object, such as inside and outside, as well as up and down, were presented simultaneously, yielding an array of geometric shapes.

Cyanotype A photographic technique invented by Sir John Herschel. It uses iron salts to produce a deep blue image, and is the source of the blueprint or dyeline process used today.

Dadaism An early twentieth-century art movement that began in Europe in the waning years of World War I, and which gained momentum and international influence directly after that conflict. Dadaists dwelled on the fragmentary and the incomplete, and instilled their work with post-war cynicism about human promise.

Daguerreotype A photographic technique taking its name from Louis-Jacques-Mandé Daguerre. It used a silver or silver-coated copper plate to register an image in a camera obscura. The daguerreotype was a unique image, not capable of making multiple copies. Daguerreotype plates were eventually standardized in terms of size (width first):

> a whole plate: 6½ x 8½ inches
> a half plate: 4½ x 5½ inches
> a quarter plate: 3¼ x 4¼ inches
> a sixth plate: 2¾ x 3¼ inches
> a ninth plate: 2 x 2½ inches

Because early daguerreotypists sometimes had cameras made to their specifications, not all plates conformed to the standard. Also, large, so-called mammoth plates of no standard size were used in specially made cameras.

Diana This inexpensive camera had several "flaws" that proved attractive to photographers by generating surprises in film development: it leaked light onto the film; the shutter could be opened repeatedly on the same frame, yielding multiple exposures; the viewfinder didn't see accurately through the lens.

Digital imaging Also termed computer-assisted imaging, this process is used to alter existing pictures, or to create images, called virtual images, which are not based on photographs taken of the real world. Digital cameras do not use film, but translate optical reality into visual bits called pixels (a new word derived from the term "picture elements") that can be stored in a computer. Electronic images may be shown on a computer screen or other visual monitors. Similarly, a scanner surveys an image and renders it into a mathematical language that can be stored and retrieved by the computer.

Direct positive (*see* NEGATIVE)

Dry-plates (also called gelatin-silver bromide, or gelatin bromide photography). Perfected in the late 1870s, from experiments begun in the 1850s, dry-plates were mass-marketed in the 1880s. They were prepared by holding a light-sensitive mixture of silver nitrate, cadmium bromide, and gelatine at a constant temperature of 32° centigrade for several days. The resulting plate was commercially produced, freeing photographers from sensitizing and developing the wet collodion plate on the spot. The exposure time of the dry-plate was so fast that it allowed photographers to record movement. Moreover, because of the quick exposure time, the camera could be held in the hands, rather than being placed on a tripod. By the early 1880s, dry-plates were manufactured throughout Europe and America.

Dye-transfer An involved process for making color prints, which allows the maker great control over the range of color at every stage of the process. It requires exposing a color transparency three times with different filters of blue, red, and green. The resulting black-and-white negatives are then used to make a matrix, a shallow-relief mold whose thickness is etched by the amount of light reaching it through the negatives. Thus the matrix is responsive to subtle color modulations. Each mold is immersed in blue, red, or green dye, respectively. After the molds have absorbed the colors, and the photographer or printer has made chemical adjustments to the tones and hues, the molds are sequentially printed on a sheet of photographic paper. The dye-transfer method produces one of the most stable, that is, permanent, color-printing processes.

Focal length The distance from the center of the camera lens to the point behind the lens where light rays from an object passing through the lens come into focus.

Fauvism An early twentieth-century art movement that arose in France and emphasized the expressive rather than the naturalistic use of color. In French, the words mean "wild beasts."

Futurism An early twentieth-century art movement, primarily in Italy, whose blurred or abstract shapes were meant to celebrate the dynamism of the machine and the promise of industrialization.

Gravure Gravure (or photogravure) is an etching process modified to reproduce photographs. A copper plate is treated with resin or bitumen powder, then exposed to a piece of carbon tissue paper that has a negative image on it. When soaked in warm water, the image transfers to the surface of the plate. It is then chemically etched with ferric chloride solution, leaving a recessed image that will accept ink. The process could be used commercially to make many copies, or with a hand-press to make a few, as was done by the Pictorialists.

Gum-bichromate process Developed in the 1850s, the process became popular with Pictorial photographers during the late nineteenth century. The technique used the photograph as the basis of the image. A sheet of paper was brushed with gum arabic into which had been mixed potassium bichromate and a colored pigment. After it dried, the paper was exposed to a negative. The photochemically sensitive materials on the paper hardened in proportion to the amount of light received. The photographer then washed away the unhardened material, leaving a positive print. During the wash, the photographer could add color, or brush the print to create painterly effects.

Half-tone process The process whereby photographs may be printed with text in a book, newspaper or magazine by relief or by lithography. It was called half-tone because it allowed the reproduction of tones between black and white. Applying a principle discovered by William Henry Fox Talbot, the half-tone uses a fine screen to break up the surface of a print into tiny dots whose size accords with the darkness and lightness of a picture. The screen is printed on a metal plate covered with gelatin mixed with bichromate. The gelatine hardens and the non-printing areas of the image are etched with acid. The half-tone process was used sporadically even before the late 1880s, when it was perfected, allowing newspapers routinely to include photographs.

Heliotype A method for reproducing photographs developed in the 1870s. It refined already existing lithographic processes for reproducing photographs in books. Like the WOODBURYTYPE, it was not compatible with type.

Hypo Originally hyposulphite of soda, a substance that dissolved silver salts and stopped the further development of the silver. Today "hypo" is the related substance, sodium thiosulfate.

Installation art As the phrase suggests, installation art involves creating an art environment composed of many objects, rather than a single object or image. The technique was used by Constructivists and Dadaists, as well as artists in the late twentieth and early twenty-first centuries.

Latent image An image registered on a photographically sensitive surface, like paper or a metal plate, but which is not visible to the eye. The latent image must be developed through a chemical process.

Lithography A printing technique in which an image is reproduced on a flat surface, originally a stone, but later a copper or zinc plate, rather than by being cut or gouged into a surface, like metal or wood. To make a lithograph, the surface is treated in such a way that the areas intended to convey an image will hold ink, and the remaining or negative areas, will repel ink.

Negative, Positive, Direct positive A negative is a photographically produced image in which the tones of the actual subject are reversed, that is, light areas are dark and darks are light. It is used to produce a positive print, in which the tones are re-reversed to create an image that reproduces optical reality. A direct positive is a unique, single image without a negative. In a direct positive print, like the daguerreotype, an image is produced on a surface and then treated chemically to imitate the tonal range of nature.

Oil-pigment process A process similar to the gum print. A piece of gelatine-coated paper was sensitized with potassium bichromate and exposed to a negative. Placed in a water bath, the print developed raised areas on the hardened gelatine. While wet, the print was brushed with pigments. The application of pigment could follow the subject of the negative, or be more expressive.

Outsider art Sometimes also called "self-taught art", the term was first used in the 1950s, but gained more prominence during the late twentieth century, as a way to recognize art produced by people who generally make their own guidelines and who work outside the conventional art world.

Pantograph An aid for copying prints and drawings. It consists of four bars, arranged in a parallelogram. A stylus is placed at the "V" joint of one set of bars and a drawing pencil is placed at the upper tip of the second set of bars. By tracing the stylus over a print, the drawing pencil makes an exact copy. The pantograph can also be used to enlarge or reduce an image.

Photogenic drawing A photographic technique developed by William Henry Fox Talbot that used light-sensitized paper to produce a negative from which multiple positive prints could be made.

Photogram Cameraless photographs made by casting light on photo-sensitive paper, or by placing objects directly on the light-sensitive surface. Some early photographers, such as William Henry Fox Talbot and Anna Atkins, made what would later be called photograms. The technique became popular with experimental photographers in Europe between World War I and World War II.

Photomontage A technique popular with experimental artists and photo-graphers in the period after World War I. Images from such sources as advertising and newspapers were cut and reassembled to form composite images. Sometimes drawing or paint was applied. The final picture might be photographed or prepared for mechanical reproduction.

Physionotrace French engraver Gilles-Louis Chrétien adapted the PANTO-GRAPH to make engravings in 1786, calling his invention the physionotrace. An artist viewed the sitter through an eyepiece, moving it to trace the sitter's profile. A stylus in the lower area of the physionotrace tracked the eyepiece movements exactly, registering them in ink on paper. The portrait was then transferred to a copper plate, etched, and used to make multiple images. The central parts of the image were then engraved by hand.

Pictorialism An early twentieth-century movement in art photography, whose photographs were characterized by a soft focus, or in which the photographer's apparent hand-manipulation of the negative aimed to give the photograph the appearance of brush stroke or other painterly effects.

Pinhole camera An extremely simple camera, sometimes constructed by children from round oatmeal containers. It is a light-tight container with a pinhole used as a lens at one end, and light-sensitive film or paper placed at the opposite end. Pinhole cameras produce wide-angle soft-toned pictures with a minimum of detail.

Platinum prints Known in the late nineteenth- and early twentieth-centuries as platinotypes after the Platinotype Company, which manufactured platinum paper, beginning in 1879. The paper was saturated with a light-sensitive mixture of potassium chloroplatinate and ferric oxalate. After exposure to a negative, the paper was washed with potassium oxalate, which precipitated out the platinum. An expensive, long-lasting, and stable process, the platinum print yields a wide range of soft-gray tones.

Positive (*see* NEGATIVE)

Precisionism An American art movement of the 1920s and 1930s in which objects were rendered as nearly abstract geometric shapes but were still recognizable.

Rayograph A term invented by the artist Man Ray, who used his own name to label the cameraless photographic images he produced by placing objects directly on to a sheet of photographically sensitive paper. The process is more widely known as a photogram.

Rotogravure An early twentieth-century printing process that allowed photographs to be printed with text. It was also the name for popular illustrated newspaper inserts, such as those found in Sunday papers. Fashion and high society were often subjects of the rotogravure.

Salt print One of the earliest photographic techniques to sensitize paper in order to make a photographic print. Paper was soaked in salt and then coated on one side with silver nitrate, yielding a light-sensitive silver chloride surface. The paper was then dried, placed under a negative, and exposed to light, producing a photographic print.

Silhouettes Drawings or cut-out profiles of the human face, derived from cast shadows.

Silkscreen A printmaking process in which a stencil is made on silk or a synthetic textile tightly stretched over a frame. The technique can be adapted to photography, in which case the photograph is imprinted on the textile, and the artist can adjust the colors.

Single-lens reflex camera (SLR) A camera that uses a movable mirror placed between the lens and the film. This mirror projects the image as it is seen through the lens onto a focusing screen.

Social Realism An inexact phrase used to describe a tendency in art to dwell on societal ills and misfortunes. The term is also associated with the anti-experimental, highly descriptive propaganda art preferred by leaders of the Soviet Union, beginning in the 1930s.

Solarization A technique that involves briefly exposing a print or negative to light during the development process. Discovered by accident in the nine-teenth-century, the result is a reversal of tones along the edges of forms. Sometimes called edge reversal, solarization is somewhat unpredictable, making it a favorite of the Surrealists. It is also known as the Sabattier effect, for French photographer Antoine Sabattier (active 1850s), who is said to have discovered it.

Stereography A technique for producing photographs that when seen through a special viewer (stereoscope) produced the illusion of depth. Two images taken from slightly different angles are printed on a card, which is put in the viewing device. Stereographs approximate the distance between the two human eyes that helps to produce depth perception.

The stereoscope was invented by Charles Wheatstone (1802–1875) in 1832, before photography was announced to the world. It was an awkward viewing apparatus that used mirrors to simulate what the right eye and the left eye see separately. In 1849, Sir David Brewster (1781–1868) perfected a smaller stereoscope, better adapted to viewing stereoscopic photographs in both the daguerreotype and calotype formats. The earliest stereoscopic daguerreotypes, such as Claudet's *The Geography Lesson* (see Fig. 2.51), were taken with two cameras, each adjusted to mimic human sight. Twin-lens stereoscopic cameras were introduced in the mid-1850s.

Strobe Fast bursts of intermittent light used to illuminate moving subjects.

Tabloid More compact than nineteenth-century broadsheets, tabloid newspapers feature many illustrations, most of them photographs or derived from photographs. From the earliest post-World War I tabloids, the genre has featured sensational pictures, which carry as much meaning as the text.

Tintype An inexpensive photographic process that rendered images on thin sheets of iron, not tin. The tintype was lightweight, making it easy to send through the postal system.

Tomography A computer-assisted process that produces cross-sections of the human body and assembles them into a three-dimensional picture.

Toning During or after the development of a print, it might be treated with a chemical solution containing silver and another ingredient, such as gold, platinum, or selenium. Toning allows the photographer to create a soft overall coloration, usually ranging from light gold to sepia.

Transparency As the word implies, a transparency is a positive film that allows light to pass through it. Transparencies may be in color or in black and white. The most familiar kind of transparency is the 35mm color slide, but transparencies can be made in larger sizes.

Waxed paper process An improvement to the CALOTYPE that allowed the light-sensitive paper to be prepared up to two weeks before exposure, and then developed a week after, though with variable results. As the name suggests, paper was coated with wax, then sensitized. It could be used wet, by being placed between two clean pieces of glass, or used dry. The prepared paper gave the photographer, especially when traveling, greater freedom and quickness.

Wet-plates *see* COLLODION PROCESS

Woodburytype A method of printing photographs for book illustrations. Woodburytype images could not be printed with text. Instead, they were tipped in, that is, pasted on separate sheets of paper in a book. Invented in 1866 by Walter Bentley Woodbury, the woodburytype used a gelatin film sensitized with potassium bichromate, which was exposed to a negative of the photograph to be copied. The resultant exposed film was then dipped in warm or hot water in a process that yielded a relief image, similar to low-relief sculpture, but much thinner. The various thicknesses of the gelatine corresponded to the different tones of the photograph. The negative was placed in a special press that transferred lead into the relief spaces. The lead mold was removed and used as the basis for printing a copy of the photograph.

PICTURE CREDITS

1 Rapho, Paris; **2** Courtesy Andrea Rosen Gallery, NY, in representation of Estate of Felix Gonzalez-Torres. © Estate of Felix Gonzalez-Torres. Photo by Peter Muscato; **3** © Bazuki Muhammad/Reuters/Corbis;
1.1 © Historical Picture Archive/Corbis; **1.2** Photo Bibliothèque Nationale de France, Paris; **1.9** © Ville de Chalon-sur-Saône, France. Musée Nicéphore Niépce; **1.15, 1.17, 1.18** Science & Society Picture Library, London; **1.19** With thanks to Douglas Nickel;
2.0 With thanks to Alison Doane; **2.6** Courtesy Hans P. Kraus, Jr., NY; **2.7, 2.9** Science & Society Picture Library, London; **2.8** Glasgow University Library, Department of Special Collections; **2.14** V&A Picture Library, London; **2.27, 2.28** Courtesy John Wood, McNeese State University, Louisiana; **2.32** Conaculta-INAH-SINAFAO-Fototeca Nacional, Mexico City; **2.33** Courtesy the Director, National Army Museum, London; **2.34** Research Library, Getty Research Institute, Los Angeles; **2.39, 2.54, 2.55** Photo Bibliothèque Nationale de France, Paris; **2.41** Courtesy George Eastman House, NY. Museum Purchase: Charina Foundation Purchase Fund; **2.47** DG-40-80 Floyd and Marion Rinhart Collection. Ohio State University Libraries. Used by permission; **2.46** © National Gallery of Canada; **2.49** With thanks to William Welling, NY; **2.53** With thanks to Peter Palmquist; **2.56** Courtesy Strong Museum, Rochester, NY

© 2005; **2.57** © National Portrait Gallery, Smithsonian Institution/Art Resource, NY; **2.58** Cincinnati Art Museum, Gift of James M. Marrs, M.D. Photo: Walsh 11/1999; **2.59** Courtesy Library of Congress, Washington D.C. Prints & Photographs Division LC-USA7-10881; **2.60** Museum of Fine Arts, Boston. Gift of Richard Parker in memory of Herman Parker 1994.124 © 2001 Museum of Fine Arts, Boston, All Rights Reserved; **2.61** Metropolitan Museum, NY. Gift of I.N.P. Stokes and the Hawes family; **3.2** LOC/P&P. LC-USZ62; **3.4, 3.11, 3.17, 3.19, 3.20, 3.21, 3.44, 3.45, 3.46, 3.49, 3.52, 3.59, 3.92, 3.98, 3.104** V&A Picture Library, London; **3.7** © Photothèque des Musées de la Ville de Paris/cliché Ladet; **3.8, 3.25, 3.64, 3.65, 3.68** Photo RMN, Paris; **3.9, 3.10** Félix Nadar/ Archives Photographiques © Centres des Monuments Nationaux, Paris; **3.14** Science & Society Picture Library, London; **3.29** © National Portrait Gallery, Smithsonian Institution/ Art Resource, NY; **3.30** LOC/P&P LC-USZ62-114481; **3.31** LOC/P&P LC-USZ62-76355; **3.33** LOC/P&P # 301949; **3.35** LOC/P&P LC-B8171-557; **3.36** LOC/P&P LC-B8171-7798; **3.38** LOC/P&P LC-USZ62; **3.41** With thanks to G.Léyris; **3.42** Illustrated London News; **3.43** Photo Bibliothèque Nationale de France, Paris; **3.47** Courtesy Library of Congress; **3.60** © Christie's Images Ltd 2005; **3.63** Courtesy the Director, National Army Museum, London; **3.61** Collection Centre Canadien d'Architecture/Canadian Centre for Architecture, Montréal PH1980:0048:04:010; National Museum of American Art, Smithsonian Institution, bequest of Sara Carr Upton/Scala, Florence; **3.70** LOC/P&P C-USZ62-22284; **3.71** National Archives, Washington, D.C. 77-KS-1-15; **3.72, 3.87** Courtesy George Eastman House, NY; **3.73** LOC/P&P LC-USZ62-50848; **3.77, 3.80** © National Anthropological Archives, Smithsonian Institution #4042; **3.79** LOC/P&P LC-USZ62; **3.81** © Smithsonian Institution; **3.82** National Archives, Washington, D.C. 77-HQ-264-809; **3.84** LOC/P&P LC-BH821-6803; **3.86** Bibliothèque de l'Institut de France, Paris/Photo RMN, Paris/Le Mage; **3.91** © Bibliothèque Centrale M.N.H.N. Paris;

3.101 © Hulton-Deutsch Collection/Corbis; **3.103** With thanks to G.Léyris; **3.106** Sotheby's Picture Library, London; **3.107** © Christie's Images Ltd 2005; **3.108** Rheinisches Bildarchiv, Cologne;
4.0 LOC/P&P LC-USZ62-64301; **4.5, 4.40, 4.44** V&A Picture Library, London; **4.6** Dayton Art Institute, Dayton, Ohio 1984.58. Gift of Mrs Lillian T. Snider; **4.7, 4.8, 4.10, 4.12, 4.13, 4.58** Courtesy Library of Congress; **4.15** Art Seal Services; **4.18** LOC/P&P LC-USZ62-76355; **4.19** Museum of Modern Art, NY. Purchase. Copy Print © 2001 Museum of Modern Art, NY; **4.21** Museum of Modern Art, NY. Gift of Mrs Hermine M. Turner. Copy print © 2001 Museum of Modern Art, NY; **4.22** LOC/P&P LC-USZ62-79452. Reprinted with permission of Joanna T. Steichen; **4.23** Museum of Modern Art, NY. Gift of the photographer, © 2001 Museum of Modern Art, NY/Reprinted with permission of Joanna T. Steichen; **4.24** Reprinted with permission of Joanna T. Steichen; **4.26** LOC/P&P LC-USZ62; **4.29** Collection Chris Mees, Design Documentation, Etchingham, East Sussex; **4.32** Museum of Modern Art, NY (Gift of Mrs Hermine M. Turner). Photograph © 2001 Museum of Modern Art, NY; **4.34** Rare Book, Manuscript & Special Collections Library, Duke University, Durham, North Carolina; **4.36, 4.37** Photo RMN, Paris; **4.39** Photographie J.H. Lartigue © Ministère de la Culture-France/A.A.J.H.L.; **4.42** LOC/P&P LC-USZ62-79449; **4.43** Museum of Modern Art, NY. Gift of Arthur Bullowa. Copy Print © 2001 Museum of Modern Art, NY/© 1971 Aperture Foundation Inc., Paul Strand Archive; **4.45** LOC/P&P USZ62/11036/301951; **4.53** © Collège de France; **4.55** © Succession Marcel Duchamp/ADAGP, Paris and DACS, London 2005; **4.60** Courtesy Smithsonian Institution, National Museum of American History; **4.61** Lancelyn Green Collection, London; **4.65** With thanks to Padre Fedele Merelli; **4.69** Préfecture de Police, Paris. All Rights Reserved; **4.70** Collection Arne Svenson © 1998; **4.73** Birmingham Central Library/John Whybrow Ltd; **4.75** Imperial War Museum # C02264; **4.77** American Museum of Natural History Library, image # 11604;

TIMELINE The Cultural History of Photography

CULTURE AND POLITICS	PHOTOGRAPHY AND IMAGING
12TH TO 16TH CENTURIES	**12TH TO 16TH CENTURIES**
Early-mid 1300s: Rise of city-states in Europe; patronage of craftsmen, inventors, artisans; religious reformation creates desire for liturgy, Bible in English; beginnings of Renaissance in Italy	Several European cathedrals used as camera obscura: holes in roof focus sun's image on floor
Early 1400s: Patronage of artisans/artists by ruling families, particularly by the Medicis in Florence, Italy, which becomes centre of Renaissance	First wood-block printing on paper in Germany
1452: Gutenberg Bible printed	c. 1436: Gutenberg invents printing press;
Rise in scientific and astronomical observation throughout Europe; exploration of other countries	1446: First dated printed engraving from metal plate
1527: Troops of Holy Roman Empire attack Rome; Pope Clement VII imprisoned; Italian Renaissance ends	Perspective machines devised to create illusion of 3D image on 2D surface; c. 1510 Leonardo da Vinci's *Draughtsman Drawing an Armillary Sphere*
1535: Reformation begins as Henry VIII declares himself head of the English church	1590: Forerunner of telescope and compound microscope invented by Zacharias and Hans Janssen
1541 Knox leads Reformation in Scotland	
1543: Copernicus publishes *On the Revolution of Heavenly Bodies*	
17TH CENTURY	**17TH CENTURY**
Exploration and annexation of other lands undertaken by Spain, France, Portugal, and England	1609: Galileo Galilei invents first effective telescope
Rise of affluent bourgeoisie and merchant class in Europe leads to more experimentation and invention; also leads to more demand for realistic domestic portraits by wealthier merchant families	Pantograph invented
	1668: Sir Isaac Newton builds first reflecting telescope
18TH CENTURY	**18TH CENTURY**
In England and France, advances in mechanization cause shift from agricultural to industrial populations; beginnings of Industrial Revolution; promotion of scientific method creates need for accurate visual record-keeping and documentation	Camera obscura perfected, then made portable
	Thomas Wedgwood and Humphrey Davy experiment with ways of fixing light-sensitive images using silver nitrate
1775: Lunar Society formed in Birmingham, England, bringing together scientific minds of the English-speaking world	1786: Gilles-Louis Chrétien adapts pantograph to engraving, creating the physionotrace, which produces multiple copies
1776: American Declaration of Independence	1794: Elizabeth Fulhame publishes *View to a New Art of Dying [sic] and Printing*; proposes capture and retention of images on cloth via light and metal interaction
1778: Captain Cook discovers Hawaii	
Silhouette portraits become commonplace	1798: Alois Senefelder perfects lithographic technique
1789–99: French Revolution ends dominance of privileged upper class; number of inventions rise in France as new entrepreneurs and middle class emerge	
1796–1815: Napoleonic Wars in Europe	
Continued exploration by Western European nations leads to early theories of racial evolution and rise in interest in ethnology	
EARLY 19TH CENTURY	**EARLY 19TH CENTURY**
c. 1800: Western European governments promote economic expansion via industry and commerce; beginnings of Industrial Revolution in England; advances in record-keeping desired; scientists and inventors encouraged; inventions and discoveries soar	1800: William Herschel discovers infrared rays; Alessandro Volta produces electricity
	1802: Humphrey Davy and Thomas Wedgwood's experiments published
1803: US negotiates Louisiana Purchase; expands	1806: William Hyde Wollaston invents camera lucida, using prisms with silver sides
1812: Napoleon invades Russia. US declares war on Britain	1816: Joseph Nicéphore Niépce experiments with lithography; silver chloride results in negative image
1815: Napoleon defeated by Wellington at Waterloo	1819: John Herschel experiments with hypo
c. 1816: scattered movements of naturalism in art across Europe, such as the Biedermeier style in Germany	1822: Joseph Nicéphore Niépce invents engraving plate
1820: Missouri Compromise: US expands again	1826: Niépce creates first positive image—*View from the Window at Gras*;
1825: First passenger-carrying railroad in England	c. 1828: Niépce meets Louis-Jacques-Mandé Daguerre
1830–40	**1830–40**
1830: French invade Algeria; Louis Philippe becomes "Citizen King"; Charles X forced to abdicate	c. 1830: Antoine Hércules Romuald Florence invents *poligraphie*; conceives photography and uses sunlight to print images
Rise of urban middle classes, commerce, and industry	Louis-Jacques-Mandé Daguerre continues Niépce's work; develops latent image
1836: Mexicans defeat Texans at the Alamo; Texas gains independence after Battle of San Jacinto	1830s: William Henry Fox Talbot develops "photogenic drawing"
	1832: Antoine Hércules Romuald Florence coins term *photographie*— i.e., "photography"
	1833–34: William Henry Fox Talbot conceives fixing light-induced images; creates contact salt prints

1830–40 CONTINUED

1837: Victoria becomes queen of Great Britain

French government generates financial support for science and invention

1839: First Opium War begins

1830–40 CONTINUED

1837: Louis-Jacques-Mandé Daguerre discovers table salt as a stopping agent. Still-life daguerreotypes created

January 1, 1839: François Arago describes Daguerre's photographic process to French Academy of Science

February 7, 1839: John Herschel presents "photographic specimens" to the Royal Society in London and prints from negative image

1839: Bayard creates direct positives; *cliché verre* invented; John Herschel suggests photographic equipment be included in British expedition to Antarctic

1840–50

Philosophy of public works and education; rights for working classes; industrial capitalism creates middle-class professionals, scientists; rapid growth of cities gives rise to shared ideas.

Western expansion into Asia, Africa and Latin America; rural subjects and countryside idealized in art

1842: First Opium War ends; Europeans gain greater trade opportunities with China

1844: Morse transmits first telegraph message, patents telegraph; five Chinese ports open to US ships

1846: Potato famine in Ireland; California and New Mexico annexed by US; ether used as anesthetic

1846–48: Mexican–American War; rise in American newspapers and new high-speed presses create demand for images of war; war correspondents used for first time by US newspapers; appetite for up-to-date news among public

The *Tableau vivant* (a "living picture" created and posed by actors) becomes popular

1848: Revolution in Paris, Vienna, Venice, Rome, Warsaw, Berlin, Milan; *Communist Manifesto* published; Livingstone crosses Africa; rise in interest in racial evolution leads to need for anthropological records

1849: California gold rush begins

1840–50

1840s: Andreas Ritter von Ettingshausen creates microscopic daguerreotype images; John Herschel creates cyanotype, used for blueprints until digital age; Demand for photographic portraits increases; E. Thiéssen shoots "portraits" of Sofala and Brazilian Botocudos; photography arrives in China

1841: William Henry Fox Talbot patents calotype, which uses reusable negative and forms basis for modern photographic reproduction

1844: William Henry Fox Talbot shoots *The Open Door*; beginnings of photography as a new art form; (1844–46): Talbot publishes *The Pencil of Nature*, one of first photo-illustrated books; beginnings of documentary photography

1845: Léon Foucault and Hippolyte Fizeau photograph sunspots; David Octavius Hill and Robert Adamson make some of earliest anthropological portraits: *Newhaven Fishwives*

c. 1846: Frederick von Maltens invents rotating camera: takes *Panorama of Paris*

1847: Albert Sands Southworth and Josiah Johnson Hawes's *Early Operation Using Ether for Anesthesia*; recreations of historic events in photographs validate the use of "artistic license"

1848–49: John McCosh, earliest named war photographer, takes calotypes in India of fellow officers, also native peoples with emphasis on racial differences; Albert Sands Southworth and Josiah Johnson Hawes create full-plate celebrity daguerreotypes and advance notion of photographer as artist

1849: Edgar Allen Poe has his portrait taken—calls photography "a positively perfect mirror"

1850–60

1850: Interest in racial qualities/differences increases

1851: *New York Times* begins publication; The Great Exhibition opens in London, including display of photographic equipment; time of social advancement; modern architecture becomes subject matter for photography; Nathaniel Hawthorne's *The House of the Seven Gables* published; increase in amateur photographers; advances in science and medicine

1853: Turkey declares war on Russia—Crimean War begins

Mid-1850s: Europeans undertake "Grand Tour"; rise of "compulsive visibility": social, scientific, and personal progress understood as dependent upon increased visibility of data; growth and expansion of scientific subjects plus colonial expansion bolsters greater desire for stereographs; rise in periodicals and newspapers using photographically derived engravings

1855: *Frank Leslie's Illustrated Newspaper* founded

1856: Crimean War ends; Second Opium War begins

1857: *Harper's Weekly* founded

Late 1850s: proposals to miniaturize and store information become more frequent; debate about differences and similarities of photography and art rages

1859: Darwin's *On the Origin of Species* published

1850–60

1850s: Gum bichromate process developed; Antoine Sabbatier thought to have discovered solarization

1850: Louis Agassiz commissions slave portraits by J. T. Zealy; Historic Monuments Commission in France chooses calotypes for architectural inventory

1851: John Jabez Edwin Mayall documents the Crystal Palace, says photography capable of "illustrating history"; Frederick Scott Archer publishes collodion ("wet plate") process; George Phillips Bond and John Adam Whipple's *Moon* photograph recognized at Great Exhibition; Sociéte Héliographique formed; William Henry Fox Talbot uses electrical sparks to provide light for photography; many sitters ascribe supernatural powers to the camera and photographic process

c. 1851: Gustave Le Gray explores photography's potential as "light work"— creates *Forest of Fontainbleau*, invents dry waxed paper process; Hugh Welch Diamond experiments with collodian process, uses glass plates to record images of mental patients

1852–53: Women photographers: Anna Atkins and Theresa Llewellyn create cyanotypes for scientific illustration; Carl Durheim creates first "police photographs" in Switzerland

1853: Photographic Society of London formed

1854: Wilhelm and Friedrich Langenheim take daguerreotypes of solar eclipse in US; André Adolphe Eugène Disdéri perfects and patents the *carte-de-viste*

Mid-1850s: Improved stereographic camera produces two simultaneous images; "stereos" create photographic boom; war photographers take images of the Crimean conflict; photography enters Japan, Middle East

1855: Alexandre Clausel's *Landscape near Troyes* shows potential of photography as art form

1856–59: Gustave Le Gray merges negatives to create *Mediterranean Sea at Sète*, uses "combination printing"

1856: Tintype developed; Hugh Welch Diamond addresses Royal Society on photography as form of permanent record-keeping

1858: William Lake Price's *A Manual of Photographic Manipulation* published

Late 1850s: Need for more documentary photographs of illness/injury results in "de-personalized" photography; photomicrography perfected and increased; many painters turn to photography; more women take up photography

CULTURE AND POLITICS

1860–70
1860s: Advancement and growth of medicine, including antiseptics and anesthesia; discovery of ether by William T. G. Martin
1861: American Civil War begins
1864: Paraguay invades Brazil; War of the Triple Alliance begins
1865: Abraham Lincoln assassinated; American Civil War ends
1866: Alfred Nobel invents dynamite
1867: US acquires Alaska; Karl Marx's *Das Kapital* published; Moscow Ethnographic Exhibition; Congress sponsors surveying expedition to Rockies
1869: First US transcontinental railroad; Suez Canal opens

1870–80
1870s: Public and scientific interest in human expression, emotion increases; (1870s–80s) Impressionist movement in art
1870: Franco-Prussian War begins
1872: Charles Darwin's *The Expression of the Emotions in Man and Animals* published
1873: Jules Verne's *Around the World in Eighty Days* published
1874: First exhibition of Impressionist paintings, Paris; increased interest in space in the sciences
1876: Centennial Exhibition, Philadelphia; Battle of the Little Big Horn: Sioux/Cheyenne defeat US Cavalry; Queen Victoria becomes Empress of India; Mark Twain's *The Adventures of Tom Sawyer* published; Alexander Graham Bell invents telephone
1877: Reconstruction collapses in US
1879: US Bureau of Ethnology established

1880–90
1880s: Symbolist movement in art; Emile Zola proclaims that "metaphysical man is dead"; debate on photography as art form continues; Arts and Crafts movement gathers strength in England
1881: President Garfield assassinated
1882: Britain invades Egypt; Germany, Austria, Italy form the Triple Alliance
1885: Berlin Conference: European expansion into Africa
1886: Frederick E. Ives develops half-tone engraving process
1887: Queen Victoria's Golden Jubilee
1888: National Geographical Society founded in US; *National Geographic* begins publication
1889: Johnstown floods in Pennsylvania; Eiffel Tower completed
Late 1880s–1890s: Newspaper editors run camera columns; urbanism increases alongside demand for more and faster information; illustrated newspapers increase worldwide, followed by rise in illustrated magazines; advertisers begin using photographs to sell products

1890–1900
1890s: Expressionist art in Germany; Samoan Islands used as US and German trade and naval bases; *Berliner Illustrirte [sic] Zeitung* founded
1890: Battle at Wounded Knee: Sitting Bull killed
1892: Diesel engine patented; Ellis Island opens
1893: Chicago World's Fair promotes "ideal city"
1894: Sino-Japanese War begins
1896: Alfred Nobel's will establishes the Peace Prize
1898: Spanish-American War; Pierre and Marie Curie discover radium
1899: Boer War begins

1900–10
1900s: International Arts and Crafts movement continues, focus on Native Americans; many artists and writers, such as Degas, Munch, Strindberg, and Zola, experiment with photography; social reform movement grows
1900: Boxer Rebellion in China

PHOTOGRAPHY AND IMAGING

1860–70
1861: American war photographers create first comprehensive visual chronicle of conflict; tintypes flourish; images copyrighted
1864–65: Gaspard Félix Tournachon, aka Nadar, takes underground photos using carbon arc lamp—also takes aerial photographs of Paris
1866: Alexander Gardner publishes *Gardner's Photographic Sketch Book of the Civil War 1865–6*; Walter E. Woodbury invents woodburytype; US Army Medical Museum publishes *Photographs of Surgical Cases and Specimens*; George Barnard publishes *Photographic Views with Sherman's Campaigns*
1867: Timothy O'Sullivan official photographer for King survey
1868: O'Sullivan takes photos in Comstock mine by igniting magnesium wire
1869: Henry Peach Robinson's *Pictorial Effects in Photography* published

1870–80
1870s: Heliotype developed; dry plates perfected, simplifying photographic process
1872: Celluloid production begins in US
1872–77: Eadweard Muybridge photographs horses in motion
1873: Jules-Bernard Luys publishes *L'Iconographie photographique des centres nerveux*; platinotype invented in Britain
1874: International competition to record transit of Venus: Pierre-César Jules Janssen develops "revolver camera" to make sequential exposures
1875: Carl Dammann publishes *Ethnological Photographic Gallery of the Various Races of Man*
1877: William Henry Jackson publishes *Descriptive Catalogue of Photographs of American Indians*; (1877–80:) Jean-Martin Charcot publishes *L'Iconographie photographique de La Salpêtrière*
1879: Karl Klick develops photogravure process; Platinotype Co. manufactures platinum paper: birth of the platinum print; Eadweard Muybridge demonstrates zoöpraxiscope

1880–90
1880s: Dry-plates mass-marketed; photographs increasingly used in law and police work; Pictorialism gathers pace
1881: Photographic roll film invented in England and US
Mid-1880s: pictorialist style in photography flourishes
1884–85: Eadweard Muybridge's *The Pole Vaulter*
1886: Photographs reproduced in newspapers
1887: Eadweard Muybridge's *Animal Locomotion* published
1888: Eastman Dry Plate Co. introduces the No 1 Kodak camera, which uses "American [roll] film"
1889: Peter Henry Emerson's *Naturalistic Photography* published;
Eastman introduces the No 2 Kodak camera which makes 3½-inch images
Late 1880s–early 1890s: Over 60 photographic journals and 161 photographic societies worldwide; press photographers and photographic agencies emerge; growth of papparazzi as demand for celebrity photographs increases; black-and-white film perfected, yielding better tonal variation; use of hand cameras leads to invention of camera shutter

1890–1900
1890s: Photographic postcards become popular; scenes of urban poor become more commonplace; increased use of photography in criminology and anthropology Jacob Riis's *How the Other Half Lives* published with half-tone prints—social reform photography gains strength; Etienne Jules-Marey's *The Flight of Birds*
1891: Wiener Kamera Klub formed in Austria
1892: Linked Ring formed in Britain
1893: James Craig Annan's *Miss Janet Burnet*
1894: Thomas Edison introduces the kinetoscope; Photo-Club de Paris formed
1895: Louis and Auguste Lumière invent motion picture projector; Wilhelm Konrad Röntgen discovers x-rays

1900–10
1900s: Cameras increasingly miniaturized; photo-postcards increasingly common; Pictorialism flourishes
1900: Eastman Co. produces Brownie camera; snapshots increase
1901: Charles H. Caffin's *Photography as a Fine Art* published; Kodak Girl advertising image introduced

1900–10 CONTINUED

1901: Guglielmo Marconi makes first radio transmission; Queen Victoria dies; President McKinley assassinated

1903: Wright brothers make first powered flight; Suffragettes campaign for vote in Britain; Henry Ford organizes Ford Motor Co.

1904: St Louis World's Fair; Russo-Japanese War begins; National Child Labor Committee founded in US; *Daily Mirror* appears in Britain

1905: Albert Einstein publishes his theory of relativity

1906: San Francisco earthquake and fire; British Labour Party founded

1907: Cubist paintings exhibited in Paris

1908: Ford Motor Co. introduces the Model T

1909: Italian Futurism in art; Lewis Hine addresses NCLC: "... photographs do not lie, but liars may photograph"

1910–20

1910–25: Art Nouveau/Deco movement gathers strength; companies produce booklets and magazines demonstrating social awareness; tabloid newspapers more common; rotogravure printing process developed

1911: First Picasso exhibit in US

1912: *Titanic* sinks

1913: Ezra Pound coins term "Vorticism" for English art movement; The Armoury Show in New York

1914: World War I begins

1916: Beginnings of Dadaism in Zurich

1917: US enters World War I; Bolshevik Revolution in Russia; Sigmund Freud's *Introduction to Psychoanalysis* published

1918: Tristan Tzara writes *Dada Manifesto*

1919: *New York Illustrated Daily News* founded; *The ABC of Communism* published: idea of utopianism through technology; Treaty of Versailles

1920–30

1920s: Increased expansion of mass media and industrialization; politically aligned periodicals appear; postwar hardships in Central Europe and Germany; rapid expansion of automobiles, radios, electricity; Modernism gains ground in art

1920: League of Nations holds first meeting; 19th Amendment ratified in US

1921: *Arbeiter Illustrierte Zeitung* launched in Germany; Communist Party of China founded

1922: Mussolini marches on Rome and forms Fascist regime

1923: Adolf Hitler writes first volume of *Mein Kampf*

Mid-1920s: Surrealism born in Paris

1925: The Scopes evolution trial in Tennessee

1927: Television demonstrated publicly; Charles Lindbergh makes first solo transatlantic flight; Joseph Stalin becomes ruler of Soviet Union; first "talking picture", *The Jazz Singer* screened

1928: *Vu* launched in France; Alexander Fleming discovers penicillin

1929: Wall Street crashes; Great Depression begins; Helen Lynd's *Middletown: A Study in Modern America* published

1930–40

1930s: Nazi Party gains power; Frank Whittle patents jet engine; unemployment rife, foreign trade with US declines

1933: Adolf Hitler appointed German chancellor; *King Kong* screened

1934: Hitler becomes Führer; USSR enters League of Nations

1935: Franklin D. Roosevelt institutes the Resettlement Administration (RA), creates Works Project Administration (WPA)

1936: *Life* magazine launched in US; Edward VIII abdicates, George VI king of Great Britain; Spanish Civil War begins; Berlin Olympics; Walter Benjamin writes "The Work of Art in the Age of Mechanical Reproduction"

1937: *Hindenburg* explodes in New Jersey; Japan invades China; RA becomes the Farm Security Administration (FSA); Chicago Institute of Design (New Bauhaus) founded

1938: *Picture Post* launched in Britain; House Un-American Activities Committee formed

1939: World War II begins; Spanish Civil War ends

1900–10 CONTINUED

1902: Alfred Stieglitz, Edward Steichen, and others found the Photo-Secession; Stieglitz sponsors *American Pictorial Photography* exhibition; Gertrude Käsebier's *Portrait—Miss N*

1903: *Camera Work* journal founded; Jack London's *The People of the Abyss* published

1904: Louis and Auguste Lumière develop autochrome color process; Robert Demachy creates *Struggle* (photogravure); photographic exhibition at Carnegie Institute, Pittsburgh; Lewis Hine begins photographing Ellis Island immigrants

1905: Little Galleries of the Photo-Secession opens

1907–30: Edward S. Curtis's *The North American Indian* published; bromoil process developed; Alfred Stieglitz's *The Steerage*

1908: Clarence White's *Morning*

1910–20

c. 1910: Annie Brigman's *The Heart of the Storm*; Shinzo Fukuhara's *Light with its Harmony 8: Pond*

Alvin Langdon Coburn adopts Vorticism, and creates Vortescope to take abstract photographs (Vortographs)

1913: Antonio Giulio Bragaglia's *Fotodinamismo futurista* published; Photodynamism grows

1914–18: Aerial photography perfected during World War I

1915: D. W. Griffiths produces *The Birth of a Nation*; c. 1915 Roso Fukuhara's *Sangaatsudo*

1917: *Camera Work*'s last issue devote to Paul Strand; Pictorialism draws to an end

1919: Hannah Hoch's photomontage *Schnitt mit dem Küchenmesser ...*

1920–30

1920s: Group f.64 formed in California; documentary photography becomes popular; term "photojournalism" enters common usage; many European art photographers turn to photojournalism to survive; photomontage becomes common in art; photography used increasingly in advertising; Ansel Adams photographs Yellowstone National Park; worker-photographers in Europe

1922: Karel Teige creates *Foto-Kino-Film*; Man Ray's *Les Champs délicieux* (photograms) published

1923: Wirephoto transmissions begin

1924: Leica compact 35mm camera introduced; El Lissitzky's *The Constructor*

1925: Flashbulb developed in Germany; Lázló Moholy-Nagy's *Malerei, Photographie, Film* published; Edward Weston's *Excusado*

1928: Eastman Kodak makes 16mm color film; Tom Howard's *Dead!* appears on cover of the *Daily News*

1929: Motion picture film standardized (24 frames/second); *Film und Foto* exhibition; August Sander's *Antlitz der Zeit* published

1930–40

1930s: Documentary photography grows; Workers Film and Photo League founded in New York

1930: Technicolor introduces full-color film

1931: Exhibition of Foreign Advertising and Industrial Photography

1933: Brassaï's *Paris de nuit* published; *Die Kamera* exhibition in Berlin: propaganda photography grows; Alfred Eisenstaedt's *Joseph Goebbels*

1934: First Salon of Pure Photography

1935: Associated Press Wirephoto formed; newsreels feature at cinemas; Roy Stryker supervises RA's photographic activities—hires Walker Evans, Dorothea Lange

1936: Dorothea Lange's *Migrant Mother*; Arthur Rothstein's *Fleeing a Dust Storm*; Margaret Burke White's cover of *Life*; Harold Edgerton's *Drop of Milk ...*; Robert Capa's *Death of a Loyalist Soldier*

1937: Museum of Modern Art exhibits *American Photographs,* exhibition of photographic history; *Indian Photography and Cinematography* launched

1938: Raoul Ubac's *La Conciliabule* (*brulage* print); (1938–39) Manuel Álvarez Bravo's *La Buena Fama Durmiendo*; Walker Evans's *American Photographs*

1939: Dorothea Lange's *An American Exodus* published; Berenice Abbott's *Changing New York* published; Harold Edgerton helps develop lighting for aerial photography

1940–50

1941: Pearl Harbor bombed by Japanese; US enters the war; Manhattan Project (atomic bomb research) begins in US; *Indian Art in the United States* exhibition, New York

1942: FSA subsumed into Office of War Information

1944: Normandy invasion (D-Day)

Mid-1940s: First exhibitions of Abstract Expressionist art

1945: Yalta Conference; Germany surrenders; FDR dies; atomic bomb dropped on Hiroshima, Nagasaki; Japan surrenders; United Nations founded

1946: Churchill's "Iron Curtain" speech

1947: Cold War established; India gains independence; HUAC investigates Hollywood motion picture industry

1948: Mahatma Gandhi assassinated; Communists seize Czechoslovakia; Berlin airlift; nation of Israel proclaimed; UN's Declaration of Human Rights; apartheid formalized in South Africa

1949: Soviets explode atomic bomb

1950–60

1950s: Pop art begins in Britain; McCarthyism expands; arms race continues

1950: President Truman orders H-bomb development; Korean War begins; Vietnam "Police Action" begins; David Reisman's *The Lonely Crowd* published

1951: Color television introduced in US; *Drum* magazine founded in Johannesburg

1952: George VI dies; Elizabeth II crowned

1953: Eisenhower becomes president of US; Stalin dies; Hillary and Norkay conquer Everest; Moscow announces explosion of H-bomb; Korean War ends; first color television broadcast

1954: Racial segregation banned in US schools; Jonas Salk inoculates children against polio; US tests H-bomb on Bikini Atoll

1955: Warsaw Pact signed

1957: Soviet Union launches Sputnik I, first space satellite; Jack Keroac's *On the Road* published

1959: Cuban Revolution; Xerox introduces the xerographic copier

1960–70

1960s: Anti-American demonstrations on US campuses; Conceptual art movement grows

1961: Berlin Wall erected; Bay of Pigs invasion; Yuri Gagarin becomes first man to orbit the earth

1962: Cuban missile crisis; James Meredith registers at the University of Mississippi

1963: Pope John XXIII dies; civil rights rally in Washington D.C.; President Kennedy assassinated

1965: Watts riots for six days in Los Angeles

1966: First artificial heart implant

1967: Anastasio Somozo president of Nicaragua; Six-Day War between Israelis and Arabs

1969: Richard Nixon inaugurated US President; first live television space broadcast; Andy Warhol founds *Interview* magazine

1970–80

1970: Rhodesia declares independence; Kent State anti-war protests and shootings

1971: Greenpeace founded

1972: *Life* magazine closes; Nixon visits Communist China; beginning of Watergate scandal; Bloody Sunday shootings in Northern Ireland; Computed Tomography (CT) invented

1973: OPEC oil crisis; Augusto Pinochet overthrows Salvador Allende in Chile; Britain, Ireland, and Denmark enter European Common Market

1974: Nixon resigns; US troops withdraw from Vietnam

1975: First US-Soviet space link-up; Pol Pot assumes leadership in Cambodia—genocide begins

1940–50

1940: Museum of Modern Art Department of Photography opens, New York, headed by Edward Steichen; *Kodak Indian Magazine* launched

1941: Walker Evans and James Agee's *Let Us Now Praise Famous Men* published; Weegee's (Arthur Fellig) *Their First Murder*

1942: *Road to Victory* exhibition

1944: Eastman Kodak introduces Kodacolor film; Eugene Smith's *US Marines with a ... Dying Infant*

1945: Lee Miller's *Buchenwald; Power in the Pacific* exhibition; Joe Rosenthal's *Iwo Jima*; Yevgeny Khaldei's *Reichstag*

1946: Edward Weston's *Waterfront, Monterey* Cibachrome print

1947: Edwin Land invents Polaroid camera; Robert Capa founds Magnum Photos

1948: Sunil Janah photographs Calcutta crowds

1949: Nacho López's *Campesino*; Aaron Siskind's *Jerome, Arizona*

1950–60

1950: Ken Domon co-founds Shudan Photo Group; David Douglas Duncan's "There Was a Christmas"; Lotte Jacobi's *Photogenic*

1952: Yosuke Yamahata's *Atomized Nagasaki* published

1953: Federation of Indian Photography founded

1954: Eastman Kodak introduces high-speed Tri-X film

1955: *Family of Man* exhibition, Museum of Modern Art; Claudia Andujar arrives in Brazil; Roy DeCarava's *The Sweet Flypaper of Life* published

1956: Richard Hamilton's *Just what is it ...?*

1958: Ken Domon's *Hiroshima* published; Robert Frank's *The Americans* published

1959: Seydou Keïta's *Two Women*

1960–70

1960: Polaroid develops high-speed film; Korda (Alberto Díaz) photographs Che Guevara; Ricardo Rangel's *Our Nightly Bread*; Harry Shrunk's *Yves Klein Leaping into the Void*

1962: Eastman Kodak invents Instamatic camera; Yasuhiro Ishimoto's *Chicago*; Minor White's *Empty Head*; Eliot Porter's *In Wildness is the Preservation of the World* published; Andy Warhol's *Marilyn Diptych*

1963: Society for Photographic Education formed; Eikoh Hosoe's *Barakei* published; Charles Moore's *Birmingham*; Bob Jackson's *Lee Harvey Oswald Shot*

1964: David Bailey's *Mick Jagger*

Mid-1960s: "social landscape" photography becomes popular

1966: *Twelve Photographers of the American Social Landscape* exhibition; Larry Burrows's *At a First-aid Centre ...*; John Szarkowski's *The Photographer's Eye* published

1967: Peter Magubane's Wanela Mine Recruiting Agency photograph; Ernest Cole's *House of Bondage. New Documents* exhibition, New York; Chuck Close's *Big Self-Portrait*; (1967–72) Martha Rosler *Bringing Home the War*

1968: Laura Gilpin's *The Enduring Navajo* published; Ernest Withers's *Workers Assembling for a Solidarity March*

1969: Eikoh Hosoe's *Kamaitachi* published; Apollo 11's moon photograph; Robert Smithson's *Seventh Mirror Displacement*

1970–80

1970: David Douglas Duncan's *War without Heroes* published; John Paul Filo's Kent State photograph; Ron Haeberle and Peter Brant's *Q. And Babies? A. And Babies.*

1971: Philip Jones Griffiths's *Vietnam, Inc.* published

1972: Daido Moriyama's *Stray Dog*; Bill Owens's *Suburbia* published; Huynh Cong (Nick) Ut *Children Fleeing a Napalm Strike*

1973: Larry Clark's *Tulsa* published; John Szarkowski's *From the Picture Press* exhibition; Judy Dater's *The Feminine Eye in Photography* published

1974: Robert Cumming's *Academic Shading Exercise*;

1975: *New Topographics* exhibition, New York; Alan Sekula's "On the Invention of Photographic Meaning"; digital camera created

1970–80 CONTINUED

1976: Jimmy Carter elected US President; civil war in Nicaragua; Mao Zedong dies

1977: First manned flight of US space shuttle; *Star Wars* appears at box office; first MRI test on a human being

1978: Karol Wojtyla becomes Pope John Paul II

1979: Shah of Iran deposed; Margaret Thatcher becomes British Prime Minister; Soviet Union invades Afghanistan; Jean-François Lyotard's *The Postmodern Condition* published

1970–80 CONTINUED

1976: Sara Facio and Alicia D'Amico's *Humanario* published; Lee Friedlander's *The American Monument* published; Marcel Broodthaers's *La Soupe de Daguerre*; Robert Mapplethorpe's *Rosie*;

1977: Susan Sontag's *On Photography* published; (1977-80): Hitoshi Nomura's *"Moon Score"*; *Pictures* exhibition in New York

1978: First Colloquium of Latin American Photographers; *Hecho en Latinoamérican* exhibition; Claudia Andujar's *Yanomami* published; John Szarkowski's *Mirrors and Windows* exhibition; Chauncey Hare's *Interior America* published; Cindy Sherman's *Untitled FIlm Stills* published

1980–90

1980s: Rise of computer-related technology, digital imagery

1980: Iran–Iraq War begins; Polish solidarity movement grows; Neo-Expressionism in art

1981: IBM creates first personal computer; Ronald Reason inaugurated as US President

1982: Compact disks introduced; Falklands War; Israel invades Lebanon

1983: Compact disks marketed; AIDS virus officially identified; US invades Grenada

1984: Apple launches Macintosh computer; Indira Gandhi assassinated; miners' strike in Britain; Canon demonstrates digital electronic still camera

1985: Mikhail Gorbachev becomes leader of Soviet Union; hole in ozone layer confirmed

1986: Space shuttle *Challenger* explodes; Chernobyl disaster; Irangate scandal in US; Fuji introduces disposable camera

1987: First personal computers sold

1989: Berlin Wall torn down

1980–90

1980: *Voyager* space probe photographs Saturn; Roland Barthes' *Camera Lucida* published

1981: Susan Meiselas's *Nicaragua* published; Sandy Skoglund's *Revenge of the Goldfish*

1982: Soviet spacecraft takes first color photographs of Venus; *Thinking Photography* published

1983: Raghubir Singh's *Shiva Temple, Jahngira*; David Hockney's *Christopher Isherwood ...*; (1983–84) Nancy Burson's *Mankind*; Mary Ellen Mark's *"Rat" and Mike with a Gun*; Barbara Kruger's *"We Won't Play Nature to Your Culture"*; Nan Goldin's *The Ballad of Sexual Dependency* published

1984(?): *Britain in 1984* exhibition

1985: Vladimir Kuprejanov's *In Memory of Pushkin* published; Christian Boltanski's *Monuments*

1986: Paul Graham's *Beyond Caring* published; Eugene Richards's *Exploding into Life* published; (1986–87) Barbara Ess's *Food for the Moon*

1987: James Clifford's *The Predicament of Culture* published; Santu Mofokeng's *Shebeen in White City, Soweto*; Kamel Dridi's *Mosque, Fes*; Andres Serrano's *Piss Christ*

1988: Chris Killup's *In Flagrante* published; Tokihiro Satoh's *Photo-Respiration*

1989: Bill Gates establishes Corbis.com; *Adbusters* launched

1990–2000

1990s: Launch of the Hubble space telescope; Gulf War begins

1990: Nelson Mandela freed

1991: Soviet Union collapses

1992: Earth Summit in Rio de Janeiro; Single European Market

1994: Russia invades Chechnya; North American Free Trade Agreement; massacres in Rwanda; Channel Tunnel connects England and France; Nelson Mandela president of South Africa;

1995: World Trade Organization formed; Oklahoma City bombings; evidence of global warming from Intergovernmental Panel on Climate Change

1996: BSE crisis in Britain; Taliban forces seize power in Afghanistan; Yitzhak Rabin assassinated

1997: Mother Theresa dies; Diana, Princess of Wales, dies in car crash; China regains control of Hong Kong

1998: Kosovo conflict begins; India, Pakistan make nuclear tests

1999: Vladimir Putin Russian prime minister; camera phone invented

1990–2000

1990s: Adobe PhotoShop software marketed (February 1990); Stanford University's *The Visible Human Project*; Sebastião Salgado's *An Uncertain Grace* published

1991: Pedro Meyer's *The Temptation of the Angel*; (1991–92) Jeff Wall's *Dead Troops Talk*; *Pleasures and Terrors of Domestic* Comfort exhibition

1992: Young Kim's *Distances*; Larry Sultan's *Pictures from Home* published; Sally Mann's *Immediate Family* published

1993: Suzanne Bloom and Ed Hill's (MANUAL) *The Constructed Forest*; *Time* magazine's "The New Face of America"

1994: Anthony Aziz and Sammy Cucher's *Dystopia*

1995: Albert Chong's *Aunt Winnie*; Garth Amundson's *Dr Kempf's Nightmare*

1996: Derek Johnston's *Havisu Falls*; Chen Chieh-Jen's *Self-destruction*; Esther Parada's *Transplant...*

1997: Gary Schneider's *Genetic Self-portrait*; (1997–98) Mariko Mori's *Pure Land*; (1997–98) Bettina Witteveen's *Hybrid Identities* published; Boris Mikhailov begins *Case Studies* series; Robert Parkeharrison's *Patching the Sky*

1998: Andreas Gursky's *Bundestag, Bonn*

1999: *Another Girl, Another Planet* exhibition

2000–PRESENT

2000: Michael Hardt and Antonio Negri's *Empire* published; human DNA sequence established

2001: September 11—World Trade Center destroyed; October 7—US bombs Kabul, Afghanistan

2002: US/Afghan Operation Anaconda in Afghanistan; *Whale Rider* screened; India and Pakistan fight over Kashmir; economic crisis in Latin America; October 12—Bali terrorist bombings; US and Russia agree to cut nuclear arsenals; Chechen rebels take hostages in Moscow

2003: Ariel Sharon elected Israeli prime minister; war and famine in Sudan; *Look-Look* magazine founded; U.S. and Britain launch war against Iraq; Dec: Saddam Hussein is captured by American troops (Dec. 13)

2004: March 11—Madrid terrorist bombings; U.S. hands over power to Iraqi interim government; Iyad Allawi becomes prime minister; Summer Olympics in Athens, Greece; December 26—tsunami devastates South Asia

2005: July 7—London bombings; Hurricane Katrina devastates US Gulf Coast; October 1—Bali terrorist bombings

2000–PRESENT

2000: Claudia Andujar awarded Lannan Foundation Cultural Freedom Prize; *Deborah Willis's Reflections in Black ...* published; Rineke Dijkstra's *Tiergarten, Berlin*

2001: Orlan's *Omniprésence Vénus*

2002: Edward Burtynsky's *Shipbreaking* series; Alfredo Jarr's *Lament of the Images*; *Documenta XI* exhibition; Wendy Ewald's *White Girl's Alphabet* series

2003: Kodak announces end of slide projector manufacture; Thomas Demand's *The Clearing*; Susan Sontag's *Regarding the Pain of Others* published

2004: Photos of US soldiers abusing Iraqui soldiers revealed; Kodak announces end of black-and-white photo paper manufacture; *Photography in Britain since 1968* conference; (2004–05) *Why Are We the Way We Are?* exhibition; (2004–06) *Between Past and Future* exhibition; *Nazar: Photographs from the Arab World* exhibition; (2004–06) *Girl's Night Out* exhibition

2005: (2005–06) *SlideShow* exhibition; *African Remix* exhibition; *White: Whiteness and Race in Contemporary Art* exhibition

NOTES

Introduction

1 Allan Sekula, "Photography: Between Labour and Capital," in *Mining Photographs and Other Pictures, 1948–1968: A Selection from the Negative Archives of Shedden Studio, Glace Bay, Cape Breton, Photographs by Leslie Sheddon*, ed. Benjamin H. D. Buchloh and Robert Wilkie (The Press of the Nova Scotia College of Art and Design and The University College of Cape Breton Press, 1983), p. 201.
2 Lady Elizabeth Eastlake, [untitled review], *The Quarterly Review*, vol. 101 (April 1857), p. 465.
3 Henry James, "The Real Thing," in *The Short Stories of Henry James*, ed. Clifton Fadiman (New York: Random House, 1945), p.194.
4 Siegfried Kracauer, "Photography," in his *The Mass Ornament*, ed. and trans. by Thomas Y. Levin (Cambridge, MA: Harvard University Press, 1995), pp. 58–61. This essay and the others in *The Mass Ornament* were published in the newspaper *Die Frankfurter Zeitung*.
5 Daniel J. Boorstin, *The Image: A Guide to Pseudo-Events in America* (New York: Harper Colophon Books, 1961), p. 240.
6 Thomas Lawson, "Last Exit: Painting," *Artforum* (October 1981), p. 45.
7 Roberta Smith, "The Art and Artists of the Year," *New York Times* (Sunday, December 28, 2003), p. AR 37
8 John Berger, *Ways of Seeing* (London and Middlesex, England: Penguin Books and the British Broadcasting Corporation, 1972), p. 7.

CHAPTER ONE
The Origins of Photography (to 1839)

1 For more information, see J. L. Heilbron, *The Sun in the Church: Cathedrals as Solar Observatories* (Cambridge, MA: Harvard University Press, 1999).
2 Oliver Wendell Holmes, "The Stereoscope and the Stereograph," *Atlantic Monthly*, vol. 3 (June 1859), pp. 738–39.
3 Eric Hobsbawm, *The Age of Revolution, 1789–1848* (New York: Vintage Books, 1996), pp. 7–28.
4 Eric Hobsbawm, pp. 7–28. The role of realistic depiction in art and science in promoting the invention of photography is discussed in Heinrich Schwarz, *Art and Photography: Forerunners and Influences: Selected Essays by Heinrich Schwarz*, ed. William E. Parker (Layton: UT: Gibbs M. Smith and Peregrine Smith Books, 1985), and Peter Galassi, *Before Photography: Painting and the Invention of Photography* (New York: Museum of Modern Art, 1981).
5 For a review of perspective machines see Martin Kemp, *The Science of Art: Optical Themes in Western Art from Brunelleschi to Seurat* (New Haven, CT: Yale University Press, 1990), pp. 163–257. My discussion of perspective and drawing machines is indebted to this excellent text.
6 Gisèle Freund, *Photography and Society* (Boston: David R. Godine, Publisher, 1980), p. 11.
7 Boris Kossoy, "Hercules Florence, Pioneer of Photography in Brazil," *Image*, vol. 20, no. 1 (March 1977), p. 17.
8 Kossoy, pp. 16–19.
9 For the circumstances of Florence's invention, I am indebted to Boris Kossoy's essay "Photography in Nineteenth-Century Latin America: The European Experience and the Exotic Experience," in *Image and Memory: Photography from Latin America, 1866–1994*, ed. Wendy Watriss and Lois Parkinson Zamora (Austin, TX: University of Texas Press, 1998), pp. 21–25.

10 Quoted in Boris Kossoy, "Photography in Nineteenth-Century Latin America: The European Experience and the Exotic Experience," in *Image and Memory: Photography from Latin America, 1866–1994*, ed. Wendy Watriss and Lois Parkinson Zamora, p. 25.
11 In 1842, Talbot wrote to Herschel that "Science is now cultivated by so many, that it is impossible that cases of simultaneous invention should not frequently arise." Quoted in Larry J. Schaaf, *Out of the Shadows: Herschel, Talbot and the Invention of Photography* (New Haven, CT: Yale University Press, 1992), p. 126.
12 Thomas Wedgwood and Sir Humphry Davy, "An Account of a Method of Copying Paintings upon Glass and of Making Profiles, by the Agency of Light upon Nitrate of Silver," reprinted in Beaumont Newhall, *Essays and Images* (New York: Museum of Modern Art, 1980), p. 16.
13 See a discussion of Niépce's processes in Helmut and Alison Gernsheim, *L. J. M. Daguerre: The History of the Diorama and the Daguerreotype*, 2nd, rev. ed. (New York: Dover Publications, Inc., 1968), pp. 51–64.
14 For a technical description of this process and many early photographic processes, see William Crawford, *The Keepers of Light: A History and Working Guide to Early Photographic Processes* (Dobbs Ferry, NY: Morgan & Morgan, 1979).
15 Quoted in Helmut and Alison Gernsheim, *L. J. M. Daguerre: The History of the Diorama and the Daguerreotype*, 2nd, rev. ed., pp. 80–81.
16 See Mary Warner Marien, *Photography and Its Critics: A Cultural History, 1839–1900* (New York: Cambridge University Press, 1997), pp. 32–33.
17 Arago's statement and Gaucheraud's newspaper article are excerpted in English in Helmut and Alison Gernsheim, *L. J. M. Daguerre: The History of the Diorama and the Daguerreotype*, 2nd, rev. ed., pp. 82–85.
18 See the discussion in Larry J. Schaaf, *Out of the Shadows: Herschel, Talbot and the Invention of Photography*, pp. 23–25.
19 See Pierre G. Harmant, "Anno Lucis 1839," a three-part article in *Camera* (May 1977, no. 5, pp. 39–43; August, no. 8, pp. 37–41; October, no. 10, pp. 40–44). Also Robert Meyer, "Hans Thøger Winther: A Norwegian Pioneer in Photography," in *Shadow and Substance: Essays on the History of Photography*, ed. Kathleen Collins (Bloomfield Hills, MI: The Amorphous Institute Press, 1990), pp. 39–48.
20 Bayard's note is reproduced in full in Michael Sapir, "The Impossible Photograph: Hippolyte Bayard's Self-Portrait as a Drowned Man," *Modern Fiction Studies*, vol. 40, no. 3 (Fall 1994), p. 623.
21 Quoted in Larry J. Schaaf, *Out of the Shadows: Herschel, Talbot and the Invention of Photography*, p. 49.
22 Schaaf, p. 130.
23 Letter by William Henry Fox Talbot, dated January 30, 1839, published in the *Literary Gazette* (February 2, 1839). Quoted in Gail Buckland, *Fox Talbot and the Invention of Photography* (Boston, MA: David R. Godine, Publisher, 1980), p. 43. It is unknown if Talbot was actually preparing a report, or whether his claim to be doing so was an attempt to respond to the announcement of the daguerreotype.
24 Gail Buckland, *Fox Talbot and the Invention of Photography*, p. 38.
25 William Henry Fox Talbot, *The Pencil of Nature* (London: Longman Brown, Green & Longmans, 1844–46), n.p. The book was reproduced in facsimile by Da Capo Press in 1969.

26 This experiment is described in Larry J. Schaaf, *Out of the Shadows: Herschel, Talbot and the Invention of Photography*, p. 40.
27 Quoted in Larry J. Schaaf, *Out of the Shadows: Herschel, Talbot and the Invention of Photography*, p. 42.
28 Quoted in Gail Buckland, *Fox Talbot and the Invention of Photography*, p. 39.
29 See Mary Warner Marien, *Photography and Its Critics: A Cultural History, 1839–1900*, pp. 6, 35.
30 Quoted in Larry J. Schaaf, *Out of the Shadows: Herschel, Talbot and the Invention of Photography*, p. 57.
31 Schaaf, p. 71.
32 Schaaf, p. 75.
33 See Mary Warner Marien, *Photography and Its Critics: A Cultural History, 1839–1900*, p. 17.
34 Quoted in Helmut and Alison Gernsheim, *L. J. M. Daguerre: The History of the Diorama and the Daguerreotype*, 2nd, rev. ed., pp. 101–2.
35 See Marien, *Photography and Its Critics*, p. 3, and the subsequent discussion.

CHAPTER TWO
The Second Invention of Photography (1839–1854)

1 "New Discovery in the Fine Arts," *The New Yorker* (April 13, 1839), excerpted in Merry Foresta and John Wood, *Secrets of the Dark Chamber: The Art of American Daguerreotype* (Washington, DC: Smithsonian Institution Press, 1995), p. 224.
2 "New Discovery in the Fine Arts," p. 223.
3 "Self-operating Processes of Fine Art: The Daguerotype [sic]," *The Museum of Foreign Literature, Science and Art*, 35, n.s. 7 (January–April, 1839), p. 341.
4 For a discussion of the range of these meanings applied to photography see Jens Jäger, "Discourses on Photography in Mid-Victorian Britain," *History of Photography*, vol. 19, no. 4 (1995), pp. 316–21.
5 Fritz Kempe, *Daguerreotypie in Deutschland: Vom Charme der frühen Fotografie* (Seebruck am Chiemsee: Heering Verlag, 1979), p. 62.
6 *The Athenaeum* (December 18, 1847), p. 1304, quoted in Jens Jäger, "Discourses on Photography in Mid-Victorian Britain," *History of Photography*, p. 317.
7 Francis Wey, "Exposé sommaire du but et des principaux éléments du journal," (1851), reprinted in Heinz Buddemeier, *Panorama, Diorama, Photographie* (Munich: Wilhelm Fink Verlag), pp. 253–54.
8 *Alexander's Weekly Messenger* (January 15, 1840), p. 38.
9 "Fine Arts," unsigned review of the Society of British Artists, *The Athenaeum* (April 17, 1847), p. 416.
10 "Self-operating Processes of Fine Art: The Daguerotype [sic]," p. 341.
11 Paul Greenhalgh, *Ephemeral Vistas: The Expositions universelles, Great Exhibitions and World's Fairs, 1851–1939* (Manchester: Manchester University Press, 1988), p. 145.
12 *The Golden Age of British Photography, 1839–1900*, ed. Mark Haworth-Booth (Millerton, NY: Aperture, 1984), p. 48.
13 William Henry Fox Talbot, *Some Account of the Art of Photogenic Drawing, or the Process by which Natural Objects May Be Made to Delineate Themselves without the Aid of the Artist's Pencil* (London: R. & J. S. Taylor, 1839), n.p.
14 Letter dated June 1839, quoted in Gail Buckland, *Fox Talbot and the Invention of Photography* (Boston, MA: David R. Godine, Publishers, 1980), p. 19.
15 William Henry Fox Talbot, *The Pencil of Nature* (1844–46; rpt New York: Da Capo Press, 1869), n.p.

16 Larry J. Schaaf, *The Photographic Art of William Henry Fox Talbot* (Princeton: Princeton University Press, 2000), p. 166.
17 Francis Wey, "Album de la Société héliographique," *La Lumière* (May 18, 1851), p. 58. Quoted in Andre Jammes and Eugenia Parry Janis, *The Art of the French Calotype* (Princeton, NJ: Princeton University Press, 1983), p. 4.
18 Sander Gilman, *Seeing the Insane* (New York: J. Wiley, 1982) p. 189.
19 Hugh W. Diamond, "On the Application of Photography to the Physiognomic and Mental Phenomena of Insanity" (read before the Royal Society, May 22, 1856), reprinted in *The Face of Madness: Hugh W. Diamond and the Origin of Psychiatric Photography*, ed. Sander L. Gilman (New York: Brunner/Mazell, Publishers, 1976), p. 19.
20 Diamond, p. 20.
21 Diamond, p. 24.
22 See Bates Lowry and Isabel Barrett Lowry, *The Silver Canvas: Daguerreotype Masterpieces from the J. Paul Getty Museum* (Los Angeles, CA: The J. Paul Getty Museum, 1998), p. 112.
23 Brian Wallis, "Black Bodies, White Science: Louis Agassiz's Slave Daguerrreotypes," *Art in America*, vol. 9, no. 2 (Summer 1995), p. 40.
24 Daniel M. Fox and Christopher Lawrence, *Photographing Medicine: Images and Power in Britain and America since 1840* (New York: Greenwood Press, 1988), p. 24.
25 Daniel M. Fox and Christopher Lawrence, *Photographing Medicine*, p. 25.
26 For further details, see the discussion in Bates Lowry and Isabel Barrett Lowry, *The Silver Canvas*, pp. 182–85.
27 See Olivier Debroise, *Mexican Suite: A History of Photography in Mexico*, trans. Stella de Sá Rego (Austin, TX: University of Texas Press, 2001), pp. 164–67.
28 Gina Rodriguez Hernandez, "Cerro Gordo, abril 18 de 1847," in *Alquimia*, vol. 1, no. 2 (April 1998), pp. 44–45.
29 See Olivier Debroise, *Mexican Suite: A History of Photography in Mexico*, p. 166.
30 Beaumont Newhall, *The Daguerreotype in America* (New York: Dover Publications, Inc., 1976, 3rd rev. ed.), p. 88.
31 James R. Ryan, *Picturing Empire: Photography and Visualization of the British Empire* (Chicago, IL: University of Chicago Press, 1997), p. 28.
32 Alkis X. Xanthakis, *History of Greek Photography, 1839–1960* (Athens: Hellenic Literary and Historical Archives Society, 1988) pp. 28–29.
33 Xanthakis, p. 30.
34 Yeshayahu Nir, *The Bible and the Image: The History of Photography in the Holy Land, 1839–1899* (Philadelphia: University of Pennsylvania Press, 1985), p. 35. I am indebted to Nir's discussion and the work of Kathleen Stewart Howe in *Revealing the Holy Land: The Photographic Exploration of Palestine* (Santa Barbara, CA: Santa Barbara Museum of Art, 1997).
35 Quoted in Kathleen Stewart Howe, *Revealing the Holy Land*, p. 23. These daguerreotypes are now lost. Also see Robert Hershkowitz, *The British Photographer Abroad: The First Thirty Years* (London: Robert Hershkowitz Ltd., 1980), p. 80.
36 For a full discussion of the commission and its work, see Jammes and Janis, *The Art of the French Calotype*, especially pp. 52–66.
37 Malcolm Daniel, *The Photographs of Edouard Baldus* (New York: The Metropolitan Museum of Art, 1994), pp. 21–22.
38 Eugenia Parry Janis and Josiane Sartre, *Henri Le Secq: Photographe de 1850–1860* (Paris: Flammarion, 1986), p. 116.
39 This image is discussed in William Welling, *Photography in America: The Formative Years* (Albuquerque, NM: University of New Mexico Press, 1978), p. 28.
40 *Daguerrean Journal*, vol. 1, no. 4 (January 1, 1851), p. 117. Quoted in Michael L. Carlebach, *The Origins of Photojournalism in America* (Washington, DC: Smithsonian Institution Press, 1992), p. 27.

41 Janet E. Buerger, *French Daguerreotypes* (Chicago, IL: University of Chicago Press, 1989), p. 28.
42 See *Photography in Russia, 1840–1940*, ed. David Elliott (London: Thames and Hudson, 1992), p. 28.
43 *Photography in Russia*, p. 27.
44 Francis Wey, "Du Naturalisme dans l'art de don principe et de ses conséquences," (*La Lumière*, vol. 1, 1851), reproduced in Heinz Buddemeier, *Panorama, Diorama, Photographie*, p. 281 The quotation reads "et leurs portraits ne ressemblent point, comme certaines épreuves daguerriennes, des merlans frits collés sur un plat d'argent."
45 Elizabeth Anne McCauley, *Industrial Madness: Commercial Photography in Paris, 1848–1871* (New Haven, CT: Yale University Press, 1994), p. 154.
46 T. S. Arthur, *Godey's Lady's Book*, 1849. Quoted in Floyd Rinhart and Marion Rinhart, *The American Daguerreotype* (Athens, GA: University of Georgia Press, 1981), pp. 113–14.
47 Quoted in Robert Taft, *Photography and the American Scene* (1938; rpt. New York: Dover Publications, 1964), p. 76.
48 Alan Trachtenberg, *Reading American Photographs: Images as History, Mathew Brady to Walker Evans* (New York: Hill and Wang, 1989), p. 26.
49 Deborah Willis, *Reflections in Black: A History of Black Photographers, 1840 to the Present* (New York: W. W. Norton & Co., 2000), p. 4.
50 Michael L. Carlebach, *The Origins of Photojournalism in America*, pp. 22–23.
51 Matthew R. Isenburg, "Southworth and Hawes: The Artists," in John Woods, *The Daguerreotype: A Sesquicentennial Celebration* (Iowa City, IA: University of Iowa Press, 1989), p. 75.
52 Albert Sands Southworth, "The Early History of Photography in the United States," in *Photography: Essays and Images*, ed. Beaumont Newhall (New York: Museum of Modern Art, 1980), p. 41.
53 Sara Stevenson, "David Octavius Hill and Robert Adamson," in *British Photography in the Nineteenth Century: The Fine Art Tradition* (New York: Cambridge University Press, 1989), p. 53.
54 Talbot quoted in Larry J. Schaaf, *The Photographic Art of William Henry Fox Talbot* (Princeton, NJ: Princeton University Press, 2000), pp. 19, 59.
55 Letter from Hill to Mr. Bicknell, dated January 17, 1848, quoted in Colin Ford and Roy Strong, eds., *An Early Victorian Album: The Photographic Masterpieces (1843–1847) of David Octavius Hill and Robert Adamson* (New York: Alfred A. Knopf, 1976), p. 321.
56 Sara Stevenson, "David Octavius Hill and Robert Adamson," p. 43.
57 See discussion in Richard Rudisill, *Mirror Image: The Influence of the Daguerreotype on American Society* (Albuquerque, NM: University of New Mexico Press, 1971), pp. 218–19.
58 Sir Francis Palgrave, "The Fine Arts of Florence," *Quarterly Review*, vol. 66 (1840), p. 326.
59 "Photogenic Drawing, or Drawing by Agency of Light," *Edinburgh Review*, vol. 154 (January 1843), pp. 160–61, 169.
60 John Ruskin, *The Works of John Ruskin*, ed. E. T. Cook and A. Wedderburn (London: G. Allen, 1903–1912), vol. 33, p. 304.
61 "Otkrytie Dagera," in *Khudozhestvennaia gazeta*, no. 2 (January 15, 1840), pp. 11–12, quoted in *Photography in Russia*, p. 26.
62 Eugène Delacroix, "Le dessin sans maître, par Mme Elisabeth Cavé," *Revue des Deux Mondes*, vol. 3 (September 15, 1850), pp. 1144–45.
63 Gustave Flaubert, *Correspondance (1850–1854)* (Paris: Louis Conard, 1910), p. 427, and C. A. Sainte-Beuve, "De la littérature industrielle," *Portraits Contemporains*, vol. 2 (Paris: Michel Lévy Frère, 1889), p. 434. The comments appeared in September 1839.
64 E.-J. Delécluze, "Exposition de 1850," *Journal des Débats* (March 21, 1851), n.p.
65 For a fuller discussion of photography's critics, see Mary Warner Marien, *Photography and Its Critics: A Cultural History, 1839–1900* (New York: Cambridge University Press, 1997), pp. 64–73.
66 For Francis Wey's discussion, see "Du Naturalisme dans l'art de don principe et de ses conséquences," (*La Lumière*, vol. 1, 1851), reproduced in Heinz

Buddemeier, *Panorama, Diorama, Photographie* (Munich: Wilhelm Fink Verlag, 1970), pp. 267–84.
67 See William Newton's address to the Photographic Society of London, printed in the *Journal of the Photographic Society*, vol. 1 (March 3, 1853), p. 6.
68 Gustave Le Gray, *Photographie: traité nouveau théorique et practique des procédés et manipulations sur papier ... et sur verre* (Paris: Lerebours et Secretan [1852]), p. 3. See also p. 3.
69 Michel Foucault, *Discipline and Punish: The Birth of the Prison*, trans. Alan Sheridan (New York: Vintage Books, 1979), p. 187.

CHAPTER THREE
The Expanding Domain (1854–1880)

1 [Lady Elizabeth Eastlake], (Untitled Book Review) *Quarterly Review*, 101 (January–April 1857), pp. 442–43.
2 Keith F. Davis, "'A Terrible Distinctness': Photography and the Civil War Era," in *Photography in Nineteenth-Century America*, ed. Martha A. Sandweiss (New York: Harry N. Abrams, Inc., 1991), p. 137.
3 See the contemporary description from *New York Review*, reproduced in William Welling, *Photography in America: The Formative Years, 1839–1900* (Albuquerque, NM: University of New Mexico Press, 1978), p. 265.
4 Oliver Wendell Holmes, "The Stereoscope and the Stereograph," *Atlantic Monthly*, vol. 3 (June 1859), p. 744.
5 Oliver Wendell Holmes, "Sun-Painting and Sun-Sculpture," *Atlantic Monthly*, vol. 8 (July 1861), pp. 14–15
6 Oliver Wendell Holmes, "The Stereoscope and the Stereograph," p. 747.
7 "Stereoscope: or Travel Made Easy," *The Athenaeum*, no. 1586 (March 20, 1858), p. 371.
8 *Revue Photographique* (1862), p. 151, quoted in André Rouillé, "The Great Photography Debate," *Impact of Science on Society*, vol. 42, no. 4 (no. 168), p. 292.
9 Elizabeth Anne McCauley, *A. A. E. Disdéri and the Carte de Visite Portrait Photograph* (New Haven, CT: Yale University Press, 1985), p. 220.
10 For information on photographic journals in the United States, see William and Estelle Marder, "Nineteenth-century American Photographic Journals: A Chronological List," *History of Photography*, vol. 17, no. 1 (Spring 1993), pp. 95–100.
11 *Art Journal* (1860), p. 221, from frontispiece of Richard J. Huyda, *Camera in the Interior: 1858, H. L. Hime, Photographer: The Assiniboine and Saskatchewan Exploring Expedition* (Toronto: The Coach House Press, 1975).
12 Andre Jammes and Eugenia Parry Jani, *The Art of the French Calotype* (Princeton, NJ: Princeton University Press, 1983), pp. 162, 185.
13 Francis Frith, "The Art of Photography," *Art Journal*, 5 (1859), pp. 71–72 (emphases Frith).
14 C. Jabez Hughes, "On Art Photography," *American Journal of Photography*, 3 (1861), p. 261.
15 Christopher Date and Anthony Hamber, "The Origins of Photography at the British Museum," *History of Photography*, vol. 14, no. 4 (1990), p. 316.
16 Valerie Lloyd, *Roger Fenton: Photographer of the 1850s* (London: South Bank Board, 1988), p. 11.
17 Abigail Solomon-Godeau, *Photography at the Dock: Essays on Photographic History, Institutions, and Practices* (Minneapolis, MN: University of Minnesota Press, 1991), pp. 158–59.
18 See Howard B. Leighton, "The Lantern Slide and Art," *History of Photography*, vol. 8, no. 2 (1984), pp. 107–18.
19 Marcus Aurelius Root, *The Camera and the Pencil* (1864; rpt. Pawlet, VT: Helios, 1971), p. 28.
20 "Stereoscopes for Amateurs—Process of Producing Stereoscopic Photographs," *Scientific American*, 2 (June 2, 1860) p. 361. For a discussion of art reproduction and visual literacy, see Mary Warner Marien, *Photography and Its Critics* (New York: Cambridge University Press, 1997).

21 "Fine Arts: New Publications" [review of the exhibition "Gems of Art Treasures"], *The Athenaeum*, 1549 (July 4, 1857), p. 856.
22 Rembrandt Peale, "Portraiture," *Crayon*, 4, Part II (February 1857), p. 44 (emphasis Peale).
23 Charles Baudelaire, "Salon of 1859," in *Art in Paris*, p. 154.
24 Rembrandt Peale, "Portraiture," p. 44.
25 A later version (1858) included drawing derived from photographs taken by Nadar.
26 Eugène Delacroix, "Le dessin sans maître, par Mme. Elisabeth Cavé," *Revue des Deux Mondes*, 3 (September 15, 1850), pp. 1144–45.
27 For an international discussion of the painters who may have been influenced by photography see Nissan N. Perez, *Focus East: Early Photography in the Near East, 1839–1885* (New York: Harry N. Abrams, Inc., 1988), pp. 66–67.
28 Plate note, in Maria Morris Hambourg, Françoise Heilbrun, and Philippe Néagu, *Nadar* (New York: The Metropolitan Museum of Art, 1995), p. 114.
29 Quoted in Maria Morris Hambourg, "A Portrait of Nadar," in Maria Morris Hambourg, Françoise Heilbrun, and Philippe Néagu, *Nadar*, p. 25.
30 See Elizabeth Anne McCauley, *Industrial Madness*, p. 124.
31 Maria Morris Hambourg, plate note, in Maria Morris Hambourg, Françoise Heilbrun, and Philippe Néagu, *Nadar*, p. 113.
32 For a history of the *tableau vivant*, see Heinz K. Henisch and Bridget A. Henisch, *The Photographic Experience, 1839–1914* (University Park, PA: The Pennsylvania State University Press, 1994), pp. 70–75.
33 For more information on Madame Warton's programs see Jack W. McCullough, *Living Pictures on the New York Stage* (Ann Arbor, MI: UMI Research Press, 1983), pp. 38–47.
34 William Crawford, *The Keepers of Light* (Dobbs Ferry, NY: Morgan & Morgan, 1979), p. 55. This book contains a useful key to the allegorical significance of the figures in *The Two Ways of Life*.
35 Mark Haworth-Booth, ed., *The Golden Age of British Photography, 1839–1900*, p. 94.
36 Anne Anninger and Julie Mellby, *Salts of Silver, Toned with Gold: The Harrison D. Horblit Collection of Early Photography* (Cambridge, MA: The Houghton Library, Harvard University, 1999), p. 116.
37 Grace Seiberling, *Amateurs, Photography, and the Mid-Victorian Imagination* (Chicago, IL: University of Chicago Press, 1986), p. 139.
38 Virginia Dodier, "Clementina, Viscountess Hawarden," in Mike Weaver, *British Photography in the Nineteenth Century: The Fine Art Tradition* (New York: Cambridge University Press, 1989), p. 145.
39 Naomi Rosenblum, *A History of Women Photographers* (New York: Abbeville Press, 1994), p. 302.
40 From a letter to John Herschel reproduced in Helmut Gernsheim, *Julia Margaret Cameron: Her Life and Photographic Work* (Millerton, NY: Aperture, 1975), p. 14.
41 Julia Margaret Cameron, "The Annals of My Glass House," in Beaumont Newhall, ed., *Photography: Essays and Images* (New York: Museum of Modern Art, 1980), p. 137.
42 See Mike Weaver, *Julia Margaret Cameron, 1815–1879* (Boston, MA: New York Graphic Society/Little Brown Company, 1984), p. 138.
43 William Culp Darrah, "Nineteenth-Century Women Photographers," *Shadow and Substance: Essays on the History of Photography*, ed. Kathleen Collins (Bloomfield Hills, MI: The Amorphous Institute Press, 1990) p. 89.
44 Jabez Hughes, "Photography as an Industrial Occupation for Women," *British Journal of Photography* (May 9, 1873), p. 223.
45 William Culp Darrah, "Nineteenth-Century Women Photographers," p. 89.
46 Oliver Wendell Holmes, "The Stereoscope and the Stereograph," p. 748.
47 [John W. Draper], "Editorial Miscellany," *American Journal of Photography*, vol. 3 (1861) p. 320.
48 Callwell's *Small Wars: Their Principles and Purpose* was published in 1899. See the discussion in James

R. Ryan, *Picturing Empire: Photography and the Visualization of the British Empire* (Chicago, IL: University of Chicago Press, 1997), p. 73. Also of related interest is André Rouillé, *L'Empire de la Photographie, 1839–1870* (Paris: Le Sycomore, 1982).
49 James R. Ryan, p. 73.
50 [Eugéne Durieu], "Rapport," *Bulletin de la Société Française de Photographie* (February 1856), p. 50.
51 Donald E. English, *Political Uses of Photography in the Third French Republic, 1871–1914* (Ann Arbor, MI: University of Michigan Research Press, 1984), p. 8.
52 Helmut and Alison Gernsheim, *Roger Fenton: Photographer of the Crimean War* (London: Secker & Warburg, 1954), pp. 12–13.
53 See the discussion in Mike Weaver, "Le Gray—Fenton—Watkins," in *The Art of Photography, 1839–1989*, ed. Mike Weaver (New Haven, CT: Yale University Press, 1989), p. 96. Indeed, it may not have been the actual spot where the tragic military offensive took place. See Jennifer Green-Lewis, *Framing the Victorians: Photography and the Culture of Realism* (Ithaca, NY: Cornell University Press, 1996), p. 126.
54 *Photographic Journal*, vol. 2 (1855), p. 221.
55 Ulrich Keller, *The Ultimate Spectacle: A Visual History of the Crimean War* (London: Gordon and Breach, 2001), p. 136.
56 Fenton may not have been the first to offer photographic instruction to Queen Victoria and Prince Albert. They may have been taught by Dr. Ernst Becker, who was appointed librarian to Prince Albert and an assistant tutor to the princes. See Francis Dimond and Roger Taylor, *Crown and Country: The Royal Family and Photography, 1842–1910* (New York: Viking, 1987), p. 14.
57 For a study of his work and reprints of his letters from the Crimea, see *Jean-Charles Langlois: La Photographie, La Peinture, La Guerre. Correspondence Inédite de Crimée (1855–1856)*, ed. François Robichon and André Rouillé (Nîmes: Éditions Jacqueline Chambon, 1992).
58 See *New York Times* (July 26, 1864), p. 4.
59 Cook's life and work are recounted in Jack C. Ramsay, Jr., *Photographer under Fire: The Story of George S. Cook, 1819–1902* (Green Bay, WI: Historical Resources Press, 1994).
60 Mary Panzer, *Mathew Brady and the Image of War* (Washington, DC: Smithsonian Institution Press, 1997), p. 103.
61 Vicki Goldberg, *The Power of Photography* (New York: Abbeville Publishing Group, 1991), p. 77.
62 Geo. Alfred Townsend ("Gath"), "The New York World Interview with Mathew Brady," in Vicki Goldberg, *Photography in Print* (New York: Simon and Schuster, 1981), p. 204.
63 Quoted in Josephine Cobb, "Photographers of the Civil War," *Military Affairs*, vol. 26, no. 2 (Fall 1962), p. 128.
64 *New York Times* (Monday, July 21, 1862), p. 5.
65 Described in Jack C. Ramsay, *Photographer under Fire*, p. 71.
66 Alexander Gardner, *Gardner's Sketchbook of the Civil War* (1865–66; rpt. New York, Dover, 1959), p. 36.
67 *New York Times* (Monday, October 20, 1862), p. 5.
68 Oliver Wendell Holmes, "Doings of the Sunbeam," *Atlantic Monthly*, vol. 12 (July 1863), pp. 11–12.
69 At one point, the photograph was credited to Timothy O'Sullivan by Gardner.
70 Kathleen Collins, "Living Skeletons: *Carte-de-visite* Propaganda in the American Civil War," *History of Photography*, vol. 12, no. 2 (April–June 1988), p. 104.
71 Collins, pp. 103–20. A *carte-de-visite* in the William C. Darrah collection shows the Elmira prison as neat and orderly rows of white tents. See his *Cartes de Visite in Nineteenth Century Photography* (Gettysburg, PA: W. C. Darrah, Publisher, 1981), p. 83, pl. 189.
72 Wendy Watriss and Lois Parkinson Zamora, *Image and Memory: Photography from Latin America, 1866–1994* (Austin, TX: University of Texas Press, 1998) pp. 7, 411.

73 For this information, and a comprehensive discussion of photography during the French Commune, I am indebted to Donald E. English, in his book, *Political Uses of Photography in the Third French Republic, 1871–1914*, for my discussion of the French Commune.
74 Albert Boime, *Art and the French Commune* (Princeton: Princeton University Press, 1995), p. 5. Boime's book is a lucid account of the reaction of artists to the events of the Paris Commune.
75 Quoted in Boime, p. 194.
76 For more discussion of this print, see English, p. 24.
77 "Photographs from the Philippine Islands," *Photographic News*, no. 61 (November 4, 1859), p. 99.
78 S. Bourne, "Narratives of a Photographical Trip to Kashmir and Adjacent Districts," *British Journal of Photography* (November 23–28, 1866), pp. 559–60.
79 *The Golden Age of British Photography, 1839–1900*, ed. Mark Haworth-Booth (Millerton, NY: Aperture, 1984), p. 104.
80 B. A. and H. K. Henisch, "James Robertson of Constantinople: A Chronology," *History of Photography*, vol. 14, no. 1 (January–March 1990), pp. 30–31.
81 Mark Haworth-Booth, ed., *The Golden Age of British Photography*, p. 104, and "Photographieren auf Forschungreisen: Robert Schlagintweit und seine Brüder erforschen die Alpen, Indien und Hochasien (1850–1857)," in *Silber und Salz: Zur Frühzeit der Photographie im deutschen Sprachenraum, 1839–1860*, ed. Bodo von Dewitz and Einhard Matz (Cologne and Heidelberg: Edition Braus, 1989), pp. 310–33.
82 Clark Worswick and Ainslie Embree, *The Last Empire: Photography in British India, 1855–1911* (Millerton, NY: Aperture, 1976), pp. 4–5. I am indebted to this book for information on the history of photography in India, as well as to Christopher Pinney's *Camera Indica: The Social Life of Indian Photography* (Chicago, IL: University of Chicago Press, 1997).
83 Vidya Dehejia, *India through the Lens, 1840–1911* (Washington, DC: Freer Gallery of Art and Arthur M. Sackler Gallery, Smithsonian Institution, 2000), p. 17.
84 See Roberta Wue, "Picturing Hong Kong: Photography through Practice and Function," in *Picturing Hong Kong* (New York: Asia Society Galleries and George Braziller, 1997), p. 28, n. 5. I am indebted to Wue for her insightful essay on early Hong Kong photography.
85 John Thomson, quoted in Roberta Wue, "Picturing Hong Kong," p. 38. For all his years in Asia, Thomson had two assistants, Akum and Ahong, the latter of whose name resembles A-Hung and Afong. For Ahong, see Stephen White, *John Thompson: A Window to the Orient* (New York: Thames and Hudson, 1985), p. 10.
86 John Thomson, quoted in Roberta Wue, "Picturing Hong Kong," p. 37. Afong was active from about 1859 to 1900.
87 Clark Worswick, *Japan: Photographs, 1854–1905* (New York: A Pennwick/Alfred A. Knopf, 1979), p. 30. Also see Terry Bennett, *Early Japanese Images* (Rutland, VT: Charles E. Tuttle Company, 1996), pp. 31–32. I am indebted to Worswick and Bennett for information on Japanese photography. Long considered lost, some of the Eliphalet Brown daguerreotypes may be held in Japanese museums. See Bennett, above, pp. 30–31, and Hugh Cortazzi and Terry Bennett, *Japan: Caught in Time* (New York: Weatherhill, 1995) p. 31.
88 Julia Meech, "Woodblock Prints and Photographs: Two Views of Nineteenth-Century Japan," *Asian Arts* (Summer 1990), p. 56.
89 Clark Worswick, *Japan*, p. 136, and Terry Bennett, *Early Japanese Images*, p. 144.
90 Bill Jay, *Victorian Cameraman: Francis Frith's Views of Rural England, 1850–1898* (Newton Abbot, Devon: David & Charles, 1973).
91 Kathleen Stewart Howe maintains that De Clercq's religious photographs are unusual among French photographs of the Holy Land. She suggests that, unlike English religious education, which stressed Bible reading and a sense of historical place, French religious study emphasized Catholic creed.

NOTES

See *Revealing the Holy Land: The Photographic Exploration of Palestine*, essay by Kathleen Stewart Howe (Santa Barbara, CA: Santa Barbara Museum of Art, 1997), p. 28. The relationship between surveys and photography is also discussed in Nissan N. Perez, *Focus East: Early Photography in the Near East, (1839–1885)* (New York: Harry N. Abrams, Inc., 1988), pp. 77–80.

92 Richard Parkhurst and Denis Gérard, *Ethiopia Photographed* (London: Kegan Paul International, 1996), p. 20.

93 Keith David, *Désiré Charnay*, p. 21.

94 See Elizabeth Anne McCauley, *Industrial Madness*, p. 306, and Keith B. Davis, *Désiré Charnay, Expeditionary Photographer* (Albuquerque, NM: The University of New Mexico Press, 1981), p. 19.

95 Quoted in Mark Haworth-Booth, ed., *The Golden Age of British Photography*, p. 114.

96 William Goetzmann, *Army Exploration in the American West, 1803–1863* (New Haven, CT: Yale University Press, 1959), p. 427–29. The border survey was not the first time that a photographer accompanied a survey team in Canada. The Assiniboine and Saskatchewan topographical and geological survey of 1858 was photographed by an engineer-photographer, Humphrey Lloyd Hime. See Richard J. Huyda, *Camera in the Interior: 1858, H. L. Hime, Photographer: The Assiniboine and Saskatchewan Exploring Expedition* (Toronto: The Coach House Press, 1975).

97 William H. Goetzmann, *Exploration and Empire: The Explorer and the Scientist in the Winning of the American West* (New York: Alfred A. Knopf, 1967), p. 231.

98 William H.Goetzmann, *Army Exploration in the American West*, p. 5.

99 William H.Goetzmann, *Exploration and Empire*, p. 303–04.

100 Gardner was not alone in associating the Leutze mural with the railroad. The artist Fanny Palmer used the title in a 1868 lithograph showing the railroad crossing the west, and painter Andrew Melrose painted *Westward the Star of Empire*, a strange view in which the train glows in a way reminiscent of J. M. W. Turner's rendering of the train as sublime in *Rain, Steam, and Speed*. For more on Leutze and on art and the railroad, see *The West as America: Reinterpreting Images of the Frontier, 1820–1920*, ed. William Truettner, (Washington, DC: Smithsonian Institution Press, 1991).

101 *New York Times* (May 8, 1867), p. 8.

102 James D. Horan, *Timothy O'Sullivan: America's Forgotten Photographer* (New York: Doubleday & Co., 1966), pp. 217–18.

103 Horan, p. 221.

104 Peter Bacon Hales, *William Henry Jackson and the Transformation of the American Landscape* (Philadelphia, PA: Temple University Press, 1988), p. 95. I am indebted to Hales's work for my understanding of Jackson.

105 Hales, p. 96.

106 Robert Bartless Haas, *Muybridge, Man in Motion* (Berkeley, CA: University of California Press, 1976), p. 51.

107 For more information on Modoc war photography, see Peter Palmquist, "Imagemakers of the Modoc War: Louis Heller and Eadweard Muybridge," *Journal of California Anthropology* (Winter 1977), p. 206–41.

108 James D. Horan, *Timothy O'Sullivan*, p. 285.

109 Alan Axelrod, *Chronicle of the Indian Wars: From Colonial Times to Wounded Knee* (New York: Prentice Hall General Reference, 1993), pp. 208–09.

110 Axelrod, p. 203.

111 Robert M. Utley and Wilcomb E. Washburn, *The American Heritage: History of the Indian Wars* (New York: American Heritage Publishing Company, 1977), p. 266.

112 Oliver Wendell Holmes, *Atlantic Monthly*, vol. 10 (May 1863).

113 It exists today as the Armed Forces Institute of Pathology. For more information on medicine during the American Civil War, see Stanley B. Burns, *Early Medical Photography in America* (New York:

The Burns Archive, 1983), pp. 1444–69, which is a reprint of the August 1980 issue of *New York State Journal of Medicine*.

114 See *Confederate States Medical and Surgical Journal* (rpt. Metuchen, NJ: The Scarecrow Press: 1976), p. 25.

115 Ann Thomas, "The Search for Pattern," in *Beauty of Another Order: Photography in Science*, ed. Ann Thomas (New Haven, CT: Yale University Press, 1997), p. 99.

116 Quoted in Ann Thomas, "The Search for Pattern," p. 100.

117 Frederic Luther, *Microfilm: A History, 1839–1900* (Annapolis, MD: The National Microfilm Association, 1959), pp. 23–46.

118 For a discussion of this book, and nineteenth-century photographically illustrated books, see Carol Armstrong, *Scenes in a Library: Reading the Photograph in the Book, 1843–1875* (Cambridge, MA: The MIT Press, 1998).

119 This event is extensively described in Ann Thomas, "Capturing Light: Photographing the Universe," in Ann Thomas, ed., *Beauty of Another Order: Photography in Science*, pp. 191–93.

120 For a full discussion, see Ann Thomas, "The Search for Pattern," pp. 86–88.

121 Oliver Wendell Holmes, "Doings of the Sunbeam," p. 15.

122 Quoted in Nancy Ann Roth, "Electrical Expressions: The Photographs of Duchenne de Boulogne," *Multiple Views*, ed. Daniel P. Younger (Albuquerque, NM: University of New Mexico Press, 1991), p. 116.

123 Paul Ekman, "Introduction," Charles Darwin, *The Expression of the Emotions in Man and Animals* (New York: Oxford University Press, 1998), p. xiii. I am indebted to Ekman's research on Darwin and his use of photography, which appears throughout his edition of the 1872 book.

124 John O'Neill, "The Question of an Introduction: Understanding and the Passion of Ignorance," in *Freud and the Passions*, ed. John O'Neill (University Park, PA: The Pennsylvania State University Press, 1966), p. 10.

125 Joan Copjec, "*Flavit et Dissipati Sunt*," in *October: The First Decade, 1976–1986*, ed. Annette Michelson, Rosalind Krauss, Douglas Crimp, and Jon Copjec (Cambridge, MA: The MIT Press, 1987), p. 300.

126 Quoted in Sigrid Schade, "Charcot and the Spectacle of the Hysterical Body: The 'Pathos Formula' as an Aesthetic Staging of Psychiatric Discourse—A Blind Spot in the Reception of Warburg," *Art History*, vol. 18, no. 4 (December 1995), p. 510.

127 Roslyn Poignant, "Surveying the Field of View: The Making of the RAI Photographic collection," in *Anthropology and Photography, 1860–1920*, ed. Elizabeth Edwards (New Haven, CT: Yale University Press, 1992), p. 51.

128 Roslyn Poignant, "Surveying the Field of View," pp. 47–48. Edwards's book is a fine source for information on nineteenth- and early twentieth-century anthropological photography.

129 "Elena Barkhatova, "Realism and Document: Photography as Fact," in *Photography in Russia, 1840–1940*, ed. David Elliott (London: Thames and Hudson, 1992), p. 42. I am indebted to the essays in Elliott's book for an understanding of Russian photography.

130 See Bernard S. Cohn, "Representing Authority in Victorian India," in *The Invention of Tradition*, ed. Eric Hobsbawm and Terence Ranger (New York: Cambridge University Press, 1983), pp. 167, 183.

131 Edward Said, *Orientalism* (London: Routledge & Kegan Paul, 1978). The application of the term Orientalism to Asia has been much criticized in recent years. But in its loosest meanings, the word has come to signal illicit looking.

132 Clark Worswick, *The Last Empire: Photography in British India, 1855–1911* (Millerton, NY: Aperture, 1976), p. 9, and Robert A. Sobieszek and Carney E. S. Gavin, *Remembrance of the Near East: The Photographs of Bonfils, 1867–1907* (Rochester, NY:

International Museum of Photography at George Eastman House, 1980), n.p.

133 Vidya Dehejia, *India through the Lens, 1840–1911*, p. 19.

134 Todd D. Smith, "Gay Male Pornography and the East: Re-orienting the Orient," *History of Photography*, 18 (Spring 1994), p. 17.

135 For a discussion of pornography, see Elizabeth Anne McCauley, *Industrial Madness, 1848–1871*.

136 Roslyn Poignant, "Surveying the Field of View," p. 45.

137 The name was later changed to the Bureau of American Ethnology (BAE).

138 For information on the American West and photography, see *Native Nations: Journeys in American Photography* (London: Barbican Art Gallery, 1998); Merry A. Foresta, *American Photographs: The First Century* (Washington, DC: Smithsonian Institution Press, 1996); and *The West as America: Reinterpreting Images of the Frontier, 1820–1920*, ed. William Truettner (Washington, DC: Smithsonian Institution Press, 1991).

139 Wendy Watriss and Lois Parkinson Zamora, *Image and Memory*, p. 43.

140 See Felicity Ashbee, "William Carrick: A Scots Photographer in St. Petersburg (1827–1878)," *History of Photography*, vol. 2, no. 3 (July 1978), p. 211.

141 Mary Bennett and Paul C. Juhl, *Iowa Stereographs: Three-dimensional Visions of the Past* (Iowa City, IA: University of Iowa Press, 1997).

142 [Robert Cecil] Unsigned, untitled review, *Quarterly Review*, vol. 116, no. 232 (July and October 1864), p. 498.

143 Cecil, p. 499.

144 Thomas Thurston, "Hearsay of the Sun: Photography, Identity and the Law of Evidence in Nineteenth-Century American Courts," http://chmn.gmu.aq/photos/essay/intro.htm (February 1, 1999).

145 *The American Law Register* 1 (January, 1869) hyper-text project http://chmn.gmu.aq/photos/text/ 17ALR1.htm

146 An exception is Captain W. W. Hooper's photographs of the Madras famine, 1876–77.

147 Maria Morris Hambourg, Pierre Apraxine, Malcolm Daniel, Jeff L. Rosenheim, and Virginia Heckert, *The Waking Dream: Photography's First Century, Selections from the Gilman Paper Company Collection* (New York: The Metropolitan Museum of Art, 1993), p. 275.

148 Carol Mavor, *Pleasures Taken: Performances of Sexuality and Loss in Victorian Photographs* (Durham, NC: Duke University Press, 1995), and Susan H. Edwards, "Pretty Babies: Art Erotica or Kiddie Porn?" *History of Photography*, vol. 18, no. 1 (Spring 1994) pp. 38–46.

149 Quoted in John Falconer, "Willoughby Wallace Hooper: 'a craze about photography,'" *Photographic Collector*, vol. 4, no. 3 (Winter 1983), p. 259.

150 For photographs of the Suez Canal, see Nissan N. Perez, *Focus East: Early Photography in the Near East, 1839–1885* (New York: Harry N. Abrams, 1988).

151 See William Newton's address to the Photographic Society of London, printed in *Journal of the Photographic Society*, 1 (March 3, 1853), p. 6.

152 John Ruskin, *The Works of John Ruskin*, ed. E. T. Cook and A. Wedderburn (London: G. Allen, 1903–1912), vol. 11, p. 212.

153 Ruskin, *Works*, vol. 20, pp. 96–97.

154 Henri de la Blanchère, *L'Art du photographe* (Paris: Amyot Editeur, 1859), p. 3.

CHAPTER FOUR
Photography in the Modern Age (1880–1918)

1 Keith F. Davis, *An American Century of Photography: From Dry-Plate to Digital*, 2nd ed. (Kansas City, MO: Hallmark Cards, Inc., 1999), p. 16.

2 Margarett Loke, ed., *The World as it Was, 1865–1921: A Photographic Portrait from the Keystone-Mast Collection* (New York: Summit Books, 1980), p. 12.

3 Loke, ed., p.16.

4 Ulrich Keller, "Photojournalism around 1900: The Institutionalization of a Mass Medium," in *Shadow and Substance: Essays on the History of Photography*, ed. Kathleen Collins (Bloomfield Hills, MI: The Amorphous Institute Press, 1990), pp. 293–94.

5 James Lawrence Breese, "The Relations of Photography to Art," *Cosmopolitan*, vol. 18, no. 2 (December 1894), p. 140.

6 See Malek Alloula, *The Colonial Harem* (Minneapolis, MN: University of Minnesota Press, 1986).

7 Michael Lesy, *Dreamland: America at the Dawn of the Twentieth Century* (New York: The New Press, 1997), pp. xi–xii.

8 H. Roger Grant, *Railroad Postcards in the Age of Steam* (Iowa City, IA: University of Iowa Press, 1994), p. 4.

9 J. Wells Champney, "Fifty Years of Photography," *Harper's New Monthly Magazine*, vol. 79, no. 471 (August 1889), p. 366.

10 Emile Zola, *Le Roman expérimental* (Paris: Bernouard, 1982), p. 52.

11 Peter Henry Emerson, "Photography: A Pictorial Art," in *Amateur Photographer*, no. 3 (March 19, 1886), p. 138.

12 Peter Henry Emerson, *Naturalistic Photography for Students of the Art*, 1st ed. (1889; rpt New York: Arno Press, 1972), p. 21, and Peter Henry Emerson, "Photography: A Pictorial Art," p. 138.

13 Peter Henry Emerson, "Photography: A Pictorial Art," p. 139.

14 J. C. Strauss, quoted in Christian A. Peterson, "The Photograph Beautiful, 1895–1915," *History of Photography*, vol. 16, no. 3 (Autumn 1992), p. 192.

15 Charles H. Caffin, *Photography as a Fine Art* (New York: Doubleday, Page & Co., 1901), pp. vii, 24.

16 Jain Kelly, "Jane Reece," in Naomi Rosemblum, *A History of Women Photographers* (New York: Abbeville Press, 1994), p. 318.

17 For James Craig Annan, I am indebted to the essay "James Craig Annan: Brave Days in Glasgow," by William Buchanan, in *The Golden Age of British Photography, 1839–1900*, ed. Mark Haworth-Booth (Millerton, NY: Aperture, 1984), pp. 170–73.

18 Frederick H. Evans, "Opening Address," *Photographic Journal*, vol. 59 (April 30, 1900), p. 238.

19 Sadakichi Hartmann, "A Plea for Straight Photography," reproduced in Beaumont Newhall, *Photography: Essays and Images* (New York: Museum of Modern Art, 1980), pp. 185–88.

20 *Photo-Secession*, no. 1 (December, 1902), quoted in William Innes Homer, *Alfred Stieglitz and the Photo-Secession* (Boston, MA: Little, Brown, and Co., 1983), p. 56.

21 For information on the Pictorialist photographic societies, see William Innes Homer, *Alfred Stieglitz and the Photo-Secession* and Margaret Harker, *The Linked Ring: The Secession Movement in Photography in Britain* (London: Heinemann, 1979).

22 Alfred Stieglitz, "The Photo-Secession," reproduced in Beaumont Newhall, *Photography*, p. 167.

23 Richard Whelan, *Alfred Stieglitz: A Biography* (Boston, MA: Little, Brown, and Co., 1995), p. 236.

24 Quoted in Whelan, p. 224.

25 Robert A. Sobieszek, *The Art of Persuasion: A History of Advertising Photography* (New York: Harry N. Abrams, Inc., 1988), p. 22, and Douglas Collins, *The Story of Kodak* (New York: Harry N. Abrams, Inc., 1990), p. 157.

26 For Käsebier, I have relied on Barbara L. Michael's monograph *Gertrude Käsebier: The Photographer and Her Photographs* (New York: Harry N. Abrams, Inc, 1992).

27 See the discussions throughout Patricia Johnston, *Real Fantasies: Edward Steichen's Advertising Photography* (Berkeley, CA: University of California Press, 1997).

28 Christian A. Peterson, "The Photograph Beautiful 1895–1915," *History of Photography*, vol. 16, no. 3 (Autumn 1992), p. 199.

29 Charles L. Mitchell, *American Amateur Photographer*, vol. 12 (December 1900), p. 567, quoted in Keith F. Davis, *An American Century of Photography: From Dry-Plate to Digital*, p. 51.

30 Quoted in Malcolm Daniel, *Edgar Degas, Photographer* (New York: The Metropolitan Museum of Art, 1998), p. 24.

31 For a description of Strindberg's photography, see Linda Haverty Rugg, *Picturing Ourselves: Photography and Autobiography* (Chicago, IL: University of Chicago Press, 1997), pp. 81–131.

32 *Bernard Shaw on Photography*, ed. Bill Jay and Margaret Moore (Salt Lake City, UT: Peregrine Smith Books, 1989) p. 90.

33 Robert Doty, *Photo-Secession: Stieglitz and the Fine-Art Movement in Photography* (New York: Dover Publications, Inc., 1978), p. 51.

34 Doty, p. 34.

35 Ulrich F. Keller, "The Myth of Art Photography: An Iconographic Analysis," *History of Photography*, vol. 9, no. 1 (January–March 1985), p. 10.

36 Ulrich F. Keller, "The Myth of Art Photography: A Sociological Analysis," *History of Photography*, vol. 8, no. 4 (October–December 1984), p. 253.

37 Keller, p. 260.

38 Alfred Stieglitz, "Pictorial Photography," *Scribner's*, vol. 26, no. 5 (November 1899), p. 528.

39 Paul Strand, "Photography," *Seven Arts*, 2 (August 1917), p. 524.

40 Alfred Stieglitz, "Our Illustrations," *Camera Work*, no. 49/50 (June 1917), p. 36.

41 Paul Strand, "Photography," p. 524.

42 Strand, p. 524.

43 Peter Bacon Hales, *Silver Cities: The Photography of American Urbanization, 1839–1915* (Philadelphia, PA: Temple University Press, 1983), pp. 243–60. I am indebted to Hales for his discussion of photography and urban reform.

44 Jacob Riis, "Flashes from the Slums: Pictures Taken in Dark Places by the Lightning Process," *Sun* [New York] (February 12, 1888), reprinted in Beaumont Newhall, ed., *Essays and Images*, p. 156.

45 Riis, p. 156.

46 For an insightful critique of Riis, see Sally Stein, "Making Connections with the Camera: Photography and Social Mobility in the Career of Jacob Riis," *Afterimage*, vol. 10, no. 10 (May 1983), pp. 9–16.

47 Quoted in *Photo Story: Selected Letters and Photographs of Lewis W. Hine*, ed. Daile Kaplan (Washington, DC: Smithsonian Institution Press, 1992), p. xxvii.

48 *Photo Story*, p. xxv.

49 Daile Kaplan, "'The Fetish of Having a Unified Thread,': Lewis W. Hine's Reaction to the Use of the Photo Story in *Life* Magazine," *exposure*, vol. 27, no. 2 (1989), p. 10.

50 Larry Peterson, "Producing Visual Traditions among Workers: The Uses of Photography at Pullman, 1880–1980," *Afterimage*, vol. 13, no. 2 (Spring 1992), p. 7.

51 Wolfgang Ruppert, "Images of the Kaiserreich: the Social and Political Import of Photographs," in *German Photography, 1870–1970: Power of a Medium*, ed. Klaus Honnef, Rolf Sachsse, and Karin Thomas (Cologne: DuMont Buchverlad, 1997), p. 25.

52 Peterson, p. 5.

53 Kevin Boyle and Victoria Getis, *Muddy Books and Ragged Aprons: Images of Working-Class Detroit, 1900–1930* (Detroit, MI: Wayne State University Press, 1997), p. 40.

54 David E. Nye, *Image Worlds: Corporate Identities at General Electric, 1890–1930* (Cambridge, MA: The MIT Press, 1985), p. 81.

55 Peter Bacon Hales, *Silver Cities*, pp. 138–39.

56 Hales, p. 143.

57 Quoted in Melissa Banta and Curtis M. Hinsley, *From Site to Sight: Anthropology, Photography, and the Power of Imagery* (Cambridge, MA: Peabody Museum Press, 1986), p. 61.

58 Linda Dalrymple Henderson's article "X Rays and the Quest for Invisible Reality in the Art of Kupka, Duchamp, and the Cubists," *Art Journal*, 47 (Winter 1988), p. 331, and Marta Braun, *Picturing Time: The Work of Etienne-Jules Marey (1830–1904)* (Chicago, IL: University of Chicago Press, 1992), p. 291.

59 Quoted in Elizabeth Johns, "An Avowal of Artistic Community: Nudity and Fantasy in Thomas Eakins's Photographs," in *Eakins and the Photograph* (Washington, DC: Smithsonian Institution Press, for the Pennsylvania Academy of Fine Art, 1994), p. 84.

60 Quoted in Marta Braun, *Picturing Time*, p. 296.

61 Marta Braun, "The Expanding Present: Photographing Movement," in *Beauty of Another Order*, ed. Ann Thomas, p. 172.

62 Marta Braun, *Picturing Time*, pp. 237–38.

63 For a discussion of the Gilbreths' work in the context of scientific management, see Martha Banta, *Taylored Lives: Narrative Productions in the Age of Taylor, Veblen, and Ford* (Chicago, IL: University of Chicago Press, 1992), pp. 160–61.

64 Michael O'Malley, *Keeping Watch: A History of American Time* (Washington, DC: Smithsonian Institution Press, 1996), p. 233.

65 Peter E. Palmquist, *Elizabeth Fleischmann: Pioneer X-Ray Photographer* (Berkeley, CA: Judah L. Magnes Museum, 1990), and Bettyann Holtzmann Kevles, *Naked to the Bone: Medical Imaging in the Twentieth Century* (Reading, MA: Addison-Wesley, 1998), p. 125.

66 Joseph J. Corn, ed., *Imagining Tomorrow: History, Technology, and the American Future* (Cambridge, MA: The MIT Press, 1986), p. 14.

67 The importance of the notion of a fourth dimension is exhaustively presented in Linda Dalrymple Henderson's *The Fourth Dimension and Non-Euclidean Geometry in Modern Art* (Princeton, NJ: Princeton University Press, 1983).

68 Giovanni Lista, "Futurist Photography," *Art Journal*, vol. 41, no. 4 (Winter 1981), p. 358.

69 Bettyann Holtzmann Kevles, *Naked to the Bone*, p. 53. My discussion of the X-ray owes to Kevles's research and writing as well as to Linda Dalrymple Henderson's article "X Rays and the Quest for Invisible Reality in the Art of Kupka, Duchamp, and the Cubists," *Art Journal*, 47 (Winter 1988), pp. 323–40, and her "Francis Picabia, Radiometers, and X-Rays in 1913," *Art Bulletin*, vol. 71, no. 1 (March 1989), pp. 114–23.

70 Umberto Boccioni, "Futurist Painting: Technical Manifesto," quoted in Stephen Kern, *The Culture of Time and Space, 1880–1918* (Cambridge, MA: Harvard University Press, 1983), p. 185.

71 Christian Brinton, "Evolution Not Revolution in Art," *International Studio*, vol. 69 (April 1913), p. 35.

72 Cosmo Burton, "The Whole Duty of the Photographer," *British Journal of Photography*, vol. 36 (1889), p. 668 [emphases Burton].

73 E. F. im Thurn, "Anthropological Uses of the Camera," *Journal of the Anthropological Institute*, vol. 22 (1893), p. 184.

74 John Thomson, "Exploring with the Camera," *British Journal of Photography*, vol. 32 (1885), p. 373, quoted in James R. Ryan, *Picturing Empire: Photography and the Visualization of the British Empire* (Chicago, IL: University of Chicago Press, 1997), p. 43.

75 See the discussion in James R. Ryan, *Picturing Empire: Photography and the Visualization of the British Empire*, pp. 131–35.

76 The saga of Stanley, Livingstone, and the images their encounter generated can be found in *David Livingstone and the Victorian Encounter with Africa* (London: National Portrait Gallery, 1996). For Kalulu, see pp. 132–33.

77 Quoted in Ryan, *Picturing Empire*, p. 31.

78 For an extensive discussion of these photographs, see James R. Ryan, *Picturing Empire*, pp. 30–44.

79 Nicholas Monti, *Africa Then: Photographs, 1840–1918* (New York: Alfred A. Knopf, 1987), p. 9.

80 For a discussion of the importation of European ways in Africa, see Terence Ranger, "The Invention of Tradition in Colonial Africa," in *The Invention of Tradition*, ed. Eric Hobsbawm and Terence Ranger (New York: Cambridge University Press, 1983), pp. 211–62.

81 See Anne Baldasarri, *Picasso and Photography* (Paris: Flammarion, 1997). Fortier is discussed throughout *Delivering Views: Distant Cultures in Early Postcards*, ed. Christraud M. Geary and Virginia-Lee Webb (Washington, DC: Smithsonian Institution Press, 1998).

82 Quoted in Nicholas Monti, *Africa Then: Photographs, 1840–1918*, p. 10.

83 Quoted in Catherine A. Lutz and Jane L. Collins, *Reading the National Geographic* (Chicago, IL: University of Chicago Press, 1993), pp. 26–27. I have used this account to describe the Society's founding.
84 Jorge Lewinski, *The Camera at War* (New York: Simon and Schuster, 1978), p. 56.
85 Roy Flukinger, *The Formative Decades: Photography in Great Britain, 1839–1920* (Austin, TX: University of Texas Press, 1985), p. 141.
86 Quoted in Alison Devine Nordström, "Photography of Samoa: Production, Dissemination, and Use," in *Picturing Samoa: Colonial Photography of Samoa, 1875–1925* (Daytona Beach, FL: Southeast Museum of Photography, 1996), p. 14. I am indebted to this work for information on Samoan photography.
87 Alison Devine Nordström, "Photography of Samoa," p. 15.
88 For a discussion of tattoos and exotic Pacific island life, see Harriet Guest, "The Great Distinction: Figures of the Exotic in the Work of William Hodges," in *New Feminist Discourses*, ed. Isobel Armstrong (London: Routledge, 1992), pp. 296–341.
89 Allan Sekula, "The Body and the Archive," in *The Contest of Meaning*, ed. Richard Bolton (Cambridge, MA: The MIT Press, 1989), p. 351. For more information on the use of photography in police work, see Sandra S. Phillips, Mark Haworth-Booth, and Carol Squiers, *Police Pictures: The Photograph as Evidence* (San Francisco: San Francisco Museum of Modern Art and Chronicle Books, 1997).
90 Eugene S. Talbot, *Degeneracy: Its Causes, Signs, and Results* (London: Walter Scott, 1901), p. 18.
91 For a history of fingerprinting, see the inventor William J. Hershel's *The Origin of Finger-Printing by Sir William J. Hershel* (1916, rpt. New York: AMS Press, 1974).
92 My discussion of Clara Sheldon Smith owes to the research and writing of photographer Arne Svenson in his book *Prisoners* (New York: Blast Books, 1997).
93 Francis Galton, "Eugenics: Its Definition, Scope, and Aims," *The American Journal of Sociology*, vol. 10, no. 1 (July 1904), p. 1.
94 Galton, p. 3.
95 Francis Galton, "Photographic Chronicles from Childhood to Age," *Fortnightly Review* (new series; vol. 31, January 1–June 1, 1882), p. 26.
96 Francis Galton, *Inquiries into Human Faculty and Its Development*, pp. 6, 222.
97 Susan D. Moeller, *Shooting War: Photography and the American Experience of Combat* (New York: Basic Books, 1989), p. 25. My discussion of the Spanish–American War owes to her analysis.
98 Margarett Loke, ed., *The World as it Was*, pp. 15–16.
99 Quoted in Lewis L. Gould and Richard Greffe, *Photojournalist: The Career of Jimmy Hare* (Austin, TX: University of Texas Press, 1977), p. 75. I have relied on this work for information on Jimmy Hare.
100 Gould and Greffe, p. 33.
101 For this dimension of the war, and for information on the British homefront, see John Taylor, *War Photography: Realism in the British Press* (London: Routledge, 1991), p. 20.
102 Peter Robertson, "Canadian Photojournalism during the First World War," *History of Photography*, pp. 39, 42–43.
103 Quoted in Bernd Weise, "Photojournalism from the First World War to the Weimar Republic," in *German Photography, 1870–1970: Power of a Medium*, ed. Klaus Honnef, Rolf Sachsse, and Karin Thomas (Cologne: DuMont Buchverlag, 1997), p. 54.
104 Nevertheless, photographs of World War I corpses were made, both by professional photographers and by amateurs with small cameras. Generally, they would not be shown until after the war.
105 Allyson Booth, *Postcards from the Trenches: Negotiating the Space Betweeen Modernism and the First World War* (New York: Oxford University Press, 1996), p. 21.
106 Quoted in Jane Carmichael, *First World War Photographers* (London: Routledge, 1989), pp. 34–35. I rely on Carmichael for her account of photography during the war.

107 The story of Canadian photographer Ivor Castle's fabricated "over the top" photographs is told in Michael L. Carlebach, *American Photojournalism Comes of Age* (Washington, DC: Smithsonian Insitution Press, 1997), p. 91, and Peter Robertson, "Canadian Photojournalism during the First World War," *History of Photography*, vol. 2, no. 1 (January 1978), p. 44. Castle was not the only photographer to fake war photographs. Jean-Baptiste Tournassou, Chief of the Photography and Cinematography Organization for the French Army, also staged photographs of soldiers.
108 Bernd Weise, "Photojournalism from the First World War to the Weimar Republic," p. 53.
109 "The Real Thing," in *The Short Stories of Henry James*, ed. Clifton Fadiman (New York: Modern Library, n.d. c.1945.), p. 196.
110 Quoted in Miles Hudson and John Stanier, *War and the Media: A Random Searchlight* (New York: New York University Press, 1998), p. 40.
111 Thomas Thurston, "Hearsay of the Sun: Photography, Identity and the Law of Evidence in Nineteenth-Century American Courts" [http://chmn. gmu.aq/photos/essay/intro.htm] (February 1, 1999).
112 Lewis Hine, "How the Camera May Help in Social Uplift," quoted in Maren Stange, *Symbols of Ideal Life: Social Documentary Photography in America, 1890–1950* (New York: Cambridge University Press, 1989), p. 86.
113 James Lawrence Breese, "The Relations of Photography to Art," *Cosmopolitan*, vol. 18, no. 2 (December 1894), p. 140.
114 Lewis Hine, "How the Camera May Help in Social Uplift," quoted in George Dimock, "Children of the Mills: Rereading Lewis Hine's Child-Labour Photographs," *Oxford Art Journal*, vol. 16, no. 2 (1993), p. 39.

CHAPTER FIVE
A New Vision (1918–1945)

1 Anton Kaes, Martin Jay, Edward Dimendberg, ed. *The Weimar Republic Sourcebook* (Berkeley, CA: University of California Press, 1994), p. 641.
2 Colin Osman and Sandra S. Phillips, "European Visions: Magazine Photography in Europe between the Wars," in Marianne Fulton, *Eyes of Time: Photojournalism in America* (Boston, MA: New York Graphic Society/Little, Brown and Company, 1988), p. 76. The word *Illustrirte* in *Berliner Illustrirte Zeitung* was idiosyncratically spelled. More correctly, it would have been *Illustrierte*.
3 Willi Münzenberg's life and career are discussed in Helmut Gruber's "Willi Münzenberg's German Communist Propaganda Empire, 1921–1933," *Journal of Modern History*, vol. 38, no. 3 (Sept. 1966), pp. 278–97.
4 Colin Osman and Sandra S. Phillips, "European Visions," p. 76.
5 Osman and Phillips, p. 78.
6 Michael L. Carlebach, *American Photojournalism Comes of Age* (Washington, DC: The Smithsonian Institution Press, 1997), p. 145.
7 Richard Guy Wilson, "America and the Machine Age," in *The Machine Age in America, 1918–1941*, ed. Richard Guy Wilson (Brooklyn, NY: The Brooklyn Museum, 1986), p. 26.
8 William Stott, *Documentary Expression and Thirties America* (New York: Oxford University Press, 1973), pp. 80–81.
9 Kurt Schwitters, translated and quoted in Maud Lavin, "Advertising Utopia: Schwitters as Commercial Designer," *Art in America* (October 1985), p. 137.
10 Edlef Köppen, "The Magazine as a Sign of the Times," in *The Weimar Republic Sourcebook*, ed. Anton Kaes, Martin Jay, and Edward Dimendberg, p. 644.
11 Christopher Phillips, "Resurrecting Vision: European Photography between the World Wars," in *The New Vision: Photography between the World Wars* (New York: The Metropolitan Museum of Art, 1989), p. 73. I am indebted to Phillips for my understanding of this period.

12 Hannes Meyer, "The New World," in *The Weimar Republic Sourcebook*, ed. Anton Kaes, Martin Jay, and Edward Dimendberg, pp. 445–46.
13 Quoted in Peter Galassi, "Rodchenko and Photography's Revolution," in Magdalena Dabrowski, Leah Dickerman, and Peter Galassi, *Alexsandr Rodchenko* (New York: Museum of Modern Art, 1998), p. 104.
14 See the extended discussion in Margarita Tupitsyn, *El Lissitzsky: Beyond the Abstract Cabinet* (New Haven, CT: Yale University Press, 1999), pp. 20–21.
15 Quoted in Margarita Tupitsyn, *The Soviet Photograph, 1924–1937* (New Haven, CT: Yale University Press, 1966), p. 11.
16 Quoted in Christopher Phillips, "Resurrecting Vision," p. 84.
17 For a discussion of the history of the idea of "making strange," see Simon Watney, "Making Strange: The Shattered Mirror," in *Thinking Photography*, ed., Victor Burgin (London, Macmillan, 1982), pp. 154–76.
18 Tristan Tzara, "Dada Manifesto 1918," in *Art in Theory, 1900–1990: An Anthology of Changing Ideas* (Oxford: Blackwell, 1992), p. 252.
19 Richard Hülsenbeck, "First German Dada Manifesto," in *Art in Theory, 1900–1990: An Anthology of Changing Ideas* (Oxford: Blackwell, 1992), p. 253.
20 The most comprehensive book on women photographers in Germany and their connection to the New Woman motif has yet to be translated into English. See *Fotografieren Hiess Teilnehman: Photografinnen der Weimarer Republik*, ed. Ute Eskilden (Düsseldorf: Richter Verlag, 1994).
21 Quoted in Dawn Ades, *Photomontage* (London: Thames and Hudson, rev. ed., 1986), p. 12.
22 Maud Lavin, *Cut with the Kitchen Knife: The Weimar Photomontages of Hannah Höch* (New Haven, CT: Yale University Press, 1993), p. 23. I owe my understanding of Höch to Lavin's scholarship.
23 Dawn Ades, *Photomontage*, p. 28.
24 László Moholy-Nagy, "Unprecedented Photography," in *Photography in the Modern Era: European Documents and Critical Writings, 1913–1940*, ed. Christopher Phillips (New York: The Metropolitan Museum of Art/Aperture, 1989), p. 84.
25 Moholy-Nagy, p. 85.
26 László Moholy-Nagy, "Photography in Advertising," in *Photography in the Modern Era*, ed. Christopher Phillips, p. 90.
27 Johannes Molzahn, "Stop Reading! Look!" in *The Weimar Republic Sourcebook*, ed. Anton Kaes, Martin Jay, and Edward Dimendberg, p. 648.
28 Quoted in Kim Sichel, *Germaine Krull: Photographer of Modernity* (Cambridge, MA: The MIT Press, 1999), p. 77. I am indebted to Sichel for my understanding of Krull.
29 "Les intellectuels allemands ne peuvent pas faire caca ni pipi sans des idéologies." Quoted in Dawn Ades, *Photomontage*, p. 114.
30 Ades, p. 115.
31 Francis Naumann, "The New York Dada Movement: Better Late than Never," *Arts* (February 1980), p. 143.
32 Maria Morris Hambourg, "From 291 to the Museum of Modern Art: Photography in New York, 1910–37," in Maria Morris Hambourg and Christopher Phillips, *The New Vision: Photography Between the World Wars*, pp. 15–16.
33 Quoted in Theodore E. Stebbins, Jr. and Norman Keyes, Jr., *Charles Sheeler: The Photographs* (Boston, MA: Museum of Fine Arts, 1987), p. 17.
34 Stebbins and Keyes, p. 25.
35 Stebbins and Keyes, p. 27.
36 See Sue Taylor, *Hans Bellmer: The Anatomy of Anxiety* (Cambridge, MA: The MIT Press, 2000), and Therese Lichtenstein, *Behind Closed Doors: The Art of Hans Bellmer* (Berkeley, CA: University of California Press, 2001).
37 Kim Sichel, *Germaine Krull: Photographer of Modernity*, p. 106.
38 Quoted in Peter Galassi, *Henri Cartier-Bresson: The Early Work* p. 39

39 Henri Cartier-Bresson, *The Decisive Moment* (New York: Simon & Schuster, 1952), n.p.

40 Peter Galassi, *Henri Cartier-Bresson: The Early Work*, p. 29.

41 Quoted in Victor Margolin, *The Struggle for Utopia: Rodchenko, Lissitzky, Moholy-Nagy, 1917–1946* (Chicago, IL: University of Chicago Press, 1997), p. 113.

42 Eleanor M. Hight, *Picturing Modernism: Moholy-Nagy and Photography in Weimar Germany*, p. 209.

43 Willi Warstat, "Photography in Advertising," in *The Weimar Republic Sourcebook*, ed. Anton Kaes, Martin Jay, and Edward Dimendberg, p. 651.

44 Dziga Vertov, "The Council of Three," in *Kino-Eye: the Writings of Dziga Vertov*, ed. Annette Michelson, trans. Kevin O'Brien (Berkeley, CA: University of California Press, 1984), p. 17.

45 James Curtis, *Mind's Eye, Mind's Truth: FSA Photography Reconsidered*, pp. 77–78.

46 Eleanor M. Hight, *Picturing Modernism*, p. 203.

47 Karel Teige, "The Tasks of Modern Photography," in *Photography in the Modern Era*, p. 319.

48 Teige, pp. 318, 319. Teige's art and his theoretical writings are reviewed in Eric Dluhosch and Rostislav Suácha, *Karel Teige,1900–1951: L'enfant terrible of the Czech Modernist Avant-Garde* (Cambridge, MA: The MIT Press, 1999).

49 Walter Benjamin, "A Small History of Photography," in his *One-Way Street and Other Writings*, trans. Edmund Jephcott and Kingsley Shorter (London: NLB, 1979), p. 255.

50 Benjamin, p. 254.

51 Quoted in Melissa A. McEuen, *Seeing America: Women Photographers between the Wars* (Lexington, KY: University Press of Kentucky, 2000), p. 37.

52 Margarita Tupitsyn, *El Lissitzky: Beyond the Abstract Cabinet*, p. 61.

53 See Christopher Phillips, "Resurrecting Vision," p. 95, and Benjamin H. D. Buchloh, "From Faktura to Factography," in *The Contest of Meaning: Critical Histories of Photography*, ed. Richard Bolton (Cambridge, MA: The MIT Press, 1989), pp. 76–77.

54 Raoul Hausmann, "Photomontage," in *The Weimar Republic Sourcebook*, ed. Anton Kaes, Martin Jay, and Edward Dimendberg, p. 652.

55 Robert A. Sobieszek, *The Art of Persuasion: A History of Advertising Photography* (New York: Harry N. Abrams, Inc., 1988), p. 66.

56 Quoted in Therese Thau Heyman, "Modernist Photography and the Group f.64," in *On the Edge of America: California Modernist Art, 1900–1950*, ed. Paul J. Karlstrom (Berkeley, CA: University of California Press, 1996), p. 252.

57 Heyman, p. 256.

58 Quoted in Michel Oren, "On the 'Impurity' of Group f/64 Photography," *History of Photography*, vol. 15, no. 2 (Summer 1991), p. 122.

59 Weston's statement for the *Film und Foto* exhibition, quoted in David Travis, "Ephemeral Truths," in Sarah Greenough, Joel Snyder, David Travis, and Colin Westerbeck, *On the Art of Fixing a Shadow: One Hundred and Fifty Years of Photography* (Washington, DC: National Gallery of Art, 1989), p. 243.

60 Leah Ollman, "The Worker Photography Movement: Camera as Weapon," in *Multiple Views: Logan Grant Essays on Photography, 1983–89*, ed. Daniel P. Younger (Albuquerque, NM: University of New Mexico Press, 1991), p. 235.

61 Forrest McDonald, *The American Presidency: An Intellectual History* (Lawrence, KS: University of Kansas Press, 1994), pp. 441–42.

62 See the extensive discussions of these media throughout William Stott, *Documentary Expression and Thirties America* (New York: Oxford University Press, 1973).

63 John Grierson, "First Principles of Documentary" (1934–36), in *Imagining Reality: The Faber Book of Documentary*, ed. Kevin Macdonald and Mark Cousins (London: Faber and Faber, 1996), p. 101.

64 John Grierson, "The Documentary Idea: 1942," in *Grierson on Documentary*, ed. Forsyth Hardy (Berkeley, CA: University of California Press, 1966), p. 249.

65 Adams was addressing Roy Stryker, head of the Farm Security Section that produced photographs. See Roy E. Stryker and Nancy Wood, *In This Proud Land: America 1935–1943 as Seen in the FSA Photographs* (Greenwich, CT: New York Graphic Society, 1973), p. 8.

66 See Leah Bendavid-Val, *Propaganda & Dreams: Photographing the 1930s in the USSR and US* (New York: Edition Stemle, 1999).

67 William Stott, *Documentary Expression and Thirties America*, p. 26.

68 Maren Stange, "'The Record Itself': Farm Security Photography and the Transformation of Rural Life," in Pete Daniel, Merry A. Foresta, Maren Stange, and Sally Stein, *Official Images: New Deal Photography* (Washington, DC: Smithsonian Institution Press, 1987), p. 1.

69 Maren Stange, *Symbols of Ideal Life: Social Documentary Photography in America, 1890–1950* (New York: Cambridge University Press, 1989), p. 111.

70 Quoted in Lawrence W. Levine, "The Historian and the Icon: Photography and the History of the American People in the 1930s and 1940s in *Documenting America, 1935–1943*, ed. Carl Fleishhauer and Beverly W. Brannan (Berkeley, CA: University of California Press, 1988), p. 39.

71 See Keith F. Davis's discussion in his *An American Century of Photography: From Dry-Plate to Digital*, 2nd, rev. ed. (Kansas City, MO, and New York: Hallmark Cards, Inc., in association with Harry N. Abrams, Inc., 1999), p. 165.

72 Quoted in Maria Morris Hambourg, "A Portrait of the Artist," in Maria Morris Hambourg, Jeff L. Rosenheim, Douglas Eklund, and Mia Fineman, *Walker Evans* (New York: The Metropolitan Museum of Art, 2000), pp. 21–22.

73 Quoted in Belinda Rathbone, *Walker Evans: A Biography* (New York: Houghton Mifflin, 1995), p. 70. The original appeared in a book review by Evans titled "The Reappearance of Photography," in *Hound and Horn*, vol. 5, no. 1 (October–December 1931), p. 127.

74 Maria Morris Hambourg, "A Portrait of the Artist," in *Walker Evans*, Maria Morris Hambourg et al., p. 9.

75 James Agee and Walker Evans, *Let Us Now Praise Famous Men* (1941, rpt; Boston, MA: Houghton Mifflin Co., 1988), p. xlvii.

76 Quoted in Sally Stein, "Peculiar Grace: Dorothea Lange and the Testimony of the Body," in *Dorothea Lange: A Visual Life*, ed. Elizabeth Partridge (Washington, DC: Smithsonian Institution Press, 1994), p. 59.

77 James Curtis, *Mind's Eye, Mind's Truth: FSA Photography Reconsidered* (Philadelphia, PA: Temple University Press, 1989), pp. 75–76.

78 Jefferson Hunter, *Image and Word: The Interaction of Twentieth-Century Photographs and Texts* (Cambridge, MA: Harvard University Press, 1987), p. 97.

79 Keith F. Davis's discussion in his *An American Century of Photography*, p. 165.

80 Quoted in Vicki Goldberg, *Margaret Bourke-White: A Biography* (New York: Harper & Row, 1986), p. 115.

81 For new information on Bubley, see Bonnie Yochelson, *Esther Bubley on Assignment* (New York, Aperture, 2005).

82 *Documenting America, 1935–1943*, ed. Carl Fleishhauer and Beverly W. Brannan; essays by Lawrence W. Levine and Alan Trachtenberg, p. 314.

83 Jefferson Hunter, *Image and Word*, pp. 14–15. In *Documentary Expression and Thirties America*, William Stott voices much the same opinion.

84 Melissa A. McEuen, *Seeing America: Women Photographers between the Wars*, pp. 58–59.

85 *August Sander: Citizens of the Twentieth Century*, ed. Gunther Sander, text, Ulrich Keller, trans. Linda Keller (Cambridge, MA: The MIT Press, 1986), pp. 8–9. I am indebted to this publication for my analysis of Sander.

86 *August Sander*, p. 19.

87 See Leah Ollman, "The Worker Photography Movement: Camera as Weapon," in *Multiple Views: Logan Grant Essays on Photography, 1983–89*, p. 226. Most articles on worker-photography have not been translated from German.

88 Leah Ollman, "The Worker Photography Movement," pp. 230–31.

89 See the discussion in Ute Eskilden, "The A-I-Z and the Arbeiter Fotograf: Working Class Photographers in Weimar," *Image*, vol. 23, no. 2 (December 1980), p. 7.

90 See Terry Dennett, "The British Film and Photo League," in *Creative Camera*, nos. 197–98, (May/June 1981), p. 91. The entire issue is devoted to worker photography. Also see Hanno Hardt and Karin B. Ohrn, "The Eyes of the Proletariat: The Worker-Photography Movement in Weimar Germany," *Studies in Visual Communications*, vol. 7, no. 3 (Summer 1981), pp. 46–57

91 Leah Ollman, "The Worker Photography Movement," p. 233.

92 See the discussion throughout Maud Lavin, "Montage, Mass Culture, and Modernity: Utopianism in the Circle of New Advertising Designers," in Matthew Teitelbaum, ed., *Montage and Modern Life, 1919–1942* (Cambridge, MA: The MIT Press, 1992), pp. 37–59.

93 Deborah Frizzell, *Humphrey Spender's Humanist Landscapes: Photo-Documents, 1932–1942* (New Haven, CT: Yale Center for British Art, 1997), p. 24.

94 Erik Barnouw, *Documentary: A History of the Non-Fiction Film* (New York: Oxford University Press, 2nd rev. ed., 1993), pp. 111–12.

95 For information on the Photo League, see Anne Tucker, "A History of the Photo League: The Members Speak," *History of Photography*, vol. 18, no. 2 (Summer 1994), pp. 174–84. Also see her "Aaron Siskind and the Photo League: A Partial History," *Afterimage*, vol. 9, no. 10 (May 1982), pp. 4–5.

96 Ute Eskilden, "Innovative Photography in Germany Between the Wars," in *Avant-Garde Photography in Germany, 1919–1939* (San Francisco, CA: San Francisco Museum of Modern Art, 1980), p. 35.

97 Ann Thomas, "The Search for Pattern," in *Beauty of Another Order: Photography in Science*, ed. Ann Thomas (New Haven, CT: Yale University Press, 1997) p. 110.

98 Peter Reichel, "Images of the National Socialist State," in Klaus Honnef, Rolf Sachsse, and Karen Thomas, eds., *German Photography, 1870–1970: Power of a Medium* (Cologne: DuMont Buchverlag, 1997), p. 72.

99 Quoted in Rolf Sachsse, "Photography as NS State Design Power's Abuse of a Medium," in *German Photography, 1870–1970*, p. 92.

100 Phillip Knightley, *The First Casualty: From the Crimea to Vietnam—The War Correspondent as Hero, Propagandist, and Myth Maker* (New York: Harcourt Brace Jovanovich, 1975), pp. 220–21.

101 Susan Moeller, *Shooting War: Photography and the American Experience of Combat* (New York: Basic Books, 1989), p. 192.

102 Mary Anne Staniszewski, *The Power of Display: A History of Exhibition Installations at the Museum of Modern Art* (Cambridge, MA: The MIT Press, 1998), p. 223.

103 Staniszewski, p. 215.

104 Staniszewski, p. 224.

105 Walter Benjamin, "The Work of Art in the Age of Mechanical Reproduction," in Walter Benjamin, *Illuminations*, ed. Hannah Arendt (New York: Schocken Books, 1969), p. 223.

106 Maud Lavin, "Montage, Mass Culture, and Modernity: Utopianism in the Circle of New Advertising Designers," in Matthew Teitelbaum, ed., *Montage and Modern Life, 1919–1942*, p. 59.

107 Phillip Knightley, *The First Casuality: From the Crimea to Vietnam*, pp. 210–12. For a recent continuation of the story, see Caroline Brothers, *War and Photography: A Cultural History* (London: Routledge, 1997), pp. 179–81.

108 See the discussion of the photograph in Vicki Goldberg, *The Power of Photography* (New York: Abbeville Press, 1993), pp. 142–47.

CHAPTER SIX
Through the Lens of Culture
(1945–1975)

1 Edward Steichen, *The Family of Man* (New York: Simon and Schuster, 1955), pp. 4–5.
2 Christopher Phillips, "The Judgment Seat of Photography," in Richard Bolton, *The Contest of Meaning: Critical Histories of Photography* (Cambridge, MA: The MIT Press, 1989), p. 28.
3 Quoted in Aline B. Saarinen, "The Camera Versus the Artist," compiled in "The Controversial Family of Man," *Aperture*, no. 3 (1955), p. 11.
4 Jacob Deschin, "Panoramic Show at the Museum of Modern Art," compiled in "The Controversial Family of Man," *Aperture*, no. 3 (1955), p. 8.
5 Barbara Morgan, "The Theme Show: A Contemporary Exhibition Technique," compiled in "The Controversial Family of Man," *Aperture*, no. 3 (1955), p. 24.
6 William Manchester, *In Our Time: The World as Seen by Magnum Photographers* (New York: The American Federation of Arts and W. W. Norton & Co., 1989), pp. 423, 430.
7 Eric J. Sandeen, *Picturing an Exhibition: The Family of Man and 1950s America* (Albuquerque, NM: University of New Mexico Press, 1995), pp. 43–49. I am indebted to Sandeen's writing for information on the exhibit.
8 Phoebe Lou Adams, "Through a Lens Darkly," *Atlantic Monthly*, no. 195 (April 1955), p. 72.
9 Roland Barthes, "The Great Family of Man," in his *Mythologies*, trans. Annette Lavers (New York: Hill and Wang, 1972), pp. 100–01.
10 The Universal Declaration of Human Rights is available on the United Nations website. See http://www.un.org/Overview/rights.html
11 Eric J. Sandeen, *Picturing an Exhibition*, p. 27.
12 Melville J. Herskovits, *Cultural Relativism: Perspectives in Cultural Pluralism*, ed. Frances Herskovits (New York: Random House, 1972), p. 8.
13 For the history of the Che Guevera photograph, see Fernando Castro, "Crossover Dreams: Remarks on Contemporary Latin American Photography," in Wendy Watriss and Lois Parkinson Zamora, *Image and Memory: Photography from Latin America, 1866–1994* (Austin, TX: University of Texas Press, 1998), pp. 57–61, and Vicki Goldberg, *The Power of Photography* (New York: Abbeville, 1991), pp. 156–61.
14 The now-classic study is Eva Cockcroft, "Abstract Expressionism, Weapon of the Cold War," *Pollock and After: The Critical Debate*, ed. Francis Frascina (New York: Harper and Row, 1985), pp. 125–32.
15 Fernando Castro, "Crossover Dreams: Remarks on Contemporary Latin American Photography," in Wendy Watriss and Lois Parkinson Zamora, *Image and Memory*, p. 61. Castro's article is one of the few in English to recount the relationship of politics and photography in Latin America.
16 John Mraz, "Cuban Photography: Context and Meaning," *History of Photography*, vol. 18, no. 1 (Spring 1994), p. 88.
17 For the late survival of itinerant photography in Latin America see Ann Parker and Avon Neal, *Los Ambulantes: The Itinerant Photographers of Guatemala* (Cambridge, MA: The MIT Press, 1982).
18 Raquel Tibol, [no title], in *Hecho en Latinoamérica* (Mexico City: Consejo Mexicano de Fotografía, 1978), p. 25.
19 Tibol, p. 28.
20 Maria Eugenia Haya (Marucha), "Photography in Latin America," *Aperture*, no. 109 (1987), pp. 68–69.
21 For a discussion of the work of Latin American women making anthropological photographs, see Naomi Rosenblum, *A History of Women Photographers*, p. 196.
22 John Mraz, "Nacho Lopez, Photojournalist of the 1950s," *History of Photography*, vol. 20, no. 3 (Autumn 1996), p. 210.
23 Quoted in Olivier Debroise, *Mexican Suite: A History of Photography in Mexico*, trans. Stella de Sá Rego (Austin, TX: University of Texas, 2001), p. 197.

24 John Mraz, "Foto Hermanos Mayo: A Mexican Collective," *History of Photography*, vol. 17, no. 1 (Spring 1993), p. 88, n. 1.
25 The literature on Álvarez Bravo is replete with references to his Surrealism. An example is Charles Hagen's review of an exhibition: "A Mexican Master Surveys the Past," *New York Times* (Sunday, March 22, 1992), H37.
26 Paul Hill and Thomas Cooper, "Manuel Alvarez Bravo," in their *Dialogue with Photography* (New York: Farrar, Straus and Giroux: 1979), p. 231.
27 Hill and Cooper, p. 226.
28 Quoted in Jane Livingston, *Manuel Alvarez Bravo* (Boston, MA: David R. Godine, Publisher, 1978), p. ix.
29 Paul Hill and Thomas Cooper, "Manuel Alvarez Bravo," p. 233.
30 I am indebted to Nissan N. Perez for this interpretation, which appeared in "Visions of the Imaginary: Dreams of the Intangible," in *Revelaciones: The Art of Manual Alvarez Bravo* (Albuquerque, NM: University of New Mexico Press, 1990), p. 18.
31 Heike Behrend, "A Short History of Photography in Kenya," in *Anthology of African and Indian Ocean Photography* (Paris, Review Noire, 1999), p. 161. I am indebted to this book and to *In/Sight: African Photographs, 1940 to the Present* (New York: Guggenheim Museum, 1996) for my understanding of African photography.
32 PMSL & JLP, [untitled section introduction] in *Anthology of African and Indian Ocean Photography* (Paris, Review Noire, 1999), p. 197.
33 Stephen F. Sprague, "Yoruba Photography: How the Yoruba See Themselves," *African Arts*, vol. 12, no. 1 (1978), pp. 52–59. I am indebted to this now classic article for my understanding of the subject.
34 Joanna C. Scherer, "The Photographic Document: Photographs as Primary Data in Anthropological Enquiry," in *Anthropology and Photography, 1860–1920* (New Haven, CT: Yale University Press, 1992), p. 37.
35 G. Thomas, *History of Photography in India, 1840–1980* (N.P.: Anhandra Pradesh State Akademi of Photography, 1981), p. 45. A comprehensive history of photography in India, especially from the years immediately preceding Independence to the present, is sorely lacking.
36 Thomas, pp. 5, 49, 51.
37 P. C. Smith, "The Colors of India: Raghubir Singh," *Art in America*, vol. 88, no. 3 (March 2000), p. 99.
38 Pinney, p. 149.
39 For a discussion of Japanese aesthetics and the camera see Robert Stearns, *Photography and Beyond in Japan* (Tokyo: Hara Museum of Contemporary Art, 1995).
40 For this discussion, I relied on the research and analyses by Christopher Pinney in his *Camera Indica: The Social Life of Indian Photographs* (Chicago, IL: University of Chicago Press, 1997).
41 Vinay Lal, "Reading between the Frames: Burden (and Freedom) of Photography," *Economic and Political Weekly*, vol. 35, no. 14 (April 1–7, 2000), p. 1170.
42 Yosuke Yamahata, *Nagasaki Journey: The Photographs of Yosuke Yamahata, August 10, 1945*, ed. Rupert Jenkins (San Francisco, CA: Pomegranate Artbooks, 1995), p. 19.
43 Mark Holborn, "Introduction," in *Eikoh Hosoe* (New York: Aperture, 1999), p. 5.
44 Shoji Yamagishi, "Introduction," in *New Japanese Photography*, ed. John Szarkowski and Shoju Yamagishi (New York: Museum of Modern Art, 1974), p. 11.
45 Mark Holborn, *Black Sun: The Eyes of Four—Roots and Innovation in Japanese Photography* (New York: Aperture, 1986), p. 10.
46 Holborn, p. 14.
47 Shomei Tomatsu, *Nagasaki, 11:02, August 9, 1945* (Tokyo: Shinchosa, 1995).
48 Edward Putzar, *Japanese Photography, 1945–1985* (Tucson, AZ: Pacific West, Inc., 1987), p. 6.

49 For this and other aspects of the postwar Japanese experience, see John W. Dower, *Embracing Defeat: Japan in the Wake of World War II* (New York: W.W. Norton & Co./The New Press, 1999), p. 293.
50 John W. Dower, *Embracing Defeat*, p. 293.
51 Quoted in Fuminori Yokoe, "The Call of the Ocean of Memory," in Colin Westerbeck, *Yasuhiro Ishimoto: A Tale of Two Cities* (Chicago, IL: The Art Institute of Chicago, 1999), p. 103.
52 Quoted in Spencer R. Weart, *Nuclear Fear: A History of Images* (Cambridge, MA: Harvard University Press, 1988), p. 110.
53 I depended on the following sources for this discussion: Peter B. Hales, "The Atomic Sublime," *American Studies*, vol. 32 (Spring 1991), pp. 5–31; Vince Leo, "The Mushroom Cloud Photograph: From Fact to Symbol," *Afterimage*, vol. 13, nos. 1 and 2 (Summer 1985), pp. 6–12; and Spencer R. Weart's study, *Nuclear Fear*.
54 Leo Rubinfien, "Investigations of a Dog," *Art in America* (October 1999), p. 134.
55 Rubinfien, p. 134.
56 Rubinfien, p. 135.
57 Rubinfien, p. 136.
58 Quoted in Helen Gee, *Photography of the Fifties: An American Perspective* (Tucson, AZ: Center for Creative Photography, 1983), p. 4.
59 Tom Engelhardt, *The End of Victory Culture: Cold War America and the Disillusioning of a Generation* (New York: Basic Books, 1995), p. 10.
60 David Riesman, with Nathan Glazer and Reuel Denny, *The Lonely Crowd: A Study of the Changing American Character* (abridged by the authors) (New York: Doubleday & Co., Inc., 1953).
61 Quoted in Lili Corbus Bezner, *Photography and Politics in America: From the New Deal into the Cold War* (Baltimore, MD: The Johns Hopkins University Press, 1999), p. 14.
62 Aaron Siskind, "The Drama of Objects," in *Aaron Siskind, Pleasures and Terrors*, ed. Carl Chiarenza (Boston, MA: Little, Brown and Co., 1982), pp. 65–66.
63 See the discussion in Daniel Belgrad, *The Culture of Spontaneity: Improvisation and the Arts in Postwar America* (Chicago, IL: University of Chicago Press, 1998), pp. 49–56.
64 Sheryl Conkelton, "Seeing and Knowing the Order of Things," in *Frederick Sommer: Selected Texts and Bibliography*, ed. Sheryl Conkelton (New York: G. K. Hall & Co., 1995), p. 11.
65 Jerry Uelsmann, "Preface," *Photo Synthesis* (Gainesville, FL: University Press of Florida, 1992).
66 Quoted in Peter C. Bunnell, *Minor White: The Eye that Shapes* (Princeton, NJ: The Art Museum, Princeton University, 1989), p. 17.
67 Quoted in Bunnell, *Minor White*, pp. 15–16.
68 Allan Sekula, "On the Invention of Photographic Meaning," in *Thinking Photography*, ed. Victor Burgin (London: Macmillan, 1982), p. 102.
69 Peter C. Mazio, "Introduction," *Robert Frank: New York to Nova Scotia* (Houston, TX: Museum of Fine Arts, 1986), p. 6.
70 Quoted in "History—His Story," in *The Pictures are a Necessity: Robert Frank in Rochester, NY, November 1988*. Occasional Papers no. 2, Rochester Film and Photo Consortium (Rochester, NY: University Educational Services at George Eastman House, 1989), p. 43.
71 Andy Grundberg, "Harry Callahan, Cool Master of the Commonplace, Dies at 86," *New York Times* (Thursday, March 18, 1999), B9.
72 Maren Stange, "'Illusion Complete within Itself': Roy DeCarava's Photography," *Yale Journal of Criticism*, vol. 9, no. 1 (1996), pp. 63–92.
73 Quoted in Keith F. Davis, *An American Century of Photography, From Dry-Plate to Digital* (Kansas City, MO, and New York: Hallmark Cards, Inc., in association with Harry N. Abrams, Inc., 2nd, rev. ed., 1999), p. 288.
74 For a comparison of *film noir* and tabloid photography, see William Hannigan, *New York Noir: Crime Photos from the Daily News Archive* (New York: Rizzoli, 1999), especially pp. 20–22.

75 The textual source, if there is one, is not mentioned. See Jonathan Green, *American Photography*, p. 99.

76 Green, p. 106.

77 Bruce Davidson, *Bruce Davidson: Photographs* (New York: Agrinde/Summit Books, 1978), p. 10.

78 Jonathan Green, *American Photography*, p. 119.

79 Joseph Marshall, "The Moral Issue of a Pregnant Woman Shooting Up," *Photo Review*, vol. 16, no. 1 (Winter 1993), p. 5.

80 David Halberstam, [Introduction] in Bill Owens, *Suburbia*, ed. Robert Harshorn Shimshak (New York: Fotofolio, 1999), n.p. (p. 5).

81 Jeffrey Kastner, "A Vision of Suburban Bliss Edged with Irony," *New York Times* (Sunday, March 19, 2000), AR36.

82 Quoted in Douglas Collins, *The Story of Kodak* (New York: Harry N. Abrams, Inc., 1990), p. 261.

83 Quoted in Maria Morris Hambourg, Jeff L. Rosenheim, Douglas Eklund, and Mia Fineman, *Walker Evans* (New York: The Metropolitan Museum of Art, 2000), p. 137.

84 Quoted in Beaumont Newhall, *Supreme Instants: The Photography of Edward Weston* (Boston, MA: Little, Brown and Company, 1986), p. 43.

85 Douglas Collins, *The Story of Kodak*, p. 289.

86 For a full discussion of the impact of space photography, see Vicki Goldberg, *The Power of Photography*, pp. 52–57.

87 Marianne Fulton, "Changing Focus: The 1950s to the 1980s," in Marianne Fulton, *Eyes of Time: Photojournalism in America* (Boston, MA: Little, Brown and Company, 1988), p. 217.

88 David Robbins, *The Independent Group: Postwar Britain and the Aesthetics of Plenty* (Cambridge, MA: The MIT Press, 1990), p. 55.

89 Robbins, p. 69.

90 Robert Smithson, "Art through the Camera's Eye," quoted in Robert Sobieszek, *Robert Smithson: Photo Works* (Albuquerque, NM: University of New Mexico Press, 1993), p. 32.

91 It is interesting to note that both Bill Brandt and Nigel Henderson photographed at Bethnal Green, a lower-class area of London, yet both also moved outside social documentary to more experimental forms of photography.

92 Quoted in Tony Godfrey, *Conceptual Art* (London: Phaidon Press Limited, 1998), p. 203.

93 Quoted in Michael Compton, *Marcel Broodthaers* (London: Tate Gallery, 1980), p. 13.

94 Robert Stearns, *Photography and Beyond in Japan* (Tokyo: Hara Museum of Contemporary Art, 1995), pp. 59–60.

95 Quoted in Reiko Tomii, "Concerning the Institution of Art: Conceptualism in Japan," in *Global Conceptualism: Points of Origin* (New York: Queens Museum of Art, 1999), p. 26.

96 John Szarkowski, *Looking at Photographs: 100 Pictures from the Collection of the Museum of Modern Art* (New York: Museum of Modern Art, 1973), p. 120.

97 John Szarkowski, *A Photographer's Eye* (New York: Museum of Modern Art, 1966), n.p.

98 See, for instance, John Szarkowski, *Looking at Photographs*, p. 10.

99 John Szarkowski, *From the Picture Press* (New York: Museum of Modern Art, 1973), p. 6.

100 Kubler—and before him, the art historians Heinrich Wölfflin (1864–1945) and Alois Riegl (1858–1905)—insisted on a large time frame, not a decade.

101 Szarkowski, *Looking at Photographs*.

102 Szarkowski, *A Photographer's Eye*.

103 Quoted in Jonathan Green, *American Photography: A Critical History 1945 to the Present*, p. 187.

104 Szarkowski, *William Eggleston's Guide* (New York: Museum of Modern Art, 1976), pp. 6–8.

105 Szarkowski, *Mirrors and Windows: American Photography since 1960* (New York: Museum of Modern Art, 1978), p. 11.

106 John Szarkowski, p. 18.

107 John Szarkowski, p. 13.

108 John Szarkowski, p. 14.

CHAPTER SEVEN
Convergences (1975–2000)

1 Cristina Vives Gutiérrez, "About the Idea, the Negative and Negation," in *Conceptual Art in Cuba* (Minneapolis: Parts, n.d. [2000]), n.p.

2 See Thomas McEvilley, "Toward a Creative Reversal," *Art in America* (January 2001), p. 41.

3 Young Kim, [untitled artist's statement] in Andy Grundberg, Rebecca Solnit, and Ronald Takaki, *Tracing Cultures* (San Francisco, CA: The Friends of Photography, 1995), p. 40.

4 For Hillman's ideas, see James Hillman, "The Practice of Beauty," in *Uncontrollable Beauty: Toward a New Aesthetics* (New York: Allworth Press, 1998), pp. 261–74.

5 Ann Thomas, "The Portrait in the Age of Genetic Mapping," in Gary Schneider, *Genetic Self-Portrait* (Syracuse, NY: Light Work, 1999).

6 Thomas, p. 32.

7 For a discussion of Delaroche's legendary comment, see Mary Warner Marien, *Photography and Its Critics* (New York: Cambridge University Press, 1997), pp. 55–57.

8 Nicholas Mirzoeff, *An Introduction to Visual Culture* (London: Routledge, 1999), p. 88.

9 William J. Mitchell, *The Reconfigured Eye: Visual Truth in the Post-Photography Era* (Cambridge, MA: The MIT Press, 1992), bookjacket. A similar, but less forceful, statement occurs in the text on p. 20.

10 Joan Fontcuberta, "Introduction," in Pedro Meyer, *Truths and Fictions: A Journey from Documentary to Digital Photography* (New York: Aperture Foundation, 1995), p. 9.

11 Fontcuberta, p. 10.

12 Fontcuberta, p. 12.

13 See David King, *The Commissar Vanishes: The Falsification of Photographs and Art in Stalin's Russia* (New York: Metropolitan Books, 1997).

14 For analyses of the Gulf War see Douglas Keller, *The Persian Gulf TV War* (Boulder, CO: Westview Press, 1992), and Michael Griffin and Jongsoo Lee, "Picturing the Gulf War: Constructing an Image of War in *Time*, *Newsweek*, and *U.S. News and World Report*," *Journalism & Mass Communication Quarterly*, vol. 72, no. 4 (Winter 1995), pp. 813–25.

15 Anthony Aziz and Sammy Cucher, "Notes from Dystopia," in *Photography after Photography*, pp. 126–28.

16 Aziz and Cucher, pp. 126–28.

17 Joan Fontcuberta, "Introduction," in Meyer, *Truths and Fictions*, p. 11.

18 Katy Siegel, "Consuming Vision," *Artforum* (January 2001), p. 106.

19 Keith Cottingham, "Fictional Portraits," in *Photography after Photography: Memory and Representation in the Digital Age* (Amsterdam and Munich: OPA and Siemens Kulturprogramm, 1996), p. 162.

20 Lynne Warren, "Miroslaw Rogala," in *Photography after Photography*, p. 52.

21 "Blood and Oil," *The Economist* (March 4, 2000), p. 68.

22 See the discussion in Victor Burgin, "The Image in Pieces: Digital Photography and the Location of Cultural Experience," in *Photography after Photography*, p. 32.

23 Weston Naef and Sebastião Salgado quoted in Matthew L. Wald, "The Eye of the Photojournalist," *New York Times Magazine* (June 9, 1991), p. 58.

24 Vicki Goldberg, "Art, Facts, and Artifacts," *American Photographer* (March 1988), p. 26.

25 Stuart Hall, *Different* (London: Phaidon Press, 2001, p. 37).

26 Susan Kismaric, *British Photography from the Thatcher Years* (New York: Museum of Modern Art, 1990), p. 12.

27 Cornell Capa, quoted in Pooley, p. 40.

28 See, for example, John Worden, "Gimme Shelter," *Afterimage*, vol. 15, no. 10 (May 1988), p. 19.

29 Eugene Richards, quoted in Eric Pooley, "The Trouble He's Seen," *American Photographer* (November 1989), p. 40.

30 David Perlmutter, "The Vision of War in High School Social Science Textbooks," *Communication*, vol. 13, no. 2 (1992), pp. 143–60.

31 Gilles Peress, *Telex Iran: In the Name of Revolution* (Zurich and New York: Scalo, 1997).

32 Donna Ferrato, *Living with the Enemy* (New York: Aperture, 1991), n.p.

33 Quoted in a 1987 interview with Marianne Fulton, in her "Changing Focus: The 1950s to the 1980s," in Marianne Fulton, *Eyes of Time: Photojournalism in America* (Boston, MA: Little, Brown and Company, 1988), p. 248.

34 Vicki Goldberg, "The Heroism of Anonymous Men and Women," *New York Times* (June 13, 1993), H35.

35 See, for example, *Anthropology and Photography, 1860–1920*, ed. Elizabeth Edwards (New Haven, CT: Yale University Press, 1992); and James Clifford, *The Predicament of Culture: Twentieth-Century Ethnography, Literature, and Art* (Cambridge, MA: Harvard University Press, 1988).

36 Allan Sekula, "Dismantling Modernism, Reinventing Documentary (Notes on the Politics of Representation)," in *Photography: Current Perspectives*, ed. Jerome Liebling (Rochester, NY: Light Impressions Corporation, 1978), p. 232.

37 Jolene Rickard, quoted in Theresa Harlan, "As in Her Vision: Native American Women Photographers," in *Reframing: New American Feminist Photographies*, ed. Diane Neumaier (Philadelphia, PA: Temple University Press, 1995), p. 115.

38 Rickard, quoted in Harlan, p. 115.

39 Michael Kimmelman, "Can Suffering Be Too Beautiful?" *New York Times* (July 13, 2001), Section E, Part 2, 27.

40 Henry Hitchings, "What's Right in Front of You," *TLS* (July 18, 2003), p. 18.

41 David Byrne, "Foreword," in Lynne Cohen, *Occupied Territory* (New York: Aperture, 1987), p. 15.

42 J. M. Roberts, *Twentieth Century: The History of the World, 1901–2000* (New York, Viking, 1999), p. 613, n. 1. The Cambodian Genocide Program at Yale University can be accessed at www.yale.edu/cgp

43 Santu Mofokeng, "Trajectory of a street-photographer," in *Anthology of African and Indian Ocean Photography* (Paris: Review Noire, 1999), p. 269.

44 Walter Benjamin, "A Short History of Photography," in *One-Way Street and Other Writings*, trans. Edmund Jephcott and Kingsley Shorter (London: NLB, 1979), p. 255.

45 Martha Rosler, *Positions in the Life World*, ed. Catherine de Zegher (Cambridge, MA: The MIT Press, 1998), pp. 32–33. For a discerning analysis of the new social documentary, see Grant H. Kester, "Toward a New Social Documentary," *Afterimage*, vol. 14, no. 8 (March 1987), pp. 10–14.

46 Rosler, *Positions in the Life World*, p. 33.

47 Abigail Solomon-Godeau, "Who is Speaking Thus? Some Questions about Documentary Photography," from *Photography at the Dock* (Minneapolis, MN: University of Minnesota Press, 1991), p. 183.

48 The poster/essay for *The Health and Safety Game* was written by Allan Sekula.

49 Fred Lonidier, "Working with Unions," in *Cultures in Contention*, ed. Douglas Kahn and Diane Neumaier (Seattle, WA: The Real Comet Press, 1985), p. 103.

50 Martha Rosler, "In, Around, and Afterthoughts (On Documentary Photography)" in *The Contest of Meaning: Critical Histories of Photography*, ed. Richard Bolton (Cambridge, MA: The MIT Press, 1989), p. 322.

51 Martha Rosler, *Positions in the Life World*, p. 44.

52 Andy Grundberg, "Two Camps Battle Over the Nature of the Medium," *New York Times* (Sunday, August 14, 1983), H 24.

53 Allan Sekula, "The Traffic in Photographs," *Art Journal*, vol. 41, no. 1 (Spring 1981), p. 20.

54 Allan Sekula, "The Body and the Archive," in *The Contest of Meaning: Critical Histories of Photography*, ed. Richard Bolton (Cambridge, MA: The MIT Press, 1989), pp. 342–89.

55 Allan Sekula, "On the Invention of Photographic Meaning," in *Thinking Photography*, ed. Victor Burgin (London: Macmillan, 1982), p. 102.

56 Allan Sekula, "Dismantling Modernism, Reinventing Documentary (Notes on the Politics of Representation)," in *Photography: Current Perspectives*, ed. Jerome Liebling (Rochester, NY: Light Impressions Corporation, 1978), p. 231.

57 Sekula, p. 239.

58 Sekula, p. 251.

59 Allan Sekula, "The Body and the Archive," p. 379.

60 Sekula, p. 249.

61 Roland Barthes, *Camera Lucida: Reflections on Photography* (New York: Hill and Wang, 1981), p. 73.

62 Douglas Crimp, *Pictures* (New York: Artists Space; Committee for the Visual Arts, 1977), p. 3. Another Crimp article, also titled "Pictures," was published in *October*, vol. 8 (Spring 1978), pp. 75–88. It expanded on the first article and brought the ideas to bear on artists not included in the original show, most notably Cindy Sherman.

63 Thomas Lawson, "Last Exit: Painting," *Artforum* (October, 1981), p. 45.

64 Sontag's book was compiled from essays she wrote in 1973, 1974, and 1977 for the *New York Review of Books*.

65 Abigail Solomon-Godeau, "Conventional Pictures," *The Print Collector's Newsletter*, vol. 12, no. 5 (November–December 1981), p. 138.

66 See, for example, the discussion in Abigail Solomon-Godeau, "Photography After Art Photography," in her *Photography at the Dock: Essays on Photographic History, Institutions, and Practices* (Minneapolis, MN: University of Minnesota Press, 1991), pp. 113–14.

67 David Rimanelli, [untitled review] *Artforum* (December 2000), p. 120.

68 See the discussion of this picture in Brandon Taylor, *The Art of Today* (London: Everyman Art Library, 1995), p. 53.

69 Craig Owens, "The Discourse of Others: Feminists and Postmodernism," in Hal Foster, *The Anti-Aesthetic: Essays on Postmodern Culture* (Port Townsend, WA: Bay Press, 1983), p. 59.

70 Owens, p. 68.

71 See Griselda Pollock, "What's Wrong with Images of Women," *Screen Education*, no. 24 (October 1977), pp. 25–31, and Janet Wolff, *Feminine Sentences: Essays on Women & Culture* (Berkeley, CA: University of California Press, 1990).

72 Deborah Bright, "Of Mother Nature and Marlboro Men: An Inquiry into the Cultural Meanings of Landscape Photography," in *The Contest of Meaning: Critical Histories of Photography*, ed. Richard Bolton (Cambridge, MA: The MIT Press, 1989), p. 139.

73 For a more complete discussion of the controversy see Steven C. Dubin, *Arresting Images: Impolitic Art and Uncivil Actions* (New York: Routledge, 1992).

74 Dubin, p. 100.

75 A. D. Coleman, "The Directorial Mode: Notes Toward a Definition," in his *Light Readings: A Photography Critic's Writings, 1968–1978* (Albuquerque, NM: University of New Mexico Press, 1998), pp. 250–54.

76 Quoted in Annette Grant, "Lights, Camera, Stand Really Still: On the Set with Gregory Crewdson," *New York Times* (Sunday, May 30, 2004), p. AR20.

77 See David Mellor, "Romances of Decay, Elegies for the Future," in Mark Haworth-Booth, et al., *British Photography: Towards a Bigger Picture* (New York: Aperture, 1988), p. 52.

78 Quoted in Gary Boas, "New Image Art," in *Artforum* (December 2000), p. 152.

79 Walker, Ursitti, and McGinniss, *Photo Manifesto: Contemporary Photography in the USSR* (New York: Stewart, Tabori & Chang, 1991), p. 63.

80 Ulf Erdmann Ziegler, "Preface" to *Contemporary German Photography* (Cologne: Taschen Verlag, 1997), n.p.

81 Interview with Wang Jinsong by Stephanie Smith, in Wu Hung and Christopher Phillips, *Between Past and Future: New Photography and Video from China* (Chicago and New York: The Smart Museum of Art and the International Center of Photography, 2004).

82 Göran Gnaudschun [artist's statement], in *Contemporary German Photography*, n.p.

83 Quoted in Jennifer Blessing, *Rrose is a Rrose is a Rrose: Gender Performance in Photography* (New York: Guggenheim Museum, 1997), p. 208.

84 Quoted in Peter Weiermair, "Photography as Fiction," in *Jack Pierson: The Lonely Life*, ed. Gérard A. Goodrow and Peter Weiermair (Zurich: Editions Stemmle, 1997), n.p.

85 See Peter Weiermair, *Japanese Photography: Desire and Void* (Zurich: Edition Stemmle, 1997), p. 12.

86 Noriko Fuku, "I am a Photographer," in *An Incomplete History: Women Photographers from Japan, 1864–1997* (Rochester, NY: The Visual Studies Workshop, 1998), p. 11.

87 Noriko Fuku, "I am a Photographer," p. 5.

88 Larry Sulton, *Pictures from Home* (New York: Harry N. Abrams, 1992), p. 114.

89 I am grateful to Elizabeth Ferrer's interpretation in *A Shadow Born of Earth: New Photography in Mexico* (New York: The American Federation of Arts, 1993), p. 85.

90 For an overview, see Laura U. Marks, "Minor Infractions: Child Pornography and the Legislation of Morality," *Afterimage*, vol. 18, no. 4 (November 1990), pp. 12–14.

91 See, for example, Carol Mavor, *Pleasures Taken: Performance of Sexuality and Loss in Victorian Photographs* (Durham, NC: Duke University Press, 1995), and Anne Higonnet, *Pictures of Innocence: The History and Crisis of Ideal Childhood* (London: Thames and Hudson, 1998).

92 For a comprehensive history of political debates involving images, see Steven C. Dubin, *Arresting Images: Impolitic Art and Uncivil Actions* (New York: Routledge, 1992).

93 See Robert Shlaer, *Sights Once Seen: Daguerreotyping Frémont's Last Expedition through the Rockies* (Albuquerque, NM: Museum of New Mexico, 2000).

94 See, for example, Bill McKibben, "The Problem with Wildlife Photography," *Doubletake* (Fall 1997), pp. 50–56.

95 Robert Adams, *Beauty in Photography: Essays in Defense of Traditional Values* (New York: Aperture, 1981), p. 13.

96 Marusia Bociurkiw, "The Transgressive Camera," *Afterimage*, vol. 16, no. 6, (January 1989), p. 18.

97 From the ACT UP flyer handed out at Nixon's 1988 show at the Museum of Modern Art, quoted in its entirety in Jan Zita Grover, "Visible Lesions: Images of the PWA," *Afterimage* (Summer 1989), p. 14.

98 Interview with David Hevey titled "A Radical Creature" [no author] *Creative Camera* (February–March 1992), pp. 28–30.

99 Bonnie Yochelson, *Esther Bubley on Assignment*, p. 72.

100 Joyce Kozloff [interview with Barbara Pollack] [www.jca-online.com/pollack.html].

101 See Abigail Solomon-Godeau, "Living with Contradictions: Critical Practices in the Age of Supply-Side Aesthetics," in her *Photography at the Dock*, pp. 134–48.

102 Jeff Rian, "On the Ground: Paris," *Artforum* (December 2004), p. 80

103 Adam Lammiman, "Whose Reality is it Anyway?", *Adbusters*, no. 30 (June/July 2000), p. 18.

CHAPTER EIGHT
Into the New Millennium

1 Daniel Zalewski, "Old Masters Cheated," *New York Times Magazine* (December 9, 2001), p. 86.

2 Deidre Stein Greben, "'The Medium of the Moment,'" *Art News Online* (February 2003), p. 1. www.artnewsonline.com.

3 Richard West, "When Dinosaurs Ruled the Earth," in *Source: The Photographic Review*, issue 41 (Winter 2004), pp. 3–4.

4 Unsigned review, "Art History," *The New Yorker* (May 3, 2004), p. 19.

5 Elizabeth Van Ness, "Is a Cinema Studies Degree the New M.B.A.?" *New York Times* (March 6, 2005), pp. 1, 15.

6 Francesco Bonami, "The Road Around (or A Long Good-Bye)," in *Echoes: Contemporary Art at the Age of Endless Conclusions*, ed. Francesco Bonami (New York: Monocelli Press, Inc., 1996), p. 13.

7 Yinka Shonibare in dialogue with others in "Global Tendencies: Globalism and the Large-Scale Exhibition," ed. Tim Griffin, *Artforum* (November 2003), p. 154.

8 Jean-Hubert Martin, "The Reception of African Art," in *Africa Remix* (Ostfildern-Ruit, Germany: Hatje Cantz Publishers, 2005), p. 29.

9 See, for example, Klaus Biesenbach, "Mexico City: An Exhibition about the Exchange Rates of Bodies and Values," in *Mexico City: An Exhibition about the Exchange Rates of Bodies and Values*, ed. Klaus Biesenbach (New York: D. A. P., 2002), pp. 41–43.

10 Gilbert Vicario, "What Makes Art Mexican?" in *Made in Mexico*, ed. Gilbert Vicario (Boston, MA: Institute of Contemporary Art, 2004), p. 9.

11 Shannon Burke, "Lonnie Graham is the Spark," *The Grizzly* [Ursinus College], November 11, 2004, p. 3.

12 Andreja Kuluncic, quoted in Carol King, "To Be Noticed, Croatian Artists Set Their Sights on New York," *New York Times* (Thursday, June 23, 2005), p. E3.

13 Okwui Enwezor in dialogue with others, in "Global Tendencies: Globalism and the Large-Scale Exhibition," ed. Tim Griffin, *Artforum* (November 2003), p. 158.

14 Eleanor Heartney, "A 600-Hour Documenta," *Art in America*, vol. 19, issue 9 (September 2002), p. 95.

15 Quoted in Catherine Elton, "500 Tragic Years of Mayan Life, Shows in an Exhibition of Outreach and Hope," *New York Times* (August 23, 2004), p. E5.

16 Michael Hardt and Antonio Negri, *Empire* (Cambridge, MA: Harvard University Press, 2000), p. 393.

17 Richard Vine, "Sixty Ways of Looking at China" (Interview with Wu Hong and Christopher Phillips), *Art in America* (June/July 2004), p. 126.

18 This synopsis of Chinese photography is drawn from the catalog by Wu Hung and Christopher Phillips, *Between Past and Future: New Photography and Video from China* (Chicago and New York: The Smart Museum of Art and the International Center of Photography, 2004).

19 Allan Sekula, "On the Invention of Photographic Meaning," in *Thinking Photography*, ed. Victor Burgin (London: Macmillan, 1982), p. 102.

20 Walter Benjamin, "The Work of Art in the Age of Mechanical Reproduction," in Walter Benjamin, *Illuminations*, ed. Hannah Arendt (New York: Schocken Books, 1969), p. 241.

21 Hal Foster, "Postmodernism: A Preface," in *The Anti-Aesthetic: Essays on Postmodern Culture*, ed. Hal Foster (Port Townsend, WA: Bay Press, 1983), p. xv.

22 Martha Rosler in dialogue with others, in "Global Tendencies: Globalism and the Large-Scale Exhibition," ed. Tim Griffin, *Artforum* (November 2003), p. 163.

23 Rineke Dijkstra, quoted in Michael Kimmelman, "An Artist Exploring an Enlisted Man's Look," *New York Times* (Friday, August 3, 2001), p. E29.

24 Craig Garrett, "Coerced Confessions: Snapshot Photography's Subjective Objectivity," *Flash Art International*, 36 (November–December 2003), p. 72.

25 Claire Daigle, "Pagan Stories: The Situations in Recent Art," *New Art Examiner*, vol. 25 (March 1998), p. 55.

26 Kenneth Chang, "How the Red Planet Came Down with Pink Blues," *New York Times* (February 10, 2004), p. F3.

27 Eric Bates, "Land of the Lost," *Rolling Stone* (October 28, 2004), p. 83.

28 David Brittain, "To Hell and Back: The Photoblog," *Source: The Photographic Review*, no. 43 (Summer 2005), p. 34.

29 Bradley Graham and David Von Drehle, "Bush Apologizes for Abuse of Prisoners," *Washington Post* (May 7, 2004), A01.

30 Susan Sontag, *Regarding the Pain of Others* (New York: Farrar, Straus and Giroux: 2003), p. 115.

BIBLIOGRAPHY

Many excellent books on individual photographers and movements have been published in recent years. This bibliography emphasizes English-language general histories, rather than monographs.

GENERAL HISTORIES OF PHOTOGRAPHY

Braive, Michel F. *The Photograph: A Social History*, trans. David Britt (New York: McGraw-Hill Book Company, 1966). Idiosyncratic, historically outdated, yet delightful array of European vernacular photography.

Campany, David ed. *Art and Photography* (London: Phaidon, 2003). An overview of photography's place in recent art history, from the 1960s onwards.

Daval, Jean-Luc. *Photography: History of an Art* (New York: Rizzoli, 1982). Oversize and beautifully printed review emphasizing European photography. Daval concentrates on the interaction of photo-grphy and other art media.

Eder, Josef Maria. *History of Photography*, trans. Edward Epstean (New York: Dover Publications, Inc., 1978). Eder's influence on the history of photography, through his chronological organization of the medium's technical developments in Europe (first translated in 1945), is still felt. No illustrations.

Freund, Gisèle. *Photography and Society* (Boston, MA: David R. Godine, 1980). Originally published in France. Freund's insistence on seeing European photography, especially French photography, in the context of political and social events, helped to shift scholarly focus from photography as art to the cultural history of photography.

Frizot, Michel, ed. *A New History of Photography* (Cologne: Könemann, 1998). Lavishly illustrated history, with articles primarily on photography in the United States and Europe. This book incorporated new directions in the field, such as research on the development of mass-media networks, fashion photography, and the use of photography in the development of ethnic stereotypes. Flawed by the excessive use of sepia in the reproductions.

Gernsheim, Helmut, with Alison Gernsheim. *The History of Photography from the Camera Obscura to the Beginning of the Modern Era*, 2nd ed. (New York: McGraw-Hill, 1969). With Beaumont Newhall (see below), the Gernsheims shaped the field of photographic history. The Gernsheim collection, now in the Harry Ransom Research Center at the University of Texas at Austin, is one of the few large private collections to remain intact.

Kevles, Bettyann Holtzmann. *Naked to the Bone: Medical Imaging in the Twentieth Century* (New Brunswick, NJ: Rutgers University Press, 1997). From X-rays to PET scans, Kevles provides an informative reflection on society's reaction to imaging the body, and frequently notes the uses to which artists put medical imaging.

Kosinski, Dorothy. *The Artist and the Camera: Degas to Picasso* (Dallas, TX: Dallas Museum of Art, 1999). Kosinski and others examine the sometimes hidden history of photography's impact on modern art. Well-researched and lavishly illustrated.

LeMagny, Jean-Claude and André Rouillé, eds. *A History of Photography*, trans. Janet Lloyd (New York: Cambridge University Press, 1987). Individual articles mostly on European photographic history, written by leading historians and curators.

Orvell, Miles. *American Photography* (New York: Oxford University Press, 2003). Ranging from portraiture and landscape photography to family albums, this book traces 150 years of the history of American photography.

Newhall, Beaumont. *The History of Photography* (New York: The Museum of Modern Art, 1982). Newhall's preference for so-called straight photography, whether in art, documentary, or photojournalism, was apparent from his first catalog, published in 1937, to this last edition. The influential historian and curator shaped the prominent collections at the Museum of Modern Art in New York City and George Eastman House in Rochester, New York.

Parr, Martin and Gerry Badger. *The Photobook: A History*, vol. 1 (London: Phaidon, 2004). A comprehensive overview of the development of the photobook from the very early days of photography to the present.

Rosenblum, Naomi. *A World History of Photography*, 3rd ed. (New York: Abbeville Press, 1997). Rosenblum led the way to the current rewriting of photographic history. Her book included long- overlooked women photographers, and reached out to report on photography in the non-Western world.

Scharf, Aaron. *Art and Photography* (Harmondsworth, Middlesex: Penguin, 1974). One of the first books to investigate interactions between the fine arts and photography. Contains a useful bibliography of primary sources.

Thomas, Ann. *Beauty of Another Order: Photography in Science* (New Haven, CT: Yale University Press, 1997). Highly informative articles by Thomas and others in a catalog to the important exhibition of the same name at the National Gallery of Canada in Ottawa.

NINETEENTH-CENTURY PHOTOGRAPHY

Baldwin, Gordon, Malcolm Daniel, and Sarah Greenough. *All the Mighty World: The Photographs of Roger Fenton, 1852–1860* (New Have: Yale University Press, 2004). A comprehensive study of the influential British photographer.

Bann, Stephen. *Parallel Lines: Printmakers, Painters and Photographers in Nineteenth-Century France* (New Haven: Yale University Press, 2001). An investigation of the interaction between painting, print-making and photography in France at a time when technological advances precipitated enormous changes in the reproduction of images.

Bartram, Michael. *The Pre-Raphaelite Camera* (New York: New York Graphic Society, 1985). Painstaking and convincing look at the shared themes and visual techniques of painting and photography.

Batchen, Geoffrey. *Burning with Desire: The Conception of Photography* (Cambridge, MA: MIT Press, 1997). A critical, philosophically aware review of the formal, cultural, and political definitions of photography in its early decades.

Buerger, Janet E. *French Daguerreotypes* (Chicago, IL: University of Chicago Press, 1989). Largely based on the Cromer collection at George Eastman House in Rochester, New York, this book elucidates the multiple directions taken by the daguerreotype in mid-nineteenth-century France.

Carlebach, Michael L. *The Origins of Photojournalism in America* (Washington, DC, Smithsonian Institution Press, 1992). An introduction to the integration of photographically-based images into nineteenth-century newspapers.

Crawford, William. *The Keepers of Light* (Dobbs Ferry, New York: Morgan & Morgan, 1979). In his mixture of history and how-to-do-it, Crawford guides novice photographers through the chemistry and techniques of early photographic processes. This book is still sought-after for its clear instructions.

Edwards, Elizabeth, ed. *Anthropology and Photography, 1860–1920* (New Haven, CT: Yale University Press, 1992). Seldom-seen images and insightful essays track the intertwined development of photographic practice and the science of anthropology.

Flukinger, Roy. *The Formative Decades: Photography in Great Britain, 1839–1920* (Austin, TX: University of Texas Press, 1985). Showcases the wealth of nineteenth-century photography housed in the libraries at the University of Texas at Austin. Accompanied by helpful notes on the works and photographers.

Foresta, Merry and John Wood. *Secrets of the Dark Chamber: The Art of the American Daguerreotype* (Washington, DC: National Museum of American Art and Smithsonian Institution Press, 1995).

Daguerreotypes from an exhibition at the National Museum of American Art in Washington, DC, accompanied by writings on the medium produced by critics and photographers throughout the nineteenth century.

Galassi, Peter. *Before Photography: Painting and the Invention of Photography* (New York: Museum of Modern Art, 1981). Like Schwarz (below), Galassi speculated on the aesthetic forebears of photography. A still controversial early essay by the director of the photography department at the Museum of Modern Art.

Gray, Michael, Arthur Ollman, and Carol McCusker. *First Photographs: William Henry Fox Talbot and the Birth of Photography* (New York: Powerhouse Cultural Entertainment, Inc., 2002). Accompanying an exhibition of the same name, this book contains several rarely seen images, together with short essays and a timeline.

Hambourg, Maria Morris, Pierre Apraxine, Malcolm Daniel, Jeff L. Rosenheim, and Virginia Heckert. *The Waking Dream: Photography's First Century: Selections from the Gilman Paper Company Collection* (New York: The Metropolitan Museum of Art, 1993). Richly illustrated review, augmented with extensive, succinct descriptions of individual works.

Hamilton, Peter and Roger Hargreaves. *The Beautiful and the Damned: The Creation of Identity in Nineteenth Century Photography* (London: Lund Humphries in association with the National Portrait Gallery, 2001. An examination of the development of portrait photography in the nineteenth century, including how the carte-de-visite conferred social status and family albums were similarly used to establish a position within society.

Henisch, Heinz Z., and Bridget A. Henisch. *The Photographic Experience, 1839–1914: Images and Attitudes* (University Park, PA: Pennsylvania State University Press, 1994) and *The Painted Photograph, 1839–1914: Origins, Techniques, Aspirations* (University Park, PA: Pennsylvania State University Press, 1996). Drawn mostly from a collection of vernacular photography started by Henisch and Henisch before studies of the photography of everyday life became popular in the late twentieth century.

Jammes, Andre, and Eugenia Parry Janis, *The Art of the French Calotype* (Princeton, NJ: Princeton University Press, 1983). Photographic history's debt to collectors is evidenced in the images from the Jammes collection of French photography, Janis's attentive history serves not only to underscore the depth of the collection, but also its loss to scholars and the public when it was dispersed by auction at Sotheby's in 1999.

Keller, Ulrich. *The Ultimate Spectacle: A Visual History of the Crimean War* (London: Gordon and Breach, 2001. Using a range of pictorial materials including scientific diagrams, press illustrations and academic painting as well as photo, this book gives an account of a war that was conducted under the eye of public scrutiny and whose aesthetic scripting was drafted on that basis.

Kemp, Martin. *The Science of Art: Optical Themes in Western Art from Brunelleschi to Seurat* (New Haven, CT: Yale University Press, 1989). Lavishly illustrated, Kemp's book incorporates detailed histories and technical data for optical instruments, such as the camera obscura, which preceded the invention of the photographic camera.

Marien, Mary Warner. *Photography and Its Critics: A Cultural History, 1839–1900* (New York: Cambridge University Press, 1997). An analysis of U.S. and European critical writing on the medium.

McCauley, Elizabeth Anne. *Industrial Madness: Commercial Photography in Paris, 1848–1871* (New Haven, CT: Yale University Press, 1994). A comprehensive look at commercial photography and its consumers.

Rudisill, Richard. *Mirror Image: The Influence of the Daguerreotype on American Society* (Albuquerque, NM: University of New Mexico Press, 1971).

Difficult-to-find social history of early photography that has survived the test of time.

Sandweiss, Martha A., ed. *Photography in Nineteenth-Century America* (Fort Worth, TX: Amon Carter Museum, and New York: Harry N. Abrams, 1991). Richly illustrated. Six scholarly essays trace the social interactions of photography. The first entry, Alan Trachtenberg's "Photography: the emergence of a key-word," is an invaluable introduction to the intricate interplay of photographic practice and cultural values.

Sandweiss, Martha A. *Print the Legend: Photography and the American West* (New Haven: Yale University Press, 2002). Tells the intertwined stories of the photography and the American West in the nineteenth century.

Schaaf, Larry J. *The Photographic Art of William Henry Fox Talbot* (Princeton: Princeton University Press, 2000). In this collection of Fox Talbot's own writings, as well as those of his contemporaries, each of the 100 plates is reproduced at the actual size of the original. This is a record of Fox Talbot's technological as well as his artistic achievements.

Schwarz, Heinrich. *Art and Photography: Forerunners and Influences: Selected Essays by Heinrich Schwarz*, ed. William E. Parker (Layton, UT: Peregrine Smith Books, 1985). Essays by the distinguished Czech museum curator, whose examination of the social and cultural forces that encouraged the invention of photography has been widely influential in photo-graphic studies.

Seiberling, Grace. *Amateurs, Photography, and the Mid-Victorian Imagination* (Chicago, IL: University of Chicago Press, 1986). Intelligent analysis of the role that photography played in defining social class among British middle- and upper-class amateurs.

Thomas, Alan. *Time in a Frame: Photography and the 19th-Century Mind* (New York: Schocken Books, 1977). An early attempt to conceive photography as the history of an idea.

PHOTOGRAPHY SINCE 1900

Amelunxen, Hubertus van, Stefan Iglhaut, and Florian Rötzer, eds. *Photography after Photography: Memory and Representation in the Digital Age* ([Amsterdam?:] G+B Arts, 1996). Individual essays elucidate suites of images by contemporary artists whose images depend on computer assistance.

Blessing, Jennifer. *Rrose is a Rrose is a Rrose: Gender Performance in Photography* (New York: Guggenheim Museum, 1997). Blessing and others underscore the philosophical unity linking early twentieth-century photographers such as Claude Cahun with contempo-rary artists such as Cindy Sherman.

Bright, Susan. *Art Photography Now* (New York, Aperture, 2005). A survey of the work of many important artist-photographers working today, grouped by theme and with a commentary on each sequence by the author.

Campany, David ed. *Art and Photography* (London: Phaidon, 2003). An overview of photography's place in recent art history, from the 1960s onwards.

Constructed Realities: The Art of Staged Photography (Zurich: Edition Stemmle, 1989/1995). Attempts to define the staged photograph through a broad survey of work by American and European artists.

Cotton, Charlotte. *The Photograph as Contemporary Art* (London: Thames & Hudson, 2004). Useful for students, this book addresses the vocabulary and debates of photographic criticism.

Doss, Erika, ed. *Looking at Life Magazine* (Washington, D.C.: Smithsonian Institution Press, 2001). A collec-tion of articles that make full use of the magazine's archive.

Doswald, Christoph, ed. *Missing Link: The Image of Man in Contemporary Photography* (Zurich: Edition Stemmle, 2000). Unfortunately titled, wide-ranging survey of the overwhelming presence of the human form in contemporary art photography.

Enwezor, Okwui, ed. *The Short Century: Independence and Liberation Movements in Africa, 1945–1994* (Munich: Prestel, 2001). Enwezor and a group of scholars exam-ine popular imagery in post-World War II liberation movements. Lavish illustrations show, among other things, the centrality of photographic practice.

Faber, Monika and Janos Frecot. *Portraits of an Age: Photography in Germany and Austria, 1900–1938* (New York and Vienna: Neue Galerie and Albertina, 2005). A survey of portrait photographs that documents the changing image of middle-class society in Germany and Austria during years in which the assertion of individuality was both vital and fraught with difficulty.

Global Conceptualism: Points of Origin, 1950s–1980s (New York: Queens Museum of Art, 1999). Not primarily about photography, but demonstrates the extent to which photography became a major medium in North American, South American, European, African, and Asian art.

Graham-Brown, Sarah. *Images of Women: The Portrayal of Women in Photography of the Middle East, 1860–1950* (New York: Columbia University Press, 1988). Comprehensive, undervalued study of stereotypes, and also the role of women as photographers.

Griffith, Bronwyn A. E., ed. *Ambassadors of Progress: American Women Photographers in Paris, 1900–1901*. (France: Musée d'Art Americain in association with the Library of Congress, Washington D.C., 2001) Over a hundred years ago, an exhibition in Paris revealed how American women photographers, both amateur and professional, influenced the international pictorialist movement. Twenty-nine photographers are discussed in this series of articles that explores this little-known exhibition.

Howarth, Sophie, ed. *Singular Images: Essays on Remarkable Photographs* (New York, Aperture, 2005). A series of commentaries by distinguished critics and photo historians on single images from photo-graphers whose work spans 150 years, from William Henry Fox Talbot to Jeff Wall.

In/sight: African Photographers, 1940 to the Present (New York: Guggenheim Museum, 1996). Scholars such as Okwui Enwezor and Olu Oguibe bring critical insights to the practice of post-war photography in Africa.

Janus, Elizabeth, ed. *Veronica's Revenge: Contemporary Perspectives on Photography* (Zurich: Scalo, 1998). Janus and others explore the scope of Marion Lambert's perceptive collection of American and European photographers and artists who use photo-graphy in their work.

Kemper, Sarah. *Virtual Anxiety: Photography, New Technologies, and Subjectivity* (Manchester: Manchester University Press, 1998). A reflection on the possible impacts of digitalization on photography.

Lahs-Gonzales, Olivia, and Lucy Lippard. *Women Photographers of the 20th Century* (St. Louis, MO: St. Louis Art Museum, 1997). International in scope and taking account of recent theoretical approaches, this book contains essays introducing the often-overlooked collection of Helen Kornblum.

McEuen, Melissa A. *Seeing America: Women Photographers between the Wars* (Lexington, KY: University Press of Kentucky, 2000). Engaging text on such photo-graphers as Margaret Bourke-White, whose images responded to and shaped American social policy.

Millstein, Barbara Head, ed. *Committed to the Image: Contemporary Black Photographers* (New York: Brooklyn Museum of Art in association with Merrell, 2001). Social commentary provided by ninety-five contemporary African-American photographers whose work has been thought-provoking and often highly politicized.

Mitchell, William J. *The Reconfigured Eye: Visual Truth in the Post-Photographic Era* (Cambridge, MA: MIT Press, 1992). Merges a technical account, now largely out-of-date, with the philosophical issues raised by digital imaging.

Phillips, Christopher, ed. *Photography in the Modern Era: European Documents and Critical Writings, 1913–1940* (New York: Metropolitan Museum of Art, 1989). Valuable resource for understanding photography between the world wars, with important articles by Gustav Klucis, Ossip Brik, and Karel Tiege.

Pultz, John. *The Body and the Lens: Photography 1839 to the Present* (New York: Harry N. Abrams, 1995). A compact introduction to late twentieth-century concerns with the body as the primary site of human identity.

Reframings: New American Feminist Photographies (Philadelphia, PA: Temple University Press, 1995). Essays and images that underscore the diversity of women's photographic practice.

Rosenblum, Naomi. *A History of Women Photographers* (New York: Abbeville Press, 1994). An encyclopedic account that has had a lasting impact on photographic studies. Especially strong on mid-twentieth-century figures.

Tupitsyn, Margarita. *The Soviet Photograph, 1924–1937* (New Haven, CT: Yale University Press, 1996). Compact look at interrelated political and aesthetic issues from the death of Lenin to the pre-war period under Stalin.

HISTORIES OF ETHNIC, REGIONAL, AND NATIONAL PHOTOGRAPHY

Alibhai-Brown, Yasmin, *Imaging the New Britain* (London: Routledge, 2001). Although not a photo-graphy book, this is a perceptive and wide-ranging analysis of contemporary multicultural Britain in the shadow of the royal family and Shakespeare. Provides useful background to contemporary British photographic practice.

Alison, Jane, ed. *Native Nations: Journeys in American Photography* (London: Barbican Art Gallery, 1998). Comprehensive look at photography of and by Native Americans, with text by many of the artists represented in the book.

Anthology of African and Indian Ocean Photography (Paris: Éditions Revue Noire, 1999). Beautifully printed images in a huge compilation devoted to recent historical scholarship, including that of the black diaspora from the point of view of Africans.

Badger, Gerry, and John Benton-Harris. *Through the Looking Glass: Photographic Art in Britain, 1945–1989* (London: Barbican Art Gallery, 1989).

Bezner, Lili Corbus, *Photography and Politics in America: From the New Deal to the Cold War* (Baltimore, MD: The Johns Hopkins Press, 1999). Bezner shows that American documentary photography cannot be separated from political reform movements and official reactions.

Billeter, Erika. *A Song to Reality: Latin-American Photography, 1860–1993* (Barcelona: Lunwerg Editores, 1998). Strong on documentary photo-graphy, and the continuing iconographic themes that inform Latin-American photography.

Daniel, Pete, Merry A. Foresta, Maren Stange, and Sally Stein. *Official Images: New Deal Photography* (Washington, DC: Smithsonian Institution Press, 1987). A close examination of the politics behind the public idealism of photographic projects such as those carried out by the Farm Security Administration.

Davis, Keith F. *An American Century of Photography, From Dry-Plate to Digital: The Hallmark Photographic Collection*, 2nd ed., rev. (Kansas City, MO and New York: Hallmark Cards, Inc. in association with Harry N. Abrams, Inc., 1999). A clearly written, well-illustrated review of photography, with an emphasis on photography as art.

Debroise, Olivier. *Mexican Suite: A History of Photography in Mexico*, trans. and rev. by Stella de Sá Rego (Austin, TX: University of Texas Press, 2001). Covers twentieth-century photography by Mexicans and non-Mexicans. Canonical works, such as those of Manuel Álvarez Bravo, are accompanied by new research, especially into the vernacular uses of photography.

Dehejia, Vidya. *India: Through the Lens, Photography 1840–1911* (Washington, DC, Smithsonian Institution, 2000). Lavishly illustrated account of colonial photography with historical essays by scholars including John Falconer, curator of photo-graphs for the outstanding Oriental and India Office Collections at the British Library in London.

Elliott, David, ed. *Photography in Russia, 1840–1940* (London: Thames and Hudson, 1992). Russian scholars and curators discuss major developments. Experimental movements in the 1920s are well-known outside of Russia, but equal space is given to early efforts.

Ferrer, Elizabeth. *A Shadow Born of Earth: New Photo-graphy in Mexico* (New York: Universe Publishing, 1993). An eye-opening review of contemporary documentary as well as art photography.

Gao Minglu ed. *Inside Out: New Chinese Art* (Berkeley, CA: University of California Press, 1998). Gao brings together Western and Chinese scholars to review recent developments in contemporary Chinese art, which is frequently photo-based. (The history of photography in China has yet to be written.)

Green, Jonathan. *American Photography: A Critical History, 1945 to the Present* (New York, Harry N. Abrams, 1984). Still influential for its taxonomy of post-war photography, as well as the publications and the institutions that promoted the medium.

Gupta, Sunil, ed. *An Economy of Signs: Contemporary Indian Photographs* (London: Rivers Oram Press, 1990). Especially interesting for an essay by Saleem Kidwai on the relationship of photography to traditional Indian arts, and for its account of feminist photographic practice.

Hales, Peter Bacon. *Silver Cities: The Photography of American Urbanization, 1839–1915* (Philadelphia, PA: Temple University Press, 1983). Explores the use of photography in creating both visual histories of American cities and so-called 'booster books' to promote commerce.

Holborn, Mark. *Black Sun: The Eyes of Four: Roots and Innovation in Japanese Photography.* Concentrates on the influential post-war images of Hosoe, Tomatsu, Fukase, and Moriyama.

Honnef, Klaus, Rolf Sachsse, and Karin Thomas, eds. *German Photography 1870–1970: Power of a Medium* (Cologne: DuMont Buchverlag, 1997). Strongest in its account of photography and the rise of National Socialism, and the aftermath of World War II.

India: A Celebration of Independence, 1947 to 1997 (New York: Aperture, 1997). Reviews the work of Indian photographers such as Sunil Janah, and Western photographers such as Mary Ellen Mark, who have worked in India. (A comprehensive account of colonial and post-colonial photography in India is long overdue.)

Kuehn, Karl Gernot. *Caught: The Art of Photography in the German Democratic Republic* (Berkeley, CA: University of California Press, 1997). Against the odds, some photographers countered photo-based propaganda with scenes of the harshness of everyday life and lyrical personal diaries that experimented with form.

Out of India: Contemporary Art of the South Asian Diaspora (New York: Queens Museum of Art, 1998). Many photo-based works by artists of Indian descent living around the world.

Pelizzari, Maria Antonella. *Trances of India: Photography, Architecture, and the Politics of Representation, 1850–1900* (Montreal and New Haven: Canadian Centre for Architecture and Yale Center for British Art, 2003). A comprehensive and analytical review of late nineteenth-century photo-graphy about Indian identity.

Pinney, Christopher. *Camera Indica: The Social Life of Indian Photographs* (Chicago, IL: University of Chicago Press, 1997). Acknowledging his debt to French theorist Roland Barthes's influential book *Camera Lucida* (see below), Pinney examines the ways in which Indian photographers broke from colonial modes of representation and invented unique forms of photographic practice.

Rencontres de La Photographie Africaine: Bamako 2003: Rites sacrés/Rites profanes (Paris: Editions Eric Koehler, 2003) [Text in French and English]. An overview of historic and contemporary African photography.

Stange, Maren. *Symbols of Ideal Life: Social Documentary Photography in America, 1890–1950* (New York: Cambridge University Press, 1986). An in-depth examination of the documentary practice of Jacob Riis and Lewis Hine, as well as others who developed the notion of documentary photography.

Stathatos, John. *Image and Icon: The New Greek Photography, 1975–1995* (Athens: Hellenic Ministry of Culture, 1997). With Aris Georgiou, whose work is included in this survey, Stathatos has worked tirelessly to make Greek photographic practice better known, primarily through the yearly international festival of photography held in Thessaloniki. The most lavishly illustrated of his recent publications, this text uses a broad definition of landscape to encompass recent mixed-media work.

Stearns, Robert. *Photography and Beyond in Japan: Space, Time and Memory* (Tokyo: Hara Museum of Contemporary Art, 1995). A brief history of enduring themes in Japanese image-making. The last section concentrates on international figures such as Yasumasa Morimura and Nobuyoshi Araki.

Stott, William. *Documentary Expression and Thirties America* (New York: Oxford University Press, 1973). Reviews the definitions of documentary that influenced government-sponsored photographic projects, such as the Farm Security Administration's work, as well as social science.

Taft, Robert. *Photography and the American Scene: A Social History, 1839–1889* (New York: Dover Publications, Inc., 1964). First published in 1938, Taft's extensive archival research and collection of anecdotes set the stage for the study of photography in the United States.

Trachtenberg, Alan. *Reading American Photographs: Images as History, Mathew Brady to Walker Evans* (New York: Hill and Wang, 1989). An insightful look

at the impact of political and cultural developments on photography from the Civil War to the Depression years. Trachtenberg pioneered the inclusion of photographic history in American Studies.

Walker, Ursitti and McGinniss. *Photo Manifesto: Contemporary Photography in the USSR* (New York: Stewart, Tabori & Chang, 1991). Profusely illustrated, with solid analytic text describing the lively condition of photography during the dissolution of the Soviet Union.

Watriss, Wendy, and Lois Parkinson Zamora, eds. *Image and Memory: Photography from Latin America, 1866–1994* (Austin, TX: University of Texas Press, 1998). Large, well-illustrated catalog for an exhibition surveying historical and contemporary work in more than a dozen countries.

Weiermair, Peter, and Gerald Matt, eds. *Japanese Photography: Desire and Void* (Zurich: Edition Stemmle, 1997). Well-illustrated account of contemporary Japanese photography, especially those figures who have acquired international reputations.

Welling, William. *Photography in America: The Formative Years, 1839–1900* (New York: Thomas Y. Crowell, 1978). What began as a compendium of nineteenth-century writings on photography was illustrated with carefully selected images, many from private or seldom-seen collections.

Willis, Deborah. *Reflections in Black: A History of Black Photographers 1840 to the Present* (New York: W.W. Norton, 2000). An extensive look at African-Americans who practiced photography by a scholar who has spent her career researching the topic. Some reproductions, especially in the first third of the book, are inexplicably blurry, but the remainder are sharp and fresh.

Wride, Tim B. *Shifting Tides: Cuban Photography after the Revolution* (Los Angeles, CA: Los Angeles County Museum of Art, 2001). Cuban photographers did not shed their experimental tendencies, but participated in the international trend toward personal photography, with diary-like images that confound the better-known revolutionary propaganda photographs.

Xanthakis, Alkis X. *History of Greek Photography, 1839–1960,* trans. John Solman and Geoffrey Cox (Athens: Hellenic Literary and Historical Archives Society, 1988). Primarily Greek photographers, with many images of classical architecture, as well as vernacular photography.

PHOTOGRAPHIC THEORY AND CRITICISM

Barthes, Roland. *Camera Lucida: Reflections on Photography,* trans. Richard Howard (New York: Hill and Wang, 1981). Barthes's meditation on a photograph of his mother as a child has become a standard reference in photographic studies, much as Proust's madeleine has come to signal the 'remembrance of things past.'

Berger, John. *Ways of Seeing* (London: British Broadcasting Corporation and Penguin Books, 1972). Influential essay, based on a BBC television series, which discusses the impact of pictures, regardless of medium or context – for example, Ingres's Odalisque is paired with a bare-bosomed figure that illustrated a girlie magazine.

Bolton, Richard, ed. *The Contest of Meaning: Critical Histories of Photography* (Cambridge, MA: MIT Press, 1989). Thoughtful anthology of writings by such critics as Allan Sekula and Rosalind Krauss, selected to demonstrate the breadth of postmodern theory.

Bourdieu, Pierre. *Photography: A Middle Brow Art,* trans. Shaun Whiteside (Stanford, CA: Stanford University Press, 1990). First published in 1965, this book is a cross between anthropology and speculative criticism, in which the author stresses the relationship between taste, photographic practice, and social class.

Burgin, Victor, ed. *Thinking Photography* (London: Macmillan, 1982). With *The Contest of Meaning* (above), a compendium of influential critical writing, including essays by Walter Benjamin and Umberto Eco, as well as articles by Burgin.

Hight, Eleanor M. and Gary D. Sampson, eds. *Colonialist Photography: Imag(in)ing Race and Place* (London: Routledge, 2002). An analysis of photo-graphy's role in the social construct of the notion of race.

Pinney, Christopher and Nicholas Peterson, eds. *Photography's Other Histories* (Durham, NC: Duke University Press, 2003). A collection of essays by leading critics on post-colonial photography.

Solomon-Godeau, Abigail. *Photography at the Dock: Essays on Photographic History, Institutions, and Practices* (Minneapolis, MN: University of Minnesota Press, 1991). A collection of writings by one of the most incisive and persuasive contemporary critics of photographic practice.

Sontag, Susan. *On Photography* (New York: Farrar, Straus and Giroux, 1973). Contains six of Sontag's seven short essays on photography that first appeared in the New York Review of Books. Widely analyzed and discussed when they were published, the essays introduced ideas about mass media that are still prevalent.

Wells, Liz, ed. *Photography: A Critical Introduction,* 2nd ed. (London: Routledge, 2000). A largely successful attempt to integrate contemporary photographic theory with a history of twentieth-century photographic practice.

WEBSITES

Websites are making historical and contemporary photography widely available. Search engines can be used to pursue the names of individual photographers as well as ethnic and national collections. The few listed below only hint at the growing richness of the World Wide Web as a resource for photographic history.

Prominent among the general websites is the well-maintained site for George Eastman House, www.geh.org, which offers a time-line of photography, and is constantly enriched with new material. The United States Library of Congress, www.loc.gov, has a rich assortment of photographs displayed in its American Memory section, and frequently directs viewers to other themed sites where photographs can be found. Likewise, many museums, such as the Smithsonian Institution http://www.si.edu/; the Getty Museum www.getty.edu; The Museum of Contemporary Photography, http://www.mocp.org/; and the Museum für Kunst und Gewerbe in Hamburg, Germany http://www.mkg-hamburg.de/; have samples of their collection and exhibits on line. The American Museum of Photography is a museum without walls at http://www.photographymuseum.com/.

Major journals devoted to photography often have on-line exhibits and articles. See, for example, *Camera Austria*, http://www.camera-austria.at/, and the *British Journal of Photography*, http://www.bjphoto.co.uk/.

Some sites, such as http://www.lightwork.org/lw.html; http://www.bjphoto.co.uk/, and www.spelthorne.ac.uk/pm/sites.htm, collect and post links to a variety of websites devoted to historic and contemporary photography. The International Directory of Photography Historians lists the interests of more than a thousand specialists: http://www.rit.edu/~andpph/hpg.html; and The Women in Photography archive can be found at http://www.sla.purdue.edu/WAAW/Palmquist/. Autograph: The Association of Black Photographers has changing exhibitions on-line at http://www.autograph-abp.co.uk/.

Websites of special interest to photohistorians include the images and related materials about the French Commune available at www.library. nwu.edu/spec/siege. Increasingly, specialized archives are being put on-line. For example, the United States Steel Gary [Indiana] Works are being digitized by Indiana University. See www.dlib.indiana.edu/collections/ steel/steel.html.

Various historical photographic techniques also have websites, for example the Daguerrian Society at http://www.daguerre.org/. Craig's Daguerrian Registry is primarily a source for collectors but also supports a list of daguerreotypists: see www.daguerreotype.com. Those interested in contemporary and former uses of the cyanotype can visit www.cyanotypes.com. The Stereoscopic Association can be found at http://www.stereoscopicsociety.org.uk/. One of the largest websites showing postcards can be found at http://www.lcfpd.org/teich_archives. Similarly, sites for persons interested in area studies or historical period have also been founded. See, for example http://interart.co.il/photography/, which is devoted to photography in the Near East. The Latin American photographic archive at Tulane University at http://www.tulane.edu/~latinlib/lalphoto. html contains fifty major collections.

540 INDEX

541

INDEX

Naptime (Mann, 1989) **470**, 470–71
Nasmyth, James (1808–90) 145–6, **146**
Nast, Mrs. Condé 193, **193**
National Child Labor Committee (N.C.L.C.) 206, 230
National Geographic (magazine) 220, 325, 354, 398
Native Americans 74, **74**, 132, 136, 138, **139**, **140**, 140–3, **141**, **142**, 155–6, 193–4, **194**, 208, 310, 337, 418, **418**
Native Son (Wright, 1940) 286
Native Woman of Sofala (Thiésson, 1845) 39, **39**
Naturalistic Photography (P. Emerson, 1889) 170
Nature, La (journal) 209, **210**
Nauman, Bruce (b. 1941) 373, **373**
Nazis 235, 266–7, 289, 295, 296–8, 300
N.C.L.C. *see* National Child Labor Committee
negatives 9
Nègre, Charles (1820–80) 60, **60**
Negretti & Zambra 116, 120
Negri, Antonio 501
Nesbitt, Evelyn 191; portrait (Käsebier, 1902) **191**
Nettles, Bea (b. 1946) 468
Neue Sachlichkeit see New Objectivity
New Deal, the 276, 277, 278, 286
New Documents (MoMA, 1967) 344, 347
New Objectivity 265, 289
New Orleans (Friedlander, 1968) 345, **345**
New Orleans (McCusker, 2005) **490**
"New Photography" 265
New Topographics (exhibition, 1975) 352–3, 372, 474
New York (Levitt, c. 1940) 349–50, **350**
New York American **167**
New York Dada 251
New York Daily News 237
New York *Journal* 226
New York Seen Through the Body (Picabia, 1913) 216
New York Times 108, 110, 133, 293, 308, 325, 332, 430, 491, 496, 511
New Yorker, The 25, 28, 332, 494
Newhall, Beaumont (1908–93) 294, 295, 385
Newhaven Fishwives (D. Hill & Adamson, c. 1845) 72, **72**
Newly Occupied Tract Houses, Colorado Springs (R. Adams, 1969) 352, **352**
newspaper photography *see* press photography
Newton, William (1785–1869) 77, 162, 170
Nicaragua (Meiselas, 1981) 413–14, **414**
Nickel Tailings No. 34, Sudbury, Ontario (Burtynsky, 1996) 475, **476**
Niépce, Claude 9, 11, 12
Niépce, Claude de St. Victor (1805–70) 37
Niépce, Isidore (1805–68) 13, 14, 15, 76
Niépce, Joseph Nicéphore (1765–1833) 9–12, **10**, **11**, 23, 76
Nightmare no. 3 (Park Bul-dong, 1985) 422, **424**
Nil, Le (Blanquart-Evrard, 1854) 56
Nine Swimming Pools and a Broken Glass (Ruscha, 1968) 379, **380**
Nipsic in Limón Bay..., *The* (O'Sullivan, 1871) 134, **135**
Nixon, Nicholas (b. 1947) 480
Nixon, President Richard (1913–94) 353, 362
Nocturne: Orangerie Staircase, Versailles (Steichen, c. 1910) 185, **185**
Nomura, Hitoshi (b. 1945) 374–5, **375**
Nonook of the North (Flaherty, 1922) 277
Nordström, Alison Devine 221
North American Indian, The (Curtis, 1907–30) 194
notan 177, 197
Notre Dame de Paris (Lerebours, 1840–44) 51, **51**
Nouveau procédé (Daumier, c. 1856) **62**
Noval, Liborio **311**
Nude (Boughton, 1909) 186, **187**
Nude (Weston, 1934) 275–6, **276**
Nude Descending a Staircase # 2 (Duchamp, 1912) 181, 211, **211**, 252
Nude Sicilian Youths (von Gloeden, c. 1885) 187, **187**
Nude Youth with Laurel Wreath... (Day, c. 1907) 178, **179**

nudity 65–6, **66**, 153, 154, 178, **179**, 186–7, **187**, **188**, 220, **220**, 221, **222**, 271, **463**, 463–4, **464**, 477; children 470–71
Oak Tree in Eridge Park (Lady Mostyn, 1856) **94**
Observation Room (Cohen, n.d.) 422, **424**
Ochre Anointment (Kurland, 2003) 504, **505**
October (Eisenstein, 1927) 262
Oehme, Gustav (1817–81) 64, **64**
oil-prints **192**, 199
O'Keeffe, Georgia (1887–1986) 181, 183, 272; portrait (van Venchten, 1936) **294**
Omaha Beach D-Day Landing (Capa, 1944) 303, **303**
Omniprésence Vénus (Orlan, 2001) 392, **394**
One in Ten (Knight, 2001) 483, **484**
On the Hillside (Kühn, 1910) 174, **174**
On the Road (Kerouac, 1957) 340
One in Ten (Knight) 483, **484**
Onion Field, The (Davison, 1907) 173, **173**
Open Door, The (Talbot, 1844) **30**, 31
Ophelia (Crewdson, 2001) 454, **454**
Ophelia, Study no. 2 (Cameron, 1867) **97**
Opie, Catherine (b. 1961) 479, **479**
Opium Wars (1839–42) 118
Organ-Grinder Couple, An (Austen, 1896) 202, **203**
Oriental Races and Tribes... (1863) 118, **119**
Orientalism 154
Orlan (b. 1947) 391–2, **394**
Orozco, Gabriel (b. 1962) 452, **452**, 453, 497, 498
Orozco, José Clemente (1883–1949) 319
Osman, Colin 236
O'Sullivan, Timothy (1840–82) 109, **109**, 134, **134**, 135, **136**
Oswald, Lee Harvey 382, **385**
Our Nightly Bread (Rangel, 1960) 321, **321**
Outerbridge, Paul (1896–1958) 177, 260, **260**, 354
outsider art 465
Owens, Bill (b. 1938) 353, **353**, 411
Owens, Craig 434, 444–5
Page, Tim (b. 1944) 364
Pair of Tumor Suppressor Genes (Schneider, 1997) 396, **396**
Palgrave, Francis (1788–1861) 76
Panorama d'Égypte et de Nubie (Horeau, 1841) **50**, 51
Panorama of Hong Kong (Beato, 1860) 120, **120**
Panorama of Paris (von Martens, c. 1846) 57, **57**
Panorama of the "Taking of Sebastopol" (Langlois, 1885) 104, **104**
Panorama of the West Face of the Taj Mahal (Murray, c. 1850s–1860s) 118, **118**
Panthéon Nadar (Nadar, 1854) **88**, 89
pantographs 4, **4**
Panzer, Mary 106
Paolozzi, Eduardo (1924–2005) 367, **368**
Papiers qui Volent, les (Faucon, 1977–95) 461, **461**
Parada, Esther (1938–2005) 406–7, **407**
Parents (Wang, 1998) 459, **459**
Paris 57, **57**, 90, **90**, 156, **158**
Paris by Night (Brassaï, 1933) 257, **257**
Paris Commune 113–15, **114**, **115**
Paris Opera Project (Henson, 1990–91) **495**, 496
Park Bul-dong (b. 1956) 422, **424**
ParkeHarrison, Robert (b. 1968) **473**, 473–4
Parker, Ann **313**
Parks, Gordon (b. 1912) 282, 283, **283**
Parlormaid and Under-Parlormaid Ready to Service Dinner (Brandt, 1932–5) 291, **291**
Parr, Martin (b. 1952) 412, **413**
Patching the Sky (ParkeHarrison, 1997) **473**, 473–4
Patiño, Adolfo (1954–2005) 468, **469**
Patronize the Disabled Soldier (anon., c. 1866) 143, **143**
Paulina with Lion (Rossell, 1999) 497, **497**
Peale, Rembrandt (1778–1860) 87
Pencil of Nature, The (Talbot) **30**, 31, 31–32, **32**, 56
Penny Pictorial Magazine 166
People of India, The (1868–75) 153, **153**
People of the Abyss, The (London, 1903) 203

Pepsi-Cola 484
Père Ubu (Maar, 1936) **256**, 257
Peress, Gilles (b. 1946) 414, **415**, 510
Perlmutter, David 414
Perry, Commodore Matthew C. 69, 124
Persistence of Memory, The (Dalí, 1931) 402
Persons Unknown (Hunter) 495
Peterson, Larry 206
Petrole Hahn Advertising (foto ringl + pit) **264**, 264
Petti, Alessandro (b. 1973) 501
Pfahl, John (b. 1939) 474, **475**
Phillips, Christopher 430, 502
Phillips, Sandra S. 236
Phinney, Christopher 472
photoblogs 507, 510
Photo-Club de Paris 176, 181
Photogenic (Jacobi, c. 1950) 337, **337**
"photogenic drawings" 18, 18–19, **20**
photograms 248, **248**, 254, 442, **443**, 473
Photograph—New York (Strand, 1917) 199, **200**
Photographer's Eye, The (Szarkowski, 1966) 376, 377
Photographers' Studios (Floyd, 1860s–1870s) **80**
Photographic Art Journal, The 85
Photographic Art Treasures (1856) 87
Photographic Exchange Club (Britain) 85, 94
Photographic Journal 101
Photographic News 116, 145
Photographic Society of London 85, 94, 100, 176
Photographic Society, French 99, 176
Photographic Society, Vienna 85
photography-by-artists 437–8
Photography as a Fine Art (Caffin, 1901) 172
photogravure 177
photojournalism 235–9, 410–17
Photo League, New York 263, 272, 292–3, 335, 347, 411
photomicrography 30–31, 144–5, **145**
photomontages **240**, 241, **241**, 244, **244**, 245, **245**, 246, 248, **248**, 260, 267–8, **325**
Photopath (Burgin, 1967) 372–3
Photo-realism 369
Photo-Respiration (Breath-graph no. 22) (Satoh, 1988) 453, **453**, 455
photo-sculptures 472, 472–3
Photo-Secession 179–81, 184, 185, 191, 196, 197, 204
Physiomythological Diluvian Picture (Ernst & Arp, 1920) 250, **251**
physionotraces 4, **4**, 5
Picabia, Francis (1879–1953) 216, 250, 251
Picasso, Pablo (1881–1973) 181, 183, 216, 219, 257, 489–90
Pictorial Effect in Photography (Robinson, 1869) 172
Pictorialism/Pictorialists 171–4, 177, 178, 179, 181, 182, 185, 186–9, 192, 196–200, 201, 231, 233, 268, 270–71, 441
Picture of Dorian Gray, The (Wilde, 1884) 229
Picture Post 236
Pictures (New York exhibition, 1977) 434, 435, 436, 487
Pictures from Home (Sultan, 1992–96) 464–5, **465**
Picturing Us (Willis, 1994) 466
Pierre et Gilles 478, **478**
Pierrot the Photographer (Nadar & A. Tournachon, 1854–55) 89, **89**
Pierson, Jack (b. 1960) 462, **462**, 482
Pietà (Frare, 1992) 484, **485**
pinhole cameras 173, 441–2
Pinkerton, Allan (1819–84) 110
Pinochet, Augusto (b. 1915) 312, 422, 433
Piper, Adrian (b. 1948) 391, **391**
Piss Christ (Serrano, 1987) 448, 448–9
Pittsburgh Survey, The (1909–14) 206
platinum prints 170, 396
Pleasures and Terrors of Domestic Comfort (MoMA exhibiton, 1991) 465, 487
Plow that Broke the Plains, The (Lorentz, 1936) 263, 271
Plumbe, John (1809–57) 68
Poe, Edgar Allan (1909–49) 28; portrait (anon., 1849) **28**

Poinsettia Girl, The (Reece, 1907) 172, **172**
Pol Pot (c. 1925–98) 426
Polaroid photography 313, 357–8, **358**, 378, **379**, 391
Pole Vaulter, The (Eakins, 1884–85) 211, **211**
police pictures 73, 159–60, 222–4, 418–19
Police Station Lodgers (Riis, c. 1898) 205, **205**
Poling the Marsh-Hay (P. Emerson, 1886) 170–71, **171**
Polke, Sigmar (b. 1941) 391, **392**
Pollack, Barbara 444, **444**, 486
Pollock, Griselda 445
Pollock, Jackson (1912–56) 337, 340
Pop art 366–9
Poppy (Atkins, c. 1852) 35, **35**
pornography 66, 84, 154; *see also* "erotic" photography
Porter, Charles H., IV **415**
Porter, Eliot (1901–90) 355, **356**, 378
Portrait (Ruff, 1987) 422, **424**
Portrait—Miss N (Käsebier, 1902) 191, **191**
portraiture 28, 61–76, 84, 87–90, 96, 106–7, 143, 155–6, 187–92, **200**, **234**, 272, 296–7, **297**, **298**, 419; *see also* cartes-de-visite; Self-Portrait...
positon emission tomograpy (PET) 396
postage stamps **490**, 490–91
postcards 154, 168–70, **169**, 187, **189**, 219, **219**, 221
Postmodernism 434–6, 438, 450, 475, 482, 483, 486–7, 496
post-mortem photographs 66, **67**
Pound, Ezra (1885–1972) 197
Powell, John Wesley (1834–1902) 155
Prangey, Joseph-Philibert Girault de (1804–92) 53, **54**
Precisionism 252
Predicament of Culture, The (Clifford, 1987) 417
press photography 44, 165–6, **167**, 208, 226, 235–8, 298–9, 410, 412, 416
Pretend no. 3 (Piper, 1990) 391, **391**
Price, William Lake (1810–96) 90–91, **92**
Priestley, Joseph (1733–1804) 8, 15
Prince, Richard (b. 1949) 435–6, **436**, 487
Professional Criminals of America (Byrnes, 1886) 224
"Projection Photography" 295
Proposiciones (Grobet, 1978) 317–18, **318**
Pullman Company 208
Punch cartoon (1855) **100**
Pure Land (Mori, 1997–8) 404–5, **405**
Puyo, Charles E. J. Constant (1857–1933) 176, **177**, 186
Pyramid and Tufa Domes... (O'Sullivan, 1878) 134, **134**
Q. And Babies? A. And Babies (Haeberle & Brant, 1970) 364, **365**
Queen's Empire, The (1897) 219
Quicker than a Wink (1940) 295
Quiet Day at the Mortar Battery, A (Fenton, 1855) **102**
Quite a Hopeless Case (Elliott, c. 1856) 90, **91**
RA *see* Resettlement Agency
Raad, Walid (b. 1967) 501
"racial types" *see* ethnography
railroads **132**, 132–3, **133**
Rangel, Ricardo (b. 1924) 320–21, **321**
"Rat" and Mike with a Gun (Mark, 1983) 410, **411**
Rauch, Neo (b. 1960) 450
Rauschenberg, Robert (b.1925) 369, **369**, 379
Ray, Man (1890–1976) 250, 253–4, **254**, **255**, 256, 257, 262, 264, 268, 287, 291, 301
Ray, Satyajit (1921–92) 325
rayographs 254, **254**
Reading Dick and Jane with Me (Sligh, 1990) 466, **467**
Reclaiming Paradise (1987 exhibition) 446
Reece, Jane (c. 1869–1961) 172, **172**
Reflection of a Man in a Dresser Mirror (Siskind, c. 1938) **292**
Refractive Hexagon (Heinecken, 1965) 379, **382**
Régnard, Paul (active 1870s) 151
Reichstag (Khaldei, 1945) 305, **305**
Reims Cathedral (Le Secq, 1851) 58, **59**

INDEX